HOSPITALITY FACILITIES MANAGEMENT and DESIGN

Educational Institute Books

UNIFORM SYSTEM OF ACCOUNTS FOR THE
LODGING INDUSTRY
Eleventh Revised Edition

PLANNING AND CONTROL FOR FOOD AND
BEVERAGE OPERATIONS
Ninth Edition
Jack D. Ninemeier

UNDERSTANDING HOSPITALITY LAW
Fifth Edition
Jack P. Jefferies/Banks Brown

SUPERVISION IN THE HOSPITALITY INDUSTRY
Fifth Edition
Jack D. Ninemeier/Raphael R. Kavanaugh

MANAGEMENT OF FOOD AND BEVERAGE
OPERATIONS
Sixth Edition
Jack D. Ninemeier

MANAGING FRONT OFFICE OPERATIONS
Tenth Edition
Michael L. Kasavana

MANAGING SERVICE IN FOOD AND BEVERAGE
OPERATIONS
Fifth Edition
Ronald F. Cichy/Philip J. Hickey, Jr.

THE LODGING AND FOOD SERVICE INDUSTRY
Eighth Edition
Gerald W. Lattin/Thomas W. Lattin/James E. Lattin

SECURITY AND LOSS PREVENTION MANAGEMENT
Third Edition
David M. Stipanuk/Raymond C. Ellis, Jr.

HOSPITALITY INDUSTRY MANAGERIAL
ACCOUNTING
Eighth Edition
Raymond S. Schmidgall

MANAGING TECHNOLOGY IN THE HOSPITALITY
INDUSTRY
Seventh Edition
Michael L. Kasavana

HOTEL AND RESTAURANT ACCOUNTING
Eighth Edition
Raymond Cote

ACCOUNTING FOR HOSPITALITY MANAGERS
Fifth Edition
Raymond Cote

CONVENTION MANAGEMENT AND SERVICE
Ninth Edition
James R. Abbey

HOSPITALITY SALES AND MARKETING
Sixth Edition
James R. Abbey

MANAGING HOUSEKEEPING OPERATIONS
Revised Third Edition
Aleta A. Nitschke/William D. Frye

HOSPITALITY TODAY: AN INTRODUCTION
Eighth Edition
Rocco M. Angelo

HOSPITALITY FACILITIES MANAGEMENT AND
DESIGN
Fourth Edition
David M. Stipanuk

MANAGING HOSPITALITY HUMAN RESOURCES
Fifth Edition
Robert H. Woods, Misty M. Johanson, and Michael P. Sciarini

RETAIL MANAGEMENT FOR SPAS

HOSPITALITY INDUSTRY FINANCIAL
ACCOUNTING
Fourth Edition
Raymond S. Schmidgall/James W. Damitio

HOTEL INVESTMENTS: ISSUES & PERSPECTIVES
Fifth Edition
Edited by Lori E. Raleigh and Rachel J. Roginsky

LEADERSHIP AND MANAGEMENT IN THE
HOSPITALITY INDUSTRY
Third Edition
Robert H. Woods/Judy Z. King

CONTEMPORARY CLUB MANAGEMENT
Third Edition
*Edited by Joe Perdue and Jason Koenigsfeld for the Club
Managers Association of America*

HOTEL ASSET MANAGEMENT: PRINCIPLES &
PRACTICES
Third Edition
Edited by Rich Musgrove, Lori E. Raleigh, and A. J. Singh

MANAGING BEVERAGE OPERATIONS
Second Edition
Ronald F. Cichy/Lendal H. Kotschevar

FOOD SAFETY: MANAGING WITH THE HACCP
SYSTEM
Second Edition
Ronald F. Cichy

SPA: A COMPREHENSIVE INTRODUCTION
Elizabeth M. Johnson/Bridgette M. Redman

REVENUE MANAGEMENT: MAXIMIZING REVENUE
IN HOSPITALITY OPERATIONS
Second Edition
Gabor Forgacs

FINANCIAL MANAGEMENT FOR SPAS
Raymond S. Schmidgall/John R. Korpi

HOSPITALITY FACILITIES MANAGEMENT and DESIGN

Fourth Edition

David M. Stipanuk

AMERICAN HOTEL & LODGING
EDUCATIONAL INSTITUTE

Disclaimer

This publication is designed to provide accurate and authoritative information in regard to the subject matter covered. It is sold with the understanding that the publisher is not engaged in rendering legal, accounting, or other professional service. If legal advice or other expert assistance is required, the services of a competent professional person should be sought.

— *From the Declaration of Principles jointly adopted by the American Bar Association and a Committee of Publishers and Associations*

The author, David M. Stipanuk, is solely responsible for the contents of this publication. All views expressed herein are solely those of the author and do not necessarily reflect the views of the American Hotel & Lodging Educational Institute (AHLEI) or the American Hotel & Lodging Association (AH&LA).

Nothing contained in this publication shall constitute a standard, an endorsement, or a recommendation of AHLEI or AH&LA. AHLEI and AH&LA disclaim any liability with respect to the use of any information, procedure, or product, or reliance thereon by any member of the hospitality industry.

Editor: Jim Purvis

Contents

Preface

As THE FOURTH EDITION of *Hospitality Facilities Management and Design* goes to print, the U.S. hospitality industry seems to have emerged from the negative economic impacts of 2008 with generally optimistic projections about the future. These projections include modest increases in ADR and occupancy, and in the construction of new hotels. The slow rate of addition of new rooms since 2008 has helped the industry to recover financially but has some other implications. For example, the average age of lodging properties is growing older. And the tough recent economic times have meant expenditures on CapEx have been delayed. The result is that 2014 will see a record expenditure of about $6 billion on CapEx within the industry.

The aging stock of lodging properties means that the core focus of this text, the management of hospitality facilities, will continue to be important. Chapter 1 ("The Role, Cost, and Management of Hospitality Facilities") continues to tell the story of facilities management in hospitality with updated data on costs. With a combination of the economic slowdown, reduced energy prices, and the success of sustainability efforts, the cost picture shows moderate increases. Chapter 2 ("Hospitality Facilities Management Tools, Techniques, and Trends") also has had data and examples updated. References to historic paper-based maintenance management methods have been modified in light of the more widespread use of computerized maintenance management systems. Links have been added that will provide an ongoing way for readers to access benchmarking information. The chapter's discussion on training and certification has been expanded to reflect the many opportunities that exist for ongoing education in the field.

Chapter 3 ("Environmental and Sustainability Management") was benefitted by the contributions of Jeanne Varney, who has taught courses in sustainability and facilities at Cornell since 2012. Jeanne has experience as a hotel asset manager and has also operated a hospitality sustainability consulting business; she is recognized as a LEED Green Associate by the U.S. Green Buildings Council. Updates to Chapter 3 have included additions to the text as well as web links that strive to capture the extensive growth and rapid changes concerning sustainability within the hospitality industry. *Hospitality Facilities Management and Design* was one of the first hospitality texts to discuss sustainability and hotels. The topic continues to grow in interest, and Chapter 3 provides a look at current sustainability efforts within the hospitality industry.

Chapters 4–8 ("Safety and Security Systems," "Water and Wastewater Systems," "Electrical Systems," "Heating, Ventilating, and Air Conditioning Systems," and "Lighting Systems") have all been updated to reflect current values and trends. Topics such as carbon monoxide issues, terrorism, and natural disasters have been highlighted in the safety and security discussion. The chapter on water and wastewater systems has had cost figures updated and information on pool safety and pool ADA requirements added. The electrical systems chapter has a new discussion of "green" power as well as some discussion of photovoltaics at hotels. Changes to building systems and a discussion of the impact of government regulations on equipment efficiency and controls are some of the updates in the HVAC systems chapter. For the lighting chapter, something new for this edition is a brief discussion of LED lamps, with links to more technical discussions of LEDs. LEDs represent a major technological change in lighting.

Updates by Tom Mara of the Victor Kramer Company to the "Laundry Systems" chapter expand somewhat the discussion of actual laundry operations and provide new material on laundry equipment and design. Today, fewer large hotels have their own laundry operations, as there has been a trend within the industry to consolidate laundry operations off-site in a facility serving multiple hotels.

The "Building Structure, Finishes, and Site" chapter has been carefully updated and includes some new material on elevator maintenance contracts and ADA requirements for parking areas.

"Lodging Planning and Design" has benefitted from the contribution of Stephani Robson. Stephani is the co-author (along with Chapter 11's original author, Richard Penner) of a leading book on hotel design (*Hotel Design, Planning, and Development*). She has taught hotel and restaurant design and planning at Cornell since 1993. Design and development data have been updated within the chapter, current design trends incorporated, technology impacts on design highlighted, and material on the need to consider "green" design aspects such as LEED has also been added.

The "Renovation and Capital Projects" chapter has been extensively revised and updated by Jeanne Varney. The chapter has greatly benefitted by the use of data from HVS Design, a source that provides annual updates of renovation costs and trends to the hospitality industry, as well as by Jeanne's perspectives from her experience in the asset management field.

Acknowledgments

The School of Hotel Administration at Cornell has a long tradition of valuing education regarding the design and operation of hospitality buildings. This legacy began with the early hire of Frank Randolph to teach hotel engineering (and a number of other courses) at the School's founding. When I joined the School's faculty in 1984, plans were underway for a major building project that eventually involved the demolition of the existing Statler Hotel and the building of a new 150-room hotel with a substantial amount of meeting space. The School's facilities underwent extensive renovations and updates as well. All of these changes occurred during the deanship of Jack J. Clark. Professor Clark had been a member of the facilities faculty in the School prior to becoming its dean. It would seem that Professor/Dean Clark had a vision for the role of facilities in hospitality! In later years, Michael Redlin from the facilities faculty served as Associate Dean of the School, and was my collaborator on the first edition of this text in 1987. Subsequent editions benefitted from the contributions of my Cornell colleagues Richard Penner and Jan deRoos, as well as students and others within the hospitality industry and in hospitality education.

In this edition of the text, two current members of the School's faculty, Stephani Robson and Jeanne Varney, have updated the material from previous editions contributed by professors Penner and deRoos. I am very pleased to have Stephani and

Jeanne involved in this update, especially since they are both former students of the Hotel program at Cornell.

This edition of the text also has benefitted from the direct and indirect input of a number of others. As mentioned previously, the laundry chapter was extensively revised by Tom Mara, President of the Victor Kramer Company. Data about hospitality facilities costs from PKF and HVS has once again been graciously provided by these companies. Interactions over the years with the members of the Engineering and Environment Committee of the American Hotel & Lodging Association have been stimulating and helpful in many ways.

Having retired from the School several years ago, I have decided that this edition will mark my last contribution to the academic world. Interactions with and encouragement from my faculty colleagues, coupled with the supportive environment of the School of Hotel Administration, made for a most enjoyable career at Cornell. Seeing former Cornell students of my colleagues and mine such as Tom Riegelman, Rick Werber, Richard Manzolina, Dina Zemke, Eric Ricaurte, and Walker Lunn with flourishing careers in facilities and sustainability-related areas has been encouraging. And hearing that what was learned in our facilities courses has proved to be valuable to the careers of others, especially those in the hospitality real estate field, was also encouraging.

Finally, I want to thank the Educational Institute for a wonderful working relationship that spanned almost three decades. The recent editing work of Jim Purvis on this text and my other EI text (*Security and Loss Prevention Management*) has been much appreciated and most professional. Tim Eaton's earlier edits of text materials and his management of the academic publications department at EI also have been outstanding. And, while with my retirement I have had fewer occasions to interact with George Glazer, over the years I certainly enjoyed and benefitted from his input and observations. My thanks also to all the others at EI who help make EI's products a success, and to the folks at Pearson as they facilitate the marketing and distribution process.

I hope the users of *Hospitality Facilities Management and Design,* Fourth Edition, will find it useful in educational settings and within the industry itself. The adoption of this text by many academic programs across the globe has been heartening and is much appreciated.

David M. Stipanuk
Ithaca, New York

About the Author

David M. Stipanuk, Professor Emeritus, taught at the School of Hotel Administration at Cornell University from 1983 to 2008. His academic degrees include a Master of Science from the University of Wisconsin-Madison and a Bachelor of Science from the University of Wisconsin-Milwaukee. His teaching responsibilities included courses in sustainable development, facilities management, hospitality risk management, and hotel development and construction. He also published articles on environmental issues for the lodging industry and on workplace safety benchmarking for the travel and tourism industry. Mr. Stipanuk authored or coauthored the following texts: *Managing Hospitality Engineering Systems, Hospitality Facilities Management and Design,* and *Security and Loss Prevention Management.* He also helped to prepare AH&LA's *Energy Management and Conservation Guide.*

During his academic career, Mr. Stipanuk was a registered Professional Engineer, a member of ASHRAE, and active with the Engineering and Environment Committee of the American Hotel & Lodging Association.

Part I

Introduction

Chapter 1 Outline

The Role of Facilities in the Hospitality
    Industry
Costs Associated with Hospitality Facilities
    The Costs of Development and
        Construction
    The Costs of Operation
    The Costs of Renovation and
        Modernization
The Impact of Facility Design on Facility
    Management
    Components and Layout
    Materials, and Quality and Types of
        Construction
    Equipment
    Systems
Management's Responsibilities
    Management Contracts and Franchise
        Agreements
Responsibilities of the Facilities
    Department
Facilities Managers in Lodging Operations
Conclusion

Competencies

1. Identify a number of important roles played by hospitality facilities. (pp. 3–6)

2. Explain why construction costs vary by facility type and why proper construction practices provide long-term benefits. (p. 6)

3. Identify the two principal categories of facility operating costs, the components of each category, and various factors that affect those costs. (pp. 6–10)

4. Define "CapEx" and explain the purpose and limitations of the reserve for replacement. (pp. 10–11)

5. Describe how facility components, layout, materials, quality and types of construction, equipment, and systems affect facility management. (pp. 11–16)

6. State management's responsibilities with regard to facility management. (pp. 16–18)

7. Outline typical maintenance requirements found in management contracts and franchise agreements. (pp. 18–20)

8. Summarize the basic responsibilities of the facilities department and the facilities manager. (pp. 20–26)

1

The Role, Cost, and Management of Hospitality Facilities

In 1877, a San Francisco reporter, evidently weary of the end-less hoopla over the city's new Palace Hotel, described the hotel's remote signaling device. Twenty-five thousand numbered bellboys, he wrote, one for each guestroom, wait in a basement for lodgers to ring. "Down goes the clerk's foot on a corresponding pedal and up shoots the bellboy ... he is put in a box, shut up in a pneumatic tube and whisked right into the room designated by the bell-dial. A door in the wall opens to receive him, an automatic clamp catches him by the coat-collar, and he is quietly dropped to the floor." This whimsy satirized a very real tradition of technological innovation in the hotel industry. In fact, the idea of luxury in a hotel had already come to be defined as much by plumbing, heating, and machinery as by rich fabrics, furniture, and architecture.[1]

FROM THE EXOTIC AND LUXURIOUS ENVIRONMENT of the fantasy resort to the gleaming stainless steel and specialty equipment of the commercial kitchen, the hospitality industry of today relies on well-designed and well-maintained facilities as a key element of its business. Guests desire a safe and comfortable environment in which to conduct business, entertain, relax, dine, and sleep. The hotel, motel, or restaurant is their home away from home, and they usually want it to be better than home.

Hospitality managers' involvement with facilities takes several forms. All departments use the facilities, relying on efficient design and proper equipment and systems to perform their duties. Department heads may be consulted for ideas concerning the design of new facilities. They are also often involved in either planning for or coping with renovations. Meetings of the executive committee at most hotels place department heads in formal contact with the maintenance/engineering/facilities manager. A hotel's managers also have day-to-day involvement with the maintenance/engineering/facilities department as they use its services. (For our purposes, the terms maintenance, engineering, and facilities will generally be used interchangeably.)

The Role of Facilities in the Hospitality Industry ────────

Facilities play critical and varied roles in the hospitality industry. Hospitality facilities play a major role in guest satisfaction. They can provide an appealing visual environment that contributes to the overall ambience, experience, and comfort of the guest. These elements, created by the artistic efforts of architects, interior designers, and craftspeople, are sustained by the diligence of the maintenance and housekeeping staff. For some components of the industry, such as destination resorts, theme restaurants, casinos, theme parks, and water attractions, the facilities themselves are the attraction that engages and entertains guests. Other elements of the facilities also contribute to ambience and comfort but in more subtle ways. Often, unseen facilities components create comfortable thermal environments by controlling indoor air conditions, while others provide needed supplies of clean water at the proper temperature for bathing, swimming, and relaxing in spas. The environment for the guest is also enhanced by the control or elimination of unwanted sounds that could disturb the guest's experience. At the most basic level, facilities provide for guest comfort by protecting guests from the elements—whether inside the building or under sheltered areas near pools. Safety is another important factor related to facilities. Guests expect to be safe. They expect to be provided an environment in which they are protected from injury and from loss of their possessions. For hospitality facilities to fulfill many of these roles, the skills of the engineer and the technician are required, although the guest (who *expects* comfort) may not directly notice their contributions.

Besides contributing to the pleasurable experience of the guest, facilities play a role as the "manufacturing plant" in the creation and delivery of services and products. Facilities house and interconnect the equipment and systems that allow the hospitality operation to function, whether it be the power and communication cabling connecting point-of-sale devices; the elevators that move guests; or the collection of utilities, equipment, and controls that make up a modern kitchen or laundry facility. In their manufacturing plant role, the hospitality operation's facilities are also the workplace for employees. Back-of-the-house as well as front-of-the-house spaces need to be efficient, comfortable, and safe. Specialized consultants in fields such as food service, laundry, and other technical areas are called upon to design these spaces.

Facilities help to define the industry and provide identity in the marketplace. Characteristic roof shapes, signage, colors, and other trademark elements create an image for various hospitality products and serve to draw customers. Travelers quickly develop the ability to identify various hospitality businesses by the characteristic appearance of their facilities. Children who can't yet read have no trouble identifying their favorite quick-service restaurant at 300 yards from a speeding auto.

It must also be recognized that industry growth largely comes as a result of additions to the number or size of facilities. In an era of e-commerce, when many services are accessed or delivered electronically via cyberspace, the hospitality industry remains a service that requires a unique space (facility) to produce and deliver its service. And while some growth is achievable by higher prices and more customers served (better occupancy), a significant portion of the growth of many hospitality enterprises comes through the addition of facilities. This is also true of restaurant operations, where most sales growth for chain operators is due largely to additional stores rather than increased sales at existing stores.

Hospitality companies such as ARAMARK and Sodexo have further recognized the potential for facilities management to be a contributor to corporate growth in another way. These **facilities management companies** provide services such as housekeeping, grounds, and physical plant management to hospitality companies, schools, universities, and various industries. Recognizing the opportunities and challenges involved in the operation of facilities provides another role for facilities management within the hospitality industry—that of business opportunity.

Hospitality (and particularly lodging) facilities provide owners with a return on investment in two basic ways. First, they are the location where the business generates operating profit. Second, hospitality firms enjoy a portion of their "return" in the change in market value of their property. In this regard, the return considerations resemble those of real estate, an industry where facilities certainly play a major role.

Finally, facilities play a key role in the amount of revenue generated at the property. On one level, this is obvious: the presence of guestrooms, meeting spaces, dining outlets, and even recreation spaces provides the appeal guests recognize in choosing a property. The proper design and mix of these facilities is important to meet customers' needs. However, the existing facility has little latitude to make extensive changes with what it has in terms of facilities except through the infusion of massive amounts of new capital. What the existing facility *can* do is maintain the facilities it has.

One study illustrates the linkage between facilities maintenance and revenue.[2] This study investigated the relationship between the defects identified in quality-assurance reports and the revenue per available room (RevPAR) of the properties. Properties with one or more "failed" items related to facilities on the quality-assurance reports showed significantly different RevPAR values than those that had no failed items. For example, "hotels with at least one defect in the exterior had a RevPAR of $3.12 less than hotels with no defects in the exterior. Hotels with at least one defect in the guest bath had a RevPAR of $1.32 less than hotels with no defects in the guest bath." These are very significant findings. The study estimated that the effect of facilities deficiencies for the chain studied amounted to lost revenue of $20 million over the three-year period studied. The study concluded by stating:

> This study demonstrates a direct relationship between product quality and an operation's financial performance, when product quality is gauged by the level of facility defects … the defective hotels in my sample recorded a RevPAR of approximately $2.80 less than hotels that did not have defects. This difference was consistent over time and represents an annual revenue shortfall of approximately $200,000 per deficient hotel. The study also indicates where hotels might best invest their capital-improvement and maintenance funds. What seems to count is the exterior, the guestrooms, and the guest bath.[3]

Successful managers recognize that maintenance, energy, environmental, and capital project expenditures are not only "costs" but also contributors to guest satisfaction, employee productivity, revenues, and profits. Delivery of effective, well-managed facilities services plays a key role in the successful operation of a hospitality business.

Costs Associated with Hospitality Facilities

Hospitality facilities generate several types of costs: initial costs, operating costs, and renovation costs. First, the facilities must be designed, developed, and constructed. Once occupied, they must be operated. And eventually, they must be renovated and modernized. Each of these phases incurs unique expenses.

The Costs of Development and Construction

The facilities of the modern hospitality industry vary greatly. Budget and economy lodging operations have relatively small and simple physical plants, while convention, resort, and luxury properties may resemble small cities. And the facilities of food and beverage (F&B) outlets can range from a simple airport kiosk to a large, elaborately themed restaurant. Such differences in complexity and in the overall luxury level of finishes and furniture contribute significantly to the differences in the construction costs of various types of facilities.

Exhibit 1 contains an overview of new hotel development costs (per guestroom) subdivided into various levels of service. As you can see, even a modest-size budget/economy property represents an investment of several million dollars, and a large luxury property could cost several hundred million dollars. The maintenance, operation, and renovation of these multimillion-dollar facilities are ultimately entrusted to the engineering staff.

The development and construction of a hospitality facility represents a commitment of capital by an owner who naturally expects a return on this investment. As mentioned earlier, this expected return is driven by two elements: operating profit (from the sale of rooms, food and beverages, and meeting services) and real estate appreciation. To provide both types of return, the facility must be operated and maintained in a manner that maximizes operating profit potential and real property appreciation.

A facility constructed with appropriate quality and good budget control should have predictable costs for maintenance, operation, and renovation. Conversely, one that is poorly designed or built with cost overruns and cost-cutting due to poor budget planning, poor project management, or poor construction practices may well face major problems within the first few years of operation. This often means larger-than-expected infusions of cash and a nightmare for maintenance personnel and other property staff.

The Costs of Operation

Following the construction of the facility, there will be ongoing costs of operation. The two principal cost entries on the operating (or income) statement pertaining to facilities operation are the *property operation and maintenance* (or **POM**) and the *utilities* accounts. In the United States, lodging properties expend more than $13 billion annually for POM and utilities.

Exhibit 1 2013/14 Hotel Development Cost per Room Amounts

	Land	Building and Site Improvements	Soft Costs	FF&E	Pre-Opening and Working Capital	Total
Budget/Economy Hotels						
Average	$12,300	$58,700	$5,800	$8,300	$3,200	$77,400
Median	$11,800	$53,300	$2,900	$8,300	$3,000	$71,200
Allocation	14%	66%	10%	11%	3%	
Midscale Hotels w/o F&B						
Average	$15,400	$77,200	$11,700	$10,300	$4,200	$109,100
Median	$14,100	$68,300	$8,500	$10,000	$4,000	$93,100
Allocation	12%	68%	9%	11%	2%	
Extended-Stay Hotels						
Average	$12,800	$83,800	$11,600	$13,400	$3,700	$141,000
Median	$11,400	$75,000	$10,200	$13,800	$3,500	$121,900
Allocation	10%	68%	9%	13%	1%	
Midscale Hotels w/ F&B						
Average	$14,600	$83,100	$13,600	$13,900	$3,900	$129,400
Median	$11,000	$88,500	$10,700	$13,000	$3,700	$110,900
Allocation	16%	63%	11%	11%	1%	
Full-Service Hotels						
Average	$36,300	$154,900	$17,200	$25,400	$17,200	$267,900
Median	$35,000	$140,600	$14,400	$24,700	$16,000	$214,800
Allocation	14%	65%	10%	11%	4%	
Luxury Hotels and Resorts						
Average	$93,600	$373,900	$81,900	$56,800	$20,800	$641,000
Median	$91,300	$324,200	$90,400	$60,700	$18,700	$576,500
Allocation	18%	58%	14%	10%	4%	

Source: HVS.

Exhibit 2 is a summary of typical POM and utilities expenditures for U.S. hotels. Hotels typically pay 7 to 9 percent of revenue for these two items, with POM usually the larger of the two. The POM account includes all labor and fringe benefit costs in the facilities department, maintenance supplies and expendables, and all contract maintenance costs. Labor and fringe benefit costs are usually about one half of the POM expenditure.

The utilities account includes electricity, fuel, steam, and water/sewer. The major element of the utilities expenditure is electricity. Fuel includes such items as natural gas, oil, and propane. A steam cost will be incurred by hotels (and a few resorts) that derive their heating energy from steam purchased from a local district heating system or from a central heating plant for those in mixed-use complexes. For most hotels, electricity will be over half of total utility costs, with the next highest cost usually being water/sewer. Hotels in very cold climates might see fuel costs comparable to water/sewer costs.

The high absolute cost of POM for various types of properties will generally correlate with initial construction costs. That is, the more you spend to build the

Exhibit 2   U.S. Hotel POM and Utilities Costs: 2013 Median Values

	Percentage of Revenue		Cost per Available Room ($)	
	POM	Utilities	POM	Utilities
Full-Service Hotels	4.5	3.5	2616	2069
Limited-Service Hotels	5.2	4.6	1231	1088
Resort Hotels	4.5	3.8	4802	4022
All-Suite Hotels w/o F&B	4.8	4.3	1575	1407
All-Suite Hotels with F&B	4.5	3.2	2196	2050
Convention Hotels	4.2	3.2	3243	2486

Source: *Trends in the Hotel Industry—USA Edition* (San Francisco: PKF Consulting, 2014).

property, the more you spend to maintain it. Utilities expenditures also vary by type of property, but not as greatly as POM expenditures.

In 2013, a U.S. full-service hotel had a median expenditure of 8.0 percent of revenues for POM and utilities, while a limited-service hotel had a median expenditure of 9.8 percent of revenues for these services. The manager who effectively controls utilities and maintenance expenses can contribute both significant dollar amounts to the bottom line (especially at large properties) and a potentially significant percentage to property profits (possibly even turning a losing operation into a profit center).

The median expenses for POM and utilities as a percentage of revenue have slightly declined over the past decade. The absolute value of these expenses have increased however. Below is a table showing the percentage increase in these expenses for four types of properties (comparisons for all-suite hotels were not possible due to changes in the categorization of these properties). Increases varied quite a bit depending on the type of property.

Utility expenses have recently declined for all categories of hotels, based on PKF data (PKF is an accounting/consulting firm). This could be due to the availability of lower-priced natural gas, which not only reduced the cost of natural gas for hotels but also served as a lower-cost fuel for electricity production. It is also possible that hotels are seeing lower energy usage as a result of sustainability efforts. It must be recognized that government legislation regarding improving the efficiency of equipment probably has also played a role.

% Increase in Costs
2005–2014

Type of Hotel	POM	Utilities
Full-Service	38	18
Limited-Service	35	31
Resort	5	25
Convention	16	8

Data from Exhibit 2 can be adapted to present the POM and utilities budgets for "typical" properties in each category. As the following table (which uses average-size data from PKF) shows, typical full-service hotels have budgets for POM and utilities that total more than $1,000,000. Resort and convention hotels have budgets for POM and utilities that near or are in excess of $2,000,000 in each category. As you can see, facilities managers in typical properties have oversight responsibilities for a large amount of property expenses.

Type of Hotel	Average Number of Rooms	Annual POM Budget	Annual Utilities Budget
Full-Service	233	$ 609,000	$ 482,000
Limited-Service	111	$ 137,000	$ 121,000
Resort	460	$ 2,209,000	$ 1,850,000
All-Suite w/o F&B	123	$ 194,000	$ 173,000
All-Suite with F&B	237	$ 520,000	$ 486,000
Convention	768	$ 2,491,000	$ 1,909,000

Factors to Consider. A sometimes-debated question concerning hotel utilities and POM expenditures is the degree to which these costs vary with hotel occupancy. Any discussion of this issue should consider a couple of points. First, utilities costs *are* influenced by occupancy, but the building is heated or cooled (at least somewhat) and much of the equipment is operated whether the building is occupied or not. Weather plays a much larger role in determining energy costs. Sometimes occupancy and energy needs are correlated, and sometimes they are not. A resort in the southwest United States may see occupancy peak in the winter, a time of lower outside temperatures and therefore lower cooling needs than in the summer. A ski resort located in Colorado may see peak heating requirements and occupancy exactly coincide. It is possible that as much as 80 percent of a facility's utilities costs can be fixed—that is, unaffected by occupancy.

Second, while the usage of the building and systems during periods of high occupancy clearly creates increasing *needs* for maintenance, the high occupancy itself may make it difficult to *perform* the maintenance. Management may choose to delay maintenance (and therefore expenditure) until periods of lower occupancy. While this tactic may frustrate managers hoping to cut costs when occupancy is low, it is hard to find the time to perform needed maintenance when occupancy is high. During such periods, rooms are occupied, equipment is heavily used, and the maintenance staff lacks the access it needs. Periods of low occupancy are a good time for maintenance staff to deal with backlogged work, shut off systems, and get "behind the walls." Management needs to be aware of this and plan accordingly, especially in budget preparation. Estimates of the percentage of fixed POM expenses range from 50 to 75 percent.

Caribbean hotels have POM expenses that are similar to continental U.S. resort hotels. However, utilities costs in the Caribbean are substantially higher (+160 percent) than in the continental United States. The table below provides some data on POM and utilities expenses for Caribbean hotels:[4]

Caribbean Hotel POM and Utilities

	Percentage of Revenue	
ADR	POM	Utilities
$176 (All Hotels)	5.4	9.4
<$150	5.6	12.1
$150-$300	5.2	9.3
$300-$600	5.3	8.4
>$600	6.5	7.3

POM and utilities data about hotel properties are often presented on a per-room basis. While this approach produces interesting comparisons, it can create problems when comparing two properties. First, despite the fact that much energy usage is fixed, some of the POM and utilities expense will be related to occupancy. Comparing properties without controlling for occupancy or other differences may lead to incorrect conclusions.

Another problem arises when large differences exist in the business mixes of the two properties. If a hotel has a large banquet business and all the related facilities, its expenditures, when expressed per available room, will look high compared to a facility with the same number of rooms but without the banquet business. The presence of an on-site laundry will also increase POM and energy expenses.

The commercial building sector expresses its costs for utilities and POM on a cost-per-square-foot basis. This is probably a better way to express these costs, in that much of these costs are more related to building area. Most hotel energy management programs use this measure, although it is somewhat rare for measuring POM expenses.

Other factors to consider when comparing two facilities are the ages of the facilities, types of building systems, local utility rates, local labor rates, and identifiable differences in construction (such as single- versus double-glazed windows).

The Costs of Renovation and Modernization

One large expenditure category that is clearly facilities-related is that of capital expenditures, or **CapEx**. CapEx includes not simply "the replacement of worn-out furniture, finishes, and soft goods... CapEx must also cover wear and tear, obsolescence, regulatory requirements such as the Americans with Disabilities Act (**ADA**) and life safety, franchise product demands, changing technology, market demand for product change, and replacement and renovations of building components and heavy equipment."[5] Recognition of the unique and expensive nature of CapEx, planning for its needs, and managing its implementation represent a significant portion of the facilities manager's duties, especially as buildings age.

Historically, management contracts for lodging properties provided for three to four percent of revenue to be placed in what was often called a *reserve for replacement* account. This percentage was sometimes lower during the first couple of years after opening, because these years were often not profitable. The low percentage level of the reserve conveyed confusing signals to ownership about the actual costs and timing of CapEx over the life of the facility. CapEx can range from near zero to as much as 30 percent of revenue in a given year, something not conveyed by a small fixed percentage number. Some industry consultants believe that "poor planning for CapEx was a major reason for the operating losses and bankruptcies the industry experienced in the early 1990s."[6] Estimates of CapEx needs for well-maintained properties (where capital expenditures do not also have to compensate for neglected ongoing maintenance) indicate that, over a full-service hotel's first thirty years of life, CapEx will approximately equal and may exceed seven percent of total gross revenues.[7]

The Impact of Facility Design on Facility Management ——

> Good design can clearly increase a hotel's top-line performance, as evidenced by the ability to command higher room rates and increased revenue. Good design also helps build a better bottom line by reducing staffing costs, energy costs, and operations and maintenance expenses.... Poor design can accelerate a hotel's physical and functional obsolescence, thereby decreasing its value. When valuing hotels, we look closely at operating costs that are out of line with the norm. If the hotel is under-performing, the problem may be inherent in the building's design.[8]

Our primary focus is on *managing* rather than *designing* facilities. Nonetheless, a facility's design will clearly dictate the scope of the facility management function. The role of facility design can be understood by focusing on such factors as:

- Facility components and layout
- Materials
- Quality and types of construction
- Equipment
- Systems

Components and Layout

The facility components dictate the needs for facility maintenance, renovation, and operation. The presence of recreational facilities, kitchens, food and beverage outlets, convention space, meeting rooms, and extensive landscaped grounds will all create maintenance needs.

Layout also affects maintenance needs. A high-rise structure generally has more complex building systems and concerns. In addition, high-rise facilities bring needs and costs for such items as elevator maintenance and window cleaning. Low-rise facilities that spread over multiple acres, such as those found at some resorts, create maintenance needs for transportation equipment and can mean long travel times for maintenance staff members as they navigate around the facility.

Materials, and Quality and Types of Construction

The materials used in a building will affect not only maintenance needs, but also renovation needs and such operating costs as energy and insurance. Most seasoned hospitality personnel (and a number of homeowners) have experienced maintenance problems caused by poor material selection—for example, slippery flooring material, siding that is not suitable for the local climate, or premature product failure due to a defect. Problems caused by materials increase maintenance costs. They often can be solved only by capital investments.

The quality of construction for a building also will affect maintenance, operation, and renovation. If the building is well-constructed, the maintenance manager's duties will in fact focus primarily on maintenance. However, if the quality of construction is substandard, the maintenance manager may quickly be forced into the construction business. Actual examples of substandard construction and its consequences include, but unfortunately are not limited to, the following:

- A poorly installed roof soon began to leak, requiring replacement of walls and ceilings as well as more cosmetic changes.

- Poor construction of the exterior skin of a hotel subject to driving rainstorms in a hot, humid climate allowed moisture to enter the skin and flow along the dividing walls between guestrooms. This led to mold, mildew, and deterioration of the walls.

- Some years ago, many hotels in the southeast United States failed to properly insulate water pipes. This resulted in massive failure due to freezing.

- A new urban hotel was built with knockdown (multi-piece) doorframes rather than one-piece doorframes. The frames sagged, aligned poorly, and caused operating problems with locks. Panicked guests often found themselves unable to leave their rooms.

- A hotel in Hawaii had moisture trapped in its building materials during construction and was not adequately dehumidified. Subsequently, extensive mold and mildew problems required that the hotel be closed and tens of millions spent on repairs.

The design and construction of hospitality facilities involves multiple individuals bringing their expertise to bear in creating the final product—a building that "works" for the owner, operator, and customer. When some element of the building doesn't work, problems can result. Owners find themselves spending money to correct the problem, operators discover they have difficulty in controlling costs and delivering service, and customers are negatively affected. While most design and construction problems with buildings are relatively minor, there are times when the problems are severe.

The Hyatt Regency in Kansas City, Missouri, provides a tragic illustration of the potential severity of design and construction problems. On July 17, 1981, two walkways suspended over the hotel's lobby collapsed, resulting in the deaths of 114 people and injuries to hundreds of others. The owner of the property (Crown Center Redevelopment Corporation) is believed to have settled various civil suits out of court for more than $100 million. In addition, various design professionals found themselves facing lawsuits and the loss of their licenses. The Hyatt Regency Kansas City had been open for almost a year when the collapse occurred. An investigation into the cause of the collapse showed that ceiling rods supporting the walkways failed, resulting in the collapse. The design and construction of the rods had been compromised during the fast-track construction process by a number of errors in calculation, communication, and coordination.[9]

Besides the problems that can result from substandard design and construction, the type of construction itself can affect the costs of the physical plant. A wood-frame structure will have higher insurance rates than a masonry one. An exterior surface that requires painting will have higher maintenance costs than one that does not. A facility with plaster walls will cost more to repair than one with drywall. The retrofit of sprinkler systems in older buildings will be easier if a drop ceiling is in place in the guestroom corridor rather than just a finished slab. Facilities with poorly insulated exterior walls and roofs and inefficient windows will have higher-than-average utility costs.

Equipment

The equipment installed at the facility will have an impact on the need for maintenance. An island resort operating its own electrical generators, desalination plant for fresh water, sewage treatment facility, and large refrigerated storage facilities will clearly have greater and more complex maintenance needs than will a suburban 100-room economy motel. Equipment concerns that will affect maintenance and operating needs involve such issues as equipment *durability, lifetime, repairability, efficiency,* and *accessibility.*

Durability and Lifetime. Some equipment is clearly designed with a throw-away mindset—a light bulb, for example. Other equipment may be suitable for residential use, but not durable enough to last under constant usage in a commercial setting. The nature of the hospitality environment mandates the use of commercial-duty equipment for such items as vacuum cleaners. Information about equipment lifetime and maintenance costs can be helpful in understanding maintenance needs and in planning equipment purchases.

Hotels make a significant investment in mechanical and electrical equipment, with the goal of having this equipment operate efficiently for extended periods of time. Major equipment such as building chillers and boilers should have lifetimes in excess of twenty years. Smaller, electrically powered, through-the-wall units providing heating and cooling for guestrooms may have lifetimes of fifteen to twenty years, while fan coil units supplied with chilled and hot water may last in excess of thirty years.[10]

Extending the lifetime of equipment can be done with proper maintenance. However, there comes a time when equipment needs to be replaced. For example, older equipment can be so inefficient that, even though it continues to operate properly, it has become too costly to operate. Obsolescence is also a factor when making replacement decisions; the decision to invest hundreds of dollars per room to purchase flat screen TVs for guestrooms is a prime example.

Repairability. The repairability of equipment involves several issues. Property staff can repair some equipment, while other equipment clearly requires the services of specially trained mechanics. This is one of the reasons 50 percent or more of the POM account is expended on items other than payroll. The decision to repair or replace an item involves several factors. Equipment near its expected life is probably not worth repairing unless the repair will result in a large extension of its life. In addition, the repair of equipment sometimes reduces the efficiency of the equipment. An electric motor, for example, is generally less efficient when it is rewound.

Repairability also depends on the availability of parts and the ability to remove equipment from service while it is repaired. Some operators have purchased imported equipment and discovered that service and parts were virtually impossible to get domestically. Though operators of off-shore facilities often face such problems, this distressing and costly experience has happened even regionally within the United States. This is one good reason to check on service and parts availability *before* you sign the purchase agreement.

The repair of equipment (and facilities) must never jeopardize safety. Equipment (and facilities) should not be repaired in a way that bypasses, disables, or compromises safety features. A repaired electric cord with the grounding plug removed, a repaired lawnmower without a discharge guard, or a repaired fan with its belt guard removed may function properly, but each is a potential safety hazard to both employees and guests. One hotel "repaired" a leaking roof by installing a false guestroom ceiling below. Eventually, the true ceiling collapsed and killed a guest sleeping in the bed below. The lesson is clear: *safety first.*

Efficiency. Selecting equipment with efficiency in mind involves being aware of the life-cycle implications of equipment decisions. Some pieces of equipment have operating costs per year that are two to four times their purchase price—for example, a water heater for the laundry. Other pieces of equipment, like incandescent light bulbs, will cost thirty to fifty times more to operate than their initial cost. Therefore, choosing a more efficient piece of equipment at a higher initial cost could provide some real payback.

Management sometimes finds itself with inefficient equipment that was purchased to keep the initial cost of the building on budget. While there may be no immediate remedy to this problem, the worst decision management can make is to choose the same inefficient equipment when a replacement is required.

Understanding the factors that contribute to the efficiency of various types of equipment can help managers make wise purchase decisions. A helpful process to use in this regard involves the total cost of ownership (TCO) approach.[11] TCO provides an approach to capital investment that strives to identify all costs and benefits from the investment as well as place these costs and benefits within a framework that considers the different time frames in which they occur. Application of TCO should be done wherever applicable.

Accessibility. Accessibility to equipment is essential to ensuring proper maintenance. Some years ago, one of the major auto manufacturers built a car that required the partial removal of the engine to change its spark plugs! Though defying common sense, these accessibility problems can and do happen, and building design and equipment location are not exempt. While it is tempting to squeeze mechanical space to reduce building costs, the result can be a near disaster for future maintenance. Maintenance staff may forget equipment located in remote areas with difficult access, either accidentally or deliberately. Burying equipment in difficult-to-access locations also can mean that the equipment is placed in areas where heat buildup can be a real problem, resulting in inefficient operation and premature failure.

Systems

The types of systems found in a building will clearly affect facility management needs. Older buildings with steam heating systems need experts who specialize in this type of equipment maintenance. Local codes may even require such buildings to have on-site boiler operators. Newer facilities often use hot water for heat distribution, reducing the need for maintenance in general and eliminating the need for boiler operators altogether.

To provide guests the option of regulating heating and cooling of their guestrooms and to avoid using through-the-wall packaged room units, many hotels choose centralized (fan-coil) heating, ventilation, and air conditioning (**HVAC**) units for guestrooms. In contrast with packaged units, centralized units have a large amount of additional equipment besides what is in the guestroom, but, from a cost-to-operate perspective, can be more efficient. Constituting these units are boilers, chillers, cooling towers, pumps, and a variety of control devices. All of these components will need specialized maintenance and will incur costs consistent with that level of maintenance expertise.

Systems installed in modern buildings can be quite complex. Computers often must interpret input from a number of sensors in order to control the operation of various pieces of equipment. In addition, the systems are themselves integrated, with the operation of one having an influence on the other. For example, a building fire control system and a building HVAC system may both want to control the operation of certain pieces of equipment, while the building energy management system may want to turn this equipment off.

Systems such as cable or satellite TV and Wi-Fi, and the addition of increasingly sophisticated entertainment venues within casino hotels and other facilities have increased facilities-related system needs. This trend is certain to continue. Today the demand for wireless connections for Internet access and the increasingly sophisticated locking and control technology for guestroom security are broadening the sphere of maintenance knowledge and activity. Landscaping features using precision-controlled (computerized) fountains and lights are increasingly being used. What the future may see in terms of new systems in buildings, and the maintenance implications of these new systems, could truly redefine the skills set of today's facilities engineer. (Imagine the buildings and other systems necessary to launch the much-discussed era of Space Tourism!)

Building System Design—The Oversizing Problem. The designers of building systems are concerned about many issues as they design the systems. Building and safety codes must be met. Owner and franchise standards need to be complied with. Aesthetic and architectural issues arise. And, obviously, the building system needs to fulfill its purpose. In the instance of HVAC systems, this means that they heat, cool, ventilate, and generally operate in a manner that provides comfort for the building's occupants. Ideally, this is done in a cost-effective manner in terms of initial development costs and operating costs. Unfortunately, this is not always the case. Building systems have at times been drastically oversized, resulting in excessive initial costs and high operating expenses. A modification to a hotel constructed in California in 1988 illustrates the oversizing issue.

This 253-room hotel in Southern California was initially designed with two 350-ton chillers, two sixty-horsepower chilled water pumps, two twenty-five-horsepower condenser water pumps, and two twenty-five-horsepower cooling towers. (It is common practice to design systems with two or more of each component to provide backup and allow for maintenance.) An energy study done in 2001 indicated that the system operated at less than 50 percent of the rated capacity almost 90 percent of the time, and the highest load on the system was only 71 percent of the capacity of one of the chillers! This would be similar to building a hotel that operated at no more than 36 percent occupancy. The owner had designed and purchased a system that was significantly oversized. A new system was installed that reduced chiller size to 185 tons, the chilled water pumps to ten horsepower, the condenser pumps to ten horsepower, and the cooling tower fans to 7.5 horsepower. The new smaller (and more efficient) equipment and controls resulted in a 68 percent reduction in energy usage, yielding savings of approximately $150,000 a year.[12]

Why was the initial design so oversized? We don't know specifically for this hotel, but we can provide some insight into how this occurs in general. First, in the interest of being sure to meet the expected loads (and future load growth) and to compensate for potential deterioration in performance, systems are generally somewhat oversized. Second, when building a new building, owners often don't want to pay for computer modeling of the building to estimate appropriate equipment size. Third, oversized systems may result from the use of "rule of thumb" designs that may be overly conservative or are just a copy of the design used on the last project. Finally, compensation for designers is sometimes based on a percentage of the system cost, resulting in a direct financial incentive to design bigger systems. Owners would be well-served to request further analysis of proposed systems and encourage (and reward) designers who can provide more optimal designs.

Management's Responsibilities

The management of facilities is not the responsibility of just the building engineer/facilities manager. While this person has budgetary responsibility for utility, POM, and often CapEx funds, these funds are really spent to provide services for guests and for all of the departments in the operation, not just the facilities department. Everyone at the property in varying degrees has responsibilities for properly using and maintaining the facilities. Since all staff members and departments are involved with facilities to some degree, understanding the responsibilities and priorities of facilities management is a shared need.

We can think of the responsibility of facilities management as involving five major areas:

- Safety and security
- Legal and regulatory compliance
- Service
- Cost control

- Asset management

"Safety is always the first concern; legality is tied for second with customer service."[13] The responsibilities of facilities managers with regard to safety and security are numerous. Facilities staff are often responsible for the proper operation of building systems installed specifically to provide a safe and secure environment. These include fire protection systems, water purification and treatment systems, and locking and security systems. In addition, proper repair and operation of a variety of building equipment and systems are required to ensure safety. Examples include such items as ensuring furniture is in good repair and that no electrical shorts exist in lamps and around pool areas. Safety and security also involve the standards, methods, and procedures used to maintain and care for the facility. Facilities employees need to safely conduct their work, following procedures that do not endanger themselves or others. With ongoing renovation at many properties, the safety of guests and staff members within renovation "construction zones" is also an important consideration.

Legal compliance includes attention to local building codes, health department regulations, emissions and environmental requirements (including such items as mandatory recycling), and such issues as Americans with Disabilities Act mandates. The need for legal and regulatory compliance is driven not only out of a need to comply with laws at a variety of levels but also by contracts entered into by the property. To remain valid, equipment warranties may mandate certain maintenance requirements. Management contracts and franchise agreements may also require specific levels of maintenance and refurbishment. Agreements with tour providers may stipulate certain levels of maintenance, environmental performance, and availability of amenities and services.

By design and in practice, the facilities department is a service operation. Facilities staff members provide services to guests, to other departments, and—directly and indirectly—to the owner of the building. The level of maintenance and care of the facility should contribute positively to the guests' experience. There are numerous ways in which a well-maintained facility can contribute in a positive manner, and possibly even more ways in which a poorly maintained facility can create a negative experience. More often than not, guests make their comments about the facility to employees of other hotel departments other than the facilities department. The impact of the facilities department is felt throughout the operation and can boost or impair productivity and quality in other departments. Properly operating equipment allows staff in departments such as housekeeping, food service, and laundry to perform their tasks quickly and efficiently. Finally, the efforts of the facilities staff in caring for the overall physical plant provide an important asset management and protection service to the building's owner. Facilities professionals represent the long-term interests of the owner by preserving his or her investment and contributing to the monetary appreciation of the building.

Cost control has high priority in the activities of the facilities department; at times, it is top priority. Costs over which the facilities manager can exercise some control are utilities (fuel, electricity, water, and related items), maintenance and operations (including labor, materials, and contracts), and capital expenditures—including furniture, fixtures, and equipment (**FF&E**) and major building equipment and systems replacement. Controlling the costs of each major category requires attention to various issues that can, at times, conflict. For example, if an operation focuses too intensely on the control of capital expenses, there may be a rise in maintenance expenses because of the need to constantly repair aging equipment and systems.

The asset management role of the facilities engineer is one in support of the broader asset management role of today's professional asset manager:

> One of the asset manager's primary responsibilities is the protection of the asset. Failure of the manager or prior owner to maintain the physical plant of the hotel adequately may—and most likely *will*—result in the need to replace key systems and components well before the end of the assets' normal lifespan. Even in the smallest hotel, HVAC (heating, ventilating, and air conditioning) units and fire alarm systems are very costly items. It is the asset manager's responsibility to understand the condition of the critical systems in the hotel and to know which systems will require repair or replacement and the cost to do so.[14]

The facilities manager needs to protect the hotel's physical asset in daily operations via the processes of maintenance and repair, as well as provide information and direction for the development of the capital plans for the facility. A facilities manager who thinks like an asset manager is a valuable asset to any hotel operation and a valued "asset manager" for the building's owner.

Finally, the management contracts and franchise agreements that characterize so much of today's lodging and food service environment often hold managers responsible for providing certain levels of facility maintenance. Let's look at this issue in more detail.

Management Contracts and Franchise Agreements

Management contracts may require management to fund reserves for future maintenance and repair needs, to solicit the owner's approval before making building-related expenditures, and to report to the owner regarding how funds are used. A requirement that the operator fund reserves for replacement of FF&E is a common provision of management contracts. Less common are reserves established for non-FF&E repairs. Exhibit 3 presents two sample clauses.

In the 1990s, management contracts underwent some significant changes, as owners were able to garner more control. These changes, as described in Exhibit 4, brought **replacement reserves** more in line with actual expenditures and required operators to analyze and document proposed expenditures.

Under the terms of most management contracts, the operator generally needs the owner's approval to spend the reserves. Getting this approval can be a difficult point of negotiation when the operator and the owner disagree over whether a certain expenditure should come from the POM budget, the reserve account, or the owner's capital. If the expenditure is categorized as a POM item, it will decrease income before fixed charges (or some other profit line) and may therefore decrease the management fee (if the management fee is based on financial performance rather than a flat fee). On the other hand, if the expenditure is categorized as a capital or reserve item, income before fixed charges is not affected and the man-

Exhibit 3   Sample Management Contract Clauses

1. **Reserve for Replacement of Furniture, Fixtures, and Equipment**

   Owner shall establish and maintain a separate account to be known as "Reserves for Capital Improvements and Replacements of and Additions to Furniture, Fixtures, and Equipment," for use solely for capital improvements and replacement of, and additions to, furniture and equipment so as to maintain the Hotel in a first-class condition.

2. **Reserve for Structural Repairs**

   Operator shall establish, in respect of each Fiscal Year during the term of this Agreement, a reserve cash amount from which shall be drawn funds for structural or extraordinary equipment repairs, replacement, or maintenance at the discretion of Owner. During each Fiscal Year of the Agreement, funds shall be transferred into the Structural Component Reserve in accordance with the following percentages: (a) None (0%) for all Fiscal Years through and including the Fiscal Year in which the Renovation Program is completed; and (b) One half of one percent (0.5%) in each full Fiscal Year thereafter.

Source: Stephen Rushmore, *Hotel Investments—A Guide for Leaders and Owners* (Boston: Warren Gorman & Lamont, 1990), pp. A3–10, A3–12.

agement fee will be higher. This is a financial basis for debate and potential conflict between owners and management.

Similar disagreement can occur regarding contract services, which are also covered in management contracts. Issuing contracts for "emergency" services may become a point of friction when operators and owners have different definitions of what constitutes an emergency. For example, the owner and operator may disagree over whether a given amount of flooding in the building should be handled by current staff or treated as an emergency calling for contract service.

The management contract will generally contain provisions specifically assigning responsibility for the operator to perform needed repairs, replacements, and improvements. These clauses may contain limitations based on dollar amounts or a percentage of revenue, may contain provisions for owner approval of expenditures, and may allow the owner the option of performing the work using outside contractors. The contract may also specify guidelines for determining whether the expenditure will be considered a POM, reserve, or capital item.

Negotiating and interpreting these clauses is a challenging task. As operating margins tighten, owners become more reluctant to authorize capital expenditures and may even question repair and maintenance expenditures. Conflict results, especially when the pressure on economic performance is caused by the entry of new or renovated facilities into the marketplace. These problems can have major effects on the condition of the physical plant and on the options available to meet perceived needs.[15]

Franchise agreements also establish important requirements for property operation and maintenance. Most franchisors require that facilities be developed

Exhibit 4   The Funding of Reserves

The basis for funding replacement reserves for furniture, fixtures, and equipment has generally increased in recent years to better match actual expenditures. Most contracts base the initial calculation of annual reserve amounts on at least three percent of gross revenues. The base is stepped up to five percent after the first several years of operation. The issue of whether the owner funds all or a partial amount of the reserve remains a topic of strenuous negotiation. Owners want the reserve funds to be on call, while operators want all or a significant portion of the funds to be placed in escrow. Often a management-discretion slush fund is established for minor expenditures for operators to use without obtaining owner approval.

Owners frequently require approval of competitive bids on all reserve-for-replacement requests and cost-benefit analyses on major expenditures over a negotiated amount. Since significant owner-operator differences can exist in classifying expenditures as repairs and maintenance on one hand or as capital expenditures on the other, recently negotiated contracts often contain appendices describing in detail what types of expenditures are to be classified in each of the two categories—with the arbitrator making the decision for items contested or not included.

Owners and operators both are negotiating for additional capital expenditure budgets separate from the reserve-for-replacement. The funding base for such capital-expenditure budgets is usually one to two percent of gross revenues. Operators seeking to spend those budgets are required to submit cost-benefit analyses for owners' approval or disapproval. Operators have the right to expend funds without owners' approval in emergencies and for situations involving health, safety, licensure, law, or brand compliance.

Many owners require that operators submit three- to five-year plans for replacement and capital improvement with the annual budgets. These plans permit the owner and the operator to focus on the upcoming year's priorities, which often compete and change during the year. The two parties agree in general terms to the expenditures at the beginning of the year, but before the expenditure is made the operator submits actual bids with supporting documentation for the owner's approval.

Source: James J. Eyster, "Hotel Management Contracts in the U.S.," *Cornell Hotel and Restaurant Administration Quarterly,* June 1997, p. 30.

and operated in accordance with the franchisors' operating manuals. These manuals establish minimum standards and requirements for constructing, equipping, furnishing, supplying, operating, maintaining, and marketing the establishment. Exhibit 5 presents sample phrasing that might be used in a franchise agreement regarding these duties.

Responsibilities of the Facilities Department

A complete discussion of the responsibilities of the facilities department in hotels can be quite involved. The following discussion briefly illustrates the potential

Exhibit 5   Sample Franchise Agreement Clause

Licensee's Duties

Operate, furnish, maintain, and equip the hotel and related facilities in a first-class manner in accordance with the provisions of this Agreement and the Operating Manual, in conformity to the high service, moral, and ethical standards of the System, and in compliance with all local, state, and federal laws, customs, and regulations, including, without limiting the generality of the foregoing, maintaining and conducting its business in accordance with sound business and financial practice.

scope of duties and responsibilities of the facilities staff. Not all operations require all of these responsibilities to be covered, and in some instances, the responsibility may be given to some other department rather than the facilities department. For large hotel corporations, the duties described below may be handled by corporate departments at various times as well.

Systems and Building Design. It is highly beneficial to have the facilities manager for a new facility provide input regarding building systems and building design from a facilities perspective. This will help to ensure that the facility has been designed with maintenance and operating costs in mind and that the facilities manager is as knowledgeable as possible about the systems and components of the building.

Systems and Building Commissioning. When the actual construction work on the building or system is complete, a commissioning and startup process should be implemented. Commissioning is the "quality assurance facet of systems installation. It is a process for achieving, verifying, and documenting the performance of each system to meet the operational needs of the building, within the capability of the documented design and specified equipment capacities, according to the owner's functional criteria. It is a process that ensures the quality of the installation."[16] Typical of the elements of commissioning HVAC and water systems is what is referred to as **TAB**—testing, adjusting, and balancing.

There has recently been interest in the use of retrocommissioning (RCx) in buildings. The RCx (sometimes called recommissioning) process involves many steps similar to the commissioning process but is applied to a building years after it is constructed. Major lodging companies such as InterContinental and Marriott have noted the value of retrocommissioning for their large hotels.[17] Improvements in building operations as well as significant costs savings are often benefits of the RCx process.[18]

Building and System Operations. Building and system operations are the day-to-day activities that ensure the building and its systems continue to operate as intended and provide needed services. To the operators of the facility, this means attention to details, such as proper operation of doors and locks, resetting circuit breakers when appropriate, making sure meeting room schedules are entered into the building management computer system, and a host of other seemingly small but meaningful activities. In the best circumstances, these activities are transparent—everything is working when it should and it becomes invisible to those receiving the resulting service.

Building Maintenance. The building structure and components are a significant investment and serve as the first line of protection for the building's occupants and contents. Facilities staff need to pay attention to the building structures' needs. Elements such as roofing, exterior surfaces, windows, driveways and parking areas, and steps all require regular inspection, maintenance, and other care. The building's exterior is the first image guests are exposed to; its appearance has a strong influence on their impression of the operation.

Guestroom, Furnishings, and Fixtures Maintenance. The importance of the guestroom, its physical condition, and the proper operation of the equipment serving it cannot be overstated. Regular guestroom preventive maintenance three to four times a year is a signature responsibility of the facilities department that helps make the guest experience a positive one.

Equipment Maintenance and Repair. Property facilities contain a vast and varied amount of equipment whose proper operation requires maintenance and repair by facilities staff or by suppliers contracted by the facilities department. Also, facilities staff members are often responsible for the maintenance and repair of equipment used in or by other departments, such as housekeeping, laundry, and food and beverage.

Equipment Selection and Installation. The equipment operated in hospitality operations changes over time. As new food service, laundry, and other equipment is acquired, it is important that facilities staff be involved in its selection and installation. Facilities staff involvement helps ensure that the equipment is suitable, that its installation can be accomplished cost-effectively, and that its ongoing maintenance can be performed efficiently and in a cost-effective manner.

Contract Management. A host of facilities services are provided by outside contractors. Managing the contracts and contractors for these services is important if costs are to be controlled and the necessary services provided. Facilities managers are central to providing contractor oversight and coordinating and negotiating contract responsibilities.

Utilities Management. The task of utilities management is one of growing complexity and growing opportunities for cost savings. Facilities professionals are increasingly finding they have a broader field of utility service vendors from which to choose. Evaluating the cost, dependability, and service levels of each utility vendor calls for even more managerial decisions than before. Moreover, decisions need to be made about how to control costs of services once they are purchased. For water in particular, some utilities managers may find they have potential curtailment or shortage issues to contend with, which may also involve regulatory restrictions with significant cost penalties for over-consumption. Finally, with utilities management now a key component of the growing environmental/sustainability arena, compliance, conservation, and communication become priority issues for facilities staff and management.

Waste Management. The facilities department usually is charged with the task of managing waste; its cost is usually in the facilities budget, facilities staff are knowledgeable about the regulatory environment, and facilities professionals have traditionally taken on this task, sometimes even viewing it as a way to reduce the operation's environmental impact.

Budgeting and Cost Control. Facilities professionals must be able to plan and budget for their financial needs (utilities, POM, and CapEx), properly explain and justify these needs, and control the expenditures in all areas under their purview. With 15 to 20 percent of property revenue budgeted for these categories, proper management skills are clearly needed.

Security and Safety. The contributions of the facilities department involving security and safety are twofold. First, the facilities department must be sure its own staff members are working in a safe manner. Second, facilities staff must do all that is appropriate to ensure a safe and secure environment for other employees and for guests. These responsibilities can range from attention to the building and grounds to the proper operation of security and locking systems.

Contractual and Regulatory Compliance. Many elements of facilities operations come under regulatory oversight. Examples include fire codes, building codes, sanitary codes, and environmental regulations. In addition, franchise agreements and management contracts—along with contracts with customers—have elements requiring action on the part of the facilities department involving the facility.

Parts Inventory and Control. The potentially large number of specialized parts and equipment needed for facilities operations requires that inventory be adequately controlled. Because much of this inventory is also usable outside the building, control of inventory is needed to prevent theft as well as to ensure that parts and materials are available when needed.

Modifications, Additions, and Renovations. Almost immediately upon opening a property, there begins an unending process of modification, addition, and renovation. These activities can range from a minor installation of a bookshelf to the addition of a new guestroom tower. The involvement of the facilities department is critical. Since adequate service to guests and other departments cannot be jeopardized, maintaining high safety levels and controlling costs during these activities are a major concern of the facilities staff.

Special Projects. Special projects include "unexpected" tasks that fall to facilities staff and those tasks that meet unique guest demands and needs. Building custom facilities for performances and special events, configuring lighting and sound systems, creating special effects, and a host of other unique demands not only provide the opportunity for facilities staff members to be resourceful and creative, but generate new streams of revenue for the property.

Staff Training. The continued education and training of departmental staff is essential to orient new employees and enable veterans to learn emerging and changing technologies. Local technical institutions and vendors may offer training services that help facilities staff to update their skills consistent with advances in technology. Another important source for upgrading skills is internal training, in which property-specific and general-awareness issues—such as OSHA requirements—can be addressed.

Emergency Planning and Response. Because of their knowledge of the facility and its systems, facilities staff members play leadership roles in the property-level emergency planning and response effort. Facilities employees are often key members of emergency response teams as well. If a catastrophe results in damage to the facility, the staff must be prepared to secure the facility from further damage and know the steps to take to restore the facility to operation.

Corporate Reporting. Documenting the activities of the facilities department is important to the success of the operation, as it provides a living history of facilities-related events. Facilities staff members will have requirements for corporate reporting and measurement via benchmarking, based on their efforts to keep the facility operating regardless of systems, environmental, or natural problems.

Staff will also be called upon to gather and report specific additional information on facility maintenance, repair, and restoration and on compliance with internal and governmental requirements. These reports serve as the basis not only for recording system and facility breakdowns and slowdowns, but as repair and restoration guides for future reference in similar circumstances. Records of maintenance actions and emergency planning and response may also be needed in legal cases.

Facilities Managers in Lodging Operations

Individuals in charge of the lodging facility may have one of a variety of titles such as Director of Engineering, Chief Engineer, Director of Property Operations, or Director of Facilities. Their responsibilities vary as well. Small economy lodging operations have Directors of Engineering (DOE) who do much of the work themselves and require more technical than managerial skills. At larger properties and those with more elegant interiors, the DOE is much more of a manager, controlling a large budget and staff and working to accommodate more complicated demands.

Facilities managers in lodging operations generally do not oversee housekeeping activities. They are also unlikely to oversee security, except at small properties. However, in the world of other commercial buildings, housekeeping and security often report to the facility manager. The separation of these activities in lodging is not universal; some operations have initiated a management structure that has engineering and housekeeping reporting to a Director of Facilities staff person, though this is unusual.

Lodging facilities managers are likely to have some technical background generated in military service, contracting firms, or trade and technical schools. Managerial skill development is largely on-the-job or derived from in-house management seminars. Most U.S. property-level managers do not hold four-year engineering or technical degrees, having gained much of their knowledge through experience. However, in countries outside the United States it is not unusual for the facilities manager to be a graduate of a college engineering program. Exhibit 6 summarizes the skills typically expected from a facilities manager or director.

The salaries of lodging facilities managers (chief engineers) are on the lower end compared with other members of the executive committee of the property. However, as the quality level of the property increases, the relative salary of the chief engineer improves as well. This is perhaps reflective of the more significant role that facilities departments play and the more significant responsibilities they have in higher-end operations.

Facilities staffing varies with the age of the property, services offered, types of systems, commitment to in-house versus contract services, and a host of other factors. Staffing levels of 2.5 to 4 facilities staff members per 100 rooms covers the likely range. However, luxury and first-class operations with large rooms and suites and extensive grounds can have significantly more facilities staff members.

Exhibit 6   Summary of a Facilities Director's Position and Required Skills

Scope of Position

Manages and coordinates the work of skilled engineering staff, placing particular emphasis on guest satisfaction and maintaining the property in good working condition.

Position is responsible for supervising, managing, and overseeing the following departments:

- Maintenance
- Engineering
- Security

Position Requirements

Technical

Current on all safety and sanitation policies and procedures that affect the property.

Familiar with chillers, cooling towers, chemical treatments, pneumatics, control systems, water systems, boilers, refrigeration, compressors, etc.

Strong energy management background.

Strong technical skills in HVAC, electrical, mechanical, plumbing, carpentry, etc.

Managerial

Participative management style.

Instill a "can do" attitude in employees.

Use a "hands-on" approach to management.

Demonstrate ability to lead by example.

Ability to sell concepts and ideas to management, peers, and employees.

Instill a guest service attitude in all employees.

Clear, concise written and oral communication skills.

Conclusion

One goal of this chapter has been to drive home the importance of facilities in the hospitality industry. Some of the material about facilities is a bit technical, but then, the industry is increasingly so—just look behind the front desk at most hotels! The manager who wants to control costs, create value for owners and stockholders, and have high departmental efficiency and productivity, happy guests, and a safe and secure operation should find this material helpful. The manager who lacks these concerns should probably look for another line of work. The services provided by a properly funded and well-run facilities department are of significant value to a hospitality property. When it comes to facilities maintenance, you can pay now or pay more later.

Endnotes

1. Molly W. Berger, "The Old High-Tech Hotel," *Invention & Technology*, Fall 1995, p. 46.

2. Cheryl E. Kimes, "How Product Quality Drives Profitability—The Experience at Holiday Inn," *Cornell Hotel and Restaurant Administration Quarterly*, June 2001, pp. 25–28.

3. If the 1990–1993 figures in this paragraph were brought up to date, the RevPAR reduction would be $4.74 and the annual revenue shortfall $338,500. Hotels with that kind of performance usually close, get sold, or otherwise "move on." Maintenance matters!

4. *Caribbean Trends in the Hotel Industry, 2013*. PKF Consulting/Hospitality Research, Atlanta, Georgia.

5. Peggy Berg and Mark Skinner, "CapEx: Do You Spend Enough?" *Lodging Hospitality*, April 1995, p. 48.

6. Peggy Berg and Tom French, "CapEx in the '90s," *Lodging*, April 1995, p. 103.

7. A detailed look at the cost of CapEx can be found in the *Hotel Cost Estimating Guide, 2011*, JN+A & HVS Design. http://www.hotelnewsresource.com/pdf11/Hotel_ Cost_ Estimating_Guide_2011.pdf.

8. Russell Kett, Managing Director of HVS International (London), quoted in Howard J. Wolfe, "Maximizing the Top and Bottom Line by Design," *Hotels Investment Outlook*, September 1999, p. 68.

9. http://ethics.tamu.edu/ethics/hyatt/hyatt1.htm and Gregory P. Luth, "Chronology and Context of the Hyatt Regency Collapse," *Journal of Performance of Constructed Facilities* (May 2000): 51–61.

10. A source for information on equipment lifetime is the ASHRAE:HVAC Service Life Database; http://xp20.ashrae.org/publicdatabase/service_life.asp.

11. http://www.business-case-analysis.com/total-cost-of-ownership.html.

12. Kent W. Peterson, "Primary-Flow: Chilled-Water-Plant Conversion," *Heating/Piping/ Air Conditioning* (March 2004): S10–S15.

13. David G. Cotts, *The Facility Management Handbook*, 2nd Ed. (New York: AMACON, 1998), p. 10.

14. John C. Boettger, "Creating the Asset Management Plan," in Paul Beals and Greg Denton, eds., *Hotel Asset Management: Principles and Practices* (Lansing, Mich.: American Hotel & Lodging Educational Institute, 2004), p. 36.

15. Further information on management contracts may be found in James J. Eyster and Jan A. DeRoos, *The Negotiation and Administration of Hotel and Restaurant Management Contracts*, 4th ed., (Ithaca, N.Y.: Cornell University, 2009).

16. ASHRAE, 1999 *ASHRAE Applications Handbook*, 1999, Chapter 41.

17. An example of the view of Marriott on this topic can be found at http://www.facilitiesnet.com/facilitiesmanagement/article/Commission-to-Maximize-Efficiency—8964. A perspective by an Inter-Continental facilities manager can be found at http://www.facilitiesnet.com/maintenancesolutionsroundtables/ article/Managers-Share-Experiences-With-Retrocommissioning--13896.

18. A useful publication regarding retrocommissioning is *A Retrocommissioning Guide for Building Owners*. The publication was developed by Portland Energy Conservation with funding from the United States Environmental Protection Agency; http://www.peci.org/sites/default/files/epaguide_0.pdf.

🔑 Key Terms

ADA—Americans with Disabilities Act. U.S. federal legislation enacted in the early 1990s mandating that owners and operators of public facilities provide certain accommodations for individuals with disabilities as specified in the legislation.

CapEx—Short for "capital expenditure." A major expenditure category in the hospitality industry covering replacement of worn-out furniture, finishes, and soft goods; wear and tear; obsolescence; regulatory requirements such as ADA and life safety; franchise product demands; changing technology; market demand for product change; and replacement and renovations of building components and heavy equipment.

facilities management companies—Companies with the expertise to provide services such as housekeeping, grounds, and physical plant management to hospitality companies, schools, universities, and various industries.

FF&E—Furniture, fixtures, and equipment; a major portion of CapEx.

franchise agreement—An agreement under which one entity that has developed a particular pattern or format for doing business—the franchisor—grants to another entity—the franchisee—the right to conduct such a business provided it follows the established pattern.

HVAC—An abbreviation for "heating, ventilation, and air conditioning." HVAC is the general term applied to a property's temperature management system. It includes heat and refrigerated air systems and attendant ductwork, airflow machinery, and control devices.

management contract—An agreement between the owner/developer of a property and a professional hotel management company. The owner/developer usually retains the financial and legal responsibility for the property, and the management company receives an agreed-upon fee for operating the facility.

POM—An abbreviation for "property operation and maintenance." One of two principal cost entries (along with utilities) in the hospitality industry detailing ongoing costs of operation following construction of the facility.

replacement reserves—Cash reserves set aside largely for maintenance and repair needs (the amount set aside is usually based on a percentage of gross revenues). Management contracts commonly require that operators fund replacement reserves for FF&E.

TAB—An abbreviation for "testing, adjusting, and balancing." In the building commissioning process, TAB is one of the verification elements that ensures the quality of the installation of systems in the facility (for example, the HVAC and water systems).

Review Questions

1. What are the roles fulfilled by facilities in the hospitality industry?

2. What are the three major categories of costs of hospitality facilities? Which of these are the responsibility of the hospitality facilities manager? Of the costs that are the responsibility of the facilities manager, which one is most variable? Why?

3. What are some advantages of gathering utility and POM data on a per-room basis? What are some disadvantages?

4. How might knowledge of equipment lifetimes affect maintenance decisions?

5. What are management's general responsibilities with regard to the maintenance function? Why is knowledge of the facility important for all managers?

6. Why is there sometimes a question over whether to allocate an expense to the POM, reserve for replacement, or capital account? When are such questions likely to arise?

Internet Sites

For more information, visit the following Internet sites. Remember that Internet addresses can change without notice. If the site is no longer there, you can use a search engine to look for additional sites.

Association of Higher Education Facilities Officers
www.appa.com

Building Owners and Managers Association
www.boma.org

Chartered Institute of Building Services Engineers—UK
www.cibse.org

Facilities Net
www.facilitiesnet.com

FMLINK
www.fmlink.com

Institute of Real Estate Management
www.irem.org

International Facilities Management Association
www.ifma.com

Today's Facility Manager
www.todaysfacilitymanager.com

Tradeline
www.tradelineinc.com

$\mathcal{O}$ Case Study

Drifting Toward the Storm

Ray Misnick was upset with himself. As the GM of a 600-room hotel, he should have known that a hotel's physical plant doesn't take care of itself. Hadn't his father always told him that? His father had owned and operated a little mom-and-pop hotel many years ago; Ray worked there during the summer while he was going through high school and college. Ray could still remember his father holding up six fingers and saying, "Your hotel takes in six dollars—" and he'd pause to start wiggling one finger before continuing—"you've got to spend this one dollar to heat it, light it, and keep it up! You may not want to spend it, but you've got to. If you don't, sooner or later you're going to run into some stormy weather."

That's exactly what had happened to Ray, except that, instead of scrimping on the funds to keep his hotel up, he had scrimped on the money necessary to *manage* the hotel's facilities. And now he was facing the consequences.

It all started eleven months ago when his director of engineering got a promotion and moved on to another hotel in the chain. That was $100,000 in salary and benefits that dropped off the payroll, so Ray thought he'd take his time hiring another director. Maybe the assistant director, Tim Francisco, could keep the hotel running. If Tim passed the test, then Ray could forget about hiring a new director of engineering and the hotel could save that money year after year.

At first, the plan seemed to be working. Tim scheduled the engineering department's employees like he'd always done, and he kept the day-to-day work orders, purchase orders, and other routine paperwork flowing smoothly. Maintenance calls were taken care of in the manner that they'd always been taken care of. That was all to the good.

But other engineering department issues began to surface. For example, several times since the director of engineering had left, Ray had gotten a call from the hotel's controller: "What's going on with engineering? Expenses are way under budget for the month." Ray would call Tim, who would say, "Oh, sorry—I've got some invoices down here that I haven't turned in yet." "Some" usually turned out to be a stack an inch thick. Guest satisfaction scores started trending downward, primarily in categories related to the hotel's facilities. Utility costs were trending upward—Ray wasn't sure why, and, unfortunately, neither was Tim. Just last month, the hotel had been fined by the city Building Department because the city's inspector certificates in the hotel's elevators had expired. Last but not least, during the budget meeting for putting next year's budget together, Tim had some good comments to make about the maintenance budget, but he had no suggestions for the hotel's capital expenditures plan. That had made Ray a little uneasy; the year before, the director of engineering had had a whole laundry list of engineering items he wanted to spend money on.

All of these issues had made Ray begin to reassess whether going without a director of engineering was such a good idea after all, but yesterday was the final straw that pushed him to the conclusion that something had to be done. Yesterday morning, a grease fire had broken out in the kitchen, causing the dry chemical fire suppression system to go off. Fortunately, the fire was put out quickly, but there was a huge mess in the kitchen. Coarse white powder was everywhere, and the kitchen had to be shut down while the cleanup was underway, so thousands of dollars of dining room and room service sales were lost. The fire department responded to the fire and slapped the hotel with a code violation, because the hood over the kitchen ranges had not been cleaned during the last six months—Tim had let the maintenance contract expire. While they were at the hotel, fire department personnel checked other elements of the building's fire safety system and discovered that other fire safety maintenance and testing activities had not been performed. More violations, more fines.

So yesterday, the alarm bells had gone off literally for Ray. It was past time for him to hire a new director of engineering. It wasn't that Tim wasn't a good employee—he had done a good job of keeping up with the engineering department's day-to-day tasks. But now Ray realized that there were a lot of other engineering duties and responsibilities associated with operating a 600-room facility properly. Without a director of engineering, the hotel was encountering costs and problems that could have been avoided if Ray had not been so intent on saving the salary costs of the director of engineering position. Dad was right, Ray thought ruefully; you have to spend that dollar.

Ray visited the HR department and picked up the job description for the director of engineering position. Reviewing it back in his office, Ray thought the job description was incomplete, so he decided to update it. Also, it might not be a bad idea to write down some interview questions in advance, he thought. If he was going to spend the money to hire someone, he wanted to make sure he found just the right candidate for the job.

Discussion Questions

1. What should Ray include in his job description for the director of engineering position?

2. What types of questions should be covered when Ray interviews job candidates?

3. How would the interview questions change if the property was much larger than Ray's 600-room property? much smaller?

4. In addition to Ray, who should be involved in the interview process? What are their likely concerns?

Case Number: 2811CA

The following industry experts helped generate and develop this case: Richard Manzolina, Director of Property Operations, Capital Hilton, Washington, D.C.; Ed Pietzak, RPA, FMA, CEOE, Director of Engineering, New York Marriott Marquis, New York, New York; and David M. Stipanuk, Associate Professor, School of Hotel Administration, Cornell University, Ithaca, New York.

Chapter 2 Outline

Facilities Maintenance and Repair
Maintenance Management Systems
    Contract Services and Outsourcing
Computerized and Internet-Based Facilities
    Management
Budgeting for POM and Utilities
Contract Services, Responsibility
    Accounting, and Facilities Costs
Capital Expenditure (CapEx) Management
Facilities Benchmarking
Personnel Management in Facilities
Training and Certification
    Building Certification

Competencies

1. Describe several types of maintenance. (pp. 33–36)

2. Discuss maintenance management systems, identify and explain the function of several important forms and documents typically used in a maintenance management system, and summarize tactics for dealing with maintenance emergencies. (pp. 36–49)

3. Discuss contract services and outsourcing. (pp. 49–52)

4. Describe computerized and Internet-based facilities management. (pp. 52–53)

5. Explain basic elements of budgeting for POM and utility costs, and discuss accounting strategies for dealing with other facilities costs. (pp. 53–59)

6. Describe the role of the facilities department in capital projects and renovations, and explain facilities benchmarking. (pp. 59–63)

7. Outline several considerations involved in managing personnel issues in the facilities department, summarize training and certification opportunities for facilities personnel, and discuss building certification. (pp. 63–66)

Hospitality Facilities Management Tools, Techniques, and Trends

The ideal [engineer] is he who sees further than the mere production of power—who also follows it to the logical conclusion: satisfactory service to the guest at the lowest possible costs to the management. The engineer to succeed must be able to work with department heads and employees in departments that consume the products he manufactures. They must be impressed with the necessity for the engineer and his associates.

Next to the manager I believe the engineer can serve as the most valuable man in the organization of a hotel that has a complete modern plant. The engineer in such an organization should be responsible for the physical upkeep of the house. Under his direction should be the electricians, plumbers, carpenters, decorators, masons, machinists, telephone men, laundry superintendent, silversmiths, and all engine room employees. He should be responsible for the inspection and maintenance of every piece of mechanical equipment in the house.

And it should be possible for him to requisition for whatever he needs in his department. His department should operate on a carefully prepared budget. He should at all times receive reports from the accounting department so that he will know where he stands.

One of the greatest weaknesses in the American hotel system is the manager's failure to work more closely with the man who is responsible for the "Heart of the House." In order to do so it is not necessary that he know all there is to know about different types of heating systems, refrigerating units, and ventilators. But he can learn the highlights about these in a few hours of study.

An engineer does not expect a manager to know as much about engineering as he does, but he appreciates a sympathetic interest in his problems—which after all are the manager's problems as well.

—*Gaston Lauryssen, 1929*[1]

WHETHER IT IS 1929 or today, "satisfactory service to the guest at the lowest possible cost" and being "able to work with department heads and employees in departments that consume the products he manufactures" remain key aspects of the facility manager's goals. Achieving them requires the use of the correct managerial and physical tools and techniques, as well as continued attention to relevant trends and opportunities. In this chapter, we will discuss the management of the facilities function, focusing on types of maintenance, maintenance management systems, budgeting, and personnel management. Our goal is that you, as a person applying "a few hours of study," will develop an understanding and appreciation of the management of operations within the "Heart of the House."[2]

Facilities Maintenance and Repair

A significant portion of the property operation and maintenance (POM) budget is consumed by maintenance and repair demands. Maintenance activities are those done to keep something in an existing state or to preserve something from failure or decline. Repair activities are those that restore something by replacing a part or putting together what is torn or broken. There is intrinsic value in functioning in a maintenance mode rather than in a repair mode. Using an appropriate mix of maintenance methods and capital expenditures is a sound approach to keeping repair to a minimum. But when repair is needed, the skills, parts, and even time should be available to allow the repair to be done in the most efficient manner, on time and within budget.

The types of maintenance at any property can be grouped under a variety of labels. One possible grouping classifies maintenance types as routine, preventive, guestroom, scheduled, predictive, reactive (emergency/breakdown), and contract.

Routine maintenance is that which pertains to the general upkeep of the property, recurs on a regular basis, and requires relatively minimal skill or training to perform. Activities such as grass cutting, leaf raking, and snow shoveling are in this category, as are such housekeeping activities as carpet and floor cleaning.

While some confusion seems to exist concerning **preventive maintenance** (often abbreviated PM), most practitioners agree that it has several common elements: inspections, lubrication, minor repairs or adjustments, and work order initiation. Preventive maintenance on equipment is generally performed using manufacturers' information concerning maintenance needs as a guideline, coupled with a healthy dose of good mechanical knowledge and common sense. Preventive maintenance may also be performed to comply with code requirements, corporate requirements, and insurance standards, as well as in response to the overall usage of the equipment and the impacts of the equipment's operating environment. Preventive maintenance may also result from test and inspection activities that indicate action is needed.

A unique category found in the maintenance manuals of most hospitality firms, **guestroom maintenance** is actually a form of preventive maintenance. It involves the inspection of a number of items in the guestroom, filter changes in air conditioning units, minor lubrication of doors and other equipment, repair of obvious small problems, and, when needed, the initiation of a work order for more substantial problems or needs.

Certain forms of maintenance clearly require advance planning, a rather significant amount of time to perform, specialized tools and equipment, and high levels of coordination between departments. **Scheduled maintenance** includes preparing equipment for changes in the seasons (such as draining cooling towers or winterizing pools) and other activities that are periodically required to keep equipment operating at an efficient level (such as descaling boilers and water heaters). Scheduled maintenance may also involve more substantial activities, such as replacing major equipment or equipment components, or replacing major elements of the building itself (such as a window).

Scheduled maintenance activities usually involve more than inspection, simple cleaning, and lubrication as their primary activities, making them somewhat different from many preventive maintenance actions. Scheduled maintenance may require that major pieces of equipment be removed from service for several hours or longer. In addition, the needed repair may be costly and may be performed by contract service personnel—for example, the repair of a leaking piece of refrigerant piping in a rooftop air conditioning unit. Scheduled maintenance activities may result from PM inspections when the maintenance worker notices a need for repair beyond the scope of PM.

Another action that could be considered a form of scheduled maintenance is the replacement of equipment. Replacement sometimes requires only a minor amount of scheduling. For example, if a through-the-wall guestroom HVAC unit needs replacing, the maintenance staff probably needs access to the room only for about half an hour to remove the old unit and install the new one. On the other hand, if the item to be replaced happens to be all the windows at the property or the roof-mounted HVAC unit for all the public space at the property, the time and scheduling issues may be critically important.

A growing emphasis is being placed on **predictive maintenance**. Predictive maintenance is similar to preventive maintenance, but generally relies on and uses more sophisticated technological methods to increase operational life and target preemptive corrective actions. Predictive maintenance replaces older rule-of-thumb or fixed-time-interval-based maintenance planning with diagnostic-based maintenance planning. Examples of predictive maintenance include infrared and ultrasonic testing of electrical equipment, vibration analysis of operating machinery, system monitoring (often integral to modern control systems), and fluid/metal analysis.

Reactive or **emergency/breakdown maintenance** is potentially the most costly and disruptive form of maintenance since it is unscheduled and (generally) unavoidable. The emergency or breakdown forms of maintenance are those that either have an immediate revenue effect (the room is out of service and cannot be rented until the problem is solved) or are likely to have a revenue effect if allowed to continue (a leaking pipe threatens the potential rentability of guestrooms if not repaired, or the poorly operating food service refrigeration system will not properly chill food). These forms of maintenance are particularly costly for the operation because:

- They are usually solved only with the application of premium pay (overtime).
- They often bypass the traditional parts or supplies purchasing system, leading to premium parts costs.
- They often have other costs associated with their solution (for example, a leaking pipe may also damage walls and ceilings).

At all properties, the maintenance effort is a mix of in-house and contract activities. **Contract maintenance** activities are undertaken for a variety of reasons, including (but not limited to):

- A desire to minimize the commitment of staff on the payroll to handle these needs.
- A recognition that special tools or licenses are required to perform the work effectively.
- A temporary staffing shortage.
- A need to deal with emergencies.
- A recognition that the complexity of the task is beyond the skills of the existing maintenance staff.

Elevator maintenance, trash haulage, window cleaning, kitchen duct cleaning, yard work, herbicide and pesticide application, water treatment, and HVAC control calibration are common contract maintenance services. Large hospitality firms will often negotiate national contracts for some of these services to reduce costs and standardize services.

Maintenance Management Systems

To effectively manage the types of maintenance outlined above, the hospitality business uses a variety of maintenance management systems. The goals of these systems are to:

- Handle the maintenance needs of the property effectively.
- Record essential information concerning the equipment and systems at the property.
- Establish standards for the performance of the maintenance workers.
- Provide the feedback necessary for management to assess the performance of the facilities department and the status of work in this department.

This discussion of maintenance management systems uses a paper systems model. While it is relatively easy to visualize these systems, maintenance management is increasingly being computerized. Computer systems are also discussed in this chapter.

The **work** or **repair order** is one of the most commonly used maintenance management forms. Used to initiate requests for maintenance services, this very simple document (usually a sequentially numbered form) provides basic information concerning the needed repair (room, nature of the problem, initiator of the request), a place for the name of the individual assigned to the task, and an area for this individual to record when the task is completed and note other pertinent information in a "remarks" or "comments" section. A work or repair order sometimes includes space for an estimate of time spent, material used, and other information that might be used for recordkeeping. Exhibit 1 is a sample work order.

At small properties, work orders may be issued from the front desk or from the housekeeping department. Front desk work orders are generally the result of comments or complaints received from guests. Housekeepers may generate work orders in response both to guest comments and to problems that come to their attention in the course of their duties. Some small properties consolidate all work orders in a log at the front desk, while others maintain separate logs in several areas of the hotel. If logs are maintained, they can identify the overall activity in maintenance, the promptness of response, and the size of any backlog.

Many maintenance manuals contain written instructions and flow charts that describe the steps to be taken when a need for maintenance arises. Exhibit 2 illustrates various potential "initiators" of a maintenance need. In this instance, guests, housekeeping, quality assurance (QA) checks, PM checks, and insurance or manager inspections may all identify the need to initiate a maintenance work order. Most of the steps result in some sort of log entry regarding repair.

Exhibit 1   Sample Maintenance Work Order

DELTA FORMS - MILWAUKEE U S A

(414) 461-0086

HYATT HOTELS ®   **MAINTENANCE REQUEST**

TIME _____   1345239

BY _____ DATE _____

LOCATION _____

PROBLEM _____

ASSIGNED TO _____

DATE COMPL. _____ TIME SPENT _____

COMPLETED BY _____

REMARKS _____

RPHK-04

HYATT HOTELS MAINTENANCE CHECK LIST
Check (☒) Indicates Unsatisfactory Condition
Explain Check In Remarks Section

BEDROOM - FOYER - CLOSET

☐ WALLS   ☐ WOODWORK   ☐ DOORS
☐ CEILING   ☐ TELEVISION   ☐ LIGHTS
☐ FLOORS   ☐ A.C. UNIT   ☐ BLINDS
☐ WINDOWS   ☐ DRAPES

REMARKS : _____

BATHROOM

☐ TRIM   ☐ SHOWER
☐ DRAINS   ☐ LIGHTS
☐ WALL PAPER   ☐ PAINT
☐ TILE OR GLASS   ☐ DOOR
☐ ACCESSORIES   ☐ WINDOW

REMARKS : _____

Courtesy of Hyatt Corporation

Exhibit 2 Maintenance Work Order Flow Chart

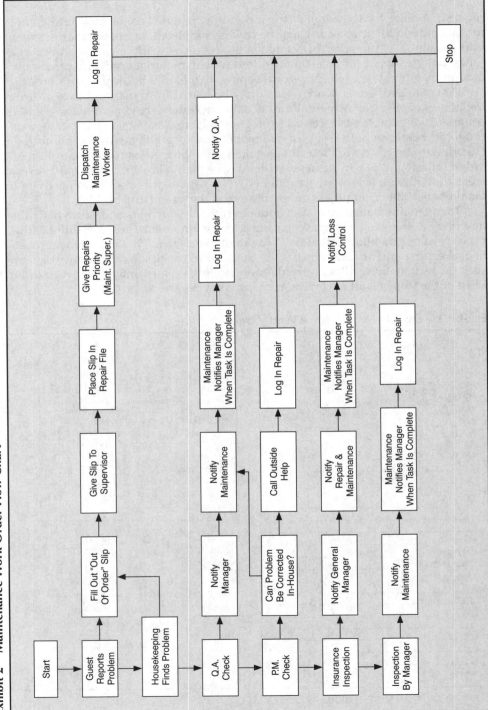

Courtesy of Days Inns of America.

A property contains many pieces of equipment. Since the continuity of information from manager to manager or employee to employee cannot be expected, several types of written records are maintained concerning the building and equipment. **Equipment data cards** are used for all major pieces of equipment to record facts and information of importance for maintenance purposes. Exhibit 3 is a sample of one such card. When a property is opened or a piece of equipment is purchased, the equipment data card is completed using information from the equipment specifications, nameplates, and other sources. The equipment data card provides maintenance staff members with a summary of key facts and specifications that will assist them in making repairs and in determining the correct operation of the equipment.

Maintenance log cards (see Exhibit 4) are used to record maintenance performed on the equipment. Information contained on these cards can be very helpful in determining if equipment is nearing (or has exceeded) its useful or design life. This information is especially helpful when making repair-or-replace decisions for a piece of equipment.

Since a key element of the guest experience in hotels is the guestroom itself, some companies maintain information specifically concerning the guestrooms. Exhibit 5 is a sample **room data card** used to record information concerning an individual guestroom. This card contains information about the basic physical characteristics of the guestroom and data on all major elements of the room, whether fixed or movable. The merit of such information usually is not apparent until the need arises to replace some element of a guestroom. Also note that there is space for scheduling and verifying the preventive maintenance dates for the room.

Besides the items contained on the first page of the room data card (usually referred to as FF&E—furniture, fixtures, and equipment), the second page of the card contains information about the major HVAC and electrical services in the room. The equipment portion of the room card contains an area for entry of warranty information (as does the equipment data card). For a new or relatively new property or for newly acquired equipment, this can be very useful and potentially valuable if maintenance problems arise during the warranty period.

Another important recordkeeping system is the **inventory record** kept by maintenance. A large number of items go into the physical plant of a hospitality facility, many of which are listed on the equipment and room data cards. The choice of *what* to put into the maintenance inventory and *how much* of the item to stock affects the responsiveness of the maintenance staff, the storage space needed for maintenance supplies, and the overall investment in the inventory.

The need to maintain an inventory of supplies must not be overlooked when facilities are designed. Failure to consider this need results in a space shortage. It also leads to difficulty in locating inventory, because the supplies that do exist often must be stored in various nooks and crannies. This contributes to inventory loss or excess inventory. Establishing a formal inventory list for maintenance, stocking target levels for these items, and conducting periodic inventories of maintenance supplies helps ensure that what is needed is in stock and that excess supplies are not acquired. Some chain establishments with relatively uniform physical plants develop inventory lists for their properties.

Exhibit 3   Sample Equipment Data Card

EQUIPMENT DATA

PROPERTY NO		EQUIP. ID NO			EQUIP. LOCATION	
EQUIP. DESCRIPTION				MANUFACTURER		
PURCHASE FROM						
DATE INSTALLED		P O NO.			COST	
WARRANTY/REPAIR AGENCY						

MECHANICAL DATA | AIR COND/REFRIGERATION DATA

ITEM:			ITEM:	
MFG	CFM		MFG	FILTERS
TYPE/MODEL	PULLEY		TYPE/MODEL	BLOWER
SER. NO.	BELTS		SER. NO.	CONTROL
SIZE	BEARING		BTU	REFRIGERANT
GPM	SHAFT SIZE		GPM	PRESSURE
RPM	BLOWERS		RPM	CAPACITY
TYPE OIL			TEMP. RANGE	
CAPACITY			COIL: HEATING	COIL COOLING

ELECTRICAL DATA

MANUFACTURER			SER. NO.		PURCHASE DATE	
VOLTS	PHASE	CYCLE	RPM	PF	HP	AMPS

MOTOR: | MOTOR: | THERMOSTAT/CONTROL

TYPE	SHAFT SIZE	TYPE	SHAFT SIZE	MFG	
FRAME	PULLEY	FRAME	PULLEY	ITEM	
FLA	LRA	FLA	LRA	MODEL	
WATTS	STARTER	WATTS	STARTER	TYPE	
CAPACITOR	HEATER NO.	CAPACITOR	HEATER NO.	VOLTS	AMPS

MAINTENANCE REQUIREMENTS

Courtesy of Days Inns of America.

Exhibit 4   Sample Maintenance Log Card

	MAINTENANCE LOG				
Property No _____			Equip. ID No _____		

Date	Work Performed	By	Cost	
			Labor	Parts

Courtesy of Days Inns of America.

Still, all properties need to develop their own lists to address the unique items needed at their facilities.

Preventive maintenance schedules and instructions are certainly the backbone of the PM system. Exhibit 6 is a PM schedule for one lodging chain. This listing illustrates several features typical of PM schedules—for example:

- Not every element of the building and physical plant is on the list to receive preventive maintenance. Elements of the building that are critical to guest satisfaction, overall property image and marketing, safety and security, and the performance of other departments' duties are often included in a PM program.

- PM frequency varies with type of equipment. Some elements of the building require PM on a weekly basis. This is likely to consist largely of an inspection or the performance of some repetitive task. Other equipment requires attention monthly, quarterly, or even less frequently. But, when attention is required, the work often involves more than just a simple inspection.

- The scheduling of PM activity is done to attempt to smooth the workload. Activities are not "bunched" into the first week of the month or in some other way accumulated, but rather are staggered throughout the months to allow for productive use of labor.

- The schedule is only a schedule. Information about what is to be done to each system, piece of equipment, or area is not found on the schedule. This information is contained in specific preventive maintenance instructions, which vary for each item on the PM list.

Preventive maintenance instructions are derived from several sources. Equipment suppliers often suggest maintenance activities and frequencies in their

Exhibit 5   Sample Room Data Card

ROOM DATA

NAME OF UNIT	UNIT NO:
LOCATION	ROOM NO:

AREA	LENGTH ×	WIDTH ×	HEIGHT =	SQ. FEET =	SQ. YARDS	P.M. DATES	
						JAN	JULY
CARPET	YARDS	COLOR	MAKER	COST	DATE INSTALLED		
DRAPES							
VINYL							
WINDOWS	SIZE		WINDOWS	SIZE			
DOORS	SIZE		DOORS	SIZE		FEB	AUG
LOCKS	MAKE	TYPE	LOCKS	MAKE	TYPE		
BEDS			HEAD BOARDS				
DRESSER			CHEST DRAWER				
NIGHT STANDS			LAMPS			MAR	SEP
TABLES			LAMPS				
CLOSETS			LAMPS				
MIRRORS			DESK				
SOFA			CHAIRS				
BATHROOM	LENGTH ×	WIDTH ×	HEIGHT =	SQ. FEET		APR	OCT
ITEM	TYPE	MAKE	ITEM	TYPE	MAKE		
TUB/ SHOWER			PLUMBING				
TOILET			FLUSH VALVE				
TOILET SEAT			TOILET TANK				
VANITY LAMP			BASIN			MAY	NOV
HEAT LAMP			FLOOR TILE				
JACUZZI			WALL TILE				
STEAM BATH							
ACCESSORIES						JUNE	DEC
ITEM	MAKE	MODEL	ITEM	MAKE	MODEL		
REFRI-GERATOR			COFFEE TABLE				
BAR			END TABLE				
TV/RADIO			EASY CHAIR				
SMOKE DETECTOR			RECLINER				
SPRINKLER			OTTOMAN				
MESSAGE CENTER			STOOL				
ARMOIRE			DR TABLE & CHAIRS				
SAFE			PICTURES				
TELEPHONE			PICTURES				

HEATING & AIR CONDITIONING ON REVERSE SIDE

Exhibit 5   *(continued)*

ADDITIONAL COMPONENT DATA

PROPERTY CONTROL NO.	MANUFACTURER	
PURCHASED FROM		
DATE INSTALLED	P.O. NUMBER	COST
WARRANTY/REPAIR AGENCY		

AIR CONDITIONING DATA

	ELECTRICAL HEATING	COILS COOLING	HEATING
MFG	MFG	CAPACITY	CAPACITY
TYPE	VOLTAGE	PRESSURE	PRESSURE
SERIAL NO.	KW	MEDIUM	MEDIUM
BEARINGS	AMPS	MFG	MFG
R.P.M.		REMARKS	REMARKS
SIZE			
BELT & NO.			
FILTER SIZE		NO. FILTERS	MFG. FILTERS
MODEL NO.		SERIAL NO.	THERMOSTAT
TYPE		COOLANT	MFG.
R.P.M.		CAPACITY	MODEL
G.P.M.		REFRIGERANT	TYPE
TEMP. RANGE	PRESSURE	DRIVE	VOLTAGE

ELECTRICAL DATA / MAINTENANCE CODES

MANUFACTURER			
SERIAL NO.		PURCHASE DATE	
H.P.		R.P.M.	
VOLTS	PHASE	CYCLE	PF

MOTOR		MOTOR	
TYPE	FRAME	TYPE	FRAME
FLA	LRA	FILA	LRA
BEARINGS	WATTS	BEARINGS	WATTS
PULLEY/SHEAVE	CAPACITOR	PULLEY/SHEAVE	CAPACITOR
SHAFT SIZE	CAPACITOR	SHAFT SIZE	CAPACITOR
STARTER	HEATER	STARTER	HEATER
PANEL	CIR #	PANEL	CIR #

Courtesy of Days Inns of America.

Exhibit 6 Sample Preventive Maintenance Schedule

Weeks 1–26:

Item	1	2	3	4	5	6	7	8	9	10	11	12	13	14	15	16	17	18	19	20	21	22	23	24	25	26
1 Air conditioners—1st floor	•				•			•				•				•				•				•		
2 Air conditioners—2nd floor		•				•			•				•				•				•				•	
3 Air conditioners—3rd floor			•				•			•				•				•				•				•
4 Air conditioners—roof																										
5 Air conditioners—service areas		•				•			•				•				•				•				•	
6 Bathroom vent filters																										
7 Boiler room		•				•			•				•				•				•				•	
8 Building exterior	•	•	•	•	•	•	•	•	•	•	•	•	•	•	•	•	•	•	•	•	•	•	•	•	•	•
9 Carpets													•													
10 Caulking/weatherstripping																		•								
11 Circulating pumps					•													•								
12 Clean hot water systems																										
13 Clean ice machines					•													•								
14 Cribs/rollaways	•								•							•								•		
15 Door closers																		•								
16 Dryers		•				•			•				•				•				•				•	
17 Elevators	•	•	•	•	•	•	•	•	•	•	•	•	•	•	•	•	•	•	•	•	•	•	•	•	•	•
18 Emergency lighting	•	•	•	•	•	•	•	•	•	•	•	•	•	•	•	•	•	•	•	•	•	•	•	•	•	•
19 Exterior lighting																										
20 Fire alarm systems																		•								
21 Fire extinguishers																		•								
22 First aid kits	•										•			•												
23 Flush hot water system						•																	•			
24 Gutters	•														•											
25 Keys/vingcard	•	•	•	•	•	•	•	•	•	•	•	•	•	•	•	•	•	•	•	•	•	•	•	•	•	•
26 Key machine	•				•																					
27 Landscaping	•	•	•	•	•	•	•	•	•	•	•	•	•	•	•	•	•	•	•	•	•	•	•	•	•	•
28 Laundry/washers					•													•								
29 Lawn mower																			•							
30 Lobby floor																										
31 Locks	•							•							•					•				•		
32 Maintenance shop		•				•			•				•				•				•				•	
33 Mattress rotation—1st floor													•													
34 Mattress rotation—2nd floor	•																									
35 Mattress rotation—3rd/4th floor																										
36 Mechanical room			•				•			•				•				•				•				•
37 Meeting room	•																	•								
38 Mini computer	•	•	•	•	•	•	•	•	•	•	•	•	•	•	•	•	•	•	•	•	•	•	•	•	•	•
39 OSHA 200 log					•																					
40 Parking lot	•	•	•	•	•	•	•	•	•	•	•	•	•	•	•	•	•	•	•	•	•	•	•	•	•	•
41 Pool area	•	•	•	•	•	•	•	•	•	•	•	•	•	•	•	•	•	•	•	•	•	•	•	•	•	•
42 Pool Filter													•													
43 Pruning/fertilizing												•										•				
44 Quik fix-it carts	•							•										•				•				
45 Roof	•				•			•										•				•				
46 Room attendants cart	•							•										•				•				
47 Signage	•	•	•	•	•	•	•	•	•	•	•	•	•	•	•	•	•	•	•	•	•	•	•	•	•	•
48 Smoke detectors		•			•			•				•			•			•				•			•	
49 Stairways, entrance & exits	•	•	•	•	•	•	•	•	•	•	•	•	•	•	•	•	•	•	•	•	•	•	•	•	•	•
50 Storage areas																										
51 Telephone room																										
52 Vacuum cleaners	•		•			•		•				•					•			•		•				
53 Van (*check oil daily)	•		•			•		•				•					•			•		•				
54 Walk off mats			•				•				•			•					•							
55 Water softener																										•
56 Water temperature	•	•	•	•	•	•	•	•	•	•	•	•	•	•	•	•	•	•	•	•	•	•	•	•	•	•

Weeks 27–52:

Item	27	28	29	30	31	32	33	34	35	36	37	38	39	40	41	42	43	44	45	46	47	48	49	50	51	52
1 Air conditioners—1st floor			•				•				•				•				•				•			
2 Air conditioners—2nd floor				•				•				•				•				•				•		
3 Air conditioners—3rd floor					•				•				•				•				•				•	
4 Air conditioners—roof			•																							
5 Air conditioners—service areas				•				•				•				•				•				•		
6 Bathroom vent filters																										
7 Boiler room			•				•				•				•				•				•			
8 Building exterior	•	•	•	•	•	•	•	•	•	•	•	•	•	•	•	•	•	•	•	•	•	•	•	•	•	•
9 Carpets																								•		
10 Caulking/weatherstripping																										
11 Circulating pumps																										
12 Clean hot water systems																										
13 Clean ice machines																										
14 Cribs/rollaways																							•			
15 Door closers																										•
16 Dryers			•				•				•				•				•				•			
17 Elevators	•	•	•	•	•	•	•	•	•	•	•	•	•	•	•	•	•	•	•	•	•	•	•	•	•	•
18 Emergency lighting	•	•	•	•	•	•	•	•	•	•	•	•	•	•	•	•	•	•	•	•	•	•	•	•	•	•
19 Exterior lighting			•																							
20 Fire alarm systems													•													
21 Fire extinguishers			•				•				•				•				•				•			
22 First aid kits													•										•			
23 Flush hot water system										•																
24 Gutters	•	•	•	•	•	•	•	•	•	•	•	•	•	•	•	•	•	•	•	•	•	•	•	•	•	•
25 Keys/vingcard	•	•	•	•	•	•	•	•	•	•	•	•	•	•	•	•	•	•	•	•	•	•	•	•	•	•
26 Key machine										•																
27 Landscaping	•	•	•	•	•	•	•	•	•	•	•	•	•	•	•	•	•	•	•	•	•	•	•	•	•	•
28 Laundry/washers																							•			
29 Lawn mower																								•		
30 Lobby floor																										
31 Locks				•				•				•				•				•				•		
32 Maintenance shop																	•									
33 Mattress rotation—1st floor																										•
34 Mattress rotation—2nd floor																										
35 Mattress rotation—3rd/4th floor	To have all mattresses rotated by the 15th of the first month in the current quarter.																									
36 Mechanical room			•				•				•				•				•				•			
37 Meeting room																										
38 Mini computer	•	•	•	•	•	•	•	•	•	•	•	•	•	•	•	•	•	•	•	•	•	•	•	•	•	•
39 OSHA 200 log																				•						
40 Parking lot	•	•	•	•	•	•	•	•	•	•	•	•	•	•	•	•	•	•	•	•	•	•	•	•	•	•
41 Pool area	•	•	•	•	•	•	•	•	•	•	•	•	•	•	•	•	•	•	•	•	•	•	•	•	•	•
42 Pool Filter									•											•						
43 Pruning/fertilizing																										
44 Quik fix-it carts	•							•										•				•				
45 Roof	•							•										•								
46 Room attendants cart	•							•										•				•				
47 Signage	•	•	•	•	•	•	•	•	•	•	•	•	•	•	•	•	•	•	•	•	•	•	•	•	•	•
48 Smoke detectors			•			•			•			•			•			•			•			•		
49 Stairways, entrance & exits	•	•	•	•	•	•	•	•	•	•	•	•	•	•	•	•	•	•	•	•	•	•	•	•	•	•
50 Storage areas																							•		•	•
51 Telephone room																										
52 Vacuum cleaners	•		•			•		•				•					•			•		•				
53 Van (*check oil daily)	•		•			•		•				•					•			•		•				
54 Walk off mats	•					•			•				•				•				•					
55 Water softener																										
56 Water temperature	•	•	•	•	•	•	•	•	•	•	•	•	•	•	•	•	•	•	•	•	•	•	•	•	•	•

Courtesy of La Quinta Motor Inns, Inc.

equipment manuals. PM instructions for FF&E, building features, and building grounds are generated through a combination of experience, input from vendors and suppliers, and information from various professional and technical organizations. PM instructions may also contain a listing of specialized parts or equipment required to perform the PM task.

The chapter appendix shows sample PM procedures for a guestroom AC wall unit, an ice machine, and laundry equipment. They are provided for illustrative purposes and are not suggested as the only recommended procedures for such equipment. Nonetheless, they verify that much of PM activity involves basic inspection, cleaning, and lubrication. PM is not a troubleshooting activity directed at diagnosing and solving a problem. The instructions for PM generally do not state how to repair a piece of equipment. Obviously, to perform PM, the maintenance person must have access to specific tools and supplies.

Like PM activities, many guestroom maintenance activities involve inspection, lubrication, and cleaning. Most hospitality firms have some form of **rooms checklist** that is used for guestroom maintenance (see Exhibit 7). The checklists used for guestroom (preventive) maintenance will usually list all the items in the guestroom and provide a brief explanation of the type of inspection, lubrication, or cleaning activity to be performed. Since the goal of guestroom maintenance is to keep the guestroom in proper operating order, completing the checklist also involves some repair and replacement activities.

To be able to handle guestroom maintenance activities efficiently and with minimal downtime for the room, the guestroom maintenance person is usually given a guestroom maintenance cart. This cart contains basic tools and supplies necessary to deal with problems or needs typically encountered. Exhibit 8 is a list of tools and supplies included in a guestroom maintenance cart for a typical motel operation. The selection of tools and supplies for any particular hospitality facility will depend on the design and contents of that facility's guestrooms.

Many operations provide detailed instructions to employees concerning the tools and methods to be used to perform maintenance. Exhibit 9 contains a sample of this type of instruction for the touch up and repair of damaged furniture. Note that the quality of the finished product is stressed. Note also that safety is addressed in the use of the paint remover. The **material safety data sheets** (MSDSs) that are referenced serve to inform employees about potentially hazardous materials used in the workplace, how to work safely with these chemicals, and what to do in case of an accident. In the United States, the Occupational Safety & Health Administration (OSHA) requires vendors and suppliers of hazardous materials to provide an MSDS for each product. The hospitality operation must then maintain these forms and make them available to employees.

Detailed instructions help maintain a standard of work. This is especially useful when personnel turnover occurs and when employees have different perceptions of how to do a task.

The best PM program will not eliminate all breakdowns and emergencies, but it will help extend the time between these events. The familiarity that the employees develop with the equipment while doing PM should prove useful when the need to repair equipment occurs. In order to have at hand the information necessary to perform equipment repairs, it is useful to maintain files of equipment specifications

Exhibit 7   Sample Rooms Checklist

ENCLOSURE #2
DAYS INN ROOM CHECK LIST

☐ OK   ☐ NEEDS REPAIR   ☐ REPAIR COMPLETE

PROPERTY _____
ROOM NO. _____

DATE INITIALS

AIR CONDITIONERS
- Thermostat controls and fan (operation)
- Knob on thermostat (secure)
- Filter (clean or replace)
- Condensation water drain (clean) add Algaecide tablet
- Grille (clean)

LAMPS
- Switches (check)
- Lamp sockets (tighten)
- Lamp shades (repair or note for replacement)
- Cord on hanging light pullswitch (check)
- Cover on hanging light (secure)
- Bulb (replace if necessary)
- Plugs (replace if necessary)

SWITCHES & RECEPTACLES
- Outlet wall plates (insect, clean, secure)
- Switches (inspect, clean, secure)
- Switches, and receptacles (replace missing screws)
- Receptacles (change if necessary)

TELEVISION
- Audio (check radio channels)
- Video (check television channels)
- Knob (replace if necessary)
- Fine tuning (adjust if necessary)
- Antenna outlet (secure plate)
- Antennae connectors (check, repair if necessary)
- Remote control
- Security mount

TELEPHONE
- Replace message light cover (if necessary)
- Dialing instructions (replace if necessary)
- Defects (report any other defects to front desk)

FURNITURE
- Drawer handles and knobs (check, replace if necessary)
- Drawer guides (lubricate if needed with WD 40)
- Stains (clean and touch up)
- Chair legs (check)
- Table tops (check, repair small defects)
- Headboards (check and secure)
- Casters or legs (check and secure)
- Chair bumpers (check, replace if missing)
- Spring on chairs (check)
- Night stands (check and secure)
- Coat racks (check and secure)

WINDOWS MIRRORS
- Window guides (lubricate with WD 40)
- Mirror hangers (check and secure)
- Window hardware (check and secure)

BEDDING DRAPERY CLOSETS
- Bedframe (check and secure)
- Inspect and secure all drapery track, rollers and pull cord
- Hangers (should be 8) clothes hanger hooks (replace if rusty)

DOORS
- Handles (check and secure)
- Lock cylinder set screw (check)
- Hings and hinge pins (oil with WD 40 and secure)
- Door chain and viewer (check, repair if necessary)
- Lock striker plates (check and secure)
- Night latch (check)
- Door frame rubber bumpers (check, replace if needed)
- Door stops (check and replace if necessary)

BATHROOM
- Toilet flush valve (check)
- Toilet cover bumpers (check)
- Seat hinges (check and secure)
- Toilet seal (check for evidence of leaks)
- Bath drain plug and pop-up (check)
- Mixing valve (secure handle)
- Mixing valve washers (replace if necessary)
- Hot and cold faucets (check/replace 'H' and 'C' buttons—leaks)
- Escutcheon plates (secure)
- Shower curtain hooks (check and replace if needed)
- P trap under basin (check)
- Drain pop-up (check)
- Faucet strainer (clean or replace)
- Basin bowl hangers (reglue or resecure)
- Toilet paper holder (check)
- Clothes hanger on bathroom wall (check and secure)
- Floor and wall tile (grout tile and caulk around tub if needed)
- Soap dish and grab bar (check and secure)
- Towel rack (check and secure)
- Lavatory counter (check and refasten)
- Non slip pads in tub
- Exhaust grill (clean)
- Tissue holder (check and replace)

GENERAL
- Baseboards (check and replace/reglue as needed)
- Carpet (check)
- Vinyl (check, reglue if necessary)
- Pictures (check)
- Ceiling (check for cracks and/or peeling paint)
- Paint (check paint on walls and door casings)
- Rate card
- Fire exit plan
- Check for air leaks under A/C units
- Cracks in sidewalks

Courtesy of Days Inns of America.

and manuals supplied by the manufacturer with the equipment. These are the same items that often contain the PM recommendations, another good reason to retain them. These specifications and manuals often contain troubleshooting lists that can help greatly in diagnosing the problem and deciding upon a solution.

Exhibit 8   Guestroom Maintenance Cart Tools and Supplies

QUICK FIX-IT PROGRAM

Required Tools:

1   3/8 Electric Drill—variable speed
1   Set Drill Bits
1   8" Pipe Wrench
1   10" Pipe Wrench
1   6" Vice Grip Pliers
1   8" Pliers
1   Linesman Pliers
1   Claw Hammer
1   Ball Peen Hammer
1   Electricity Tester 0-250 V. AC/DC
1   Hand Sander
1   7 Piece Punch and Chisel Set
1   6 Piece Combination Wrench Set
    ($\frac{7}{16}$, $\frac{1}{2}$, $\frac{9}{16}$, $\frac{5}{8}$, $\frac{11}{16}$, $\frac{3}{4}$)
1   Putty Knife
1   6" x 10" Clear Plastic Tray for
    assorted bolts, nuts, screws
1   3" Paint Brush
1   2" Paint Brush
1   6" Three Cornered File
1   6" Tailed File
1   6" Flat File
1   Set Allen Wrenches
3   Phillips Screwdrivers (small,
    medium, large)
3   Regular Screwdrivers (small,
    medium, large)
1   Package Assorted Sandpaper
1   Large Sponge
1   Plumber's Friend
1   Plumber's Snake
1   Wire Stripper
1   Utility Knife

Supplies for Cart:

1   Commode Seat
2   #1 Wax Toilet Bowl Gasket
6   Hinges, Pins, Nuts for Commode
    Seats
1   Can Rossite Drain Opener
1   Can Tile Grout
1   Elmers Contact Cement #1602
1   Can Elmers Carpenter Wood Filler
3   Lamp Sockets
2   Showerheads
2   #782 Double Hooks for Bathroom
    Doors
4   Rate Cards and Holders
4   Liability Law Cards
4   Aerators
2   Shower Cartridge Assembly
3   Drain Release Assembly
2   Tub Drain Stoppers
2   Tank Balls
4   Plug Bottoms
4   Faucet Handle Caps
3   Toilet Water Control Repair Kits
3   Ballcock Repair Kits #41071
1   Smoke Detector
1   Carpet Repair Kit
1   Furniture Touch-up Kit

Courtesy of La Quinta Motor Inns, Inc.

Another useful item is a **control schematic**, which shows the relays, timers, fuses, switches, and basic wiring of controls within electrical equipment.

When maintenance staff must deal with renovations, the building itself, and equipment installed as part of the building, the plans and specifications for the building are key. *Structural plans* allow the maintenance staff to determine locations of key building structural elements, a most important piece of information

Exhibit 9   Sample Task Breakdown: Refinishing Wood Furniture

TASK BREAKDOWN		ADDITIONAL INFORMATION
WHAT TO DO:	**HOW TO DO IT:**	
Refinish wood furniture.	Refinish wood furniture when scratches cannot be covered.	Formby's paint remover is recommended.
	a. Brush paint remover on the damaged part of the furniture. See MSDS #25.	Use caution while working with paint remover. Read and follow the container instructions carefully.
	Allow the paint remover to set for at least 20 minutes.	
	When the finish begins to bubble and blister, use a putty knife to scrape the finish off the furniture.	Be careful to keep the putty knife parallel to the surface to avoid damaging the wood.
	Wipe off the remaining finish with a clean rag.	
	b. When sanding upholstered furniture, insert a broad knife between the wood surface and the upholstery to protect the upholstery.	
	Use a vibrating sander with #180 fine grade sandpaper to sand heavily damaged areas.	
	If nicks are still present after sanding,	
	Place a damp, heavy cloth on the area.	The moist heat will cause the wood to swell and the nick to pop out.
	Place a hot, flat iron on the damp cloth for about 5 seconds.	
	c. Apply a stain that matches the furniture.	The longer the stain is allowed to set before wiping, the darker it will become.
	Wipe along the wood grain.	
	Allow the stain to set.	
	Wipe off excess with a dry rag.	
	d. Spray the repaired area with the clear lacquer. See MSDS #86.	A stained piece can be immediately sprayed with a polyurethane spray that will give a gloss finish and dry faster, approximately 1½ to 2 hours. Minwax is recommended.
	Let the lacquer dry completely to avoid smudges, fingerprints, etc.	

Courtesy of La Quinta Motor Inns, Inc.

for certain proposed modifications. *Mechanical plans* identify flow patterns for air and water, control schemes, equipment and system interconnections, and basic operating parameters. *Electrical plans* provide information about circuit capacities, wire sizes, circuit connections and routing, and emergency power circuits. Plans for specialty services such as laundry, telecommunications, lighting, and sound systems assist the maintenance staff or outside contractors in repairing or updating these systems.

How you store plans is very important. Plans should always be accessible to the technician needing them when he or she needs them and stored such that they remain in good condition over time. Purchasing a suitable plans storage unit can be well worth the investment. It is also very helpful to update the plans as changes and modifications are made to the building and systems. When the time arrives to renovate, the lack of updated, current plans often leads contractors either to over-bid or to request numerous change orders in the project. Both can result in excess cost and delays.

As mentioned earlier, emergency and breakdown maintenance activities are costly. The use of the maintenance management systems outlined so far in this chapter will help to greatly reduce the need for emergency and breakdown maintenance. Still, it will be impossible to eliminate this need entirely. Because of the inevitability of emergencies, a property should be prepared. The following are some tactics that can help make a difference during maintenance emergencies:

- Keep a current listing of all telephone numbers for maintenance staff. This list should be available to the facilities manager and the general manager.

- Train the appropriate night staff concerning procedures to be followed in the event of the more common emergencies. In the context of maintenance emergencies, this would include knowing the location of key water valves and electrical shutoffs.

- Maintain an ongoing relationship with contract maintenance and cleaning firms. Know their telephone numbers (day and night numbers). Adequate resources of people and equipment during a maintenance emergency (such as a windstorm that damages a roof) can make a major difference in the extent of damage that might follow and the cost of repairs.

- Consider appropriate backup systems for use during emergencies. This could include using multiple pieces of equipment for key system components (for example, two pumps on the building's chilled or hot water circulation systems, so that a backup exists) or stocking replacement items for key system components (for example, one pump on the system and a spare in stock).

Contract Services and Outsourcing

Contract maintenance services are commonly used to supply various services for hospitality properties (see Exhibit 10). Managing these services begins *before* the contract is put out for bid. The following were identified by two authors as some key provisions in drafting a maintenance contract:

Exhibit 10   Sample Maintenance Contract Services and Expenses

Maintenance Contracts	
Generator Maintenance	$4,100
Fire Alarm—Clubhouse	3,200
Water Treatment	8,300
Window Washing—Ground Level	12,900
Window Washing—Guestrooms	7,400
Chillers	11,600
Pest Control	18,100
Fire Alarm Monitoring	400
Sprinkler and Alarm Testing	5,300
Electronic Locks	2,900
Plants—Interior	3,200
Energy Monitoring	1,200
Metal Maintenance	11,600
Hood Cleaning	16,500
Drain Cleaning	3,300
Grease Trap Pumping	4,600
Total	**$114,600**

- *Insurance:* The contract should require that the contractor have adequate insurance coverage and specify both the type and limits of coverage. The property owner and management company should be a named insured on the contractor's insurance policy.

- *Term:* The contract should be for a specific term with no automatic renewal provision.

- *Cancellation:* The property manager should have the right to cancel the agreement on short notice for lack of performance, and either party should be able to cancel the contract in 30 days for no cause. Penalties for nonperformance may also be included.

- *Contractor not an employee:* The agreement should state that the contractor is not an employee or agent of the property owner or management company.

- *No assignment of contract:* The contractor should be prohibited from assigning the contract.

- *Specifications:* The contract should include very detailed specifications of the work to be performed and the frequency of each task. The specifications should be attached as an addendum to the agreement.

- *Contract fee:* The contract should be specific on the fees for the services named and address fees for extra services. A retention fee would be advisable if the contract is for a one-time maintenance job.

> A 10-percent retention fee payable after the work has been inspected and approved is appropriate.
>
> All non-technical maintenance, such as janitorial service, snow removal, parking lot sweeping, and most landscaping maintenance, can be negotiated on a property's standard maintenance contract. Have all contract forms reviewed by an attorney before use. However, technical maintenance, such as elevator or HVAC, requires a maintenance agreement designed specifically for that service.
>
> Most [hospitality] companies do not have specific technical maintenance agreements and must use the contractor's agreement. When this is the case, the property manager must thoroughly review the contract and negotiate provisions out of the agreement that might be detrimental to the property or its owner.[3]

In addition, it is suggested that properties use a relatively short contract term, especially in the early stages of a relationship with a contractor, and take great care with the form of the insurance and indemnification wording found in the contract. A current certificate of insurance should be required and kept on file for all contractors.

Once a contract is signed, it is the responsibility of the facilities manager or some other responsible individual at the property to ensure that the work that has been contracted and billed for has been performed. One property had contracted and been billed for boiler water treatment from one firm for several years. When failures in the heating system began to occur, an inspection of the system revealed major corrosion and a need to replace the boiler and several elements of the piping system. The contractor had never performed the specified work and no one at the hotel had ever followed up to ensure that it was performed.

A growing trend in commercial real estate is **outsourcing**, a process by which facilities services are provided not by in-house staff but by contract service firms. This is an extension of a common practice in real estate and the lodging industry of what is sometimes referred to as "out-tasking," purchasing specific facilities services (such as window washing and elevator maintenance) from outside contractors. Hospitality industry firms such as ARAMARK and Sodexo are active in providing facilities outsourcing.

The U.S. lodging industry has not embraced facilities outsourcing to any significant degree, though there are indications that outsourcing activity is on the rise. Outside of the United States, lodging facilities are outsourcing at a somewhat greater level. U.S. outsourcing is primarily associated with large building complexes, either individual large hotels or hotels that are part of larger complexes. Outsourcing of energy services occurs when steam or chilled water is purchased from a local utility or from a centralized plant serving a building complex of which the hotel is a part. Of course, the use of contract services for a variety of needs is commonplace in the lodging industry.

Facilities outsourcing can go in both directions. A lodging property could decide that it will, in effect, go into the facilities management business for other properties. This generally involves offices, retail space, or apartments, rather than other hotels, because of proprietary and competitive issues. It is certainly reasonable that hotels occupying portions of buildings (for example, with retail on the ground floor and apartments either above or below the hotel) could provide facilities services to these other spaces. This could turn the typical facilities cost center into a revenue center.

Computerized and Internet-Based Facilities Management

A number of lodging companies use various computerized and Internet-based facilities management systems. In most instances, these are systems operating separately from the existing "property management" systems, a term that in commercial real estate often includes a facilities management element. Lodging's use of this term does not generally include facilities management, a subtle but important difference.

Computerized maintenance management systems (CMMSs) in lodging are used for a variety of functions. Large operations often control primary building systems (HVAC, for example) by computer. The capability of these systems varies, with the most sophisticated not only controlling equipment operation and building comfort but also fire protection interfaces, security, and electric power management. Even freestanding restaurants have versions of these systems, with varying degrees of "smart" electronics for operating the building's HVAC system and often other equipment.

The management of the "paperwork and dispatch" of maintenance and repair is also increasingly being handled by computerized systems. Preventive, scheduled, and guestroom maintenance and work orders can all be established on computerized systems. These systems can also direct this work to the appropriate staff, account for the time and materials used on the task, and establish a record of the work. In some cases, this feature is a part of a computer package that provides for building systems operations and management. More commonly today, however, it is a stand-alone system (a CMMS module). While a computer does central coordination and recordkeeping, a variety of other technologies and tools are also used. Work orders can be printed, faxed, or dispatched via pager or personal digital assistant (PDA). Communication can be via phone, pager, or PDA as well. Data can be input by way of keyboard, electronic transfer, or barcode reader.

CMMSs have provided a way to help bridge the gap that sometimes exists between the housekeeping and facilities departments. Maintenance management packages can provide multilingual precoded information for housekeeping that allows housekeepers to have information in their native language via pre-recorded messages. Housekeeping responds to a given problem with an appropriate telephone signal (a code 555, to mean "light bulb needs replacing," for example, and, depending on the system, the guestroom number may also be shown). When the computer system receives the signal, it generates a work order to the appropriate employee and sends it via a pager. The employee completes the task and enters the work order number (if not already displayed) to indicate the task is done. One light bulb is deducted from the inventory records. All of the interim steps of the former manual system (housekeeping reports bulb outage to floor supervisor, supervisor writes work order, supervisor sends work order to dispatcher, dispatcher logs and dispatches work order, employee picks up work order, employee completes the work, employee makes a record of completed work, employee makes manual inventory entry) are done automatically in a fraction of the time.

CMMSs not only improve productivity and provide for more complete records, they also provide the basis for more knowledgeable and well-advised decisions up and down the chain of operation. These systems generate information in ways that former systems could not. A ready overview of maintenance backlogs, average time to respond, employee productivity, types of repairs, location of repairs, and a host of other databases can be created. Managers now can actually use maintenance data to help influence decision-making—a much talked-about wish in the era of manual systems, but one often difficult to achieve.

CMMSs are being used both at the unit level and the regional and corporate level. It is possible for access to be set up to these systems in a remote mode. In this manner, a regional or corporate manager can oversee unit-level facilities activity. Or a manager in charge of multiple operations can access the data for them without having to be physically at each location. Under the best of scenarios, this could mean that an engineering manager is able to connect with the CMMS and "solve" an operational problem with a piece of equipment without having to drive an hour each way in an ice storm.

An additional feature of some CMMS packages, though one not widely used in lodging, is the integration of building plans and specifications with the facilities management software. Managers of office buildings, universities, corporate headquarters, and even manufacturing plants are finding this a particularly helpful tool to effectively and efficiently manage, plan, and allocate the space they occupy. Lodging properties have not seen a particular need for this type of usage, but the application potential is apparent and such a feature may become a common tool for hoteliers in the future.

Today, many CMMS implementers are not loading their systems into individual computers at the property level; they are using an Internet connection. Some interesting capabilities and activities are emerging in building monitoring and energy management, thanks to the Internet. By using a CMMS in Internet mode, facilities professionals and outside vendors alike have access to historical and (at times) real-time information about the building and its systems.

Budgeting for POM and Utilities

The facilities department's expenditures for property operation and maintenance (**POM**) and utilities are 8 to 9 percent of a U.S. property's revenue. In this section we will discuss the components of these two elements of the budget, some considerations for budget development, and some of the factors that may result in variations from the budget. The discussion uses the "standard" form of the POM and utility accounts as found in the *Uniform System of Accounts for the Lodging Industry (USALI)* and an actual listing of these accounts for a sample property.

The POM and utility accounts as defined by the *USALI* are shown in Exhibits 11 and 12. For most operations, salaries, wages, and employee benefits constitute approximately 40–50 percent of the POM expenditure. Note that contract expenditures may be found in several areas of the POM account. Contract maintenance costs can constitute 25 percent or more of the non-labor element of the

Exhibit 11   POM Schedule

	Period Of												
	Current Period						**Year-To-Date**						
	Actual		**Forecast/ Budget**		**Prior Year**		**Actual**		**Forecast/ Budget**		**Prior Year**		
	$	%	$	%	$	%	$	%	$	%	$	%	
EXPENSES													
Labor Costs and Related Expenses													
Salaries, Wages, Service Charges, Contracted Labor and Bonuses													
Salaries and Wages													
Management													
Non-Management													
Sub-Total: Salaries and Wages													
Service Charge Distribution													
Contracted, Leased and Outsourced Labor													
Bonuses and Incentives													
Total Salaries, Wages, Service Charges, Contracted Labor and Bonuses													
Payroll-Related Expenses													
Payroll Taxes													
Supplemental Pay													
Employee Benefits													
Total Payroll Related Expenses													
Total Labor Costs and Related Expenses													
Other Expenses													
Building													
Cluster Services													
Contract Services													
Corporate Office Reimbursables													
Dues and Subscriptions													
Electrical and Mechanical Equipment													
Elevators and Escalators													
Engineering Supplies													
Entertainment—In-House													
Equipment Rental													
Floor Covering													
Furniture and Equipment													
Grounds Maintenance and Landscaping													
Heating, Ventilation, and Air Conditioning Equipment													
Kitchen Equipment													
Laundry Equipment													
Licenses and Permits													
Life/Safety													
Light Bulbs													
Miscellaneous													
Operating Supplies													
Painting and Wallcovering													
Plumbing													
Swimming Pool													

Exhibit 11 *(continued)*

	PERIOD OF											
	CURRENT PERIOD						YEAR-TO-DATE					
	ACTUAL		FORECAST/ BUDGET		PRIOR YEAR		ACTUAL		FORECAST/ BUDGET		PRIOR YEAR	
	$	%	$	%	$	%	$	%	$	%	$	%
Training												
Travel—Meals and Entertainment												
Travel—Other												
Uniform Costs												
Uniform Laundry												
Vehicle Repair												
Waste Removal												
Total Other Expenses												
TOTAL EXPENSES												

Source: *Uniform System of Accounts for the Lodging Industry,* 11th Rev. Ed. (Lansing, Mich.: American Hotel & Lodging Educational Institute, 2014).

Exhibit 12   Utility Cost Schedule

	PERIOD OF											
	CURRENT PERIOD						YEAR-TO-DATE					
	ACTUAL		FORECAST/ BUDGET		PRIOR YEAR		ACTUAL		FORECAST/ BUDGET		PRIOR YEAR	
	$	%	$	%	$	%	$	%	$	%	$	%
UTILITIES												
Electricity												
Gas												
Oil												
Water/Sewer												
Steam												
Chilled Water												
Other Fuels												
Contract Services												
TOTAL EXPENSES												

Source: *Uniform System of Accounts for the Lodging Industry,* 11th Rev. Ed. (Lansing, Mich.: American Hotel & Lodging Educational Institute, 2014).

POM budget; rubbish removal is a quickly growing cost for many operations. Utility costs include not only what is typically considered to be energy (fuels and electricity), but also water (and sewer) charges. While the fuel and electricity portions of this account have been relatively stable in most areas in recent years, the water and sewer component has substantially increased due to water shortages and/or increased costs of sewage disposal.

Electricity prices vary widely from state to state (and even within states) in the United States. While the commercial electricity price within the United States averages about $0.10 per kwh, the state of Hawaii has an average commercial price of almost $0.35 per kwh and the next highest state (New York) has a price of about $0.15 per kwh. On the lower end, the state of Idaho has an average commercial price of just under $0.07 per kwh. While the nationwide average price increased by only 7 percent from 2006 to 2012, the price in Hawaii increased 63 percent and in West Virginia by 51 percent. Texas, on the other hand, saw average prices decrease by about 17 percent over the 2006–2012 period. Natural gas prices also vary by state, and they also vary significantly by month, due to the higher demand for not only space heating but increasingly for electrical power generation. Recent years have seen price reductions in natural gas as new sources have been developed.[4]

Exhibit 13 presents sample annual budget information for the POM and utility budgets. The process of preparing the POM and utility budgets should use data from several sources. For POM, the labor portion should be approached as it would be for any department, using expected staffing levels, projected hourly wages, and estimated benefit costs. The non-labor portion of the POM account requires a somewhat different treatment. While many operations budget this portion by adding a percentage to the previous year's amount, this approach can create problems. In particular, when either the base year or the year being budgeted involves extraordinary expenditures, this method may produce unreliable figures. For example, a renovation, whether it is upcoming or just finished, will probably reduce the need to expend resources on basic repairs. Conversely, as a property ages, costly repairs may be needed in some years.

Budgeting the utility portion is best handled by dealing with the actual units of energy purchased (kwh, gallons, liters, or whatever is appropriate) and attempting to secure price estimates for these fuels for the coming year from suppliers. Global political events can cause major changes in oil prices, which have some indirect impact on utility costs when oil is used in electricity production. This is one reason for the high price of electricity in Hawaii, where 75 percent of the electricity is produced using oil as the fuel. With the United States producing more oil and natural gas in recent years, the sensitivity of continental-U.S. energy prices to global events has lessened to some extent. Hotels have benefitted from the lower energy prices enjoyed in recent years. While this may continue, attention to what is happening in local energy markets is still important when developing budgets.

Contract Services, Responsibility Accounting, and Facilities Costs

There was a time when many contract services were charged to the POM budget, regardless of which department used those contract services. The *Uniform System of Accounts for the Lodging Industry* has rejected this approach since 1996. In the 1996 edition, *USALI* made a change to include "any contracted service expense within the department that is responsible for the contract."[5] Such charges are now assigned to the Contract Services line of the affected department or cost center. While properties are not required to follow the *USALI*, most do.

Exhibit 13   Sample Facilities Department Budget Information

315-Room Resort Hotel

POM Payroll Budget

Cash Payroll	$560,400
PTO	37,400
Sick Pay	9,300
Bonus	17,300
Employee Meals	9,900
Health Insurance	63,100
401K Match	7,400
FICA	47,800
FUTA	5,000
SUI	6,200
Workers Comp	7,200
Total	**$771,000**

Other POM Expenses

A/C & Refrigeration	$68,300
Building	80,900
Electrical and Mechanical	19,400
Elevators and Escalators	52,900
Equipment Repairs—Kitchen	58,800
Equipment Repairs—Laundry	41,700
Floor Coverings	7,400
Furniture	5,300
Grounds and Landscaping	212,900
Information Technology	1,300
Light Bulbs	23,300
Locks and Keys	3,800
Maintenance Contracts	114,600
Painting and Decorating	8,800
Personnel—Development	5,300
Plumbing	31,900
Postage and Overnight Mail	400
Supplies—Office	1,300
Supplies—Operating	10,100
Swimming Pool	24,200
Telecommunications	3,800
Travel	1,900
Uniforms	12,100
Vehicle	3,200
Waste Removal	40,300
Total	**$833,900**

Utilities

Electricity	$974,200
Natural Gas	111,700
Water/Sewer	191,300
Total	**$1,277,200**

The income of a revenue department (for example, rooms, food and beverage) is computed by subtracting from departmental revenue a number of expenses that are traceable to the department. Other expenses are not charged directly to revenue departments, even when those departments benefit from the expenditures. For instance, undistributed operating expenses (such as marketing, and property operation and maintenance) and expenses that are charged against gross operating profit such as rent, insurance, depreciation, and property taxes are not charged against individual revenue departments. This approach to departmental income is chosen to help ensure account uniformity. Uniformity is important for the comparability of operating units.

However, because of this approach to departmental income measurement, departmental expenses omit a number of significant costs that a revenue department may incur indirectly. To get a complete and legitimate measure of departmental performance, it may be necessary to ascribe many of the undistributed operating expenses and deductions from gross operating profit to the revenue departments. For example, there may be times when managers wish to know the overall cost of operating a department. This information is useful for assessing the profitability of a department, for determining prices for services and goods, and for determining whether outsourcing for the services is practicable. Identifying the true full costs incurred by a department is also useful for making managers responsible for the consumption of resources that drive costs. Managers who are charged for resources may use them more judiciously than those who do not feel responsible for certain costs. Charging costs to revenue departments may also provide departmental managers with more incentive to monitor the costs of service departments, since these costs will be assigned to their departments.[6]

It is certainly possible to submeter utilities within hotels and track specific information on the usage of utilities by various areas. This is most readily done during property construction, since the installation of the meters is easiest at that point. There are also methods to allocate utility costs based on area or other factors. With the growth of food and beverage (F&B) outsourcing within hotels, there may be a growth in interest among both hoteliers and the F&B operators in getting metered information about utility usage.

Arguably, the easiest facilities expense to charge to areas using the service is that of POM. Computerized maintenance management systems can readily account for the POM activity of the major revenue areas of the property as well as other areas (such as the laundry). The *USALI* indicates that expenses incurred by the facilities department for providing special customer services (such as for trade shows or weddings) are to be charged to the department receiving the revenue for these events.

Finally, although not addressed in the *USALI*, an additional cost-tracking opportunity is to allocate the capital expenditure costs to departments. This large expenditure could shed some most interesting (and possibly unwelcome) light on the actual costs and profitability of various activities in the hotel.

Charging costs to "tenants" in a building is not a new idea. Many lodging companies already do this within their timeshare/condominium divisions and, when the hotel is part of a mixed-use complex, a central plant with submetering often supplies utility services. There is increasing interest in this activity for all utility services, since it is generally acknowledged that submetered customers paying directly for their own usage are more frugal than those who are not metered. There is little reason to believe that the same would not be true for departments in a hotel.

Capital Expenditure (CapEx) Management

The management of capital expenditures is a significant task. At the unit level, the magnitude of responsibility will vary with the size of the property and the corporate organizational structure. At small properties, the owner or general manager may be extensively involved in the planning decision and implementation of capital expenditures. This responsibility at large properties may again be in the hands of the owner or general manager, or the facilities manager may play a more significant role. In any event, two major managerial functions related to capital expenditures must be addressed: (1) planning and budgeting, and (2) execution.

Planning and budgeting for **CapEx** requires knowledge of the expected lifetime of various elements of the facility and the cost of their replacement. Lifetime is defined as a function of the item itself (for example, kitchen equipment lasts longer than office equipment), the durability of the item (commercial grade lasts longer than residential), the care of the item (periodic and proper cleaning of items such as carpeting extends their lifetimes), the degree of use (a space with 90 percent usage will wear faster than one with 50 percent usage), the degree of abuse (items cannot withstand high levels of guest or employee abuse), and the overall level of appearance expected by management and guests (a "worn and tired" piece of FF&E unacceptable at a five-star property could be quite acceptable at a two-star hotel).

Property-specific data tailored to the unique issues facing the property itself is the most pertinent to CapEx planning. Generally speaking, CapEx activity becomes heightened beginning approximately in year five of a property's existence. A property should have a CapEx plan that addresses at a minimum its near-term needs (two to five years), with the management team at least being aware of expected longer-term needs (six to twenty-five years). A study conducted by the International Society of Hospitality Consultants is useful in further understanding CapEx issues. The most recent version of this study is titled *CapEx 2007 — A Study of Capital Expenditures in the U.S. Hotel Industry.*[7]

Exhibit 14 is the capital budget for a 315-room resort hotel. The "Building and Engineering" and "Site and Landscaping" elements of this budget will certainly be directly managed by the facilities department, and other areas of the CapEx budget will also likely get input from the facilities department.

What are some of the major elements that make up the Building and Engineering expenses? In Year 1, the resort has over $300,000 budgeted for roofing, all three years have almost $150,000 budgeted for HVAC expenses, and in Year 3, elevator expenses are budgeted at $400,000. In the Site and Landscaping category, the parking lot is scheduled for repair and resurfacing in Year 1, requiring expenditures in excess of $500,000 for that one item alone. It is quite likely that all of the estimated expenses for Year 3 will grow higher as that year gets nearer. What is illustrated in these figures is the potentially "lumpy" nature of CapEx, with some

Exhibit 14   Sample Capital Budget

Capital Budget for a 315-Room Resort Hotel			
	\<Year 1\> Budget	\<Year 2\> Budget	\<Year 3\> Budget
Total Building and Engineering	$734,000	$626,000	$807,000
Total Rooms Division	178,1000	270,000	24,000
Total Site and Landscaping	684,000	45,000	45,000
Total Food and Beverage	351,000	2,137,000	0
Total Meeting/Conference Center	1,096,000	138,000	61,000
Total Public Areas	113,000	0	0
Total Recreation and Health	400,000	432,000	212,000
Total Information Technology	399,000	43,000	76,000
Sub-total Capital Expenditures	5,558,000	3,690,000	1,225,000
Annual Escalation	5,558,000	3,801,000	1,299,000
Project Management	222,000	152,000	52,000
Total Property Expenditures	$5,780,000	$3,953,000	$1,351,000

years seeing dramatically higher expenditures than other years. That lumpy or roller-coaster nature of CapEx expenses is due to the reality that some CapEx costs can't be spread over a number of years. When the parking lot is repaired and resurfaced, for example, the entire cost for that work appears in the year the work was done; the same goes for when the roof is replaced. So, if too many major CapEx items are allowed to pile up, delays in taking care of these items will almost always occur, because the needed funds won't be there to take care of them all at once. To avoid this budget problem, proactivity rather than reactivity is needed, and this means planning.

The execution of CapEx plans is in many ways similar to the process of facilities construction. Detailed plans and specifications may need to be prepared. These are placed out to bid and vendors and contractors must be selected. Contracts must be negotiated and signed. Timelines and plans must be coordinated with hotel operations. When construction begins, conformance to budget and timetable must be monitored, along with the quality of the work and materials supplied. Often, the responsibility for overseeing a CapEx project is given to the facilities manager. Depending on the size of the task, the size and skills of the staff, and the preferences of the owner-operator, the actual execution of the CapEx activity may be by in-house staff, outside contractors, or a combination of the two.

In some cases, the planning and even the execution of CapEx at hotels is under the oversight of an **asset manager**, an employee of the owner who serves as a combination of owner representative, investment manager, financial and marketing consultant, and project manager. The asset manager position evolved during the late 1980s and early 1990s, as owners of lodging properties recognized that their interests might not have been adequately served in CapEx projects.[8]

CapEx expenditures are made by the building owner and represent large outflows of cash. While a large portion of CapEx expenditures is related to issues of physical appearance of the building and its interior finishes, expenditures are also made to replace mechanical equipment and building systems. Investing in energy-efficient equipment and systems can result in significant operating cost savings. Purchasing energy-efficient equipment and systems may even result in rebates or credits of a portion of the costs. Facilities personnel and asset managers clearly need to be aware of such rebates or credits to take advantage of them.

Rebates or credits can come from several sources. One source is the local utility providing electric and sometimes even gas services. Many utilities provide rebates for the purchase of energy-efficient equipment, and some provide partial or total payment for the cost of energy-efficiency audits as well. A second source for rebates and similar assistance are programs of state and local governments. For example, the New York State Energy Research and Development Administration, a state agency funded by a charge on utility bills, provides a wide array of rebates and energy-efficiency funding.[9] Various other organizations periodically accumulate information about special rebate opportunities such as renewable energy. The federal government also offers some tax rebates for energy efficiency.[10] Hospitality managers in other countries are encouraged to investigate sources of rebates or credits within their local settings.

Facilities Benchmarking

The concept of **facilities benchmarking**—developing numerical (and other) standards that allow comparison of a given facility to itself and to other facilities—is not new. Facilities costs and utilities usage have long lent themselves to this concept. And, with the right tools in place, it is also possible to benchmark facilities service itself, providing insights into areas in which the facilities department is providing guest service and those areas that need improvement. The desired result is improved cost control and better service.

Given the accounting system used by the industry, it is not unusual to attempt to benchmark utilities based on cost per room as a percent of revenue. As was indicated previously, facilities-related costs and other measurements are best compared on a per-square-foot or -square-meter basis. This is how benchmarks are developed for other types of commercial real estate.

A number of tools to assist hotels in benchmarking their energy and, in some instances, environmental practices have emerged in recent years. Within the United States, the Environmental Protection Agency has launched the Energy Star Portfolio Manager program, which scores the energy performance of buildings on a 1 to 100 scale.[11] Use of benchmarking via Energy Star is encouraged or required by many environmental certifications and "best practices" programs.[12]

Other benchmarking activities have occurred in industry associations at the national level in other countries. One notable service is provided by the Federation of Hotel & Restaurant Associations of India (FHRAI). Hotels in India are able to use this service to obtain environmental benchmarking of their performance as a free service of their membership in FHRAI.[13]

One challenge with many energy and water benchmarking efforts outside the hotel is that the underlying support for continuing these efforts often disappears. For example, the U.S. federal government discontinued a program called the Commercial Building Energy Consumption Survey, which resulted in the loss of a source of information that was used for energy benchmarking. Various hotel and tourism groups have initiated benchmarking activities over the years as well, only to see these activities cease after a short time.

The most readily used benchmarking data source is the property itself. Comparing performance with similar time periods in previous years or monitoring long-term trends in performance is readily done. Internal benchmarking gets around the challenge of comparing like with like that exists when outside comparisons are made. However, looking only internally for benchmarks and best practices may result in a complacent attitude and a failure to strive for significant improvements in performance.

The creation of benchmarks for the POM budget can be expressed in total expenditures per room or as a percent of revenue. Facilities labor per room could also be compared, as either staff per 100 rooms or rooms per staff member. As with utilities, a per-room benchmark can make comparisons between properties misleading. Commercial real estate firms might use a value such as facilities staff full-time equivalents (FTE) per unit area.

Exhibit 15 contains sample benchmarks from one major lodging corporation. Numeric values for each of these benchmarks will vary depending on the age of the property; extent of services; local costs of utilities, labor, and materials; and a variety of other factors.

The introduction of computerized maintenance management systems has significantly increased the ability of managers to use other benchmarks. Benchmarks readily available in these systems are:

- Work orders completed per unit of time—total by trade, location, piece/type of equipment, and employee.

Exhibit 15   Sample Benchmarks for Commercial Hotels

Benchmark

Rooms per Person
Sq. Ft. per Person
POM% of Revenue
POM Cost per Room
POM Cost per Sq. Ft.
Energy % of Revenue
Energy Cost per Sq. Ft.

- Work order backlog—total by trade, location, age, and employee.

- Work order response time—total by trade, location, age, and employee.

- Work orders created—total by location, employee, department, and time of day.

Benchmarking can be a useful tool to the hotelier, and there are indications that its use will become even more widespread, especially as environmental issues develop. However, caution must be used when applying this tool. The needs and even abilities of properties vary significantly due to climate, facilities, systems, and age. A good first step to initiating benchmarking as a management tool is to use a property's own parameters. After this, comparison with other facilities is appropriate when done with care. The result should help create a measurable path for improved service and reduced costs.

Personnel Management in Facilities

Key concerns in the management of facilities department personnel include job qualifications, on-the-job supervision, and employee productivity. Depending on the size of the property and the complexity of the equipment, the way in which the departmental organization is structured will vary, as will the needs for management.

Management personnel for the facilities department will need to have some level of mechanical and electrical skill. The smaller the property, the more the engineering manager will have a "hands-on" role with regard to maintenance. As staff size grows and departmental responsibilities increase, the engineering manager becomes much more a manager and much less a line worker.

Line staff members in the facilities department need very broad skills in maintenance at the small property level, where they perform a varied list of tasks. Usually, these staff members need an education in the electrical, mechanical, and plumbing trades beyond that available in high school. Ideally, they would have several years of experience in these fields. As a screening technique, many operations develop a set of technical questions about maintaining the types of equipment they own. Applicants then must try to answer these questions. In addition, since maintenance staff members are sometimes required to lift heavy objects, they should be in good health and physical condition. Properties should consider using a physical examination as part of the hiring process. If physical examinations are required, in the United States they must be required of everyone applying for a given job; requiring physical examinations selectively violates the Americans with Disabilities Act.

Since facilities staff members work all over the property, often under minimal direct supervision, they need to be reliable and capable of working on their own. In addition, they need to be aware of what constitutes good workmanship and proper safety procedures and of what complies with local codes. While their trade training should provide much of this knowledge, the property still needs to establish and communicate its own standards regarding, for example, appearance and how to address guests and fellow employees.

Training and Certification

Providing the necessary training for facilities staff and management is not difficult, but it does require commitment, time, and money. With low turnover common within a facilities department, little is invested over time in recruitment and job familiarization training of staff. A "fair share" approach suggests that money and time be budgeted to the department to allow long-term facilities staff members to continue upgrading their skills. This is especially important for staff members holding positions and performing tasks that require licensing and certification.

The American Hotel & Lodging Educational Institute (AHLEI) offers a Maintenance Employee Hospitality Skills Certification program. Employees who complete this program will have received information about basic maintenance skills and knowledge, including information concerning preventative maintenance, HVAC systems, maintenance tools, environmental issues, and OSHA regulations.[14] Also available from AHLEI are several training videos appropriate for facilities staff, including *Hospitality Fire Prevention, Hazard Communications,* and *Preventive Guestroom Maintenance.*

Facilities line staff can benefit from programs offered by local technical schools and a host of trade associations. Groups such as the International Facilities Management Association (IFMA) and Building Owners and Managers Association (BOMA) offer course and certification sequences geared toward developing the skills and knowledge of the technical staff.[15] Also, most equipment suppliers offer a variety of technical training that may be a requirement of new equipment acquisition. Such training is either included in the purchase price of the equipment or offered for a fee.

Training for the facilities department's management staff is also widely available. Not only can these managers benefit from the programs for line staff, they can take advantage of certification programs offered for facilities managers. Both IFMA and BOMA have certification sequences of various types oriented toward corporate and speculative office building managers and not-for-profit building managers. AHLEI offers the Certified Hospitality Facilities Executive certification program that recognizes individuals possessing a specified combination of experience and knowledge in the field. Also available through AHLEI is the Certified Director of Engineering (CDOE) certification. This certification is from the National Association of Hotel & Lodging Engineers (NAHLE). NAHLE also offers a Certified Chief Engineer (CCE) Program for Select Service Properties that is administered by AHLEI.

A good source for technical skills and knowledge is the Energy University offered by Schneider Electric. "Energy University is a FREE online, educational resource, offering more than 200 vendor-neutral courses on energy efficiency and data center topics to help you identify, implement, and monitor efficiency improvements within your organization."[16] Schneider has partnered with AHLEI to include and recognize Energy University courses as education points toward recertification for the Certified Hotel Administrator (CHA) and the Certified Hospitality Facilities Executive (CHFE) certifications.

While the facilities manager/director of engineering (FM/DOE) needs knowledge regarding the technical aspects of facilities, he or she also needs managerial skills. At the property level, FM/DOEs need to continually interact and communicate with other managers and recognize that they are in the service business and therefore must know how to deal graciously with customers. And, particularly with regard to CapEx issues, the FM/DOE also will need to communicate with asset managers and owners. Professionalism during all of these interactions is important. Providing services in ways that add value to all aspects of the hotel is also important. For example, being aware of the total cost of ownership (TCO)[17] of various building components and encouraging the use of the TCO concept in facilities decisions is one valuable service that can be provided by the FM/DOE.

Communication and coordination needs extend beyond the individual hotel. When hotel companies have multiple properties in cities, they will sometimes designate the FM/DOE of one hotel as the "cluster leader." The cluster leader can assist managers at other properties in addressing questions which may arise, as well as encourage those managers in the performance of their duties and even perform evaluations of other hotels. Cluster leaders can also receive training and information from corporate or other sources and then share these with others. For individual hotels lacking a larger corporate base, the FM/DOE may find that a local hotel engineers association may be a good place for ideas and information.[18] Of course, hotel engineering associations have also been established in countries outside the United States. An example of such an organization is the Australian Institute of Hotel Engineering.[19] Local chapters of groups such as BOMA and IFMA[20] may also be good places for information and professional development. BOMA and IFMA have chapters in many countries as well.

Many of the issues facing hotel facilities managers are also faced by restaurant owners and operators. The Restaurant Facility Management Association (RFMA) was formed to "advance industry awareness of restaurant facility management while promoting professional and ethical standards to serve the customer with added value."[21] In 2010, RFMA launched its official publication, *The Facilitator*, which is currently published bi-monthly. RFMA offers conferences, educational activities, certification programs, and career services, and serves as an advocate for facilities issues in restaurants.

Building Certification

In recent years there has been increasing interest in establishing standards for "green" or "sustainable" products of many types. This interest has included buildings. One early program in this regard was the Building Research Establishment's Environmental Assessment Method (BREEAM) in the United Kingdom. "BREAM sets the standard for best practice in sustainable building design, construction, and operation and has become one of the most comprehensive and widely recognized measures of a building's environmental performance."[22] BREEAM also has a presence in various European Union countries and elsewhere around the globe. Assessments are made by BREEAM of buildings, points awarded, and performance rated on a star system. New and existing structures can be rated.

In the United States, the U. S. Green Buildings Council (USGBC) has developed a certification program for new and existing buildings referred to as LEED (Leadership in Energy and Environmental Design). LEED is "a green building certification program that recognizes best-in-class building strategies and practices. To receive LEED certification, building projects satisfy prerequisites and earn points to achieve different levels of certification."[23] As of this writing, there are almost 400 LEED-certified hotels listed on the USGBC website.

Endnotes

1. Gaston Lauryssen, "Proved Plans that Have Reduced Engineering Costs," *Mid-West Hotel Reporter*, 1929, reprinted in *Hotel Engineering* 1 (1941).

2. The suggested modifications to this chapter, made during the revision of the third edition, of Professor Carolyn Lambert of Pennsylvania State University and Mr. Dennis Peete of Servidyne Corporation are acknowledged and appreciated.

3. Richard F. Muhlebach and Frank E. Ryan, "Developing the Maintenance Agreement," *Journal of Property Management,* March/April 1988, p. 40.

4. http://www.eia.gov/dnav/ng/NG_PRI_SUM_A_EPG0_PCS_DMCF_M.htm.

5. *Uniform System of Accounts for the Lodging Industry*, 9th Rev. Ed. (Lansing Mich.: American Hotel & Lodging Educational Institute, 1996), p. ix. (Note: The 11th revised edition came out in 2014.)

6. *Uniform System of Accounts for the Lodging Industry,* p. 183.

7. *CapEx 2007* is published by the International Society of Hospitality Consultants, 515 King, Street, Suite 420, Alexandria, VA 22314; www.ishc.com.

8. Further information about asset management can be found in Greg Denton, Lori E. Raleigh, and A. J. Singh, eds., *Hotel Asset Management: Principles & Practices,* 2nd ed. (Lansing, Mich.: American Hotel & Lodging Educational Institute, 2009).

9. www.nyserda.org/incentives.asp.

10. Refer to the Database of State Incentives for Renewable & Efficiency for information on the variety of rebates and incentives that are available at http://www.dsireusa.org/.

11. http://www.energystar.gov/buildings/tools-and-resources/energy-star-score-hotels.

12. An example of a "best practices" program using Energy Star is the "14 Minimum Guidelines for Going Green" program of the American Hotel & Lodging Association; http://www.ahla.com/Green.aspx?id=35740.

13. www.dainet.org/benchmarking/about_this_model.asp.

14. https://www.ahlei.org/CME/.

15. For further information, visit www.ifma.org and www.boma.org.

16. http://www2.schneider-electric.com/sites/corporate/en/products-services/training/energy-university/energy-university.page.

17. http://www.business-case-analysis.com/total-cost-of-ownership.html.

18. An example of such a group is the Hotel Engineers Association of New York; http://hotelengineers.org.

19. http://www.aihe.com.au/.

20. http://www.breeam.org/about.jsp?id=66.

21. www.rfmalonline.com.

22. http://www.breeam.org/about.jsp?id=66.

23. www.usgbc.org.

🔑 Key Terms

asset manager—An official of the property who serves as a combination of owner representative, investment manager, financial and marketing consultant, and project engineer.

CapEx—An abbreviation for "capital expenditure"; capital expenditures are expenditures for items such as FF&E and building systems.

computerized maintenance management system (CMMS)—A computerized maintenance scheduling, recordkeeping, and archiving system that streamlines the "paperwork and dispatch" of maintenance and repair.

contract maintenance—Maintenance performed by contract service companies.

control schematic—A document showing the relays, timers, fuses, switches, and basic wiring of controls within equipment.

emergency/breakdown maintenance—Maintenance required for problems that either create an immediate negative revenue effect or are likely to create a negative revenue effect if allowed to continue. Also called reactive maintenance.

equipment data card—A card used for each major piece of equipment to record facts and information of importance for maintenance purposes.

facilities benchmarking—A continuous-improvement initiative of developing numerical and other standards to allow the comparison of a given facility to itself and to other properties or facilities.

guestroom maintenance—A form of preventive maintenance involving the inspection of a number of items in the guestroom, minor lubrication of doors and other equipment, repair of obvious small problems, and, when needed, the initiation of work orders for more substantial problems or needs.

inventory record—A recordkeeping system that keeps track of the equipment and other items in physical inventory.

material safety data sheets (MSDSs)—OSHA-mandated forms that inform employees about potentially hazardous materials used in the workplace, how to work safely with these materials, and what to do in case of an accident. Vendors and suppliers of hazardous materials must provide an MSDS for each product. These forms must be available to employees.

outsourcing—A practice in which facilities services are provided by contract service firms rather than by in-house staff.

POM—An abbreviation for "Property Operation and Maintenance." One of two principal cost entries (the other being utilities) in the hospitality industry detailing ongoing costs of operation following construction of the facility.

predictive maintenance—Maintenance that uses sophisticated technological methods to increase the operational life of equipment and systems, and target preemptive corrective actions by using diagnostic-based maintenance planning.

preventive maintenance—Maintenance stressing inspections, lubrication, minor repairs or adjustments, and work order initiation, generally performed using manufacturers' information as a guideline.

preventive maintenance instructions—Maintenance instructions derived from experience, input from vendors and suppliers, and information from various professional and technical organizations. May contain a listing of parts or equipment required to perform each task.

preventive maintenance schedule—A schedule for maintaining elements of the building that are critical to guest satisfaction, overall property image and marketing, safety and security, and the performance of other departments' duties.

reactive maintenance—See *emergency/breakdown maintenance.*

repair order—A document used to initiate requests for maintenance services. Also called a work order.

room data card—A card used to record information concerning the basic characteristics and major elements of an individual guestroom.

rooms checklist—A checklist used for guestroom (preventive) maintenance, usually listing all of the items in the guestroom and providing a brief indication of the type of inspection, lubrication, or cleaning activity to be performed.

routine maintenance—Maintenance that pertains to the general upkeep of the property, recurs on a regular basis, and requires relatively minimal skill or training to perform (for example, grass mowing, leaf raking, snow shoveling, carpet and floor cleaning, etc.).

scheduled maintenance—Significant maintenance requiring advance planning, a significant amount of time to perform, specialized tools and equipment, and high levels of coordination among departments.

work order—See *repair order.*

Review Questions

1. What are the basic activities associated with preventive maintenance?

2. Under what circumstances might it be appropriate for hospitality managers to use contract maintenance services?

3. How are equipment data cards similar to and different from room data cards?

4. Why is it important to consider inventory needs when designing a facility? What problems can arise if these needs are ignored at this stage?

5. How does preventive maintenance contribute to the productive use of labor?

6. What are the possible consequences of failing to update building plans as changes are made?

7. What is the best way to determine the energy budget? the labor portion of the POM budget?

8. How does property size affect the facilities department's role in capital projects and renovations?

9. What factors affect the size of the facilities staff?

10. What are some possible measures of facilities department productivity? What are the pros and cons of using these measures? What steps can be taken to improve productivity?

11. What are the principal benefits of a CMMS?

12. What is facilities benchmarking? How can benchmarking aid the facilities manager?

13. What is submetering? How does it help in managing costs?

14. What is CapEx management?

15. What are the tasks of the asset manager?

Internet Sites

For more information, visit the following Internet sites. Remember that Internet addresses can change without notice. If the site is no longer there, you can use a search engine to look for additional sites.

American School & Hospital Facility
www.facilitymanagement.com

Buildings
www.buildings.com

Building Operating Management
www.facilitiesnet.com/bom/

FacilitiesNet
www.facilitiesnet.com

Facility Maintenance Decisions
www.facilitiesnet.com/ms

FMLINK
www.fmlink.com

Institute of Real Estate Management,
Journal of Property Management
www.irem.org/sechome.cfm?sec=jpm

International Society of Hospitality
Consultants
www.ishc.com

Maintenance Solutions
www.facilitiesnet.com/ms

United States Department of Energy,
Energy Information Agency, Commercial Buildings Energy Consumption Survey
www.eia.doe.gov/emeu/cbecs

Case Study

How Many Calls Does It Take to Change a Light Bulb?

The phone was ringing. Again.

The tonal buzz was insistent and, at 5:15 P.M., was not likely to be good news. Abel Wallington, the director of engineering for a 1,000-room downtown hotel, hit the save hotkey on the report he was preparing for his general manager. Maia Bounacas, the general manager, had asked him to detail the benefits the property had been experiencing since installing the new computerized maintenance management system. A sister property was considering installing the same system and Abel wanted to help them make the most of it.

He picked up the phone and had barely gotten out his greeting when the strident voice of Daphne Remonstra, the front office manager, interrupted him. "Is anyone working down there? Abel, what is going on in your department? This is the fourth time this week that we're sitting on forty-eight out-of-order rooms right before the height of my check-in time. I've got a convention coming in and they're all going to be sitting in the lobby waiting for rooms. Our coat-check room is full of luggage and our bell attendants can barely move in it."

Abel clicked onto the work order system, grateful that the system put the status of all work orders at the tips of his fingers. "I couldn't have done this six months ago," he thought to himself. "Of course, six months ago, we weren't having these problems."

He quickly sorted the work orders and saw that thirty-nine of the forty-eight out-of-order rooms were due to burned-out light bulbs and that his only electrician was currently working on them.

"We should be getting them in pretty quickly, Daphne," he said. "But you know Maia has a zero-tolerance policy on burned-out light bulbs and won't let us release a room until they're changed."

"What I know is that I've got to comp drinks for a lobby-full of weary travelers!" Daphne said as she slammed the phone down.

Abel sighed and set aside his report to go help his skeletal evening staff replace light bulbs and get the rooms back into order more quickly. Ninety minutes later, he was walking back to his office with his swing shift engineer, Vernon.

"I dunno, boss," Vernon said as he shrugged into his jacket and punched his passcode into the system to clock out. "Days like today are becoming awful common. It's slow for hours and then we get slammed with more work orders than we can turn before check-in time. Sure would be nice if we could get the orders a little earlier in the day."

"That it would," Abel agreed. "Have a good night and I'll see you tomorrow." He went into his office and pulled up his report again.

The maintenance software allowed room attendants to call in requests directly to the work order system. The automated response walked them through the reporting process in the language of their choice. The hotel had installed modules for English, Spanish, Chinese, French, and German. The system then generated a work order, prioritized it, and sent it to the alphanumeric pager that each engineering department employee carried. They knew they'd get a lot of great benefits with a computerized work order system, but this went far beyond their expectations.

Abel quickly reviewed the system's other features:

- It creates a history of closed work orders.

- It allows assignment of work order priority.

- It tracks "who, what, where, and when" for each work order, including who identified the problem, whether a guest initiated the request, who corrected it, time reported, time closed, where the order was initiated from, and where the deficiency was.

- It allows for all employees to call in work orders with simple codes from any in-house phone.

- It sorts data by room, floor, and building.

- It records labor and materials costs on each work order.

- It can view open, overdue, and on-hold work orders for any asset.

- It creates data tables for employee records.

- It creates a variety of reports based on user-input sorts.

He'd already detailed the benefits for the first two features in his report and had just started on the third one when he'd been interrupted. He re-read the paragraph he'd just finished:

> Tracking data has allowed us to do things we've never been able to do before. For example, by sorting orders according to repeat calls, we discovered that the bathroom ceiling in Room 455 had been re-painted six times in one year. Each time a different maintenance employee had performed the work and no one realized that this was a repeat problem. This data raised a red flag for us. We investigated and found that the real problem was a slow leaking toilet in a low-occupancy room above it. This time, we fixed the real problem instead of applying a Band-Aid.

Abel consulted his outline. In his report he wanted to address four additional issues of how the system had helped to change the way the department worked. His plan was to write about how the system helped them to:

- Evaluate a proposed incentive program for the engineering and housekeeping departments.

- Benchmark their performance against other properties of their size within the chain.

- Identify tasks that could be cost-effectively outsourced.

- Prepare a budget for property operations and maintenance costs and a staffing guide.

As Abel began a new paragraph, Vernon's parting words suddenly struck him and he again pulled up the work order system. He quickly reviewed the data for the past week, sorting work orders by the time of day. Things were starting to become much clearer. He shot an e-mail off to the executive housekeeper Amber Limpieza, asking for fifteen minutes of her time the next morning. He then decided to call it a night.

At 8:30 the next morning, Abel sat down in Amber's office. "I'm hoping you can help me solve a problem we've been having. Lately we've had a lot of rooms that are still unavailable at check-in time. This creates a back-up at the front desk as well as greater-than-expected numbers in the lounge as they are serving comped guests." He took out a spreadsheet and set it in front of her. "Take a look at this, Amber. It's all the work order requests called in by housekeeping. Notice that 85 percent of the calls are coming in at either 11:30 A.M. or at 3:30 P.M. This means my staff has little to do for hours and then they get hit right before their lunch and right as most of their shifts end."

"Well, of course," she said. Abel waited for her to explain further. Amber sighed and rolled her eyes, "That's when the room attendants go on break or end *their* shift."

"I still don't get it," Abel said. "Why would we get more calls when they're on break then when they're working?"

"Because that's when the room attendants give their floor supervisors the list of all the out-of-order items," Amber replied, as if stating the obvious.

Abel was dumbfounded. He sputtered for a moment and then asked, "Why are they doing that? Why don't they just pick up the guestroom phone and call it into the system themselves?"

"Come on, Abel," she answered. "Most of my staff has been working here fifteen years or more. Do you really think they're going to change the way they do things? Besides, most say they don't understand how to use the system."

Discussion Questions

1. How does the issue of having all the work orders hit the system at once affect both internal and external customers?

2. What is the root cause of the problem and what other factors contribute to it?

3. What are some of the ways the problem can be solved?

4. How can a computerized work order system provide information to address the four issues Abel mentions in his report:

    *   Evaluate a proposed incentive program for the engineering and housekeeping department.

    *   Benchmark their performance against other properties of their size within the chain.

    *   Identify tasks that could be cost-effectively outsourced.

    *   Prepare a budget for property operations and maintenance costs and a staffing guide.

Case Number: 2812CA

The following industry experts helped generate and develop this case: Richard Manzolina, Director of Property Operations, Capital Hilton, Washington, D.C.; Ed Pietzak, RPA, FMA, CEOE, Director of Engineering, New York Marriott Marquis, New York, New York; and David M. Stipanuk, Associate Professor, School of Hotel Administration, Cornell University, Ithaca, New York.

Case Study

To Certify or Not to Certify?

The board of directors of the Gold Standard hotel chain is considering expanding the chain's market reach by adding a group of existing limited-service hotels currently owned by another chain to its portfolio. During the due diligence process, top management from Gold Standard toured several of the properties and found some serious infrastructure issues across all of them, including substandard preventive maintenance programs and malfunctioning life safety systems. The board is now in the process of researching solutions to these problems and deciding whether Gold Standard should continue to pursue the acquisition.

Kate Allen, a high-level executive at Gold Standard, is on her way home from an American Hotel & Lodging Association (AH&LA) conference. At the conference, she heard a presentation about a major competitor's recent implementation of a program to require all engineering management staff members to earn a Certified Hospitality Facilities Executive (CHFE) designation in order to move up through the ranks. The designation is attained through AH&LA's Educational Institute, which offers programs based on education, experience, or early entry. Candidates must also successfully complete a comprehensive examination at the end of their program.

Kate has earned a CHA designation from AH&LA, and feels that it has been useful throughout her career. She thought this sounded like at least part of the solution to Gold Standard's potential infrastructure woes among the limited-service properties. "You know," she thought, "I bet most of these issues stem from the fact that the engineering managers at these properties simply lack experience or haven't been given the chance to continue their educations." As she continued to think about the potential of implementing a certification requirement at Gold Standard, she realized that the company already required all engineering managers at its properties to participate in forty hours of training each year. Why not standardize the training so everyone gets the most out of their time and the company knows exactly what it is getting? "And," Kate thought, "if we require the same training for everyone, every manager at every property will be on the same page with regard to engineering tasks and how they need to be done."

As soon as her plane landed, Kate placed an excited phone call to Keith McGarry, the board's chairman, to tell him about her ideas for implementing the certification requirement. He said, "Well, it certainly sounds like you heard a convincing presentation, but board members are going to want more information before they sign off on such a drastic change in policy. I'd like you to prepare a report for our next meeting that includes the costs and benefits of implementing such a program, as well as ways to address any concerns our engineering staff might have."

Kate knew she had a daunting task ahead of her, but she was confident that she would be able to convince the board that a certification requirement was just what the company needed.

Discussion Questions

1. What are some of the benefits and costs for Gold Standard to consider when deciding whether to require certification for its engineering managers?

2. What concerns might engineering managers have about such a requirement? How might these concerns be addressed?

Case Number: 2812CB

The following industry experts helped generate and develop this case: Richard Manzolina, Director of Property Operations, Capital Hilton, Washington, D.C.; Ed Pietzak, RPA, FMA, CEOE, Director of Engineering, New York Marriott Marquis, New York, New York; and David M. Stipanuk, Associate Professor, School of Hotel Administration, Cornell University, Ithaca, New York.

Chapter Appendix:

Sample Preventive Maintenance Procedures

What follows are sample preventive maintenance procedures for a guestroom AC wall unit, an ice machine, and laundry equipment. They are provided for illustrative purposes and are not suggested as the only recommended procedures for such equipment.

TASK 5

Inspect and Service Guestroom AC Unit

STEPS:	HOW-TO'S:	TIPS:
To complete all steps, you will need new AC unit filters; lubrication; dry, clean cloths; a coil cleaner; a coil comb; and sandpaper.		
1. Inspect filter.	❑ Unplug the AC unit.	
	❑ Remove the AC unit grill or front.	*Some AC units in guestrooms may have grills that are screwed on while others may be attached with the use of clips or tabs.*
	❑ Inspect the filter for excessive dirt and dust.	*Most AC units can accommodate both disposable and reusable filters.*
	❑ Replace disposable filters if necessary. If replacing the filter, make sure it is properly installed.	*Filters should be cleaned at least once a month during the warmer seasons. In areas where dust or sand is more prevalent, it may be necessary to replace or clean filters more frequently.*
2. Inspect the AC drain pan and drain lines.	❑ Inspect the drain pain to make sure that condensation from the unit is properly draining.	
	❑ Remove any debris, sludge, or other kinds of build-up from the drain pipe. Wipe it clean if necessary.	*It may be necessary to remove the drain pipe in order to clean it. Use a cloth and running water to clear out the drainpipe.*
	❑ Determine that water is properly moving through the drain lines and supply/return lines.	
	❑ Check that the drain lines and the supply/return lines are clear from clogs and other obstructions.	*When clearing clogs in the drain pan or lines, use a chemical approved for the prevention of **legionella** and other diseases developed in air conditioning and ventilating units.*
3. Inspect the fan blowers and motor.	❑ Check that the fan blowers are functioning properly.	
	❑ Check that the blades are free from dust or dirt.	
	❑ Wipe the blades if needed.	
	❑ Make sure the blades are not cracked or broken.	

Continued

Task 5: Inspect and Service Guestroom AC Unit *(continued)*

STEPS:	HOW-TO'S:	TIPS:
	❑ Lubricate the fan motor bearings.	*There should be an oil port on the motor for dropping lubricant into the motor. Many newer AC units are self-lubricating and care should be taken to avoid adding oil to the casing. Consult the manufacturer to determine which type of unit you have at your property.*
4. Check the AC unit coils.	❑ Clean the coils free of debris or rust. ❑ Use a coil cleaner solution to clean the coils, if necessary. ❑ Remove and steam clean the coils if they are excessively dirty or clogged. ❑ Straighten bent coils using a coil comb.	*The AC unit coils are also known as vacuum evaporator fins.*
5. Sand and prime any rusted or corroded parts of the AC unit.		
6. Calibrate the AC unit thermostat according to the thermostat manufacturer's instructions.	■ **AT YOUR PROPERTY** The instructions for calibrating the AC unit thermostats are as follows:	
7. Test the AC unit.	❑ Plug the AC unit in and make sure that it cools properly. ❑ Clean up the work area before exiting.	

TASK 22

Maintain and Service Ice Machines

STEPS:	HOW-TO'S:	TIPS:
To complete all steps, you will need a dolly or cart, a bristle brush, lubricant, a refrigeration manifold gauge, and ice machine cleaner.		*Cleaning and maintaining the ice machines at your property should be included on your preventive maintenance schedule.*
1. **Service ice machine condensing unit.**	❑ Turn off power to the ice machine unit.	
	❑ Remove the condensing unit from the ice machine and transport it to the maintenance shop on a dolly or cart.	
	❑ Perform steam cleaning on the condenser.	
	❑ Clean all the electrical contacts and switches with a contact cleaner solution.	
	❑ Check the door on the condenser. Make sure it opens and closes properly and that the door seals aren't worn.	
	❑ Check that the evaporator is functioning properly.	
	❑ Flush out the condensing unit's long drain lines with water or appropriate chemicals to guard against development of bacteria.	
	■ **AT YOUR PROPERTY**	
	Use the following chemicals when flushing out ice machine drain lines:	
	❑ Inspect the water pump. It should be sufficiently lubricated.	

Continued

Task 22: *Maintain and Service Ice Machines* (continued)

STEPS:	HOW-TO'S:	TIPS:
2. **Service ice machine compressor.**	❑ Remove the compressor cabinet cover to gain access to the condenser coil.	
	❑ Use a bristle brush to remove dirt or debris from the condenser coil.	
	❑ Check that the condenser fan motor is in good condition.	
	❑ Insert lubricant into the bearing service tubes.	
	❑ Check that the refrigerant pressure is at an appropriate level using a refrigeration manifold gauge.	*If the pressure reading is too low, the unit may require recharging.*
	❑ Clean the condenser coil cabinet of any leftover dirt with a damp cloth.	
	❑ Turn on the ice machine and check its operation by timing one cycle.	*One ice machine cycle is the amount of time between one defrost cycle and the next.*
	❑ Shut the compressor cabinet.	
3. **Service the ice machine water circulating system.**	❑ Open the cover on the water circulating system to gain access.	
	❑ Pour the proper amount of ice machine cleaner into the water circulating system. Turn on the ice machine's wash cycle and allow it to run for 30 minutes.	*The wash cycle allows water and cleaner to circulate through the system and remove sludge and impurities.*
	❑ Flush the wash water from the system and allow it to refill with fresh water.	
	❑ Turn the ice machine back on and allow the ice machine to produce a batch of ice cubes.	
	❑ Discard the first batch of ice cubes.	*Discarding the first batch of ice will ensure that no residual cleaner or water impurities are consumed by guests.*

TASK 42

Maintain and Service Laundry Equipment

STEPS:	HOW-TO'S:	TIPS:
1. **Perform daily dryer maintenance.**	❑ Turn off the dryer and make sure the tumbler has stopped turning. Disconnect power to the dryer. Perform lockout/tagout procedures.	*See Task 38: "Perform Lockout/Tagout Procedures During All Repairs."*
	❑ Open the dryer lint panel and remove any accumulated lint in the lint storage area.	
	❑ Inspect the lint screen to make sure it is not torn. If the lint screen is torn, replace immediately.	*A torn lint screen will allow lint to leave the tumbler and enter the ductwork system, leading to a restriction in proper air circulation during dryer use as well as a potential fire hazard.*
	❑ Clean lint off of the thermostat sensing probe, the cabinet hi-limit thermostat (if applicable), or the thermistor (if applicable).	*Keeping the heat sensing dryer components lint-free will enable them to function properly and protect the tumbler from overheating.*
	❑ Check that no flammable materials are in the dryer area.	
2. **Perform seasonal dryer maintenance.**	❑ Turn off the dryer and disconnect power to the dryer.	
	❑ Remove lint from the dryer's drive motor air vents.	*The dryer's motor is cooled by air circulating through the vents. Lint can cause a decrease in air circulation and become a fire hazard.*
	❑ Clean the exhaust duct: • Remove the exhaust duct from the exhaust thimble. • Remove any lint buildup in the exhaust duct. • Reattach the exhaust duct.	
	❑ Check the tension of the dryer motor belt. Adjust, if necessary.	
	❑ Inspect the tumbler thoroughly. Make sure no nuts or bolts are loose and that all electrical connections are secure.	

Continued

Task 42: *Maintain and Service Laundry Equipment* (continued)		
STEPS:	**HOW-TO'S:**	**TIPS:**
	❑ Check that no flammable materials are in the dryer area.	
3. Perform monthly washer maintenance.	❑ Turn off the washer and disconnect the power source. Perform lockout/tagout procedures.	*See Task 38: "Perform Lockout/Tagout Procedures During All Repairs."*
	❑ Add grease to lubricate the washer motor, as needed.	
	❑ Check the washer motor brakes for wear. Adjust or replace the brakes if required.	
	❑ Inspect the washer belts and pulleys for wear. Replace if needed.	
	❑ Inspect the washer hoses, clamps, and connections for leaks, cracks, or bulges. Replace if necessary.	
	❑ Inspect the washer door and door latch. Lubricate the door hinges and latches if necessary.	

Chapter 3 Outline

Motivations for Environmental Concern
    Economic Considerations
    Regulatory Issues
    Market Factors
    The Social Responsibility Dimension
Waste Minimization and Management
Energy Conservation and Management
Management of Fresh Water Resources
Wastewater Management
Hazardous Substances
Transport
Land-Use Planning and Management
Involving Staff, Customers, and
    Communities
Design for Sustainability
Partnerships for Sustainable Development
Measurement Tools
Conclusion

Competencies

1. Describe economic, regulatory, market, and social responsibility factors that have led hospitality businesses to take action on environmental issues. (pp. 83–88)

2. State some of the principal measures facilities managers can take to minimize and manage waste. (pp. 88–92)

3. Describe the liabilities of poor energy management in terms of its effect on both the hotel's bottom line and the local/world community. (pp. 92–95)

4. Outline the issues involved with proper fresh water and wastewater management. (pp. 95–97)

5. Describe the dangers inherent in commonly recognized hazardous substances and ways to safeguard against them. (pp. 97–99)

6. Explain the negative aspects of operating a diverse fleet of vehicles and what measures the facilities engineer can take to reduce or eliminate them. (pp. 99–100)

7. Explain the economic and social nuances of appropriate land-use planning and management. (pp. 100–101)

8. Describe the benefits of involving staff, customers, and communities in a hospitality company's environmental and sustainability concerns, and discuss how lodging properties can design for sustainability. (pp. 101–106)

9. Discuss partnerships for sustainable development, and identify measurement tools hospitality companies can use to evaluate their impact on the environment. (pp. 106–110)

Environmental and Sustainability Management

Significant contributions to this chapter for this edition have been made by Jeanne Varney, M.B.A., LEED Green Associate, Green Globes Professional, and Lecturer at the School of Hotel Administration, Cornell University, Ithaca, New York.

Sustainability: A method of harvesting or using a resource so that the resource is not depleted or permanently damaged. (Webster's Dictionary)

AWARENESS OF THE SIGNIFICANT IMPACT that lodging operations may have on the environment has become prevalent today. This awareness evolved over approximately the last fifty years through a combination of environmental research, scientific findings, and "cause and effect" evidence from operational practices. In 1972, the United Nations Environment Program (UNEP) was created to study the linkage between the environment and development. In 1987, the World Commission on Environment and Development published *Our Common Future* (also known as the Brundtland Report), which defined sustainable development as "development that meets the needs of the present without compromising the ability of future generations to meet their own needs." This definition remains widely used today.

In 1992, the United Nations Conference on Environment and Development (UNCED) held the Earth Summit in Rio de Janeiro. At this summit, *Agenda 21*—a 300-page document outlining a non-binding action plan for sustainable development—was presented. (The "21" is an allusion to the twenty-first century.) In 1995, three international organizations (the World Travel & Tourism Council, the World Tourism Organization, and the Earth Council) joined together to create an action plan customized for travel and tourism businesses entitled *Agenda 21 for the Travel & Tourism Industry: Towards Environmentally Sustainable Development*. *Agenda 21* is the foundation on which many international hospitality companies have formed their environmental policies.[1]

In the United States, recognizing a need for more attention to the environment, the American Hotel & Lodging Association (AH&LA) in the early 1970s formed a standing Committee for a Quality Environment. The committee's charter was to study the potential effects of industry operations on the environment and devise methods and procedures to address them. Within AH&LA today there is a Sustainability Committee that addresses environmental issues.

Internationally, hospitality leadership at both the association and corporate levels has emerged to evaluate and reduce environmental impacts. The International Hotel and Restaurant Association, World Travel & Tourism Council, and International Hotels Environment Initiative have introduced a host of programs to heighten awareness in both identifying and reducing environmental impacts. Local and regional travel and tourism associations have also been active, providing training materials, technical assistance, and awards programs for best practices. Accor, InterContinental, Scandic, and Canadian Pacific Hotels were early innovators in this effort.

Environmental issues often are limited to only the natural environment and tend to focus on issues of global climate change (especially CO_2 emissions and CFCs), pollution (air, water, noise, visual, and other forms), habitat/ecosystem degradation, and resource consumption (including issues of solid waste). Closely related but broader in context is **sustainability**. Sustainability embraces not only typical environmental concerns but also recognizes the need to balance the basic business components of people, planet, and profit. This is commonly referred to as the Three P's (see Exhibit 1).

The Three P's are cited as the pillars of the triple bottom line of sustainability. The triple bottom line represents the balance that is required among social ("people"), environmental ("planet"), and financial ("profit") factors to sustainably manage a company. The triple bottom line "aims to measure the financial, social, and environmental performance of the corporation over a period of time.

Exhibit 1   The Three P's of Sustainability

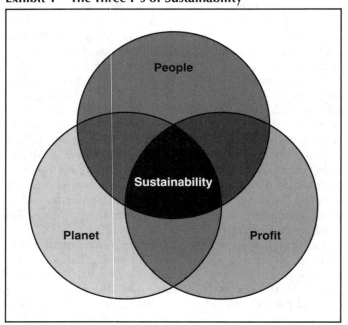

Only a company that produces a triple bottom line is taking account of the full cost involved in doing business."[2] The theory is that if one or two of the P's are given resources at the cost of one of the other P's, then the business model will be ultimately unsustainable.

The hospitality industry has addressed financial, environmental, and social sustainability concerns in a variety of ways. Financial sustainability has always been a major concern and a major challenge for all hospitality businesses. Correcting environmental problems can prevent hospitality firms from "killing the golden goose,"[3] a concern of resort operations and others whose main attraction is the natural environment. Lodging operations can look for ways to not only minimize environmental damage but also make positive contributions to the environment. Social equity aspects of sustainability are potentially more challenging. How to measure a business's impact on local communities and cultures, and how a business can be socially responsible in dealing with its various constituencies are just a few of many social equity issues.

Sustainability is a major theme pervading the global business community, and its importance to the success of the hospitality industry continues to grow. (More detailed discussions of this topic are available in references in the chapter's endnotes.)

Motivations for Environmental Concern

Hospitality corporations and individual hospitality operations have various motivations for environmental concerns and actions. Among these motivations are economic considerations, regulatory issues, market factors, and social responsibility dimensions.

Economic Considerations

The economic dimensions of environmental actions are often both compelling and significant. Many environmental initiatives have significant economic benefits. For example, converting incandescent lamps to more efficient and longer-lasting compact fluorescent or LED lamps results not only in an environmental benefit—a reduction in energy use—but also, by extension, a reduction in energy costs. These longer-lasting lamps also reduce maintenance costs for a property, since they don't need to be replaced as often. To cite another example, recycling is good for the environment, but it also reduces a property's waste disposal costs.

Regulatory Issues

Environmental legislation requirements are tightening more and more around the world. Requirements for energy consumption reporting, recycling, restrictions on water use due to shortages, emission and discharge regulations, and other regulations mean that concern for environmental issues is not only good business, it is the law. Environmental impact must be addressed from the feasibility stage of new project development through operations (including renovations)—all within the context of regulations. Failure to do so can jeopardize new developments and result in fines and penalties. Hotel companies are meeting the challenge in various

Is Your Green Property Tour-Worthy?

Is your property tour-worthy? Interestingly, an increasing number of "green" properties are becoming tourist attractions because of their investments in sustainability. The Hilton Fort Lauderdale Beach Resort, for example, has launched a Sustainability Property Tour series to provide the public with a behind-the-scenes look at the resort's progressive environmental sustainability practices and initiatives. The complimentary program series is hosted weekly and made available to hotel guests, area schools, community groups, and local businesses in an effort to raise awareness about the innovations and initiatives that the property has implemented to address waste reduction, resource conservation, and energy efficiency.

The Alexander, a LEED Silver–certified hotel in Indianapolis, Indiana, offers building tours with detailed explanations on how certain green initiatives (waterless urinals, the hotel's storm water collection system, etc.) came to fruition.

At Grande Lakes Orlando, guests have the opportunity to learn about the resort's natural surroundings from six certified Florida Master Naturalists who are experts in the areas of local wildlife, ecosystems, and environmental stewardship. These naturalists conduct educational eco-tours at the resort, providing guests with a unique glimpse into the resort's natural surroundings, which include bird habitats and nature trails.

During its Summer Honey Festival last year, The Ritz-Carlton, Charlotte offered registered guests guided Saturday morning tours of the hotel's rooftop herb garden and beehives. The tours allowed guests to see the green, vegetated roof's 18,000 sedum plants in their full summer bloom, the hotel's two beehives, and the 100,000 resident honeybees that have called the rooftop home since early 2010.

These are just a few examples of the sustainability tours that some of today's hotels have created to get the word out about their efforts to protect and preserve the environment. While it is not likely that these tours are having a huge impact on increasing the number of "heads in beds" in these hotels, the tours can certainly help sway the booking decision of some groups and individuals. Such tours also are a great way to connect with the local community and can be an essential part of an overall corporate citizenship strategy. Guests may take home some of the sustainability lessons learned at the hotel, and visiting hoteliers can implement similar green initiatives at their own properties. Sustainability tours can also be excellent public relations tools, especially when members of the media are invited to take part.

Source: Adapted from a blog by Glenn Hasek, Editor-in-Chief, www.greenlodgingnews. com, July 2014.

ways; for example, on the hotel development side both Marriott and Starwood have developed LEED Volume[4] prototype hotels for developers to use to build "green" hotels.

Market Factors

There is little debate that both businesspeople and their customers have become more educated on environmental issues and best practices. This has caused a shift in hotel selection priorities for some customers which, in turn, has prompted many hotels to become more aggressive in their sustainability efforts and in the marketing of those efforts. Some global hospitality companies have actually branded their sustainability programs. Examples include Hilton LightStay, Wyndham Green, and Accor Planet 21, to name a few.

Increasingly, the RFP (request for proposal) process from meeting planners and other hospitality customers looking for bids from hotels now includes requests for information about a hotel's environmental practices. Lodging operators heretofore unconcerned about environmental issues may change their minds when major customers refuse to do business with them because of their failure to address environmental issues. The increasing requirements by the global business community for supplier/vendor environmental certification through the **ISO 14000 standards** series (Environmental Management Systems) means that many hospitality customers will be looking to see if the hospitality companies they wish to patronize have ISO certification, and hospitality companies will be looking for this certification from their vendors.[5] Hilton Worldwide earned this certification for their entire system of hotels globally. It's possible that in the near future, certification of high environmental performance will be a requirement of doing business, just as adequate credit and insurance coverage is today.

AH&LA has developed significant resources to assist hotels in their "green" efforts. There is also a growing "green meetings" movement that is striving to reduce the environmental impact of meetings and conventions.[6] Green meetings initiatives have ranged from recycling to sustainable menu choices and even to methods to offset the environmental impacts of travel.[7]

In the food service sector, too, companies have become more sensitive to environmental issues. For example, Starbucks has established a sustainable business model that includes building greener stores, implementing aggressive recycling programs, using sustainable materials, and instituting environmentally conscious product sourcing (including assisting farmers to lower their environmental impact).[8]

The Social Responsibility Dimension

Many firms both within and outside the hospitality industry recognize the interaction of environmental policy with corporate **social responsibility**. InterContinental Hotels Group includes its environmental activities and other social responsibility actions on its website, as does Hyatt.[9] The actions of these companies exemplify the attention given within the lodging industry to environmental and other social responsibility issues.

In food service, Starbucks has developed significant community-based programs at both the local and global levels that include youth programs, community outreach events, international farm community programming, and initiatives for supporting local economies (see Exhibit 2).

The items considered to be part of an environmental program can and will vary depending on the company, location, and a host of other factors. For guidance regarding the content of environmental programs, managers can look to efforts such as the International Hotels Environment Initiative and *Agenda 21 for the Travel & Tourism Industry*. Exhibit 3 contains summary information about

Exhibit 2   Starbucks' Community Commitment

Community Service	Each year Starbucks launches "Global Community Service Month" where each store focuses on making a positive impact on its local community through service projects.
Youth Leadership	The Starbucks Foundation supports programming to develop youth ages 15–24 in three areas: Business Savvy, Social Conscience, and Collaborative Communication.
Community Stores	Starbucks collaborates with local nonprofits to play a central role in supporting revitalization efforts to address employment, education, health, housing, and safety issues.
Farming	This is a collaborative program that renders economic and social development for local farming communities, while caring for the environment.
Diversity & Inclusion	Starbucks has robust diversity programming in place starting with leadership commitment and using a wide network of partners in both employment and in their supply chain.
Create Jobs for USA	This program assists underserved community businesses through loans, housing project financing, and microfinance activities.
Starbucks Foundation	Established in 1997, this foundation supports a wide variety of causes.

Source: http://www.starbucks.com/responsibility/environment.

Agenda 21 for the travel and tourism industry. More details for each priority area listed in Exhibit 3 are included in the appendix at the end of the chapter.

Waste Minimization and Management

Waste minimization and management involves reduction, reuse, recycling, and waste transformation, as well as overseeing the cost structure and management of waste haulage contracts. These efforts combine to minimize the amount of waste disposed and the cost of its disposal, and help ensure that final disposal is done in an approved and environmentally suitable manner.

A lodging property's waste stream obviously varies with the type of services provided and the scope of the facilities. Economy lodging operations without food service, having a small and minimally landscaped site and lacking conference facilities, will have a relatively small amount of waste per room. Full-service resort/conference facilities with extensive food service, large areas of highly landscaped grounds, and customers making purchases of a variety of types during their more extended stays can produce more waste per room. Quick-service

Exhibit 3   Agenda 21 for the Travel and Tourism Industry

Priority area 1: waste minimization
Objective: to minimize resource inputs, maximize product quality, and minimize waste outputs.

Priority area 2: energy conservation and management
Objective: to reduce energy use and reduce potentially damaging atmospheric emissions.

Priority area 3: management of fresh water resources
Objective: to protect the quality of water resources and to use existing resources efficiently and equitably.

Priority area 4: wastewater management
Objective: to minimize wastewater outputs in order to protect the aquatic environment, to safeguard flora and fauna, and to conserve and protect the quality of fresh water resources.

Priority area 5: hazardous substances
Objective: to replace products containing potentially hazardous substances with more environmentally benign products.

Priority area 6: transport
Objective: to reduce or control harmful emissions into the atmosphere and other environmental effects of transport.

Priority area 7: land-use planning and management
Objective: to deal with the multiple demands on land in an equitable manner, ensuring that development is not visually intrusive and contributes to conserving environment and culture while generating income.

Priority area 8: involving staff, customers, and communities in environmental issues
Objectives: to protect and incorporate the interests of communities in developments and to ensure that the environmental lessons learned by staff, customers, and communities are put into practice at home.

Priority area 9: design for sustainability
Objective: to ensure that new technologies and products are designed to be less polluting, more efficient, socially and culturally appropriate, and available worldwide.

Priority area 10: partnerships for sustainable development
Objective: to form partnerships to bring about long-term sustainability.

Source: *Agenda 21 for the Travel & Tourism Industry—Towards Environmentally Sustainable Development;* WTTC, WTO, The Earth Council, 1997.

restaurants have a waste stream consisting largely of disposable final product packaging (cups, plates, napkins, and similar materials), with food production waste minimized by pre-processing activities. Full-service restaurants dispose of smaller amounts of final product packaging but have more food production waste.

The potential economic benefits of waste minimization and management are significant. Waste haulage contracts can be a large part of the property operations and maintenance budget of hotels, with costs in excess of $100 per room per year not uncommon. Supervision and inspection of trash container contents can also reduce unnecessary losses by, for example, recovering tableware or other materials that should not have been discarded. Management of waste haulage contracts can minimize the cost of disposal by ensuring that:

- Only full waste containers are removed (haulage contracts often pay for the "pull" of the trash container as well as for the weight of the contents).

- Weight tickets are submitted with bills to verify waste quantities (where costs are based on weight rather than volume).

- Competitive bidding determines the contractor.

Reducing or minimizing waste generation begins with the purchasing function. Purchasing products in bulk, using products manufactured from recycled materials, controlling the usage of products to avoid waste, and working with suppliers to minimize product packaging are all proven ways to minimize waste generation. Selecting products with greater durability (and hence a longer lifetime) and employing proper maintenance and housekeeping procedures reduces the products' deterioration and extends their functional life.

Reuse or repurpose as a means of waste reduction has been practiced in the hospitality industry for many years; beer kegs and beverage containers such as those holding syrup concentrate are typical reuse items. Administrative areas commonly reuse printer cartridges and water cooler bottles. And operators have long returned shipping trays and pallets to suppliers for reuse. Reuse does not have to happen on the property itself—used linens can be donated to shelters or other charitable organizations for reuse. Furniture and equipment items from renovations are often sold to liquidators or in other ways reused and given an extended life.

Recycling as a means of conservation can be turned into a revenue stream. The price paid for a lodging property's recyclable materials varies geographically and over time. Geographic variations are due to the proximity to potential processors and users of recycled materials as well as to the degree of development of recycling in the area. Variations over time occur due to market forces that are related not only to the varying supply of recyclable materials but also to the demand for recycled products. The real economic value to a property of a recycling program is usually in the savings in waste haulage rather than in the money received for the recycled products. When fewer tons of trash are hauled to the landfill, the property saves money (see Exhibit 4).

A recycling effort will generally focus on the following materials:

- Glass
- Metals
- Plastics
- Paper
- Cardboard
- Yard waste

Exhibit 4   University of Maryland University College Inn Recycling Results

	2008	2009	Percentage saved
Tons of trash sent to landfill per year	444	336	24%
Recycling and composting efforts generated savings that totaled over $6,000 per year.			
Note: Of the waste generated in 2008, 10 percent was glass, metal, paper, and cardboard, and 32 percent was organic materials (food waste and plant materials).			

Source: Adapted from "Hotel Reduces Costs by Recycling," *Environmental & Energy Management News,* March 2009.

Purchasing records are a rich source for identifying the potential volumes of recyclable materials. Knowing the quantity of various products purchased and the packaging used allows for a quick estimate of the potential volume to be recycled.

With glass recycling, it may be necessary to separate the containers by color to receive the best prices. To reduce the volume of the glass, a glass crusher may be a worthwhile investment (depending on the volume of glass waste generated). Some glass recycling, occurs when reusable bottles are used for beverages. Metals recycled in the hospitality industry are usually from metal beverage containers (generally aluminum) and food cans (containing steel and tin). Aluminum has the higher value, making separation important. In certain areas, aluminum and glass beverage containers have a deposit, providing a significant incentive for their return. Food cans need to be clean and in some instances stripped of their paper labels in order to be accepted for recycling. Crushing food cans helps to reduce their volume and therefore the space required for storage.

Plastic recycling can be more challenging—particularly in developing countries—since not all locations have the capability to handle recycled plastics. As is true for other materials that are recycled, cleanliness of the product and separation of the various types are keys to receiving a good market price for the plastics.

Paper recycling is an option available to many operations. Separation of various types of paper—newsprint, office copy paper, and other paper—is sometimes appropriate if large enough amounts exist, since the prices for mixed paper are significantly lower than those for separated paper. Cardboard has long been recycled. There is generally a stable market for this material and, because of its characteristics, it lends itself to on-site collection, compression, and baling. If large quantities of cardboard are collected, the purchase of a baler may be warranted. Besides the day-to-day accumulation of scrap cardboard from receiving department activities, a potentially large amount can also be generated when renovations or replacements of furniture and other items are undertaken. Working with vendors at these times can help ensure that the cardboard involved is recycled. Many composting companies will now take cardboard.

Yard waste and seaweed from beach cleanups is non-existent at some lodging operations but can be 40 percent or more of the waste stream for others. If space and time permit, on-site composting of these wastes, along with non-meat kitchen waste, can not only reduce the cost of waste disposal but also provide a valuable soil and fertilizer source. For those operations that elect not to compost this waste on-site, haulers are available to take it to locations for composting.[10]

Waste transformation is an opportunity that may be worth considering under certain circumstances. Incineration of wastes was once common and is still used today in some locations; incineration can be done at the unit level or in a large waste-to-energy facility. Unit-level incineration is often the option of choice where landfill disposal is not feasible—for example, at locations in or near national parks where animals would be drawn to landfills. If heat recovery is combined with incineration, the process is highly efficient and, if recyclables and potentially toxic materials are removed from the waste before burning, it is viewed as minimally harmful to the environment.

Pulping is another method of transforming waste, in which a pulping machine mixes food waste with water, grinds it up (much like a garbage disposal), presses it (which extracts water from the tank in which the waste is ground), then expels the resulting pulp into a holding bin. The waste does not enter the sewage system, and the pulper recycles the water it used during the grinding process. Pulpers can handle typical food service waste such as plastic utensils and containers, paper napkins, aluminum foil, straws, milk cartons, and corrugated cardboard. Garbage volume is reduced by 75 to 80 percent, which dramatically lowers the waste disposal costs for this material. It is also possible to transform food service wastes with a pulper and make them easier to handle for eventual composting.

Composting is becoming a common form of organic-matter waste disposal. With composting, hotels and restaurants separate their food waste (and many times cardboard) into separate containers from non-compostable waste. The compostable waste is often retrieved by larger composting operations. In most cases, the cost of hauling away composting waste is less than regular waste removal costs, thus making it an attractive economic option while producing a positive impact on the environment. There are options for on-site composting machines; these machines require employees to separate the compostable items and deposit them into the machine directly.

Energy Conservation and Management

Energy conservation and management has long been a concern to the hospitality industry, especially to facilities managers. Energy (sometimes referred to as utilities) typically represents four to six percent of hotel revenues for U.S. hotels. In the U.S. lodging industry, this translates into an annual expenditure for energy of $4 billion.

Energy includes usage of electricity, fossil fuels, water and sewer (according to the *Uniform System of Accounts for the Lodging Industry*), certain vehicle fuel, and in some instances, purchased steam, hot water, and chilled water. By-products of energy usage include carbon dioxide, nitrous and sulphur oxides, and particulate matter. Efforts directed at energy conservation and management attempt to reduce energy usage with resultant cost savings and reduction in environmental pollutants.

Composting and Environmental Entrepreneurship

As a student at Cornell University, Walker Lunn recognized that there was great potential for reducing the amount of composting waste that was entering our landfills. While at Cornell, he was hired to consult for the World Bank to develop a composting program for their buildings. He understood that the same process he developed for analyzing compostable waste removal in these buildings applied to hotels as well.

Upon graduation, Lunn set upon his goal to "try to get hotels to be green from the inside." During his work with the World Bank, he realized that there was inadequate infrastructure in place to handle the potential volume of composting from hotels, schools, office buildings, etc. That was the genesis for the launching of his composting company, Envirelation.

Envirelation developed the infrastructure, tools, and training programs necessary to allow clients to separate out their compostable waste. Envirelation's business model is based on both environmental and economic benefits. The environmental benefits are obvious, since, with composting, less waste is heading to landfills. The economic benefits are present as well, since it costs less to send waste to composting companies than to landfills. Notably, restaurants have the most to gain from a composting program, with Envirelation estimating a minimum of 60 percent waste diversion for most restaurants. Envirelation also offers cooking oil recycling, with the cooking oil being sent to facilities that make bio-fuel.

Source: Adapted from "Pure Genius: Envirelation Tackles Hospitality Industry Waste Through Composting," *Smart Planet,* Issue 19, January 2011; www.smartplanet.com.

Good facilities management practices involve actions that will control energy usage. Examples of the kinds of management actions that help control energy usage are:

- Keeping records of energy usage and energy costs.
- Benchmarking for improvement.
- Properly maintaining equipment.
- Using proper operating methods and records.

To monitor the usage of energy, it is necessary to keep adequate records of energy used and the amounts paid for the energy. Unfortunately, the process used by some operations does not provide the facilities manager with the needed information. If bills for utility services are not provided to the facilities manager for review, not only does the operation lose a needed check on charges being incurred, but the facilities manager is denied the opportunity to maintain a record of the quantity and cost of the energy. On the other hand, some operations have developed sophisticated methods to know how much energy is being used at a facility. Many hotel operators today have developed extensive and proprietary databases of energy and water consumption information and use this information to measure and benchmark a given hotel's performance. Using computerized controls at the building (commonly referred to as building management systems or energy management systems), the facilities manager is able to not only obtain records of energy usage over time but also to monitor real-time usage.

Another helpful option is to actually submeter energy usage (including water) within the building. This allows for usage to be accurately matched to specific operations (the laundry, for example) and, if the property wishes, charged to those operations. This can help offset the problem of the way information is typically recorded in the hotel industry. Costs and consumption are often viewed on a per-room basis. This conveys the impression that the actual usage of energy occurs in the guestroom. For many operations, this is not the case. Energy is used by a host of hotel systems, and energy management needs to focus on those systems and the areas they serve. **Submetering** is relatively inexpensive during new construction. As operations conduct more outsourcing of on-site operations such as food and beverage, submetering may become more common.

Proper operation of equipment and systems by facilities department staff members and other employees is also an important component of energy management. Facilities staff members need to know the factors that affect equipment performance and operation. This involves issues such as what equipment to operate during periods of low usage or demand to maximize efficiency. It also involves controlling the operation of equipment so that unnecessary operation does not occur—for example, there is no need to provide full air conditioning to unoccupied meeting rooms. Other employees need to understand the impact of their actions on energy usage and costs as well. Using hot water to melt ice from buffets, not fully loading washing machines, failing to turn off lights in unoccupied rooms, and a host of similar practices can, in total, waste a significant amount of energy.

Opportunities for energy conservation and cost savings include:

- Improving equipment efficiency.
- Reducing operating hours.
- Reducing energy loads.
- Recovering and reusing waste energy.
- Using the least-costly fuel source.

The amount of energy used by any equipment is significantly influenced by the efficiency of the equipment. A vivid (and visual) example is lighting. An incandescent lamp has a typical efficiency of less than 20 lumens per watt. A fluorescent lamp may have an efficiency of 60 lumens per watt. This means three times the energy is required to produce the same amount of light from an incandescent versus a fluorescent lamp. Knowing the way in which efficiency is expressed for various pieces of equipment, the cost of energy, and the amount of energy used by the equipment, a manager can conduct an economic analysis to assess the feasibility of purchasing more efficient equipment. Or the manager may simply decide that the combination of economics and environmental benefits from more efficient equipment are enough of a justification.

Another way to reduce energy usage is reducing operating hours—that is, turning the equipment off. Operating storage area lighting twenty-four hours a day, leaving computers/copiers/printers running at all times, operating parking lot lighting on time clocks rather than on photocells, and a host of other all-too-common practices result in excessive and unnecessary energy usage.

Reducing energy loads is an often-overlooked option. Window films or double pane windows can reduce solar heat gain. Providing additional roof insulation or "green" roofs cuts down on heating and cooling loads. The opportunities to reduce energy loads are extensive.

Hospitality operations have a number of opportunities to recover and reuse waste energy. One option for all commercial buildings is recovery of heat or cold from exhaust air. Pre-heating or cooling the building's incoming air via the exhaust air is a way to recover and reuse waste energy. The laundry provides further opportunities for recovery of heat, from both exhaust air and from discharged water. For resourceful managers, the opportunities are almost limitless. Imagine using water to cool refrigeration equipment, then using that heated water in the laundry operation. Not only is water recovered that might have been discharged, but so is heat.

Using the least-costly fuel source can require careful recordkeeping and research. Consulting historic consumption records and information about prices provides the data necessary to consider fuel cost options. This can involve looking into the electric utility tariff under which electricity is purchased as well as the electricity supplier. It could also involve evaluating whether to purchase a dual-fueled boiler (operators installing such a system become eligible for what are known as interruptible gas rates) and evaluating the cost-effectiveness of purchasing steam from a local distribution system rather than running a boiler at the property. Researching the available options can be daunting, but the results can be highly rewarding. Some firms have found it worthwhile to contract with companies to audit utility bills for errors or for the correct tariff. The fact that such companies provide this service for a portion of the savings they find suggests this may be an area of substantial opportunity.

A number of resources are available to assist facilities managers and hotel owners in reducing and managing energy usage (see Exhibit 5). Many U. S. lodging corporations are members of the U.S. Environmental Protection Agency's Energy Star Buildings program.[11] The Portfolio Manager program is used to determine which hotels qualify for Energy Star building certification and offers benchmarking and other improvement resources.

There may be on-site energy generation opportunities, with the most common being solar panels. Installing on-site renewable energy technology may be logistically challenging or not financially feasible; however, that does not mean that properties can't purchase "clean energy" from their utility providers. Most utility providers have renewable-energy-source options available for the asking.

Management of Fresh Water Resources

Because global supplies of fresh water are limited—they represent less than one percent of the total water on the earth—hospitality firms need to be good stewards of this valuable resource by using as little as possible and helping to protect the quality of what remains. As with other environmental initiatives, a reduction of fresh water use can bring potential cost savings. With hotels using 100 to 200

Exhibit 5   Energy Reduction Resources

American Hotel & Lodging Association— Green Home	www.ahla.com/Green.aspx?id=24988
U.S. Environmental Protection Agency's Energy Star Program	www.epa.gov
Association of Energy Engineers	www.aeecenter.org
American Society of Heating, Refrigerating and Air-Conditioning Engineers	www.ashrae.org
International Facilities Management Association	www.ifma.org
Building Owners and Managers Association	www.boma.org
National Association of Hotel & Lodging Engineers	www.nahle.org
Green Lodging News	www.greenlodgingnews.com
Energy User News	www.eetd.lbl.gov

gallons (380 to 760 liters) of water per room per day (36,500 to 73,000 gallons [138,000 to 276,000 liters] per room per year) and fresh water costing $2.00 to $4.00 per 1,000 gallons ($0.50 to $1.00 per 1,000 liters), and sometimes that much again for wastewater disposal, efforts to reduce water usage may potentially affect the bottom line significantly and positively.

Hospitality operations may find themselves subject to regulations limiting water usage because of supply shortages caused by dry weather, high consumption, or water system breakdowns. Regulations can also prohibit certain uses of water or the time of its use; for example, lawn watering may be prohibited or limited to the evening hours. Regulations may also set maximum usage levels, with fines imposed for exceeding them.

Resort operations are the most likely to pay particular attention to social responsibility as it relates to fresh water. Resorts proposing to build in any area need to be conscious that their large demands for fresh water will affect water supplies in the local community. These demands may also create needs for costly increases in water infrastructure that could raise the price of water for local people. During construction and in subsequent ongoing operations, resorts need to pay attention to sustaining the quality of fresh water supplies by not allowing site run-off or hazardous wastes to be discharged into water supplies.

Low-volume showerheads and toilets can greatly reduce the amount of fresh water a hotel uses. There are many other opportunities that exist for effective management of fresh water resources. For example, rainwater capture is widely used in locations with limited water supplies. Directing refrigeration condenser cooling water to the laundry for reuse is another option. Staff creativity at the unit level plays a huge role in identifying other opportunities to save water.

Wastewater Management

Most of the fresh water used by hospitality operations ends up leaving the operation as **wastewater**, the notable exceptions being water used in cooling towers and for landscape irrigation. Operators pay for wastewater disposal as a component of their "water bill," as a separate charge, or in the form of their own wastewater treatment plant (when no wastewater treatment facility exists in the local community). Costs can range from $75 to $200 per room per year for wastewater treatment.

Most commonly, local regulations govern the quality levels of water discharged from wastewater treatment plants. Moreover, there may be regulations governing the content of wastewater discharged to the wastewater system.[12] These regulations were the impetus for creating grease traps in kitchen areas. In many locales, regulations also require that receiving dock drainage be routed to sanitary rather than storm sewers, and prohibit the discharge of site runoff and general storm runoff to the sanitary sewer system.

Market factors can clearly be influential in wastewater management. Coastal lodging operations with poor wastewater management have contaminated beaches, resulting in at best an unpleasant environment and at worst the illness of guests and local people. From a business perspective, this is disastrous. Circumstances such as these have prompted tour operators to refuse to bring groups to affected destinations until assurances were given that the problems had been corrected. Even when guests do not directly react to the problem, the local flora and fauna do. Reef areas severely damaged by sewage discharges lose their attractiveness, which severely reduces the appeal of the lodging operation and other local businesses, and negatively affects residents who depend on the reef for their livelihood.

Discharge of untreated wastewater to the environment is socially irresponsible. While guests may be exposed to this wastewater during their stays at the lodging property, it is the local population that is most exposed both to the water itself and to the possible diseases the water may carry. Hotel owners and managers need to ensure that wastewater treatment plants in their area are operating properly—not only their own on-site plants, but also those of other businesses in the area. Owners and managers also should take responsibility to ensure that waste processing by municipal agencies is not harming the environment. Failure in doing this could mean that the clean environment so essential to business survival will be irreparably damaged.

Those lodging operations exhibiting proper responsibility regarding wastewater treatment will help to ensure the ongoing environmental health of their destination for guests, employees, and local residents.

Hazardous Substances

Hospitality businesses generally do not create or use large quantities of **hazardous substances**.[13] However, there are operations and activities in the industry that *do* use hazardous substances. By definition, hazardous substances include those that are:

- **Toxic**—substances that cause damage to health, physical or mental impairment, or death when inhaled, ingested, or absorbed; for example, pesticides and herbicides.

- **Flammable**—substances that can be easily ignited by sparks or flames and cause fires. Of particular concern are those liquids with low flash points; for example, solvents and fuels.

- **Explosive**—substances capable, by chemical reaction, of a sudden release of energy accompanied by the production of light, heat, sound, and pressure, causing damage to the surrounding area.

- **Corrosive**—materials that destroy other materials by chemical reaction. When in contact with human tissues, these substances may cause burns and destroy tissue. At greatest risk are skin, eyes, the lungs, and stomach. Oven and toilet cleaners are usually corrosive.

- **Infectious**—substances that contain viable microorganisms and their toxins, capable of causing disease. Examples of infectious items are medical waste or contaminated food (botulism, *salmonella*, and *legionella*).

An action plan related to hazardous materials is needed and should include the following objectives:

- Minimize the use of hazardous materials.

- Use more environmentally acceptable alternatives.

- Limit the use of hazardous materials to trained personnel.

- Ensure that hazardous materials are stored, labeled, used, handled, and disposed of in accordance with local and international standards and regulations.

Recommended steps to include in the action plan are:

- Identify and record where hazardous materials are being used, what they are being used for, and the reasons for their use.

- Assess the hazards associated with their use.

- Identify, where possible, environmentally preferable alternatives.

- Review handling, storage, labeling, and disposal procedures.

- Compile a hazardous materials manual, including Material Safety Data Sheets).

The use of Material Safety Data Sheets is required in the United States through the Occupational Safety & Health Administration (a federal agency), and similar forms are required in many other countries internationally. These data sheets contain extensive information related to each chemical used in a commercial building. This information includes, but is not limited to, ingredients, safe handling procedures, storage requirements, potential reactions, how to treat spills, poison control, and more.[14]

During the 1980s and 1990s, particular attention was given to two hazardous substances: PCBs and asbestos. PCBs (polychlorinated biphenyls) were in transformers and certain other electrical devices. Ensuring that PCBs do not leak from these devices and that PCB-contaminated products are disposed of in an approved manner continues to be a concern, especially in developing countries.

Asbestos problems center primarily on the potential for this material to become airborne and then inhaled by building occupants. Proper procedures to identify and manage asbestos are well developed and should be followed.[15]

On-site storage of the fuels needed for vehicles and possibly to fire boilers is common in the industry. Fuel leaks and discharges can be highly damaging to the environment. Proper procedures and regular inspection of tanks and supply pipes are critical to maintaining the integrity of these storage systems. Fuel storage tanks should be located above ground to help minimize undetectable leaks and to contain fluids that do leak.

In lodging establishments, common corrosive materials include cleaning chemicals, chlorine for pool water treatment, and bleach used in laundry operations. Replacing chlorine with ozone-based cleaning systems should be considered as a way to reduce the use of, and exposure to, this potentially corrosive chemical.

Food service operators in the United States and elsewhere often use the HACCP (Hazard Analysis Critical Control Points)[16] approach to managing potentially infectious food products. A source commonly used by U.S. operators for training in HACCP and other best practices is the ServSafe program.[17]

Transport

Transportation is inherently one of the largest environmental challenges for the hospitality industry. The hospitality industry obviously would not exist without means of transport for customers, employees, and supplies. The combustion of fuel by autos, buses, trucks, trains, planes, and ships clearly contributes to emissions and air pollution. Building the infrastructure to meet transportation needs, such as roads, airports, and terminals, requires alterations to the landscape and contributes to environmental concerns. Congestion resulting from transportation gridlock further contributes to a less-than-pleasurable experience for guests and employees.

To help curb vehicle emissions at the unit level, lodging operators can purchase hybrid or fuel-efficient vehicles, consider powering these vehicles with clean fuels such as natural gas or bio-fuels, and encourage car-pooling and public transportation by employees. Kimpton Hotels offers either free or significantly discounted parking for guests driving fuel-efficient vehicles to their hotels. In select cities, Kimpton also offers free charging stations for guests' electric cars.[18]

Coordinating the ordering of supplies to help ensure a minimum number of deliveries and looking to purchase supplies produced locally can also help to reduce the environmental impact of transportation.

Finally, with environmental programs focusing not only on the natural (non-human) environment but on the human environment as well, an active program to encourage safe transportation is important, which might entail encouraging seat belt use and the safe operation of vehicles, and calling attention to transportation hazards such as the overcrowding of buses and other transport.

Transportation-related injuries and deaths are all too prevalent and clearly represent an area where improvements are needed.

Land-Use Planning and Management

Probably tens of thousands of hospitality facilities are developed each year if one includes restaurant, lodging, and amusement facilities. The tenets of sustainable development—"development that meets the needs of the present without compromising the ability of future generations to meet their own needs"[19]—are widely known in the development, design, and construction fields.

From an economic perspective, appropriate **land-use planning** and management can result not only in development that is environmentally sensitive but also in reduced or, at the very least, more controlled costs for the development and subsequent operation of a lodging property. Reuse of existing buildings (either existing hotels and restaurants or other structures that have been converted to these uses) is just one example of appropriate land-use planning and management that can reduce initial costs. Reusing existing structures also helps to retain a cultural and social fabric for a location that could be significantly affected by a demolish-and-build approach. Proper site orientation of newly constructed buildings and retention of existing landscaping can result in lower energy costs and reduced costs for landscaping, both initially and in the long term.

From a regulatory perspective, attention to land-use planning and management has become an integral part of the project approval process and is often included in the broader context of the **environmental impact statement (EIS)**. The EIS process can be expedited by addressing land-use issues in the planning stages. Appropriate attention to land-use planning and management can create a lodging product with a greater sense of place, which can result in greater customer appeal.

In fact, customers *do* respond to careful land-use planning and management. A well-designed facility that integrates the setting in which it is located to maximum advantage is a marketing plus. There are subtle issues here as well, such as the concept of xeriscaping. Xeriscaping is a technique that uses plant-life that needs little to no supplemental water to survive in its location; choosing indigenous plants for landscaping minimizes the need for fertilizers, insecticides, and other chemical treatments, which is a big plus for the environment and can lower landscaping maintenance costs for the property.

Social responsibility means that land-use planning and management considerations should not stop at the property boundaries. For example, the development of a new resort in a remote location can create additional demands on the local community to provide land and services to accommodate transportation needs, staff housing, and general community services (particularly schools and medical care). Supporting initiatives in the local community to meet environmental good practice should be given due consideration. The quality of service to guests depends largely on the employees rendering the service; therefore, a property should attend to the well-being of its employees to the extent that it can. Employees should have access to good housing, good health services, proper sanitary conditions, and in general live in an environment that is somewhat comparable to the environment they are in while at work.

Describing the practices of operations exhibiting social responsibility helps to define the concept. Nihiwatu Resort, a luxury resort in Indonesia, balances providing luxury service with support of the local community (see Exhibit 6). As a Conde-Nast Traveler World Savers Award winner in the "Doing It All (Small Resort)" category and a runner-up in the "Health" category, Nihiwatu demonstrates how a resort can successfully improve the infrastructure, health care, and education in its destination area.[20]

Applying sustainable land-use planning and management strategies to local situations is the responsibility of not only the hotel's owners and managers, but also of the design professionals involved in the creation and/or modification of the facility. A willingness to curb development when appropriate can often help create a location that is more desirable to all concerned, resulting in sustainable economics as well as environmental and equity benefits.

Involving Staff, Customers, and Communities

The development and operation of a hospitality business can benefit from the involvement of staff, customers, and the community in environmental issues. A staff empowered and involved with a property-level environmental program can be a positive contributor to the program itself and take the program's ideas and concepts into their homes and communities. Saunders Hotel Group in Boston, Massachusetts, was an early innovator in getting its staff involved in its environmental program. Saunders' SHINE program (Saunders Hotels Initiative for the Environment) engaged and rewarded employees for their environmental initiatives and involvement. HEI Hotels in Norwalk, Connecticut, has a robust Energy Enhanced Program that rewards employees for environmental recommendations and participation in the property's environmental efforts.

Some hospitality managers believe that certain environmental actions may result in a negative customer reaction. In those cases, market testing of environmental initiatives is needed just as it is with any new guest service. Providing some guest education to go along with the testing is also appropriate. Some hotels even look to have fun with their environmental and educational initiatives. For example, the InterContinental New York Barclay Hotel adopted a sustainability mascot, the Barclay Bee. The hotel hosts a roof-top bee farm that includes a Bee Cam which allows viewers to observe the bees during the honey-making season. The hotel blogs a comic book series featuring different bee characters that deliver various environmental messages.[21] But the hotel is very serious about its environmental responsibilities, as can be seen in its "Responsible Business Policy" (see Exhibit 7).

By stimulating staff, customer, and community involvement and sensitivity to environmental concerns, a property can encourage greater buy-in to its environmental initiatives and help to create a more sustainable world for everyone.

Design for Sustainability

Significant potential exists for improving the design of hospitality facilities to incorporate more sustainable elements. This potential resides at all levels of the

Exhibit 6   Social Responsibility in Action

Nihiwatu: Building Clinics, Wells, and Forests

What: Twelve luxury bungalows on a gorgeous beach.

Where: Sumba Island, Eastern Indonesia.

Because: It is bringing clean water and medical care to local communities—while educating guests.

You might call him the accidental philanthropist. Unlike other sustainability pioneers, Nihiwatu's co-founder, Claude Graves, didn't set out to build a hotel to do good. He wanted a good beach. He found one in 1988 on the Indonesian island of Sumba—and then discovered the dire local needs, from clean water to medical care. "It was quite a wake-up call," he says. In 2001, Graves turned to his guests for help and established the Sumba Foundation to oversee the charity work and provide transparent reports to donors. More than $4.9 million has been donated to the foundation to date, with guest gifts averaging about $5,000. In each community it enters on the beautiful but impoverished island, the foundation first digs wells, then launches a malaria control program, and finally builds a clinic so that no one has to walk more than two miles for care. The amazing results so far: sixty wells supply clean water to 20,230 people and sixteen schools in 205 villages. More than 20,000 people in 400 villages have benefited from free malaria testing; 9,000 have been treated and provided with free mosquito nets; and 286 infants and children have been saved from malaria-related deaths at the five foundation clinics.

Here's the real magic: The hotel is everything a luxury traveler has come to expect from a remote getaway—thatched-roof villas with private plunge pools overlooking the Indian Ocean and elegant fixtures handcrafted from local stone and teak. The emphasis on comfort doesn't stop Graves from encouraging guests to get involved. A ten-page booklet in each guestroom highlights initiatives that need funding, and in the bar, the property shows a short film about the foundation's efforts. In addition to diving, fishing, surfing, and indulging in spa treatments, guests are encouraged to tour the foundation's charitable projects. You can take a horseback ride through the jungle, for example, and visit villages along with employee Data Daku—who has sent his brothers, sisters, and children to college thanks to the foundation's scholarships.

What's next? A reforestation project that is planting 15,000 teak trees a year. Each season the nursery distributes some 5,000 saplings to thirty families that have joined the project. With the first harvest projected to take place in 2025, these families may share in an income distribution program of as much as $3.5 million each year.

Source: Adapted from *"World Savers Awards," Conde-Nast Traveler,* September 2013.

industry and applies not only during new construction but also during renovation planning and when making other capital decisions. To help realize this potential, research is needed to develop new products that have minimal environmental impact. Research results then need to be communicated within the industry and

Exhibit 7 Sample Responsible Business Policy—InterContinental New York Barclay Hotel

We, as a team, adhere to the following commitments:

Profit and Governance

- We follow all rules, policies, and regulations stipulated by the authorities and our owning and managing company.
- We are transparent in what we do.
- We communicate as much as we can and when necessary with all stakeholders.
- We continuously review our way of working to improve all costs.

Social Responsibility

- We advocate socially responsible business practices.
- We treat all our employees on the same level and give them equal opportunities.
- We support fundamental human rights.
- We respect New York Hotel & Motel Trades Council, AFL-CIO as a partner.
- We incorporate our business into our community as much as possible and work closely with local organizations, associations, and entities.
- We encourage our employees to be socially responsible through education and training.

Environmental Protection

- We advocate environmentally responsible business practices.
- We comply with all applicable environmental laws and regulations.
- We are conscious of our responsibility toward the environment and continuously work to improve our environmental performance in reducing the impact of our activities.
- We invest in equipment that helps reduce energy consumption.
- We incorporate a waste management program to mitigate waste production by diminishing waste creation. We recycle as much as possible and compost wet waste.
- We are committed to preventing pollution due to our activity.
- We encourage our supply chain partners to implement a Triple Bottom Line strategy.
- We promote Triple Bottom Line ideals to our local community.
- We communicate our initiatives to our guests and employees, to create awareness and inspiration for their personal and professional lives.

Source: Excerpt taken from the InterContinental Barclay Hotel's Responsible Business Policy; www.intercontinentalnybarclay.com.

the educational community, and hospitality corporations need to incorporate the new concepts arising from the research into their policies and mission statements.

Leadership in sustainability within the hospitality industry has come in many forms. Companies such as Scandic Hotels, a company with more than 100 hotels throughout Scandinavia, illustrate ways in which corporations are responding to the challenge of sustainability. Scandic has received a number of awards for its environmental programs and has pioneered what it refers to as *ecorooms*—guest-rooms built in an environmentally friendly way. Scandic takes the environment into consideration as well as its guests when it designs its hotels, choosing the most sustainable design and construction solutions in partnership with its archi-tects, builders, and suppliers.

A variety of resources have recently become available to assist operations interested in designing for sustainability. The International Tourism Partnership and Conservation International have published *Sustainable Hotel Siting, Design and Construction*, which provides comprehensive guidelines for sustainable development. "Sustainable tourism is about preserving popular destinations, the environment, and its resources," said Ed Fuller, former chair of the International Tourism Partnership.[22] The United States Green Buildings Council (USGBC) has developed the **LEED** (Leadership in Energy and Environmental Design) rating system, "a voluntary, consensus-based national standard for developing high-performance, sustainable buildings."[23] Within the United States, the LEED rating system provides an opportunity for new and existing buildings to review their design and operation and evaluate these against sustainability principles. The LEED certification program has gained significant traction in hotel development and is deemed a credible green building certification program by governmental bodies as well as developers.

Although to date there are ten different LEED certification systems, histori-cally hotels could only use three of them: LEED for New Construction, LEED Core and Shell, and LEED for Existing Building Operations and Maintenance. However, LEED v4 will now include a new certification category, LEED for Hospitality.

The LEED certification point system is based off of a 100 point scale, with a potential for earning ten extra points. Certification levels are:

- Certified: 40–49 points
- Silver: 50–59 points
- Gold: 60–79 points
- Platinum: 80+ points

Typically there are seven credit categories:

- Sustainable Sites
- Water
- Energy and Atmosphere
- Indoor Air Quality
- Materials and Resources

How One Hotel "Went Green"

The Washington Marriott at Metro Center in Washington, D.C., received the city's Environmental Excellence Award for "Outstanding Achievement by a Hotel" because of its efforts to reduce its energy and water usage, reduce the waste it produced, and find other ways to "go green." Its green accomplishments and initiatives include the following:

Featured Accomplishments

- The hotel saved 745,685 kWh in electricity from the previous year, with the implementation of energy-efficient lighting with programmable and dimmable automation, and utilization of the Energy Management System controlling the heating/cooling and lighting of our banquet space.
- The hotel will save an estimated 600,000 gallons of water a year, through recently converting all restroom urinals to water-free urinals.
- The Fire & Sage Restaurant installed recycled wood flooring and uses linenless dining tables.
- All lighting within the hotel uses energy-efficient bulbs.
- Guestroom bathrooms have low-flow showerheads and toilets.
- Guestroom keys are made from 50 percent recycled materials.
- The hotel offers Marriott's newspaper program, in which guests are asked to choose one newspaper or decline newspapers entirely.

Green Meetings

- 100 percent of the hotel's meeting space is on an Energy Management System, ensuring that energy usage (lights, temperature) is minimized during vacancy.
- The hotel uses linen-less tables for meeting sets and serves filtered water in glass pitchers instead of bottled water for meetings.
- The hotel provides organic meeting room candy, sustainable menus, and organic floral options upon request.
- Meeting note pads are made from 100 percent recycled materials, pens from 75 percent recycled materials; meeting planners can take advantage of a recyclable box lunch program.
- The hotel uses Earthwise® recycled beverage napkins.

Recycling

- The hotel offers a centralized recycling program for guest participation: meeting space, lobby, and guest floors.
- The hotel's kitchens recycle used oil into biofuel.
- The hotel recycles used fluorescent bulbs, batteries, lighting ballasts, metals, computer components, and used refrigerants.
- The hotel reuses damaged linens as cleaning rags.

(continued)

(continued)

Chemical Reduction/ Earth Friendly Solutions

- The hotel's pool uses saline water instead of chlorine.
- The hotel purchases from strategic eco-friendly vendors.
- The hotel uses environmentally friendly cleaning products.

Energy & Water Conservation

- Variable frequency drives installed in 50 percent of the hotel's air handling units (the remaining 50 percent is projected to be completed next year).
- Guestroom windows are secured to reduce the loss of conditioned internal air.

Source: Adapted from an article by the Marriott International News Center, "Washington Marriott at Metro Center Receives Mayor's Environmental Excellence Award," August 2010.

- Innovation and Design
- Regional Priority Credits

Each of these categories has specific environmental measures and intended benefits. Within each of the categories there are specific prerequisites a project must satisfy, plus a variety of credits that a project can pursue to earn points. The number of points the project earns determines its level of LEED certification.[24]

Whatever a lodging property's development goals, understanding the issues involved in designing for sustainability is an important element in meeting environmental regulations and the expectations of a growing number of guests who favor companies that are environmentally responsible. A property's owners and managers should also keep in mind that designing for sustainability often requires a willingness to adopt creative sustainability ideas from other industries.

Partnerships for Sustainable Development

Creating coalitions to encourage sustainable development is integral to the concept of sustainability. Input and cooperation of all stakeholders is needed to achieve the economic, environmental, and equity concerns inherent in sustainability. Though individual operations have scored significant sustainability gains, guidance has been provided through the leadership of various industry organizations.

As mentioned earlier, AH&LA has extensive resources for hoteliers' sustainable development needs. Although it has not authored a green certification for hotels, AH&LA provides resources within a three-tiered progressive program ("Green," "Greener," and "Greenest") for hotels wishing to adopt sustainability practices, products, and policies.[25]

The Green Globe organization, founded in 1994 to promote environmental awareness, provides a location for coordinating information and conducting dialogue related to sustainability issues throughout the world. Green Globe was founded to:

- Encourage companies and communities of all sizes to join Green Globe to show their commitment to sound environmental practice.

- Promote the truth that adopting good environmental practice makes good long-term business sense.

- Collect, explain, and distribute examples of industry best practices to businesses and governments.

- Sustain the quality of our vacations for our children—and our children's children.

Another partnership focusing on sustainability issues has emerged in the Caribbean: The Caribbean Alliance for Sustainable Tourism (CAST) has as its goals to:

- Expand the awareness of the region's hotel and tourism operators by providing high-quality education and training related to sustainable tourism.

- Promote the industry's sustainability efforts and success to the traveling public and other stakeholders.

- Serve as a vital link to all stakeholders with an interest in sustainable tourism in the Caribbean region.

Formed as a subsidiary company of the Caribbean Hotel Association, CAST has an advisory board consisting of industry and public sector members. CAST is illustrative of a regional grassroots effort to improve the overall environment for tourism as well as the environmental impact of tourism. Further information on CAST can be found on its website.[26]

The United States Environmental Protection Agency operates Energy Star, "a government-backed program helping businesses and individuals protect the environment through superior energy efficiency."[27] A number of U.S. hospitality firms have participated in Energy Star and have been recognized for their achievements in this voluntary partnership between business and government. Among these are the following:

Year	Firm
1998	Walt Disney World
2000	La Quinta Inns
2001	Hilton Hotels Corporation
2002	Starwood Hotels
2003	Starwood Hotels
2004	American Hotel & Lodging Association
2005	Marriott International
	Saunders Hotel Group
2006	Marriott International
2007	Marriott International*
2008	Marriott International*
2009	Marriott International*

2010   HEI Hotels

2011   HEI Hotels

2012   HEI Hotels*

*Also received the Energy Star Partner of the Year—Sustained Excellence Award.

Both Marriott International and HEI Hotels have received repeated recognition from Energy Star and have earned the Energy Star Partner of the Year—Sustained Excellence Award. To earn the award for sustained excellence, companies must earn the Energy Star Partner of the Year Award for three consecutive years.

Clean the World is a global organization whose mission is to save lives by providing hygiene products to people in impoverished areas of the world. The organization collects partially used amenities from hotels, sanitizes the products, and repackages them for use. This organization provides economic, environmental, and social benefits to many individuals and corporations.[28] Over 1,000 individual hotels participate in the program; the Starwood Hotels & Resorts chain has a corporate agreement with Clean the World to recycle its partially used hygiene products.

Establishing partnerships with other organizations involved in the environmental effort can significantly enhance a lodging property's environmental initiatives. These partner organizations not only provide affiliation opportunities but also valuable resources to help a property achieve progress and success in its sustainability efforts. In the process, properties may well find they have also made a positive economic contribution to their bottom line.

Measurement Tools

There are a variety of tools available to assist hospitality businesses evaluate their impacts on the environment. Most of these tools require businesses to measure outputs such as energy, water, and waste, and then complete the tools' templates. A widely used industry tool for carbon footprint measurement is the **Hotel Carbon Measurement Initiative (HCMI)** that was spearheaded by the International Tourism Partnership and the World Travel and Tourism Council. These organizations brought together over twenty large hotel companies representing millions of guestrooms in more than 100 countries to agree to a methodology for measuring carbon emissions. According to the International Tourism Partnership:

> The aim of the methodology is to provide transparency and clear communications for the growing body of corporate clients who require [carbon emission] information as part of the annual RFP [request for proposal] process. Developed together with consultants at KPMG, under the guidance of a Working Group comprised of experts from WTTC and ITP member companies, the methodology is a first step in ensuring a common approach across the [lodging] sector. The methodology was road-tested at a number of diverse properties across the world, ranging from boutique hotels to resorts, casinos, and major conference hotels.[29]

The easy-to-use tool provides an estimated carbon footprint for hotels and meeting planners that measures the approximate footprint per occupied room and per square meter.

Statler Hotel Recycles Soap to Boost Global Hygiene

Something we casually throw away can save lives. In 2013, Cornell's Statler Hotel recycled thousands of tiny bars of used soap through its partnership with Clean the World, a nonprofit organization that seeks to bolster better global hygiene. "That's a lot of soap," says Rebecca Rypkema, the Statler Hotel's director of rooms, who has headed the recycling initiative. The used soaps are melted (and thus sanitized), made into new soap bars, and distributed to communities in more than fifty-five countries. By simply making this recycled soap available to people in developing countries, conditions like diarrhea—a major cause of death among children worldwide—can be alleviated. (Diarrhea kills about 760,000 children annually around the world, according to the World Health Organization. This preventable and treatable condition is the second leading cause of death among children under five years old.)

Clean the World, however, doesn't limit itself to soap. Clean the World also helps the Statler recycle its unused shampoo and lotion amenities as well as recycle plastic bottles. Current data shows that, thanks to Clean the World, the Statler has recycled more than 988 pounds of shampoo and lotion, and 388 pounds of plastic.

"We have had a great response. Our housekeeping staff is very excited [about the Clean the World initiative]," Rypkema said. Roger Soule, who works in the hotel's housekeeping department, said that room attendants separate the soap bars and bottle products into two separate bins during the course of their duties. Then, every week the bins are sent to Clean the World, which redistributes the products.

Next semester, the Statler Hotel plans to take part in Clean the World's "ONE Project," which distributes hygiene kits to members in the local community. Rypkema said that the hygiene kits, which will be funded by the Statler and packed by Cornell students working in an assembly line, will include soap, shampoo, conditioner, lotion, a toothbrush, toothpaste, a washcloth, and an inspirational note card for people in need.

Clean the World helps more than 320,000 hotel rooms in North America recycle. Since its founding in February 2009, the company has recycled more than 750 tons of soap, shampoo, and other amenities. Clean the World provides a recycling solution for the tremendous amount of unused soap and plastic bottles generated by the hotel industry. "Most guests stay one and a half days, and during that time they don't use up the entire bar of soap," says Rypkema. Soule adds, "I think this is a good program, because at the Statler, we don't like to throw anything out when it can be reused or recycled."

Source: Adapted from Hanna Zdrnja, "Statler Hotel Recycles Soap to Boost Global Hygiene," *Cornell Chronicle*, December 2013.

A tool for measuring recycling benefits was developed by EcoRewards Recycling. With this tool, a hotel inputs the various weights of its recycled waste stream matter, and the tool calculates the savings of landfill weight, greenhouse gas emissions, energy, and water.[30]

Energy Star's Portfolio Manager is a free benchmarking tool for energy and water consumption. A lodging property's individual data is uploaded annually and benchmarked according to property type.

There are numerous other tools available that measure various environmental inputs and outputs, some free and some available for a fee. Choosing the right tool requires managers to match up what the tool is designed to measure with what the property needs to measure in order to help it meet its environmental and sustainability goals.

Conclusion

A large number of properties, companies, and organizations around the world are working to improve the sustainability of travel and tourism. Space does not permit a full discussion of even a small fraction of the many commendable approaches being taken to improve the hospitality industry's environmental record. That so much is happening is heartening. However, while many hospitality properties are making great strides with their environmental efforts, others have not yet answered the challenge.

Recognition of the economic, regulatory, market, and social responsibility aspects of environmental/sustainability issues should be sufficient to motivate most hospitality managers to take some action. As the topics discussed within the chapter illustrate, there is a wide variety of approaches within the industry to address a wide variety of environmental and sustainability issues. Sustainability is more about a process than an ultimate destination. Some development and operational activities within the industry are more sustainable than others, and some practices are more environmentally sound than others. Perhaps the only way to achieve perfect performance in the sustainability arena is to avoid consumption completely. Since that is not practical, the challenge for hospitality owners and managers is to work to minimize their businesses' detrimental impacts on the environment and strive to achieve an ethical balance in the social costs and benefits of doing business, while still operating in a manner that provides an acceptable economic return.

Endnotes

1. For more information on Agenda 21 see: http://www.unep.fr/shared/publications/pdf/3207-TourismAgenda.pdf.

2. See http://www.economist.com, Idea: Triple bottom line, November, 2009.

3. See also E. W. Manning and T. D. Dougherty, "Sustainable Tourism: Preserving the Golden Goose," *Cornell Hotel and Restaurant Administration Quarterly,* April 1995.

4. For more information on USGBCs LEED Volume program see: http://www.usgbc.org/leed/certification.

5. ISO standards are developed by the International Organization for Standardization. Another ISO series with which the hospitality industry has experience is the ISO 9000 series dealing with quality.

6. See www.conventionindustry.org/projects/green_mtgs.htm and www.epa.gov/oppt/greenmeetings.

7. See www.sustainabletravelinternational.org/documents/op_carbonoffsets.html.

8. See http://www.starbucks.com/responsibility/environment.

9. See www.ihgplc.com/environment/index and http://thrive.hyatt.com/interactiveMap.html.

10. Information on composting can be accessed at www.cfe.cornell.edu/compost.

11. See www.energystar.gov.

12. Standards from organizations such as the World Bank and World Health Organization may be used as references when local regulations are lacking.

13. This discussion is based on *Environmental Management for Hotels: The Industry Guide to Best Practice,* Third Edition, by Claire Baker (2008), "Hazardous Materials" chapter.

14. See https://www.osha.gov/dsg/hazcom.

15. For an example of asbestos management policies and procedures, see *Environmental Management for Hotels,* "Hazardous Materials" chapter.

16. See www.haccpalliance.org.

17. See www.nraef.org. Another resource is Ronald F. Cichy, *Food Safety: Managing the HACCP Process* (Lansing, Mich.: Educational Institute of the American Hotel & Lodging Association, 2004).

18. See https://www.kimptonhotels.com/promotions/hybrid-parking.aspx.

19. From the World Commission on Environment and Development (the Brundtland Commission) report *Our Common Future* (Oxford: Oxford University Press, 1987).

20. See http://www.cntraveler.com/world-savers/2013.

21. See http://blog.intercontinentalnybarclay.com/#.

22. See http://www.tourismpartnership.org/what-we-do/products-programmes/publications.

23. See www.USGBC.org.

24. See www.usgbc.org.

25. See www.ahla.com/green.

26. See www.caribbeanhotelandtourism.com/CAST.php.

27. See www.energystar.gov.

28. See: http://www.cleantheworld.org/Hotel-Program.asp.

29. See http://www.tourismpartnership.org/what-we-do/products-programmes/hotel-carbon-measurement-initiative.

30. See http://www.ecorewards.com/infostore/ECalculator.asp.

🔑 Key Terms

compost—Organic material that decomposes and can be used for soil amendment or material to grow plants.

corrosive—Any materials that destroy other materials by chemical reaction. When in contact with human tissues, these substances may cause burns and destroy tissue.

environmental impact statement (EIS)—A document stating the effect a planned construction project will have on the surrounding community.

explosive—Any substance capable, by chemical reaction within itself, of producing an explosion causing damage to its surroundings.

flammable—Any substance that can be easily ignited by sparks or flames and cause fires.

hazardous substances—Any substances that have the potential to damage health or property.

Hotel Carbon Measurement Initiative (HCMI)—A tool to measure hotel meeting and group carbon footprint impacts.

infectious—Any substance that contains viable microorganisms and their toxins, capable of causing disease.

ISO 14000 standards—A set of environmental guidelines established by the International Organization for Standardization that is recognized as the global standard for environmental management. Certification by the ISO to the ISO 14000 standards is acknowledged in the industry as a benchmark achievement.

land-use planning—A facilities development function in which careful and appropriate planning and management is applied to existing real property, structures, and natural resources to preserve the cultural and social fabric of the surrounding community.

LEED—Stands for "Leadership in Energy and Environmental Design," which is a green building certification system.

pulping—A method of transforming waste (such as that generated in kitchens) from solid form into a type of slurry by adding water and processing the waste through a pulping machine. The pulping machine grinds the waste, presses out the water, and expels the pulp into a holding bin.

recycling—Separating certain items of refuse for eventual shredding or melting to their basic materials, which will then be used to make new products.

reuse—The practice of using items more than once, thereby substantially reducing trash and throwaways. Beverage containers, beer kegs, shipping trays, and pallets are typical reuse items.

submetering—A method of tracking and recording energy usage by hotel department or function such that usage can be accurately matched to specific operations (such as the laundry) and charged to those operations (if desired).

sustainability—A broad approach to environmental consciousness in which environmental issues are addressed within the context of economics, ecology, and ethics.

social responsibility—The recognition by hospitality owners and managers of an obligation to protect the environment for their associates, guests, and communities.

toxic—Any substance that causes damage to health, physical or mental impairment, or death when inhaled, ingested, or absorbed.

waste minimization—An approach to environmental good practice involving reduction, reuse, recycling, and waste transformation to minimize the amount of waste disposed and the cost of its disposal. The ultimate goal of waste minimization is to ensure that disposal is done in an approved and environmentally suitable manner.

waste transformation—The practice of converting waste products into another usable form, such as incinerating burnable items and capturing the heat energy thus created to generate power.

wastewater—The majority of water leaving a hospitality operation (exceptions being cooling tower water lost to evaporation and irrigation water for the grounds).

 Review Questions

1. What are potential motivations for initiating environmental programs?
2. Why is waste management important to hotel operators?
3. What are examples of re-use? recycling? waste transformation?
4. What is pulping, and what are its benefits to the hotelier?
5. What does good energy management contribute to environmental good practice? to the bottom line?
6. What is submetering, and why is it a good management practice?
7. What are some examples of energy load reduction? What five broad areas of opportunity are available for energy conservation and cost savings?
8. Why is fresh water resource management a critical issue to hoteliers, especially those managing resort operations? How does the nature of wastewater management affect the market appeal of a given hotel/resort operation?
9. What are the five commonly recognized hazardous substances? What danger potential does each present?
10. What are some of the business-related benefits of appropriate land-use management?
11. Why is employee involvement important to the success of an environmental program?
12. What is sustainability and what impact does it have on the success of a property?

Internet Sites

For more information, visit the following Internet sites. Remember that Internet addresses can change without notice. If the site is no longer there, you can use a search engine to look for additional sites.

Agenda 21 for the Travel and Tourism Industry (PDF)
www.unep.fr/shared/publications/
pdf/3207-TourismAgenda.pdf

American Hotel & Lodging Association Green Guide
www.ahla.com/Green.aspx?id=24560.

American Solar Energy Society
www.ases.org

Association of Energy Engineers
www.aeecenter.org

Blue Flag
www.blueflag.org

Business Enterprises for Sustainable Travel
www.sustainabletravel.org

Caribbean Action for Sustainable Tourism
www.cha-cast.com

Ceres
www.ceres.org

Corporate Social Leadership in Travel & Tourism by the World Travel and Tourism Council
wttc.org/publications/pdf/cslreport.pdf

Energy & Power Management
www.energyandpowermanagement.com

ENERGY STAR
www.energystar.gov

Foundation for Environmental Education
www.fee-international.org

GEMI—Global Environmental Management Initiative
www.gemi.org

GBCI—Green Building Certification Institute
www.gbci.org

Green Globe
www.greenglobe.org

Green Seal
www.greenseal.org

Global Sustainable Tourism Council
www.gstcouncil.org

International Tourism Partnership
www.tourismpartnership.org

ISO 9000 and ISO 14000
www.iso.org/iso/en/iso9000-14000/
index.html

National Renewable Energy Laboratory
www.nrel.gov

Project Planet
www.projectplanetcorp.com

The United Nations Commission on Sustainable Development
www.un.org/esa/sustdev

United Nations World Tourism Organization
www2.unwto.org/

U.S. Green Building Council
www.usgbc.org

WTTC—World Travel & Tourism Council
www.wttc.org

🔍 Case Study ⎯⎯⎯⎯⎯⎯⎯⎯⎯⎯⎯⎯⎯⎯⎯⎯⎯⎯⎯⎯⎯⎯⎯⎯⎯⎯

Greening the Excelsior

Susan Sayles, Director of Marketing for the Excelsior Hotel and Conference Center, was not happy. She had just heard that one of her competitors, Natural Lodging, had booked some business that she had hopes of getting. The annual conference of CERES was going to Natural Lodging rather than the Excelsior. Not only was the CERES business good—300 rooms for three nights plus conference rooms, lunches, and a major banquet—but Susan was hoping the conference would get her property on the radar screen of those attending the conference. Several Fortune 100 businesses were among the companies represented at the conference, and many of these companies had substantial local operations that could generate a lot of business for the Excelsior.

When a local historic but underperforming hotel had reopened as Natural Lodging a few years earlier, Susan and a number of marketing directors at other area hotels had viewed its "green hotel" concept with skepticism. She had heard of green marketing and knew it worked for companies such as Whole Foods and Body Shop, but doubted it would work in the hotel business. She had been a little surprised that Natural Lodging's certification under the *Leadership in Environmental and Energy Design—Existing Building* program (administered by the U.S. Green Buildings Council) had generated a lot of press when it was announced, and she sensed that some business had come to Natural Lodging as a result. When the hotel had operated under the flag of a well-known lodging brand, it had been a below-average performer in the market. Now, as Natural Lodging, the latest Smith Travel Research information showed it was outperforming its competitive set in occupancy with rates that were comparable and edging higher. Natural Lodging seemed to be doing quite well.

When Susan had prepared the bid for the CERES conference, it required that someone from the Excelsior complete the CERES Green Hotel Initiative Best Practice Survey. She had asked the rooms division director to complete this survey, verified that it had been done, and included it in her bid. Wondering if this might have influenced her bid's failure, she pulled out her copy and looked it over.

Ouch! Excelsior scored a 0 ("no activity in this area") or a 1 ("budgeted initiative, planned for implementation within one year of submission date") in most areas. Nothing had scored a 5 ("well-established practice/equipment installed throughout property"). She had a feeling Natural Lodging's scores were a lot higher.

A year later, Susan was asked to take the Director of Marketing position with another Excelsior Hotel in another city. Coincidentally, CERES was looking to have its annual convention in this city in a little over a year. She decided to have a talk with her new GM about the lost bid and the potential value of greening the hotel in light of the CERES opportunity. Susan indicated that Natural Lodging did not have a property to compete with in this city, and she thought the CERES business was a really good one to pursue. The GM was cautiously supportive of the idea and asked her to put together a group of staff to pursue it. Susan found herself leading the Excelsior "green team," except she didn't yet have a team and she wasn't really sure what was involved in a hotel's environmental performance.

Discussion Questions

1. What items might Susan present to the GM regarding the value of a green program in addition to the potential for business such as CERES?

2. Who do you think Susan should involve in the group of staff to pursue the green program? Why?

3. If you were Susan, how would you involve the group members in the green program? Do you think she should focus them on the CERES bid and Best Practice Survey or should they be given more latitude to develop their own approach?

4. What should Susan do to investigate other green market opportunities for the hotel?

Case Number: 2813CA

Chapter Appendix:

Agenda 21 for the Travel and Tourism Industry

In 1987, a landmark document in the field of sustainability was released—*Our Common Future,* also known as the Brundtland Report, named for Gro Harlem Brundtland, the head of the United Nations World Commission on Environment and Development, the organization that developed the report. *Our Common Future* strongly influenced the formation of *Agenda 21,* which was a document released at the Earth Summit held in Rio de Janeiro in 1992. In 1996 the World Travel & Tourism Council (WTTC), the United Nations World Tourism Organization (UNWTO), and the Earth Council collaborated to launch *Agenda 21 for the Travel & Tourism Industry: Towards Environmentally Sustainable Development* (Agenda 21 TTI). Agenda 21 TTI outlines ten priority areas for governments and organizations to target to implement sustainable development for the travel and tourism industry; these priority areas (and the supporting implementation information) serve as the foundation for many corporate sustainability programs within the travel and tourism industry:

Priority area 1: waste minimization

- Reduce the waste burden by selecting products that have minimal waste implications.

- Select suppliers who agree to minimize the waste implications of their products or insist that manufacturers minimize or reuse non-essential packaging.

- Reuse products wherever possible.

- Recycle where reduction and reuse is not possible or where more environmentally sound waste disposal routes (e.g., biomass) are not appropriate.

- Dispose of unavoidable wastes responsibly.

- Encourage staff to employ the principles of waste minimization at home.

- Work with governments and other authorities to establish labeling schemes that provide realistic environmental information about products and disposal.

- Open recycling or disposal facilities to employees and local communities to improve overall destination quality.

Priority area 2: energy conservation and management

- Implement programs to reduce energy wastage; simple measures such as switching off equipment when not in use can bring substantial financial and environmental benefits as the first step in an energy management program.

- Research alternative, environmentally benign methods of energy generation, such as solar, wind, or biomass power.

- Develop, use, and disseminate energy-saving technology.

- Integrate energy efficiency considerations into all new developments.
- Train staff about the environmental benefits of initiatives to save energy.
- For trans-national corporations, employ energy-efficient technologies in all facilities in developed and developing countries.

Priority area 3: management of fresh water resources

- Take all possible measures to protect the quality of fresh water reserves and establish appropriate emergency procedures should reserves be under threat.
- Provide fresh water facilities for use by local communities in communal areas or pay for water infrastructure to be installed to serve the needs of both tourists and local communities.
- Minimize wastage of water by undertaking regular maintenance checks.
- Work with customers to reduce water demand; placing notices explaining to guests the importance of conserving water is just one example of a commonly used and effective initiative.
- Use water-saving devices to reduce water consumption while maintaining service quality.
- Plant drought-resistant species in landscaped areas.
- Develop appropriate environmental impact and design criteria to ensure that water conservation is a key element of new projects and, if water is scarce and construction may result in local shortages, be prepared to make the decision not to build.
- For trans-national corporations, disseminate water-saving technologies and techniques to facilities in developing countries.
- Reuse and recycle water wherever possible.
- Encourage staff and customers to incorporate components of the water management program into daily procedures at home.

Priority area 4: wastewater management

- Use wastewater treatment facilities in all outlets around the world to ensure that all effluent is treated to match WHO standards as a minimum and reused for secondary purposes where appropriate.
- Where wastewater facilities do not exist, work with other companies and governments to establish appropriate facilities and procedures.
- Establish appropriate catchment ponds to ensure that potentially damaging chemicals do not enter the waste system through runoff.
- Establish programs with staff, tourists, and communities to clean up degraded aquatic environments.
- Establish emergency procedures to ensure that the aquatic environment is protected from disasters within the facility.

- Wherever possible, avoid products containing potentially hazardous substances which may eventually find their way into the water system.
- Dispose of wastewater responsibly.

Priority area 5: hazardous substances

- Examine the necessity for use of products containing potentially hazardous substances and, where possible, use more environmentally benign products.
- Assess the full environmental as well as financial implications of new products prior to purchase.
- Where environmentally benign alternatives do not exist, form partnerships with governments and manufacturers to develop them.
- Reduce use of products containing hazardous substances to the lowest possible quantity and recycle or reuse any residue that can be captured.
- Dispose of any unavoidable wastes responsibly.
- Set up inventories and storage procedures to guard against theft/accidents.
- Ensure that all appropriate staff are trained in handling of hazardous substances and in emergency procedures.
- Start routine emissions of toxic substances to the environment as part of a "right-to-know" program for employees and host communities.
- Transfer benign technologies and know-how to developing countries.

Priority area 6: transport

- Use well-maintained and modern transport technology, thus minimizing emissions into the environment; this is particularly important for airlines, which should seek to operate the most efficient fleet possible.
- Help developing countries to acquire relevant technological skills or equipment.
- Develop and manage car-share, cycle, or walk-to-work schemes for employees and provide incentives to ensure success.
- Provide information to customers to help them use public transport, cycle ways, or footpaths.
- Work with planning authorities to ensure that coach stops and other drop-off points are well located.
- Work with suppliers to ensure that purchases are not delivered at peak times (congestion contributes to emissions) and that deliveries are fully loaded.
- Work with local farmers and other local businesses to purchase supplies locally whenever possible.
- Work with governments to implement measures to reduce congestion and hence pollution; this is particularly relevant to the air transport sector and to city environments.

- Work with governments to integrate transport modes and thus reduce reliance on the private car.
- Consider transport as a part of development plans.
- Operate demand management to reduce the need for polluting modes of transport in favor of less polluting modes and activities.

Priority area 7: land-use planning and management

- Assess the potential environmental, cultural, social, and economic impacts of new developments.
- Take measures to avoid negative impacts or minimize unavoidable impacts.
- Monitor the impacts of all new processes and procedures.
- Use local materials (from substantially managed sources) and labor when constructing new facilities.
- Employ technologies and materials appropriate to local conditions in new developments and refurbishments.
- Work with regional and national authorities to ensure that adequate infrastructure is in place for new developments and refurbishments; this may include making provision for wastewater treatment facilities or electricity supply within the development or ensuring support for local craft industries.
- Involve the local community in major development decisions (see priority area 8).
- Consider overall carrying capacity and resource restraints when developing new products, especially on small islands.
- Work with other sectors to ensure balanced and complementary development patterns.

Priority area 8: involving staff, customers, and communities in environmental issues

- Take into account the opinions of all sectors of the community in the management of tourism developments; this can be facilitated by a local tourism forum or by formal meetings between staff and community members.
- Provide economic outlets for local tradespeople.
- Discuss development plans and opportunities with local communities.
- Open company recycling, water, or waste disposal facilities to the local community.
- Tell communities about the risks and environmental benefits of the business.
- Ensure that all members of the community, including women, indigenous people, the young, and the old, have access to employment and promotional opportunities within the company.
- Improve the local environment by staff sponsored clean-ups, etc.

To realize travel and tourism's potential for educating communities, customers, and staff and raising public awareness, companies should:

- Train all staff, from top management to temporary employees, in environmental issues.

- Provide specialist training to staff in key positions.

- Tell customers about company environmental initiatives, both to inspire product loyalty and to ensure that the environmental messages learned on holiday are put into practice at home.

- Work with local schools and colleges to integrate environmental issues into primary and vocational education.

- Encourage or sponsor training for community members to enable them to participate in the environment and development process.

- Involve employees' families in environmental activities and events.

- Offer training opportunities to other businesses in the area.

Priority area 9: design for sustainability

- Establish company-wide policies on sustainable development.

- Increase research and development activities.

- Examine the potential environmental, social, cultural, and economic impacts of new products.

- Seek solutions to environmental problems in developed and developing countries.

- Within the transport sector, strengthen efforts to collect, analyze, and exchange information on the relation between transport and the environment.

- Provide information and support to schools and colleges about environmental issues to help build up institutional, scientific, planning, and management capacities.

- Make adequate preparations for natural disasters, including designing and building new tourism facilities to withstand such disasters.

- Exchange information on solutions to environmental problems through resource centers such as the World Tourism Organization and the World Travel & Tourism Environment Research Centre.

- When developing facilities in other countries, ensure than environmental standards are as high as those in the country of origin.

Priority area 10: partnerships for sustainable development

- Contribute to the economic development and improve the well being of the local community.

- Use representative sectoral bodies to host jointly funded initiatives to test the constructs of sustainable development.

- Foster dialogue between industries, based on formulating solutions to joint problems.

- Work with small and medium-sized enterprises to exchange management skills, market development, and technological know-how, especially as regards the application of cleaner technology.

- Work with governments to establish an enabling framework for the achievement of sustainable development.

- Promote interaction between tourists and host communities and so enhance the industry's potential to contribute to increased understanding of other cultures.

- Promote and support access to markets for the wide range of interests involved in the Travel & Tourism industry.

- Incorporate the concerns of communities—especially indigenous communities—in the planning process so that they effectively participate in sustainable development.

Part II

Facility Systems

Chapter 4 Outline

Competencies

1. Describe how to reduce occupational injury rates in the hospitality industry. (pp. 125–132)

2. Outline how building design and maintenance affect safety. (p. 132)

3. Identify several safety concerns with regard to the guest bathroom. (pp. 132–135)

4. Cite evidence that concern over fire safety is growing. (pp. 136–140)

5. Identify critical elements of fire prevention, fire detection, and fire notification. (pp. 140–144)

6. Identify components of fire suppression and fire control devices and systems. (pp. 145–152)

7. Outline several elements that should be addressed in evacuation plans. (pp. 152–155)

8. Describe various ways in which facilities design and management can enhance a property's security efforts. (pp. 155–157)

9. Identify the elements of key control and guestroom locking systems. (pp. 157–163)

10. List several protective measures that can help mitigate the risk of terrorist attacks, and discuss other extraordinary events that can affect hospitality properties. (p. 164)

Safety and Security Systems

When you lay your head on a pillow at night, you're statistically safer from fatal fire when that pillow is in a hotel or motel than virtually any other place—safer than in a single-family house, a duplex, a manufactured home, an apartment, a townhouse, rooming house, boarding house, or lodging house.

The current situation (re: hotel fires) is a result of an industry transforming itself. While the number of people the lodging industry serves continues to grow, fires have been cut by more than half in the past 15 years, and fire deaths by more than three-fourths, because the industry responded to major disasters with determination and sustained efforts to make their properties safe.[1]

THE HOSPITALITY INDUSTRY has long been expected to provide guests with a reasonably safe and secure environment. This safe environment has changed from the stout walls and barred doors of the travelers' inns of hundreds of years ago to the electronic locks, fire sprinklers, smoke detectors, and closed-circuit television systems of many modern lodging properties. Today's hospitality manager must understand safety and security needs as they affect the well-being of both guests and employees and how they influence the financial success of the business.[2]

Managers should be motivated to address safety and security issues by several factors, including:

- A sense of moral and ethical responsibility for the welfare of guests and employees.

- Concern over the cost of losses associated with safety and security problems.

- Concern over potential legal liability for failure to exercise "reasonable care."[3]

The contributions to this chapter of April Berkol (Director, Environmental Health, Fire, and Life Safety, Starwood Hotels and Resorts Worldwide, Inc.), Chad Callahan (Vice President, Enterprise Loss Prevention, Marriott International, Inc.), and Jerry LaChapelle (Director of Risk Management, Harrah's Entertainment, Inc.) are not only acknowledged but applauded. Their greatly appreciated input and comments illustrate the commitment of the lodging industry to providing safe and secure operations for customers and employees.

- Corporate policies and procedures that establish standards.
- Contractual responsibilities related to union contracts.
- Governmental regulations.
- Concern for employee welfare, productivity, and retention.
- Market issues related to safety and security standards expected by guests.

Safety and the Hospitality Industry

Our discussion of safety in the hospitality industry will begin with a focus on employees and then move on to items that involve guests (and often employees as well). Safety involves avoiding those causes of injury and damage that we might call accidental—slips and falls, cuts, burns, and other personal injuries, as well as related property damages. Safety issues are important for their impact not only on guests and employees but on profitability as well.

Exhibit 1 shows data on occupational injury and illness from the Bureau of Labor Statistics from 2004 and 2012. All three of the hospitality segments in the exhibit have shown a reduction in the total cases of injuries and illness per 100 workers. However, the rate of more severe cases of injury and illness that involve days away from work have declined relatively little or not at all from 2004 to 2012.

Some U.S. lodging companies have achieved injury and illness rates that are lower than the national averages and have lead the industry in establishing a safer work environment. They have achieved this by implementing programs of loss prevention as part of their overall corporate risk management efforts. Risk management and loss prevention programs are designed to pinpoint major potential risk areas and identify options to reduce either the frequency or the severity of their losses. Implementation of restricted duty programs, as evidenced in the data in Exhibit 1 (see the "Cases with Job Transfer or Restriction" category), is an effort by hospitality companies to reduce the severity of losses. Exhibit 2 lists fourteen elements that the U.S. National Safety Council suggests are necessary for a successful safety and health program. The emphasis a property places on each of the individual elements is dependent on its type of business or unit.

Exhibit 1   Occupational Injury and Illness Incidence Rate per 100 Workers

	Total Cases		Cases with Days Away from Work		Cases with Job Transfer or Restriction	
	2004	2012	2004	2012	2004	2012
Traveler Accommodation	5.8	5.3	1.6	1.6	1.5	1.3
Full-Service Restaurants	4.1	3.4	1.0	0.9	0.3	0.3
Limited-Service Eating Places	4.3	3.2	0.8	0.8	0.5	0.2

Source: http://www.bls.gov/iif/oshwc/osh/os/ostb3581.txt.

Exhibit 2   The 14 Elements of a Successful Safety and Health Program

The 14 Elements

The U.S. National Safety Council established the following 14 Elements as the standard for a successful safety and health program. All effective programs contain these elements, but the emphasis on each will vary according to individual company needs. For example, a service organization might place less emphasis on some activities that receive top priority in a heavily regulated manufacturing company.

Element 1: Hazard Recognition, Evaluation, and Control

Establishing and maintaining safe and healthful conditions require identifying hazards, evaluating their potential effects, developing ways to eliminate or control them, and planning action priorities. This process is the essence of successful safety and health management.

Element 2: Workplace Design and Engineering

Safety and health issues are most easily and economically addressed when facilities, processes, and equipment are being designed. Organizations must incorporate safety into workplace design, production processes, and equipment selection. They also need to evaluate and modify or replace existing processes, equipment, and facilities to make them safer.

Element 3: Safety Performance Management

As in all areas of operations, standards must be set for safety performance. They should reflect applicable regulatory requirements, additional voluntary guidelines, and best business practices.

Element 4: Regulatory Compliance Management

The Occupational Safety and Health Administration (OSHA), the Mine Safety and Health Administration (MSHA), and state safety and health agencies establish and enforce safety and health regulations. Other agencies, such as the Environmental Protection Agency, also issue and enforce regulations relating to safety and health in the United States.

Element 5: Occupational Health

Occupational health programs range from the simple to the complex. At a minimum, such programs address the immediate needs of injured or ill employees by providing first aid and response to emergencies. More elaborate medical services may include medical surveillance programs and provision for an in-house medical capability. In addition, some companies are beginning to focus on off-the-job safety and health through employee wellness and similar programs.

Element 6: Information Collection

Safety and health activities, including inspections, recordkeeping, industrial hygiene surveys and other occupational health assessments, injury/illness/incident investigations, and performance reviews, produce a large quantity of data. Safety and health professionals must collect and analyze this data. Small incidents often provide early warnings of more serious safety or health problems. Complete and accurate records can be used to identify hazards, measure safety performance and improvement, and, through analyses, help identify patterns. The recording, analysis,

(continued)

Exhibit 2   *(continued)*

and communication of safety and health data are greatly simplified through the use of computers and commercially available software.

Element 7: Employee Involvement

Design and engineering controls are limited in their ability to reduce hazards. Companies now understand that their real assets are people, not machinery, and they also realize that employees must recognize their stake in a safe and healthful workplace. As employees become more involved in planning, implementation, and improvement, they see the need for safer work practices. Solutions to safety and health problems often come from affected employees.

Element 8: Motivation, Behavior, and Attitudes

Motivation aims at changing behavior and attitudes to create a safer, healthier workplace.

Element 9: Training and Orientation

New and transferred employees must become familiar with company policies and procedures and learn how to perform their jobs safely and efficiently. The use of on-the-job, classroom, and specialty training can contribute to a successful safety and health program. A complete program includes hazard recognition, regulatory compliance, and prevention. The training is reinforced through regular follow-up with both new and veteran employees.

Element 10: Organizational Communications

Effective communication within the organization keeps employees informed about policies, procedures, goals, and progress. Effective two-way communication among employees and managers is critical, as is publicizing safety and health information in the community.

Element 11: Management and Control of External Exposures

Today's safety and health programs must address risks beyond the organization's walls. Contingency plans and "what if" worst-case scenarios are part of planning for disasters, contractor activities, and product and other liability exposures.

Element 12: Environmental Management

Environmental management often requires a complete program of its own. Many companies, however, address environmental issues along with safety and health as part of their comprehensive programs.

Element 13: Workplace Planning and Staffing

Safety and health considerations are important when planning for and staffing the company's work force. Issues include work safety rules, employee assistance programs, and requirements resulting from the Americans with Disabilities Act.

Element 14: Assessments, Audits, and Evaluations

Every organization needs tools to measure conditions, monitor compliances, and assess progress. A variety of evaluative tools can be used to meet the needs of the organization, including self-assessments, third-party assessments, and voluntary regulatory assessments.

Establishment of a safety committee is a key to encouraging a safe workplace. Involving employees in the development of safety policies, reviewing details of accidents, recommending corrective action, and participating in safety inspections and other safety functions helps ensure employee interest and buy-in. It is helpful for managers to draft a policy statement that outlines the organization, responsibility, and procedures for the property's safety committee. Numerous resources exist to assist in this endeavor, ranging from those of the corporation itself, to the American Hotel & Lodging Educational Institute,[4] to the National Safety Council.[5]

Occupational injuries and lost workdays affect the capability of operating departments to function properly. This degraded functionality in turn affects the operation's profit picture. In addition, injuries affect employees and their families. A property with a good safety program should be able to reduce both the rate at which injuries occur and the severity of the injuries that do occur.

Some hospitality operations have reduced their injury rates below the industry average by implementing comprehensive safety programs. Such programs are often part of an overall program of **risk management**, an integrated effort to reduce the causes and effects of safety- and security-related incidents of all types. One of the most important factors in risk management programs is having the support and involvement of top management. One researcher has noted:

> The effectiveness of a risk management program depends greatly on the support of top management, both at the property and corporate level.... The most effective programs held property managers accountable for losses, either through charge backs for losses or incentives for safety. Moreover, properties that have implemented ongoing training programs as part of their culture have better risk management programs. In these litigious times, a solid risk management program is a sound investment.[6]

It is also very important to place either an individual or a safety committee in charge of safety. This person or committee should have the authority to enforce compliance with safety rules. The membership and leadership of a safety committee should be rotated among management employees and perhaps key line employees as well. One study found that the most effective safety committees included the general manager, certain department heads, and some line employees. This study found the seemingly least effective technique to be that reported by one manager:

> We meet every month, review the accident records, and make recommendations. The minutes are sent to the GM, but nothing ever really changes unless corporate [management] calls screaming that we've got to lower our accident rate. Then the GM has us start contests and do more training. This lasts for about two or three months, and then it's back to business as usual.[7]

A note of caution is needed. *Responsibility* for safety and security cannot be delegated to a committee or to a department. Safety and security must be viewed as a responsibility of all employees—line and management. However, without accountability, there can be no responsibility. A method of measuring how employees and managers are doing with regard to safety must be implemented.

The Legionnaires' Disease Risk

In 1976, an American Legion Convention in Philadelphia had an outbreak of a mysterious disease that killed thirty-four people and debilitated nearly another 200.* The disease was traced to the air-handling system at a hotel where a bacterium, previously unknown and now referred to as *Legionella,* was entering the building from the building's cooling tower exhaust plume. Issues associated with *Legionella* have continued to occur globally, with some of these happening in hotels. And, while locations such as cooling towers can contain this bacteria, most *legionellosis* is the result of potable water in buildings. This includes areas such as showers, taps, pools, spas, decorative fountains, and food preparation areas as well as utility water for cooling and heating.

It has been suggested that the Hazard Analysis Critical Control Point (HACCP) system that has been widely accepted for preventing foodborne disease can be a model for dealing with *Legionella*-related problems. In the modified form of a Water Safety Plan, HACCP-related approaches have been promoted by the World Health Organization to address *legionellosis*.

The role of property systems design and maintenance in reducing risks from *Legionella* is quite significant. The case below illustrates the potential seriousness of an outbreak.

Consequences of a *Legionella* Lawsuit

Five family members and a family friend were in town for a wedding. The group visited the pool/spa area in their hotel to let their kids swim.** The adults sat by the whirlpool. They did not enter the water. The group dispersed to two different states immediately after the wedding.

Within days, the entire group was sick. The grandmother ended up in a coma, diagnosed with *legionellosis*. She spent a month in the hospital and two additional months recovering. The rest of the group, including a five-week-old infant who had been in his mother's arms while she sat in the pool area, suffered milder *legionellosis*, which was diagnosed as Pontiac Fever.

No one would have known about this outbreak if not for the family's tenacity. They had been together for only a short time, which allowed them to pinpoint where they had been exposed. The family notified the Centers for Disease Control and Prevention (CDC). The CDC reported that the outbreak was "identified only because the indexed cases occurred in an extended family from two states that stayed at a Georgia hotel, and family members brought the outbreak to the attention of public health officials."

The response from the CDC was impressive and thorough. It tested the hotel water system and collected information about pool and spa maintenance. The CDC reported that the hotel spa had been "poorly maintained." Review of the maintenance records at the hotel indicated that the condition of the whirlpool spa was "frequently below optimal throughout the time period examined."

Maintenance did not improve even after hotel management knew people had nearly died from *legionellosis* contracted from the spa. One water treatment chemical remained chronically outside regulated ranges. Less than three months after the spa was reopened, tests showed the pool/spa was infested with *Legionella* again.

During the discovery phase of the lawsuit, public health records in every county in every state where this hotel chain had a property revealed that eighteen health departments had shut down twenty-five of the chain's pools or spas. The case was settled before reaching trial.

In a tort case, plaintiffs typically claim two types of damages: economic (such as medical bills and lost wages) and non-economic (pain and suffering). In this case, the grandmother had incurred nearly $100,000 in medical bills. The family had been through a terrible ordeal, enduring significant non-economic damages.

A claim for punitive damages was brought because of corporate management's failure to respond to mounting evidence that better maintenance of building water systems was necessary to prevent serious disease.

Aside from ethical issues, it makes financial sense for a company to take steps to prevent this disease. The amount budgeted for water system management may seem to be a waste, but legal action can be much more expensive.

---

* The discussion is derived from William F. McCoy, "Legionellosis—Why the Problem Continues," *ASHRAE Journal*, January 2006, pp. 24–27.

** This information is the result of several interviews with Lee T. Wallace, Esq., the lawyer who handled the family's case. Wallace is an attorney for The Wallace Law Firm in Atlanta.

This measurement can be in the form of behavioral issues, such as conducting training sessions and tracking the number and quality of accident investigations, safety inspections, and so forth, or it can be measured against expressed goals to reduce all accidents, lost-time accidents, the number of a specific kind of accident, and so forth.

Attention to safety issues related to employees is legally mandated in the United States under the Occupational Safety and Health Act. The act created the Occupational Safety and Health Administration (OSHA), which performs inspections of workplaces and reports the results of these inspections. The citations resulting from these inspections can provide some insights into areas possibly warranting additional attention at hospitality properties.

Some key elements of safety programs that have helped reduce employee injuries include:[8]

- Composing and communicating to all employees a written policy relating the organization's commitment to safety and what it expects of its employees.

- Soliciting and using the input of line employees on safety matters.

- Conducting regular safety inspections of the property.

- Setting realistic goals for accident reduction, closely monitoring progress, and rewarding reductions.

- Requiring accountability for accident reduction.

- Offering a modified—or transitional—duty program in order to return injured employees to work sooner.

- Creating a heightened sense of safety awareness through signs, contests, rewards, and health fairs.

- Training, retraining, and then training some more.

- Establishing specific safety-oriented behaviors as a performance consideration for management.

Building Design, Maintenance, and Safety

The proper design and maintenance of the physical plant are important contributors to employee and guest safety. Properly maintained and adequately illuminated walkways, stairs, and parking lots reduce the likelihood of falls and related injuries. Using slip-resistant flooring materials and finishes helps protect employees and guests from injury due to slippery surfaces. Another important design consideration is the Americans with Disabilities Act of 1990 (and its periodic updates), which spells out accommodations to be made for people with disabilties.

The glass installed in sliding doors to balconies, other patio doors, and exit/entrance doors is another potential source of safety problems. Tempered glass should always be installed in such locations. Tempered glass is harder to break and, when shattered, breaks into rounded pieces, reducing the chance of injury. Staff should take care when replacing glass that the correct type is used. In addition, when glass doors may be mistaken for open doorways, the glass should have decals affixed or bars of some type placed across the glass to alert people to the doors' presence.[9]

Besides the physical plant, the furniture, fixtures, and equipment also need attention as part of a safety program. When these items are cleaned, they also should be inspected for loose connections and worn or frayed parts. This is yet another example of the need for a close working relationship between maintenance and housekeeping. If any problems are noted, the item in question should be either repaired immediately or removed from service until it is repaired.

Attention should also be paid to product recall and defect notices. In recent years, defective sprinkler heads and high chairs were among a host of product recalls. More recently, a new Federal Crib Standard was passed that requires hotels to only supply cribs that comply with the new federal standards.[10]

Safety in the Guest Bath

An area of particular concern in guest safety is the guest bathroom. Some of the safety concerns are:

- Hot water temperatures.

- Slip resistance of bathtubs, showers, and bathroom floor coverings.

- Electrical shock.

- Proper bathroom construction.

Safety and Security Systems and the ADA

Guests with disabilities may often be at greater risk in emergency situations due either to a diminished ability to hear warning signals or an inability to exit a building quickly. Guests with hearing or cognitive disabilities may be unable to perceive some types of emergency warnings, while guests with some types of mobility impairments may be unable to independently evacuate floors that are above or below grade if the elevators are out of service. Although such potential situations have been recognized for many years, possible solutions have only recently been addressed by accessibility standards.

To alert guests who cannot readily hear audible alarms, Title III ADA Standards for Accessible Design require the installation of visual fire alarms (strobe lights) in various areas, especially where an individual might be isolated, such as in restrooms, meeting rooms, and guestrooms. The strobe lights are required to meet certain minimum requirements such as spacing, installation heights, flash rates, intensity, and synchronization.

All wheelchair-accessible guestrooms plus a percentage of other guestrooms are required to have audible/visual alarms that are triggered by a local smoke detector and the building's general fire alarm. Accessible guestrooms are required to be configed and distributed to provide choices of room types and amenities comparable to those offered to the general public, including room types, levels of service, smoking/no-smoking rooms, views, etc.

The ADA Standards for Accessible Design require that new hotels be fully sprinklered or that each floor have either direct at-grade egress or an area of rescue assistance. Areas of rescue assistance are designated protected spaces that connect directly to a means of egress (usually a fire stair), are large enough to accommodate two wheelchairs out of the path of normal egress, and have a two-way audible and visual communications system that connects to a fire command location. In these protected areas, guests who are unable to use stairs are expected to wait to be evacuated. Unfortunately, areas of rescue assistance can cause collateral security problems in hotels/motels. Spaces with immediate access to an exit, where persons are out of sight of security personnel, can potentially cause a threat to other hotel guests. Also, if storage space is at a premium, it typically becomes an ongoing management challenge to ensure that areas of rescue assistance are kept clear *at all times.*

It is important that hoteliers establish backup operational procedures to ensure the safety of guests with disabilities. The simple task of flagging the folio of each guest with a hearing or mobility impairment at the time of check-in can provide an effective means of identifying rooms that staff should take special care to notify in case of an emergency or that fire professionals should check to ensure that guests have been safely evacuated.

The scalding of guests in lodging bathrooms has resulted in injury and death. This problem occurs primarily in older establishments due to outmoded system design and operation. A hotel shower safety study published in 2007 reported the results of a survey of 350 guestrooms in 101 individual hotels representing fifty-two different hotel chains. The study found about 88 percent of these hotels had showers that delivered water in excess of 115°F (46°C), 53 percent in excess of 125°F (52°C), and 12 percent in excess of 140°F (60°C). The highest recorded shower temperature was 171.5°F (77.5°C)! The lawsuits that can result from scalding guests with these high-temperature water supplies can bankrupt small operations and significantly affect the bottom line of larger ones, not to mention the ethical considerations involved. To prevent scalding, it is suggested that operators:

- Set guest-use water temperatures no higher than 120°F (49°C) at the source and 110°F (43°C) at the tap.

- Separate hotel water systems supplying commercial facilities, guestrooms, and locker rooms from those supplying kitchens and laundries.

- Install bath and shower valves that provide pressure and temperature compensation. These valves maintain a preset mix of hot and cold water and automatically adjust to system changes.

The slip resistance of bathtubs is also a concern, since slippery bathtubs can cause injuries. The American Society for Testing and Materials (ASTM) has defined indices of "slipperiness." When purchasing new bathtubs and showers, lodging managers should ask for a nonslip surface per ASTM F462.

The slip resistance rating of a bathroom tub and shower can decrease over time due to wear and the effects of cleaning chemicals. Tub and shower suppliers can recommend cleaning materials and methods to help alleviate this problem. When resurfacing these fixtures, managers should be sure to specify the required slip resistance as part of the contract; the contractor should be required to submit test results per ASTM F462 on samples of the finished product.

The location and installation of grab bars is also important in bath safety. Suggested guidelines for positioning and mounting grab bars appear in Exhibit 3. All wall-mounted items need to be installed with adequate blocking to ensure secure anchoring. The Americans with Disabilities Act also contains important provisions regarding grab bars.

Water Temperature Is a Safety Issue

When conducting a water conservation and energy audit some years ago, one hospitality industry consultant encountered a roadside motel (carrying the flag of a well-known limited-service franchise) that supplied water to guestrooms at 175°F (79°C)! When the hot water tap was opened in the bathroom sink, it released a stream of excessively hot water that looked like steam pouring from an opened steam line. Why was the water so hot? It turned out that this motel was heating water electrically. The motel had two water heaters. The owner was concerned about his high electric bill, specifically the demand charge. Therefore, to ensure a sufficient amount of hot water but have only one water heater contributing to the demand charge, the owner had disconnected the electric supply to one water heater and used it only as a storage tank for the 175°F (79°C) water produced by the other heater. Saving money on the electric bill while increasing the potential for guest injury and a costly lawsuit is not good business.

Exhibit 3   The Position and Mounting of Grab Bars

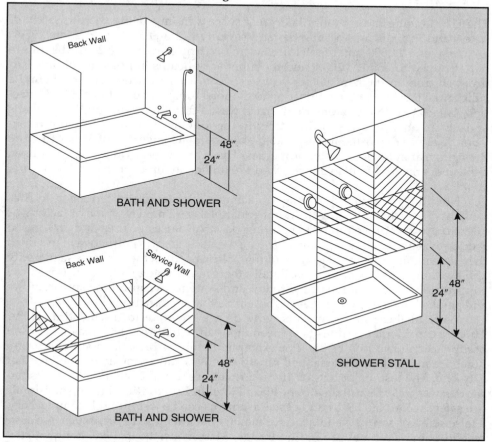

Source: Robert L. Kohr, "The Safety Factor in Bathroom Design," *Lodging,* May 1989, p. 28.

Any glass used in shower stalls and mirrors should be safety glazed. Shower stall doors should be of tempered glass to reduce the possibility of cuts should the door break.

Bathroom flooring should also have proper slip resistance. When specifying floor surfaces, managers should require the manufacturer to submit certified copies of slip resistance test results from independent laboratories. The test results should represent conditions appropriate to the expected use of the flooring material. The manufacturer can also recommend cleaning materials that will maintain the floor's slip resistance. Taking these steps will help minimize slips and falls.

To reduce the hazard in the guest baths due to electrical shocks, managers should furnish ground fault protection on selected electrical outlets. If a lodging property provides hair dryers, the fan and coil should be mounted on the wall with a built-in GFCI capability.

Fire Safety

The U.S. lodging industry has had great success in improving the fire safety of hotels and in reducing the number and severity of hotel fires. In the late 1970s, an average of 11,500 hotel/motel fires were occurring yearly. By 2002, this figure had dropped to about 4,200,[11] and the number of deaths in hotel/motel fires had dropped from more than 100 per year to sixteen. This reduction occurred amid a substantial increase in the number of hotel/motel rooms. The National Fire Protection Association (NFPA) remarked that it was in fact a milestone in the dramatic and remarkable progress of fire safety in the lodging industry.[12] In more recent years, U.S. fire departments responded to an estimated average of 3,900 structure fires per year at hotel or motel properties. These fires caused an average of fifteen civilian deaths, 150 civilian injuries, and $76 million in direct property damage per year.[13]

How did the industry manage to achieve this significant reduction in fires while also greatly increasing the number of hotels and motels? A major factor was attention to fire prevention—identifying possible causes of fires and striving to reduce or eliminate them. Hotels have also greatly improved the ways in which they detect the presence of a fire and the policies and methods they use to notify and evacuate building occupants. Finally, there is technology. Vastly improved fire suppression systems are installed today, and systems to control the spread of fire and smoke effectively control even those fires that do flare up.

With all these improvements, why do we continue to discuss fire safety? Though considerable strides have been made in hotel fire safety, major fires still occur that involve loss of life. For example, Exhibit 4 presents a summary of a hotel fire in Thailand that claimed ninety-one lives and seriously injured another fifty-one. The last major loss of life in a hotel fire in the United States or its territories was in 1986 at the Dupont Plaza Hotel in Puerto Rico, but the admirable fire safety record of U.S. lodging establishments can be lost through complacency, a false sense of security, and a lack of managerial attention to fire issues. A classic case in point is a hotel fire in Cambridge, Massachusetts, in 1990. Banquet staff brought a twenty-pound propane tank into a function room to operate a buffet warming grill. The grill created smoke and set off the room's smoke detector. To dissipate the smoke, the staff set up fans. Later, when the staff disconnected the propane tank, they failed to notice that the fuel line was still open. The escaping propane was circulated around the room by the fans. When it encountered an ignition source, a fireball surged across the room. Amazingly, only one person died; ten others were hospitalized. In a news story reporting the fire, the writer stated, "Fire safety know-how may or may not trickle down to the people who need it most—the banquet staff."[14] This incident is a reminder that management not only needs to know what to do, it needs to convey this information to the staff and ensure that policies and procedures are followed.

Continued attention to fire safety is mandated also by rapidly advancing fire detection and suppression technology. New technology, systems, and devices require continued maintenance and testing and, unfortunately, may be subject to operational problems. The greatly reduced numbers of lodging fires, coupled with the presence of increasingly sophisticated fire technology, can give managers a

Exhibit 4   Hotel Fire in Thailand

At approximately 10:20 A.M. on July 11, 1997, a fire began in a ground-floor coffee shop at the Royal Jomtien Resort at Jomtien Beach in Thailand, approximately 200 kilometers (124 miles) southeast of Bangkok. The fire killed ninety-one hotel guests and staff and seriously injured fifty-one.

The fire was first reported by a crew from the local beach rescue foundation, which was patrolling nearby.

The nearest fire station crew, monitoring the radio traffic, overheard the first call and responded immediately, arriving on the scene in seven to ten minutes. At the hotel, they saw a well-advanced fire with flames emanating from the third-floor [of the seventeen-story structure] roof of the discotheque. Smoke was also visible from the top of the hotel towers, and fire was visible on the third floor.

The first-arriving crews also noticed that fourteen people had climbed out a second-floor window onto a canopy above the hotel foyer and that they were exposed to the fire.

During the early stages of their operations, firefighters concentrated on rescuing and protecting those exposed to the fire. Once the first on-scene apparatus had exhausted its water, firefighters had to leave the scene to replenish its supply.

An aerial apparatus with a turntable ladder that arrived with the second wave of responders positioned itself near the hotel entrance, and its crew rescued the fourteen people from the canopy above the foyer.

Once inside the hotel, firefighters tried to mount an attack using the standpipe, but they found it dry. The post-fire investigation revealed that no standpipe connections existed to permit the fire brigade to boost the standpipe system, and that an electric fire pump would have been needed to do so.

The only external city water source at the resort was in the southwest section of the complex near the hotel's swimming pool, where it was used to maintain the pool's water level. It was impossible to position a piece of apparatus close to the valve outlet, and when firefighters tried to connect [a] hose to it, they discovered that the connection wasn't compatible with that of their hoses.

The firefighters' only alternative water supply on the property was the swimming pool, which contained approximately 336,000 liters (88,763 gallons) of water. They suctioned the water from the pool using a floating pump and five portable pumps. Tankers were refilled at water sources outside the property.

Fire cause and origin

Before the fire started, approximately eight staff members smelled what they thought was gas emanating from the buffet area of the coffee shop. Investigating its source, a male staff member noticed that gas was leaking from the valve assembly of a nine-kilogram (twenty-pound) liquid propane gas cylinder. The cylinder was connected at the valve assembly to a Y-shaped breaching piece connected by [a] flexible rubber hose to two wok-type burner jets. The jets were regularly used to cook breakfast for the hotel guests.

Noting the leak, the man tried to shut down the cylinder's main control valve. However, he inadvertently turned the valve the wrong way and, instead of shutting off the flow of gas, actually increased it. The vapor, expanding as it was released, quickly ignited.... The fire, which grew rapidly as it consumed combustibles near the cylinder, soon became too big to contain with a portable extinguisher.

(continued)

Exhibit 4 *(continued)*

> According to the local police officers responsible for the initial investigation, the sister of one of the hotel's senior managers had fled the area of the fire before she realized that no one had begun to evacuate the resort's guests. When she re-entered the complex to do so, she was overcome by the fire.
>
> Combustible interiors, the westerly breeze, and the lack of fire separation, compartmentation, and active suppression systems allowed the fire to spread rapidly through the lower levels of the complex. As the fire grew, the lack of pressurization in the stairwell, the lack of self-closers on many of the upper-level doors, and the lack of firestopping in the service shafts allowed smoke to penetrate the upper levels, causing the hotel to fill with smoke.
>
> According to NFPA Chief Fire Investigator Ed Comeau, the lessons learned from this disaster are those that have been repeated time and time again, both in the United States and throughout the world.
>
> "While significant progress has been made through code adoption and fire safety education, there's still much work to be done," says Comeau.

Source: Adapted from *NFPA Journal,* March/April 1998. Written by Garry J. Martin, inspector for the Fire Investigative and Analysis Department of the Metropolitan Fire and Emergency Services Board of Melbourne, Australia.

false sense of security. Smoke detectors and sprinkler heads do require maintenance; they cannot be installed and then forgotten. Moreover, various components of fire safety systems need periodic checking and, possibly, replacement.

Market factors favor operations with the proper technology and systems related to fire safety. For example, the federal government continues to follow the Hotel and Motel Fire Safety Act, which stipulates minimum fire protection standards for the lodging establishments at which federal employees stay. Federal employees will not be reimbursed for stays at properties not complying with federal fire safety requirements. Since the federal government is the largest employer in the United States, it represents a huge market for the lodging industry.[15]

A fire safety program involves fire prevention, detection, notification, control, suppression, and evacuation. No fire safety program will ever totally eliminate the possibility of a fire. However, a well-conceived and well-managed fire protection program can reduce the frequency and severity of fires.

Major hotel companies have improved their fire safety records through design of new facilities, retrofitting fire protection features into older facilities, and developing and implementing various fire safety procedures. The use of property-level checklists to identify and remedy hazardous situations is one feature of these procedures. Exhibit 5 is a checklist from the NFPA that identifies a number of key concerns in fire safety at the property level. Checklists such as these should be prepared and used to help maintain a fire-safe facility.

One key fire safety provision is that all fire protection equipment must be able to operate during a power outage. Therefore, checking the connection and operation of fire protection equipment under conditions of a simulated power outage is very important.

Exhibit 5   NFPA Hotel Fire Safety Checklist

To be completed by Chief Engineer, Director of Safety or Equivalent:

1. Is there a fire alarm system to alert the attendees of a fire? What does it sound like?

   a. Bell   b. Horn   c. Slow whoop   d. Other:

2. Are exit doors and routes to them indicated by illuminated EXIT signs?

3. Is there emergency lighting for the exit ways and exit stairs?

4. Are there any obstructions in corridors, exit doorways, exit stairs, and other routes that constitute exit ways for occupants?

5. Do exit doors from meeting, food service, or casino areas swing out?

6. Are exit doors locked or secured in any way that would prevent ready use of the door?

7. Are doors which could be mistaken for an exit marked properly? At least, DO NOT EXIT.

8. Do doors to exit stairs close and latch automatically after use and remain properly closed?

9. Are you able to access the guestroom floor from the exit stairs?

10. Are instructions prominently displayed in each attendee's room giving details of the fire alarm signal and indicating locations of the nearest exits?

11. Are attendees' room doors self-closing and free of transoms or louvers that might permit penetration of smoke into the room?

12. Is there a sign clearly visible in each elevator lobby station that states "Elevators are not to be used during a fire"?

13. Are there signs posted at the principal entrance to meeting and facility rooms, specifying maximum number of occupants?

14. Are the provided exits remote from each other so that occupants are able to use alternatives if one exit becomes unusable in an emergency?

15. Are folding partitions or air walls arranged so as not to obstruct access to required exits?

16. Are there mirrored surfaces near exits that might create confusion for evacuees?

17. Do meeting rooms have sufficient exits to allow the number of occupants to leave readily, based on the following rate?

More than 1,000	4 exits (minimum)
300–1,000	3 exits
50–300	2 exits

18. Are all corridors, stairways, and aisles free of temporary or permanent storage, including laundry, chairs, tables, room service trays, and trash?

19. Is there a designated senior staff person responsible for on-site fire-safety inspections?

   Name: _____   Title: _____

Exhibit 5   *(continued)*

20. Are you subject to a fire code? If so, which one?

21. Are any violations related to fire safety inspections outstanding or uncorrected? If so, please list.

22. Does your facility have an established operating emergency procedure in case of fire? Please include a copy with this completed checklist.

23. Is your facility fully sprinklered? If no, indicate where sprinklers are located.
    a. Meeting Rooms   b. Corridors   c. Public Lobbies   d. Guestrooms
    e. Public Washrooms   f. Other

24. Are smoke detectors located in all areas of the facility? If no, indicate smoke detector locations.
    a. Meeting Rooms   b. Corridors   c. Public Lobbies   d. Guestrooms
    e. Other

25. Are all smoke detectors hard-wired into a central signaling system or directly to the fire department? If no, which are not?

Fire Prevention

Fire prevention is *everyone's* job. It is clearly linked with the facilities department, but fire safety itself pervades all departments and tasks. An "It's not my job" attitude toward fire safety just isn't acceptable.

Many links exist between maintenance activities and fire prevention. Establishments with on-site laundry facilities need to clean dryer ductwork regularly and remove lint from filters frequently to minimize the risk of fire. If a linen chute is used, it should also be cleaned periodically as needed. In addition, all linen chutes should be kept locked and provided with automatic fire sprinklers. Regularly scheduled inspections of the building's electrical systems (and especially thermal scanning of electrical wiring) also help prevent fires. Critically important, especially in the lodging industry, is a well-informed staff. Managers should make fire prevention and response training a priority in their operation. Materials are available from a host of sources, including fire prevention agencies, local fire departments, government agencies, and trade associations.

Kitchen areas pose great risks for fire. Attention to proper housekeeping practices in the kitchen and regular cleaning of ductwork can help prevent fires and reduce their severity if they do occur. Quick attention to problems with poorly operating kitchen equipment will help to prevent the outbreak of fire.

Particularly important from both a fire safety and sanitation perspective is the kitchen ventilation or hood system.[16] This system must be properly designed and maintained. Cleaning a hood system is a major maintenance task, the extent and nature of which depends on the type of hood system and the filtering method used. Some old hood systems are difficult to clean, yet require frequent cleaning. New designs incorporate automatic wash cycles, minimize potential pockets and crevices where grease can accumulate, and incorporate grease extractors rather than mesh or baffle filters. Periodic cleaning of ductwork and fans is also required

Exterior Fires

The January 2008 fire at the Monte Carlo Resort and Casino in Las Vegas resulted in property and revenue losses of something in the range of $90 to $100 million. There were no serious guest injuries in the fire and, given the challenges of extinguishing the fire, it is surprising that no firefighters were injured. The fire was at a hotel with state-of-the-art fire protection systems. The fire was as serious as it was because it involved the exterior of the building, where no fire suppression system existed.

How did the fire start? Contractors were working on the roof of the hotel with welding equipment. Sparks from the welding are believed to have been the ignition source. For fuel, the fire used the exterior insulation system on the hotel, a plastic material. This material burned and melted from the heat of the fire, which allowed the fire to spread down the exterior of the building. Firefighters fought the fire from the interior of the building by breaking windows and directing hoses on the flaming exterior. Water damage to the hotel was extensive.

Four days after the Monte Carlo fire, an exterior fire also occurred at the Foxwoods Resort in Connecticut. This time the ignition source was a malfunctioning heating cable in the gutters of the building. While the exterior insulating material did not catch fire in this instance, it contributed to the difficulty of fighting the fire. As with the Monte Carlo fire, firefighters had trouble accessing this fire from the exterior.

In both of these fires, the installed fire suppression system in the hotel had little impact on putting out the fires because of the fires' location on the exterior of the buildings. In both instances, the fire department faced some challenges in suppressing the fire due to the design of the building itself.

One lesson from these fires (and others that could be cited) is that hotels are at risk of fire due to the action of people or things not in their direct control beyond arson—e.g., contractors or malfunctioning equipment. Another lesson is that fire risk is not confined to the interior of a building; fires may start on a building's exterior where there is little or no fire suppression equipment.

No matter where a hotel fire starts, an evacuation plan is very important. Getting guests and staff out of the building to a safe location and being sure all are accounted for is critical. Fires will happen. Preparation for coping with fires when they occur also needs to happen.

A final comment on the financial cost of fires in hotels and restaurants. While the property loss of most of these fires may be relatively small due to fire suppression equipment, large losses can and do occur. And the losses extend beyond the damaged property. A large amount of lost business can occur while a property is partially or fully closed to rebuild after the fire, which can be particularly devastating for small operations that may lack adequate insurance coverage or financial resources.

to reduce the risk of fire and avoid a "grease dump" on the roof or wall area near the fan outlet. This cleaning is often done by a contract service.[17]

Trash storage and disposal should also be viewed with the possibility of fire in mind. Storing combustible trash near the building (on the loading dock, for example) provides an arsonist with a supply of fuel for which only a match is needed. Failure to secure trash rooms and other storage areas in the building may also provide an arsonist with a relatively isolated location loaded with fuel.

Fire prevention is also a key issue during renovation. Renovation may involve nothing more than replacing interior finishes, or it may consist of substantial changes to the building. When replacing interior finishes, managers should be sure to consider the relative flammability and smoke development potential of the new materials. Local fire codes and corporate standards usually establish minimum requirements for these finishes. If such standards do not exist, managers can refer to publications of the NFPA such as *NFPA 101 — The Life Safety Code.* Also, staff should be careful about where new furniture, carpeting, and other combustible items are stored. No one wants to create an opportunity for either an arsonist or a carelessly thrown cigarette to create a fire. Some major hotel fires have started this way.

More extensive renovations sometimes create additional risks. To demolish and remove portions of the building, contractors often bring equipment on-site that may create a fire risk (cutting torches and fuel tanks, for example). Managers should stress fire safety with their contractors, specify designated smoking areas and storage locations for hazardous materials, inspect their work for unsafe practices, and be sure that both the property and the contractors have the necessary insurance coverage. It is also important for managers to know if any elements of the property's fire detection, notification, or suppression systems have been disabled during the renovation. A system for scheduling notification and a fire watch must be determined prior to any shutdown.

Fire Detection

Fires are often first detected by human observation. Nonetheless, methods of fire detection that operate independently of human presence are needed. These methods include heat detectors, smoke detectors, and sprinkler activation detectors.

Heat detectors react to the absolute temperature in a location (fixed temperature detectors), to a change in the temperature of a space (rate-of-rise detectors), or to a combination of the two (rate-compensation detectors). They are likely to be used where the use of smoke detectors would be problematic, such as in dusty locations.

Smoke detectors are of two types. Photoelectric detectors are triggered when smoke particles either scatter or obscure light. Ionization detectors contain a small amount of radioactive material that establishes a flow of ionized air between charged electrodes in the conductor. The presence of smoke changes this flow of ionized air and triggers the detector.

Dust buildup on smoke detectors can result in "nuisance alarms." Therefore, periodic cleaning of detectors is required. In addition, detector sensitivity changes over time; too large a change can either compromise system operation or result in nuisance alarms. Because of this drift in detector sensitivity, it is necessary to calibrate detectors from time to time. Some detection systems monitor detector sensitivity, adjust this sensitivity automatically, and signal operators when detectors exceed allowable changes so that maintenance can be performed. For other systems, periodic calibration is necessary. Managers should consult manufacturers' information for testing methods and frequencies.

Many lodging establishments now contain sprinkler systems. Besides their contribution to suppression, these systems also detect fires and trigger an alarm.

The alarm is triggered by flow in the sprinkler piping, which is sensed by piping flow sensors connected to the building alarm. The alarm also identifies the particular flow sensor involved, making it possible to identify the approximate location of the fire. In newer fire alarm and detection systems, each device has a unique address that indicates its exact location. These systems are referred to as "addressable" systems.

Fire Notification

Notification involves all means used to inform guests and employees not only of an existing fire, but also about the correct procedures to follow in case of a fire. Notification is accomplished in several ways, each of which requires some maintenance attention and consideration. Common elements of a fire notification system are:

- Emergency instructions and floor plans.
- Building horns and alarms.
- Voice alarms, visual alarms, and communication systems.
- Single-station smoke detectors.

Local fire codes will dictate minimum standards with regard to all aspects of building fire protection. Most fire codes will address the items listed above.

Emergency instructions are typically posted on each guestroom door. They tell guests what to do in case of a fire or other emergency. Floor plans should be part of these instructions and should show the locations of the nearest exits. If elevators are present, guests should be instructed not to use them during a fire. Typically, guests are also instructed to keep their room keys with them (to allow them to get back into their rooms either after an all-clear signal is given or if the fire has them trapped). If stairwell doors are self-locking, guests should be warned of this. Other property-specific emergency instructions should be included as well. With the growing number of international travelers, management should

---

Carbon Monoxide Detectors

Twenty-five states have mandated the installation of carbon monoxide (CO) detectors in certain residential properties, while a few states (six as of this writing) require CO detectors in some hotels as well.[18] Hotels have experienced instances of CO poisoning resulting in serious injuries and deaths due to a variety of problems, including a lack of adequate venting of combustion gases when using oil or gas space heaters in interior areas as well as maintenance issues (cracks in combustion gas venting or blocked venting on furnace equipment). Since CO is odorless and invisible, hotels operating fossil-fuel heaters must be particularly vigilant. CO poisoning has been caused by faulty operation of indoor pool heaters, space-heating equipment, and water heaters; it can also be caused by faulty installations and modifications made during building maintenance.

include graphic instructions and instructions in languages commonly spoken by the hotel's guests.

Some hotels have created videos that provide safety and security information. These are commonly shown on an information channel on the guestroom television. The guestroom television may be set to tune to this channel automatically when the television is turned on. At some lodging properties, there are several such channels, each in the language of a major guest group.

Building alarms should be checked regularly, in accordance not only with local codes but also corporate standards. Special testing and inspection is also warranted whenever work is performed on or near these circuits. Alarms must be clearly audible inside guestrooms; codes usually specify some noise level that the alarm must produce inside the guestroom. Adjustments may be necessary to meet these standards.

Some alarms have test switches or reset keys that are used during testing. Other alarms are activated only when the user breaks a glass panel. When these alarms are tested, the glass should be removed; afterward, the glass should be replaced. The maintenance staff should have the replacement links needed to restore the system following activation.

To provide better information to guests, lodging properties have been installing more voice and visual alarms and communication systems. **Emergency voice alarm communication (EVAC) systems** usually integrate a warning alarm with a pre-recorded message providing guests with information about proper procedures in case of a fire. The systems normally allow property staff or the fire department to override the recorded message so that additional instructions can be given. Keep in mind that those who speak foreign languages may not understand these spoken instructions. Just as multilingual written information about emergency procedures may be needed in the guestrooms, multilingual spoken instructions may be needed when appropriate. Voice alarms and other communication systems should be tested periodically for proper operation.

To notify hearing-impaired guests of fires and other emergencies, visual signaling devices are now required. Strobe alarms are required to be installed in hotel guestrooms, in hallways, and on the exit signs in hallways. These visual devices may go off in all rooms or only in rooms identified as having hearing-impaired guests, depending on local codes.

As already discussed, smoke detectors are a key feature of fire detection systems. Some detectors also serve as local notification devices—that is, they do not sound a general building alarm. Called **single-station smoke detectors**, these devices are similar to those used in residences in that they contain both a smoke detector and an integral alarm. They differ from most residential types in that they are powered by a dedicated electrical circuit, not by batteries. This type of detection device is found in guestrooms. There is a growing trend today to install system-connected addressable guestroom detectors that are monitored by the main fire alarm panel. System-connected addressable guestroom detectors do not sound a building alarm. When they are activated, they send a signal to the main fire alarm panel, which then alerts hotel staff to investigate the room. This allows for early detection and suppression of a fire before the occupant of the room is seriously harmed.

Fire Suppression

Despite the successful initiatives by designers and operators to reduce the number of fires, outbreaks of fires in hospitality establishments still occur. It is therefore necessary to have adequate fire suppression and control equipment, to know how to use this equipment, and to keep it in proper operating condition. Fire suppression equipment includes such items as sprinklers, standpipes and hose systems, portable extinguishers, and all related equipment (such as fire pumps, emergency generators, and hoses).

Sprinkler systems are becoming much more prevalent in hospitality applications as their effectiveness becomes better known and as fire codes are modified to require them. Wet-pipe sprinklers are commonly found in hospitality applications. These systems consist of pipes filled with water, individual temperature-activated sprinkler heads, and a water source with sufficient pressure. For low-rise buildings, the water source is generally the local water supply, which provides adequate pressure without a supplemental pump. For high-rise buildings (usually those higher than five to seven stories), a fire pump is generally installed to provide the necessary water pressure and quantity.

A 2004 survey by AH&LA and Smith Travel Research revealed that installation of sprinkler systems, while widespread, is still not universal in lodging establishments.[19] Exhibit 6 depicts the results of this survey. Many small establishments are not required by code to install sprinklers, particularly if their guestrooms open directly to the outside. While lodging establishments associated with major lodging chains are likely to have sprinklers, it is also true that many non-chain properties (and some very old chain-affiliated properties) may lack sprinklers. For example, a survey of lodging properties in the greater Birmingham, Alabama, area showed that one-third of them lacked sprinklers. The lack of sprinklers (in a franchise lodging product) was a factor contributing to the death of four college-age women in an area hotel in January 2010.[20]

Properties with sprinkler systems are required by code to stock a supply of spare sprinkler heads to replace those damaged or needing replacement after a small fire. If these are not on hand, occupants may be denied re-entry to the building after a small fire. This causes at best an inconvenience for guests and employees and at worst a significant revenue loss.

Portable fire extinguishers are useful for extinguishing fires in their early stages. To be effective, however, an extinguisher must be the correct type and must be operated properly. Exhibit 7 summarizes the types of extinguishers suitable for use on various types of fires. The extinguishers in a given area should be appropriate for the type of fire likely to be encountered in that area (that is, a water extinguisher should not be located in an electrical room, for example). Some extinguishers are labeled for multi-purpose application (the ABC extinguisher, for example), while others are labeled for a specific type of fire.

Two recent developments regarding portable fire extinguishers should be noted. First, a new type and classification of extinguisher has been added—the Class K. This new extinguisher was created to cope with fires in large fryers and other appliances using large quantities of vegetable or animal fats. The new extinguisher reduces the potential for fire flashback. Before development of the Class K,

Exhibit 6 Percentage of Hotels with Sprinklers in Room

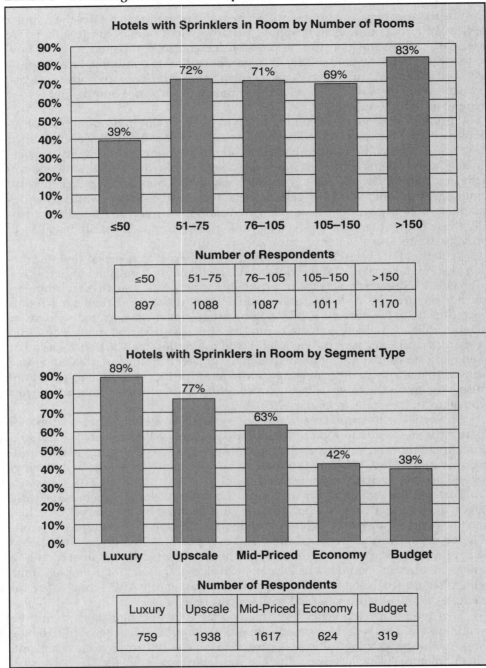

Source: AH&LA and Smith Travel Research, 2004.

Exhibit 7 Types of Portable Fire Extinguishers

There are five different types of portable fire extinguishers, each type with its own unique extinguishing agent. Most fire extinguishers display symbols to show the kind of fire on which they are to be used.

Types of Fire Extinguishers

 Class A extinguishers put out fires in ordinary combustible materials such as cloth, wood, rubber, paper, and many plastics.

 A
Ordinary Combustibles

 Class B extinguishers are used on fires involving flammable liquids, such as grease, gasoline, oil, and oil-based paints.

 B
Flammable Liquids

 Class C extinguishers are suitable for use on fires involving appliances, tools, or other equipment that is electrically energized or plugged in.

C
Electrical Equipment

 Class D extinguishers are designed for use on flammable metals and are often specific for the type of metal in question. These are typically found only in factories working with these metals.

 D
Combustible Metals

Class K fire extinguishers are intended for use on fires that involve vegetable oils, animal oils, or fats in cooking appliances. These extinguishers are generally found in commercial kitchens, such as those found in restaurants, cafeterias, and caterers. Class K extinguishers are now finding their way into the residential market for use in kitchens.

K
Combustible Cooking

There are also multi-purpose fire extinguishers—such as those labeled "B-C" or "A-B-C"—that can be used on two or more of the above types of fires.

Source: U.S. Fire Administration, http://www.usfa.dhs.gov/citizens/home_fire_prev/extinguishers.shtm.

auto-ignition was a problem because, though other extinguishers smothered the fire initially, heat retained in the fat could re-ignite the fire. Class K extinguishers are designed to effectively prevent re-ignition. (Class K extinguishers are used in addition to and following activation of the kitchen's installed fire protection system.)

The second new development is an expansion of the extinguisher ratings. A numerical value has been added to the previously used letter value. The number now appearing before the "A" letter classification denotes the amount of fire suppression material contained in the extinguisher. An extinguisher rated 2A has approximately 2.5 gallons (9.5 liters) of extinguishing agent. The number before the "B" letter classification denotes the total square feet of a Class B (flammable liquid) fire that the extinguisher is rated to cover. A unit rated 20B is suited for suppression of approximately twenty square feet (1.9 square meters) of surface of a Class B fire. No numbers are assigned to the "C" and "K" letters.

All portable extinguishers should be included in the operation's preventive maintenance program. Maintenance staff should regularly inspect hoses, fittings, gauges, pressure levels, and the weight and condition of the extinguishing media. Staff should also ensure that the correct type of extinguisher is readily available. If managers hire outside contractors to service portable extinguishers, then a manager or some other person at the property should monitor their work.

For many years, the standard fire suppression system in kitchens used dry chemicals discharged through a set of nozzles located over key equipment and sometimes in ductwork. Dry chemical hood systems are particularly sensitive to pipe runs, so any change in piping should be done only after an engineering study. Property staff should check chemical levels in the systems periodically and inspect all plumbing for propellant leaks. These systems are activated manually or by a fusible link (that melts to activate the system) in the hood or ductwork. In several restaurant fires, the fire protection equipment did not operate properly because of problems with its installation, the installation of food service equipment, or maintenance-related failings. A study by the NFPA of fires in restaurants where the suppression system failed to operate showed that, in 44 percent of the cases, the failure resulted from a lack of maintenance; in another 25 percent of the cases, the system's failure was due to manual intervention (someone shut off the system).[21]

Because of the need to suppress and control vegetable oil and animal fat fires, recent code changes require food service operations to use wet agents in their kitchen hoods. One version of the wet agent system uses a mixture of potassium salts and water spray. These extinguishing agents are used on Class K fires (those involving large quantities of cooking oils in appliances such as fryers). These wet chemical extinguishing systems create a foam layer on the surface of the hot or burning grease, thereby smothering the fire and preventing reflash. In addition, the liquid spray provides a cooling effect. The cooling effect is important to reduce the potential for re-ignition of the fire. Advantages of the wet agent system include its easy cleanup and low corrosiveness. Dry agents use sodium bicarbonate, which is not only quite messy, but also somewhat corrosive if left in contact with kitchen equipment. Wet agents result in more localized application of the agent and can be cleaned up with sponges and towels. Agents used in these systems must pass UL 300 tests.[22]

Many different types of kitchen hood systems exist, several of which are designed to reduce energy usage. Unfortunately, some of these energy-saving

Five Common Fire Code Violations

The following are five common fire code violations that lodging managers should make sure to avoid:

1. **Painted sprinkler heads.** Sprinkler heads should not be painted (they're not meant to be pretty) or covered in any way. In addition to regular yearly inspections, sprinkler systems must be inspected internally every five years to ensure that they are free of buildup that would restrict water flow.

2. **Fire extinguishers that do not meet requirements for hazard type.** Different hazards require different types of extinguishers, and using the wrong extinguisher can sometimes make the fire worse. The type and number of fire extinguishers needed change with the use and contents of a building. Lodging managers should make sure that their properties have the appropriate extinguishers available based on the hazards present at their properties.

3. **Failures in emergency lighting and exit signs.** OSHA 1910.37 and NFPA 101 require emergency lights and exit signs to be tested for thirty seconds monthly and ninety minutes annually, along with other important but easy-to-miss vitals that a trained technician will know to check.

4. **Alarm systems not tested at required intervals.** Lives are at stake when a fire occurs, and an alarm system won't do its job if it's not properly maintained. NFPA 72 outlines required testing intervals for automatic fire alarm systems. Proper maintenance of a fire alarm system will greatly improve the chances that it will detect a fire, notify the building's occupants, and alert first responders.

5. **No inspection paperwork.** If no paperwork exists, did the inspection really take place? Lodging managers should work with a fire protection provider that offers complete, easy to understand inspection reports. This will help managers keep track of all completed inspections and quickly reference them when needed.

Source: Adapted from *Lodging,* March 3, 2014; http://www.lodgingmagazine.com/five-common-fire-code-violations/.

designs fail to provide adequate kitchen ventilation. Maintenance and food service managers considering energy-saving ventilation systems should make sure that these systems provide ventilation adequate to meet all applicable code requirements.

For any kitchen hood system, maintenance staff should check that (1) the hood system is properly connected, (2) the nozzle caps are in place to protect nozzles from grease, (3) the nozzles are aimed correctly, and (4) the fusible links are not covered with grease and dirt. Fusible links may need to be replaced on a regular (usually annual) basis per manufacturer's instructions. Spare fusible links should be in continuing inventory. Cable connections for manual activation should also be inspected.

When the kitchen fire suppression system is activated, it should also shut off the supply of fuel to equipment. Care should be taken when installing new equipment or modifying equipment installations so that the shut-off valve is not affected. One operation connected a new range to two gas lines but installed a shutoff on only one, resulting in a problem when a fire occurred. This can easily happen when maintenance staff replace equipment or modify installations to reflect changing needs. Regular inspection of the fire suppression system by a qualified contractor can help to ensure its proper operation when needed.

On the other hand, not all equipment needs to be shut off automatically. Managers should not connect such equipment to automatic shutoffs, because this may interrupt some equipment unnecessarily—for example, a kitchen alarm that shuts off all gas in the building. Management should either provide a separate gas line for the kitchen or use another fuel (such as electricity) as the primary or backup energy source for the rest of the building.

Studies of restaurant fires indicate that sometimes the plumbing connecting the dry chemical tanks, piping, and spray nozzles either was never completed or was disconnected for maintenance and not reconnected. In other instances, the fusible links were replaced with wires, bolts, or other inappropriate items. The result was suppression systems that failed when needed. Management must be aware of these problems and should never compromise the operation of the fire suppression system. Work done by outside contractors on a hotel or restaurant's fire suppression system should always be inspected.

Maintenance staff members are often part of the emergency response team—particularly at small properties—and should be instructed in the proper operation of extinguishers and other fire suppression equipment. Exhibit 8 contains information concerning the discharge time and distance of several common types of portable extinguishers. Familiarity with such data is important for any operator of extinguishing systems.

Kitchen staff should also be trained to use portable fire extinguishers. Particular emphasis should be placed on instructing the staff on how to use them on grease fires. An improperly handled Class K extinguisher can spread a grease fire

Exhibit 8   Portable Fire Extinguishers: Typical Discharge Times and Distances

Type and Capacity	Discharge Time	Discharge Distance	UL Classification
Water 2.5 gal. (9.4L)	60 seconds	30–40 feet (9–12 m)	2-A
Dry Chemical, 2.75 to 5 lb (1.2 to 2.3 kg)	8–25 seconds	5–20 feet (1.5–6.1 m)	5 to 20-B:C
Wet Chemical, 2.5 gal. (9.4L)	45–85 seconds	8–12 feet (2.4–3.7 m)	1-B;C or 2-A:1-B:C
Carbon Dioxide 2.5 to 5 lb (1.1 to 2.3 kg)	8–30 seconds	3–8 feet (0.9–2.4 m)	1- to 5-B:C
Halon, 2 to 3 lb (0.9 to 1.4 kg)	8–10 seconds	6–10 feet (1.8–3 m)	5-B:C

rather than smother it. Also, employees should practice removing extinguishers from wall mountings. Managers should ensure that extinguishers are not located in places that are too high or that otherwise make access difficult. Employees should become familiar with handling extinguishers *before* there is a fire. Training in extinguisher operation can be obtained from most local fire departments, corporate training resources, or the NFPA.[23]

Fire Control

Fire and smoke control equipment includes such items as fire and smoke dampers in air handling systems, smoke sensors in HVAC ductwork, stairwell pressurization systems, automatic guestroom door closers, and alarm-initiated fire and smoke control door closers. Fire control also involves elements of building construction and operation that control the spread of fire and smoke. Understanding the role of these elements is important when conducting building maintenance and renovations.

Fire dampers are installed in ductwork where the duct penetrates walls and floors. The dampers, which limit the spread of fire, are activated by the melting of a link that holds them in their normally open position. Maintenance workers have been known to wire these dampers open when links break or are lost. This seriously compromises the fire control built into the building by the designers. Investigation of one of the major hotel fires of the 1980s showed dampers held open with wires and steel straps so they could not close. Whether done by in-house personnel or outside contractors, such changes to the building's fire control design clearly increase the risk of damage, injury, and death due to a fire. Maintenance staff members need to be attentive to the design intent of these features and not compromise this intent.

Smoke dampers are installed to inhibit the movement of smoke through ductwork. **Smoke sensors** control smoke dampers. Smoke sensors may also control smoke by shutting down the air handling system when smoke is detected. **Stairwell pressurization systems** increase the air pressure in stairwells, thereby keeping the stairwells relatively smoke-free.

The automatic door closers on guestroom doors should be inspected as part of guestroom preventive maintenance. One major deadly hotel fire would probably have been a minor incident if a self-closing door had been able to operate properly. Fire and smoke control doors should never be blocked or have their complete closure inhibited.

Some doors are connected to automatic release devices. These doors are normally held open by the release devices, but are designed to close automatically when a fire alarm is sounded. Unfortunately, they will also close if a power outage occurs. Since these doors are installed for fire and smoke control, they must meet certain minimum construction standards—for example, any glass used in these doors must be fire tested (which usually means it must be wired glass).

The walls that surround any means of egress (such as the guestroom corridor or the fire stairs) must meet a minimum fire resistance rating. Renovations must be done with this in mind. Any replacements of walls, doors, or windows that involves spaces along a means of egress will need to have the proper fire resistance rating. In addition, smoke and fire stops (means of sealing gaps that result from construction work) should be installed in plumbing chases and other penetrations of walls and floors. Maintenance clearly has a role in keeping these features operational.

The importance of replacing smoke and fire stops when performing mainte-nance and the need to close fire doors are illustrated by another hotel fire from the early 1980s. A fire on the second floor of a Toronto hotel resulted in deaths on the sixth, twelfth, and twenty-third floors of the building. Smoke and fire were able to spread throughout the building because a fire door was held open by a doorstop, and fire stops were not replaced in pipe chases when maintenance work was per-formed. These factors facilitated the vertical movement of fire and smoke in the building. Pipe chases and other vertical shafts that extend, uninterrupted, for the full height of a building act like chimneys to move smoke and heat up throughout the building.

Most hotel corporations have standards for building design that incorporate fire safety concerns. Many have developed corporate training materials to assist in keeping staff informed of fire safety issues and systems on their properties. Exhibit 9 is an excerpt from a sample maintenance schedule for fire protection systems. Such a schedule should be developed for each lodging property on the basis of the equipment installed at that property. The schedule should use information from the building designer and equipment suppliers. Another source of maintenance information is the NFPA, which includes maintenance suggestions as a compo-nent of its standards for various pieces of fire protection equipment.

Evacuation Plans

The probability of facility evacuation is real and must be planned for accordingly. The process of evacuation and re-entry should occur as easily as possible. Though a detailed discussion of all aspects of evacuation plans is not possible here, plans should include:

- Designation of staff members to supervise the movement of guests down exit stairwells, out exit stairs, and to pre-arranged locations of assembly.

- Designation of locations of assembly for hotel staff outside the building.

- Preparation of lists of registered guests and their room numbers, as well as on-duty staff in case there is a need to account for all building occupants.

- Designation of staff members to ensure that special-needs guests, such as those with physical handicaps, receive information and special care as needed.

- Designation of individuals to meet fire department personnel and provide whatever assistance and information they require.

- Instructions for the securing of cash and other valuables.

Egress

Since most hotel guests are only slightly familiar with the physical layout of the building they are staying in, the role of exit signs and lighting in a fire is very

Exhibit 9   Periodic Test Requirements: Fire Protection Systems

Device	Frequency	Comments	NFPA Code
Private Hydrants	Annually	Flow water minimum of 1 minute, until water has cleared. Close and observe for proper drainage.	25
Control Values	Annually	Physically verify open position quarterly, annually operate valve through full range—shut and re-open.	25
Main (2") Drain	Annually		25
Back Flow Prevention Devices	Annually	Per code requirements, must measure flow and calculate friction loss.	25
Dry Pipe Valves	Annually	Annual trip tests, full flooding every 3rd year. Test quick opening devices.	25
Fire Pump	Weekly	Churn (no flow) test of motor driven pump—10 minutes minimum. Engine driven—30 minutes minimum.	25
Fire Pump	Annually	Full flow test.	25
Fire Pump Alarms		Verify pump running alarm in conjunction with weekly test run. Other alarms to be verified in conjunction with annual pump test.	
Water Flow Alarm	Quarterly		25
Standpipe		Hydrostatic test and water supply test—5 years. Pressure-reducing valves (hose connection)—5 years.	25
Valve Supervisory Switch	Semi-Annually	Verify alarm signal after two turns of the valve or after it has been moved one-fifth of the distance from its normal position.	25

(continued)

Exhibit 9   *(continued)*

Device	Frequency	Comments	NFPA Code
Smoke Detectors	Annually	Distance from its normal position.	
Heat Detectors	Annually	For nonrestorable type, test electrically. For restorable type, use listed aerosol acceptable to the manufacturer.	72
Fire Alarm Pull Stations	Annually		72
Alarm Notification —Audible & Visual	Annually		72
Elevator Capture/Return		Falls under ASME/ANSI A17.1. Required monthly operation and written records on premises.	101
Electromechanical Door Releases	Annually	In conjunction with Pull Station Tests.	
Stairwell Pressurization	Semi-Annually	All operating parts must be tested semi-annually by "approved" personnel— recorded results.	101
Restaurant Hood Extinguishing System	Semi-Annually		96
Engine-Driven Generator	Weekly	Inspect/exercise weekly. Exercise monthly under load.	110

Refer to latest editions of these codes for updates:

NFPA 25   Standard for Inspection, Testing, and Maintenance of Water-Based Fire Protection Systems.

NFPA 72   National Fire Alarm and Signaling Code.

NFPA 96   Standard for Ventilation Control and Fire Protection of Commercial Cooking Operations.

NFPA 101 Life Safety Code.

NFPA 110 Standard for Emergency and Standby Power Systems.

important. In addition, exit signs are almost always included in a fire department inspection. Management has the clear responsibility to keep exit signs illuminated and clear of obstruction. Emergency lighting should be properly installed and operational at all times. Inspecting and maintaining emergency lighting often involves using emergency test switches and checking battery fluid levels (for battery lighting systems). Systems powered by emergency generators should always be checked with the generator under load. Doors and hallways that are dead ends should be clearly marked "NOT AN EXIT." Changes in exit patterns as a result of ongoing renovations must also be noted.

Managers should be sure to never override the protection devices of fire doors or allow exit passages to be blocked. Far too often when a new hotel is opened, wooden wedges are placed to hold open every fire door in the hotel. This compromises the fire protection designed into the building. Fire and smoke control doors should *not* be held open by anything other than an approved device that will release the door in the case of a fire. Similarly, exit passages should *not* be used to store equipment and furnishings (or anything else, for that matter). Doing so not only reduces their ability to serve as exit passages, but also may provide a fuel source for a fire.

Security

As mentioned previously, market issues stand as one of the motivating factors of managerial concern for safety and security. Guests care about security!

A hotel that maintains a high level of security does so through a mix of facility design and managerial practices. Physical facilities designed with security in mind help restrict hotel access to guests only. They are designed to inhibit forced entry, allow supervision of entrances and exits, and provide adequate lighting. Managerial practices that increase security range from instituting procedures to ensure guest privacy, to keeping adequate records to support security-related decisions, to training employees to recognize and deal effectively with security-related issues, and to adhering to procedures that enhance the security of the property.

To reduce the potential for security problems at hotels, several design and operational features should be considered. These include:

- Installing electronic locks.
- Providing guests with information about property security and safe behaviors for guests. Using AH&LA's "Guest Safety Tips" or equivalent material is one way to do this (see Exhibit 10).
- Equipping guestrooms with phones to enable guests to make emergency calls.
- Installing guestroom doors that self-close and lock automatically. They should also be provided with deadbolt locks, view ports or the equivalent, and security chains or bars that allow the door to be partially opened and yet secure.
- Installing deadbolt locks on both sides of connecting doors between guestrooms.
- Ensuring that operable guestroom windows and sliding glass doors have a means of being locked. Windows should not open wide enough to allow a

Exhibit 10   AH&LA's Guest Safety Tips Card

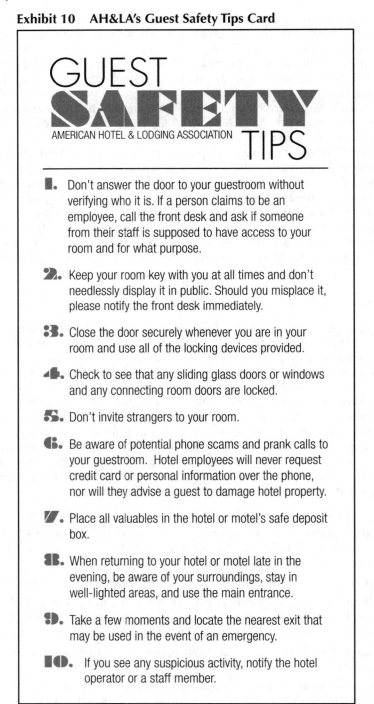

GUEST
SAFETY
AMERICAN HOTEL & LODGING ASSOCIATION   TIPS

1. Don't answer the door to your guestroom without verifying who it is. If a person claims to be an employee, call the front desk and ask if someone from their staff is supposed to have access to your room and for what purpose.

2. Keep your room key with you at all times and don't needlessly display it in public. Should you misplace it, please notify the front desk immediately.

3. Close the door securely whenever you are in your room and use all of the locking devices provided.

4. Check to see that any sliding glass doors or windows and any connecting room doors are locked.

5. Don't invite strangers to your room.

6. Be aware of potential phone scams and prank calls to your guestroom. Hotel employees will never request credit card or personal information over the phone, nor will they advise a guest to damage hotel property.

7. Place all valuables in the hotel or motel's safe deposit box.

8. When returning to your hotel or motel late in the evening, be aware of your surroundings, stay in well-lighted areas, and use the main entrance.

9. Take a few moments and locate the nearest exit that may be used in the event of an emergency.

10. If you see any suspicious activity, notify the hotel operator or a staff member.

person or object to pass through. For sliding glass doors at ground level (and others where access may be possible via the balcony) consideration should be given to the installation of secondary access-restricting devices as well (hinged bars, metal or wood placed in the door channel, or additional locks).

Operations such as casinos have used security cameras for many years. The use of security cameras in hotels has grown during the past few decades and they are now quite common (see Exhibit 11). It is important for staff to monitor what the security cameras are observing if safety or security breaches are to be dealt with as they occur. A record must be created if what the cameras observe is to be used for apprehension and prosecution. Maintenance of security camera systems is relatively easy for digital recording systems.

Hotel guests may have valuables that they wish to secure during their visit. Historically, this was done via a safe-deposit box near the front desk. A variety of procedures and regulations cover the use of safe-deposit boxes; the safe-deposit box responsibilities of the facilities department are often limited to drilling out box locks when guests lose their keys.[24] Today, a growing number of properties are installing in-room safes for guests to use to secure their property. Several factors are involved in this trend. First, guests are often interested in a secure place to store personal computers, and many existing safe-deposit box systems do not have the space to store these computers. Second, many guests prefer the convenience of an in-room storage location for computers (and other items) to a front desk location. Finally, hotels have been able to realize some revenue from the in-room safes. It is likely that the in-room safe will become a more common amenity in the future. Exhibit 12 shows in-room safe availability by hotel size and segment type.

All employees should keep security in mind with each decision they make. Training employees to recognize and report suspicious individuals and unsafe conditions is also strongly recommended. AH&LA's Educational Institute has addressed these issues in a video titled *Eye on Awareness—Hotel Security Training* as well as in other video resources.

A 2004 *Dateline NBC* hidden-camera investigation into hotel security highlighted the importance of staff training and vigilance in security. The investigation documented instances of theft from a conference room, a guest raped in her room after her cries for help were ignored by the hotel operator and security guard, and a hotel employee who helped the unauthorized reporter and camera crew use the freight elevator to get access to an exclusive guest tower, among other security breeches. All of these instances occurred in high-end hotels. "In the end, it seemed, it wasn't whether hi-tech security equipment worked. It was whether hotel employees were watching—whether they were doing their jobs. It all came down to the human factor."[25]

Key Control

Central to security for hotels is **key control**. Key control for locking systems is critical to establishing and maintaining security at any lodging facility. Whether mechanical or electronic locks are used, the need for key control is essentially the same. Mechanical systems rely more on continuous management involvement,

Exhibit 11   Percentage of Hotels with Security Cameras in Lobby

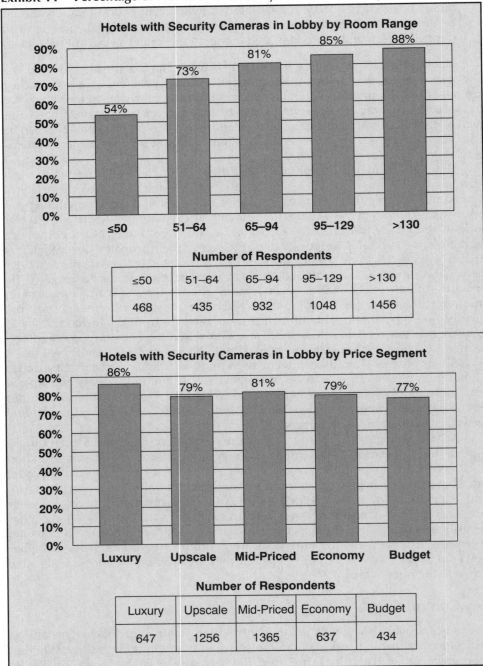

Hotels with Security Cameras in Lobby by Room Range

≤50	51–64	65–94	95–129	>130
54%	73%	81%	85%	88%

Number of Respondents

≤50	51–64	65–94	95–129	>130
468	435	932	1048	1456

Hotels with Security Cameras in Lobby by Price Segment

Luxury	Upscale	Mid-Priced	Economy	Budget
86%	79%	81%	79%	77%

Number of Respondents

Luxury	Upscale	Mid-Priced	Economy	Budget
647	1256	1365	637	434

Source: AH&LA and Smith Travel Research, 2012.

Exhibit 12   Percentage of Hotels with In-Room Safes

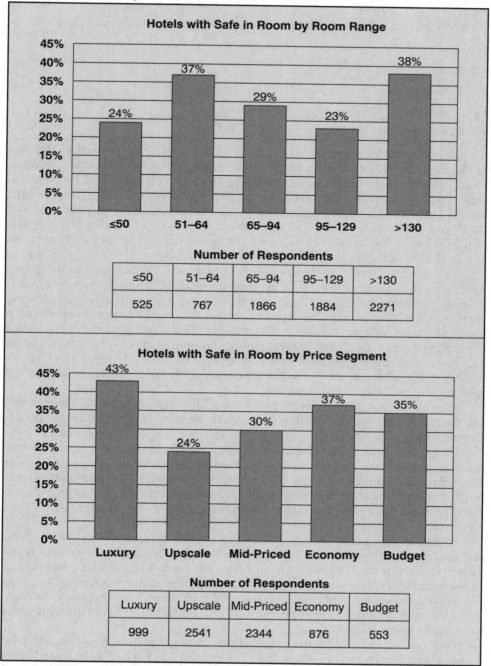

Hotels with Safe in Room by Room Range

≤50	51–64	65–94	95–129	>130
24%	37%	29%	23%	38%

Number of Respondents

≤50	51–64	65–94	95–129	>130
525	767	1866	1884	2271

Hotels with Safe in Room by Price Segment

Luxury	Upscale	Mid-Priced	Economy	Budget
43%	24%	30%	37%	35%

Number of Respondents

Luxury	Upscale	Mid-Priced	Economy	Budget
999	2541	2344	876	553

Source: AH&LA and Smith Travel Research, 2012.

while electronic systems embody a large amount of key control within the system itself.

One approach to this topic is to remember "the five R's of key control":

- Rationale
- Records
- Retrieval
- Rotation
- Replacement

The *rationale* of a key control system includes the criteria used to develop the keying schedule and to identify who will have what level of access. In other words, the rationale determines how many keying levels there will be and who gets what keys. Considerations include the physical layout of the building, departmental needs for access, the interaction of these needs with the productivity and staffing of these departments, the needs of guests, and the overall security needs of the facility. A rationale lets you develop a coherent hotel keying schedule such as that shown in Exhibit 13.

Key control *records* involve a number of elements. With regard to the guestroom, effective key control calls for keeping information about the status of guestroom keys, the names of room occupants, and the names of any others having access to the room. Guestroom keys should be given out only to guestroom occupants, and then only after their identities are verified. With regard to keys issued to employees, records should indicate which employees have which keys. Hotels also need to maintain records of problems with guestroom and other locks (maintenance and incidents) and of actions taken to enhance security, including the rotation and replacement of locks.

Mechanical key blanks need to be kept under control. Information concerning the number of blanks and their disposition should be recorded and checked. Records of the lock cores installed in each guestroom should also be made.

One practice of recordkeeping that some hotels do but that is not recommended is recording the guestroom number on the key itself. This practice—or a similar one of attaching a tag with the room number to the key—has far too much potential for compromising guest security. It is much better to provide the guest with the room number separate from the key itself—on a key envelope, note paper, etc.

Retrieval involves all actions to retrieve keys from guests who are checking out and from employees when they leave the building. Asking for room keys when guests check out and providing drop boxes for room keys at exit points assist in this process. (This is more important for properties using mechanical locks, as electronic systems can render plastic key card guestroom keys inoperative once a guest has checked out.) Housekeeping staff should be told what to do with guest keys found in the room.

It is also important to retrieve keys from employees. Employees should take no keys off the premises, mechanical or electronic. Keys needed for the work shift should be signed out at the start of the shift and returned at the end. They should

Exhibit 13   Sample Hotel Keying Schedule

Master Key	Submaster Key	Privacy Key
Administration	Executive offices Sales and catering offices Accounting offices Personnel	Cashier's office (safe) Accounting files Safe-deposit area
Rooms division	Front office Entrances Guestrooms (by floor)	Retail shops

Food and beverage	Kitchens
	Food outlets
	Beverage outlets
	Food and beverage
	  storage
	Food and beverage
	  offices, purchasing
	Receiving area
		Wine and liquor storage
		Refrigerators and freezers
		China and silver storage
		Entertainers' dressing rooms

Function areas	Function rooms Function storage	Audiovisual equipment storage

Housekeeping	Guestrooms (by floor or
	  other maid unit)
	Linen/housekeeping
	Lockers and employee
	  dining
		Lost and found

Laundry	Laundry Linen storage	
Engineering	Engineering offices Engineering shops Mechanical areas Electrical areas	Electric transformer room
Recreation	Health club and pool Remote facilities (tennis club, golf club, pool)	

Source: Walter A. Rutes and Richard H. Penner, *Hotel Planning and Design* (New York: Whitney School of Design, 1985), p. 220.

be placed in a secure location, whether in use or not. Housekeepers should keep keys on their person, not on their carts. Keys are all too often not retrieved from employees who have been terminated, as they should be. Annual surveys of hospitality students continue to find that they still possess keys to hotels or restaurants at which they previously worked.

Pay particular attention to keys given to outside contractors for access to a portion of the building. Avoid this practice if at all possible.

Rotation involves moving locks from room to room to maintain security—a sort of preventive security action. Some properties still using mechanical locks for their guestrooms rotate these locks on a regular basis (every six months or every year), while others rotate when a given number of guestroom keys have been lost. Rotation is also a good practice when it appears guestroom security has been compromised. A system should be implemented to avoid creating guest dissatisfaction due to rotation. For example, when locks are rotated for occupied rooms, use a "lock change" notice card on the guestroom door. Even properties with electronic lock systems may find it necessary to rotate mechanical locks used in back-of-the-house areas.

Despite efforts to deal with proper key control, the *replacement* of part or all of the locking system will eventually be necessary. Locks for food and beverage storage areas and other back-of-the-house locations should be replaced if it is believed that security has been compromised to the point where rotating the locks will not solve the problem. The loss of master keys may trigger the replacement of all locks at a hotel still using mechanical locks. Replacement of mechanical locks also should be considered when the property is sold, especially when there is a major change in staff.

The replacement process for those operations currently using mechanical locks will likely involve the installation of electronic locks. Operations currently using electronic locks will also find that changing technology will probably cause them periodically to consider updating or replacing these systems as well.

Electronic Locks

Electronic locks inherently perform many of the elements of key control described already. The process of purchasing and installing an electronic lock system includes developing a rationale for key issue and the master/submaster hierarchy. The central computer for the locking system maintains records of keys issued. The need to retrieve guestroom keys from guests is greatly reduced, since the combination for opening a guestroom's door is changed for each new guest. In essence, guestroom locks are "rotated" automatically for each new room occupant. If a master key is lost, the costly replacement of all locks is not necessary, since the central computer and individual units can be reprogrammed. In addition, the cost of most keys used in electronic lock systems is much less than that of mechanical locks.

Some individual locks maintain records of the keys used to gain entry to the room. The ability to "interrogate" these locks when security problems are encountered is a clear benefit. It has not only assisted in the investigation of thefts, but also has served a significant preventive role. Employee theft from guestrooms has been greatly reduced at properties installing these systems. Since every entry is recorded and every key used for entry is identified, employees know that they can neither enter a room without leaving recorded evidence nor blame some nonexistent unseen intruder.

Electronic locks have greatly improved guestroom security. Although these systems add some unique maintenance responsibilities (for example, battery changes), these added duties are more than offset by the systems' overall savings and convenience.

Electronic lock technology continues to change. Some locking systems now automatically engage the dead bolt when the door is closed, reducing the potential for forced-entry room thefts. Some electronic locks now incorporate "smart card" technology that allows guestroom key cards to be used throughout a hotel to charge to the room account. Moreover, there are locking systems that integrate with other systems in the hotel to provide information on the status of room occupancy. These systems may interact with the guestroom HVAC control system, notify housekeepers of room occupancy, and communicate with the front desk.

While electronic lock systems for lodging properties are a big improvement over mechanical locks, they are not perfect. For example, in 2012, after a series of hotel burglaries, it was found that Onity electronic locks could be opened by computer hackers using a $50 homemade electronic device. Onity, a major supplier of electronic locks to several big hotel chains, had to replace or retrofit more than four million locks in order to rectify this serious security breakdown.[26]

Hotel Safety and Security Lapses

During recent visits to the Caribbean, one hospitality industry consultant encountered newly constructed high-rise hotels that had a single exit stairwell centrally located within the hotel with no fire doors or any other means of separation from the guestroom floors. This meant that fire and smoke could readily enter the stairwell and render it essentially useless as a means of escape should a large-scale fire occur. At another property, there were no view ports or safety chains on guestroom doors, making it impossible for guests within their guestrooms to see the person at the door without opening it. Finally, at a property at which a major regional tourism meeting was being held, the hotel doors were of highly combustible wooden construction and were not self-closing; guestroom keys had the room number on the key tag; and there was no dead bolt on the guestroom doors. In addition, the door providing outside egress from one fire exit was locked during the night, the exit stairwell doors were propped open, one exit stairwell was used to store furniture and debris, and the unused upper level of the property (used for additional storage) was open to the exit stairwell.

Of course, safety and security problems are not limited to locations outside the United States. For example, an investigative news team visited a motel in the southeast United States where attacks and guestroom robberies had occurred. Despite these incidents, the motel did not rotate or replace door locks even when it was obvious that the assailants had keys to gain access. At another motel, the same news team videotaped motel security guards sleeping in their vehicles in the motel's parking lot—and this motel had a history of security problems! Another security shortfall uncovered by this investigative effort was that, in spite of having electronic locks and locked exterior doors, some area motels were failing to code expiration dates on guestroom key cards, leaving cards valid long after guests had checked out.

Terrorism and Other Extraordinary Events ────────────

Over the past dozen years, terrorists have conducted several mass-casualty attacks on so-called "soft targets," including hotels. Their methods have employed vehicle bombs, suicide bombs, and explosives in briefcases. These attacks suggest that facilities with minimal physical security measures have become more attractive targets as military and government buildings have become better secured. Some factors that put hotels at more risk of terrorist attacks are location, clientele, and the iconic status of the building itself. Hotels meeting any of these criteria should conduct risk assessments to evaluate vulnerabilities and ways to reduce risk.

The following are some protective measures that hotels can take to mitigate the risk of terrorist attacks:

- Encourage personnel to be alert to suspicious behavior or unusual activity and to report any actions that appear to constitute a threat.

- Use vehicle barriers or bollards, or rearrange traffic patterns to move vehicle traffic farther from the building.

- Control access to the building. Restrict access to registered guests and patrons, if possible.

- Deploy visible security cameras and security personnel. Review surveillance tapes regularly.

- Be aware of persons who are wearing clothing that is wrong for the weather or visibly loose.

- Regularly train personnel on terrorism prevention.

Terrorism is just one item in the category referred to by some as *extraordinary events*. Extraordinary events include accidental events (e.g., toxic chemical leaks), intentional events (e.g., war and terrorism), and natural disasters (e.g., hurricanes and floods). When events such as these occur, facilities staff and others face extraordinary challenges. The American Society of Heating, Refrigerating and Air-Conditioning Engineers (ASHRAE) has a publication that provides some guidance for facilities professionals in dealing with threats affecting air, water, and food systems under circumstances of extraordinary events.[27] One natural disaster that hotels in some regions of the world are very familiar with is the hurricane (or typhoon in the Pacific). The Caribbean Hotel Association and the Caribbean Tourism Organization have prepared a Hurricane Procedures Manual to assist hotel operators in dealing with these natural disasters.[28] In December of 2004, numerous seaside locations in the Pacific experienced a massive tsunami that killed hundreds of thousands of people and destroyed billions of dollars of property. Given the current political and environmental challenges, coping with extraordinary events may, unfortunately, become more ordinary in the years ahead.[29]

Endnotes ────────────────────────────────

1. "Top to Bottom Hotel Fire Safety," *NFPA Journal*, March/April 2001, pp. 72–76.

2. The American Hotel & Lodging Educational Institute offers several safety and security resources on its website, including the videos *Guest Safety Tips, Hospitality: Fire Prevention,* and other resources. For more information, contact AHLEI at 1-800-349-0299 or www.ahlei.org.

3. In the United States, hotel operators are generally responsible for providing "reasonable care"—a legal concept—for guests at their establishments. However, the legal dimensions, implications, and limitations of this responsibility are not the subject of this chapter. For more information on this aspect of hospitality safety and security, see David M. Stipanuk and Raymond C. Ellis, Jr., *Security and Loss Prevention Management,* Third Edition (Lansing, Mich.: American Hotel & Lodging Educational Institute, 2013); and Jack P. Jefferies and Banks Brown, *Understanding Hospitality Law,* Fifth Edition (Lansing, Mich.: American Hotel & Lodging Educational Institute, 2010), Chapter 10.

4. See *Security and Loss Prevention Management,* Third Edition, published by the American Hotel & Lodging Educational Institute; information about this book and other safety and security resources can be found at www.ahlei.org or by calling 1-800-349-0299.

5. Of particular interest is the National Safety Council publication *Accident Prevention Manual for Business,* a three-volume set dealing with several aspects of workplace environmental health and safety.

6. Jamelia Saied, "Approaches to Risk Management," *Cornell Hotel and Restaurant Administration Quarterly,* August 1990, pp. 45–55.

7. Saied, pp. 54–55.

8. Saied, pp. 45–55.

9. While recently visiting Poland, the author stayed in a relatively new hotel with an interesting design feature from a safety standpoint. The windows in the guestroom functioned both as windows (they could be opened inward to the room from the top) and as sliding doors creating large openings to the outside. A small ledge was outside the guestroom with a railing up to about one meter (a bit more than three feet). It was a little disorienting to peer out the window/door onto the street below. More than disorienting was the fact that a small child could pass under the lowest level of the railing. If it *can* happen, it *might* happen. From a safety standpoint, the railing design was flawed and posed a potential danger.

10. Regular updates on product recalls can be found at www.cpsc.gov/en/recalls for English and at http://www.cpsc.gov/es/Noticias-y-retiros-del-mercado/ in Spanish.

11. Marty Ahrens, *U.S. Fires in Selected Occupancies—Hotels and Motels* (Quincy, Mass.: National Fire Protection Association, 2006).

12. An excellent source of information about hotel fires can be found at http://www.iklim-net.com/hotelfires/mgmhotel2008fire.html.

13. http://www.usfa.fema.gov/downloads/pdf/statistics/v10i4.pdf.

14. Nichole Bernier, "Hotel Cited in Blaze," *Meeting News,* July 1990, pp. 21–23.

15. For further information on the Federal Hotel and Motel Fire Safety Act and how to get on the Master List, refer to http://apps.usfa.fema.gov/hotel/.

16. Safety aspects of kitchen ventilation equipment are addressed in *NFPA 96— Standard for Ventilation Control and Fire Protection of Commercial Cooking Operations.* Contact the National Fire Protection Association, 1 Batterymarch Park, Quincy, Massachusetts; or go online at www.nfpa.org.

17. Further information on kitchen ventilation system cleaning and maintenance is available from the International Kitchen Exhaust Cleaning Association (IKECA), www.ikeca.org.

18. "Carbon Monoxide Detectors State Statutes," National Conference on State Legislatures, updated December 2012; www.ncsl.org/issues-research/env-res/carbon-monoxide-detectors-state-statutes.aspx.

19. This is the latest survey information available; AH&LA and Smith Travel Research no longer include questions about sprinklers in their surveys.

20. http://blog.al.com/spotnews/2010/02/one-third_of_hotels_in_area_la.html.

21. https://www.nfpa.org/Assets/files/AboutTheCodes/17A/DRY-AAA_ROPagenda_07-11%20Report.pdf.

22. See National Fire Protection Association 17A, "Standard for Wet Chemical Extinguishing Systems."

23. The National Fire Protection Association has a number of videos that may prove useful for training purposes; for a listing, see http://www.nfpa.org/training/training-videos/fire-and-life-safety-videos.

24. Stipanuk and Ellis, Chapter 3.

25. Lea Thompson, "How Safe Is Your Hotel?" *Dateline NBC*, www.msnbc.msn.com/id/5114121, 4 June 2004.

26. http://www.forbes.com/sites/andygreenberg/2012/12/06/lock-firm-onity-starts-to-shell-out-for-security-fixes-to-hotels-hackable-locks/.

27. *Risk Management Guidance for Health, Safety and Environmental Security Under Extraordinary Incidents* (Atlanta: ASHRAE, 2003).

28. *Hurricane Procedures Manual* (Washington, D.C.: Organization of American States, 1998), available online at www.oas.org/cdmp/document/chaman/chaman.html.

29. The U.S. Federal Emergency Management Agency has published a Risk Management Series that addresses a number of areas of potential concern to hotels and hotel facilities professionals facing extraordinary events. Within this series are the following titles: *Communicating with Owners and Managers of New Buildings on Earthquake Risk; Incremental Seismic Rehabilitation of Hotel and Motel Buildings;* FEMA 426, *Reference Manual to Mitigate Potential Terrorist Attacks Against Buildings* (2003); FEMA 427, *Primer for Design of Commercial Buildings to Mitigate Terrorist Attacks* (2002); FEMA 452, *A How-To Guide to Mitigate Potential Terrorist Attacks Against Buildings* (2005); and FEMA 543, *Design Guide for Improving Critical Facility Safety from Flooding and High Winds: Providing Protection to People and Buildings.* For access to these and other resources, see http://www.fema.gov/media-library/resources-documents/collections/3?page=1.

Key Terms

emergency voice alarm communication (EVAC) system—A system integrating some sort of warning alarm with a pre-recorded or live message providing guests with information about proper procedures in case of a fire.

fire damper—A device installed in ductwork that limits the spread of fire, usually activated by the melting of a link that holds it in its normally open position.

heat detector—A device that reacts to the absolute temperature in a location (fixed temperature detectors), to a change in the temperature of a space (rate-of-rise detectors), or to a combination of the two (rate-compensation detectors). Likely to be used where smoke detectors function poorly, such as in dusty locations.

key control—The coordinated effort to establish and maintain the security of a property's locking systems.

risk management—An integrated effort to reduce the causes and effects of safety- and security-related incidents of all types.

single-station smoke detector—A smoke detector containing an integral alarm powered by a dedicated electrical circuit.

smoke damper—A device installed in ductwork that inhibits the movement of smoke.

smoke detector—A photoelectric or ionization device that reacts to the presence of smoke.

smoke sensor—A device that controls smoke by operating smoke dampers and by shutting down the air handling system when smoke is detected.

stairwell pressurization system—A system that increases the air pressure in stair-wells, thereby keeping the stairwells relatively smoke-free during a fire.

 # Review Questions

1. What actions might help reduce employee injuries?

2. What steps can be taken to reduce the chance that guests and employees will injure themselves in the guest bathroom?

3. What are some of the challenges facing lodging and food service operators with regard to fire safety? How can an operator deal with these challenges?

4. What are the five basic elements of a fire safety program? How do these elements fit together into a coherent whole?

5. What are the purposes of a fire notification system? How might this system differ from property to property? What elements of the system will depend on the types of guests that typically visit the operation?

6. Why is it critical that in-house and contract maintenance personnel understand the design intent of the fire control system? What sorts of maintenance actions all too often compromise this design intent?

7. How do physical facilities and managerial practices combine to create a high level of security? How can facility design help to prevent crime?

8. What are the "five R's of key control"? What role does key control play in a hotel's security efforts? What problems can arise when key control is lax?

9. What are the advantages of using electronic locks? Are there any disadvantages?

Internet Sites

For more information, visit the following Internet sites. Remember that Internet addresses can change without notice. If the site is no longer there, you can use a search engine to look for additional sites.

Federal Emergency Management
  Administration
www.fema.gov

Loss Prevention Management Bulletin
  Database
http://losspreventionbulletin.com

National Fire Protection Association
www.nfpa.org

U.S. Department of Labor—Bureau of
  Labor Statistics
www.bls.gov

U.S. Department of Labor—Occupational Safety & Health Administration
www.osha.gov

Case Study

We're in Hot Water Now

Andre whistled cheerfully as he slipped his screwdriver back into his tool belt. The shower valves were now fixed and the water running fine. He picked up the phone and put Room 933 back into service. It had been a busy day, with extra pressure to get all open guestroom orders completed.

The 400-room hotel was gearing up for the start of a convention being held at the property for the first time ever. The thirty-year-old hotel was at 100 percent occupancy and the maintenance staff had been working hard all day to make sure all guestrooms were in service so no one would have to be turned away.

Andre's whistling stopped abruptly as he entered the unusually chaotic maintenance plant where Joshua, the engineer on duty, was in a panic. When Andre had last been down, Joshua had been reviewing bids for a long-overdue tub resurfacing project. Now he'd pushed the papers aside and was banging on the side of a water tank.

"What's up?" Andre asked.

"One of our guestroom water heaters is down," Joshua said. "This entire tank is cold and our demand is going to be incredible tonight. I just called our contractor and they can't get anyone out here until tomorrow morning."

"Don't we have a backup?" asked Andre.

"We do," Joshua answered, "but it'll never provide enough hot water for this evening, much less tomorrow morning—the demand will be way too high."

"This could be bad," Mora, the department's administrative assistant, said. "You already had to turn the thermostat on the tank up this morning from 120 degrees to 130 because of all the complaints we were getting about cold water."

"Have you called Marty yet?" one of the other engineers asked, referring to the director of engineering who had left the day before to go on a two-week honeymoon.

"I can't call him on his honeymoon," Joshua said. "He left me in charge; I've got to figure out a way to solve this. Man, I told him we needed to fix it."

"If they hadn't deleted it from the capital plan in favor of new art for the hotel lobby, we wouldn't be in this fix," said Mora.

Andre scratched the back of his head and looked over at the heater. "Say, I bet we could do a temporary fix. It's only a couple feet away from the water heater for the laundry. With a little bit of piping, we could connect the two, open up a valve and start moving the water over. The laundry will be closed tonight and they won't need any of the water."

"Now that's some creative thinking!" Joshua said. "And the laundry tank is set at 160 degrees. That should be hot enough to cover any extra demand we get tonight."

"I'll go get the piping and start working on it," Andre said. "I should be able to get that fixed up in less than a half hour."

Joshua smiled and slapped Andre on the back. "You're a lifesaver. It's easy to see why you were named our department's employee of the month three times running."

"By the way," Mora said, "housekeeping just turned in a work order on the room you just left. Apparently the room attendant noticed that the grab bar was loose."

"Really?" said Andre as he left the room, "I didn't notice. It probably wasn't too bad—I'll get on it tomorrow."

Elsewhere in the hotel, Solomon Alvi signed his credit card slip at the front desk, raising his eyebrows slightly as he listened to the two front desk representatives discussing all the complaints they'd been receiving about cold water in the guestrooms. He made a mental note to be sure to use more hot than cold water in his shower.

The bell attendant appeared promptly at his side and accompanied him to room 933, an executive suite where a gift basket sat on the desk thanking Solomon for bringing the convention's business to the hotel. Solomon plugged in his laptop and spent a few hours making final preparations for his opening speech the next morning. Finally, in need of a break, he decided to take a relaxing, hot shower before calling room service for his dinner.

Solomon began running the water, letting it heat up while he prepared for his shower. He was pleasantly surprised that the water felt immediately warm, despite the grumblings he'd heard at the front desk. "This will be good," he thought to himself.

Murmuring lines to his speech, he stepped into the tub and began soaping up.

Back in the maintenance shop, Andre had finished the connections between the hot water heaters and Joshua threw the switch to start pushing the laundry's hot water into the system. "There's one crisis averted," Joshua said. "Let's finish up our paperwork and call it a day, shall we? I'll take you out for a drink."

In room 933, Solomon was halfway through his speech when he was shocked out of his reverie by a burst of scalding hot water. He yelped, took a quick step backward, and slipped on the tub floor. He reached for the grab bar as he began to fall, but it ripped out of the wall, smacking him in the eye and spraying him with chunks of tile and drywall as he fell and hit his head on the tub's side. The scalding water continued to rain down on him.

Solomon managed to roll out of the tub and pour the half-melted ice from the ice bucket over his now-red body. He caught his breath and wrapped some ice in a washcloth and applied it to his eye, "Great, I'll be sporting a shiner when I address our members tomorrow," he thought as he put on his robe and left the bathroom.

He picked up the phone and called the operator, requesting emergency medical care. After tossing the receiver down, Solomon Alvi, the president of the National Association of Safety Regulators, grimly began looking for his lawyer's phone number.

Elsewhere in the hotel, Andre was putting on his coat to head out with Joshua for that drink. He turned to see the color drain from Joshua's face as he listened silently to a voice on the phone. Joshua hung up and swallowed hard.

"I think I'd better call Marty and tell him his honeymoon is over."

Discussion Question

1. What factors contributed to Solomon Alvi's injuries?

Case Number: 2814CA

The following industry experts helped generate and develop this case: Richard Manzolina, Director of Property Operations, Capital Hilton, Washington, D.C.; Ed Pietzak, RPA, FMA, CEOE, Director of Engineering, New York Marriott Marquis, New York, New York; and David M. Stipanuk, Associate Professor, School of Hotel Administration, Cornell University, Ithaca, New York.

Chapter 5 Outline

Water Usage in the Lodging Industry
Water Systems
Water Quality
    Discharge/Sewage Water
    Legionnaires' Disease
Water Heating
    Water Heating Options
Water System Maintenance Concerns
Water for Entertainment and Recreation
    Swimming Pool Water Systems
Water Conservation
    Helpful Resources

Competencies

1. Outline water usage levels and patterns in the lodging industry, and describe the basic structure of water and wastewater systems. (pp. 173–181)

2. Identify various potential water quality problems, outline major water heating concerns and options, and identify various water system maintenance concerns. (pp. 181–188)

3. Explain how lodging properties can use water for entertainment and recreational purposes, describe issues associated with swimming pool water systems, and summarize water conservation issues pertinent to the lodging industry. (pp. 188–195)

Water and Wastewater Systems

Outside of a few private homes, hotels were the bastions of luxury and comfort—and indoor plumbing. In 1829, the brilliant young architect, 26-year-old Isaiah Rogers, sent ripples of awe throughout the country with his innovative Tremont Hotel in Boston. It was the first hotel to have indoor plumbing and became the prototype of a modern, first-class American hotel.

The four-story structure boasted eight water closets on the ground floor, located at the rear of the central court. The court was connected by glazed corridors to the bedroom wings, dining room, and rotunda.

The bathrooms in the basement were fitted with cold running water which also went to the kitchen and laundry. The bathtubs were copper or tin and probably had a little side-arm, gas furnace attached at one end. Perhaps shaped like a shoe as the French and English models, the water in the tub would flow and circulate backwards until the entire bath was heated to satisfaction.

In the Tremont, water was drawn from a metal storage tank set on top of the roof, the recently invented steam pump raising the water on high. A simple water carriage system removed the excretal water to the sewerage system. As with other individual buildings of the time, each had its own source of water and removal.

Five years later in New York City, Rogers surpassed his achievements of the Tremont Hotel. He built the Astor House with six stories, featuring 17 rooms on the upper floors with water closets and bathrooms to serve 300 guest rooms. The Astor and the Tremont were the first modern buildings built with extensive plumbing. (In contrast, the Statler Hotel in Buffalo caused a sensation in 1908 by offering "A room with a bath for a dollar and a half.")

—The History of Plumbing[1]

WATER IS USED at lodging establishments for bathing and sanitary purposes in guestrooms, for drinking, and for cleaning activities in and about the facility. In addition, water is used for sanitizing purposes and cooking in restaurants, for cleaning in laundry operations, for recreational or landscaping purposes (such as in swimming pools or decorative ponds), for fire safety systems, and as a cooling medium for various pieces of equipment. Most of the water "used" at a property is disposed of through the property's sewer system. Exceptions to this are the makeup water used in cooling towers and swimming pools, and the water used on lawns and shrubs.

An important subcategory of water usage is hot water usage, which costs the property not only for the water but also for the energy used to heat the water. Depending on the fuel sources used for water heating, the cost of the heat can range from four to twenty times the cost of the water.

The hospitality industry is clearly concerned about water and wastewater issues. Many resort operations rely on access to pristine bodies of water as major guest attractions. The expansion of hospitality facilities is limited in some areas by the availability of adequate water supplies or the capacity of wastewater treatment systems. In other locations, water shortages have led to water rationing. Even where water sources are adequate, water treatment costs sometimes skyrocket or water quality deteriorates significantly as more marginal supplies must be used. For resorts and other facilities that rely on wells or non-municipal water supplies, the quality of these sources is a major concern.

Water Usage in the Lodging Industry

Annual water usage by the lodging industry in the United States is in the hundreds of billions of gallons and the total annual water and sewer bill for the U.S. lodging industry is probably in excess of $1 billion. Water usage is dependent on a number of factors, including type of hotel, location, facilities, and managerial attention to water usage. Exhibit 1 shows the median water consumption data for different types of lodging properties. These data show that:

- As service levels increase, hotels use more water per room.

- Hotels in the same market segment exhibit a rather wide variation in water usage per room (as evidenced by the large standard deviation values).

- Resorts represent the largest users of water per room, while extended-stay properties represent the smallest.

Previous studies have shown that the presence of on-site laundry, kitchens, extensive irrigation, and cooling towers can significantly affect total water consumption. Hotels with on-site laundry operations showed laundry water consumption ranging from 5 to 29 percent of total water usage. Similar ranges existed for the percentage of total consumption represented by kitchens and cooling towers. For some properties, landscaping represented 20 percent or more of total water usage.

Without the installation of submeters, it is difficult to determine how much water is used by various areas of the hotel. Exhibit 2 shows the results of submetering of two hotels in quite different climates. Operation of cooling towers in the Jakarta property results in significant water usage for this purpose—something that is not needed in the colder climate of Germany. And, while we often talk about water usage in terms of usage per room, this exhibit shows that the usage actually occurs in many locations throughout the property in addition to the guestroom.

Exhibit 1   Water Consumption in the Lodging Industry

	Median Usage per Available room		Standard Deviation per Available Room	
	Annual	Daily	Annual	Daily
In Gallons:				
Economy/Budget (N=112)	39,137	107	19,643	54
Extended-Stay (N=154)	33,910	93	17,818	49
Midscale with F&B (N=37)	40,147	110	16,774	46
Midscale w/o F&B (N=140)	36,694	101	23,916	66
Luxury/Upscale (N=224)	58,783	161	28,454	78
Resorts (N=42)	107,873	296	65,868	180
In Liters:				
Economy/Budget (N=112)	147,938	405	74,251	203
Extended-Stay (N=154)	128,180	351	67,352	185
Midscale with F&B (N=37)	151,756	416	63,406	174
Midscale w/o F&B (N=140)	138,703	380	90,402	248
Luxury/Upscale (N=224)	222,200	609	107,556	295
Resorts (N=42)	407,760	1,117	248,981	682

Exhibit 2   Water Submetering Results

Moderate Climate: Fully submetered 300-room property in Germany

Guestrooms	34%
Kitchens	22%
Lockers/Public toilet	20%
Laundry	17%
Steam generation	4%
Pool	2%
HVAC	1%

Tropical Climate: 800 rooms, 100 apartments, 25 acres of gardens, sports center, Olympic-size pool in Jakarta

Guestrooms	34%
HVAC	16%
Kitchens	14%
Laundry	11%
Water treatment	7%
Pool	5%
Staff lockers	5%
Public areas	4%
Others	2%
Boilers	1%
Garden	1%

Source: Energy and Water Management Manual, Bass Hotels & Resorts, 2000.

The property manager will probably be most concerned about water costs. These costs are composed of two components: water purchase and water disposal (or potable water costs and sewer or wastewater costs). About 50 percent of water costs are potable water costs, 50 percent are sewer/wastewater costs. Potable water utilities and sewer utilities have a different tariff system for billing. A recent study of water and sewer costs in 100 U.S. cities found that fully one-third of these cities had seen their water rates increase by 100 percent from 2002 to 2012. In Atlanta and San Francisco, the price of water and sewer was up 200 percent.[2]

In recent decades, there has been tremendous growth in the consumption of bottled water products. Some of these are nothing more than tap water that has had some level of filtering, while others are bottled "spring" water. It is interesting to compare the costs of bottled water with that of tap water. A twelve-ounce bottle of water can retail for anywhere from $1 to $4, depending on brand and setting. At $1 per bottle, the cost of this water is $10.67 per gallon or $10,667 for one million gallons of water. This is over 1,000 times the cost of "tap" water. The growth in bottled water products has also had an impact on the waste stream, since the bottles must be disposed of. For this reason, "green meetings" advocates encourage the use of pitchers of water rather than bottled water at meetings, with leftover water from the pitchers being used for things such as watering plants.[3]

Utilities often assume for billing purposes that the amount of water disposed of in the sewer system matches the amount of water purchased. However, not all water used at hospitality facilities enters the sewer system—for example, water used for cooling towers and irrigation does not end up in the sewer system. In consideration of this fact, many water utilities do not charge for the disposal of water that can be shown not to have entered the sewer system. The high cost of water disposal highlights the potential benefit of using a **deduct meter** on the water supply to cooling towers, irrigation systems, and (to a lesser extent) the swimming pool, which together can constitute 50 percent or more of a facility's total water usage (although about 20 percent is more typical). The deduct meter submeters water used for these purposes so that this water can be deducted from the sewer bill—this can mean significant savings.

In recent years, water and sewer costs have been rising at a rate much greater than inflation (or guestroom rates!). The water and sewer bill for a hotel may now be larger than its natural gas bill (especially in warmer locations). Familiarity with the utility rate structure, tracking of water usage, and attention to opportunities to reduce water usage and costs are becoming more important as rates rise and supplies of water grow shorter in many areas of the country. To encourage hotels to save water, in February 2014 the U.S. Environmental Protection Agency launched the H$_2$Otel Challenge program as part of its WaterSense initiative (see Exhibit 3).[4] Hotel managers may wish to participate in this program or at least utilize some of its resources.

Water Systems

Water may be supplied from a variety of sources, including rivers, lakes, wells, rainwater collection, and the ocean (via desalination). Operations may purchase water from a water utility or get it from a facility they operate. There has also

Exhibit 3   EPA's H₂Otel Challenge

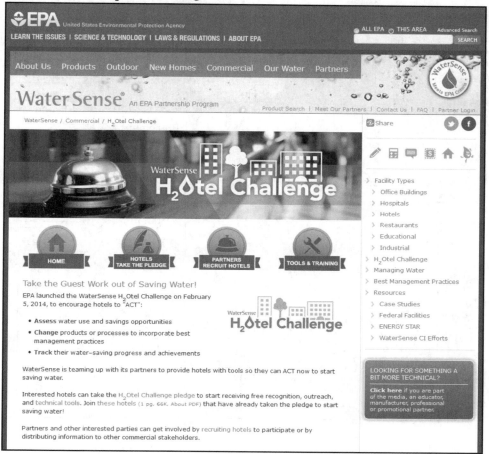

recently been renewed interest in the potential for on-site recovery of water and reuse of treated wastewater.

Building water and wastewater systems actually consist of a number of subsystems with appropriate isolation devices between the subsystems. Exhibit 4 illustrates the more common of these various subsystems. Each subsystem may have special equipment installed to create water conditions appropriate for the use being served. For example, in providing hot water for use in the laundry, the property will often put the water through a softener and then a water heater dedicated to the laundry application.

The subsystems shown in Exhibit 4 often have their own subsystems. The chilled and heated water circulated in the building cooling and heating systems is *not* part of what is typically considered the building water system. The water in such systems is *not* potable (drinkable).

Exhibit 4   Building Water Subsystems and Uses

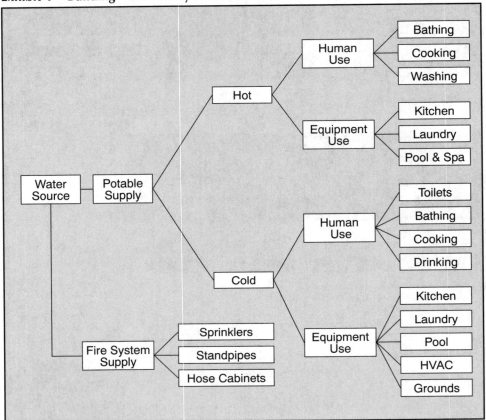

In the building water system, pipes made of galvanized iron, steel, copper, or plastic (PVC or CPVC) contain water under pressure. The pressure is supplied by the water utility, pumps at the property, or a combination of these. The pipes contain valves that may be used to isolate various elements of the system, shutting off the supply of water to these elements or to the entire system. Other valves, called **backflow preventers**, are used to prevent water from flowing from one subsystem to another—for example, a backflow preventer on an outside hose connection can prevent water standing in the hose from re-entering the building water system.

Proper water pressure is needed for proper operation of equipment and general usage. While there has been a lot of investment by hotels in the quality of their beds, one marketing consulting firm found that the shower—specifically the water pressure of the shower—was the most talked about factor when guests discussed their hotel experiences in social media.[5] In general, a water pressure for the building of between 30 and 80 psi will be suitable. However, some equipment will not operate properly at pressures lower than 50 or even 60 psi. Having too high a pressure can also be a problem in high-rise structures. High-rise structures may use pressure-reducing valves to lower water pressure on long vertical piping runs. A column of water that is 200 feet high creates a pressure at its base of 86 psi.

Building wastewater systems and their subsystems are shown in Exhibit 5. The **storm sewer system** is involved in the disposal of rainwater. Rainwater flows directly to some discharge location where the water enters a river, lake, or other drainage system. In contrast, the **sanitary sewer system** is involved in the removal of waste products from the facility. This system carries waste products to a sewage treatment facility.

In recent years, interest in water conservation and improved sanitation has resulted in several changes in plumbing fixtures. Battery-operated faucets have become relatively common in public-space sinks, where they help reduce water-usage and improve sanitation, since guests do not touch the handles of faucets. Battery-operated flush valves in public restrooms are also commonly found. In the guestroom, tank-type toilets (which do not lend themselves to battery-operated valves) are still the most common type. In order to reduce the water usage of guestroom toilets, new toilets are designed to use a smaller amount of water (typically 1.6 gallons) for flushing. To improve the performance of toilets while using a smaller amount of water, some hotels have begun specifying pressure-assisted toilet valves. These use the existing water pressure to create compressed air that is then injected to assist with waste removal. While this approach creates more noise than traditional tank toilets, the performance of the pressure-assisted units is generally more satisfactory, albeit at a higher initial cost.

Building wastewater systems are generally designed to use a gravity flow system; pumps are used only when necessary. This is the reason the bathroom

Exhibit 5   Primary Subdivisions of Property Wastewater Systems

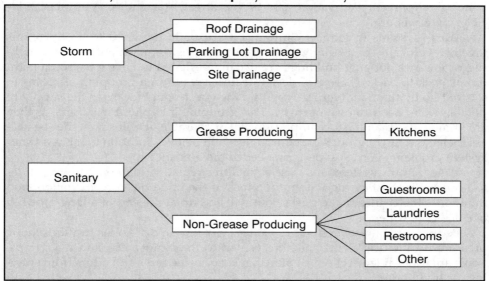

ceilings in lodging facilities are often lower than the ceilings in other parts of the guestrooms—the facilities in the rooms above need space to run waste lines which rely on a gravity flow. Piping systems for wastewater use cast iron or plastic piping (usually PVC) and are designed to withstand lower pressures than water systems. Valves are rarely found in wastewater systems at the property level. Anything that slows or constricts flow in gravity flow systems should be avoided.

Wastewater system components dealing with grease will have the wastewater flow through a **grease separator** (also known as a grease trap). Most municipal sewage treatment systems require the removal of grease, because of its negative effect on waste treatment system operation. Grease separators are mounted either in the floor area or attached to a piece of equipment. Wastewater enters the top of the unit; the unit slows the water's flow in a holding tank (which encourages separation of grease), and then moves the water toward the outlet, where it is filtered before discharge to the sanitary sewer. Grease separators should be periodically cleaned or pumped to remove the grease buildup; this task is often performed by a contract service. If additional filters are present in the separator, these should be checked, cleaned, and replaced as needed.

A few lodging properties operate their own sewage treatment facilities. While some small operators function with a septic tank under these circumstances, most others operate wastewater treatment plants. Proper operation of these facilities is extremely important because of the potentially adverse environmental consequences that can result from malfunctions. However, the extremely specialized operating and maintenance issues involved in operating a wastewater treatment plant are beyond the scope of this chapter. Operators with on-site sewage treatment facilities are encouraged to contact their state office of environmental protection, their state health department, or their equipment supplier for operating suggestions and guidelines. (One good source for operating instructions is the Water Environment Federation, 601 Wythe Street, Alexandria, Virginia 22314-1994; www.wef.org.)

Water systems in lodging buildings are usually designed to group rooms together vertically, particularly in high-rise designs. In addition, whether high-rise or low-rise, lodging buildings are usually designed to have guestroom bathrooms back-to-back. These two design features result in a grouping of rooms in sets of two by floor and vertically within the guestroom blocks for the supply of potable water and removal of waste. This grouping into plumbing **risers**, as they are known, has maintenance implications. For example, it will sometimes be necessary to shut down groups of rooms above and below a location that has a water system problem in order to perform needed maintenance.

Water supply systems may use a small recirculation loop on hot water lines to keep hot water flowing within the pipes of the building. A recirculation loop minimizes the chance that a guestroom will end up at the end of a long pipe full of cold "hot" water.

Because wastewater systems rely on gravity flow and are open to atmospheric pressure on the user's end, they are vented to the atmosphere and have **traps**. Traps are water-filled sections of pipe that keep sewer gases and odors from entering the building.

Both water and wastewater systems may utilize insulated pipes. Water system pipes are insulated to prevent heat loss from hot water piping and to prevent condensation on cold water piping. Roof drain piping is also often insulated to prevent condensation that can lead to wet walls and ceilings. When maintenance or renovation involving water systems is performed, replacement of this insulation is very important.

Water systems for fire protection include sprinklers and fire standpipes. Standpipes are used for hose systems installed at the property and for supplying hoses brought by the fire department. These fairly simple systems require little maintenance, relying on water supplied from the water main or the hydrant and pump of the fire truck.

It is much easier to meet maintenance and emergency needs related to water systems if the elements of each subsystem are clearly identified. Each pipe, valve, and pump should indicate the subsystem it belongs to and the water flow direction within the piping. Since pipes are also used to circulate water for HVAC applications, a code is sometimes developed to identify piping. Often, the code is alphabetic (CWR for chilled water return, for example); sometimes a color code system is used. Maintenance staff and key management personnel should know the location of water system shutoffs in order to reduce potential damage during emergencies.

Water Quality

Water quality involves a number of elements that differ in importance, depending on how the water is used. The most important concern is clearly related to **potability**—that is, suitability for drinking. Potability is of specific concern to guests and employees. It involves examining a variety of criteria, including the presence in the water of bacteria, nitrates, trace metals, and organic chemicals. Other water quality concerns not directly related to potability include color, odor, taste, clearness, mineral content, and acidity/alkalinity.

Any property relying on wells, lakes, streams, or water supplied by small water utilities should regularly test the quality of its water source. The Environmental Protection Agency (EPA) estimates that as many as 20 percent of the public water systems in the United States do not meet minimum water quality standards. The number of private systems failing to meet these standards is probably higher.

Potability concerns were at one time largely limited to concerns about coliform bacteria (which indicate the presence of human or animal feces in the water supply). Such contamination can occur when a well is used and the well becomes contaminated by a nearby septic system. Treatment via chlorination is the common solution, although iodinization or ultraviolet radiation is applied in some instances.

More recent potability concerns have extended to fertilizers, pesticides, herbicides, gasoline and other hydrocarbons, and a variety of heavy metals. These contaminants may have little effect on guests (because their stays are short). However, if present in sufficient quantities, they may well affect employees. Removing most of these contaminants is possible with the installation of rather expensive treatment systems, such as reverse osmosis. Because some water quality tests offered by local health departments and by vendors selling water treatment equipment are not comprehensive, specific testing for these contaminants should be requested.

Within the United States, the EPA has established National Primary Drinking Water Regulations that set forward maximum permissible levels of contaminants in public water systems. These standards are periodically revised as new data become available on the effects of these contaminants. Lodging personnel can refer to the EPA for detailed information on these standards.[6] In other countries, national and local governments are likely to have their own standards for water quality. Many of these are based on the standards of the World Health Organization.[7]

In some locations around the globe, potable water is not available, and hotels must clearly inform guests of that fact and tell them to use bottled water only. This information should be prominently displayed at each tap and probably in the shower as well. One would think that under such circumstances the hotel would provide bottled water to guests free of charge, but this is not always the case. One hotel in an Asian country, part of a major hotel brand, provides bottled water to guests for a very expensive price, a price not disclosed up front. In addition, at least two other hotels in the same area—where the consensus is that the tap water is not potable—do not post signs indicating that fact. Such negligence is inexcusable and poses a health hazard to guests.

Water quality concerns also involve a number of issues not directly related to potability. These problems may be largely aesthetic (odor and turbidity, for example), or they may be relevant for water-using equipment (such as the problem of water hardness—that is, the presence of dissolved minerals). These problems are generally solved through the use of firms specializing in water treatment. Specialists are particularly required when the problems involve microbial growths in locations such as cooling towers (a topic we will return to later).

Water softening is a common treatment method to reduce high levels of calcium, magnesium, and low levels of manganese and iron in the water supply. Calcium and magnesium will create scale (a buildup of minerals) in boilers and water heaters and on heating elements. In addition, hard water makes it difficult to generate a lather with soap, creates an irksome soap scum, and leaves mineral spots when it evaporates—which can reduce linen quality and life. Iron and manganese stain plumbing fixtures and linens. A water quality expert should determine the level of softening required, because over-softening can create problems with pipe and equipment corrosion. Since softening involves the replacement of the hardness-causing minerals with sodium, softened water should not be used for potable purposes except under special circumstances.

Water softening systems are generally low-maintenance. Refilling the brine tank with salt and checking the backwash circuit timing may be all that is required. Periodically, the zeolite (that is, the material in the softener that actually removes iron and so forth from the water) will need replacing. This decision requires input from the supplier.

Discharge/Sewage Water

There was a time when hotels and restaurants did not pay much attention to the amount of water or the condition of the water they discharged into the sewer system. Managers only had to make sure that storm water was not entering the system and that grease traps were functioning. But times have changed.

Because of the high cost of waste treatment and the costs of enlarging water treatment plants, local governments are taking a closer look at the wastewater of hotels and restaurants. Of particular concern can be the water's discharge temperature and the BOD, FOG, and TSS values of the discharge. "BOD" stands for Biochemical or Biological Oxygen Demand—the quantity of oxygen used in the biochemical oxidation of organic matter under standard laboratory procedures for five days. "FOG" stands for Fats, Oils, and Grease—the amount of free-flowing and/or emulsified vegetable-, animal-, or petroleum-based fat, oil, and/or grease detected in standard laboratory test procedures. Total Suspended Solids—TSS—is the total suspended matter that floats on or is suspended in water and is removable by laboratory filtering. In addition, discharges of ammoniacal nitrogen and *Escherichia coli* (E. coli) can be of concern. Allowable levels of these elements are established by the local sewage treatment authority.

Water conservation at hotels and restaurants can result in a more concentrated waste, with higher BOD levels. Poorly performing grease traps can increase the amount of FOG being discharged. Use of garbage disposals and pulpers can increase TSS values. Restaurants can find their annual sewer charges significantly affected by high BOD, FOG, and TSS levels in their wastewater. Data on 134 food service outlets in one region of the United States showed surcharges as high as $50,000 per year for quick-service restaurants; the average surcharge for the region's restaurants was $4,500 per year. Well-designed wastewater systems, properly maintained, along with chemical and biological treatments all can help to control wastewater costs.[8]

Legionnaires' Disease

Another important aspect of water treatment for operations with cooling towers involves Legionnaires' Disease (formally called *legionella pneumophila*). First diagnosed in 1976 at the Bellevue-Stratford Hotel in Philadelphia, this potentially deadly disease has since been encountered at a number of other buildings, including, but not limited to, hotels. The bacteria involved in this disease are widespread in the environment. A cooling tower, with its warm, wet, algae-containing environment, is a good place for bacterial growth. The cooling tower plume provides a means to introduce the bacteria into the air, where people may inhale them. A professionally designed and implemented cooling tower treatment program is among the best preventive tactics available for this disease.

Some hotels that have faced major lawsuits associated with Legionnaires' Disease have been shown to have had essentially no cooling tower treatment program. Locating the cooling tower discharge near an air intake for the building has also been a contributing factor to outbreaks of the disease. While most major outbreaks in the U.S. lodging industry have been linked to cooling towers, the potential exists for transmission via showers, humidifiers, and spas as well. In fact, many non-U.S. outbreaks have involved facilities other than cooling towers.

While *Legionella*-related illness is rare, it can create nightmares for hotels. As of this writing, a Las Vegas hotel is being sued for more than $300 million by guests claiming *Legionella* exposure.[9] A Dubai hotel, part of a major lodging chain, is being sued for $16.7 million.[10] While the underlying validity and outcomes of these lawsuits are yet to be determined, such lawsuits illustrate a hotel's potential liability. One legal decision involving *Legionella* awarded a woman almost $500,000 for a *Legionella* case involving a water system (this award contributed to the affected hotel's bankruptcy);[11] another case involving a hotel hot tub saw an award of $307,000.[12] It appears that none of these cases involved a loss of life.

In addition to its harmful effects on guests and employees, an outbreak of *Legionella* can also cause long-lasting, extremely negative publicity. The Bellevue-Stratford, site of the first U.S. outbreak, was forced into bankruptcy as a result of guest cancellations and abandonment. Clearly, it is very important that management be aware of, and take action regarding, the Legionnaires' Disease problem.[13]

Water Heating

Hotels require large amounts of hot water for uses ranging from guest showers to laundry. The cost to heat water almost invariably exceeds the cost of the water that is heated. Hot water needs for guestrooms, laundry, and kitchen applications are probably the largest at a lodging facility. Employee locker rooms and health club facilities can also be significant users. All of these needs for hot water are potentially different and should be approached separately. Guidelines for the design of service water heating systems are provided by various organizations and agencies. These include franchisors (in their franchise specifications), local code authorities, and national engineering associations.[14]

Guestroom hot water needs exist at all hotels. These needs may be rather concentrated at some properties, occurring primarily during the early morning wakeup time. Properties generally try to meet these needs by using a combination of hot water storage and production equipment. In order to meet these concentrated needs, some hotels have resorted to increasing the supply temperatures of the hot water. This is a potentially risky method, since water temperatures above 115°F (46°C) at fixtures can scald users.

Mixing valves are commonly installed to control hot water temperatures. These valves are connected to hot and cold water lines and modulate the flow of these two water sources to deliver water at a constant temperature. These devices are often an integral part of a guestroom water system or a system component, such as a shower control valve. If installed properly, mixing valves serve to protect hot water users from high water temperatures and the resulting burns and scalds.

Hotels have faced major lawsuits as a result of high temperature water supplies. A burn case in Texas led to an award to the burn victim of over $3.5 million! In this case, a high water temperature and an improperly installed mixing valve combined to severely burn a guest who had taken care to test the water temperature before entering a shower. The operation of the hot water system was so erratic that, even with this level of care, the guest was seriously injured. There are at least two lessons hotel managers can learn from this example. The first is that hotels need to keep safety in mind when establishing operating conditions for equipment and building systems. The second is that the installation of safety equipment must be done properly if this equipment is to function correctly. The failure to do this at the Texas hotel not only created great pain and suffering for a guest, but also cost the hotel a large amount of money. There is no substitute for the proper design, installation, and operation of building systems.

Since kitchens require water at 180°F (82°C), most system designers include a separate water heater or booster heater for kitchen needs. This sometimes involves a booster heater in a dishwasher. Laundry operations have such large needs for hot water over relatively short periods of time that they generally have a dedicated water heating system. The kitchen and laundry are sometimes provided with hot water from the same hot water system. This water is usually softened to help achieve proper equipment operation.

Keeping kitchen and laundry hot water systems separated from guestroom hot water systems is important. In one hotel hot-water-scalding case, there appeared to be a cross connection between the high-temperature water heater serving the kitchen and the lower-temperature heater serving the hotel's guestrooms. Building plans and measured temperatures by the health department over time showed a connection probably existed. However, after the scalding incident, both water heaters were quickly removed and new equipment installed, making verification of the cross connection impossible. The hotel settled the lawsuit out of court for a low-six-figure settlement.

Water Heating Options

Choosing from among the various available water heating options involves making decisions about equipment and fuel sources. Exhibit 6 illustrates equipment options and their accompanying fuel source options. **Directly fired water heaters** are probably the most common. These are the typical water heaters found in many homes, restaurants, and lodging establishments. A fuel is burned and heat is transferred to the water. For all fuel sources but electricity, a source of combustion air is required; the combustion gases are sent up a flue. Directly fired units may have integral or separate storage tanks.

Indirectly fired water heaters are more likely to be found at facilities with steam. The steam enters a coil or heat exchanger that transfers heat from the steam

Exhibit 6   Water Heating Equipment and Fuel Options

Water Heating Equipment	Fuel Source(s)
Directly Fired	Natural Gas, Oil, LPG (liquefied petroleum gas), Electricity
Indirectly Fired	Natural Gas, Oil, LPG, Electricity
Heat Pump	Electricity
Waste Heat Recovery	Waste Heat (from refrigeration equipment or other waste heat source)
Solar	Sun

to the water. The steam is generally kept separate from the water in these devices. Since a flue is required only where the steam is produced (rather than at the water heater), indirectly fired units can be placed in basements without access to outside air or at similar locations.

Heat pump water heaters (HPWH) extract heat from the air within a space, the outside air, or a water source. HPWHs use a refrigeration cycle to remove heat from the air (or water) and transfer it to the water being heated. Since the refrigeration system operates on electricity, there is no combustion or need for a flue. HPWHs can produce relatively cheap hot water because the refrigeration cycle uses less energy than electric resistance heating. Also, the refrigeration cycle *transfers* heat with greater efficiency than electric resistance and gas-fired water heaters *create* heat. HPWHs can pay for themselves very quickly, sometimes in less than one year.

HPWHs can be especially cost-effective installations in hotels operating central chilling plants, particularly in warmer locations. In these installations, heat is removed from the chilled water return by the HPWH and transferred to heat the potable water. It is also possible to use heated water exiting the condenser of the chiller as the heat source for the HPWH. Most efficient operation results if the water is only partially heated by the HPWH—say, up to a temperature of approximately 100°F (38°C), but temperatures of up to 140°F (60°C) are achievable. In the United States, a number of hotels in Hawaii make use of HPWH technology.[15]

With regard to operating costs, waste heat recovery and solar energy are probably the least expensive types of water heating equipment in terms of operating costs. However, the capital investments associated with each of these options can be rather substantial. Waste heat recovery water heating is most commonly done from the condenser of a refrigeration system, where as much as 15,000 Btu of energy are rejected for each ton (or 12,000 Btu per hour) of cooling capacity.[16] Managers should consider installing waste heat recovery devices on equipment with long operating hours per year, such as large food service refrigeration systems. Waste heat recovery water heating is also done at operations that have on-site electric power production.

Use of solar energy to heat water is certainly an option for hotels, and, in recent years, there has been a small but growing number of solar water heating installations at hotels. Solar water heating systems usually are installed to warm the incoming water to the hotel; the water is then heated to its final temperature by a conventional water heating system. Solar systems are usually roof mounted, although other areas providing sun access can be used. In the United States, the economics of solar water heating systems are strongly influenced by a variety of national and state tax credits associated with the systems. The environmental benefits of solar water heating systems lie in the reduction of natural gas, oil, or electricity that is needed to heat water to the desired temperature.

All water heating systems will have their costs of operation dictated by the efficiency of the water heating appliance, the cost of the fuel, the amount of hot water used, and the overall temperature rise of the water. Electric resistance water heating is generally the most expensive option. Heat pump water heating systems (which use electricity) can be competitive from an operating standpoint with oil or gas water heating systems. Waste heat recovery units incur little or no energy cost for their operation, but they do have a capital cost greater than that of conventional water heating units. They are often used with a conventional water heating system as a backup, either because they are a retrofit item or because the backup is needed to ensure adequate supplies of hot water when hot water demands are very high. Operations receiving steam from district heating systems may find that they can recover heat from their steam condensate. Operations with on-site laundry facilities may be able to reuse the discharge water from their operations to help heat their water.

Water System Maintenance Concerns

Although water systems require periodic maintenance, they are generally not a major consumer of maintenance time or cost unless they deteriorate to the point of needing major work or replacement. The preventive maintenance activities involved with water systems include such tasks as:

- Treating water to make it appropriate to the application or need.
- Replacing sacrificial anodes (which decrease pipe corrosion) in water heaters.
- Cleaning filters and strainers.
- Lubricating pumps.
- Checking hot water temperature settings.
- Checking pressure relief valves on water heaters for proper operation.

In addition, guestroom maintenance related to water consists of the repair of leaking valves and general caulking and sealing around fixtures.

A facility manager (and owner) should be aware of the potential for corrosion and erosion of water piping systems. Corrosion is the destruction of a metal or alloy by chemical or electrochemical reaction with its environment; erosion is a literal wearing of a pipe's inner surface due to friction.

There are many types of corrosion possible; leading causes include:

- The pH of the water.
- The amount of oxygen in the water.
- The chemical makeup of the water.
- The amount of galvanic corrosion from the use of dissimilar metals within (or in contact with) the piping system.
- The temperature of the water.

Facility managers can test the water's pH to determine whether the supply is overly acidic (or, in rare cases, overly alkaline) and requires treatment. Highly oxygenated water (say, in recirculating fountains) may also have a higher tendency to create corrosion. Salts are corrosive; managers and others involved with maintaining swimming pools recognize the corrosive potential of the chlorinated water used in pools. Galvanic corrosion occurs when different metals come in contact with each other. Finally, any corrosion will occur at a faster rate as the temperature of the water increases. Corrosion is also possible on the exterior of pipes, particularly those that are buried underground. In these instances, there may be a reaction between the pipe and the soil/fill around the pipe, or there may be a leakage of groundwater into the soil/fill around the pipe (especially troublesome is the salt-laden runoff from streets and parking areas that have been salted to clear them of snow and ice).

Erosion of the piping system is another concern. Turbulence in water systems (resulting from water flowing at high velocity, pipe turns, and obstacles) causes a wearing of pipe surfaces and of protective oxides produced on the inside of copper piping. Water velocities in excess of four feet (1.22 meters) per second should be avoided. A factor that can accelerate pipe erosion is the presence of particulates (sand, metal filings, and so on) in the water itself. Adequate filtering of the water should help to keep particulates at a minimum.

The flame of fossil-fueled water heating appliances should be inspected periodically to ensure that proper combustion is taking place. The flue should also be checked for any blockage. All water heating units should be inspected regularly for water-side mineral buildup and periodically cleaned and drained to reduce this buildup. If this is not done, the unit's efficiency and lifetime will be reduced.

Wastewater systems may require periodic clearing to reduce the chances of blockages and resulting backups. Traps may require periodic filling with water at some locations (such as floor drains in generally dry areas). Gutters, roof drains, and site drainage components, all related to the storm sewer system, should be inspected and cleaned of debris. This can be particularly important before times of the year when heavy rains occur and when debris is likely to have built up (leaves in the fall season for hotels in temperate climate zones, for example).

Guestroom maintenance generally involves the repair of leaking faucets and valves and the cleaning of clogged filters in aerating faucets (that is, faucets that spray water through a screen that spreads the flow). When problems occur, clogged drains need to be cleared either chemically or mechanically. When maintenance staff work on plumbing in guestrooms, they should also inspect the tile and caulk around plumbing fixtures and perform any necessary repairs.

Emergency and breakdown maintenance of water systems requires knowledge of the key water shutoff valves, the piping layout for both potable and waste water, and the appropriate cleanup equipment. Such equipment includes, at a minimum, a wet/dry vacuum and usually a pump as well.

Water for Entertainment and Recreation

Water is more than just a utility; at some hotels, it is a key element of the entertainment and recreational facilities of the property. Water is commonly used in exterior landscaping treatments—ponds, flowing streams, fountains, and more. Sometimes these elements are brought indoors. For example, at the Wilderness Lodge at Walt Disney World, a stream emerges in the lodge's lobby and flows to the outside. This is only the beginning. Outside, the stream becomes a waterfall; a geyser erupts as well. Disney also makes extensive use of water features in its theme parks.

Some hotels and casinos in Las Vegas use water for entertainment purposes. For example, the Bellagio resort created the "Fountains of Bellagio."[17] Completed in 1998 and taking up most of a small lake, the fountains employ 1,200 water jets (many of them motorized and synchronized) and more than 5,400 individually programmed underwater lights, choreographed to the music of Luciano Pavarotti, Aaron Copland, Frank Sinatra, and others. Designers, musicians, and performance artists helped mesh the movement of the water with the music. For many observers, the fountains seem to be alive, with a heart, soul, and emotions of their own. The fountains were designed to express the romantic spirit of the Bellagio.

Water features on the scale of those at Walt Disney World and Bellagio are certainly impressive and unusual. More common is the use of water for recreational facilities such as water parks, slides, and surf pools. These features are becoming more and more elaborate and more and more common. A major use of water as a central feature of the hotel experience has led to the emergence of a new lodging niche: water park hotels. These hotels feature large indoor (and sometimes outdoor) water parks; the indoor water parks of hotels located in cold climates can draw guests wanting an escape from the cold weather. Hotel water parks require very large and specialized water heating, treating, and pumping systems as well

The Fountains of Bellagio are a spectacular water attraction. (Courtesy of Bellagio, Las Vegas, Nevada.)

as systems to maintain warm and not overly humid indoor air conditions. The Wilderness Hotel & Golf Resort in the Wisconsin Dells in Wisconsin has seven water parks encompassing 470,830 square feet; most hotel water park facilities are more modest. Of the top twenty waterparks in the world, fourteen are located outside the United States, illustrating the global appeal of this concept.[18]

For those operations taking advantage of natural water features such as oceans and lakes, the water quality of these bodies of water is obviously very important. Blue Flag is a European organization formed to improve and maintain the quality of beaches, marinas, and other marine environments. It concentrates on the following areas:

- Water quality
- Environmental education and information
- Environmental management
- Safety and services

Blue Flag works with local communities as well as the operators of beaches and marinas; it recognizes that businesses and communities must work together to improve and sustain their marine environments. Blue Flag is currently expanding globally.

Swimming Pool Water Systems

Many lodging facilities have swimming pools. Maintaining a safe and comfortable pool environment is an ongoing challenge requiring a significant amount of time and labor. The failure to do so can result in major problems.

Exhibit 7, which presents a schematic of a typical swimming pool piping, filtering, and heating system, helps to illustrate the areas of concern in pool maintenance and operation. Pool maintenance involves cleaning the pool, the equipment, and the water.

Pool cleaning involves skimming to remove floating debris and vacuuming to remove debris on the bottom. Walls, steps, and other areas by the pool should be brushed or swept to remove dirt. Tile at and near the water level of the pool should be cleaned periodically (using an appropriate tile cleaner and the right equipment) to remove lime buildup.

Pool equipment is specially designed for the pool environment. Pumps are usually factory-lubricated and require little maintenance other than cleaning of the strainer and skimmer basket, which should be done daily. When the strainer is cleaned, various valves must be closed to avoid either draining the pool (if the strainer is located below pool level) or draining the pump suction line of the strainer (if the pump is located above pool level). The filter requires regular cleaning or backwashing (depending on the type of filter) in order to keep the water clean and to ensure sufficient flow in the piping system.

The cleanliness of pool water involves maintaining a proper balance of water temperature and acidity/alkalinity. Since the number of bathers, the intensity of the sunlight, and wind and rain (for outdoor pools) can all affect pool chemistry and conditions, maintaining proper pool conditions can be challenging. Failure to

Exhibit 7   Typical Swimming Pool Piping, Filtering, and Heating Schematic

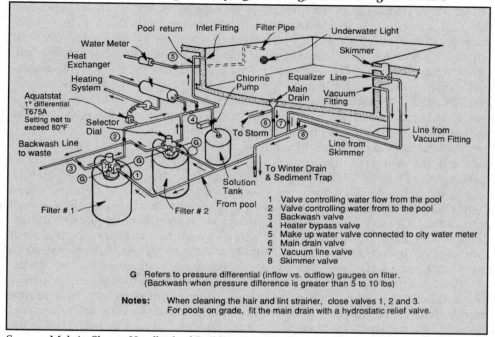

Pool return   Inlet Fitting   Filter Pipe   Underwater Light
Water Meter
Heat Exchanger
Heating System
Aquatstat 1° differential T675A Setting **not** to exceed 80°F
Selector Dial
Backwash Line to waste
Chlorine Pump
Main Drain
Equalizer Line
Vacuum Fitting
Skimmer
To Storm
Line from Skimmer
Line from Vacuum Fitting
Filter # 1
Filter # 2
From pool
Solution Tank
To Winter Drain & Sediment Trap

1 Valve controlling water flow from the pool
2 Valve controlling water from to the pool
3 Backwash valve
4 Heater bypass valve
5 Make up water valve connected to city water meter
6 Main drain valve
7 Vacuum line valve
8 Skimmer valve

G Refers to pressure differential (inflow vs. outflow) gauges on filter. (Backwash when pressure difference is greater than 5 to 10 lbs)

Notes: When cleaning the hair and lint strainer, close valves 1, 2 and 3. For pools on grade, fit the main drain with a hydrostatic relief valve.

Source: Mel A. Shear, *Handbook of Building Maintenance Management* (Reston, Va.: Reston Publishing, 1983), p. 318.

maintain proper conditions can result in disease or discomfort for swimmers, corrosion of metal pool parts, and leaching of plaster pools.

The balance between acidity and alkalinity is established by measuring the pH of the pool with a test kit. The pH should be between 7.2 and 7.6 (slightly alkaline). Pools naturally tend to become more alkaline than is desired. The pH can be controlled by treatment with muriatic acid or sodium bisulfate. Testing of pH levels should occur before chlorine is added, since residual chlorine levels can affect pH readings.

Another problem with pool water quality involves algae. Algae will clog filters and impart a disagreeable odor or taste to the water. In addition, algae interfere with disinfectants and can create slippery floors and steps. While normal chlorine levels are generally effective in controlling algae growth, they do not completely kill the algae. Killing of algae requires use of an algaecide on a regular basis.

Pool water treatment is also possible using ozone, ionization, or with chemicals other than chlorine. These methods may be used to supplement or replace chlorine or bromine. All pool chemical usage should be done in a safe manner, complying with the recommendations of suppliers and with local laws and ordinances.

Some pool operators have switched to providing pool sanitization by using saline treatment methods. Saline treatment involves the use of electrolysis to create sodium hypochlorite from a salt (sodium chloride) solution to treat pool water, resulting in a very mild saline condition in the pool. The continuous introduction of sodium hypochlorite in this process avoids the formation of chloramines and other chlorine compounds produced in other treatment methods. With these compounds eliminated, the smells and other issues (such as irritated skin, damaged hair, etc.) associated with usage of chlorine chemicals are also essentially eliminated. Additional benefits include improved safety due to the elimination of chlorine usage, reduced or eliminated needs to "shock" the pool due to algae growth, and significantly reduced costs for chemicals, since the salt is much less expensive than chlorine and actual usage of salt is minimal. The resulting saline levels in the pool are less than the levels present in human tears.

Pool heating is necessary in many locations and is usually provided for all indoor pools. A temperature range of 70–80°F (21–27°C) for pool water and air conditions of 75–80°F (24–27°C) and 50–60 percent relative humidity are comfortable to most people. Pool water may be heated by a directly or indirectly fired dedicated pool heater or by a type of heat pump designed specifically for pool applications. Directly fired heaters for indoor pools have been implicated in incidents of carbon monoxide poisoning. This is caused by inadequate provision of combustion air and/or inadequate venting of exhaust gases. Managers need to check pool heaters for these conditions and rectify any problems they may find.

Heat pumps have seen increasing use as a means to control the interior environment around indoor pools, conserve pool water and chemicals, and reduce energy costs. Some units are installed in the pool exhaust airstream where they extract water (which is returned to the pool) and heat (which is used to keep the pool air comfortable). Others are located within the pool area and dehumidify and heat the air in this area. However heat pumps are installed, their overall effect is to reduce the humidity around the pool. This helps reduce corrosion, odor, and other problematic effects of humid, chlorine-laden pool air.

Pools and similar water-based recreational facilities pose some unique safety risks. One suggested checklist for pool safety is given in Exhibit 8.

The 2010 revisions to the Americans with Disabilities Act (ADA) included items related to pool accessibility. The 2010 Standards established two categories of pools: large pools with more than 300 linear feet of pool wall, and smaller pools with less than 300 linear feet of wall. Large pools must have two accessible means of entry, with at least one being a pool lift or sloped entry; smaller pools are only required to have one accessible means of entry, provided that it is either a pool lift or a sloped entry. Public accommodations must bring existing pools into compliance with the 2010 Standards "to the extent that it is readily achievable to do so." Managers can go online at www.ada.gov to find information on specific pool requirements and exceptions.[19]

Water Conservation

With rising water costs, decreasing water availability, and governmental restrictions on water usage, hospitality businesses have several reasons to reduce water usage. The chapter appendix illustrates some possible water conservation methods as suggested by one governmental agency. In addition to these suggestions, proper

Exhibit 8   Swimming Pool Safety Checklist

- *Review applicable state, county, and municipal regulations.* These provide the minimum standards you must comply with under the law.

- *Hire a certified, trained lifeguard.* If you choose not to have a lifeguard present, post a sign warning guests to swim at their own risk. Have an employee trained in emergency first aid present during pool hours.

- *Post a diagrammatic illustration of artificial respiration procedures.* Provide clear instructions to indicate when resuscitation should begin and advise that it should continue until professional aid arrives.

- *Make safety equipment, such as a life pole, immediately available.*

- *Make breaks between shallow water and deep water obvious.* Use ropes, floats, or a different color on the floor of the pool.

- *Enclose the pool with a fence.* This will control access and may prevent child-drowning incidents.

- *Clean, inspect, and repair the pool regularly.* Make sure all ladders are secure.

- *Install slip-resistant surfaces around the pool.*

- *Provide an emergency telephone.* Have emergency phone numbers posted.

- *Clearly mark water depth.* If your property attracts many foreign visitors, consider marking the pool in meters as well as feet.

- *Post a sign prohibiting diving.*

- *Post a sign prohibiting swimming solo.*

- *Post a sign with the pool's hours.* Make sure pool hours are strictly enforced.

- *Prohibit intoxicated guests from swimming.* Consider a ban on alcoholic beverages near the pool. If this is unrealistic, keep a close eye on intoxicated guests and restrict them from swimming.

- *Prohibit rough-housing at the pool.*

- *Keep a log.* Document the times you stop unacceptable behavior in and around the pool.

Source: Adapted from *Hospitality Law,* July 1999.

maintenance and operation of valves on dishwashers and washing machines can help keep water usage at acceptable levels by reducing leaks.

The lodging industry has already taken action to reduce water usage. Some actions, such as installing low-flow shower heads, are common, due in part to the fact that they also save energy used to heat water.[20] Actions to reuse water (known as *gray water*) are less common (but growing). With increased pressure to reduce water usage, we may see further use of water recycling. But the need to have local officials approve such actions (in some instances) and to modify existing plumbing connections (calling for capital expenditure) are two major obstacles to water recycling.

Growing applications for gray water include landscaping and golf course irrigation. Water-short regions such as California, Hawaii, Florida, Arizona, and Nevada (to name a few) have found that treated wastewater can be used for irrigation, often at a cost that is a fraction of that of existing potable water; this approach has the added benefit of potentially recharging underground aquifers. One of the largest hospitality industry applications of water reuse is Disney World in Florida. Reedy Creek Utilities provides reclaimed water for irrigation of landscaped areas within the Walt Disney World Resort Complex. Five golf courses, landscaped areas at five hotels, highway medians, and a water park are irrigated using reclaimed water. Reclaimed water is also used to wash Disney tour buses and irrigate a 110-acre tree farm that produces horticultural materials for use throughout the Disney complex. A network of eighty-five rapid infiltration basins is used for ground water recharge. The permitted capacity of the reuse system is fifteen million gallons per day (mgd). About 4.6 mgd of reclaimed water was used for irrigation and 5.2 mgd was used for groundwater recharge in 2003.[21] Further information on water reuse can be found at the WateReuse Association (www.watereuse.org).

One potentially significant use of water at many hotels is the laundry operation. In recent years, a number of hotels have been shifting to using ozone laundry technology to replace the use of (most) chlorine bleaches. The resulting change in the washing process yields a reduction in chemical and water usage. In addition, it is possible to substantially reduce—even completely eliminate—the use of hot water. Lodging operations using this technology appropriately have achieved reductions in chemical usage of 30 to 40 percent, hot water usage of 80 percent or more, and overall water usage of 30 to 40 percent.[22] Further reduction in water (and energy and chemical) usage for laundry operations can occur if towel and linen reuse programs are put in place.[23]

Incorporating submeters on water lines and regularly reading water meters can help in water conservation programs. Submeters on irrigation lines can help identify leaks that are often difficult to find because they are buried and may run some distance around the property. Submeters on cooling tower makeup water can help managers measure and monitor water usage in the towers. As mentioned earlier in the chapter, both cooling tower water and irrigation water (if submetered) may qualify for exemption from payment of sewer fees, providing a further cost benefit.

Initiating water conservation practices that may affect guests should be done cautiously. One operation that installed low-volume shower heads received so many guest complaints that it chose to reinstall the previous shower heads. Another operation discovered—*after* it had installed new low-volume shower heads—that the poor condition of its piping did not allow it to raise water pressure high enough to operate the shower heads properly! Managers who are contemplating using water conservation devices should try a few as a test, monitor results, and evaluate the test before installing the devices throughout the property.

Water usage can often be reduced with little effort. Controlling landscape irrigation, installing foot-operated faucets in kitchens, and doing basic maintenance on water systems can be very effective conservation measures. Being observant of what is going on at the property is also important. For example, in one hotel in Cancun, the float valve controlling the water level in the hotel cooling tower's sump had failed and was stuck in the open position, so that water was continuously flowing over the side of the tower sump, onto the roof, and down a roof drain. Judging from the amount of algae on the roof, this problem had been going on for quite some time before finally being discovered. It pays to keep a close eye on water usage and quickly investigate if usage levels seem abnormally high or spike.

Helpful Resources

A classic book on water conservation is the *Handbook of Water Use and Conservation* by Amy Vickers (Amherst, Mass.: WaterPlow Press, 2012). The American Water Works Association calls it "the most thorough resource ever published on water use and conservation." Hotel managers and others are encouraged to refer to this publication for more ideas and information concerning water conservation. Further information on water management at hotels and resorts is also available in *A Manual for Water and Waste Management: What the Tourism Industry Can Do To Improve Its Performance* (United Nations Environmental Program, Division of Technology, Industry and Economics, 2003).[24]

Endnotes

1. "The History of Plumbing—Part Two—Plumbing in America," *Plumbing and Mechanical Engineer,* July 1996.

2. http://www.usatoday.com/story/money/business/2012/09/27rising-water-rates/1595651/.

3. Refer to groups such as The Green Meeting Industry Council (www.greenmeetings.info) and BlueGreen Meetings (www.bluegreenmeetings.org).

4. www.epa.gov/watersense/commercial/challenge.html.

5. http://www.brodeur.com/wp-content/uploads/2013/02/Brodeur_Hospitality-Relevance-Audit-2.14.13.pdf.

6. www.epa.gov/safewater/mcl.html#mcls.

7. International hotel managers and others can refer to the World Health Organization (http://www.who.int/en/) for detailed information on its various water quality standards.

8. Data provided by Foodservice Wastewater Consultants Inc., to the multi-unit architects, engineers, and construction officers' group of the National Restaurant Association, May 2000.

9. Kitty Bean Yancey, "Former guests at Aria Las Vegas resort sue over Legionnaires' disease," *USA TODAY,* August 25, 2011; http://travel.usatoday.com/destinations/dispatches/post/2011/08/former-guests-at-aria-las-vegas-resort-sue-over-legionnaires-disease/416618/1.

10. "Dubai hotel faces $16.7m lawsuit over legionnaires," *ArabianBusiness.com,* April 12, 2011; www.arabianbusiness.com/dubai-hotel-faces-16-7m-lawsuit-over-legionnaires-393411.html.

11. "Jury awards woman nearly $500,000 in Cortina Inn Legionnaires' disease case," *Rutland (Vermont) Herald,* January 8, 2010; www. rutlandherald.com/article/20100108/THISJUSTIN/100109944.

12. "Hotel guest contracts Legionnaires' disease from a hot tub: Records indicate bromine content poor, allowing for *Legionella* spore to thrive," *Michigan Lawyers Weekly,* March 11, 2011; http:// milawyersweekly.com/news/2011/03/11/hotel-guest-contracts-legionnaires-disease-from-a-hot-tub/.

13. Further information on this topic is available at EWGLI Technical Guidelines for the Investigation, Control and Prevention of Travel Associated Legionnaires' Disease, September 2011 (http://ecdc.europa.eu/en/activities/surveillance/ELDSNet/Documents/EWGLI-Technical-Guidelines.pdf). Additional information is available from the World Health Organization in its publication *Legionella and the Prevention of Legionellosis* (http://www.who.int/water_sanitation_health/emerging/legionella.pdf). A U.S. source for information is the *Legionella* homepage for the Centers for Disease Control and Prevention at http://www.cdc.gov/legionella/index.html.

14. An example of such an organization is the American Society of Heating, Refrigerating and Air-Conditioning Engineers, which sets forward design information for service water heating in Chapter 39, "Service Water Heating," of the 3 *HVAC Applications Handbook.*

15. *Guide to Heat Pump Water Heating for Condominiums, Commercial and Institutional Facilities,* Energy Services Department, Hawaiian Electric Company, Inc. (http://www.heco.com/vcmcontent/StaticFiles/pdf/heatpumpguide_sept03.pdf).

16. A Btu, or British thermal unit, is a measure of heat defined as the amount of heat required to raise one pound of water by one Fahrenheit degree. To convert Btu to kilocalories, multiply Btu by 0.252.

17. Information in this paragraph was pulled from J. Koski, "Going Where No Fountain Has Gone Before," *Plumbing and Mechanical Engineer,* July 1999.

18. http://www.waterparks.org/otherArticles/Waterpark%20Industry%20General%20Facts%202013Rev.pdf.

19. Further information about pools and the ADA can be found at http://www.ada.gov/pools_2010.htm and at http://www.ada.gov/qa_existingpools_titleIII.htm; there is also an ADA Information Line: 800-514-0301.

20. For information on how one hotel in San Antonio, Texas, saved seven million gallons of water per year, 330,000 kilowatt-hours of electricity per year, and $68,000 in water, sewer, and energy costs per year by installing water-efficient fixtures, see the EPA's *WaterSense at Work: Best Management Practices for Commercial and Institutional Facilities* at http://www.epa.gov/watersense/commercial/docs/watersense_at_work/#/282/zoomed.

21. www.dep.state.fl.us/water/reuse/project.htm.

22. For further information on ozone technology and suppliers, do a search on industry search engines such as Hotel Online (www.hotel-online.com) or on general Internet search engines.

23. One widely used towel and linen reuse program is Green Suites Hotel Solutions' Project Planet Program; for more information about this program, see http://www.greensuites.com/Environmentally-Friendly-Hotel-Programs/Project-Planet-Program.

24. This publication can be accessed at http://destinet.eu/resources/...-various-target-groups/individual-puplications/A_Manual_for_Water_and_Waste_Management_What_the_Tourism_Industry_Can_Do_to_Improve_Its_Performance_l1.pdf. Some interesting case studies in water conservation at hotels can be found at the following

Internet sites: http://www.seattle.gov/util/groups/public/@spu/@water/documents/webcontent/HOTELWATE_200407081359093.pdf;http://greenlodgingnews.com/Water-Conservation;andhttp://www.epa.gov/watersense/commercial/types.html#tabs-hotels.

 ## Key Terms

backflow preventer—A valve used to prevent water from flowing from one subsystem to another—for example, to prevent water standing in a hose from re-entering the building water system.

deduct meter—A device that submeters water that is used by a property but does not flow into the sewer system (for example, water used in cooling towers, irrigation systems, and swimming pools) so that this water can be deducted from the sewage disposal bill.

directly fired water heater—The most commonly found type of water heater, in which a fuel is burned and heat is transferred to the water. For all fuel sources but electricity, a source of combustion air is required; the combustion gases are sent up a flue. A directly fired water heater may have integral or separate storage tanks.

grease separator—A device used to capture grease in wastewater before it enters the sewer system. Also called a grease trap.

heat pump water heater (HPWH)—A water heater that extracts heat from the air within a space, the outside air, or a water source and, using a refrigeration cycle, transfers it to the water being heated.

indirectly fired water heater—A water heater in which steam enters a coil or heat exchanger that transfers heat from the steam to the water.

potability—Suitability for drinking.

riser—A grouping of rooms in sets of two by floor and vertically within the guest-room blocks that share piping for the supply of potable water and removal of waste.

sanitary sewer system—A system that removes waste products from a facility and carries them to a sewage treatment facility.

storm sewer system—A system for the disposal of rainwater; the system makes sure that rainwater flows directly to some discharge location where the water enters a river, lake, or other drainage system.

trap—A water-filled section of pipe that keeps sewer gases and odors from entering the building.

water softening—The removal of calcium, manganese, and iron from the water supply.

Review Questions

1. What are the two major subcomponents of a "water" bill for hotels? Why might water bills for the same quantity of water usage differ from location to location?

2. What factors could cause large variations in water usage for hotels of similar size?

3. When is using a deduct meter a good idea? What should you know before installing a deduct meter?

4. What is the difference between the storm sewer system and the sanitary sewer system? Which water subsystems flow into each?

5. How does the organization of plumbing risers affect maintenance needs?

6. What is the most important water quality concern? What are several secondary quality concerns?

7. What is Legionnaires' Disease? What steps should be taken to help avoid an outbreak of this disease?

8. When selecting a water heating fuel source for a new property, what factors besides price might be involved?

9. What safety concerns must be addressed when directly fired water heaters are used to heat indoor swimming pools? What advantages might heat pump water heaters have in such a setting?

10. What water conservation measures are widely applicable to, and used by, hospitality properties?

11. What is "gray" water? What are applications for its use in hospitality?

12. Why might hotels consider using an ozone technology in laundry operations?

 **Internet Sites**

For more information, visit the following Internet sites. Remember that Internet addresses can change without notice. If the site is no longer there, you can use a search engine to look for additional sites.

American Water Works Association
www.awwa.org

Association of Pool & Spa
  Professionals
www.theapsp.org

Consulting-Specifying Engineer
www.csemag.com

HPAC Engineering Interactive
www.hpac.com

Plumbing & Mechanical
www.pmmag.com

PM Engineer
www.pmengineer.com

Water Online
www.wateronline.com

WaterWeb Consortium
www.waterweb.org

Chapter Appendix:

Water Conservation Checklist

General Suggestions

Increase employee awareness of water conservation.

Seek employee suggestions on water conservation; locate suggestion boxes in prominent areas.

Conduct contests for employees (e.g., posters, slogans, or conservation ideas).

Install signs encouraging water conservation in employee and customer restrooms.

When cleaning with water is necessary, use budgeted amounts.

Read water meter weekly to monitor success of water conservation efforts.

Assign an employee to monitor water use and waste.

Determine the quantity and purpose of water being used.

Determine other methods of water conservation.

Building Maintenance

Check water supply system for leaks and turn off any unnecessary flows.

Repair dripping faucets and showers and continuously running or leaking toilets.

Install flow reducers and faucet aerators in all plumbing fixtures whenever possible.

Reduce the water used in toilet flushing by either adjusting the vacuum flush mechanism or installing toilet tank displacement devices (dams, bottles, or bags).

As appliances or fixtures wear out, replace them with water-saving models.

Shut off water supply to equipment rooms not in use.

Minimize the water used in cooling equipment, such as air compressors, in accordance with the manufacturer recommendations.

Reduce the load on air conditioning units by shutting air conditioning off when and where it is not needed.

Keep hot water pipes insulated.

Avoid excessive boiler and air conditioner blow down. (Monitor total dissolved solids levels and blow down only when needed.)

Instruct clean-up crews to use less water for mopping.

Switch from wet or steam carpet cleaning methods to dry powder methods.

Change window cleaning schedule from periodic to an on-call/as-required basis.

Pools

Channel splashed-out pool water onto landscaping.

Lower pool water level to reduce amount of water splashed out.

Use a pool cover to reduce evaporation when pool is not being used.

Reduce the amount of water used to clean pool filters.

Kitchen Area

Turn off the continuous flow used to clean drain trays of the coffee/milk/soda beverage island; clean the trays only as needed.

Turn dishwasher off when not in use. Wash full loads only. Replace spray heads to reduce water flow.

Use water from steam tables to wash down cooking area.

Do not use running water to melt ice or frozen foods.

Use water-conserving ice makers.

Recycle water where feasible, consistent with state and county requirements.

Recycle rinse water from the dishwater or recirculate it to the garbage disposer.

Presoak utensils and dishes in ponded water instead of using a running water rinse.

Wash vegetables in ponded water; do not let water run in preparation sink.

Use water from steam tables in place of fresh water to wash down the cooking area.

Bar

Do not use running water to melt ice in the sink strainers.

Laundry

Reprogram machines to eliminate a rinse or suds cycle, if possible, and if not restricted by health regulations.

Reduce water levels, where possible, to minimize water required per load of washing.

Wash full loads only.

Evaluate wash formula and machine cycles for water use efficiency.

Exterior Areas

Convert from high-water-using lawns, trees, and shrubs to xeriscape—landscape design incorporating plants providing beautiful color and requiring less water. In the future, design landscapes requiring less water.

Inventory outdoor water use for landscaped areas.

Do not water landscape every day; two to three times a week is usually sufficient.

Stop hosing down sidewalks, driveways, and parking lots.

Wash autos, buses, and trucks less often.

Avoid plant fertilizing and pruning that would stimulate excessive growth.

Remove weeds and unhealthy plants so remaining plants can benefit from the water saved.

In many cases, older, established plants require only infrequent irrigation. Look for indications of water need, such as wilt, change of color, or dry soils.

Install soil moisture overrides or timers on sprinkler systems.

Time watering, when possible, to occur in the early morning or evening when evaporation is lowest.

Make sure irrigation equipment applies water uniformly.

Investigate the advantages of installing drip irrigation systems.

Mulch around plants to reduce evaporation and discourage weeds.

Remove thatch and aerate turf to encourage the movement of water to the root zone.

Avoid runoff and make sure sprinklers cover just the lawn or garden, not sidewalks, driveways, or gutters.

Water in winter only during prolonged hot and dry periods. (During spring and fall, most plants need approximately half the amount needed during the summer.)

This checklist provides water conservation tips successfully implemented by industrial and commercial users. This list has been revised from the original copy first published and distributed by the Los Angeles Department of Water and Power. The ideas presented are not intended as an endorsement by the California Department of Water Resources of any method, process, or specific product but are merely suggestions.

Source: California Department of Water Resources, "A Checklist of Water Conservation Ideas for Hotels and Motels."

Chapter 6 Outline

A Brief Introduction to Electrical Systems
System Design and Operating Standards
System and Equipment Maintenance
    Electrical Plans
    Training in Operating and Safety
      Procedures
System Components
    Fuses and Circuit Breakers
    Distribution Panels and Wiring
    Electric Motors, Controls, and Drive
      Elements
    Electronic Equipment
    Emergency Power Systems
    Electrical Maintenance Equipment
Electric Utility Billing and Building
    Operations
    Reading Electrical Utility Meters
    Checking the Bill for Errors
    Choosing the Best Rate Schedule
Electric Utility Deregulation
Telecommunications Systems

Competencies

1. Describe briefly various aspects and components of electrical systems, and cite important considerations regarding system design and operating standards. (pp. 203–208)

2. Identify elements of an effective electrical system and equipment maintenance program. (pp. 208–215)

3. Describe electrical system components: fuses and circuit breakers; distribution panels and wiring; electric motors, controls, and drive elements; electronic equipment; emergency power systems; and electrical maintenance equipment. (pp. 215–226)

4. Explain the billing methods of electric utilities, describe how to read electrical utility meters, state why electric bills should be checked for errors, summarize issues involved in deciding on a tariff (rate) for electric service, and discuss electric utility deregulation. (pp. 226–236)

5. Outline important elements of the telecommunications system and the management of that system in hotels today. (pp. 236–239)

6

Electrical Systems

If the electric current is to be generated on the premises, it should be, by all means, direct current. There is no possible point in using an alternate current generating plan for this character of building, unless it be to conform to the characteristics of an outside service. The cost of generating and distributing direct and alternating current for the building is approximately the same, but direct current is somewhat better for motors which require speed variation, and very much better for elevator work.

With current from an outside source, it is a case of take what you can get; but if this happens to be 25-cycle, alternating current, something has to be done about it. This low frequency gives a constant flicker in the lights which is noticeable, and in fact objectionable, to anyone who has not been educated down to it. If the frequency is 60-cycle, the character of the illumination and the wiring for lighting are the same as with direct current, and the lighting of the building can be thrown at pleasure from a direct current plant to an alternating service. In this case the converter equipment need be only large enough for the direct current motors, while with a 25-cycle service it will be called on to convert the total load of power and light.[1]

OBVIOUSLY, THE WORLD OF ELECTRICITY has changed since this excerpt, taken from a 1923 magazine article, was written. Today, alternating current and 60-cycle power are the rule in the United States rather than the exception, and most operations purchase their electric power rather than produce their own. The world of hotels has changed as well. Much more so than did hotels in the 1920s, modern hotels rely quite extensively upon electricity to provide for the needs of their guests and their employees.

Electricity is the most costly and widely used energy source within the hospitality industry. A high-quality, reliable source of electrical energy is required for the operation of equipment ranging from lights to computers to kitchen equipment to the air conditioning system. With the electric bill accounting for potentially as much as 90 percent of a property's utility costs, it is clear that controlling utility costs involves controlling electricity consumption in particular. Correct design, proper operation, and attention to the maintenance of electrical systems all contribute to a safe and comfortable environment for both guests and employees. And, as hoteliers in California were forcibly reminded during California's energy crunch in 2000 and 2001, and as many eastern U.S. hotels were reminded in the Northeast Blackout of 2003, reliable electrical supplies are crucial to daily operations.

A Brief Introduction to Electrical Systems

As illustrated in Exhibit 1, electrical systems consist of a source, a distribution system, and control devices connected to various pieces of equipment. A proper understanding of these components will help a building operator have a safe and efficient electrical supply system.

Some hospitality businesses produce their own power. Internationally, the term "combined heat and power" (CHP) is used to describe one mode of on-site power production.[2] In the United States, the term "cogeneration" is also used. Both of these terms refer to a situation where both a usable thermal output and electrical power are produced. This is done mostly with an engine generator, where the heat from the engine is used to heat water or as a heat source for a heat-driven (absorption) refrigeration system. Other variations exist as well.

Most hospitality operations, however, have their electricity delivered by a local utility. For some facilities located within larger complexes, the electricity may be provided by the building owner (who in turn generally gets it from the local utility). The utility is responsible for providing power at a correct voltage and frequency. The utility provides power through an electric meter that measures the rate and amount of power consumed. These data are used to generate the electric bill.

The utility services the building with electricity at a specified voltage and number of phases, with the capacity to deliver a rated amount of current at a given frequency. The **voltage** of the system is a measure of the electrical potential provided by the utility (often compared with water pressure in a water system). **Frequency** refers to the rate at which an alternating current (AC) power supply alternates the direction of the current flow. This frequency is 60 hertz, or cycles per second, for North American electric utilities, but is different elsewhere in the world; many countries use a 50-hertz system. The number of **phases** (which is almost always either one or three) refers to the number of energized or "hot" wires in the electrical supply. The ampere capability of the service refers to the maximum current flow (measured in **amperes**) for the system. It is essentially defined by the wire size feeding the building. When facilities are expanded or significant amounts of electrical equipment are added, it may be necessary to increase the size of the electrical wires, thus increasing the ability of the service to deliver more amperes. Rewiring is a common need during renovations of older buildings.

In practice, a small U.S. restaurant might have a 120/208 volt, 500-ampere, three-phase electrical service at a frequency of 60 hertz. Larger hotels, motels, or

Exhibit 1   Conceptual Diagram of Electrical Systems

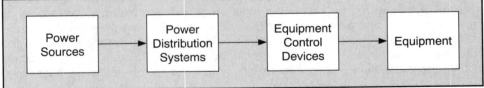

Power Sources → Power Distribution Systems → Equipment Control Devices → Equipment

On-Site Power Generation:

ICHP Microturbines at The Embassy Suites, Brea, California

Overview

The Embassy Suites Brea Hotel is a full-service hotel located in the central retail district of Brea, California. The hotel has 228 guestrooms, a 400-seat restaurant and lounge, conference and meeting rooms, an exercise area, an outdoor pool, and a spa. The hotel provides concierge, professional, and business services, and employs over 200 full- and part-time professional and service personnel. Challenged by rising energy costs and the strict environmental standards of the South Coast Air Quality Management District, the hotel provided an excellent opportunity for on-site power generation.

The Embassy Suites Brea Hotel management team collaborated with Power-House Energy (PHE) to reduce the expense of the hotel's electrical demand, as well as hot water and pool heating requirements. After a review of the technical and economic merits of a distributed generation (DG) energy system, the hotel management team approved a PHE-recommended Integrated Combined Heat and Power (ICHP) microturbine system. The microturbine system was installed and commissioned for use in June of 2003.

Technical Application

The microturbines were installed in parallel with the hotel's existing electrical utility connection provided by So Cal Edison. The microturbines run continuously to provide approximately 115 kw of electrical power to offset the hotel's average 300 kw electrical demand. Approximately 750,000 Btu/hr thermal heat output of the microturbines is recovered and circulated through a Unifin heat recovery unit and supplied to the domestic hot water storage tanks to offset the guestrooms, laundry, and kitchen thermal requirements. The captured thermal heat, using a 40° F temperature rise in the water that is pumped at 80 gpm through the heat recovery unit of the turbines and into the domestic hot water storage tank, reduces the operational run time of the hotel's two existing 1.2 million Btu/hr water heating boilers. The boilers remained in a reserve or backup capacity to the ICHP system, running only a couple hours per day in the winter months. The ICHP system provides virtually all of the domestic water heating needs during the summer months.

The outdoor pool heating is integrated to the DG energy system by a thermal heat exchanger, tying the domestic and pool hot water heating loops. The excess thermal heat, not utilized by the day or nighttime domestic demand of the hotel, is diverted to preheat the pool hot water loop. This uses about 90 percent of the thermal heat generated by the microturbines 100 percent of the time.

The installation uses two (2) 60 kw microturbines, one (1) Copeland natural gas compressor, and one (1) Unifin heat recovery unit. Installed inside an existing mechanical room with connections to a 200-amp electrical sub-panel and extended gas service, there is no impact to the operation of the hotel. Inlet air and exhaust fans are located in the exterior walls of the mechanical room to ensure proper ventilation and air circulation for the distributed generation energy system.

(continued)

Financial Results

PowerHouse Energy provided the "turn-key" installation under an Energy Service Agreement that guarantees an energy savings on the hotel's electrical and thermal energy costs over a 15-year period. PowerHouse Energy is responsible for the total installed cost, service, and maintenance for the 15-year energy contract. The hotel is billed on a monthly basis for the energy delivered at a savings over current utility costs, net of all operating costs and natural gas used in the operation of the system. The ICHP energy system provides over 35 percent of the hotel's electrical demand and over 64 percent of the thermal demand. Operating reliability, including start up and commissioning, in June has been 95 percent and 100 percent since July.

The microturbines' electrical output is reduced by about 10 percent in the extremes of summer temperatures; any decrease in electrical output in hot weather resulted in an *increase* in thermal output. The microturbines return to peak electrical output during the cooler temperatures throughout the year. The ICHP application qualified for the State of California's rebate of 30 percent on the total installed cost. Energy savings to the hotel has been very good, and will produce a net savings of about $18,000 per year, or $270,000 during the Energy Service Agreement. This savings to the hotel is net of natural gas and life-cycle maintenance costs. PHE had a total installed cost of $170,000, including the 30 percent state rebate.

Thanks to Sam Samsone of Embassy Suites Hotel for the opportunity to spotlight this distributed generation application!

PowerHouse Energy, 145 N. Sierra Madre Blvd. #4, Pasadena, California 91107

Source: www.powerhouseenergy.ws/ES_Brea_Final.pdf. Reprinted with permission.

restaurants would be served with a 277/480 volt, three-phase, 60-hertz system with a current capability of up to several thousand amperes.

After the electricity is metered, it enters the distribution and control system at the property. Exhibit 2 illustrates the layout of a building's electrical system. This

Exhibit 2   Diagram of a Building Electrical System

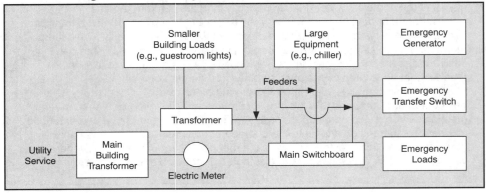

system splits the electrical supply into what are called **feeders**. Feeders deliver electricity to various portions of the building and to major equipment.

If the voltage supplied by the utility is not appropriate for all uses, the system will include **transformers**, which are devices that change (technically, *step up* or *step down*) the voltage of the electrical supply. In most large hospitality facilities, the major equipment is operated at 208/277 or 480 volts. When guestroom applications require (for example) 120 volts, a transformer is used to step down the voltage. The main service transformer for a building may be owned by either the utility or the operation. Utility ownership saves the operation the cost of the transformer and the energy it consumes and relieves the operation of the responsibility for its maintenance. On the other hand, the business owning its own main service transformer usually pays a lower utility rate. A hospitality business may also own and operate other transformers to meet its electrical needs.

As we will discuss later in the chapter, certain loads are considered to be emergency loads. These are supplied from the utility service under normal circumstances and from an emergency generator or battery backup in other circumstances. The emergency transfer switch in Exhibit 2 serves to detect the interruption of utility power. When utility power is interrupted, the switch activates the emergency power source and transfers the emergency loads to this source.

U.S. hotels should be aware that electrical equipment brought in by guests from other countries may not work at all, may work erratically, or may even be damaged when connected to a typical domestic electrical system. For example, equipment that requires a 240-volt power supply sometimes can be connected to a 120-volt system, but with a large decrease in performance. In addition, since most such equipment is expecting a 50-hertz signal, the use of the equipment at 60 hertz may create other problems. Any device using the 50-hertz signal for speed or time control will run faster on a 60-hertz signal, even when a transformer has changed the voltage to 240. There are also problems with the reverse situation—U.S. travelers staying in hotels abroad. A U.S. traveler who puts a plug adapter on something like a hair dryer (manufactured for the U.S. market) and tries to use it abroad may be greeted by sparks and a destroyed unit; this may even trip a circuit breaker in the hotel.

Plug configurations throughout the world are varied on purpose in an attempt to avoid the problems that can occur when equipment designed for one electrical system is plugged into another. Exhibit 3 shows plug configurations for electrical equipment in various countries.[3]

System Design and Operating Standards

The electrical distribution system at the property should be designed and maintained according to all relevant codes and standards. These codes and standards are established to provide safe and reliable sources of electrical power. Failure to follow the codes and standards can result in problems ranging from equipment failure to a major fire.

In the United States, electrical system codes are established by local governments. Generally, these codes are patterned after the ***National Electrical Code (NEC)*** developed by the National Fire Protection Association. The *NEC* and other

Exhibit 3   Plug Configurations Used in Overseas Locations

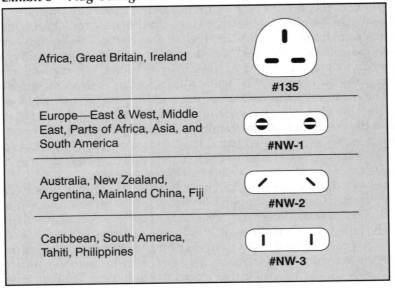

codes are primarily concerned with safety. Their provisions should be viewed as minimum standards. The *NEC* and similar local codes cover such topics as proper wire size and type (depending on the load and location), methods to determine circuit loading and capacity, proper wiring conventions, and so forth. The codes change over time as new information is discovered and new materials are developed.[4] An older facility making major renovations may need to extensively upgrade its electrical system—both to meet current electrical needs and to meet the current code. Safety issues for employees operating or maintaining electrical systems are covered in the National Fire Protection Association's "NFPA 70E—Electrical Safety in the Workplace."

Further legal requirements for electrical systems and safety are contained in the Occupational Safety and Health Act (OSHA). OSHA contains a large number of provisions for electrical safety. Major areas of concern include design safety standards for electrical systems, safety-related work practices, safety-related maintenance requirements, and safety requirements for special equipment. OSHA standards should be consulted when maintenance procedures are developed. They should also be included as minimum standards for electrical safety during maintenance.

System and Equipment Maintenance

Keeping electrical equipment from breaking down is particularly important, since this equipment is so critical to the ability to occupy the building. For an effective electrical maintenance program, the following are needed:

- A current set of plans for the building's electrical system

- Good knowledge of electrical practices and the building's electrical system by maintenance personnel (and others when appropriate)

- Good housekeeping practices in areas containing electrical equipment

- Knowledge of and adherence to proper safety procedures

- Incorporation of electrical maintenance procedures into the facility's preventive maintenance program

Electrical Plans

A number of building electrical systems have terminals in the guestrooms of a lodging facility. Therefore, the electrical plan of a guestroom provides a good reference for viewing a number of elements of the system. The electrical plan and the interior design plan must be closely coordinated to ensure that electrical services are provided at key locations.

Exhibit 4 is a copy of the electrical plan for a king guestroom. It also provides an introduction to some of the symbols used on electrical plans. This plan shows not only the electrical power systems, but also the location of the telephone, smoke detector, TV antenna, and thermostat. The wires of the electrical system are generally not shown on the plan, since they would clutter the representation.

Exhibit 5 is an electrical plan for a ballroom area. There are several differences between the electrical service of guestrooms and ballrooms. In this exhibit, Salon 3 is provided with a 208-volt, three-phase electrical receptacle. This provides a power source for larger equipment. Each salon has a "fused disconnect, 400 A total" that provides three-phase electrical service access for special needs such as entertainment lighting needs. In addition, each salon also has a 120-volt, 30-amp receptacle to provide for possible large single voltage power requirements (a typical guestroom receptacle would most likely be only capable of providing 15 or 20 amps). The ballroom area also provides additional audiovisual support in each salon area, including provisions for ceiling connections used by theatrical lighting or ceiling mounted projectors.

A building's electrical plans will be quite extensive. A major challenge is to keep them current as modifications are made to the building. While updating plans is sometimes not thought of as a maintenance activity, it should be. Operations that do not update plans are essentially relying on the memories of their maintenance personnel. Such operations invariably find that, as the years pass, their maintenance employees leave or retire, taking important information about the building with them. A good set of plans on file can greatly speed the solution of a problem and may save a lot of money during renovations or other modifications to the building.

Training in Operating and Safety Procedures

Maintenance staff and other key personnel should receive training in those aspects of the building's electrical system that are pertinent to their jobs. Their performance evaluations should then be based in part on their knowledge and

Exhibit 4   Sample Electrical Plan for a King Guestroom

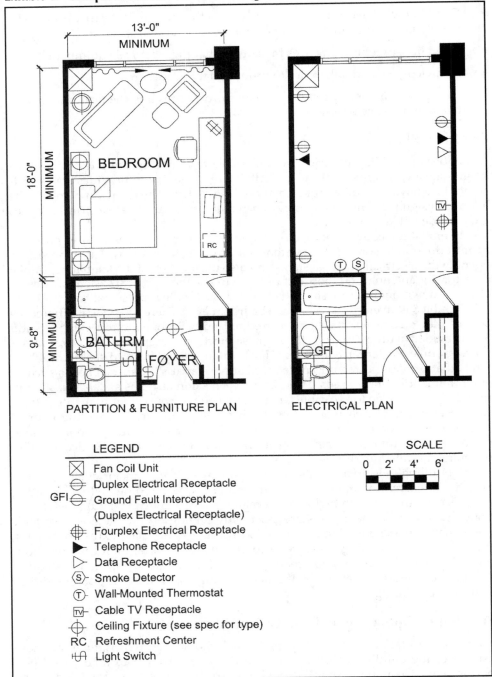

Exhibit 5   Sample Electrical Plan for a Ballroom

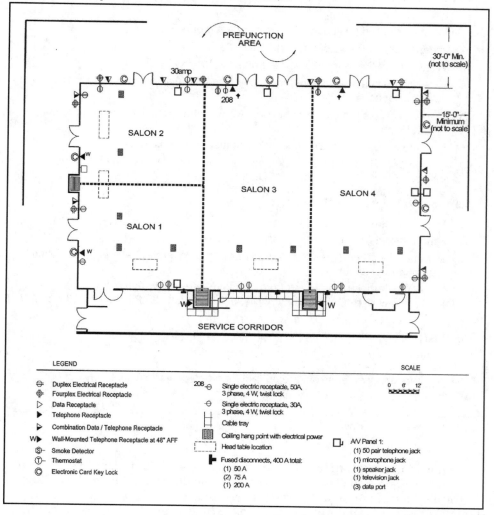

understanding of the system. Maintenance staff should be given a set of questions related to the building's electrical system. These questions should be part of their training program. The questions can also be used to test employees being considered for retention and/or promotion. It may also be advisable for the property to receive a magazine that covers electrical practices that can be read and referred to by engineering personnel.[5]

Basic questions about electrical system practices could also be included as part of an employment questionnaire for prospective maintenance staff in order to verify an applicant's competence with electrical systems (see Exhibit 6). Competence can be further verified by asking an applicant to demonstrate basic skills, such as wiring a circuit or testing a circuit for problems.

Exhibit 6   Screening Questions for Prospective Maintenance Staff

1. What color of wire is used for an equipment ground?
2. What color of wire is used for your power source?
3. What causes a hermetic motor compressor burnout?
4. How do you check a compressor to see if its windings are grounded to the compressor case?
5. If a three-phase motor is running backwards, what should you do to correct the problem?
6. How much voltage drop does it take to cause problems to a motor?
7. How many terminals does a domestic hermetic motor usually have? Name them.

Answers to Above Questions*

1. Green or bare.
2. Any color but green, white, or bare.
3. Moisture, high head pressure, single phasing on a three-phase unit, start winding not dropping out.
4. With an ohmmeter, you check for grounding between the case of the compressor to the start, run, and common windings and between the start and the run.
5. Switch any two legs of power to the motor.
6. Ten percent.
7. Three—(1) Start, (2) Run, (3) Common (Neutral)

*Note: Although these answers are correct for many countries, they may not be correct in every country.

Courtesy of Hampton Inns, Inc.

While most hotel staff members do not need specific training in electrical fundamentals, certain staff clearly need to have some understanding of the building's electrical system. Staff on duty at the front desk, especially in the evening hours, should know the location of circuit breakers and controls for various electrical systems, especially if an engineer is not always on duty. Staff should also know the location of the electrical disconnect switch for the building and the emergency generator. Staff responsiveness to guest and staff needs can be enhanced by clear labeling of breakers and controls.

Hotel staff members should also have a familiarity with the characteristics of the hotel's electrical system (voltage, frequency) and be able to answer guest inquiries as to the basic compatibility of foreign electrical equipment such as shavers, hair dryers, computers, and so on. Staff should also know where guests can find adapter plugs, either in the hotel or in nearby stores.

All staff members should be made aware of the importance of reporting needed electrical repairs and of not operating equipment that has become unsafe due to electrical (or other) problems. Staff-caused electrical maintenance needs can be reduced if staff members observe good operating practices, which include the following:

- Keep equipment that uses electricity clean.

- Avoid storage of this equipment in damp or wet locations.

- Use a firm grip on the plug when unplugging equipment rather than pulling on the electrical cord.

- Match the equipment to the task. Overloading equipment may result in motor failure or other problems.

- Promptly report malfunctioning electrical equipment so that needed repairs can be performed.

- Do not perform do-it-yourself repairs or modifications to electrical systems and equipment.

- Do not use electrical rooms for the storage of items that block access to electrical panels, reduce air circulation to transformer rooms, or otherwise create potential safety problems or contribute to premature equipment failure.

When electrical maintenance is performed, safety concerns are very important. Lockout/tagout procedures should *always* be followed when work is performed on electrical equipment. (In the United States, OSHA mandates their use.) This involves locking out of service those circuits to be worked on so that another individual cannot accidentally energize the circuits while someone is working on them. Exhibit 7 presents excerpts from the procedures and forms used at one hospitality firm.

Electrical safety can often be an issue even in non-electrical maintenance. Because electrical service is needed for so many uses, electrical wiring can be found almost everywhere. Care must be taken when performing other maintenance tasks to avoid accidental contact with electrical lines. The following are some key safety tips:

- When performing on-site excavations, refer to a site map for the location of any buried electrical cables (or other utility services). This is one more reason to keep a good set of as-built and modified drawings. If any questions exist, use a cable locator to determine the exact location. Anyone using on-site cranes, hoists, and front end loaders should always watch for overhead electrical lines. It is often easy to overlook these while concentrating on the load or the ground.

- Avoid electrical service locations when painting eaves and drain troughs or doing other work on the roof or sides of buildings.

- Avoid downed electric wires. Keep people away from these and call the electric company immediately.

- Avoid any tree or limb touching electrical wires. If a tree or limb falls over the wires, don't attempt to remove it. Call the electric company.

- Wear safety glasses and rubber-soled and -heeled safety shoes when working.

Exhibit 7   Sample Safety Lockout Procedures

SAFETY LOCKOUT SHUTDOWN PROCEDURES

Depending on the type of equipment that is shut down for service or repair, the employee responsible for the shutdown must do one of the following:

Lockout the electrical disconnect and apply the appropriate lockout tag,

or

Throw the breaker at the electrical panel and attach the appropriate lockout tag,

or

Shut off the valve or equipment at the service location and apply the appropriate lockout tag.

If any piece of equipment is removed from service for a period of eight (8) hours or more, the reason for the lockout MUST be recorded in the Engineer's Log Book.

Failure to comply with the safety lockout procedures will result in the issuance of a written warning or possible employee termination.

THE ONLY PERSON AUTHORIZED TO REMOVE A WARNING TAG OR SAFETY LOCK IS THE EMPLOYEE WHO LOCKED OUT THE EQUIPMENT OR THE MAINTENANCE ENGINEER/AGM FACILITIES.

ELECTRICIAN'S BLOCKING TAG

FRONT   BACK

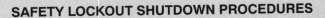

DANGER

ELECTRICIAN'S BLOCKING TAG

SWITCH HAS BEEN BLOCKED TO PROTECT MY LIFE WHILE WORKING ON THIS CIRCUIT. TAG TO BE REMOVED ONLY BY ME.

Signed by _____

Date _____

DANGER

ELECTRICIAN'S BLOCKING TAG
DO NOT OPERATE THIS EQUIPMENT
I HAVE TAKEN THE FOLLOWING STEPS BEFORE WORKING ON THIS CIRCUIT

1. _____
2. _____
3. _____
4. _____
5. _____

Signed by _____

Date _____

Courtesy of Hampton Inns, Inc.

One other concern warrants attention. Older electrical transformers that contain oil as an insulating/cooling medium may contain PCBs (polychlorinated biphenyls). If an electrical fire occurs involving these transformers, dangerous chemicals can be produced. The U.S. government (through the Environmental Protection Agency) has issued numerous rules and regulations that establish conditions for the continued use of these transformers in commercial buildings. These rules and regulations cover such topics as registration with the local fire department, limitations on where these transformers can be located within the building, procedures for their removal and disposal, and a variety of other matters. A failure to comply with these rules and regulations may result in significant fines and other penalties, so management should know and comply with them. Hotel managers should contact the EPA for a complete set of regulations if they believe that PCB-containing transformers are present at their properties.

System Components

We have already looked briefly at transformers and feeders. Other components of the electrical system are fuses and circuit breakers; distribution panels and wiring; electric motors, controls, and drive elements; electronic equipment; emergency power systems; and electrical maintenance equipment.

Fuses and Circuit Breakers

Some elements of the electrical system—i.e., fuses and circuit breakers—are quite literally designed to "break down." Fuses and circuit breakers serve to interrupt the electrical supply when a current flow in excess of safe levels is detected. Safe levels are determined by the carrying capacity of the wires and local code requirements.

Fuses, more common in old properties, are designed and sized to fail when the current in the circuit in which they are installed is too great for the circuit capacity. The fuse failure indicates either an existing safety problem due to a short circuit or a potential safety problem due to wire overloading. Some fuses have a replaceable element and reusable fuse body, while others are completely disposable. Fuses may be screw-in plugs or cylindrical cartridges with either cylindrical ends or (knife) blade ends.

When fuses are used, care should be taken to replace them with units of the correct amperage and type. When installed on circuits with electric motors, fuses are often of a time-delay type. Such fuses allow a brief flow of higher current without burning out; this is necessary because a higher current is needed to start the motor than to keep it running. If regular fuses are used in place of time-delay fuses, they may fail whenever a motor starts.

Circuit breakers serve a similar function, but differ from fuses in that the circuit breaker may simply be reset, while the fuse or fuse element must be replaced. Normally, a tripped circuit breaker merely must be turned off and then back on. The ease of resetting these devices and their inherent safety make them the device of choice for many applications today.

One type of circuit breaker is the **ground fault circuit interrupter (GFCI)**. This device, which provides a much higher level of protection than a standard circuit breaker, is largely designed to protect people. GFCIs are installed in such areas as bathrooms, outside receptacles, swimming pools, spas, and other areas where required by code, usually where electricity and water may both be found. A GFCI may be part of the wall receptacle or it may be a separate breaker in the breaker box. A built-in testing device is included. GFCIs should be tested as part of regular preventive maintenance activities.

Fuses or circuit breakers should never be replaced with items of a larger capacity (amperage) unless an analysis of the circuit reveals that the wiring and other elements are capable of handling the larger load.

The burning out of fuses or tripping of circuit breakers—especially if it is frequent—is a sign of a potential problem with the electrical system that should not be ignored. Maintenance personnel should inspect fuse and breaker boxes, looking for debris and dirt; moisture; and discoloration, a burnt odor, or other evidence of overheating or short circuits.

To avoid potential problems with vandalism and with electrical system tampering, fuse and breaker boxes should be kept locked. The key should be in the control of maintenance personnel or otherwise secured. Of course, it should always be readily available when needed.

Distribution Panels and Wiring

Next to the fuse and breaker boxes are the panels and wiring that distribute electricity to the building and its equipment. While these elements generally do not require much maintenance, there are preventive maintenance activities that may be undertaken with panels and wiring. Loose connections or overloaded wires can create safety hazards—for example, overheating can cause a fire. In addition, overheating and overloading can cause equipment to operate at conditions of voltage and current that lead to inefficient operation and even damage or failure.

Diagnosing problems in distribution panels and wiring is made easier when the following preventive maintenance actions are carried out:

- Check the tightness of all wiring connections to ensure adequate electrical contact.

- Measure the current flow in electrical circuits to be sure it is within acceptable limits.

- Measure supply voltages to electrical equipment to be sure proper voltage levels exist. This should be done under load (operating) conditions.

- Check the operating temperatures of wires, motors, and other elements of the electrical system. These should be within the rated limits of the equipment.

- Check the temperature rise in wires, terminal blocks, and motors. Values of 15 to 25 Fahrenheit degrees (8 to 14 Celsius degrees) above ambient may indicate potential problems, while those in the range of 45 to 90 Fahrenheit degrees (25 to 50 Celsius degrees) above ambient warrant immediate attention.

- Check the flow of electricity in three-phase circuits and supplies to ensure that the load on the three phases is approximately balanced.

Some older hotels may have aluminum electrical cables in lieu of the more common copper wires. Aluminum is a good conductor of electricity and is less expensive than copper. For these reasons, its use enjoyed a period of popularity some years ago. Unfortunately, aluminum suffers from a physical phenomenon called "creep" or cold flow that causes connections, especially those using set screws or crimps, to loosen. Loose connections cause temperature buildups and can be very dangerous. Properties with aluminum wire need to enforce a regular maintenance schedule to ensure tight connections. Later in the chapter the use of thermal imaging will be discussed as a diagnostic tool for overloaded electrical circuits. This is also a very useful tool to identify loose connections in aluminum wiring systems.

Electric Motors, Controls, and Drive Elements

Electric motors are found in many devices in a hospitality operation—for example, air conditioning equipment, vacuum cleaners, dishwashers, and the laundry. In addition, large motors power major pieces of building equipment such as the compressors in the chillers, air handling fans, and chilled water pumps.

Electric motors that are integral parts of other equipment, such as motors in dishwashers and guestroom air conditioning equipment, will be included in the overall preventive maintenance instructions for the equipment. Some equipment with hard-to-access electric motors may have little or no preventive maintenance performed. The level of preventive maintenance performed will vary significantly with motor size and the motor's importance to the operation. Remember, the goal of preventive maintenance is to help keep the *overall* cost of maintenance as low as possible while promoting proper and reliable equipment operation.

The preventive maintenance process will involve regular inspections during which operating conditions (such as voltage, current, and operating temperatures) are measured and noted; general conditions, noise, and vibration are observed; and cleaning and lubrication are performed. Operating conditions may indicate a need to change the frequency of maintenance. For example, a particularly dirty environment may warrant more frequent cleaning and inspection.

Exhibit 8 contains a sample preventive maintenance procedure for electric motors from one lodging chain. Quarterly activities involve inspection, cleaning, and lubrication. Annual actions include those normally performed quarterly, plus additional inspections, the measurement of key operating parameters, and some parts replacement. Because of the variety of electric motors and their applications, it is very important to write preventive maintenance procedures for each motor based on its type, its usage (especially its operating hours), and the manufacturer's recommendations for maintenance. Equipment warranties can often be voided if the purchaser does not follow the manufacturers' established maintenance procedures.

When electric motors are used to power larger devices, they do so via some sort of drive mechanism. This may be a belt and pulley, a drive chain, or some

Exhibit 8 **Sample Preventive Maintenance for Electric Motors**

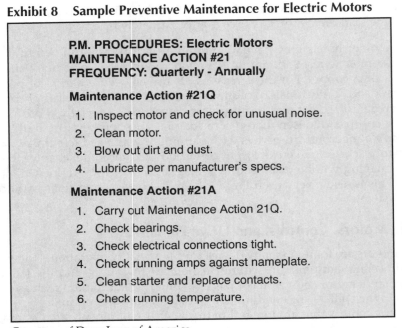

P.M. PROCEDURES: Electric Motors
MAINTENANCE ACTION #21
FREQUENCY: Quarterly - Annually

Maintenance Action #21Q

1. Inspect motor and check for unusual noise.
2. Clean motor.
3. Blow out dirt and dust.
4. Lubricate per manufacturer's specs.

Maintenance Action #21A

1. Carry out Maintenance Action 21Q.
2. Check bearings.
3. Check electrical connections tight.
4. Check running amps against nameplate.
5. Clean starter and replace contacts.
6. Check running temperature.

Courtesy of Days Inns of America.

sort of drive coupling. Preventive maintenance inspections of this equipment will involve not only the motor but also the drive mechanism.

In addition, the motor controls will need periodic attention. Motor controls are devices that provide an interface between an electric motor and the electrical system. They control the motor's operation, generally by turning it on and off, but sometimes by changing its operating speed. Relays also serve a control function; they open and close circuits in response to signals from control equipment.

When motors wear out or malfunction and cease operation, managers face a "repair or replace" decision. Generally, the best choice is probably to replace the motor, especially if it is an older motor in a critical location or is difficult to remove.

Electric motors can operate for a long time, and over their lifetime they can use a large amount of electricity. Operating costs of an electric motor can be ten to fifty times the motor's purchase price. For this reason, purchasing energy-efficient electric motors should be a high priority for facilities managers.[6]

Another way to reduce the operating costs of electric motors is to install variable-speed drives on the motors. Variable-speed drives match the speed of the motor to the needs of the connected load, making the motor run more efficiently. The result is reduced energy usage, increased life of the connected equipment, and a better matching of motor output to the application.[7]

Finally, when considering electric motors and their operation, attention to the motors' power factors is appropriate. "Power factor" is another measure of motor efficiency, having to do with the motor's use of alternating current and voltage. The goal should be to operate equipment with power factors in excess of 90 percent.

Electric Motor Replacement Issues

Hospitality operations use numerous electric motors, some contained in equipment and others connected to equipment such as fans and pumps. When purchasing equipment, the efficiency of the electric motor used in the equipment is a contributing factor to the equipment's overall efficiency. However, it is often the case that there are few or no motor options to choose from when purchasing equipment; a piece of equipment tends to come with a standard motor, and no choice is given. It is when electric motors are up for repair or replacement that the operation has the opportunity to make a decision about motor efficiency.

In the United States, new government regulations have established minimum efficiency levels for electric motors. The motors sold today are therefore more efficient than those sold fifteen to twenty years ago. It is possible to purchase motors that exceed these minimum efficiencies. This especially makes sense when the hotel is in a location with high electricity rates or when it is purchasing motors that are expected to have a large number of operating hours.

When purchasing a replacement for an electric motor, it is a very good idea to inquire as to whether the motor being replaced was correctly sized to begin with. Unfortunately, motors are often significantly oversized, and conservation efforts can make this situation worse by reducing the load served by the motor. If investigation reveals an oversized motor (that is, a motor that always operates at a current draw of approximately 85 percent or less of its full load amperage), managers should consider replacing it with a smaller motor. The property will not only save money on the motor, but also on the operating cost of the motor.

When motors are operated below about 65 percent of rated capacity, their power factor suffers. Making the right decision on motor size helps to keep the power factor as high as possible. The result can be reduced electric bills.

Electronic Equipment

Although electric motors have long been subject to various power supply problems, the proliferation of electronic equipment in the modern hospitality industry has heightened the need for a high-quality electrical supply system. Electronic equipment is especially sensitive to such power-quality problems as voltage transients, momentary voltage sags and surges, momentary power loss, electrical noise, and harmonic distortion. (To a somewhat lesser degree, these power-quality problems can also harm electric motors.)

Transients involve high voltage, short, fast electrical pulses that can destroy electronic equipment instantly or over a period of time. Sags and surges involve lower- or higher-than-normal voltages. Sags may cause motor heating and disk drive problems, while surges may cause incandescent lights and computer circuits to burn out. Momentary power losses can disrupt data processing, electronic memory, and program functioning. Electrical noise and harmonic distortion are electrical signals injected into the electrical system by faulty equipment or certain types of electric equipment. They give wrong "signals" to sensitive electrical equipment, resulting in erratic operation and possible equipment damage.

The sources of these problems include natural phenomena (for example, lightning), normal utility operations (for example, equipment maintenance), neighboring utility customers (for example, a faulty electrical system in the business next door), and a business's own internal electrical problems. There are various possible solutions to electrical quality problems.[8] These include:

- Wiring-intensive solutions such as wiring upgrades, grounding/bonding upgrades, and isolation of equipment loads.

- Equipment-intensive solutions such as surge-suppression equipment, voltage regulators, isolation transformers, and battery backup units.

Wiring upgrades involve the installation of large wires capable of handling the larger starting and operating loads of equipment. Such upgrades should help to eliminate voltage sags. Upgrading of grounding/bonding involves establishing good connections within the building to the electrical ground system and of the ground to the earth. This will help reduce stray voltages that can create noise problems. Load isolation places sensitive loads on separate circuits where the possibility of their being influenced by noise, sags, and other problems caused by other pieces of equipment is minimized. Exhibit 9 shows suggested equipment isolation where the "victim" is the electronic equipment and the "culprit" is another type of electrical equipment. Also, operations should not operate portable equipment such as vacuum cleaners and other cleaning equipment on circuits that supply electronic equipment.

The equipment-intensive solutions will generally be the more expensive option, although extensive rewiring can also be costly. Surge suppression equipment limits the magnitude of voltage transients in order to avoid damage to sensitive electronic equipment. Installation of surge suppressors may be necessary at the electrical service entrance itself, at the electrical panel where the circuit feeding the electronic equipment is located, or at the electronic equipment itself. Data lines feeding the equipment and such items as antenna leads are also candidates for this type of protection. Equipment purchased for this purpose should be UL (Underwriters Laboratories) listed as a transient voltage surge suppressor and should have indicators that reveal whether it is functioning.

Voltage regulators address both sag and surge problems by providing automatic voltage adjustment. Response times of 1.5 cycles or less and operating efficiencies of 90 percent or better are recommended. Isolation transformers help remove noise from the system, but provide no protection against sags or surges. The device's ability to reduce noise is expressed in a dB (decibel) rating. A rating of 80 dB or higher should be chosen for adequate noise reduction.

Battery backup units help to supply power during utility power outages. These units are discussed in the emergency power systems section which follows below.

Exhibit 10 is a summary of the more common symptoms associated with electrical system disturbances, the problems that may cause them, the solutions, and a range of costs. The cost-effectiveness of any particular solution is clearly dependent on how likely the problem is to occur and the cost of the symptom. Many operations find that some form of protective equipment is warranted due to

Exhibit 9   Equipment Isolation Chart

Do not connect equipment shown in the victim column of this chart into the same circuit as devices in the corresponding culprit column.		
PROBLEM	**VICTIM**	**CULPRIT**
SAGS and SURGES	Check/Credit Approval System Main/Personal Computer Order-Entry Terminal	Air Conditioning Unit Conventional Oven HVAC Equipment Industrial Mixer Refrigeration Equipment Water Cooler
TRANSIENTS	Bar Code Scanner Check/Credit Approval System Digital Scale Fax Machine Fire/Security System Main/Personal Computer Order-Entry Terminal Phone System Point-of-Sale Terminal Video Product Display	Conventional Oven HVAC Equipment Industrial Mixer Lighting Control Refrigeration Equipment
NOISE	Audio System Energy Management System Fax Machine Fire/Security System Phone System	Copy Machine HVAC Equipment Industrial Mixer Refrigeration Equipment

Source: Edison Electric Institute, *Quality Power in Your Restaurant,* p. 13.

the large losses of time and money that can result from problems with electronic equipment.

Emergency Power Systems

Emergency power systems are present to provide power during temporary interruptions in the electrical supply to the building. Emergency power supplies and equipment include such items as generators and batteries to provide lighting, and uninterruptible power supplies for computer systems. Although these devices are (one hopes) seldom used, they are greatly needed when called upon; therefore, their proper operation is very important.

The impact of power outages on hotel operations could be seen during the Northeast Blackout of 2003, a power outage affecting large areas of the northeastern and midwestern United States and the province of Ontario in Canada. Affected hotels found themselves without electricity for (on average) sixteen hours, with some forced to function without power for days. Fortunately, there was no serious injury of people or damage to property, in part because this outage occurred on a warm summer day. If the outage had happened on a subfreezing, snowy winter

Exhibit 10   Power Problem Ready-Reference

SYMPTON	PROBLEM	SOLUTION	COST
Scanner Lockup Scanner Damage Inventory Data Lost Frequent Service Calls Digital Scale Damage	Transients (Spikes)	Transient Suppression	$1,000 to $7,000
Computer Reboots Early Compressor Failure Dim or Flickering Lights Early Lamp Failure	Sags and Surges	Upgrade Wiring Rearrange Loads Line Conditioner	$500 to $20,000
Order Files Lost Scanners and Computer Must be Restarted	Power Loss (Blackout)	Battery Backup System Reduce Exposure	$500 to $30,000
Unexplainable Order Errors Noise on PA System Random Data Error	Noise	Line Conditioner Battery Backup System Relocate Equipment Isolation Transformer	$500 to $20,000
Compressor Heating	Harmonic Distortion	Harmonic Filtering	$500 to $5,000

Source: Edison Electric Institute, *Quality Power in Your Restaurant,* p. 15.

day, the results might well have been more serious. As it was, hotel guests and employees could still comfortably settle outside without fear of freezing, and the buildings had no risk of frozen pipes due to lack of heat. While the consequences could easily have been worse, the performance of hotels during this period of time clearly indicated gaps in their ability to function during a serious power outage. A study of the blackout provided some interesting information. Exhibit 11 shows the impact of the outage on various building systems. Only half of the hotels studied indicated they had anything more than a battery backup for emergency power.

Hoteliers also recognize that having power when others don't can lead to an amazing boost in business. During 2013 there were a number of extended power outages in various parts of the United States. News coverage of these outages included interviews with hotel managers whose hotels had power and were suddenly filled with people attempting to either escape the heat (in the case of summer outages) or the cold (during winter outages). When serious power outages occur, hotels within the outage area that are still operating under emergency

Exhibit 11   Effect of the Northeast Blackout of 2003 on Hotel Facilities and Processes

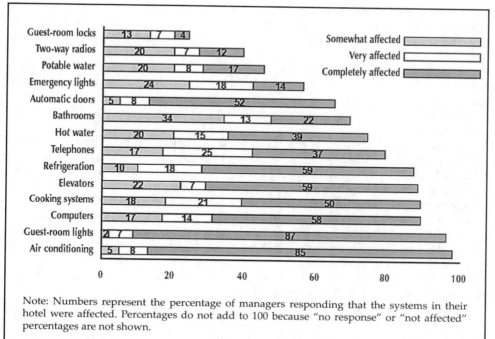

Note: Numbers represent the percentage of managers responding that the systems in their hotel were affected. Percentages do not add to 100 because "no response" or "not affected" percentages are not shown.

Source: Robert J. Kwortnik, *CHR Reports (When the Lights Went Out: Hotel Managers' Perceptions of the Blackout of '03)* 4, no. 4 (2004): 15.

power or those hotels near but outside the affected area (that is, hotels still operating normally because their electrical power supply was not disrupted) can expect to attract a lot of business.[9]

The *National Electrical Code* provides for specific types of businesses in which emergency power is required and the types of loads that must be connected to this power. Local code authorities may adopt this code or may modify it. Emergency systems are generally required in all types of hospitality businesses, with the possible exception of very small food service establishments. Among the items generally required to be connected to an emergency power system are artificial illumination, fire detection and alarm systems, fire pumps, and public safety communications systems.

Battery backup units may be either standby power supply (SPS) units or uninterruptible power supply (UPS) units. SPS units switch from utility power to battery backup when the utility power is interrupted; there is therefore a momentary power outage. One selection criterion for such equipment is the transfer time, which should be no more than fifteen milliseconds. Another criterion involves voltage regulation, which should be within 8 percent of the rated equipment operating voltage.

In contrast, a UPS unit is always on line. Power from the utility feeds the UPS, which stores this power in batteries and supplies the equipment with a "clean" power source using the batteries and electronics that create AC power. For UPS selection, efficiencies of 70 percent or more should be specified. For both UPS and SPS systems, the quoted prices of the systems should include the necessary batteries.

Emergency power may be provided by batteries alone in small buildings. Batteries will generally power lights in corridors, stairwells, and certain interior spaces such as meeting and conference rooms. If more than this level of power is needed, the operation will generally install an on-site emergency generator powered by an engine.

On-site engine generators may be installed to operate only essential or code-required loads (such as emergency lighting and fire protection systems) or may be installed to provide power to additional loads. Among these additional loads could be the uninterruptible power supply for the computer systems, food service refrigeration, and key building heating systems (especially in colder climates). Engine generators are usually diesel-fired and require on-site fuel storage. Various provisions should be made to prevent the unit from transmitting noise and vibration to the building. Emergency loads are connected to the emergency generator by an automatic emergency transfer switch (as was seen in Exhibit 2). This device supplies these loads from the utility service when it is present and switches to the emergency source when utility service fails.

Because code requirements usually call for a fuel supply capable of providing only two hours of full-load operation, the generator is of limited usefulness during long outages unless provision is made for extended operation. Battery-powered lighting systems provide light for even shorter periods of time.

Maintenance of emergency power systems is often a weekly task that involves the following:

- Checking fluid levels on battery systems. (Note: Batteries may be installed to provide emergency lighting or to provide starting energy for an engine generator.)

- Checking the charge level in batteries.

- Checking proper ventilation of battery rooms.

- Cleaning and lubricating battery terminals to retard corrosion.

- Testing engine generator systems under load. Because of the noise generated, maintenance staff should generally wear ear protection when doing this and should choose a time of day least likely to disturb guests.

- Observing and recording appropriate data regarding each engine generator test. This will include information required by local code authorities and for maintenance records, such as fuel supply, oil and coolant levels, switch settings, oil and water temperatures and pressures, and positions of any key indicator lights or gauges.

- Ensuring that the engine generator is put back on line after any testing or work where the emergency generator must be disconnected.

A properly functioning emergency power system provides insurance in the event of a power failure. The testing and maintenance of the system ensures that this insurance will be available when needed.

While it is not required by code, many operations install an uninterruptible power supply on key pieces of computer equipment. The UPS may be designed to allow either continued operation or an orderly shutdown of equipment. UPS units must be matched with the load being served and the time of operation desired. Computer operation during prolonged outages will be ensured only if the UPS is also connected to the emergency power system.

Installation of an emergency generator can also result in cost savings for hotels. It is possible for a hotel to configure its emergency generator to operate during peak electrical demand periods and thus reduce the peak power demand of the hotel. This can result in a substantial reduction in the hotel's demand charge (and sometimes in the energy charge as well). In some areas where the power grid is heavily loaded, electric utilities have requested that hotels and other commercial businesses use their emergency generators for this purpose, and have offered a reduced electricity rate for those businesses that comply.

Electrical Maintenance Equipment

The various maintenance activities discussed so far require appropriate equipment. This equipment should include the following somewhat specialized items:

- *Multimeter*—A device capable of measuring volts, ohms, and current over a wide range. Usable on both major electrical circuits and control and other lower-voltage circuits.

- *Wall receptacle analyzer*—Used to determine the condition of wall outlets (sometimes called convenience outlets). This device plugs into a wall outlet and indicates the circuit condition. Reversal of the neutral and ground wires, the quality of the ground path, and the presence of multiple wiring errors are identified if present. This is a quick diagnostic for these components.

- *Fuse pullers for cartridge fuses*—These devices allow safe removal of cartridge fuses.

- *Rubber boots, gloves, and insulated ladders*—Safety equipment designed to reduce the contact with electrical equipment and the resulting flow of current to earth if contact should occur.

- *Hydrometer*—A device that measures specific gravity and is used to check the charge level in batteries.

Other electrical maintenance equipment that may be needed, depending on the complexity of the facility and the expected duties of the staff, could include cable fault locators, transformer oil test kits, and vibration analyzers.

Because of the difficulty in accurately measuring temperatures in all elements of electrical systems, it is becoming more common for properties to use a thermal scan of the electrical systems as part of their preventive maintenance program. This scan involves the use of an infrared (IR) video imaging system that represents the object being scanned as an image whose color indicates the temperature of the object. The scan identifies overheating electrical components. Hence, it is possible to inspect the operating electrical system for potential safety or operating problems.

A thermal imaging inspection is generally a contract service. It may be implemented as part of commissioning a new building or as an element of the preventive maintenance program of an existing building. It can be particularly useful for older buildings having extensive wiring modifications that make the connected loads, wire size, and so forth difficult to evaluate. Chains and large hotels may elect to purchase IR scanning guns in order to have them available when needed.

Electric Utility Billing and Building Operations

As was indicated at the start of the chapter, the electric bill represents the bulk of a property's utility costs. Understanding the billing methods of electric utilities and their impact on building operations and operating costs can be very helpful.

First of all, there are thousands of electric utilities in the United States and throughout the world. Virtually every one will have a slightly different way of converting electrical usage into an electric bill. Almost all of these utilities will generate a bill for a commercial establishment such as a hotel, motel, or restaurant in a somewhat different manner from that used for a residence. The major difference lies in the use of both an **energy** (or consumption) **charge** and a **demand** (or capacity) **charge** when commercial bills are determined. Residences typically only have an energy charge.

Sample Electric Bill Calculation

Let's use the sample electric utility rate sheets found in the appendix to this chapter to calculate a monthly utility bill for a hotel. The meter reading for the hotel shows it has a peak demand of 700 kw and uses a total of 300,000 kwh in a summer month. According to this rate sheet, the hotel will be billed for time-of-day usage, so we need to know how much energy is used during peak and off-peak periods. Peak periods run from 9 A.M. to 10 P.M. on Monday through Friday except on holidays. The utility will meter usage in each period. Our hotel uses 200,000 kwh off peak and 100,000 on peak.

Customer Charge	$ 39.93	
Demand Charge	9,968.00	700 kw × $14.24 per kw
Off-Peak Energy	4,682.00	200,000 kwh × $.02341 per kwh
On-Peak Energy	5,599.00	100,000 kwh × $.05599 per kwh
Total	$20,288.93	

This calculation illustrates the potentially large amount of a commercial building's electrical bill that may come from the demand charge (almost half in this instance). The calculation does not show another charge generally present: sales tax. In addition, a variable fuel charge is sometimes added to the bill.

The energy charge is based on the amount of electricity used by the customer over the billing period. This electricity is measured in *kilowatt-hours* (abbreviated kwh). The kwh may be thought of as the amount of energy used by a 100-watt light bulb burning for ten hours. As you can guess, the kwh isn't a very large unit of energy. A commercial establishment can use tens or hundreds of thousands of kwh in a thirty-day period (the typical billing period used by utilities). The charge is usually in the range of $.06 to $.10 per kwh for business accounts. However, the cost per kwh can be substantially higher. In Hawaii and Puerto Rico, for example, this cost is approximately $.30 per kwh, and in a number of East Coast states and California, prices range from $0.12 to $0.15 per kwh. The cost for electricity outside the United States can be double the U.S. cost. European countries may have average electricity costs in the $.10 to $.20 per kwh range.

The demand charge is something that residential customers generally do not pay (although they pay a higher charge per kwh than business customers do). The demand charge is based on the business's highest *rate* of energy usage. This rate, measured in *kilowatts,* or kw, is usually determined by breaking the billing period up into a series of fifteen- or thirty-minute windows and measuring the energy usage in each window. The bill is then calculated using the highest average rate of energy usage or demand in these windows during the billing period. Demand charges range from $3 per kw per month to as high as $20 per kw per month.

One way to think about the demand and energy charges is to think about the way rental car agencies bill for their product. Among the options is usually one that charges you a fee per day for the auto and a fee per mile. The fee per day is analogous to the demand charge. Just as the larger the auto, the higher the fee, so the bigger the demand, the higher the demand charge. The fee per mile is analogous to the energy charge. The more you use the auto, the more you pay, just as the more energy you use, the more you pay.

Just as there are variations in rental car rate structures, there are variations in the structures of utility rates. Some utilities have rates that vary according to the time of year or time of day. Others have variations that depend on the relationship between the demand level and the energy used. Yet others will impose a minimum demand charge based on demand during some peak period of the year (rather than just during the current billing period). Under this billing practice, known in utility jargon as a **ratchet clause**, a high demand during one month can result in a high demand charge for the next eleven or twelve months. Often, the peak periods on which ratchet charges are based are months in which utility services are heavily used—summer months in cities and the southern United States, and winter months in northern locations.

Because the demand charge is based on peak demand during fifteen- or thirty-minute windows, operating practices can have a major impact on costs. One seasonally operated hotel that was up for sale turned on all the building's systems, lights, and so forth to prove to a prospective buyer that everything worked properly. This action established a high peak demand during a ratchet period and led directly to higher charges for several months. A more common scenario involves the start-up of building equipment following a shutdown or a power outage. Starting everything at once leads to high demand. Starting such equipment up in phases helps avoid an unusually high demand charge. One way to do this is to station an employee at the electric meter. This employee can follow the effect of equipment operations and communicate with other staff by phone or radio. Of course, operators with demand control equipment should be able to use it in this instance, provided the power loss or shutdown does not cause the demand control equipment to need re-setting or re-programming.

The energy and demand charges represent by far the largest portion of the utility bill. The mix between the two varies with the utility and the building. Some utilities have billing methods that weight the energy portion, while others weight the demand. It is not unusual for the demand charge to equal 25 percent or more of the total bill; locations such as Boston and Minneapolis may see demand charges comprising in excess of 50 percent of the total electric bill.

Two other charges are usually found on the utility bill. Most utilities use a fuel clause adjustment to adjust their rates in response to variations in the price of the fuels used to produce electricity. This adjustment takes the form of an additional charge or credit per kwh used in a billing period. The other rather common bill component is sales tax.

If a charge for a poor *power factor* appears on the electric bill and is a significant dollar amount, managers should call the utility and ask for help to understand the basis of this charge and what to do to lower it.

This discussion of electricity rates is somewhat similar to discussions of how hotels set their guestroom rates. Many hotels today practice revenue management: that is, they change their guestroom prices depending on their expectations of the demand for guestrooms during a specific time period. Setting electricity rates based on time of use is a form of revenue management originally developed to provide price signals to customers about the cost of their consumption of electricity. This idea was promoted for electric utilities in the early 1970s as a means of trying to control the growth in demand for electrical energy, especially during peak periods. Airlines and, later, hotels picked up this pricing strategy as a way to enhance their revenue as well as control demand.

Reading Electrical Utility Meters

The utility usually sends a meter reader to record the energy and demand values off the property's meter. A well-run operation will take its own meter readings, usually once per day and sometimes once per shift. This should be part of the shift engineer's daily responsibility. The readings should then be given to the director of engineering or the general manager. The purpose of taking these readings is to diagnose any problems before they become severe—for example, a surge in consumption caused by a theft of electric service. These readings may also prove useful if a dispute arises with the utility over the meter readings used for billing purposes.

Various types of meter dials are shown in this chapter.[10] The actual types or styles of meters used in different properties may vary, but the method of reading the meters will be the same. In general, quantities of energy consumed are determined by subtracting the beginning meter readings from the end-of-period readings. If a multiplier is shown on the dial face, you must multiply the difference between the two readings by the number shown to determine the actual quantity of energy used.

How Much Electricity Does a Hotel Use?

The table below shows results from a study of hotel electricity usage in over 600 hotels of various types. While the data is from 2000 and 2001, it is unlikely that there has been a substantial change in the median values shown. Given the rather large standard deviations for this data, especially for resort and luxury products, these values should only be seen as ballpark figures for electricity usage.

Annual Electricity Usage in Hotels

Type of Hotel	Median kwh per room	Standard Deviation	Median kwh per square foot	Standard Deviation
Midscale with F&B	8163	2552	15.5	4
Midscale without F&B	7082	1622	N/A*	N/A
Economy/Budget	6590	1412	16.4	3.8
Extended-Stay	8294	1391	14.3	2.4
Resorts	22246	9746	23.7	6.6
Luxury/Upscale	15749	5487	19.2	5.8

*N/A = Not available

Where do hotels use electricity? The pie chart below provides some information as to what applications require electricity in hotels. The actual distribution of electricity usage in a particular hotel depends in large part on the type of heating and air conditioning system in the hotel. If the hotel is conditioned using a PTAC unit, all heating is done via electricity. If the hotel is conditioned with a fan coil unit, all heating is done via a boiler probably using natural gas. If the hotel is located in a very warm climate, there is essentially no heating costs but a large amount of cooling is necessary.

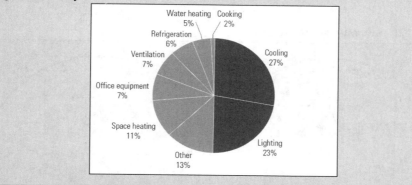

Sources: Table adapted from Energy Management and Conservation Guide, "Hotel Energy and Water Consumption Benchmarks," (New York: American Hotel & Lodging Educational Foundation, 2001), pp. 10, 14, 17, 20, 21, 24, 27; the pie chart is from the United States Environmental Protection Agency, *Energy Star Building Upgrade Manual*, Chapter 12, "Facility Type: Hotels and Motels," p. 3; http://www.energystar.gov/sites/default/files/buildings/tools/EPA_BUM_CH12_HotelsMotels.pdf.

There are two general types of electric meters: the kilowatt-hour meter and the kilowatt-hour meter with kilowatt demand meter.

Kilowatt-Hour Meter. This type of meter is used to determine the number of kilowatt-hours of electricity used. On a kilowatt-hour meter, the meter dials are read in sequence from left to right. The number recorded should be the lower of the two numbers that the hand is between in each dial.

In Exhibit 12, Example A, the first dial is read as 4, the second as 5, the third as 1, and the fourth as 9. Thus, the meter reading is 4519. In Example B, the reading of the same meter at a later time is 4628. To calculate the number of kilowatt-hours used during the time period, subtract the first reading (4519) from the second reading (4628). The difference between the two readings is 109. Since the meter face has the words "multiply by 100," you must multiply 109 by 100 to obtain the kilowatt-hours that were actually used (10,900).

Kilowatt-Hour Meter with Kilowatt Demand Meter. In a combination meter, the row of dials on the meter face marked "kilowatt-hours" is read the same way as the dials on a kilowatt-hour meter. There are many types of demand meters and each is read in a different way. When a meter is installed at your property, ask the utility company how to read it. The following section describes three common types of combined meters and provides guidelines for reading each type.

Maximum demand. The pointer in Example A in Exhibit 13 indicates maximum demand on the outer scale ring. The scale may be read directly or a multiplier may be required. The demand indicated is 0.4 kw. The pointer will be reset to zero by the meter reader. This type of meter only shows maximum demand since the previous reading and billing period.

Demand dials. Example B in Exhibit 13 depicts another type of demand meter that has demand dials below the meter dials. These dials are read from left to right

Exhibit 12   Kilowatt-Hour Meter

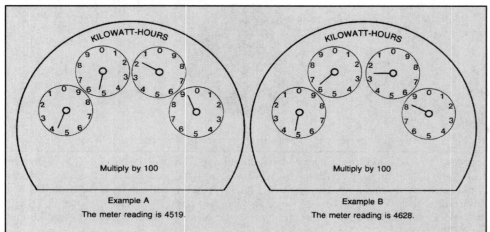

KILOWATT-HOURS

Multiply by 100

Example A
The meter reading is 4519.

KILOWATT-HOURS

Multiply by 100

Example B
The meter reading is 4628.

Exhibit 13   Combination Kilowatt-Hour and Demand Meters

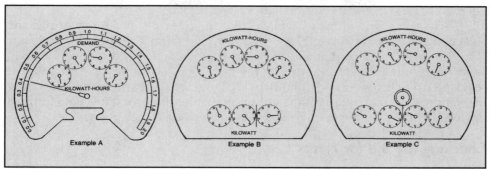

just like those on kilowatt-hour meters. The vertical line between the dials indicates where a decimal point should be placed. If there is a multiplier shown on the dial face, the reading must be multiplied by that number. The demand indicated in Example B is 96.2 kw. Demand dials of this type are also reset to zero by the meter reader after the reading is taken.

Cumulative demand register. A demand register—like that shown in Example C in Exhibit 13—looks and works somewhat like a kilowatt-hour meter. The dials are again read from left to right. The vertical line again indicates where a decimal point should be placed. The demand in this example is 13.15 kw.

In the cumulative demand register, the meter dials show the sum of the maximum demands up to the time the meter was last read. The meter reader determines the maximum demand for the current period by taking the dial reading, inserting a key in the meter that advances the dials to the new meter indication, and taking the new reading. The maximum demand for the period is the difference between the two readings. The new dial setting then remains fixed until the next meter reading.

The meter reader must use his or her key to advance the meter before the demand for any billing period can be calculated. However, by recording the meter reading just before the meter reader arrives, and by reading the meter after the reader departs, you can have a way to check on the demand number that is reported by the utility company during each billing period.

Recording demand meters. With the advent of time-of-day rates, it has become necessary for the utility company to know *when* energy consumption occurs in addition to the number of kilowatt-hours. In its simplest form, this has required the installation of more than one meter to record during certain periods of the day or year. In other instances, especially in larger commercial facilities, recording demand meters are used.

Recording devices also may be required when the rate is based on something other than the maximum demand during the month. For example, the rate schedule might stipulate that the maximum demand will be the average of the two, three, or four highest demands during the month. In another case, recording devices may be used when an individual consumer's load is large in relation to the system load. This enables the utility to determine whether the consumer's intervals of high demand coincide with system peaks.

There are several forms of demand recording devices, including strip charts and circular charts. However, these devices are giving way to those using magnetic tape. The magnetic tape demand recorder records the demand for every fifteen- or thirty-minute time interval during the month on a cassette tape. This tape is removed from the meter each month and fed into the utility company's computer for computation and billing. Some utility companies can access this data through devices that transmit meter information to a computer via telephone lines.

Checking the Bill for Errors

While the electric bill is usually given to the accounting department, it is important for the maintenance department to receive a copy to review. This makes sense because the bill will be paid out of the utility budget, which is the responsibility of maintenance. Next, the maintenance department should record the information on the bill in an energy consumption log. Engineering should review the readings taken by the utility and compare them with their own readings. Sometimes the utility company makes an error. Errors in demand readings are particularly hard to detect when the demand meter is reset to zero after it is read. Finally, engineering staff members are sometimes the only ones who understand how the electric bill is calculated. The bill should *always* be checked for errors.

In fact, billing errors are common enough that some independent contractors offer to monitor and check bills, often simply for a percentage of the savings they find. These firms maintain extensive data files on utility tariffs. They check for errors in both calculation and classification (for example, a company paying residential rather than commercial rates or paying a wrong or less advantageous commercial rate; there may be different commercial rates that apply to the same business and the utility is under no obligation to state which rate is more advantageous). Because billing errors can take many forms, some properties prefer to use the services of these outside contractors. However, with a little care, each property should be able to discover the same errors on its own.

Choosing the Best Rate Schedule

Deciding on a tariff or rate for electric service can be a somewhat confusing decision. There are often a number of options available, and it's up to the utility customer to decide which option is best. The utility provides rate information and leaves the decision up to the customer.

Some hospitality companies hire firms to identify the most advantageous electric rate for them and to audit their utility bills for errors, as just mentioned. Some of these firms provide this service "free"; they are paid by collecting a percentage of the dollars they save the hospitality companies they are working for.

It is appropriate to review the rate a property is paying when any of the following occur:

• Managers are considering replacing the building's electrical transformer.

- Managers are considering making significant additions to the building or making other changes that could increase the amount of electricity being used.

- Energy conservation measures are being implemented.

- The utility company announces changes in its rate structure. (Properties should have a copy of the current electric utility rates on file.)

The chapter appendix provides sample rate sheets from Commonwealth Edison Company, the electric utility serving Chicago. These rate sheets illustrate a number of common features of electric utility bills. For example, the demand charges vary with the time of year, the energy charges with the time of day. Some utilities vary both of these charges according to both the time of year and the time of day. Because these charges vary, the marginal cost of electricity (the cost of one additional unit of electricity used or saved during a given time period) is sometimes substantially different than that of the average cost. Knowledge of the rates will allow managers to calculate potential energy savings using marginal costs rather than average costs.

Knowledge of the rate schedule, coupled with an automated building control system, can help managers create opportunities for significant electricity savings. For example, the Marriott Marquis Hotel in New York participated in a real-time pricing (RTP) experiment with Con Edison, its electricity supplier. Con Edison was investigating the potential response of its customers to electric rates that could vary every day by the hour, with rate information transmitted to customers a day in advance, so they could prepare to adjust their electricity consumption accordingly. The director of engineering at the Marriott saw real-time pricing as a great opportunity for savings.

The Marriott Marquis controlled various building loads (primarily air-handling system fans) and other deferrable non-guestroom loads, allowing these to be shut down or reduced during the hours of high electricity prices. The results were amazing. Key results included the following:

- With automatic control responses to RTP rates, the hotel saved more than $1 million in four years, which represented cost savings of approximately 8.3 percent when compared to conventional time-of-use electric rates.

- Average yearly kilowatt consumption dropped by more than two million kilowatts, from approximately 38 million kilowatts during the baseline period to less than 36 million kilowatts during the monitored period. This represented an energy savings of about 5.2 percent compared to conventional time-of-use rates.

- Peak electric load was reduced by up to 1,400 kilowatts during high-price hours.

- These savings were achieved without compromising guest comfort or service.[11]

Exhibit 14 shows the energy savings that the Marriott Marquis enjoyed during one calendar year of the experiment, and the types of building equipment that contributed to these savings.

Exhibit 14   Kilowatts Saved, by Equipment Type, Using Real-Time Pricing

Month	Air-Handling Systems	Chillers	Exhaust Fans	Lighting	Misc. Loads	RTP kWh Reduction
January	74,386	0	18,498	0	0	92,884
February	174,472	207	38,100	0	0	212,779
March	194,880	1,979	44,115	17,600	11,000	296,574
April	120,140	11,445	4,255	0	0	135,840
May	126,704	28,253	4,485	0	0	159,442
June	132,786	68,652	6,095	0	0	207,533
July	234,648	145,683	40,655	7,200	4,500	432,686
August	145,588	79,152	13,405	3,200	2,000	243,345
September	141,554	49,293	1,035	0	0	191,882
October	150,904	17,222	2,875	0	0	171,001
November	197,254	14,136	28,840	5,280	3,300	248,810
December	173,382	1,589	11,200	800	500	187,471
Totals	**1,866,698**	**417,610**	**213,558**	**34,080**	**21,300**	**2,553,246**

Electric Utility Deregulation

The electric utility system in the United States operated for many decades as a regulated monopoly. A single electric utility served a given region, and its prices were largely fixed by filed rates approved by a state utility commission. Choice of utility companies and rates did not exist for customers. However, starting in the mid-1990s, electric utilities began to be deregulated, just as the telephone companies had been.

The result? Deregulation of electric utility companies has presented managers with another decision to make: What company should we choose to provide us with electricity? This can be a hard and potentially risky decision. First, it can be confusing because of the number of companies to choose from; figuring out which companies are reliable and reputable sometimes is not easy. Second, the rates are not fixed in some contracts; the rates are set to vary along with the market price of electricity. Experiences with market prices for electricity have shown that large, short-term jumps in power prices can occur.

Utility deregulation occurs on a state-by-state basis with different (and changing) provisions depending on the electric utility involved. The U.S. Energy Information Administration maintains an Internet site providing an overview of deregulation activities as well as links for additional information (such as to state public utility commissions). Managers can refer to the Energy Information Administration's Internet site (http://www.eia.gov/electricity/policies/restructuring/) for the latest information and issues associated with deregulation.

Deregulation has introduced another concern for managers operating hotels in states with a deregulated electric utility industry. With the electricity market deregulated, the oversight that was provided by regulatory agencies has been reduced, and the more-or-less guaranteed fixed return for utilities is gone. Deregulation has opened the door for larger profits, which has encouraged companies

Green Power

"Green power" is electricity produced by renewable, environmentally friendly sources such as solar, wind, geothermal, biomass, and low-impact small hydro-electric generators. A growing number of hotels are turning to solar power and producing their own electricity by using photovoltaic (PV) panels. PV panels (and their connected control equipment) are able to convert the solar energy striking the panels into a flow of electrons. These electrons are then collected and converted from direct to alternating current at a voltage compatible with the building's electrical voltage. The electricity produced is generally used to supplement or offset a portion of the building's electricity usage and, potentially—if the building's power needs are low—electricity may be sent out into the utility grid. Below is a schematic of a PV system:

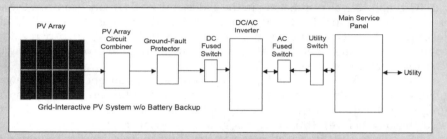

There are a number of tax credits and other incentives that improve the economics of solar PV. As a result of these incentives and a growing interest in the environmental benefits of electricity produced by PV systems, hotels and other businesses have been installing PV systems in increasing numbers.

It is possible for hotels to use green power without actually installing a solar panel on the building or a wind turbine somewhere on the property. In many areas of the country, green power can be purchased from third parties. While typical on-site solar power installations may provide 10 to 30 percent of a property's total energy usage, it is possible in some localities to purchase a much larger percentage (up to 100 percent in some instances) from a green power source. For example, the Fairmont Hotel in Washington, D.C., and the InterContinental Miami in Florida both purchase 100 percent of their power from wind sources. For the InterContinental, this is more than sixteen million kwh per year. Other InterContinental properties in the United States purchase wind power as well. Hilton Worldwide hotel properties in the United States purchase 94 percent of their electricity (315 million kwh) from green sources that include small-hydro and wind sources.

Information on green power in the United States can be found at www.epa.gov/greenpower/gpmarket/index.htm. Many other countries have a green power market as well; hotels located outside the United States should inquire about the green power options in their locations.

Sources: "InterContinental Miami Hotel Powers Up with 100 Percent Wind Energy," *Green Lodging News,* February 26, 2013 (http://www.greenlodgingnews.com/intercontinental-miami-hotel-powers-up-with-100-percent); "Hilton Once Again Among Top Green Power Users," *Green Lodging News,* January 29, 2013 (http://www.greenlodgingnews.com/hilton-once-again-among-top-green-power-users); and *A Guide to Photovoltaic Design and Installation,* California Energy Commission, 2001; http://www.energy.ca.gov/reports/2001-09-04_500-01-020.PDF.

to enter the electric utility industry that are primarily interested in quick, large profits. Other companies, under pressure to increase profits, have reduced maintenance activities and system reserve capacities. This has led to more frequent power outages and power-reliability problems. The past few decades saw brownouts (voltage reductions) and requests for voluntary power-usage curtailments (power shutdowns) in many regions. Whether these problems will recur and even worsen is yet to be seen.

Hotel and restaurant chains as well as state hospitality associations have responded to the emerging deregulated electricity markets by collecting information and negotiating new electricity purchase agreements. Some hospitality companies have negotiated directly with power companies; others have used the services of firms specializing in purchasing electricity. It is too early to tell what the overall electric-bill savings for the hospitality industry will be, but, if the experience with natural gas purchasing in the 1980s and 1990s is any example, the savings could be substantial. After the natural gas industry was deregulated, some hotels, through efficient purchasing, saw savings of from 10 to 25 percent and even higher. (Of course, natural gas users have an alternative in oil, something that electricity users do not have.)

An analysis of power purchasing options can be complicated but rewarding. For example, as mentioned earlier, Commonwealth Edison (serving Chicago, among other locations) offers a pricing option that changes hourly (with prices posted the day before). If a hotel has good historical usage information and is aware of ways to shift its usage patterns (say, by running laundry operations at lower-priced times), it might benefit from such variable prices. However, making the right determination requires a great deal of data on the hotel's energy usage as well as careful analysis. Hiring a consultant may be warranted; hotel chains may have their own corporate programs for analyzing and saving on electrical usage.

Telecommunications Systems

The widespread use of cell phones and personal computers with high-speed (often wireless) Internet connections has significantly reduced the overall revenue and profit that hotels generate from telecommunications. Full-service hotels, resort hotels, and convention hotels currently generate less than .5 percent of total revenue from telecommunications sales, with telecom expenses consuming more than the revenue.[12] The percentage of revenue from telecommunications has been declining over recent years. For this reason, telecom often does not capture management's attention as it once did. Nonetheless, the telecommunications function has not disappeared altogether. The discussion that follows provides a very brief overview of telecom systems. Readers with further interest in this topic are encouraged to refer to various telecommunications-specific publications.[13]

Telecommunications systems use equipment within the hotel itself to provide telecom services to guests and operations. The equipment must also be able to interface with service providers outside the hotel that provide local and long distance services. In addition, telecommunications equipment must be able to integrate with various pieces of equipment within the hotel, such as property management systems.

Hotels operate private branch exchanges (PBXs) that switch calls between the internal users on lines within the hotel, while all users share a certain number of external lines (also referred to as trunks). The PBX was introduced into hotels to address the need for guestrooms to have their own private extensions, with a centralized operator to process the calls for those extensions and to provide guest services. The following features of a hospitality PBX show how it differs from a conventional office or business PBX:

- *Enhanced attendance backup.* This allows multiple PBX attendants to be able to answer incoming calls.

- *Answer detection.* This is the ability to determine if a call made by a guest was actually answered. This is especially important in assessing charges for calls made by guests, but it's also useful for tracking administrative calls.

- *Crisis alerting.* Hotels have a responsibility to provide necessary assistance in an emergency. Most hotel telecommunications systems can notify and alert various departments, such as the front desk and security, as soon as an emergency 911 call has been placed, and can identify the specific extension making the call.

- *Call center.* Features such as automatic calling number identification and integration with automatic call distributors are especially useful in maximizing the effectiveness of hotel reservations departments.

In addition, hospitality PBX systems can be designed to interface with the property management system to provide the following capabilities:

- Allow guestroom telephone access to outside lines after check-in and restrict access upon check-out.

- Display guest information, specifically name and room number.

- Generate reports on guestroom telephone activity.

- Check and report on the status of a room from a housekeeping standpoint.

- Program or allow guest wake-up calls.

- Block calls between rooms and restrict internal/external calling by room.

At the present time, most guestroom phones are analog phones. Analog phones may have features such as message-waiting lights, data ports, speed-dial buttons, optional displays, cordless handsets, and speakers. Digital phones are also in use with features such as digital displays, conferencing, phantom extensions, multiple lines, programmable function keys, and message waiting.

Hotels use call accounting systems to resell telecommunication services to guestrooms, meeting rooms, event spaces, and other common guest areas. These systems enable hoteliers to independently capture and analyze guest telephone activity and then independently control profit margins and pricing methods. Some call accounting systems are built into the PBX system, while others are external to the system. Call accounting systems involve a large number of options that are beyond the scope of this discussion.

Telecommunications systems require some special design consideration. The PBX unit should be connected to an uninterruptible power supply (UPS) to ensure electricity is available should a power failure occur. UPS systems for this purpose can be standby or "off-line" units that sense a drop in main power and switch the device to the UPS, or in-line units that reside between the outside power and the telecommunications equipment. These take power from the outside sources and "clean" it, thereby ensuring that the PBX and other telecommunications equipment receive constant, clean power.

Telecommunications rooms may have unique electrical power requirements. The equipment often must be located on dedicated electrical circuits. Adequate cooling of these rooms is also needed and, if prolonged power outages are anticipated, running this cooling equipment off emergency power supplies should be considered. Managers should obtain from telecommunications services providers the specifications for telecom room physical dimensions, so that adequate space is provided for equipment connections and maintenance.

It is unlikely that property staff will perform maintenance on telecom systems. However, due to the critical nature of telecommunications services, it is important to establish a support contract with the equipment vendor to ensure that the system is supported in the event of failure. Contracts for telecom maintenance should address the following items:

- *Response times.* When a call for support goes out, a rapid response time is essential. Contracts usually stipulate a two- to four-hour emergency on-site response time. In addition, the contract should define what constitutes an emergency and establish the protocols for the various support calls. The contract also should include remedies for failure on the part of the vendor to comply with the response time.

- *New versus used parts.* Vendors often will use refurbished parts to support their telecommunications systems. Although this can be common practice in a number of environments, property managers need to determine if this is an acceptable policy as it pertains to the support of the hotel's telecommunications system. At the very least, the contract should stipulate that if the number of instances of failure exceeds a certain threshold, then the property has the right to insist on having new replacement parts placed in its system.

- *Use of certified technicians.* The contract may state that the vendor is required to use certified technicians when supporting the system.

- *Use of subcontractors.* The contract should stipulate whether third-party vendors will be used to support the system. If so, those vendors need to be listed and the property should check their references as well. The subcontractors should be governed by the same rules and requirements that govern the main vendor.

- *Limitations on liability.* In most cases, the support contracts will not cover damage from lightning, political riots, and so forth. The property should be aware of those limitations and, where possible, provide UPS equipment to try to protect against them.

- *Support of guestroom phones.* Guestroom phones can either be supported by the PBX support contract or by the hotel's own maintenance department. In some cases, it may be more cost-beneficial to maintain guestroom phones in-house, or to just keep a stock of spare phones and swap them out as necessary. In either case, the contract should detail the various responsibilities.

- *Support of telecom services.* In many situations, the telecom vendor is responsible for maintaining all the communication lines coming into the property. As such, these vendors need to maintain a relationship with the local exchange companies. Should this be part of the telecom vendor's responsibility, then it needs to be clarified in the contract.

Endnotes

1. J. F. Musselman, "Power Plant and Refrigeration Equipment," *The Architectural Forum,* November 1923, p. 257.

2. A source of information on CHP in the United States can be found at http://www.epa.gov/chp/. Also, information on two hotels that installed CHP technology can be found at http://www.epa.gov/chp/documents/presentations_sept06/dominguez.pdf and http://www.pgwenergysense.com/downloads/CHP_FourSeasonsCaseStudy.pdf.

3. Additional information on electrical plug and socket variations throughout the world can be found at http://users.pandora.be/worldstandards/electricity.htm.

4. Particularly useful sources of updated information include *Electrical Construction & Maintenance* magazine, published by Primedia Business, P.O. Box 12914, Overland Park, KS, 66282-2914; and the National Fire Protection Association, 1 Batterymarch Park, P.O. Box 9101, Quincy, MA, 02269-9101.

5. One magazine that can be helpful in this regard is *Electrical Construction & Maintenance.*

6. Lodging managers and others can find information to help them buy energy-efficient electric motors at http://www1.eere.energy.gov/manufacturing/tech_assistance/pdfs/mc-0382.pdf.

7. The *Motor Systems Tip Sheet #11* at this source provides further information on adjustable/variable speed drives; see http://www1.eere.energy.gov/manufacturing/tech_assistance/pdfs/motor_tip_sheet11.pdf.

8. These solutions are suggested in two publications of the Edison Electric Institute, *Quality Power in Your Restaurant* and *Quality Power in Your Motel,* 701 Pennsylvania Ave. N.W., Washington, D.C., 20004-2696. These publications guide the reader through a process of diagnosing and solving electrical quality problems.

9. The United States has averaged more than 3,000 power outages per year from 2010 to 2013; these outages affected 14 to 41 million people. The costs of these outages were estimated in the tens of billions of dollars per year. California had the most outages in each of the past three years. More information on power outages can be found at http://powerquality.eaton.com/blackouttracker/default.asp.

10. This section on meter reading is drawn from Robert E. Aulbach, *Energy and Water Resource Management,* 2d ed. (Lansing, Mich.: American Hotel & Lodging Educational Institute, 1988), pp. 124–126.

11. S. D. Gabel, L. Carmichael, and G. Shavit, "Automated Control in Response to Real-Time Pricing of Electricity," *ASHRAE Journal,* November 1998, pp. 26–29.

12. Robert Mandelbaum, "U. S. Hotel Guests Hanging Up and Logging In," *Hotel Online*, January 25, 2013; http://www.hotel-online.com/News/PR2013_1st/Jan13_Telecom-Revenue.html.

13. This discussion of telecommunications has been abstracted from *Telecommunications in the Hospitality Industry* (2003) developed by the American Hotel & Lodging Association's Technology Committee. For those interested in more in-depth information on telecommunications, see Annabel Z. Dodd, *Essential Guide to Telecommunications*, 4th ed. (Upper Saddle River, N.J.: Prentice-Hall, 2005).

🔑 Key Terms

ampere—A measure of the current flow in an electrical system. One ampere represents 6.251×10^{18} electrons per second passing through a cross section of the conductor.

demand charge—That part of a utility bill based on the highest rate of energy use, measured in kilowatts. Also called a capacity charge.

energy charge—That part of a utility bill based on the amount of energy used, measured in kilowatt-hours. Also called a consumption charge.

feeder—Element of a building's electrical system that supplies electricity to various portions of the building and to major equipment.

frequency—With regard to electricity, the rate at which an alternating current (AC) power supply alternates the direction of the current flow. Measured in hertz, or cycles per second.

ground fault circuit interrupter (GFCI)—A particularly sensitive circuit breaker designed to protect people from electrical shocks, usually used in areas where water may be found.

National Electrical Code (NEC)—A publication of the National Fire Protection Association that details recommended safety code standards for electrical systems.

phase—With regard to electrical service, the number of energized wires in the electrical supply. Almost always either single-phase or three-phase.

ratchet clause—A utility billing structure that bases the demand charge on the highest demand over a given period extending beyond the current billing period.

transformer—A device that changes the voltage of the electrical supply.

voltage—A measure of the electrical potential of an electrical system. Electricity flows between two points of different electrical potential. Comparable to pressure in a water system.

❓ Review Questions

1. What factors might lead a hospitality property to choose to produce its own power supply?

2. What are the potential advantages and disadvantages to a hospitality operation of owning its own transformer?

3. What is the purpose of the *National Electrical Code*?

4. Why is it important to update electrical plans as changes are made to a facility?

5. What are lockout/tagout procedures? Why are they critical to electrical safety?

6. Should preventive maintenance be performed on every piece of electrical equipment at a facility? Why or why not?

7. What steps can be taken to reduce the likelihood of electrical problems interfering with electronic equipment?

8. When is the use of battery backup systems most appropriate? What is the difference between a standby power supply and an uninterruptible power supply?

9. What is the difference between a demand charge and an energy charge? Why is it important to know the difference?

10. If a hospitality facility qualifies under more than one rate schedule, how should it select from among the available options?

Internet Sites

For more information, visit the following Internet sites. Remember that Internet addresses can change without notice. If the site is no longer there, you can use a search engine to look for additional sites.

Consulting-Specifying Engineer
www.csemag.com

Edison Electric Institute
www.eei.org

Electrical Construction & Maintenance
http://ecmweb.com/

Electric Power Research Institute
http://my.epri.com

Case Study

When Darkness Falls

Ed Watts felt he had finally recovered from the nightmare of the power outage a week ago. What started out as a sunny pleasant summer day deteriorated to an absolute disaster as the city faced a blackout that started at 10 A.M. and lasted for almost a day. As the director of engineering at the 300-room Edison Hotel, Ed had never experienced such a challenge. The hotel emergency generator was sized only for the power requirements of emergency lighting in stairwells and corridors, fire alarm systems, and other items required by code. And the fuel supply for the generator allowed for operation for only the code-mandated two hours. At noon, the generator stopped running and the hotel went dark. Now lacking the needed life safety systems and without any water in the building (no pumps to circulate it), the hotel had to be evacuated, putting guests out on the street with occupants from other buildings in the downtown area. Evacuating guests from the ten-story building in the dark stairwells and corridors without elevators was not fun. Ed was worried about all the candles that seemed to appear all over the hotel as well.

Staff pitched in in dozens of ways to assist and care for guests, including putting out food and bottled water (until they ran out) in the porte cochere. As night fell and guests realized they were going to be stranded for the night (nothing was moving due to the power outage), the hotel provided some blankets and pillows, since people had to sleep outside. Luckily, it was a pleasant night and everything went reasonably well. Even better was having the power come back on around 10 A.M. the following day. And then began the process of getting the hotel back to normal operations. Because all the door openings to get food had allowed the temperatures to warm in the refrigerators, the food and beverage staff decided they needed to dispose of a lot of stored food. The front desk was buried trying to handle folios for the rooms and handle billing issues. Housekeeping was trying to get all the rooms into ready status, encountering day-old room service trays and other things guests had left behind and resetting all the clocks that were flashing 12:00. It seemed like a million other items needed attention from every department.

Even though the Edison's daily operations recovered from the blackout, Ed's work was not done. At a staff meeting held to recap responses to the outage, it became apparent that the hotel was lucky. No one had been hurt during the blackout and, so far, it looked like there would be no lawsuits or major issues (other than dealing with the insurance carrier). But leading people around in the dark with candles and hauling luggage down staircases was not something the GM wanted repeated. Each department head was tasked with putting together a "quick-fix" list of things that the hotel could do to better respond to the next outage and that could be funded from the operations budget. Department heads were also asked to put together a long-term solution list.

So, it looked like Ed's recovery from the outage was still underway. Lots of work appeared to be ahead.

Discussion Questions

1. What should Ed include on his "quick-fix" list for engineering that will help the Edison to better handle a future power outage? How will his quick-fix items help solve some of the issues the hotel faced in the outage?

2. What might Ed include on his long-term solution list for engineering that will help the Edison to better handle a future power outage? How will his long-term solution items help the Edison? What challenges does he face in getting these approved?

3. In what ways might items on Ed's long-term solution list also serve to reduce the normal operating costs of the hotel?

4. What should other departments (rooms division, housekeeping, F&B) put on their quick-fix and long-term solutions lists?

Case Number: 2816CA

Chapter Appendix:

Sample Electric Utility Rate Sheets

RATE 6
GENERAL SERVICE

APPLICABILITY.

Except as provided in Rate 6L, this rate is applicable to any commercial, industrial, or governmental customer with a Maximum Demand of less than 1,000 kilowatts who uses the Company's electric service hereunder for all requirements. Direct current requirements provided under another rate immediately prior to September 2, 1975, will, however, also be provided hereunder.

GENERAL SERVICE – TIME OF DAY.

Time of day charges shall apply to (1) any customer with a Maximum Demand of 500 kilowatts or more, but less than 1,000 kilowatts, in three of the twelve months preceding the billing month, one of which occurs during the three months preceding the billing month, (2) successors to customers served under these charges immediately prior to the date of succession whose estimated Maximum Demands meet the demand requirements in clause (1) above, (3) new customers whose estimated Maximum Demands meet the demand requirements in clause (1) above, and (4) any customer previously billed hereunder pursuant to clauses (1) or (2), except as otherwise provided below.

These charges shall not be applicable to customers or their successors with electric space heating taking service under the Heating with Light provision of Rider 25 prior to November 23, 1977, except upon written application by the customer to the Company.

If a customer at one time was served pursuant to (1) above on General Service – Time of Day and has a Maximum Demand which (A) has not exceeded 400 kilowatts in any month of the 16-month period preceding the billing month, or (B) has not equaled or exceeded 500 kilowatts in any month of the 24-month period preceding the billing month, such customer may elect, in written application to the Company, to be served on General Service – Non-Time of Day. General Service – Time of Day shall not again be applicable until such customer meets the requirements of General Service – Time of Day.

GENERAL SERVICE – NON-TIME OF DAY.

General Service – Non-Time of Day charges shall apply to all other customers qualifying for service under this rate.

CHARGES.

General Service – Time of Day.
  Monthly Customer Charge.
  The Monthly Customer Charge shall be: $39.93

  Demand Charge.
  Charge per kilowatt for all kilowatts of Maximum Demand for the month:
    For Summer Months $14.24
    For All Other Months $11.13

For the purposes hereof, the Summer Months shall be the customer's first monthly billing period with an ending meter reading date on or after June 15 and the three succeeding monthly billing periods.

  Energy Charge.
  Charge per kilowatt-hour for kilowatt-hours supplied in the month:
    For kilowatt-hours supplied
    during Energy Peak Periods .... 5.599¢
    during Energy Off-Peak Periods .... 2.341¢

General Service – Non-Time of Day.
  Monthly Customer Charge.
  The Monthly Customer Charge shall be: $8.83

  Demand Charge.
  Charge per kilowatt for all kilowatts of Maximum Demand for the month:
    For Summer Months $14.24
    For All Other Months $11.13

In accordance with the Application of Demand Charge provisions of this rate, there shall be no demand charge as such for certain small customers, but in lieu thereof, such customers shall pay a charge per kilowatt-hour in addition to the energy charges of this rate.

The in-lieu of demand charge per kilowatt-hour for kilowatt-hours supplied in the month:
    For Summer Months .... 6.057¢
    For All Other Months .... 4.798¢

RATE 6
GENERAL SERVICE

(Continued from Sheet No. 24)

CHARGES. (CONTINUED)
  General Service – Non-Time of Day. (Continued)
    Demand Charge (Continued).
    For the purposes hereof, the Summer Months shall be the customer's first monthly billing period with an ending meter reading date on or after June 15 and the three succeeding monthly billing periods.

    Energy Charge.
    Charge per kilowatt-hour for kilowatt-hours supplied in the month:

        For the first 30,000 kilowatt-hours .... 4.247¢
        For the next 470,000 kilowatt-hours .... 3.167¢
        For all over 500,000 kilowatt-hours .... 3.118¢

  Late Payment Charge.
  The late payment charge provided for in the Terms and Conditions of this Schedule of Rates shall be applicable to all charges under this rate.

  Minimum Charge.
  The minimum monthly charge shall be the Monthly Customer Charge.

  Maximum Charge.
  For customers with demand meters, the average cost of electricity hereunder in any month, exclusive of the Monthly Customer Charge, shall not exceed the Maximum Charge per kilowatt-hour, provided, however, that such guaranteed charge shall not operate to reduce the customer's bill to an amount less than the Minimum Charge.

    The Maximum Charge per kilowatt-hour shall be: .... 20.502¢

MAXIMUM DEMAND.
For General Service – Time of Day customers, the Maximum Demand in any month shall be the highest 30-minute demand established during the Demand Peak Periods in such month.

For General Service – Non-Time of Day customers, the Maximum Demand shall be the highest 30-minute demand established at any time during such month.

APPLICATION OF DEMAND CHARGE.
The Company shall provide a demand meter and the demand charge shall apply when a customer's monthly kilowatt-hour use exceeds 2,000 kilowatt-hours in three of the twelve months preceding the billing month; or if either his Maximum Demand or monthly kilowatt-hour use is estimated to exceed 10 kilowatts or 2,000 kilowatt-hours, respectively, for at least three months of the next 12-month period. Any customer to whom the demand charge would not ordinarily apply under the preceding sentence may, at his request and upon payment of appropriate meter rentals, be provided with a demand meter and be billed the demand charge rather than the charge in lieu thereof. In such case, meter rentals shall be payable for the period during which the customer elects to retain the meter, but not less than twelve months, unless he becomes entitled to a demand meter prior to the end of the 12-month period. A customer who is entitled to a demand meter shall not be required to pay rental or other separate charges for such meter.

Where a demand meter is installed, the demand charge shall apply when the customer's monthly use exceeds 2,000 kilowatt-hours or his demand exceeds 10 kilowatts in three of the twelve months preceding the billing month. The demand charge shall continue to apply until the customer's monthly use has not exceeded 2,000 kilowatt-hours and his Maximum Demand has not exceeded 10 kilowatts in any month of the preceding 16-month period, at which time the in lieu of demand charge shall apply, except for a customer who has requested a demand meter and has elected to be billed the demand charge.

Prior to application of the demand charge, the customer being billed in lieu of demand charges will receive notification on the customer's bill each time the above 2,000 kilowatt-hours or 10 kilowatt requirement has been exceeded and the significance of it.

Chapter 7 Outline

Factors Influencing Building Comfort
    Building Loads and Comfort
    Indoor Air Quality
Heating Sources and Equipment
    Heat Sources
    Furnace and Boiler Operation and
        Maintenance
Cooling Sources and Equipment
    The Refrigeration Cycle
    Cooling Systems Operation and
        Maintenance
    CFCs, HCFCs, and the Environment
Guestroom HVAC System Types
    Centralized Systems
    Decentralized Systems
    Other Systems
    Guestroom Ventilation
    Guestroom HVAC Occupancy Control
    Guestroom HVAC Maintenance
HVAC Systems for Other Building Areas
    System Types and Configurations
    Maintenance Needs
Other HVAC Components
    Controls
    Cooling Towers
    HVAC Thermal Storage
Conclusion

Competencies

1. Describe the basic elements of human comfort and how HVAC systems affect this comfort. (pp. 247–255)

2. Identify heating sources, types of heating equipment, and operating and maintenance concerns for this equipment. (pp. 255–259)

3. Discuss cooling sources and equipment; explain how the vapor compression refrigeration cycle operates; and summarize cooling system operation, maintenance, and environmental concerns. (pp. 259–264)

4. Describe several guestroom HVAC systems, including centralized, decentralized, and hybrid systems, and summarize other guestroom HVAC concerns. (pp. 264–275)

5. Identify the system types and maintenance needs of HVAC systems for other building areas. (pp. 275–279)

6. Outline the nature and maintenance needs of HVAC controls. (pp. 279–281)

7. Identify various maintenance concerns with regard to cooling towers and discuss HVAC thermal storage. (pp. 281–285)

7

Heating, Ventilating, and Air Conditioning Systems

Air conditioning is the science of mechanically controlling the (1) temperature, (2) humidity, (3) purity, and (4) movement of the air within buildings and other enclosures, thereby controlling the effects of such air upon the persons and materials exposed to it.

The effects of air upon comfort and health are due to the reactions of the human being to variations in air temperature, humidity, purity, and motion. The sense or feeling of warmth is dependent upon the moisture content of the air, rather than upon its mere temperature, and for this reason comfortable and healthful heating requires coincident regulation of humidity. The purity of the air breathed by the human being is, of course, primarily important to his physical well-being. His personal efficiency is materially depressed by air that is contaminated with foreign matter, particularly in congested centers, manufacturing districts, or in proximity to any source of pollution. Drafts, due to improper distribution of air, are dangerous to health, and subversive to comfort. Air conditioning is a sure and sane means of insuring comfort and of eliminating the personal inefficiencies resulting from improper air qualities in spaces enclosing human beings. Just as surely as the first invigorating days of spring bring to you a pulsating sense of new energy, so will conditioned air, duplicating those same conditions perhaps, bringing new energy and comfort to all it reaches. Manufactured weather makes "Every day a good day," so that the increased satisfaction rather than discomfort of the hotel guest and the increased efficiency rather than indifference of the employee yields a day-after-day dividend on the operating cost and investment in air conditioning equipment.[1]

Heating, ventilating, and air conditioning (HVAC) systems create and maintain the levels of comfort required by guests and employees. HVAC systems must be properly selected, operated, and maintained if they are to provide an appropriate level of comfort. To maintain comfort, you need to understand the basic elements of comfort. The capabilities, limitations, and operating costs of various types of HVAC systems are important as well, especially as they relate to decisions about equipment selection and overall cost control.

Proper maintenance of HVAC systems not only will create comfortable conditions, but also will help control the operating costs associated with the equipment. Knowledge of fuel and equipment options can help management to make decisions for new and retrofit applications. In addition, certain elements of the HVAC system need special care to avoid potential safety and health problems.

While there are many types of HVAC systems, the underlying ways in which they operate are somewhat similar. Knowing how a property creates heating and cooling and provides ventilation will help you understand the ways in which each of these is used to help produce a comfortable building for guests and employees.

Factors Influencing Building Comfort

The concept of comfort involves a number of factors. HVAC systems maintain thermal comfort by modifying and controlling the factors that influence comfort. These systems use equipment such as furnaces and boilers to produce heat, air conditioners and chillers to produce cold, fans and ductwork to move air, and filters and air washers to clean the air. The mention of clean air is a reminder that indoor air quality is also a factor in building comfort. (The discussion that follows is largely an abridgement of the appendix at the end of this chapter. For further information and explanation of issues regarding thermal comfort and psychrometrics, refer to this appendix.)

Factors influencing thermal comfort include:

- Room air temperature.
- Room air movement.
- Relative humidity of room air or wet bulb temperature.
- Activity level in the room.
- Clothing worn by room occupants.
- Temperature of the room surfaces.

Most of these factors will seem quite obvious to you. A room's comfort level can be greatly changed by providing air movement—such as with a fan in the summer. A humid environment can be much less comfortable in summer than a dryer environment at the same temperature. If we are actively exercising, we find cooler conditions more comfortable. An individual wearing a suit or sweater will be warmer than he or she would be in a thin short-sleeved shirt and shorts.

An individual's comfort is the result of balancing the heat produced by his or her body with the surrounding environment. Body heat is lost by **convection**, **radiation**, and **evaporation**. Convection involves the transfer of heat due to the movement of air over a person's skin and a difference in temperature between the air and the skin. The more rapid the air movement or the colder the air, the more rapid is the transfer of heat. Transfer of heat by radiation occurs when two surfaces are at different temperatures. Energy is transferred in the form of thermal radiation from the warmer to the colder surface. Evaporation transfers heat because, in order to turn water from a liquid to a vapor, heat must be added to the water. With regard to human comfort, this heat is removed from a person's body as perspiration evaporates from his or her skin.

Radiative heat loss is particularly influenced by the temperature of room surfaces. This effect is illustrated when you sit near a window on a cold winter day. The cold glass of the window causes your body to radiate heat in that direction, making the side of your body near the window feel cold. Most building heating systems locate heat discharge points below windows so the heating system can warm the window surface. This reduces the radiative cooling effect the window has on room occupants.

The HVAC industry has provided a simplified way to view thermal comfort by defining a region of temperature and relative humidity known as the **comfort zone**. Through testing of human response to various indoor air conditions, a range of conditions in which 80 percent of the population tested was "comfortable" has been defined. Exhibit 1 illustrates this zone on what engineers call a psychrometric chart. Temperatures and relative humidity levels within the ranges specified represent desired conditions for occupied spaces. The zones numerically express what we intuitively understand. In summer we are comfortable at warmer conditions than in winter. As the air temperature rises, no matter what the season, the range of comfort shifts somewhat to lower levels of humidity.

Interpreting the comfort zone on the chart in Exhibit 1 also provides some background in interpreting the psychrometric chart itself. The lines ascending

Exhibit 1   ASHRAE Summer and Winter Comfort Zones

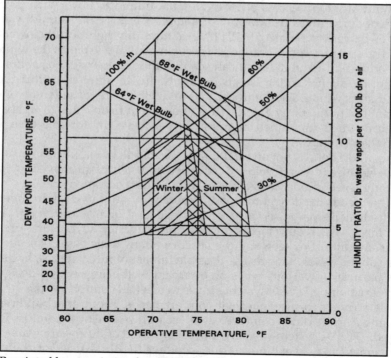

Reprinted by permission from ASHRAE.

from left to right and labeled *rh* with a % sign are relative humidity lines. Relative humidity is a measure of the relative amount of moisture the air is holding, with values ranging from 0 percent to 100 percent. These are labeled from 100 to 30 percent in the exhibit, with most of the comfort zones lying between 60 and 30 percent rh—common internal building conditions. The lines ascending from right to left are **wet bulb temperature** lines. If you move vertically from the 64°F (18°C) wet bulb line to the 68°F (20°C) wet bulb line you can see that this also results in the relative humidity increasing. The left (Y) axis is the **dew point temperature**—the temperature at which water condenses. The right axis is a measure of the absolute amount of water in the air, expressed in pounds of water vapor per 1000 pounds of dry air. The bottom (X) axis is the dry bulb temperature, referred to as the operative temperature.

The dry bulb temperature is what we commonly refer to as "the temperature" and measure with a thermometer. The wet bulb temperature is the value that would be measured if the bulb of a thermometer was surrounded by a small swatch of wet cloth. The wet bulb temperature and relative humidity are often used interchangeably. If we have a dry bulb temperature of 85°F (29°C) we can talk of a relative humidity of approximately 30 percent or of a wet bulb temperature of 64°F (18°C). And if we cooled this air to approximately 50°F (10°C) it would reach its dew point and condensation would result. All of these relationships can be illustrated using illustrations similar to Exhibit 1.

The winter comfort zone ranges from approximately 68°F (20°C) at 60 percent relative humidity to in excess of 76°F (25°C) at humidity lower than 30 percent. Summer comfort ranges from a low of about 73°F (23°C) at humidity levels in excess of 60 percent to a high of 81°F (27°C) at humidity significantly lower than 30 percent. The summer comfort zone is approximately the same as the winter zone with 5°F added (in Exhibit 1, you can see that the summer zone is shifted 5°F to the right of the winter zone). This is primarily due to different clothing levels in summer than in winter. The comfort zones in Exhibit 1 are for sedentary individuals who are not particularly elderly. (It is known that people at age eighty require temperatures three Fahrenheit degrees warmer to be comfortable than those of people in their twenties.)

The comfort zone is not an infallible guide. It will not apply universally in all situations because it was developed for specified levels of air movement, activity, and clothing levels. Nonetheless, it is useful for most occupied spaces.

Further needs in the comfort and acceptability of indoor environments concern such elements as noise, odor, and the general quality of the air. Air quality must meet basic requirements for human occupancy, such as the presence of adequate amounts of oxygen and the absence of any toxic gases. Air quality also involves subtler issues, such as the possible impact of mold spores, bacteria, and airborne particles of various types on occupant well-being. A well-designed and properly functioning HVAC system strives to meet all comfort needs.

While striving to meet thermal comfort needs, room and building HVAC systems must meet other comfort needs as well. Acoustical comfort is one of these needs. HVAC systems usually move some kind of fluid—air, water, or both. This movement may make noise, due to either the fluid itself or the pump or fan moving the fluid. Sometimes, a low level of noise is intentionally designed into equipment—for example, an air distribution system—because it can serve to mask other sounds. This is known as the "white noise" approach. Also, air that is discharged at too high a rate can make unwanted noise. Controlling ventilation airflow rates is necessary.

Additional noise and vibration can be generated by the equipment used to move the fluid. A poorly balanced fan, a lack of adequate vibration isolation of fans or pumps, bearing deterioration, and related problems can result in the transmission of vibration to the ductwork, the piping, or the building itself. While these problems should be dealt with in the design of the systems, all of them can occur because of a faulty maintenance program.

Building Loads and Comfort

Exhibit 2 illustrates some of the challenges facing an HVAC system operating in a guestroom. (A similar diagram can be drawn for other spaces.) The exterior wall, windows, and ceiling of the guestroom may add heat to or subtract heat from the space, depending on the season. The windows allow solar energy to enter and add heat to the room. The guest(s) as well as the television, lights, and other equipment add heat to the room. The shower and bath also add heat. Air leakage around the windows (and the door, if the guestroom opens to the outside) can add cold or hot air to the room, depending on the season. Moisture is added by the bath and shower, and by the breath of, and skin evaporation from, room occupants. The bathroom vent fan removes air that must be replaced. This replacement air

Exhibit 2   Guestroom HVAC Loads

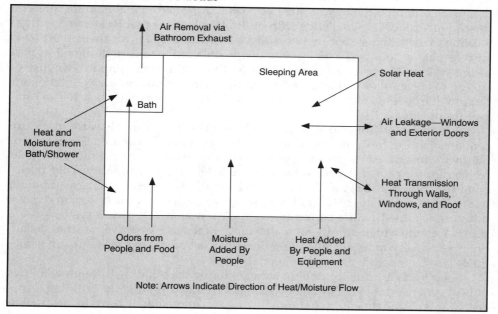

eventually enters the building from the outside, which means it must be heated or cooled somewhere. The HVAC system is ideally able to deal with all of these variable inputs to and outputs from the space (referred to as **loads** by engineers).

Building loads can be broken down into various categories. The simplest are those loads that are sensible and latent. **Sensible loads** involve heat addition (and removal) with resulting increases (or decreases) in dry bulb temperature only. **Latent loads** involve moisture addition or removal with resulting increases or decreases in the relative humidity only. If you move horizontally within Exhibit 1 you'll see the sensible load process; if you move vertically, you'll see a latent load process. Many heating loads involve sensible and latent elements—the air needs to be cooled and moisture removed as well. Sometimes failure to create comfort is a matter of overly addressing one load (usually sensible) without also addressing the other load (usually latent). One contributor to mold and mildew in guestrooms can be too much sensible cooling and not enough latent.

Building loads can also be broken down in other ways. HVAC designers talk about transmission/conduction, ventilation, infiltration, solar, and internal loads. Transmission or conduction loads involve the transfer of heat through walls, ceilings, windows, and other structural elements of the building. Heat transfer always occurs from warmer to colder locations. This means transmission loads can be heat lost (in the winter) or heat gained (in the summer). Transmission loads are reduced by increasing the insulation value of walls, ceilings, and windows.

Ventilation and infiltration loads are similar in many ways. Ventilation loads are deliberately designed into buildings to meet comfort and safety needs. Infiltration loads are not designed into the building but rather are a function of leakage of air either from the outside in or the inside out. If from the outside in, the entering air must be cooled or heated to maintain the space in the comfort zone. If from the inside out, replacement air must be cooled or heated to maintain the space in the comfort zone. One challenge with infiltration loads is that these may occur in locations where the system is not designed to compensate for them—locations such as near a door or a leaking window. Ventilation loads are designed as part of the system. However, in either instance, the load usually requires the use of energy for heating or cooling. Under the right circumstances, the ventilation air can provide cooling if needed and eliminate the need for energy usage to run cooling equipment.

A major ventilation load in hot and humid climates involves the moisture contained in the fresh air introduced to the building. Conventional methods of removing this moisture involve passing the humid air over coils that have cold refrigerant (or chilled water) in them and condensing the humidity. Cold refrigerant (or chilled water) requires the operation of mechanical cooling equipment with a large electricity cost. Another option is to use a desiccant system to remove moisture, coupled with a conventional HVAC system.[2] Desiccant systems use a substance with a high affinity for water vapor to remove water vapor from the air. Energy-recovery units, installed to reduce the cost of cooling make-up air, sometimes also incorporate desiccant materials.[3]

Solar loads are due to sunlight either entering the building through windows or heat generated into a building by surfaces on the exterior of the building (especially roofs). Sunlight entering through windows immediately turns to heat within the space. Sunlight striking building surfaces also immediately turns to heat, but the effect is first to raise the temperatures of these surfaces above the air temperature. Then, the heat produced works its way through the surface to the interior. This process can take several hours. The result is that a solar roof load may not show up in the guestrooms until 6:00, 8:00, or even 10:00 P.M. Solar loads are one good reason to paint roofs white or some other reflective color in hot climates. To illustrate, consider the difference in the temperature of the hood of a white car versus that of a black car when exposed to bright sunlight. In winter periods, solar loads can reduce the energy needed for space heating.

Internal loads involve anything inside a space that provides heat or moisture. People, a coffee pot, overhead projectors, or computers provide heat or moisture or both. In some unusual circumstances, there can be things that remove heat and moisture—a large urn of iced beverage or an ice sculpture, for example,

To maintain comfort, the HVAC system must remove the loads at the rate they are created. This can be a challenge. Imagine the change in load of an auditorium or convention space at a "comfortable" 77°F (25°C) and 40 percent relative humidity (rh) when a thousand people suddenly enter from outside where the temperature is 95°F (35°C) and 80 percent rh. Not only do the people themselves generate heat (internal loads) but their movement brings with it a large amount of outside air (infiltration). The sensible and latent loads that result are large and sudden. The good news is that the system is usually configured to handle these loads.

More of a problem in meeting a load can occur when guestroom HVAC systems, designed for a small number of occupants and minimal internal loads, are called upon to meet the needs of a large number of people and large internal loads. This can be the case when guestrooms are converted to meeting space or to provide concierge or executive lounge areas on guestroom floors. If no changes are made to the HVAC system, it is almost guaranteed that the system will be unable to meet the peak loads created by these conversions. The result will be uncomfortable guests and complaints about the comfort in these spaces. Without HVAC system changes costing many dollars, there is little that can be done.

Indoor Air Quality

Indoor air quality (IAQ) has become a subject of increasing attention in the lodging industry in the last few decades, perhaps beginning when hotel operators recognized the need to provide no-smoking guestrooms. Today, entire hotels have been designated no-smoking buildings, and IAQ issues now include mold and mildew as well as volatile organic compounds in newly installed indoor finishes and furniture. In addition, hotels seeking certification from organizations such as LEED will need to address IAQ considerations.[4]

Mold and mildew problems in the lodging industry have long existed in a limited form in areas such as guest bathrooms. Mold and mildew issues throughout the hotel can derive from problems with building design, construction, and operation. Design and construction factors affecting mold and mildew can range quite widely, from the location of air intake ducts and cooling towers, to excess amounts of humid outside air, to the protection of construction materials from moisture.

Mold and Mildew Concerns in Hotels

In the summer of 1988, construction of a large luxury resort was coming to a close. The resort was designed with vinyl wall covering on the interior side of the exterior walls. Because the wall covering had an impermeable finish, it functioned as a vapor retarder. The HVAC system consisted of a continuous toilet exhaust and packaged terminal air conditioner (PTAC) units. The outside air exchange rate in each guestroom averaged six times an hour, all from infiltration.

The combined effect of excessive outside air infiltration and a misplaced vapor retarder caused $5.5 million in moisture and mildew damage, even before the facility was opened. If these same design combinations had occurred in a more temperate climate, the problems would have been limited to increased energy consumption and possibly to complaints about guest comfort.*

Mold and mildew issues similar to those described above continue to occur in hotels, resorts, and other commercial and residential buildings. And, while not all problems result in costs in the millions of dollars, there continue to be large problems with large costs. In 2002, Hilton Corporation closed its $95 million Kalia Tower addition in Hawaii due to mold and mildew, then spent an estimated $55 million on mold remediation.**

What are the causes of mold and mildew problems and how can they be prevented? Many causes often work together to create the problem. These include:***

- High indoor humidity
- Condensation
- Poor or non-existent maintenance
- Improper operation
- Poor building stewardship
- Leaky building envelope

- Improper pressurization
- Uncontrolled ventilation
- Inadequate water management of HVAC systems
- Plumbing leaks, overflow, storm drainage
- Occupant activity
- Weather

As can be seen from this list, mold problems can result from problems with the design, construction, or operation (and sometimes all three) of the building. For example, high indoor humidity may be the result of allowing moisture to enter the building exterior due to poor design, enclosing moisture during construction, or failing to keep HVAC drains operating properly. Given the potential severity of the problems, it is generally advisable to consult information prepared by experts in the topic. ASHRAE is certainly a major resource in this area. The firm CH2M Hill has also been widely referenced in this area and has recently released a publication based on its work. Further information about air conditioning equipment can be found at http://home.howstuffworks.com/ac.htm.

* J. David Odom and George DuBase, eds., *Commissioning Buildings in Hot Humid Climates: Design and Construction Guidelines* (Lilburn, Ga.: CH2M Hill and Fairmont Press, 2000).

** www.wbdg.org/resources/hvac_humidclimates.php.

*** "Minimizing Indoor Mold Problems through Management of Moisture in Building Systems," ASHRAE Position Document, 30 June 2005.

Operational issues include proper maintenance of HVAC equipment, attention to levels of humidity in the supplied air, and general employee education.

Government and professional organizations have developed publications and resources to assist in the identification, management, and prevention of IAQ problems. Examples of these are the *Building Air Quality Action Plan* from the U.S. Environmental Protection Agency, and *The Indoor Air Quality Guide: Best Practices for Design, Construction and Commissioning* from ASHRAE.[5]

The potential severity of mold and mildew problems is illustrated by what happened in 2002 to the Hilton Kalia Tower in Hawaii. This 453-room hotel closed in July of that year and did not reopen until August 2003—more than one year later—due to a mold infestation. The cost of remediation and lost revenue was estimated at $55 million.[6] Discussions of the causes of the Kalia Tower outbreak centered on design issues associated with the building's HVAC system, structural air leaks, and wet building materials. Severe problems such as this illustrate one aspect of potential loss that hotels are exposed to involving building construction.

Because of the wide-ranging nature of, and wide-ranging human responses to, IAQ components, hotels need to be aware of a variety of possible variables affecting IAQ. Cleaning supplies and volatile organic compounds from paints, adhesives, carpets, and other interior finishes and furniture are all potential sources of chemicals that may adversely affect guests. To this list of IAQ components we could add allergens—those substances that cause allergic reactions. Hotels have identified technologies to install in guestrooms to help remove allergy-triggering materials such as dust and pollen. The resulting hypoallergenic rooms have proven popular with guests, so much so that hotels have found that they can generate rate premiums of up to $30 per night for these rooms. The potential market for hypoallergenic rooms appears to be substantial, considering the increasing number of individuals who have allergies.[7]

In regard to IAQ and smoking, anti-smoking organizations have argued that employers may be legally liable for exposing employees to smoke in the workplace and that provisions of the Americans with Disabilities Act of 1990 may apply.[8] Many locales have passed legislation prohibiting smoking in, and even near, public buildings. As a result of these and other factors, many hotels have initiated no-smoking rules that have included penalizing guests who violate the rules with substantial additional charges. Most hotels and restaurants have discovered that business has not been negatively affected by smoking prohibitions and that the change has brought actual benefits to the business as well as employees and guests.[9, 10]

Heating Sources and Equipment

The major space conditioning need of guestrooms and many other hotel spaces involves cooling. For lodging operations in colder climates, there are times when spaces must be heated; it is especially important to keep up with the maintenance associated with heating equipment, and to perform all maintenance tasks with safety in mind. Heating equipment usually creates more safety concerns than does cooling equipment, due to the flame and flue gases that are generally present. In addition, a failure of the heating system can have disastrous effects on the building because of freezing; in contrast, a failure of the cooling system generally has much less adverse effects on the building itself.

Heat Sources

Options for heating fuel are shown in Exhibit 3. The type of fuel selected for a location will be dictated by factors such as availability, relative cost of the fuel, cost of equipment and systems to use the fuel, environmental constraints, and safety concerns.

While electricity is almost always available and is generally a safe and clean fuel source, its cost is among the highest of the fuel sources. Electricity can be an economical choice when overall needs for heat are low or the cost of equipment needed to use the other fuel sources is high. Electricity might also be chosen if a reliable supply of an alternative fuel is not available. Electrical space heating equipment most commonly passes electricity through a resistance device that converts electrical energy to heat. Another way to use electricity is to operate a heat pump, a method of heating described later in the chapter.

Natural gas, LPG (liquefied petroleum gas—usually liquefied propane), and fuel oil all produce heat as a result of combustion. This combustion requires

Exhibit 3   Heating Fuel Options

Fuel Types	Heat Content/Unit Purchased	Comments
Electricity	3413 Btu/kwh	Used in all electric heaters. Requires no flue since there are no products of combustion. Usually the most expensive form of heat.
Natural Gas	1000 Btu/cubic foot (approx.)	Clean burning. Flue required. Complete condensing units very efficient. Delivered to building by underground pipe.
Liquefied Petroleum	95,000 Btu/gallon (approx.)	Relatively clean burning. Requires on-site storage tank located outside of building. Slow vaporization of fuel in winter. Delivered by truck. May also be used for cooking fuel.
Fuel Oil	140,000–150,000 Btu/gallon	More tendency to create dirt and smoke than natural gas. Requires on-site storage tank. Delivered by truck. Various grades of fuel oil with differing energy content and combustion characteristics.
Steam	1000 Btu/lb (approx.)	More common in urban areas where steam is purchased from local steam utility. May also be supplied from central boiler plant in large complexes. Supply line for steam and return line for condensate.

sufficient supplies of oxygen and produces heat, carbon dioxide, water, and other products. Combustion occurs in a furnace or boiler. A furnace is a device that produces hot air. Furnaces may be found in small restaurants and in individual lodging units such as some timeshares and condominiums. Boilers produce steam or hot water that may be used both for space heating and for other heating needs.

During the combustion process, the proper mixing of the fuel and air is required. Generally, the fuel is pressurized and injected into the air. This process both mixes and (in the case of liquid fuels) atomizes the fuel, resulting in the potential for more efficient combustion. Combustion is then initiated by either a pilot flame or a spark.

Furnace and Boiler Operation and Maintenance

The maintenance needs of furnaces and boilers are similar. They include actions that promote efficient and safe operation and that prolong the operating life of the equipment. There is an overlap in actions taken in these areas. Actions to improve efficiency can also help prolong life and vice versa. Because furnaces and boilers are important in meeting guest and employee needs, their proper and safe operation is critical.

Furnace and boiler efficiency involves two aspects—the efficient combustion of the fuel and the efficient transfer of that combustion heat to the air or water being heated. Efficient fuel combustion requires the correct mix of combustion air and fuel. Too little combustion air will cause the fuel to burn incompletely, which leads to waste. Too much combustion air will reduce the temperature of the combustion gases and, therefore, the amount of heat that can be removed from these gases.

Maintenance staff or outside contractors should check combustion efficiency as part of the semi-annual or annual maintenance of the furnace or boiler. More frequent checks are warranted when on-site personnel are used and when large furnaces or boilers are installed.

Combustion efficiency is checked by measuring the oxygen or carbon dioxide content and temperature of the flue gas. Measuring the oxygen or carbon dioxide content of the flue gas will show whether the unit is receiving the correct amount of oxygen. Most large commercial units now use a controlled combustion process in which air (oxygen) use is controlled and adjustable. The flue gas temperature may also indicate efficiency problems. A low flue gas temperature may indicate that too much air is being supplied. A high flue gas temperature may indicate that combustion heat is not being transferred efficiently. Both situations call for maintenance attention.

Besides adjusting air and fuel for proper combustion efficiency, regular maintenance should include cleaning of all heat transfer surfaces on both sides. Burner nozzles should be inspected and carefully cleaned of dirt, debris, carbon, and other buildup. Furnaces require the removal of soot and dirt from the combustion side and the cleaning of the air side. Usually a stiff brush and vacuum are required for this cleaning. Boilers require similar combustion-side cleaning and sometimes extensive water-side cleaning.

The degree of water-side cleaning required by boilers will depend on the water quality in the boiler loop water. If water in this loop contains minerals such as calcium or magnesium, there may be a problem with boiler **scale**. Scale is a buildup of calcium or magnesium carbonate on the walls of the boiler. Scale insulates the walls, thereby reducing heat transfer and increasing the operating temperature of these portions of the walls. This can lead to premature failure of these portions of the boiler. The scale problem is addressed by treating and removing calcium and magnesium from (or *softening*) boiler system water and by periodically cleaning the boiler to remove any buildup. The frequency of cleaning should be based on the needs of the individual operation and incorporated into the preventive maintenance (PM) instructions.

Further issues of boiler water quality involve maintaining the proper pH in the boiler to avoid acidic attacks on boiler components and keeping oxygen out of the boiler when adding makeup water. Operations using steam boilers, especially when this steam is also used for laundry operations, may introduce significant amounts of makeup water. Some of this water is required to compensate for blowdown water—water deliberately vented from the boiler to remove mineral buildup and debris.

Some systems provide makeup water automatically in order to avoid dangerous low water conditions in the boiler. You should install a meter on the makeup water line to the boiler system and keep records of the amount of makeup water added. Should a leak occur in a boiler water line or elsewhere, it would be shown by an increased meter reading. In a large property, such leaks could be difficult to identify readily by another means.

Because of the potential for soot buildup and other blockages in the flue, flue inspections and cleaning should be included in the PM program. Failure to remove blockages and buildups may force combustion gases back into the boiler room, leading the boiler to operate with a reduced supply of oxygen. Besides reducing efficiency, this situation can produce carbon monoxide—a potential killer if inhaled for an extended time.

All fossil-fuel-fired heating equipment should be inspected for leakage. Furnaces should receive particular attention in the area of the combustion chamber/ heat exchanger, where building air comes closest to the combustion products. All joints and seams should receive particular attention, especially on older units. Flue ductwork should also be inspected for leaks. Any problems with the exhaust of combustion products should be corrected immediately.

Close attention should also be paid to the location of flue outlets in relation to building air intakes—especially as buildings are modified over the years. Obviously, flue gas should not enter the building's fresh air intake. There are other concerns as well. One operation located its boiler exhaust quite close to the air inlet for the cooling tower. Since the boiler was used year-round for water heating, the air entering the cooling tower was always abnormally warm. In addition, combustion products were introduced into the cooling tower water. The tower's efficiency was impaired and its life was shortened.

Since the delivery of heat from the boiler or furnace usually requires the operation of various pumps or fans, maintenance considerations for such equipment should be included in boiler or furnace PM instructions. These include basic lubrication, checking of alignment and vibration, and cleaning. Furnaces usually have a filter bank installed on the air inlet side. The filters should be changed regularly; most operations do so monthly. More frequent changes may be necessary under particularly dirty or dusty conditions, such as during building startup or renovation. Filters on water systems should also be included in PM instructions.

For boiler systems to operate properly, all controls and safety devices need to function correctly. The boiler pressure relief valve and low water cut-off switch should be checked. Control systems may use compressed air as a means of operating valves and other devices. If compressed air is used, these controls should also be calibrated. In addition, the air dryer on the compressed air system should be checked and replaced if necessary, pressures checked and adjusted, air intake filters cleaned or changed, and all connections checked for leakage.

If steam above fifteen psi (pounds per square inch) is produced, the operation of boilers may require a licensed boiler operator. Most facilities have multiple boilers to provide backup during maintenance outages and to match boiler capacity to the load. Because boiler loads vary and the standby losses that occur when unused or underused boilers are kept on are potentially high, management should shut off unneeded boilers, matching the capacity of units on line to the loads.

There are different methods of rating or expressing boiler capacity. Boilers may be rated in boiler horsepower. A boiler horsepower is equivalent to a heat output rate from the boiler of 33,475 Btu/hr, 9.8 kw, or 34.5 lb. of steam per hour at standard pressure.[11]

Cooling Sources and Equipment

Mechanical cooling equipment is used to provide the cooling required in many climates. This equipment extracts heat from either air or water and uses this cooled air or water to absorb heat in the building spaces, thereby cooling the spaces. The equipment may use the **vapor compression** process or the absorption process. Since vapor compression is much more common, the absorption process will not be discussed in this chapter. However, concerns over the impact of vapor compression refrigerants on the environment (discussed later in the chapter) may create a resurgence of absorption systems. Absorption processes are used in some guestroom refrigerators and mini-bars.

The Refrigeration Cycle

Exhibit 4 shows the basic components of the vapor compression cycle. In this cycle, a circulating refrigerant removes heat from one location and transfers this heat to another location where it is rejected. Heat removal occurs in the **evaporator**, while the heat is rejected in the **condenser**. The **compressor** provides the energy necessary to accomplish this heat transfer. The **expansion valve** controls the flow of refrigerant through the system.

In the vapor compression process, the refrigerant is boiled, or converted from a liquid to a vapor, in the evaporator. The energy used to boil the refrigerant is taken from the air or water being cooled. The refrigerant vapor then leaves the evaporator and enters the compressor, which raises the temperature and pressure

Exhibit 4   Basic Vapor Compression Refrigeration Cycle

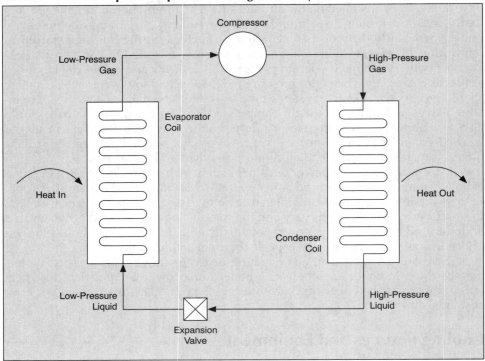

of this gas. The compressor is powered by an electric motor; it is the major energy-using component of the cycle.

The high-temperature and high-pressure refrigerant gas then leaves the compressor and enters the condenser. In the condenser, it releases heat to the condenser's cooling medium—either air or water—and reverts to a liquid. The liquid refrigerant then moves to the expansion valve, where its pressure is reduced, which causes its temperature to drop. The cold low-pressure liquid refrigerant then enters the evaporator and the cycle repeats. (The refrigeration cycle is somewhat difficult to understand looking only at a written description and static drawing. There are a number of online videos on locations such as YouTube that may prove helpful.)

Cooling Systems Operation and Maintenance

All refrigeration system components need to function properly. Maintenance activities with regard to these systems include the following:

- Inspect equipment for refrigerant leaks. These can be identified by the presence of oil carried outside the system by the leaking refrigerant. Special devices are also available to test for leaks.

- Check refrigerant dryers for indications of water contamination. (Dryers are devices installed in refrigerant lines that collect and hold moisture.) Replace all dryers showing signs of water and re-inspect these dryers again shortly afterward to be sure the problem has not recurred.

- Clean air-cooled condensers and evaporators.

- Clean condensate drip pans and drain lines from evaporators. Replace algae-cide tablets in drip pans and reapply protective paints.

- Check equipment operating conditions to be sure each unit is operating correctly. Refer to equipment manuals.

- Perform all recommended drive motor maintenance, paying particular attention to operating temperatures and motor starting controls. High operating temperatures and repeated starting and stopping are major factors in refrigeration system motor failure.

Space cooling equipment uses three different types of compressors: reciprocating, centrifugal, and rotary. Each has unique maintenance concerns. Reciprocating compressors use a cylinder moving within a chamber to compress the refrigerant. Maintenance needs resemble those of automotive engines, and on-site staff can sometimes handle these needs. Since they may be relatively small and designed to be replaced, reciprocating compressor units may be exchanged for rebuilt or other replacement units. Operating efficiencies are often already low, and poor maintenance can degrade these values to even lower levels.

Centrifugal units are generally larger compressors and require more care in maintenance and shutdown. Particular care is needed to avoid the introduction of air and water, which can cause many components to fail. Because of the complexity of centrifugal units, maintenance contracts are often used to provide the necessary services.

Rotary compressors are among the smaller compressors found at a lodging property. They are often used in through-the-wall guestroom units and may be used in other similarly sized applications. Because of the applications for these units and their small size, they are often replaced with an exchange unit rather than repaired at the property.

Cooling equipment capacities are expressed in several ways. The cooling rate of equipment might be expressed in Btu/hour (or BTUH). A unit installed in a guestroom might have a capacity rating of 7,000 to 14,000 Btu/hr. Cooling rate or capacity is also expressed in *tons*. A ton of cooling is equivalent to a cooling rate of 12,000 Btu/hr. A large hotel could have several chillers rated at several hundred tons each. All equipment ratings use a standard rating point to allow for comparison among equipment. The cost of equipment operation depends on the load on the equipment, the equipment efficiency, and the cost of electricity (the usual source of power for chilling equipment).

CFCs, HCFCs, and the Environment

During the 1980s, concern about ozone depletion in the stratosphere and global warming began to grow. Investigation determined that a major contributor to ozone depletion was probably the discharge of chlorofluorocarbons (CFCs) and, to a much lesser extent, hydrochlorofluorocarbons (HCFCs). CFCs and HCFCs are chemical compounds manufactured for use as solvents and refrigerants.

In past decades, a number of CFCs and HCFCs were commonly used in air conditioning and refrigeration equipment. The CFCs R-11 and R-12 were used in centrifugal chillers. Reciprocating chillers used R-12. HCFC R-22 was used in refrigeration equipment as well as some chillers, packaged air conditioning systems, and window units.

Depending on the type of equipment, age, and specific recommendations of suppliers, various options are available to retrofit more environmentally friendly refrigerants to existing equipment. However, some equipment does not lend itself to retrofitting, so new equipment should be purchased that use HCFCs with lower ozone depletion or use alternative refrigerants such as the hydrofluorocarbons (HFCs) having near zero ozone depletion ratings. Information on potential substitute refrigerants and other issues of interest regarding refrigerants can be found on the United States Environmental Protection Agency[12] and United Nations Environmental Program websites.[13] Decisions about refrigerant changes should be made only after careful evaluation and consultation with equipment suppliers. Changing refrigerants is not as easy as changing the oil in your car.

New refrigerants may also introduce some safety concerns. There may be a need for refrigerant monitoring devices in mechanical spaces because of potential toxic effects of exposure to refrigerants. Operations may have to purchase breathing apparatus to protect staff in the instance of leakages. These issues should be addressed with the equipment suppliers and the local health and building code authorities.

One possible solution to the potential costs and uncertainty of HCFCs and CFCs is to use an absorption (heat-driven) chiller. Exhibit 5 illustrates one application of an absorption chiller, showing the variety of issues and opportunities that arise when considering this technology.

The Montreal Protocol, signed in 1987 with subsequent modifications over the years, provides a schedule for the phase-out of ozone-depleting refrigerants as well as other rules and regulations, including provisions for global taxes on these materials. Many countries are signers of the Protocol and therefore are legally obligated to ensure compliance by their citizens. The Protocol represents a major global action to address environmental change caused in this instance by ozone depletion. This depletion is partially caused by refrigerant emissions.

Hospitality chains and individual properties should have monitoring programs in place to ensure they are following applicable local laws related to the Montreal Protocol and should be considering the implications of the CFC and HCFC regulations when performing maintenance and purchasing new equipment. One side benefit of the Protocol has been that new equipment purchased using refrigerants with lowered or zero ozone depletion potential has generally been more efficient than the old equipment it is replacing. Responding to an environmental problem has in this instance turned out to be good business—providing more reliable equipment with reduced operating costs.

There are increased costs associated with CFC/HCFC issues. First, the cost of CFCs has risen substantially due to new taxes and restricted availability. The

Exhibit 5 Gas-Fired Cooling for the Philadelphia Marriott

Over 1,400 rooms totaling about one million square feet are air-conditioned mainly by a natural-gas-fired absorption chiller at the Philadelphia Marriott hotel. Philadelphia Gas Works (PGW) developed an economically attractive equipment package, which was selected by the customer based on cost savings and energy efficiency.

The hotel's hybrid cooling system design minimizes operation costs, since the gas chiller provides most of the air-conditioning while an electric unit assists only on hot, humid summer days. The Philadelphia utility benefits from additional gas load year-round and especially during the summer, when sales volumes are lower. PGW's gas cooling load now totals about 250,000 Mcf/season.

Background

The 23-floor Philadelphia Marriott, occupying a city block in the business district, opened in early 1995. The hotel offers 11,000 square feet of meeting space, four ballrooms, four restaurants and lounges, retail space, and many other amenities.

The heating, ventilation, and air-conditioning (HVAC) system was designed by Giovanetti-Shulman Associates (Drexel Hill, Pennsylvania), which analyzed the economics of various fuels and equipment including city steam, electric chillers, heat pumps, and fan coils. Marriott's choice, based on economics and energy efficiency, was a 1,000-ton Thermachill™ unit manufactured by The Trane Co. The lower gas rate compared to electricity, along with an equipment rebate, were factors in the hotel chain's decision.

Implementation

The Trane Thermachill unit at the Marriott hotel is a direct-fired, double-effect chiller that runs primarily on natural gas. At the height of the cooling season, the gas-fired chiller is assisted by a Carrier Corp. 1,000-ton electric centrifugal chiller. The two units were piped in series to ensure that the absorption equipment takes preference.

For additional operating cost savings, the HVAC system features variable-flow pumping, water- and air-side economizers, and variable-air-flow equipment.

Advantages

As with most gas cooling systems, the biggest advantage of absorption chillers is low operating costs. Commercial electric rates penalize consumption during peak demand periods, mainly hot summer days requiring air conditioning. In hybrid cooling systems, gas-fired chillers give operators more flexibility to minimize costs by selecting the most economical combination of energy sources (gas and electricity).

Demand charges are pegged at $12.72/kw, and electric rates range up to 8.9 cents/kwh in an extremely complex rate structure. Due to a ratchet clause, a high peak demand charge for electricity is enforced year-round. Even during the winter, the customer pays 80% of the worst (highest) 15-minute summer peak demand charge.

PGW offers a very competitive gas cooling rate of $4/Mcf from May through September for interruptible service. Marriott selected a dual-fuel chiller (gas/ #2 fuel oil) to take advantage of this interruptible rate, but during four years of operation, the system has never been interrupted during the cooling season. PGW also offered a rate on the absorption chiller cost, which the utility views as a worthwhile means of increasing summer gas load.

Other advantages of gas absorption technology include quiet operation, low maintenance, and environmentally harmless refrigerants. Brian Mazuk, Marriott's Chief Engineer, says, "We have very few problems. The chiller operates efficiently, even at part-load capacity. We use natural gas as the primary fuel because it is cheaper and cleaner."

Source: "Municipal Case Studies: Philadelphia Gas Works—Absorpton Chillers," August 1999.

production of CFCs was essentially eliminated by the year 2000. Production and consumption of HCFCs will be reduced by 90 percent by 2015 and by 99.5 percent by 2020. Therefore, only recycled forms of CFC/HCFC products will likely be available for replacement needs. Scarcity and the cost of recycling will be reflected in a higher price for these products.

A large amount of the refrigerant discharged from equipment in past years was discharged due to either poor equipment maintenance or poor maintenance practices. For the sake of efficiency and to protect the environment, refrigerant leaks clearly must be eliminated or reduced to their lowest possible level. In the past, leaks were sometimes tolerated because refrigerants were relatively inexpensive and perceived to be inert and safe. These conditions no longer apply. Maintenance employees will require retraining and certification concerning appropriate practices. Venting of refrigerants as a standard purging method must be eliminated. Proper equipment must be used to remove refrigerants from equipment and either recycle it on site or store it for eventual reclamation at an off-site reclamation plant.

The decision to repair, modify, or replace existing refrigeration equipment will be more difficult due to stricter environmental legislation. An operation with an existing chiller may wish to continue to use a CFC refrigerant but take steps to minimize the possibilities of refrigerant release. This could mean installing equipment to facilitate the recovery and reuse of refrigerant. Another option would be to change refrigerants. Finally, careful analysis may lead management to decide to replace the chiller completely. New equipment is very likely to be more efficient, and potential maintenance needs and even breakdowns are likely to be fewer.

Repair, modify, or replace options require managers to evaluate a number of issues. Managers will need to collect a significant amount of data and consult knowledgeable individuals before making their decisions. A good source for current information is the American Society of Heating, Refrigerating and Air-Conditioning Engineers, located in Atlanta, Georgia.

Guestroom HVAC System Types

Exhibit 6 is a summary of the possible options for providing HVAC to guestrooms. The two major types of systems are centralized and decentralized. All modern centralized systems use pipes to distribute hot or chilled water to fan coil units in the guestrooms. The hot or chilled water is produced by large boilers and chillers. Most decentralized units use electrically powered equipment in the guestroom itself to provide heating and cooling. The "other" systems in Exhibit 6 are less frequently found, but they may be used in some applications.

Exhibit 7 contains simplified schematics of the fan coil systems found in hotel guestrooms. Guestrooms in many lodging establishments use what are called packaged terminal air conditioning units (PTAC), which are also referred to as through-the-wall units. These units are capable of providing cooling and, in many instances, heating for guestrooms. The only energy source used by these units is electricity, which makes them relatively easy to install, maintain, and replace since the unit itself slides into a "sleeve" through the exterior wall of the building and plugs into electric service within the guestroom. Exhibit 8 contains a schematic of

Exhibit 6 Guestroom HVAC Options

Centralized Systems

- Two-Pipe System
- Three-Pipe System
- Four-Pipe System

Decentralized Sytems

- Baseboard Electric Heater/Wall-Mounted Electric Heater
- Through-the-Wall and Split Units

  Cooling Only

  Cooling with Electric Heating

  Cooling with Heat Pump Heating

Hybrid and Other Systems

- Water Source Heat Pumps
- Furnace with or without Cooling

Exhibit 7 In-Room Terminal Systems

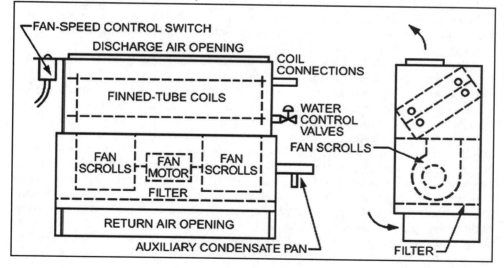

a PTAC unit. Room air is drawn into the unit by the fan through the front of the unit, is filtered and then is drawn through the cooling or heating coil. The heated or cooled air is then returned to the room through the discharge grill at the top of the unit. Heat extracted from the air is rejected in the condenser coil to air outside the guestroom.

Exhibit 8   PTAC Unit

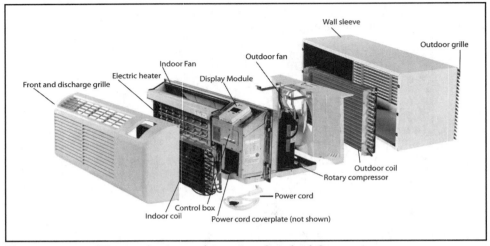

Photo courtesy of Trane, a business of American Standard Companies.

Centralized Systems

Centralized systems use boilers to create hot water and chillers to create cold water. The hot or cold water is circulated to fan coil units in the guestrooms. Air is blown through the fan coils, where heat is transferred either to or from the water, and heating or cooling occurs. Because the only devices operating in the guestroom are small fans, centralized systems are relatively quiet.

Because fan coils require no connection to the outside of the building, they can be placed in a variety of locations in the guestroom. These include under the exterior window, horizontally above the ceiling in entry areas, and vertically on adjoining walls. Vertical units are usually installed back to back; this reduces installation costs by sharing pipe and electrical runs vertically in the building.

The **two-pipe system** allows both heating and cooling, but only one of these at a time. In the two-pipe design, someone must decide whether to provide heating or cooling on a given day. Converting from one option to the other usually takes several hours or even a day or two, so it is important to choose wisely. Since only one mode is possible, the two-pipe system is not capable of dealing with situations requiring both heating and cooling over the course of a day. The operating costs of two-pipe systems are relatively low, since they limit guest HVAC options, allow shutdown of the boiler or chiller during seasons of the year, and provide fuel economies due to the operation of fossil fuel heating and an efficient central chiller.

The guests and management of facilities with two-pipe systems may be frustrated by these systems' lack of flexibility in meeting varying conditions in the building. If a building has cool outside air temperatures but abundant sunshine or widely varying outside temperatures from night to day, it will be very difficult to maintain comfortable conditions in all guestrooms. While little can be done to rectify this in the operating mode, it may be possible to make relatively minor modifications to the building piping layout that will zone the building, allowing portions to be connected to a chiller and others to the boiler. Another option is to install water source heat pumps when guestroom fan coils are replaced, if the existing electrical supply to the fan coils will allow this.

To increase the comfort provided by the two-pipe system, some operations install units that contain small electric resistance heaters. This allows the guest to select heating or cooling. This is often done in locations that have a relatively short heating season, where the expense of a boiler is not warranted. If a boiler is installed as well, the electric heater will have a sensor that disables it when the building heating system is operational.

While modern two-pipe designs use hot water, steam may be used in some older designs. When this is the case, it is not possible to connect the fan coil to a chiller. If needed, space cooling will have to be provided by another means.

The **three-pipe system** is relatively uncommon, especially in recent construction. This system provides both hot and cold water to the fan coil units at all times and mixes the return water from the fan coils. The three-pipe system can provide good guestroom comfort, since heating and cooling can be provided as needed. However, since the boiler and chiller both use this lukewarm return water as input water, their efficiencies are reduced, causing their operating costs to rise. That is, this system must use energy to bring the lukewarm return water back up or back down to proper boiler or chiller temperatures.

The **four-pipe system** provides the same level of comfort as the three-pipe system, but keeps the cold and hot water returns separated. This leads to greater boiler and chiller efficiency, since much less energy is needed to reheat or re-cool the return water. The four-pipe system is the most expensive central system option to install, since it requires more extensive piping and two coils in the fan coil unit.

The control of comfort in the guestroom can involve several different methods, depending on the system. For those systems with a wall-mounted thermostat, the thermostat generally controls one or more valves in the fan coil unit. If a combination heating and cooling thermostat is used, it will activate either the heating or cooling mode of operation (hot or cold water valve setting), depending on the thermostat setpoint (the desired room temperature) and the actual room temperature. Fan operation and speed may be selected by using a switch located with the room thermostat. The thermostat usually controls only the heating or cooling operation; it is rare that the thermostat also controls the fan. Units lacking wall-mounted thermostats have controls on the units themselves, which allow selection of heating or cooling, fan speed, and temperature.

Decentralized Systems

Decentralized systems place the heating and cooling sources within the guestroom itself or along the outside wall. An electric baseboard heating system is a decentralized heat source. Electric heaters may also be wall-mounted with a fan, an arrangement found in some bathroom areas. Electric baseboard or fan-forced units generally do not incorporate any method of providing or delivering cooling. For operations in cold climates or those operating seasonally, it may be satisfactory to provide heat only. However, most guestrooms require both heating and cooling, and some require only cooling.

Decentralized systems that provide cooling use a small refrigeration system (compressor, condenser, evaporator, and expansion valve) located within a cabinet that extends through the outside wall of the guestroom. "Split" decentralized systems locate only the evaporator and distribution fan in the guestroom and put the condenser and compressor outside the building on a balcony, roof, or on the ground. The condenser has access to outside air, which it uses for heat rejection. The evaporator is located within the room. Room air is circulated through the evaporator, where it is cooled and dehumidified.

Split systems result in a quieter operation than typical decentralized systems. In addition, split systems allow more flexibility in the placement of the in-room unit because it can be placed in an interior location along an inside wall (or in a dropped ceiling area). Split systems can be highly efficient as well. Split systems can also be purchased to function as heat pumps (discussed below).

Decentralized systems (that is, through-the-wall units or PTACs) for guestrooms are widely used in small hotels. The units are relatively inexpensive to purchase and easy to install. Their only energy source is electricity. Most of these units require penetrations through the outside wall of the building and, within the guestroom, they must not be blocked by furniture or drapery if they are to operate properly. In humid locations, units with a higher latent cooling capacity are often installed to reduce the potential for mold and mildew.

An understanding of the factors that define and influence the efficiency of cooling systems can be helpful in achieving optimal performance of these systems, in controlling operating costs, and in evaluating equipment for purchase.

The efficiency of cooling equipment involves measuring the ratio of the amount of cooling achieved (the output) to the amount of energy used to operate the system (the input). This ratio can be expressed in several ways. For small equipment, such as PTACs used in guestrooms, the ratio may be expressed as the **energy efficiency ratio**, or **EER**. The EER is calculated by dividing the rated cooling output of the unit in Btu/hr by the watts drawn by the unit. The higher the EER, the more efficient the unit.

Exhibit 9 contains information abstracted from manufacturers' specifications for PTACs. Units of approximately the same cooling capacity were selected and the capacity chosen is one suitable for many guestroom applications. The amps value is for operation in the cooling mode; the EER values measure each unit's efficiency. Many building HVAC components have their efficiencies established by rather rigorous testing. The Air-Conditioning, Heating, and Refrigeration Institute (AHRI) certifies products that pass its tests and maintains a listing of these products and their performance on its website.[14] Managers should refer to AHRI's website for information about the efficiency of the products they are considering purchasing and compare them with alternatives.

Exhibit 9 illustrates the potential value and cost of making decisions involving higher efficiency in PTAC units. Comparing Unit A and Unit D (from different manufacturers), we see that the efficiency of Unit A as measured by the EER is 12.3, while that of Unit D is 11.4. This will mean that Unit A will consume approximately 8 percent less energy than Unit D. A unit such as Unit D in a southern U.S.

Exhibit 9   Specifications of Guestroom PTAC Units (230/208 volts)

	Unit A	Unit B	Unit C	Unit D	Unit E
Type of Unit	A/C + Elec. Heat	A/C + Elec. Heat + Extra H$_2$O Removal	Heat Pump	A/C + Elec. Heat	Heat Pump
Cooling Capacity (BTUH)	9450/9250	9000/8800	9400/9200	9000	8500/8300
Cooling Amps	3.6/3.9	3.6/3.9	3.6/3.8	3.6/3.9	3.7
EER	12.3/12.3	11.8/11.8	12.7/12.7	11.4	10.5
Moisture Removal (pints per hour)	2.7	3.4	2.7	3.4	2.1
Heating Capacity Heat Pump Operation			8300/8100		8000
Elec. Resistance-KW	2.4–4.7	2.4–4.7	2.4–4.7	3.4–2.8	3.4–2.8
Elec. Resistance-BTUH	(8200–16000)	(8200–16000)	(8200–16000)	(11600–9500)	(11600–9500)
Heat Pump COP	n/a	n/a	3.8/3.8	n/a	3
Approx. Cost (unit only)	$925	$1,100	$1,100	$720	$770

location might cost $160 per year to operate, while Unit A would cost about $13 less per year to operate. The higher-efficiency unit (Unit A) costs about $200 more than the lower-efficiency unit (Unit D). Is slightly higher efficiency worth purchasing in this situation? Possibly not, but managers need to consider more than just efficiency when making a PTAC purchase. Product quality is also important, as are a host of other issues, including appearance, noise, and maintenance history. In recent years, rising government efficiency standards for all equipment have closed the "efficiency gap" between products, so that in many instances it is tougher to justify a given purchase on just greater efficiency alone.

Unit size should be matched to the cooling needs of the space; larger is not always better. Large PTAC units typically have a lower efficiency, cost slightly more, and may contribute to more humid conditions in the guestroom. Optimum service to guests and efficient operation are best provided by units matched to the peak needs of the room or slightly-less-than-the-peak needs, the latter units trading off a little capacity on the warmest days for higher efficiency the rest of the time. Operators who have reduced the heating and cooling needs of their guestrooms via installation of reflective window treatments, energy-efficient windows and doors, insulation, and energy-efficient lighting should not need to replace heating and cooling units with units of the same capacity. Smaller, less expensive units should be satisfactory, resulting in savings in initial costs as well as in energy costs.

Choosing heat pump through-the-wall units rather than resistance heat units can be a good choice. Heat pump units can cost 15 to 20 percent more than resistance heat units. However, their annual heating energy usage can be half or a third that of resistance heating units. Paybacks could be as short as one heating season.

One final element of comfort related to PTAC and PTHP units involves noise. Purchasers of these units are encouraged to test the noise generation of the units at all fan switch settings and while the compressor is cycling to determine whether the levels of noise produced are acceptable. A unit that only has an ON switch for the fan (no choice of speeds) may generate excessive noise. A unit that cycles the fan along with the compressor may create an unpleasant sleepless night for guests, as the unit's cycling may be far too noisy. Managers must remember that guest comfort includes acoustic comfort.

Larger cooling equipment, such as a building chiller, may have its efficiency expressed as an EER value or, more commonly, as a value of kilowatts per ton of cooling. The kw per ton value is really an inverse efficiency (input divided by output); that is, efficiency increases as the kw per ton value decreases.

Recent advances in the equipment rating methods for large equipment have improved the way in which efficiencies are defined. Ratings can now consider performance at various load levels. Ratings compiled in this manner are known as **integrated part load values (IPLV)** and **non-standard part load values (NPLV)**. The IPLV calculation involves testing at prescribed levels of cooling load, while the NPLV value is derived from analysis of the actual expected operating loads of the chiller, using these estimates to calculate the chiller's expected operational efficiency. The information gained using the IPLV/NPLV approach can be significant, since equipment operates for much of the time at partial loads. Selecting equipment with these part-load efficiencies in mind can result in lower operating costs. However, it has also been shown that real-world chiller operation may not agree with the theoretical operation used to develop IPLV and NPLV values. Investing in engineering studies and modeling existing chiller operation may be the best choice.[15]

Many decentralized units provide space heating with an electric resistance heater. This may create rather high costs for space heating. One way to reduce the cost of space heating may be to use a **heat pump** unit instead of electric resistance heating.

A heat pump unit uses the refrigeration cycle not only for space cooling, but also for space heating. Reversing the direction of refrigerant flow in a heat pump causes the components functioning as the evaporator and the condenser to switch functions. As a result, heat can be removed from the outside air and added to the inside (and vice versa). The heat pump uses the refrigeration cycle to do this at an efficiency two or more times greater than that of electric resistance heat.

Heat pump efficiency (output divided by input) is defined as heat delivered in Btu/hr (output) divided by the heat equivalent of the electric energy input (with each watt of input the equivalent of 3.413 Btu/hr). This ratio is defined as the **coefficient of performance (COP)**. A unit capable of delivering 8200 Btu/hr (2.4 kw) while drawing 645 watts has a COP of 3.7.

The COP is less of a constant than the EER because the temperature conditions of operation vary considerably over the heating season. The evaporator will face outside conditions ranging from temperatures in the fifties to the twenties Fahrenheit (twelve to minus seven Celsius), or possibly less. Equipment vendors are able to calculate seasonal performance values for heat pump units and compare these with the performance of electric heat-only units to determine potential savings. Managers should keep in mind the expected operating mode for the units when considering this. If occupancies are low in the winter months and the hotel keeps temperatures relatively cool in unoccupied rooms, the vendor's savings figures for replacing an existing unit with a heat pump may be somewhat overstated.

A factor affecting heat pump operation involves the defrost cycle on the evaporator. Since the evaporator extracts heat from the outside air, cold temperatures may result in frost buildup. The unit will go through a defrost cycle to remove this buildup. The controls governing the defrost cycle must operate properly if the heat pump is to function efficiently.

The efficiency of cooling equipment will vary, depending on the conditions at the evaporator and the condenser. The lower the evaporator temperature or the higher the condenser temperature, the less efficiently the equipment operates and, therefore, the less cooling it delivers. While managers may think they have little control over evaporator or condenser temperatures, maintenance actions can make a difference. If the evaporator is starved for air as a result of a clogged filter, its temperature will drop and efficiency will suffer. The same is true when the evaporator or condenser is "insulated" by a layer of dirt and dust. Heat transfer is reduced and efficiency suffers.

The operation of virtually any HVAC system in the cooling mode produces condensate on the evaporator. Therefore, a means of condensate removal must be provided. Some older units just drip the condensate outside the building. The current standard involves either using some sort of evaporation or ejection system (that, ideally, vaporizes the condensate) or draining the condensate from the drip pan to a drain system.

Other Systems

Hybrid systems have characteristics of both centralized and decentralized systems. The water source heat pump system is the most obvious choice for this category. Rather than using outside air as the heat source or location for heat rejection, the water source heat pump is connected to an internal water circulation loop from which it takes, or to which it adds, heat (in the heating or cooling mode, respectively). This allows the heat pump to operate with an evaporator (or condenser) temperature that better maximizes unit efficiency. It also eliminates the need to locate the unit on the outside wall of the building and allows the operator to recover and use waste heat within the building.

In one hotel application, the water source is well water circulated through the pump and then returned to the ground—a "free" source of heat or cooling. In another hotel application, the water pipe connected to the heat pump is also the supply pipe for the sprinkler system, thereby reducing installation costs through dual use of the piping. In addition, this system cools all refrigeration equipment with the same water, providing a heat source for the heat pump throughout the winter months. Supplemental heating is provided by a boiler, and the water loop is cooled in summer by the building's cooling tower. The result is a potentially very cost-effective application of heat pump technology.

Still another application emerging in some areas is geothermal heating and cooling. Geothermal has the potential to provide significant cost savings to hoteliers and in most applications to date has proven to be a very reliable technology.

Geothermal Heating and Cooling at the Galt House

Al Schneider is the owner and designer of the Galt House, a complex that now contains over 1.7 million square feet that includes 100 apartments, 600 hotel rooms, 150,000 square feet of conference space, and 960,000 square feet of office space. Mr. Schneider engaged Marion Pinckley, of Pinckley Engineering, Inc., to look into using a GeoExchange system (geothermal) to heat and cool the Galt House East hotel. That 1,700-ton project was completed in 1984. Based on the success of the GeoExchange system in the Galt House East hotel, Mr. Schneider has since completed the Waterfront Office Building in 1993, and the 4,700-ton combined office/hotel/apartment complex Galt House has become the world's largest GHP project.

What made GeoExchange appealing is its economy of installation and operation, ease of maintenance, and environmental benefits. System cost was $1,500/ton. A conventional system (centrifugal chillers, cooling towers, insulated pipes) for such a complex could cost from $2,000 to $3,000/ton. And maintenance is favorable due to heat pump technology, which does not require specialized procedures.

The system is controlled by a combination of thermostats and an energy management system. Each heat pump unit in the public and meeting areas has a normal thermostat with a sensor placed in it reporting to the EMS [energy management system]. The EMS kills the thermostat when it is energized; however, if the EMS fails, the thermostats take over control.

There are four 130-foot deep wells that each can provide up to 700 gpm [2,650 lpm] with 15-hp variable-speed pumps from the aquifer under Louisville. Ground water at 58° F [14.4° C] is pumped into a 150,000-gallon reservoir under the mechanical room. Water from the reservoir flows into the Ohio River. Water from the reservoir is circulated through plate and frame heat exchangers which separate the ground water from closed loop circulation systems in the buildings. There is a total of 65,000 gallons of water flowing through the entire loop system: 25,000 gallons in the hotel loops, and 40,000 gallons in the office building loops.

During a typical summer, water is stored at an approximate temperature of 80° F [27° C] while maintaining an average temperature of 55° F [13° C] in the winter. During spring and fall, energy can be simply removed from the buildings during the day and put into the loops and 140,000-gallon reservoir to be used at night. The Galt House East has a high internal load due to its occupants; therefore, incorporating GHPs with the use of thermal storage has proven to be very efficient. The use of thermal storage allows the controls to shut down the well pumps (sometimes for as long as a week) and use the Btus stored in the reservoir during the day, with a net cooling load, to heat the building during the night if necessary.

The office buildings are conditioned with package heat pumps of 10- to 20-ton capacity for interior areas. The exterior is conditioned by stacked vertical units for each bay. Exterior zones are defined as approximately the outer twelve feet.

The Galt House East hotel energy cost is approximately 53 percent of the adjacent original Galt House, when subjected to the same rented room/meeting room occupancy. The adjacent Galt House has heat pumps in the first three floors, which include meeting and public space. The remainder is served by electric heat from air units and packaged air conditioning units with electric heat. An EMS and better insulation in the Galt House East contribute to the total savings, but the all-GeoExchange system contributes the major portion of the savings.

Due to water-regulating valves and variable-frequency drives on the Galt House East circulating pumps, the pumps most often operate at 25 to 30 percent of full load. The office buildings are not filled, but similar savings are expected on that system.

Each 4-foot tall [1.2 meter], 15-hp, 700-gpm [2,650 L] pump provides the HVAC system with 3.5 MMBtu/hr of heating or cooling, equivalent to a 300-ton chiller/cooling tower combination and a 4-MMBtu/hr input boiler. The well pump and a heat exchanger pump will cost approximately $1.50/hr to operate, versus $15 to $20 for the conventional system.

Maintenance cost and personnel requirements have been very favorable. A heat pump package does not require the skill and experience required by a centrifugal system with four pipe controls or other systems common in large complexes.

In addition to saving approximately $25,000/month in energy costs, the GHP has been very reliable because each space has its own system. Such a system also has reduced capital requirements during construction, since the major portion of the equipment need not be purchased until required. And, of course, it was not necessary to furnish a 4,000-ton cooling tower, or its space and support. The GHP system saves 25,000 square feet in space that would have been used for equipment rooms with a conventional system.

All of this adds up to lower initial cost, lower operating cost, and a very friendly system for the owner, occupants, and maintenance personnel.

Source: GeoExchange Heat Pump Consortium, Inc. (www.geoexchange.org/pdf/cs-001.pdf).

Another emerging option is the use of variable refrigeration volume (VRV)/variable refrigeration flow (VRF) systems. VRV/VRF systems look like a typical split system (evaporator inside the room and condenser outside when in cooling mode) but instead of having a condenser for each evaporator, the evaporators share a condenser. The result is potentially a more efficient system where the noisy condenser can be located away from the guestrooms. In addition, it is possible to capture waste heat at the system's individual, larger condenser as well.[16]

The furnace systems mentioned in the "other" category in Exhibit 6 are sometimes found in condominium or timeshare units. In essence, a residential furnace is located within the unit. The unit may have an air conditioning capability as well. This is a type of decentralized system, but it relies on combustion of a fuel in the furnace and a remote condensing unit for the air conditioner. Therefore, it is rather different in design, appearance, and location from the typical decentralized through-the-wall unit.

Guestroom Ventilation

Providing fresh air to guestrooms can be a problem. Most guestrooms operate at a slight negative pressure due to the bathroom ventilation fan. The air removed by this fan must be replaced from somewhere. Guestrooms with central HVAC systems may rely on airflow under the guestroom door from a corridor to provide makeup air. If air does not enter the room under the door, it must migrate from somewhere and will leak in wherever it can, often along windows and through any opening. PTAC/PTHP units have vents to the outside that mix outside air with conditioned air in the unit. Some PTAC/PTHP units have adjustable doors on these vents, and some even have doors that only open when the unit operates. A smart facilities manager should know how the units at his or her property operate and evaluate the best vent settings for the property's needs. If the outside vent opening is in use, periodic cleaning of the air filter on this vent is needed.

If the outside air admitted to the room is not conditioned and controlled, operational problems can result. During the summer, hot and humid outside air leaking into guestrooms around windows and through the building exterior can result in moisture condensation in, and deterioration of, walls. In the winter, warm, moist interior air can deposit moisture in the walls as it migrates through the walls. Other related problems include mold growth on wall coverings and carpet. Some of these problems can be reduced by sealing and caulking, but the ultimate solution to many problems requires a redesign of building systems and often a resizing and reselection of the guestroom HVAC units as well. Coping with these types of problems can be a real headache for management and staff.

Guestroom HVAC Occupancy Control

While hotels are twenty-four-hour-per-day, seven-day-per-week types of businesses, guestrooms are generally not occupied 24/7. Typical hotel occupancies are often 70 percent or so. This means that on a given day many guestrooms are not occupied at all. Even when a guestroom is rented, typically the guest or guests sleep in or otherwise occupy the room perhaps ten or so hours out of the twenty-four-hour day. Conditioning guestrooms 24/7 uses large amounts of energy. One option for reducing this energy usage is occupancy control of HVAC equipment.

Occupancy control of guestroom HVAC equipment adjusts the temperature in the room depending on room status (rented or not rented) and on whether a guest (or some other person) is present. In summer, the setpoint for room temperature is raised. In winter, the setpoint is lowered. Both of these actions reduce the amount of energy used to condition the room.

Some guestroom occupancy controls can also act to turn off the electricity in the guestroom when a guest is not present. Controls of this type have been used for years by four- and five-star hotels in a number of countries around the world. In one of the simpler versions of guest occupancy control, the guest places his or her "key" into a holder upon entering the room. This engages the electrical circuits for television, lighting, and sometimes HVAC (mini-bar and entry room lighting are on a separate circuit that is always energized). With this system, guests always know where their key is, and the hotel reduces guestroom energy usage. Control of guestroom HVAC operation by occupancy controls is becoming more widely used as managers respond to cost and environmental concerns. In 2013, the State of California mandated that all hotel guestrooms constructed after July 1, 2014, have occupancy sensors that control the operation of HVAC equipment and all lighting fixtures, including plug-in lighting.[17] Actions taken by California are often followed by similar actions elsewhere in the United States.

Occupancy sensors can do more than just assist in energy conservation. This technology can also be integrated with security systems to provide enhanced security of guestrooms. When connected to the front desk, occupancy sensor systems can inform the hotel when guestroom doors are not closed properly or when unrented rooms are entered. Occupancy sensors can also create a signal that will tell housekeepers whether the guest is in the room, thus reducing the instances of those sometimes unpleasant encounters between sleepy, partially clad guests and housekeepers anxious to clean a room.

Guestroom HVAC Maintenance

Guestroom fan coil units are relatively simple devices. Maintenance of these units is generally part of the preventive maintenance (guestroom maintenance) activity. A common PM checklist for these units would include:

- Checking the operation of all valves and control knobs.
- Checking the thermostat for proper operation, appearance, and physical connections.
- Cleaning the filter inlet grill and physical connections.
- Replacing or cleaning the air filter. (Note: This may be done monthly, while guestroom preventive maintenance may be only quarterly.)
- Cleaning the condensate drain and replacing algaecide tablets.
- Inspecting fans and cleaning and tightening connections.
- Checking the condition and fit of electrical plugs and connections.
- Checking and cleaning the outside air vent.
- Cleaning all coils.
- Lubricating blower motors.
- Painting locations such as the condensate pan and any deteriorated surfaces. Reapplying corrosion treatment if in coastal areas.

HVAC Systems for Other Building Areas

The fan coil and heat pump systems used in guestrooms may be used elsewhere in the building. Units similar to these are found in office spaces, some corridor and lobby locations, small meeting rooms, and similar areas. Other areas may use HVAC systems that differ from those found in the guestroom. Most of these systems operate with an air delivery system.

System Types and Configurations

The HVAC systems for building areas other than the guestroom areas generally involve some form of all-air system. Some all-air systems use **air handling units**, while other all-air systems use **packaged air conditioning units**. Air handling units (AHUs) consist of coils (through which steam/hot water or chilled water is circulated from central boilers and chillers), filters, fresh air intakes, exhaust air discharges, and sometimes humidification equipment. AHUs are generally located in building mechanical spaces, often somewhat remote from the areas actually being served. They are connected to these areas via duct systems.

Packaged air conditioning units are generally mounted on the roof. Each packaged air conditioning unit operates separately and is essentially self-contained. A fuel provides heat and a refrigeration system produces cooling. Refrigeration systems of this type are called **direct expansion** (abbreviated DX) **systems** because the evaporator is located directly in the conditioned airstream. Duct-work for these systems is usually less extensive than that for AHUs.

Exhibit 10 shows a very simplified view of an air conditioning system for a space such as a meeting room or restaurant. Within the box representing the conditioned space, people, food, and equipment generate heat, moisture, odors, and pollutants. In addition, heat may be added or lost through the building structure and via air leakage. The air conditioning system in Exhibit 10 removes air from the space, exhausts some of this air, mixes fresh air with the remaining return air, filters this mixed air, and then either heats or cools the air. This "conditioned" air is moved to the space being conditioned, where it either warms or cools the space. It will also pick up moisture and odors as it moves through the space.

Packaged units often supply conditioned air for restaurants and various public areas in low-rise lodging facilities. The self-contained and factory-assembled nature of these units mean they can be installed quickly with relatively little on-site labor. On the other hand, their rooftop location means they may be somewhat neglected and not receive proper maintenance. One corporate director of engineering tells the story of a property in Texas that was unable to cool its ballroom. After numerous attempts to troubleshoot the system by phone failed, the director visited the property. Upon climbing on the roof to view the unit, he discovered

Exhibit 10   Air Conditioning System for a Meeting Room or Restaurant

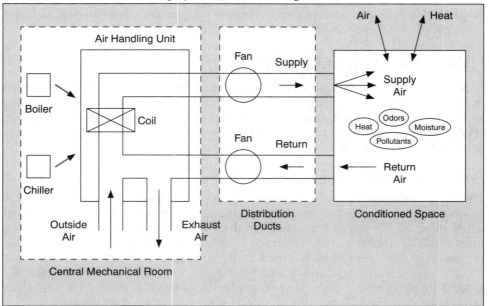

Kitchen Ventilation

The need to provide adequate ventilation in commercial kitchen areas has always been an HVAC challenge. Meeting this need can be expensive. "Conditioning the outdoor air to replace air exhausted from a commercial kitchen (along with the associated fan energy) imposes a significant energy burden—typically more than half of the total HVAC load in a commercial food-service facility."[18] However, as more is known about ventilation needs and equipment operation, kitchen ventilation can be provided more effectively and in a more cost-efficient manner.

Reporting in the *ASHRAE Journal*,[19] researchers outlined the field test results of demand-controlled ventilation (DCV) in a variety of commercial kitchens. DCV systems may take into account one or more of the following components of the kitchen environment to provide efficient ventilation:

- *Time of day.* The time of day controls in a DCV system help ensure that ventilation equipment is only operated when it is actually needed.

- *Appliance energy use.* By monitoring the amount of energy being used by kitchen appliances, a DCV system can provide the appropriate amount of ventilation.

- *Exhaust temperatures.* A DCV system can use the temperature of the exhaust hood air as an indicator of ventilation need.

- *Cooking process.* DCV systems can monitor conditions during the cooking process itself (temperatures, smoke, steam, etc.) to regulate ventilation.

- *Equipment control settings.* Some DCV systems have direct communication from kitchen equipment controls to the DCV processor, with ventilation decisions based on the equipment control settings.

As reported in the journal, hotels have the potential to see significant savings by employing DCV systems because of the typically large size of hotel kitchen fans and their operation for long hours each day. Three hotels studied saved 76,300, 35,700, and 150,800 kwh annually with DCV, and these were only the savings associated with the fan operation; additional savings would also come from the reduced need for heating and/or cooling air. Earlier studies of DCV performance in hotels showed similar savings were possible, with one hotel saving just over 150,000 kwh per year and another just over 60,000.[20]

The "Statler Hall Energy Savings Table" below shows the energy and cost savings that were realized by addressing primarily kitchen ventilation operation in the Statler Hall building complex at Cornell University. The Statler complex is the home of Cornell's School of Hotel Administration as well as the 153-room Statler Hotel. By controlling the exhaust air quantity from kitchens (and some other spaces) so that it more closely matched the true need for ventilation, impressive savings were achieved.

While investments in DCV systems can be costly, the paybacks can be impressive. Too many kitchen hoods are needlessly operated 24/7, consuming electricity and exhausting vast quantities of treated air (and creating a noisy environment in

(continued)

the process). Simply turning ventilation systems off when they are not needed is a good first step to greater efficiency and cost savings. An investment in DCV technology might be a good next step for many hospitality operations.

Statler Hall: Energy Savings Table

Utility	Historical Energy Use (MMBtu)	Est. FY 2012 Energy Use (MMBtu)	Energy Savings (MMBtu)	% REDUCTION	Historical Cost (billed rates)	*Est. FY 2012 Cost (billed)	Annual Savings $
Electric	16,900	14,200	2,700	16%	$347,000	$290,000	$55,000
Steam	16,500	12,700	3,800	23%	$373,000	$287,000	$86,000
Chilled Water	22,600	18,300	4,300	19%	$414,000	$335,500	$79,000
Totals	56,000	45,200	10,800	**19%**	$1,134,000	$914,000	$220,000

Energy use based on project scope

that the access doors and ductwork on the unit had come loose. The unit was functioning on 100 percent (hot) Texas outside air.

Maintenance Needs

The maintenance needs of HVAC systems supplying public areas are derived from the maintenance needs of their individual components. These needs include filter changes, fan cleaning and lubrication, cleaning of heat transfer surfaces, cleaning of drain pans, checking of refrigerants for moisture and leakage, belt checking and replacement, and a variety of other maintenance actions. The equipment supplier should also supply a list of suggested maintenance actions, which should then become part of the units' maintenance program.

Filter replacement (or, in some instances, cleaning) may be done on a regular schedule or on an as-needed basis, with need determined by the degree of pressure drop occurring across the filter. When a manometer (a device that records differential pressure) is installed, it is possible to determine this pressure drop and, with input from fan suppliers or the system engineer, to establish an optimal filter replacement point.

Belt checking and replacement is a key maintenance item. Replacing a worn belt with a new one can reduce the potential for future failure not only of the belt, but also of other fan components whose life may be compromised by a worn or broken belt. When belts are replaced, the entire set should be replaced, because worn belts have stretched and no longer have the tautness and alignment of a new set of belts.

Cleaning fans and heat transfer surfaces will help the system to operate efficiently at rated capacity and will reduce problems with fan imbalance caused by dirt accumulation. For badly neglected systems, it may be necessary to clean ducts as well to remove the buildup caused by neglect.

Other HVAC Components

With the exception of the most basic guestroom HVAC systems, a large number of components make up a hotel's HVAC system. We have discussed chillers, boilers, pumps, fans, and coils. Two other HVAC components warrant discussion. These are the building controls and the cooling tower.

Controls

Various forms of controls allow HVAC systems to operate properly, efficiently, and safely. Early HVAC controls consisted of a manually operated steam valve in a guestroom, an operable window, and a boiler operator who manually adjusted the firing rate of the boiler and kept the steam pressures within acceptable limits. Controls today are often electronic. They may interface with many computers and may be self-correcting and self-adjusting to changing conditions.

The most commonly encountered HVAC control is the thermostat. The thermostat, whether in a guestroom or meeting room, performs several tasks. First, it senses the temperature at the thermostat. It then converts the temperature into a signal (usually on or off) that is sent to the HVAC unit conditioning the space. The signal can be an on/off type or it can be proportional to the measured temperature. An "on" signal tells the HVAC unit to do something—usually to provide either heat or cooling. Some thermostats provide more control, such as time-of-day control, startup and shutdown, and staged heating. Thermostats may also have adjustable "dead bands" that establish a range over which neither heating nor cooling will be required. Units will also have some sort of differential control that establishes the range of likely operation around the setpoint. For example, a room thermostat set at 70°F (21.1°C) that has a two Fahrenheit degree control differential will need to sense room temperatures of 69°F (20.6°C) to initiate heating and 71°F (21.7°C) to stop heating. An appropriate differential will avoid excessively rapid cycling of the unit, while still maintaining the room temperatures within acceptable limits.

Various control devices help operate many other pieces of HVAC equipment. The simpler devices only turn equipment on and off. Others sense not only air temperature, but also relative humidity. The "enthalpy" or "economizer" control found on some HVAC systems determines when the temperature and humidity of outside air make it a potential source of cool air for the building. At such times, the mechanical cooling system can be turned off and cooling accomplished using outside air.

Older control sensors rely upon some sort of mechanical sensing and response to parameters being measured—for example, temperature measured by the degree of thermal expansion of a metal or a liquid. Some more modern systems use sensors that measure changes in electrical properties, relying on an electrical rather than a mechanical connection between the sensor and the controller. Sensors that provide an electrical signal proportional to the value being measured allow the operation of digital control systems. Digital systems use a control algorithm in the processing unit to analyze the signals and control the operation of equipment and systems.

Digital control systems allow the building operator to change the operation of the building from the central control computer. The building operator can also monitor system operation from the computer, determining the operating status and conditions of various pieces of equipment or systems. Digital control also makes variable output operation of equipment more feasible. The widespread use today of **variable air volume (VAV) systems** is largely due to advances in digital control. VAV systems vary the amount of air flowing into a zone based on sensor input of the load in the zone. Often accompanying VAV systems is a control that senses the CO_2 level in return air; the higher the CO_2 level, the more fresh air is supplied to the space. CO_2 is a by-product of human respiration, so increasing levels indicate that the space is occupied. A high CO_2 level can result in room occupants becoming drowsy; very high levels pose a health threat.

Building Automation Systems. Large, modern hotels can have relatively complex HVAC systems with system components distributed throughout the building. Effective operation of these systems requires a large amount of information and the coordination of a number of system components. To collect this information and effectively coordinate the operation of the components, hotels are increasingly installing (and updating) various forms of **building automation systems** (BAS).

Exhibit 11 shows a sample screen from a hotel building automation system depicting an air handling unit serving a ballroom area. The graphic shows the operator a large amount of information regarding the air handling unit. A large amount of other information is available by accessing other screens regarding equipment operation.

Building automation systems generally use a digital signal that provides information about the operating status and conditions of a system. Signals could show not only the operating status of a fan but also how much air the fan was moving and the temperature of the air. Information could also be generated on the amount of energy being consumed.

The information collected is then used by the BAS to make decisions as to system operation. For a fan system, the BAS might monitor the outside air temperature, the temperature of the return air from the space, and the amount of air supplied to the space. As the return air temperature rises above a setpoint, the BAS might increase the airflow to the space to provide more conditioned air to keep the space at comfortable conditions. The BAS could monitor the outside air temperature and, if that air is cold enough to provide the cool air needed, shift from mechanically chilling the air to providing it via increased amounts of outside air. Decisions can be made by the BAS itself or an operator can provide control of systems. The operator does not have to be on-site—remote control via the Internet is possible as well. BAS systems attempt to use graphics to represent the system components and their operations.

Maintenance needs for control systems depend on the type of system. Cleaning of sensors may be necessary. Proper calibration of controllers, transmitters, and gauges is important, since incorrect signals will compromise system operation.

Exhibit 11 Sample Screen from a Hotel Building Automation System

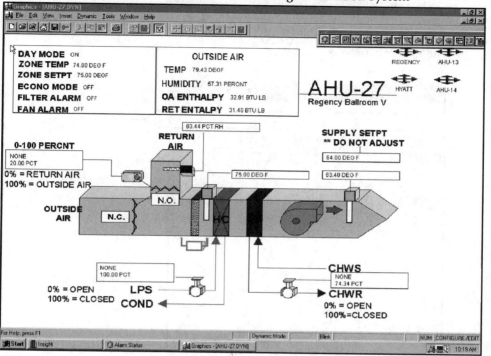

Calibration may reveal failed sensors that need to be replaced. The sensing device needs to "know" how to correlate a given signal with the condition of a piece of equipment.

Maintaining modern control systems is often beyond the capabilities of property-level maintenance staff. Maintenance contracts for these systems are common.

Cooling Towers

When a centralized HVAC system is used, the cooling of the refrigeration system is usually accomplished by circulating water through a **cooling tower**. The cooling tower cascades this water over various forms of tower fill and, at the same time, pulls or pushes air through the tower. As a result, some of the water evaporates, thereby cooling the remaining water. This cooled water is then circulated back to the cooling system to remove more heat from the condenser. Exhibit 12 is a sample cooling tower schematic.

Cooling towers have rather specific operating and maintenance needs. Because not all operations need year-round cooling, there can also be startup and shutdown considerations. Since these towers are often located in out-of-the-way (out-of-sight) places, it can be easy to forget about them until something goes wrong or it is time to start operation again.

Exhibit 12   Sample Cooling Tower Schematic

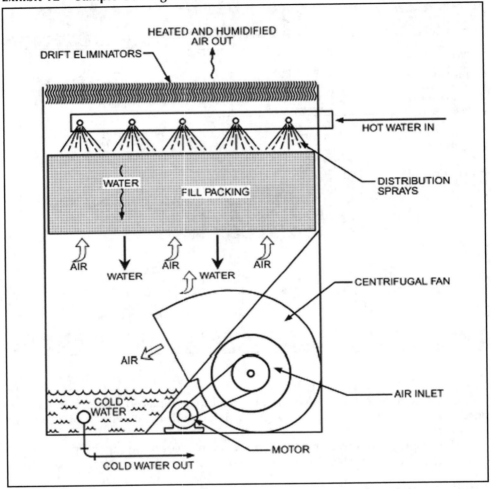

Even when functioning properly, cooling towers are large consumers of water. Water usage via evaporation and "blowdown" to adjust mineral content can result in millions of gallons of use per year at large hotels. Poor or forgotten maintenance can add significant waste to that total. One facility was discovered to have a burst makeup water line (the result of a failure to drain the line when the unit was shut down for the winter) and badly corroded fan supports and other tower components. These problems, which were not found until startup began, resulted in an unknown but potentially significant water leak, a "rush" replacement of the tower, and unhappy guests while the building cooling system was out of service. Another hotel that had implemented many water conservation efforts belatedly discovered that the float valve controlling automatic makeup of water to the tower had failed; water was continuously being added to the tower, only to cascade out into a drain.

In a hotel that took water conservation seriously, thousands of gallons of water a day had been wasted due to inattention to operation and lack of maintenance. In contrast, a hotel in Puerto Rico decided to install a system to send wastewater from its laundry operation for use in the hotel's cooling tower. Almost six million gallons of this laundry water per year was reused in this way, resulting in an annual savings of $47,000 on the hotel's water bill and a payback of 2.7 years. The added value to the community was making almost six million gallons of municipal water available for other uses in this water-short location.[21]

Since motors are used to power a cooling tower's pumps and fans, all necessary motor lubrication needs to be performed. Electrical connections on all motors and controls should be periodically inspected, cleaned, and tightened. Controls for the tower's water supply should be tested for proper operation. If controls fail to operate properly, the tower may consume excess electrical power, have excessive water usage, or fail to provide adequate heat rejection.

Because the tower uses outside air, dirt and other debris will be caught in the tower water. This debris needs to be removed from the tower basin and other locations where it may accumulate. Tower water is a potential breeding ground for various forms of algae and bacteria. Proper chemical treatment is necessary to control the buildup of these contaminants. Treatment is also applied to reduce the buildup of scale—dissolved salts that concentrate in the tower due to the evaporation of the water. Tower water treatment therefore involves using scale and corrosion inhibitors, dispersants to disperse sediments, biocides to kill or prevent multiplication of bacteria, and disinfectants of a variety of types.

Chemical treatment for cooling towers may be provided as a contract service. The manager's job is to ensure that the proper treatment is being provided, whether by in-house personnel or by a contractor. Failure to provide proper treatment can result in a significant decline in tower performance, increased operating problems and energy usage, and premature tower failure. In addition, the potential for Legionnaires' Disease due to bacteria in the tower entering the building ventilation system could pose a real danger to human health.

The metal in cooling towers should be inspected for corrosion, and any corrosion treated. Tower components need periodic cleaning and painting with corrosion inhibitors to avoid premature failure.

The startup and shutdown of towers requires attention to special concerns. Exhibit 13 contains suggestions for dealing with these special concerns. Some towers must be operated during subfreezing winter conditions because they provide heat rejection for computer rooms or food service equipment. These towers require attention to ensure that ice does not form in the tower. Some of these towers have mechanisms for adding heat to the water to melt ice, while others use tower fan shutdown or fan reversal to accomplish deicing. Large amounts of ice formation can be very damaging to the tower and the building structure itself. Management supervision is required to keep these problems from occurring.

Dissipating heat via cooling towers discards something of potential value—the heat itself. It is possible to capture this heat before it is lost in the cooling tower and use it for the property's benefit. For example, resorts in Hawaii and elsewhere have used heat rejected from air conditioning systems to pre-heat domestic water and to heat swimming pools.[22]

Exhibit 13   Shutdown and Startup Considerations for Cooling Towers

---

Shutdown Considerations

- Disassemble, clean, and reassemble float and ball-cock valves.
- Wash down interior of the cooling tower.
- Clean perforated heat pans and spray nozzles.
- Drain and flush tower pans.
- Drain and flush pipelines.
- Drain and flush pumps.
- Lock closed automatic "fill" valves.
- Remove and clean strainers and screens.
- Inspect tower fans and drives for wear, cracking, and corrosion.
- Cover fan and louver opening subject to airborne dirt.
- Check pump motor bearings and lubricate.
- Paint all metal parts subject to alternate wetting and drying.

Startup Considerations

- Remove all debris from within and around unit, then flush as required.
- Check and clean strainers, bleed, overflow, and drain.
- Lubricate fan and motor bearings per manufacturer's recommendation.
- Change oil in gear reducer assembly per manufacturer's recommendation.
- Check belts, motor pulley, and motor mounts. Replace and adjust as required.
- Inspect electrical connections, contactors, relays, and operating/safety controls.
- Check motor operating conditions.
- Clean float valve assembly and check for proper operation.
- Check operating conditions. Adjust as required.

Source: Johnson Controls, Inc. "Fall Maintenance Checklist" and "Spring Maintenance Checklist."

Before concluding this discussion, it should be noted that cooling towers are not the only way to reject heat from refrigeration/cooling equipment. For example, some hotels located near lakes or other bodies of water take water from these sources, use the water to directly or indirectly cool condensers, and then return the water to its source. In some locations around the globe, water from natural sources is available year-round at temperatures cold enough to be used directly or indirectly for building cooling.[23]

HVAC Thermal Storage

Because the cooling of buildings requires a large amount of energy, building operators and designers sometimes look to thermal storage as a means of reducing the cost of cooling. Thermal storage involves the storage of cold in the form of ice or chilled water and the use of this stored cold during periods of high energy cost. The ice or chilled water is produced at times of lower energy cost, typically during the late evening and early morning hours. During these times, not only are the costs of electrical energy (kwh) lower but also the costs of electrical demand (kw) can be lower or even non-existent. The additional cost of the chilled water storage systems can sometimes be partially offset by a reduced size of the chillers themselves and of other elements of the chilled water system.

Conclusion

The astute reader can identify in the discussions in this chapter the four major areas of HVAC responsibility for facilities managers—safety and security, legal and regulatory compliance, service, and cost control. Proper selection, operation, and maintenance of HVAC equipment is a major objective in providing a comfortable and safe environment for guests and employees. Legal and regulatory compliance requires attention to the variety of regulations that cover HVAC equipment and its operation. The operational costs of HVAC equipment can be substantial, meaning that controlling these costs can make significant bottom-line contributions. Maintaining proper indoor conditions also helps to preserve the physical condition of the building and its contents, thus protecting the interests of the owner and the operator.

Endnotes

1. Frank H. Randolph, "Air Conditioning," *Hotel Engineering Bulletins*, 1931, Cornell University, Ithaca, N.Y.

2. http://www.advantixsystems.com/pdf/Case_Study_Hotel.pdf.

3. http://www.drirotors.com/pages.php?pageID=36.

4. John J. Lembo, "Hotel Indoor-Air Quality: Balancing Comfort, Health, Efficiency," *HPAC Engineering* (Cleveland, Ohio: July 1, 2008); http://hpac.com/ventilation-iaq/hotel_indoorair_quality/.

5. U.S. Environmental Protection Agency, *Building Air Quality Action Plan*, June 1998, www.epa.gov/iaq/largebldgs/pdf_files/baqactionplan.pdf; and ASHRAE, *Indoor Air Quality Guide: Best Practices for Design, Construction and Commissioning* (Ashland, Ga.: American Society of Heating, Refrigerating and Air-Conditioning Engineers, Inc., 2009), www.ashrae.org/resources--publications/bookstore/indoor-air-quality-guide.

6. Dan Nakaso, "Kalia Tower, rid of mold, opens Monday," *The Honolulu Advertiser*, August 30, 2003; http://the.honoluluadvertiser.com/article/2003/Aug/30/bz/ bz02a. html.

7. AllerPassMD provides "unbiased information for allergic travelers" at www.aller-passmd.com.

8. Americans for Nonsmokers' Rights, "Legal Requirements to Protect Nonsmokers" (Berkeley, Calif.: October 15, 1998; updated 2005). www.no-smoke.org/search.php?q=l egal+requirements+to+protect+nonsmokers.

9. "Hospitality Industry Guest and Employee Health: Studies of 'Smoke-Free' Law in Wisconsin Show 'No Adverse Economic Effects.'" Hospitality Risk Solutions, January

31, 2011; http://hospitalityrisksolutions.com/2011/01/31/hospitality-industry-guest-health-studies-of-smoke-free-law-in-wisconsin-show-no-adverse-economic-effects/.

10. World Bank. *Smoke-Free Workplaces* (Washington, D.C., 2002); https:// openknowledge. worldbank.org/handle/10986/9764.

11. The heat content of steam as listed in Exhibit 3 is an approximate value, as are the values for natural gas, fuel oil, and LP/LPG. Specifically, the latent heat of vaporization of water is 970 Btu/lb. If you divide 33,475 by 970, you will get 34.5 lb of steam. Use of the 1000 Btu/lb figure is a common "rule of thumb" which is easy to remember and makes for simple math.

12. Visit www.epa.gov/ozone/snap. This is the U.S. EPA's Significant New Alternatives Policy (SNAP) webpage. Substitute refrigerant information can be found at this site. Other information on refrigerants and ozone depletion can also be found on the EPA site.

13. Visit www.unep.org.

14. http://www.ahridirectory.org/ahridirectory/pages/home.aspx.

15. W. R. Geister and M. Thompson, "A Closer Look at Chiller Ratings," *ASHRAE Journal*, December 2009, pp. 22–32.

16. S. F. Cendon, "New and Cool: Variable Refrigerant Flow Systems," *AIArchitect This Week*, April 10, 2009.

17. http://www.energy.ca.gov/title24/2013standards/. The California legislation cited some supporting reports that are rather interesting. Occupancy sensors were evaluated for PTAC operation in various climatic zones in California. The California modeling results indicated that, while electricity was saved (from 75 to 181 kWh per guestroom) by having occupancy sensors, the dollar savings from HVAC control alone were unlikely to offset the cost of the occupancy sensor. However, when lighting control was added, a satisfactory payback was identified. Hence, the California inclusion of lighting as well as HVAC control.

18. Don Fisher, Rich Swierczyna, and Angelo Karas, "Future of DCV for Commercial Kitchens," *ASHRAE Journal*, February 2013, pp. 48–54.

19. http://www.nxtbook.com/nxtbooks/ashrae/ashraejournal_201302/index.php#/0.

20. Demand Control Ventilation for Commercial Kitchen Hoods. ET07.10 Southern California Edison http://www.etcc-ca.com/sites/default/files/OLD/images/stories/ et_07_10_dcv_com_kitch_hoods_final_report.pdf.

21. http://grummanbutkus.com/projects/laundry-water-recovery-system/hotel.

22. http://grummanbutkus.com/projects/heat-recovery-for-domestic-water-and-pool-heating1/hotel.

23. http://honoluluswac.com/casestudies.html.

 # Key Terms

air handling units—An all-air HVAC system consisting of coils (through which steam/hot water or chilled water is circulated from central boilers and chillers), filters, fresh air intakes, exhaust air discharges, and sometimes humidification equipment.

building automation system (BAS)—A control system that uses a digital signal to provide information about the operating status and conditions of the HVAC system. Information collected by the BAS is used to make decisions as to system operation and automatically adjust for optimum operation.

coefficient of performance (COP)—A measure of heat pump efficiency defined as heat delivered in Btu/hr (output) divided by the heat equivalent of the electric energy input (with each watt of input the equivalent of 3.413 Btu/hr).

comfort zone—A range of conditions in which 80 percent of the population tested is "comfortable."

compressor—The component in a vapor compression refrigeration system that raises the temperature and pressure of the gaseous refrigerant coming out of the evaporator.

condenser—The component in a vapor compression refrigeration system in which a gaseous refrigerant releases heat and reverts to liquid form.

convection—The transfer of heat due to the movement of air over a surface and a difference in temperature between the air and the surface.

cooling tower—In a central HVAC system, the place at which refrigeration occurs. Water is cascaded over fill, causing some of the water to evaporate, which cools the remaining water.

dew point temperature—The temperature at which water condenses.

direct expansion (DX) system—A refrigeration system in which the evaporator is located directly in the conditioned airstream.

energy efficiency ratio (EER)—A measure of the efficiency of cooling equipment calculated by dividing the rated cooling output of the unit in Btu/hr by the watts drawn by the unit.

evaporation—With regard to human comfort, a method of heat removal that occurs when a person's perspiration evaporates from his or her skin.

evaporator—The unit in a vapor compression refrigeration system in which the refrigerant is converted from liquid to vapor.

expansion valve—The component in a vapor compression refrigeration system that reduces the pressure and temperature of the liquid refrigerant just before it enters the evaporator.

four-pipe system—An HVAC system that provides both hot and cold water to the fan coil units at all times and keeps the return water lines from the fan coils separate.

heat pump—A device using the vapor compression refrigeration cycle to deliver either heating or cooling, depending on the direction of the refrigerant flow.

integrated part load values (IPLV)—Equipment efficiency ratings that take into account equipment performance at various prescribed levels of cooling load (100 percent, 75 percent, 50 percent, and 25 percent).

latent loads—Addition or removal of moisture with resulting increases or decreases in the relative humidity only.

loads—In HVAC systems, variable inputs to and outputs from a space (i.e., sources of heat gain or loss and humidity).

non-standard part load values (NPLV)—Equipment efficiency ratings using estimates of the equipment's actual operating loads to calculate its expected operational efficiency.

occupancy control—A component of certain HVAC systems that adjusts the temperature in guestrooms depending on room status (rented or not rented) and on the presence of a guest (or some other person) in the room.

packaged air conditioning units—Essentially self-contained air conditioning units in which a fuel provides heat and a refrigeration cycle provides cooling; generally roof-mounted.

radiation—The transfer of heat that occurs when two surfaces are at different temperatures. Energy is transferred in the form of thermal radiation from the warmer to the colder surface.

scale—A buildup of calcium or magnesium carbonate.

sensible loads—Heat addition and removal with resulting increases or decreases in dry bulb temperature only.

three-pipe system—A relatively uncommon HVAC system that provides both hot and cold water to the fan coil units at all times and mixes the return water from the fan coils.

two-pipe system—An HVAC system that allows both heating and cooling, but only one of these at a time.

vapor compression—A refrigeration cycle in which a circulating refrigerant removes heat from one location and transfers this heat to another location, where it is rejected.

variable air volume (VAV) system—An HVAC system that varies the amount of air flowing into a zone based on sensor input of the load in the zone.

wet bulb temperature—In measuring temperature, the value that would be measured if the bulb of a thermometer was surrounded by a small swatch of wet cloth.

Review Questions

1. What factors affect guest and employee comfort? What is the comfort zone and how is it useful?

2. What are the two elements of furnace and boiler efficiency? How can you determine whether a furnace or boiler is operating efficiently?

3. How is the efficiency of cooling equipment measured? Is using integrated part load values a good way to define the efficiency of large cooling equipment? Why or why not?

4. What types of managerial decisions might be affected by growing concerns with ozone depletion in the earth's atmosphere?

5. What are the operating characteristics, advantages, and disadvantages of two-pipe, three-pipe, and four-pipe centralized HVAC systems? Are guests likely to know the differences between these systems? Why or why not?

6. How can heat pumps be used to provide both heating and cooling in guest-rooms? What is the difference between an energy efficiency ratio and a coefficient of performance?

7. Why is makeup air required in a guestroom? What problems may result if the ventilation system provides insufficient makeup air to a guestroom?

8. How are air handling units different from packaged air conditioning units?

9. What sorts of controls are needed on HVAC systems? What is the difference between mechanical and digital controls?

10. Why is chemical treatment of cooling towers needed? What kinds of treatment are needed?

11. What is a building automation system (BAS)? What benefits does it provide the hotelier?

Internet Sites

For more information, visit the following Internet sites. Remember that Internet addresses can change without notice. If the site is no longer there, you can use a search engine to look for additional sites.

American Society of Heating, Refrigerating and Air-Conditioning Engineers
www.ashrae.org

Air-Conditioning, Heating, & Refrigeration Institute
www.ahrinet.org

Consulting-Specifying Engineer
www.csemag.com

Cooling Tower Institute
www.cti.org

Energy University (Schneider Electric)
http://www2.schneider-electric.com/sites/corporate/en/products-services/training/energy-university/energy-university.page

Gas Technology Institute
www.gastechnology.org

Heating/Piping/Air Conditioning (HPAC) Interactive
www.hpac.com

U.S. Environmental Protection Agency—Building Air Quality
www.epa.gov/iaq/largebldgs/baqtoc.html

U.S. Environmental Protection Agency—ENERGY STAR Business Improvement
www.energystar.gov/index.cfm?c=business.bus_index

Chapter Appendix:

Psychrometrics and Human Comfort

Psychrometry

Psychrometry is the study of the thermodynamic properties of a combination of dry air and water vapor. A lodging manager should be aware of this subject because the comfort of guests and the comfort and productivity of employees is highly dependent on the conditions of the air inside a hospitality building. In order to maximize guest satisfaction and employee productivity with minimal cost, the conditions of the environment within the facility must be controlled properly and carefully. Knowledge of the appropriate conditions and of the best methods for control is based on the scientific properties of moist air, the mixture of dry air, and water vapor.

The properties of moist air that are important to the understanding of psychrometrics are dry-bulb temperature (°F db), wet-bulb temperature (°F wb), moisture content (pounds of water vapor per pound of dry air), relative humidity (percent rh), dew point (dp), specific enthalpy (h in Btu/lb of dry air), and specific volume (ft³/lb of dry air). The definitions for each property are developed in the following sections.

Temperature

Dry-bulb and wet-bulb temperatures are best defined by a simple experiment in which two identical common thermometers are used to measure the temperature of a sample of moist air. One of the thermometers measures the dry-bulb temperature and the other the wet-bulb temperature. A wick or piece of fabric that is soaked with water is attached around the mercury reservoir of the wet-bulb thermometer, while nothing is attached to the reservoir of the dry-bulb thermometer. When the mercury reservoir of the dry-bulb thermometer is exposed to the air sample, the reading obtained from the scale is called the dry-bulb temperature—the temperature of the air as reported in weather reports. The wet-bulb temperature is read from the scale on the wet-bulb thermometer in exactly the same manner.

The two temperature readings are usually different because of the effect of the soaked wick on the reservoir of the wet-bulb thermometer. If the air sample is able to absorb some of the water in the wick, then the water in the wick evaporates into the air sample. When this evaporation occurs, the necessary heat of vaporization is extracted from the wick and the mercury reservoir, thus cooling the reservoir. Therefore, the reading from the wet-bulb thermometer is lower than the reading from the dry-bulb thermometer. This difference between the dry-bulb and wet-bulb temperatures is inversely related to the amount of water vapor that is in the air sample. If the air sample contains a substantial amount of water vapor, then the amount of water that can evaporate from the wick is reduced, reducing the cooling effect and the temperature difference between the two temperature readings. Conversely, if the air sample contains little or no water, then the amount of water that evaporates is increased, increasing the cooling effect and the temperature difference.

Thus, the two temperature readings together indicate both the actual temperature of the air and the amount of water vapor in a sample of moist air. These two temperatures are the bases for defining the other important properties of moist air.

Moisture Content

The following experiment assists in the development of the definition of moisture (or water) content. A one-pound sample of dry air at standard atmospheric pressure and a specific temperature is exposed to a source of water at the same temperature. The water is allowed to evaporate into the sample of air and heat is added to maintain the specified temperature. After some time, the air sample cannot absorb any more water from the water source. The moist air in the sample at this condition is defined as *saturated* because no more water can be evaporated into it. The amount of water that was evaporated in the process is recorded. The same experiment is run several times at various specific temperatures. The data from such an experiment is plotted in Exhibit 1. Note that the amount of water that can be evaporated into a sample of dry air increases as the temperature of the dry air increases. Since this curve represents the maximum amount of water that can be evaporated into dry air, it is called the saturation line. On this line, the air is 100 percent saturated or is in a state of 100 percent relative humidity.

At a given dry-bulb temperature, the relative humidity of the moist air is determined by the amount of water vapor that is actually evaporated into the air compared to the maximum that could be evaporated. If the actual amount is one half the maximum, then the relative humidity of the moist air is 50 percent. For

Exhibit 1   The Saturation Line

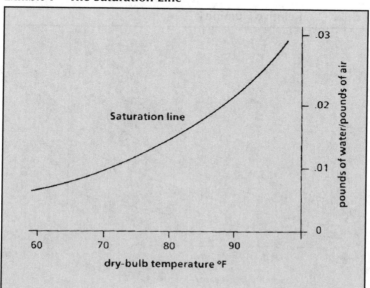

each dry-bulb temperature, the necessary amount of water for 50 percent relative humidity can be determined by comparison with the saturation amount of water at that given temperature. These amounts of water can be plotted on a graph as shown in Exhibit 2. This line is labeled as the 50 percent relative humidity line. Likewise, the lines for all other possible relative humidity levels can be plotted and labeled.

The moisture content of a sample of moist air is defined as the amount of water vapor actually held in the sample measured in pounds of water per pound of dry air. Since this parameter represents only the numerator of the ratio that determines the relative humidity of the moist air, the distinction between the moisture content and the relative humidity is very important. The moisture content measures the actual amount of water vapor in the air in an absolute sense, while the relative humidity measures this amount in a relative sense in comparison to the maximum that could be present. Notice in Exhibit 2 that the moisture content of air at a condition of 95°F db and 50 percent relative humidity actually is greater than the moisture content of air at a condition of complete saturation at 70°F db, even though the relative humidity of the former is lower.

Psychrometric Chart

The graphs plotted in the previous section are the basis for the development of the psychrometric chart, a graphical presentation of the important parameters of moist air. The three parameters—dry-bulb temperature, moisture content, and relative humidity—have already been included on the first two exhibits as shown. The four remaining important parameters—wet-bulb temperature, dew point,

Exhibit 2   Relative Humidity

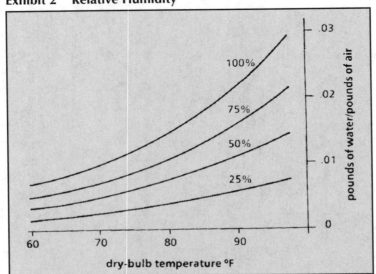

specific enthalpy, and specific volume—can be added through their relationship to the present parameters in the following ways.

The wet-bulb temperature and the dry-bulb temperature of saturated air are the same as explained in the definition of the wet-bulb temperature. Therefore, the saturation line on the graph can be labeled with wet-bulb temperatures for every dry-bulb temperature, as shown in Exhibit 3.

With this new temperature scale, the definition of wet-bulb temperature can be extended to all conditions of moist air shown on the graph. When the moist air is at a condition of less than saturation, the wet-bulb temperature is always lower than the dry-bulb temperature and the reading depends on the amount of water vapor in the air. Therefore, the relative humidity and the wet-bulb temperature of a sample of air are interrelated and lines of constant wet-bulb temperature can be added to the graph to show this interconnection. These straight parallel lines slope from the upper left region to the lower right region of the graph. For example, moist air at the condition of 80°F db and 50 percent relative humidity has a wet-bulb temperature of approximately 67°F wb.

Another of the parameters, dew point, can be added to the graph by referring to a common occurrence in everyone's experience. When warm moist air is brought in contact with a cold surface such as a cold glass of water or a cold windowpane in the winter, some of the water vapor in the moist air condenses on the cold surface, forming water droplets. This occurs because the moist air is cooled below saturation by the cold surface and the water is forced to condense because the air is no longer able to hold it. This process can be traced on the graph as follows. Warm moist air at 75°F db and 50 percent rh is cooled as it contacts the cold surface through convection of heat from the air to the surface. As the air cools, the condition of the air changes initially by a lowering in the dry-bulb temperature

Exhibit 3   Wet-Bulb Scale

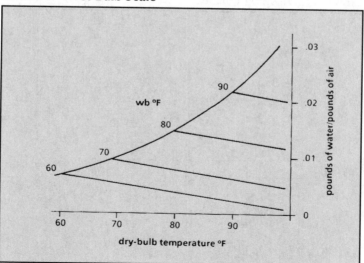

without any reduction of the moisture content. Therefore, the initial trace of the process on the graph is a horizontal line moving to the left from the beginning condition of the air. As the air continues to cool, this horizontal line intersects the saturation line. At this point, the air holds the maximum amount of water that it can contain at this temperature. This temperature is designated as the dew point for the condition of the original air because if the air is cooled below this temperature, water droplets or dew will form.

Lines of constant dew point and a dew point scale that has exactly the same values as the wet-bulb temperature can be added to the graph as shown in Exhibit 4. These straight parallel lines are horizontal on the graph and each is related to a moisture content. Therefore, the dew point of air at a specific condition is determined by the moisture content and not the relative humidity.

The final two parameters—specific enthalpy and specific volume—can be added by the measurement of two properties of the moist air. The total energy that is contained in the moist air, from both dry air and water vapor, is determined in Btu/lb of dry air and is called specific enthalpy (h). The values of specific enthalpy are based on a reference of zero specific enthalpy at 0°F. The scale for this quantity of energy is added above the saturation line and the wet-bulb temperature scale. Lines of constant specific enthalpy are essentially parallel to the lines of constant wet-bulb temperature and for common usage they are considered the same lines. Specific volume (v) is the volume of one pound of dry air at a given condition. Although the value for this parameter varies over the range of conditions normally associated with air mixtures on hospitality properties, an approximate value of 13.5 ft³/lb is used. This value corresponds with a specific density of dry air of .075 lb/ft³. Lines of constant specific volume are overlaid on the graph as shown in Exhibit 5.

Exhibit 4   Dew Point Scale

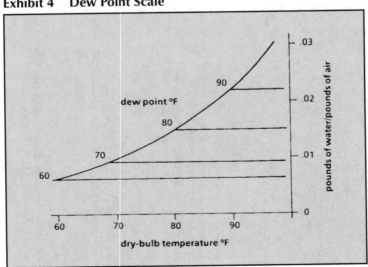

Exhibit 5   Specific Volume Scale

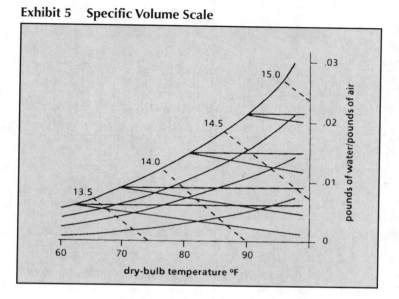

The completed graph as shown in Exhibit 5 contains all of the important information about the parameters of the mixture of dry air and water vapor and is called the psychrometric chart. A similar chart that is published by the Carrier Corporation is shown in Exhibit 6. This chart or similar charts are the basis from which all calculations regarding heating, ventilation, and air conditioning systems and determinations about human comfort are made.

Applications

Changing the conditions of moist air is accomplished through four distinct processes, which are differentiated by their direction of movement on the psychrometric chart. The process that moves the condition of the air horizontally while increasing its dry-bulb temperature is designated *sensible heating*, because the air is being heated without changing its moisture content. Likewise, the process that moves the condition of the air horizontally while decreasing its temperature is called *sensible cooling*. A process that increases the moisture without changing the air temperature is designated *humidification*, while one that decreases the moisture without changing the air temperature is called *dehumidification*.

In practice, the conditioning of the air in hospitality facilities is usually a combination of these four basic processes. In the summer, warm and moist air is both dehumidified and cooled in order to maintain the guests' and employees' comfort. In a northern location in the winter, the cold and dry outdoor air is heated and sometimes humidified to maintain desirable inside comfort conditions. In extremely dry and hot locations, the cooling of hot outside air is accomplished by allowing the air to humidify itself.

Exhibit 6   Psychrometric Chart

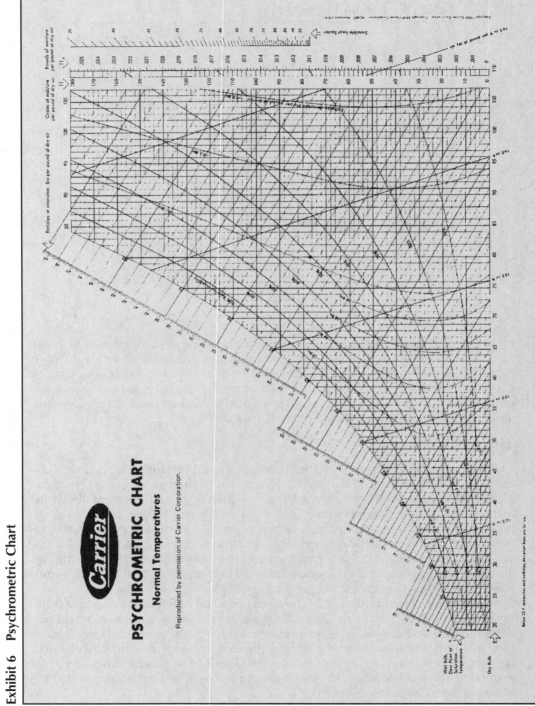

PSYCHROMETRIC CHART
Normal Temperatures

Reproduced by permission of Carrier Corporation.

The characteristic of the dew point of moist air is demonstrated in numerous situations within hospitality facilities. The condensation of water on the inside of windowpanes in the winter, the condensation of water on a glass containing a cold beverage, the formation of an ice coating on cooling coils of a freezer, the formation of water droplets on the inside surfaces of a walk-in refrigerator, and the condensation of water on the outside of cold water pipes are all examples of this phenomenon.

Human Comfort

A guest's opinion of a hospitality property is extremely dependent on the condition of the thermal environment. When the thermal environment makes the guest feel comfortable, then he or she completely forgets about it and enjoys the other attractions and amenities of the facility. However, when the thermal environment makes the guest feel uncomfortable, then he or she usually focuses on the negative sensations and does not notice the positive attributes of the facility. Consequently, the operator of a facility should strive to maintain environmental conditions within the range of comfort while minimizing the costs of providing them.

There are several factors that influence the environmental comfort of a guest: (1) the dry-bulb temperature of the air, (2) the humidity of the air, (3) the velocity of the air moving over the guest, (4) the temperature of the surfaces of the room, (5) the volume of fresh air that is supplied to the guest, and (6) the quality of the air. The first four factors affect the thermal comfort of the guest, while the last two factors are considered primarily life-safety aspects of the environment.

Thermal Comfort

The thermal comfort of a guest is defined as that condition of the mind which expresses satisfaction with the thermal environment. It is the mind's interpretation—a very subjective judgment—of the body's physiological reactions to those factors that influence the energy balance for the human body. The human body automatically attempts to maintain a constant deep body temperature by keeping a balance between the energy produced by the body and the energy dissipated by the body to the surrounding environment, while the mind registers the reaction to the environment in categories such as cold, cool, slightly cool, neutral, slightly warm, warm, and hot.

For the body to remain at a constant temperature, the heat that is produced by the body's metabolic process must be transferred away from the body. This heat balance, expressed by $M + C + R + E = 0$, is dependent on the metabolic production of energy (m), the heat absorbed or dissipated through convection with the surrounding air (c), the heat transferred through radiation with the surrounding structures (r), and the heat lost through the evaporation of perspiration (e). When the air temperature is below 98.6°F, C always has a negative sign, and when the air temperature is above 98.6°F, the sign is positive. As with C, the sign of R depends on the surface temperatures of the surrounding structures compared to 98.6°F, because heat always flows from the region of higher temperature to the region of lower temperature. E always has a negative sign because the body can only lose energy through evaporation.

The body's metabolic production of heat energy is extremely dependent on the activity level of the individual. The relationship is shown in Exhibit 7 where the amount of heat production is expressed in *met units*. A met unit is the energy produced by a seated person at rest. For an average individual, a value of 1.0 met is equivalent to an energy production of 360 Btu/hr. For hospitality employees, the metabolic heat production ranges from a low of 1.0 met for seated work up to 3.4 met for heavy housecleaning tasks; for guests, the range is from .7 met for sleeping up to 7.2 met for playing squash.

The body's thermal control systems regulate the amount of energy dissipated through convection, radiation, and evaporation in order to balance the amount of heat production so that the body has no net heat gain. Within the normal comfort region, this control is accomplished by changing the surface temperature of the body through the control of blood flow near the surface of the skin and by changing the amount of sweat secreted from the skin. The body's surface temperature affects the transfer of heat through convection and radiation because these mechanisms are dependent upon a temperature differential between the heat source and the region that absorbs the heat; the amount of sweat secretion affects the quantity of water and corresponding heat of vaporization that is removed from the body.

Environmental factors also affect these three mechanisms. The air temperature of the room has an effect on the amount of heat that is convected from the body; a lower air temperature increases the heat flow, while higher air temperature decreases the flow. The temperatures of the surfaces in a room (that is, ceilings, walls, floors) influence the amount of radiation heat transfer; a higher average surface temperature allows less heat transfer, while a lower surface temperature requires more heat flow. The humidity of the air affects the amount of evaporated heat loss; air with a lower relative humidity permits a faster rate of evaporation than does air with a higher relative humidity.

When the body's thermal control systems respond to changes in metabolic rate or environmental factors, the body first relies on the convective and radiative mechanisms before it uses the evaporative mechanism. In the case of a seated person at rest who produces 1.0 met or 360 Btu/hr in a room at 60°F and 45 percent rh, the body is dissipating almost all of the 360 Btu/hr of heat through convection and radiation. As the air temperature in a room increases, the amount of heat transferred through these two mechanisms decreases because there is a lower temperature difference between the body and its surroundings. Therefore, the body must dissipate an increasing amount of heat through evaporation in order to maintain the total dissipation rate of 360 Btu/hr. This trend continues until the room temperature is 98.6°F, at which point the entire 360 Btu/hr is being lost through evaporation. Exhibit 8 summarizes this effect.

In the case of a similar person in a room in which the temperature is lowered, the body takes action to maintain the total heat loss at 360 Btu/hr even though the temperature difference is increased. First, it shuts down the evaporative mechanism. If that does not have enough of an effect, the body begins to lower its surface temperature in order to reduce the temperature difference. If that is not sufficient, the body attempts to produce more metabolic energy to offset the increased rate of heat loss by inducing involuntary muscle action or shivering.

Exhibit 7   Metabolic Rate at Different Typical Activities

Activity	Metabolic Rate in Met units
Resting	
Sleeping	0.7
Reclining	0.8
Seated, quiet	1.0
Standing, relaxed	1.2
Walking	
On the level mph	
2	2.0
3	2.6
4	3.8
Miscellaneous Occupations	
Bakery (e.g., cleaning tins, packing boxes)	1.4 to 2.0
Brewery (e.g., filling bottles, loading beer boxes onto belt)	1.2 to 2.4
Carpentry	
Machine sawing, table	1.8 to 2.2
Sawing by hand	4.0 to 4.8
Planing by hand	5.6 to 6.4
General Laboratory Work	1.4 to 1.8
Machine Work	
Light (e.g., electrical industry)	2.0 to 2.4
Heavy (e.g., steel work)	3.5 to 4.5
Shop Assistant	2.0
Teacher	1.6
Watch Repairer, Seated	1.1
Domestic Work, Women	
House cleaning	2.0 to 3.4
Cooking	1.6 to 2.0
Washing by hand and ironing	2.0 to 3.6
Shopping	1.4 to 1.8
Office Work	
Typing	1.2 to 1.4
Miscellaneous office work	1.1 to 1.3
Drafting	1.1 to 1.3
Leisure Activities	
Stream fishing	1.2 to 2.0
Calisthenics exercise	3.0 to 4.0
Dancing, social	2.4 to 4.4
Tennis, singles	3.6 to 4.6
Squash, singles	5.0 to 7.2
Golf, swinging and golf cart	1.4 to 1.8

Reprinted by permission from 1985 ASHRAE Handbook—Fundamentals.

Exhibit 8   Distribution of Heat Loss for a Human

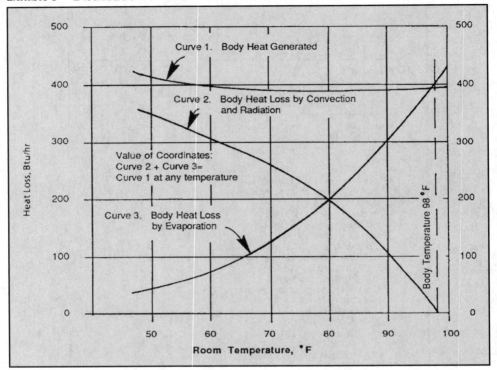

The Comfort Zone

From this discussion, it is obvious that the thermal comfort of the guest is con-nected to several factors that have an interrelated effect on the guest's perception of the thermal environment. The aggregate effect of these factors has been com-bined into a concept called the *comfort zone*. This zone is defined as containing all the combinations of air temperature and relative humidity that satisfy at least 80 percent of the population with regard to their thermal comfort.

In Exhibit 9, the comfort zones for typical winter and summer clothing are plotted separately on a portion of a psychrometric chart. The almost vertical boundaries (that is, the left and right sides) of the zones were determined by exten-sive testing of samples of people exposed to different air conditions. Each bound-ary represents those combinations of temperature and relative humidity that are perceived by the guest to be equivalent to one another and that are comfortable to exactly 80 percent of the people.

The steep downward slope of the boundaries shows an inverse tradeoff between the temperature of the air and its relative humidity in determining the comfort of a guest. For example, air at 68.5°F and 30 percent rh offers the same level of comfort as air at 67.0°F and 70 percent rh. This tradeoff is a result of the interaction of the heat transfer mechanisms that depend on a temperature

Exhibit 9   The Comfort Zone

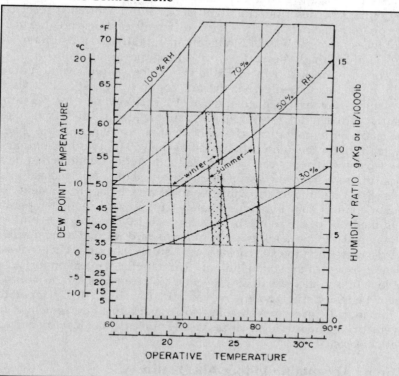

Reprinted by permission from ASHRAE Standard 55—1981.

difference (convection and radiation) with the mechanism that depends on the humidity in the air (evaporation). The loss in evaporative heat transfer due to the increase in relative humidity must be offset by an increase in the convective and radiative losses accomplished by a lower air temperature.

The horizontal boundaries of the comfort zones (that is, the top and bottom) are set for considerations that partially relate to thermal comfort as well as to other practical considerations. Air that contains less moisture than is in the air at the lower boundary (a dew point temperature of 35°F) causes people to exhibit symptoms of very dry skin, dry throats, and repertory problems. The same air also contributes to the excessive drying and deterioration of wood furniture, some building materials, and painted surfaces. Air that is wetter than the air at the upper boundary (a dew point temperature of 62°F) causes mold growth and condensation of water droplets on cool building parts such as cold water lines which are not insulated or the inside surfaces of windows in the winter. Consequently, air that is either too dry or too wet is undesirable for the successful operation of a facility.

The primary difference between the comfort zones for the winter and the summer is the amount of clothing worn by the test subjects. For the winter, the typical description of the clothing is heavy slacks, long-sleeve shirt, and sweater; for the summer, the description is light slacks and a short-sleeve shirt. Therefore, the apparent distinction between two different seasons is not due to intrinsic aspects of the seasons such as acclimatization, but rather to the differences in the amount of clothing that is normally worn during these seasons.

The comfort zones shown in Exhibit 9 are based on several assumptions regarding the factors that affect the thermal comfort of guests. The activity level is light, mainly sedentary with a met value of 1.2. The average temperature of the room's surfaces (mean radiant temperature, abbreviated as MRT) is assumed to be the same as the air temperature. The velocity of air movement is less than 30 feet per minute (fpm) for the winter zone and less than 50 fpm for the summer zone.

The two comfort zones can be extended to include situations that have characteristics different from the assumptions listed above. An increase in activity level for each 0.1 met moves the winter comfort zone by approximately 1.0°F and the summer comfort zone by approximately 0.8°F toward cooler temperatures. A change in the MRT of the room surfaces for each 1.0°F moves the comfort zones approximately 0.5°F; the comfort zones move toward warmer temperatures when the MRT decreases and toward cooler temperatures when the MRT increases. Air movement in excess of the stated limit of 30 fpm for the winter comfort zone is not acceptable, while an increase in air movement is acceptable for the summer comfort zone, when the comfort zone is moved 1.0°F toward warmer temperatures for each 30 fpm increase in air movement up to a maximum air movement of 160 fpm. Air movement beyond this level causes visible movement of loose paper, hair, and other light objects.

Maintaining Acceptable Indoor Air Quality

Both the physiological and psychological needs of humans require that an adequate supply of outside air of acceptable quality be circulated through a building. For physiological reasons, the air circulation system must supply the necessary amount of oxygen for metabolism and remove the by-products of metabolism that are present in the exhaled air, as well as control the amount of carbon dioxide in the air so that minimum standards are met. The system also must control the level of various contaminants that enter the air from either outside sources (such as general industrial pollution) or inside sources of pollutants (such as formaldehyde from insulation or carbon monoxide from faulty heating systems). For psychological reasons, the body odor of occupants and the moisture contributed to the air either by humans or other sources (for example, cooking, taking showers) must be removed from the occupied space.

Except in the locations where the quality of the outdoor air is unacceptable, the ventilation system of a building could in theory maintain acceptable indoor air quality just by circulating massive amounts of outdoor air. However, this is not a viable practical solution because the circulated outdoor air must be conditioned when it is brought into the building. When the outside air is cold, the heating system must heat the air to an acceptable temperature; when the outside air is hot and humid, the air conditioning system must cool and dehumidify the air to an acceptable temperature. Both of these processes consume substantial amounts of energy.

In addition, large circulation fans powered by electric motors consume energy just to circulate the air. Therefore, the designers of building ventilation systems specify the minimum ventilation rate, which will provide desirable indoor air quality in order to minimize the construction and operating costs of the building. There are two methods—the *ventilation rate procedure* and the *indoor air quality procedure*—that indicate how to achieve acceptable air quality. The first procedure is prescriptive in nature in that specified minimum ventilation rates of acceptable outside air are provided. This method assumes that this "clean" outside air should dilute and remove the contaminants from interior sources so that their levels in the interior air are acceptable. The second procedure is performance-oriented in that the maximum allowable levels of contaminants are provided for acceptable indoor air quality. No specified ventilation rates are provided, however; their actual choice is at the discretion of the designer of the ventilation system as long as the allowable levels of contaminants are not exceeded.

Ventilation Rate Procedure. The acceptable level of pollutants for outdoor air can be obtained from several sources.[1] If the outdoor air in a specific location satisfies these levels, then the air may be used directly to ventilate a building. However, if the outdoor air contains contaminants that exceed these levels, then the air must be treated before it may be used in a building's ventilation system.

Exhibit 10 shows the outdoor air requirements for ventilation for various types of businesses or buildings. The requirements are stated in cfm/person, cfm/ft^2 of floor area, or cfm/functional unit (for example, a room in a hotel or a bed in a hospital). By the application of this method, indoor air quality is considered acceptable if the required rates of acceptable outdoor air are provided for the occupied space and no unusual contaminants are present.

Higher ventilation rates are specified for the spaces in which smoking is permitted, because tobacco smoke is one of the most difficult contaminants to control at the source. When smoking is not permitted in designated spaces, the lower values of ventilation rates may be applied. In numerous applications, this reduction in ventilation rates can substantially affect the operating cost of the heating, ventilating, and air conditioning (HVAC) system. Therefore, use of no smoking areas in lodging properties should be strongly encouraged because of its desirable effect on the operating costs of the building. In many areas of the country, state and/or local laws prohibit smoking in public buildings such as lodging properties.

Indoor Air Quality Procedure. Under this method, acceptable indoor air quality is provided by the ventilation system if the level of contaminants in the *indoor* air does not exceed the levels as specified for *outdoor* air. In addition, acceptable levels of contaminants from indoor sources must also be met.

There are, however, numerous substances for which no regulations have yet been developed (for example, mercury), substances that have not yet been identified as harmful to humans (for example, unknown environmental carcinogens), and substances for which no regulations are likely to be developed because they are such complex mixtures (tobacco smoke). In order to respond to these substances, this method allows a subjective evaluation of the indoor air quality.

The following steps should be used to ensure the validity of the subjective evaluation. A panel of at least twenty untrained observers should enter a space

Exhibit 10   Outdoor Air Requirements for Ventilation—Commercial Facilities

	Estimated Occupancy, persons per 1000 ft.³ or 100 m² floor area. Use only when design occupancy is not known.	Outdoor Air Requirements Smoking	Non-Smoking	Comments
Food & Beverage Services		cfm/person		
Dining rooms	70	35	7	
Kitchens	20	--	10	
Cafeterias, fast food facilities	100	35	7	
Bars and cocktail lounges	100	50	10	
Hotels, Motels, Resorts, Dormitories, & Correctional Facilities		cfm/room		
Bedrooms (single, double)	5	30	15	Independent of room size
Living rooms (suites)	20	50	25	
Baths, toilets (attached to bedrooms)		50	50	Independent of room size; installed capacity for intermittent use.
		cfm/person		
Lobbies	30	15	5	
Conference rooms (small)	50	35	7	
Assembly rooms (large)	120	35	7	
Gambling Casinos	120	35	7	
Offices				
Office Space	7	20	5	
Meeting & waiting spaces	60	35	7	
Public spaces		cfm/ft² floor		
Corridors & utility rooms		0.02	0.02	
		cfm/stall or urinal		
Public restrooms	100	75	--	
		cfm/locker		
Locker & dressing rooms	50	35	15	
Sports & Amusement Facilities		cfm/person		
Ballrooms & Discos	100	35	7	
Bowling alleys (seating area)	70	35	7	
Playing floors (e.g., gymnasiums, ice arenas)	30	--	20	When internal combustion engines are operated for maintenance of playing surfaces, increased ventilation rates will be required.
Spectator areas	150	35	7	
Game rooms (e.g., cards & billiards rooms)	70	35	7	
Swimming pools		cfm/ft² area		
Pool & deck areas	--	--	0.5	Higher values may be required for humidity control.
		cfm/person		
Spectators area	70	35	7	

in the manner of a normal visitor and should render a judgment of acceptability within fifteen seconds. Each observer should make the evaluation independently of the other observers and without influence from a panel leader. The air can be considered acceptably free of annoying contaminants if at least 80 percent of the observers deem the air to be not objectionable.

Endnote

1. See, for example, ASHRAE Standard 62.1-201—*Ventilation for Acceptable Indoor Air Quality* (Atlanta, Ga.: American Society of Heating, Refrigerating and Air-Conditioning Engineers, 2013), and *2013 ASHRAE Handbook—Fundamentals* (Atlanta, Ga.: American Society of Heating, Refrigerating and Air-Conditioning Engineers), Chapter 11.

Chapter 8 Outline

Competencies

1. Define basic lighting terms, explain how natural light can be used to meet a building's lighting needs, and describe common artificial light sources. (pp. 307–317)

2. Describe the following lighting system design elements: light levels, luminaires, color rendition, safety, and emergency lighting. (pp. 317–322)

3. Describe lighting system maintenance and identify energy conservation opportunities. (pp. 322–327)

8

Lighting Systems

The designer should consider hotel lighting more a design element than a building science. Lobbies, atriums, restaurants, entertainment areas, meeting and banquet rooms, and guestrooms owe their success to comfortable and creative lighting as much as to any other single design element. As in other disciplines, the requirements are often based on common sense. For example, guestroom lighting needs to be adequate for reading in bed, working at the desk or table, and shaving or applying makeup. If the lighting for any of these is poor, the guest registers at least subconscious irritation. Meeting room lighting also must be highly adaptable. It should combine incandescent lighting for ambience with fluorescent fixtures for meeting use and track lighting for displays or accents. Special decorative restaurant lighting is essential in creating the desired mood in food outlets.[1]

LIGHTING SYSTEMS AFFECT SEVERAL ASPECTS of physical plant management. The character and direction of light influence building colors and textures. Light's optical characteristics affect the appearance of surface finishes and ceilings. Some properties make major use of lighting to attract customers and create an image; casino hotels are obvious examples. The nature and level of illumination affect employee efficiency and customer comfort. A building's lighting system influences HVAC system design and operation (because of the heat given off by the lights), a building's interior design (because of the dimensions of the lighting fixtures), electrical design, and the economics of investment (because the lamps and their controls are part of the initial investment in the hotel). Finally, lighting plays an important part in safety and security.

Basic Definitions

Before we begin our discussion of light sources and systems, we should briefly introduce some basic terms.[2] **Visible light** is defined most simply as radiated energy that can be seen by the human eye. Light is made up of various wavelengths and frequencies interpreted by the eye as color. At the low end of the spectrum, violet, indigo, blue, and green light are produced by shorter wavelengths, with violet the shortest; at the high end, yellow, orange, and red are produced by longer wavelengths, with red the longest. Sources of visible light contain some or all of these colors.

When light shines on a surface, some of the colors in the light are absorbed and disappear, while others are transmitted or reflected. The transmitted or reflected light is what gives objects their color. For example, a red napkin absorbs almost all light except red; a yellow flower absorbs all light except yellow.

Since an object's color is partially determined by the light that shines on it, a light source's color rendition is important. **Color rendition** refers to a light source's ability to provide a perceived color similar to that which results from sunlight. A lamp's color rendering index (CRI) is a number from 0 to 100 that states how closely a given light source approaches the color rendering capability of daylight or incandescent lighting, both of which have an index of 100.

The color appearance of light can also be referred to as the color temperature or, more specifically, as the Correlated Color Temperature (CCT). CCT is measured in degrees Kelvin or "K" (see Exhibit 1). Lamps with a CCT below 3500K are considered "warm" and give out a yellow or reddish light; lamps above 4000K are considered "cool" and give out a white or bluish light. Color temperature creates the mood or ambience of the space you are lighting and can influence customer behavior and employee performance. Lamp specifications generally include a CRI value and a CCT value.

Standard light-level units and measurement methods have been developed in order to have some objective means of determining relative light levels. The **lumen** is a commonly used unit of light. Light that strikes a surface is known as **illumination.** Illumination is typically measured in **footcandles;** one footcandle is a light intensity of one lumen per square foot. In countries using the metric system of measurement, light is also measured in lumens, but levels of illumination are measured in **lux,** a lux being a light intensity of one lumen per square meter.

Light Sources

Light is either natural or artificial. Both sources can be used to meet a building's lighting needs.

Exhibit 1   Correlated Color Temperature/Kelvin Ranges

Color Temperature	Warm	Neutral	Cool	Daylight
Kelvin Range	3000K	3500K	4100K	5000K
Associated Effects and Moods	Friendly Intimate Personal Exclusive	Friendly Inviting Non-threatening	Neat Clean Efficient	Bright Alert Exacting coloration
Appropriate Applications	Restaurants Hotel lobbies Boutiques Libraries Office areas Retail stores	Public reception areas Showrooms Bookstores Office areas	Office areas Conference rooms Classrooms Mass merchandisers Hospitals	Galleries Museums Jewelry stores Medical examination areas Printing companies

The Opryland Hotel makes dramatic use of natural light. (Courtesy of Opryland Hotel, Nashville, Tennessee.)

Natural Light

Natural light, or sunlight, is by far the most common and least expensive light source. The use of natural light is currently of great interest to designers of commercial buildings, especially offices and schools where lighting energy is a significant fraction of total energy use. Since clear-sky outdoor illumination levels can approach 1,000 footcandles for over 85 percent of the working day in some locations, natural light's contribution to meeting a building's overall lighting needs is potentially great. It should also be recognized that natural light has drawbacks: it can create substantial solar heat gain, be a source of glare and distraction, and contribute to the fading and physical deterioration of fabrics.

Using natural light for interior hotel and restaurant lighting is generally appreciated by guests and employees. The chance to look through a window, possibly at attractive hotel grounds or some other pleasant scene, is psychologically pleasing and helps employees avoid eye strain because they can occasionally focus their eyes on distant objects. Natural light must be used with care, however. Designers of a building's lighting system have to consider a lot of variables to make natural lighting pleasing—the type of glass used in the windows, whether or to what extent to use window treatments such as drapes or blinds, how reflective the surfaces are in the space being lit, the nature of the view outside, and others.

Artificial Light

Artificial light is light other than sunlight. Artificial light sources can be categorized by many measures, including their efficiency (measured in lumens per watt) and their color-rendering index. The three basic sources of artificial light commonly used today are incandescent lamps, electric-discharge lamps, and light-emitting diode lamps (see Exhibit 2).

Incandescent Lamps. An **incandescent lamp** consists of a filament inside a sealed glass bulb. Electric current passing through the filament heats it to incandescence, producing light. The lamp is usually etched or coated to diffuse the light produced by the filament. The electrical connection for the lamp is through the base.

Incandescent lamps are characterized by relatively short lifetimes (2,000 hours or less) and relatively poor efficiencies, defined for lamps as the **efficacy** (expressed in lumens per watt). The efficacy for incandescent lamps is 15 to 20 lumens per watt. However, they are capable of instant starting and restarting, are low in cost, and are readily dimmed. The light from these lamps is "warm" (high in reds and yellows) and color rendition is considered good. As a result, they do not "shift" or change the color of fabrics or finishes.

Because of their poor efficiency, incandescent lamps contribute a large amount of heat to a building and have relatively high operating costs. Their short lamp life results in potentially high maintenance costs, since employees must replace them often. Lamp life refers to the time it takes half of the lamps in a given sample to fail. If a lamp is rated as having a **lamp life** of 1,000 hours, for example, 1,000 hours is the expected lifetime for this type of lamp, although a given lamp might burn for more or fewer than 1,000 hours.

The higher the wattage of an incandescent lamp, the more efficiently the lamp operates. Long-life or extended-service lamps (which produce 10 to 20 percent less light per watt of power consumed) are generally less efficient than standard lamps, but have longer lifetimes and should be used where replacement is difficult. Any incandescent lamp will have its efficiency increased (and its life decreased) if it operates at higher than its rated voltage.

Besides the conventional incandescent lamp, other types of incandescent lamps are used for special applications:

- Rough service or vibration incandescent lamps are built to withstand rough handling and vibration.

- Tungsten halogen lamps are incandescent lamps that produce a slightly "whiter" light (higher CCT) and have a longer lamp life (3,000 hours) than standard incandescent lamps. These lamps are used as longer-life replacements for standard incandescent lamps as well as for special applications.

Exhibit 2 Types of Incandescent, Electric Discharge, and Light-Emitting Diode Lamps

	Standard Incandescent	Tungsten-Halogen	Fluorescent	Compact Fluorescent	Mercury Vapor	Metal Halide	High-Pressure Sodium	Low-Pressure Sodium	Light-Emitting Diode (LED)*
Wattage	3-1,500	10-1,500	4-215	4-55	40-1,250	32-2,000	35-1,000	18-180	4-28
Average System Efficacy (lm/W)	4-24	8-33	49-89	24-68	19-43	38-86	22-115	50-150	30-100
Average Rated Life (hrs)	750-2,000	2,000-4,000	7,500-24,000	7,000-20,000	24,000+	6,000-20,000	16,000-24,000	12,000-18,000	25,000-50,000
CRI	100	100	49-92	82-86	15-50	65-92	21-85	0	40-90
Life Cycle Cost	high	high	low	moderate	moderate	moderate	low	low	moderate
Fixture Size	compact	compact	extended	compact	compact	compact	compact	extended	compact
Start to Full Brightness	immediate	immediate	0-5 seconds	0-1 min	3-9 min	3-5 min	3-4 min	7-9 min	immediate
Restrike Time	immediate	immediate	immediate	immediate	10-20 min	4-20 min	1 min	immediate	immediate
Lumen Maintenance	good/excellent	excellent	fair/excellent	good/excellent	poor/fair	good	good/excellent	excellent	good/excellent

*LEDs can also be called solid-state lighting (SSL). Technological advances in LED/SSL lighting are occurring quite quickly, so data in this column is likely to change rapidly as the technology matures.

- Reflector lamps (PAR, ER, and R-type bulbs) are incandescent lamps that contain a reflector coating to give the lamps a more directed light output. These lamps are also called spot or flood lamps. They may be installed over food counters with filters to limit the amount of heat in the light beam. They provide interesting options for merchandise and accent lighting, but care is needed because of their high operating temperatures.

In many countries, including the United States, the use of incandescent lamps is being gradually phased out in favor of more energy-efficient lamps.

Electric Discharge Lamps. Electric discharge lamps generate light by passing an electric arc through a space filled with a special mixture of gases. This lamp category includes fluorescent, mercury vapor, metal halide, and high- and low-pressure sodium lamps.

Electric discharge lamps can't be operated directly from a power supply, as can incandescent lamps. Therefore, all electric discharge lamps require an additional piece of equipment, a **ballast,** that controls their starting and operation and acts as a current-limiting device. The ballast for most tube-type fluorescent lamps (the four-foot or eight-foot lamps commonly used) is a separate item from the tubes. It is usually mounted on top of the light fixture and is replaceable. Some compact fluorescents—small fluorescent lamps developed as energy-efficient alternatives to incandescent lamps—have the ballast and tube as one piece; others have separate ballasts. For many hospitality applications, having a separate ballast is preferable because replacement costs are lower.

Ten to fifteen percent of the energy used by an electric discharge lighting system is consumed in the ballast and given off as heat. Ballasts are rated by their operating temperature, type of overheating protection (those that are thermally protected, self-resetting, and generally specified for commercial uses are denoted as type "P" ballasts), and noise level (rated A through F, with A the quietest). Some recent trends in ballast design have included the development of electronic ballasts that consume up to 25 percent less energy than standard ballasts and can provide a dimming capability.

Ballasts should also be chosen with an eye on how they will affect the building's electrical system. In many applications it is preferable to have ballasts with a high power factor (above .9) to reduce the possibility of electric bill surcharges (for low overall power factor) and to improve electrical system operation. Selecting ballasts with a low total harmonic distortion (under approximately 35 percent) can also help to reduce the potential for electrical equipment problems.

Fluorescent lamps. Fluorescent lamps are the most common type of electric discharge lamp. They are characterized by a longer lifetime (7,000 to 20,000 hours) and a higher efficiency (40 to 100 lumens per watt) than those of incandescent lamps. They also put out less heat than incandescent lamps, which means less heat needs to be removed by the HVAC system. Fluorescent lamps come in circular and "U" shapes as well as long tubes.

The development of various types of compact fluorescents since the 1980s has greatly expanded the potential applications of fluorescent lamps. Compact fluorescent lamps are now commonly used in hotels and restaurants for corridor lighting, in guestroom lamps, and for downlight applications in dining rooms and

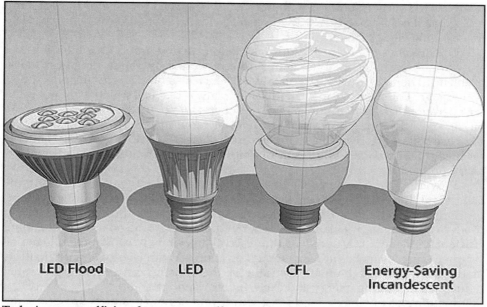

LED Flood **LED** **CFL** **Energy-Saving Incandescent**

Today's energy-efficient lamps are small enough to fit into fixtures and spaces that only incandescent lamps fit in before. Source: Energy.gov at http://energy.gov/energysaver/articles/tips-lighting.

elsewhere. Compact lamps with electronic ballasts can be used with dimming systems. When replacing incandescent lamps with compact fluorescents, managers must attend to the compact lamps' CRI and CCT values to make sure light quality is approximately the same; otherwise, the space being lighted will not look the same in terms of color and light, and the interior designer's intended look for the space will be lost.

Generally, the color rendition of fluorescent lamps is poorer than that of incandescent lamps, although some fluorescent lamps have been developed to produce a "warmer" light. Fluorescent lamps come in a variety of "whites"—for example, cool white and warm white. A cool white lamp has a color temperature of approximately 4100K; a warm white lamp has a color temperature of 3000K. Improved-color-rendition whites have red added to their light to help them bring out the full range of colors. What type of fluorescent lamp should be used in a hotel or restaurant? It depends on the space, the decor, the activities that go on in the space, the desired atmosphere, and other variables. Generally, fluorescent lamps in the "warm" group blend more successfully with incandescent lighting.

The label on a fluorescent lamp defines several of the lamp's characteristics. A lamp labeled F15T12WW is a fluorescent (F) lamp with 15 watts, a tubular (T) shape, a $^{12}\!/\!_8$ inch diameter, and a warm white (WW) color.

Fluorescent lamp life decreases as the average number of burning hours per start decreases. This has led some people to believe that it is cheaper to leave a fluorescent lamp on continuously than to switch it on and off as needed. However, this is not true, especially in areas with high-cost electrical energy. When a room or area is left vacant, fluorescent lights should be turned off. The additional lamp replacement costs associated with the reduced lamp life should easily be repaid by the resulting energy savings.

Operation of fluorescent lamps in locations in and around the building that are warmer or colder than the lamps' recommended operating range can cause problems. The same can be true of ballasts, which also have a recommended operating range. For example, in a cold location, lamps and ballasts that are not rated for operation in cold conditions may not operate, may take a long time to come on, or, once operating, may produce light at reduced levels. Hot locations will decrease ballast life, resulting in premature ballast failure. Using a ballast suitable for higher temperatures will result in longer ballast operation and fewer maintenance problems.

Providing a dimming capability for fluorescent lamps requires an electronic ballast and dimming equipment suitable for the size and type of lighting system.

During much of the late twentieth century, the standard fluorescent lamp in use was the T12 lamp—a lamp 1.5 inches in diameter. At the present time, a more efficient and commonly specified fluorescent lamp in new construction is the T8 lamp—a lamp 1.0 inches in diameter. When coupled with energy-efficient ballasts (and, ideally, with high-efficiency fixtures), the T8 lamp can provide substantial reductions in lighting energy and excellent cost savings.

Lighting technology continues to improve and new products are emerging. An example is the T5 fluorescent lamp. Providing approximately the same lumens as a similar T8 lamp, the T5 does so while consuming 10 percent less energy and doing a better job of maintaining its light output over time. With these advantages, the T5 might become the standard for tubular fluorescent applications in the future.

Other electric discharge lamps. Mercury vapor, metal halide, and high- and low-pressure sodium lamps operate on the same principle as fluorescent lamps and require ballasts for operation. These lamps are sometimes listed in a general category called **high-intensity discharge (HID) lamps**. Each type of HID lamp has possible uses within the hospitality industry.

While incandescent and fluorescent lamps light almost immediately upon being energized, the **strike time** (the time required for a lamp to reach full output from a cold start) for HID lamps can be several minutes. In addition, the time required for a hot HID lamp to restrike is usually longer than the strike time. These longer strike and restrike times can be a problem in certain applications, such as locations that need emergency lighting.

Mercury vapor lamps have long been used for lighting streets and parking lots. They have an efficiency of 15 to 60 lumens per watt and a lifetime of 12,000 to 24,000 hours. Strike times for these lamps are three to five minutes and restrike times are three to eight minutes. White mercury vapor lamps have somewhat better color rendition than clear lamps.

Metal halide (MH) lamps basically are mercury vapor lamps modified by the addition of metallic halides to improve the lamp's color rendition and increase efficiency (80 to 100 lumens per watt). Lamp life is 7,500 to 15,000 hours—less than that of mercury vapor lamps. **Lumen maintenance**—the lamp's ability to maintain its output—is also significantly reduced later in the lamp's life. Newly introduced

MH lamps have improved CRI values (80+), improved lumen maintenance, and higher energy efficiency. MH lamps have relatively short strike times of two to three minutes, but can have restrike times of up to ten minutes.

High-pressure sodium (HPS) lamps are highly efficient light sources (85 to 140 lumens per watt) that have long life (16,000 to 24,000 hours) and a high lumen maintenance over their lifetimes. Strike times are three to four minutes, with a relatively short restrike time of about one minute. Color rendition is poor. HPS lamps are typically used to light parking lots and garages, building exteriors, and entry areas. HPS lamps can be used indoors if color-corrected lamps are selected or the HPS lamps are mixed with other light sources that together produce an appropriate color rendition.

Low-pressure sodium (LPS) lamps also are highly efficient light sources, with efficiencies in excess of 150 lumens per watt possible. They have lifetimes of up to 18,000 hours and a high lumen maintenance. Their color-rendering characteristics are generally poor, since they produce a very yellow light. They are primarily used for parking lots and security lighting such as after-hours lighting in restaurants.

Light-Emitting Diode Lamps. Light-emitting diode lamps, or LEDs, are semiconductor devices that produce visible light when an electrical current is passed through them. LEDs are a type of solid-state lighting (SSL), as are organic light-emitting diodes (OLEDs) and light-emitting polymers (LEPs). LED lighting can be more efficient, durable, versatile, and longer-lasting than incandescent or fluorescent lighting.[3]

Common LED colors include amber, red, green, and blue. There is no such thing as a "white" LED. To get white LED light, the kind typically used for lighting homes and businesses, lamp manufacturers place red, blue, and green diodes in close proximity in order to create white light, or the lamp is covered with a phosphor material that shifts the color of the light into the white spectrum (the phosphor is the yellow material you can see on some LED products). Colored LEDs are widely used as signal lights and indicator lights, like the power button on a computer.

LEDs are now being incorporated into bulbs and fixtures for general lighting applications. LEDs are small and provide unique design opportunities. Some LEDs look like familiar incandescent light bulbs. Some LED light fixtures have LEDs built in as a permanent light source.

The useful life of LED lighting products is defined differently than that of other light sources. This is because LEDs typically do not burn out or fail. Instead, they experience lumen depreciation, where the amount of light produced decreases and light color appearance can shift over time. Instead of basing the useful life of an LED lamp on the time it takes for 50 percent of a large group of lamps to burn out (as is the case with traditional light sources), the product lifetime for an LED lamp is set based on a prediction of when the LED's light output will have decreased by 30 percent.

Because LEDs do not radiate heat the way incandescent or halogen light bulbs do, the heat produced by LEDs must be drawn away. This is usually done with a heat sink—a passive device that absorbs the heat produced by the LED's operation and dissipates it into the surrounding environment. This keeps LEDs from

Labels for Lighting Products

Purchasers of lighting products will see the following type of label on all lighting products, placed on the front of the product's package. This label is required by the Federal Trade Commission (FTC):

Brightness	Estimated Energy Cost
820 lumens	**$7.23** per year

A Lighting Facts label (also required by the FTC) must appear on the side or rear panel of the package. What follows are Lighting Facts labels for a compact fluorescent lamp (left) and an incandescent lamp. As you can see, not all products qualify for the Energy Star logo:

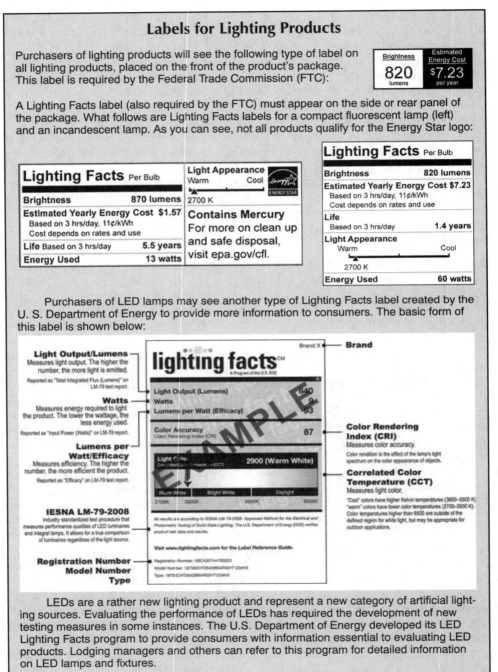

Lighting Facts Per Bulb

Brightness	870 lumens
Estimated Yearly Energy Cost	**$1.57**

Based on 3 hrs/day, 11¢/kWh
Cost depends on rates and use

Life Based on 3 hrs/day	5.5 years
Energy Used	13 watts

Light Appearance
Warm — Cool
2700 K

ENERGY STAR

Contains Mercury
For more on clean up and safe disposal, visit epa.gov/cfl.

Lighting Facts Per Bulb

Brightness	820 lumens
Estimated Yearly Energy Cost	$7.23

Based on 3 hrs/day, 11¢/kWh
Cost depends on rates and use

Life Based on 3 hrs/day	1.4 years

Light Appearance
Warm — Cool
2700 K

Energy Used	60 watts

Purchasers of LED lamps may see another type of Lighting Facts label created by the U. S. Department of Energy to provide more information to consumers. The basic form of this label is shown below:

Light Output/Lumens
Measures light output. The higher the number, the more light is emitted.
Reported as "Total Integrated Flux (Lumens)" on LM-79 test report.

Watts
Measures energy required to light the product. The lower the wattage, the less energy used.
Reported as "Input Power (Watts)" on LM-79 report.

Lumens per Watt/Efficacy
Measures efficiency. The higher the number, the more efficient the product.
Reported as "Efficacy" on LM-79 test report.

IESNA LM-79-2008
Industry standardized test procedure that measures performance qualities of LED luminaires and integral lamps. It allows for a true comparison of luminaires regardless of the light source.

Registration Number
Model Number
Type

lighting factsCM
A Program of the U.S. DOE

Light Output (Lumens)	840
Watts	9
Lumens per Watt (Efficacy)	93
Color Accuracy Color Rendering Index (CRI)	87

Light Color
Correlated Color Temperature (CCT) — 2900 (Warm White)

Warm White	Bright White	Daylight
2700K	3000K	4500K	6500K

All results are according to IESNA LM-79-2008. Approved Method for the Electrical and Photometric Testing of Solid-State Lighting. The U.S. Department of Energy (DOE) verifies product test data and results.

Visit www.lightingfacts.com for the *Label Reference Guide*.

Registration Number: ABC435TH4792023
Model Number: 1875ICHT56428954RGHT1234H3
Type: 1875 ICHT56428954RGHT1234H3

Brand

Color Rendering Index (CRI)
Measures color accuracy.
Color rendition is the effect of the lamp's light spectrum on the color appearance of objects.

Correlated Color Temperature (CCT)
Measures light color.
"Cool" colors have higher Kelvin temperatures (3600–5500 K). "warm" colors have lower color temperatures (2700–3500 K). Color temperatures higher than 6500 are outside of the defined region for white light, but may be appropriate for outdoor applications.

LEDs are a rather new lighting product and represent a new category of artificial lighting sources. Evaluating the performance of LEDs has required the development of new testing measures in some instances. The U.S. Department of Energy developed its LED Lighting Facts program to provide consumers with information essential to evaluating LED products. Lodging managers and others can refer to this program for detailed information on LED lamps and fixtures.

Sources: http://www.lightingfacts.com/Library/Content/Label; and http://www1.eere.energy.gov/buildings/ssl/ledlightingfacts.html.

overheating and burning out. Thermal management is probably the single most important factor in the successful performance of an LED product over its lifetime, because the higher the temperature at which LEDs are operated, the more quickly the light will degrade and the shorter the useful life will be. LED products use a variety of unique heat sink designs and configurations to manage heat, so they may look very different from each other. Regardless of their heat sink design, all LED products that have earned the Energy Star rating have been tested to ensure that they properly manage heat so that the light output of the LED is maintained through the end of its rated life.

Lighting System Design

Lighting system design is an important element of the overall design of any hospitality facility. Interior and exterior lighting are crucial design components that:

- Help attract guests and make them comfortable.

- Communicate a concept (your intended position in the market).

- Establish an atmosphere.

- Highlight artwork or interior features.

- Improve employee productivity.

In addition, lighting can substantially affect safety and energy costs, both directly and indirectly.

Design Factors

Factors in designing a lighting system include light levels, luminaires, color rendition, safety, and emergency lighting.

Light Levels. One of the first questions a designer must ask is: How much light should there be in a given space? This question is usually answered by determining what activities or tasks are being or will be performed within the space. Sometimes widely varying levels of light need to be available in a single space. For example, a meeting room may only need five footcandles of light during an audio-visual presentation, but 100 footcandles during a workshop. The meeting room may need several different types of lamps and fixtures with lots of light switches and perhaps dimming capabilities to accommodate the various lighting needs.

Light levels can be measured with portable light meters that indicate the available light in footcandles. These devices are accurate to plus or minus 5 percent when properly calibrated. Portable light meters will often have multiple scales allowing designers to measure light levels over a fairly wide range.

The Illuminating Engineering Society (IES) lists, for various hotel and restaurant spaces, minimum lighting levels that incorporate a number of task, space, and occupant considerations (see Exhibit 3). These levels are recommended minimum levels, not standards, and designers may want to use more light than these levels.

The design of hotel lighting systems, as with all other building systems, must comply with local and state building codes. Local and state codes often

Exhibit 3   Minimum Footcandles for Hotel and Restaurant Applications, Based on IES Standards

Hotels		Food Service Facilities	
Bathrooms	20–50	Cashier	20–50
Bedrooms (for reading)	20–50	Cleaning	10–20
Corridors, elevators, and		Dining	5–20
stairs	10–20	Food displays	30–100
Front desk	50–100	Kitchen	50–100
Lobby (general lighting)	10–20		
Lobby (reading and working			
areas)	20–50		

Source: Adapted from http://www.electrical-knowhow.com/2012/12/lighting-design-by-using-quick-estimate.html.

incorporate portions of, or adopt in total, the model standards developed by engineering and design organizations. With regard to light levels, the standards of the American National Standards Institute (ANSI), American Society of Heating, Refrigerating and Air-Conditioning Engineers (ASHRAE), and Illuminating Engineering Society (IES) are of interest for U.S. properties. The ANSI/ASHRAE/IES standards can be found in ANSI/ASHRAE/IES Standard 90.1—Energy Standard for Buildings Except Low-Rise Residential Buildings. Another useful publication regarding hotel lighting is the IES *Design Guide for Hotel Lighting* (Product ID: DG-25-12, Illuminating Engineering Society).

Publications such as ANSI/ASHRAE/IES Standard 90.1 address lighting standards in a rather unusual way. Lighting standards are presented in a "building area method" and "space-by-space method." The building area method defines various building types (e.g., convention center, hotel, or office) and then gives a lighting power density (LPD) for the whole building, expressed in watts per square foot. The space-by-space method looks at individual spaces within a building (e.g., guestrooms, corridors, offices, meeting rooms) and assigns each of these spaces an LPD, also expressed in watts per square foot. LPDs can range from lows of 0.5 in corridors to 3.0 in locations such as performing arts theaters. The designer of the lighting system must determine how much light is needed (expressed in footcandles) and then select lamps and fixtures that will deliver appropriate light levels while at the same time not consuming too much electrical power.

With the rapidly changing technology today in lighting and the desire for reduced energy usage, many lighting standards are changing (as are other building equipment and design standards). However, while standards are changing rapidly, local building codes may not be keeping pace. For example, over a twenty-year span ANSI/ASHRAE/IES Standard 90.1 set building area method values for hotels of 1.15 (1989), 1.7 (1999/2001), 1.0 (2004/2007), and 1.0 (2010); for motels, the values were 1.15 (1989), 2.0 (1999/2001), 1.0 (2004/2007), and 0.88 (2010). Local codes may or may not have kept up with all of those changes, and local codes in different localities may vary, depending on which value of ANSI/ASHRAE/IES

Standard 90.1 a local code is based on. This presents challenges to lighting designers, who may choose to design to less stringent local codes or exceed those codes using updated model standards.

Light levels within a given space can be manipulated through the use of dimming controls. Some systems use photosensors wired directly to dimmable electronic ballasts, so that light levels can be adjusted automatically. Spaces that are exposed to natural light (such as atriums and other interior spaces with extensive glazing) are candidates for this technology; as the sun goes down and the natural light dims, the system can be programmed to adjust artificial light levels upward. Many dimming systems rely on manual switches; light levels are adjusted manually depending on the task at hand or the ambience or "mood" that management wants to convey or support through lighting.

Luminaires. **Luminaires,** also known as fixtures, consist of the following components:

- Lamps
- Lamp sockets
- Ballasts (for luminaires that use electric discharge lamps)
- Reflective material
- Lenses or louvers
- Housing

The main function of a luminaire is to deliver the light produced by the lamp(s) to a space or surface in a way that is visually appealing and comfortable for people. Luminaires are used for direct lighting, indirect lighting, spot or accent lighting, flood lighting, and task lighting.

Lamps must be correctly matched to luminaires for optimal and safe operation; a lamp's geometry, heat generation, and size are all issues that must be addressed. Lamp sockets hold the lamps. Ballasts are often mounted above the luminaire. The reflective material is very important to the overall efficiency of the luminaire, because it affects the amount of light that actually exits the luminaire. Another element that affects a luminaire's efficiency is the lens or louver that is used. Lenses are generally made from translucent, ultraviolet-stabilized acrylic plastic; louvers are used when a reduction in the luminaire's glare is desired. The more translucent the lens or the more open the louver design, the more efficient the luminaire in delivering light.

The degree to which the luminaire achieves a glare-free delivery of light is measured by the visual comfort probability (VCP) rating of the luminaire. VCP values range from 0 to 100, with 70 considered to be the lowest acceptable value for a high-performance luminaire. VCP values refer to the percentage of people who would not find the light from a particular luminaire objectionable due to glare.

The overall efficiency of a luminaire is called the **coefficient of utilization (CU).** This value integrates the efficiency of the luminaire's reflective material and reflector design, the efficiency of its lens/louver, and how well the luminaire's lamp interacts with these elements. High CU values can approach or exceed 90 percent.

All luminaires have basic maintenance requirements—they must be cleaned, replacement items (such as decorative globes or safety covers) must be stocked, and repairs must be made. Whenever possible, designers should choose luminaires that are easily cleaned. For most applications, this means that a fixture should have no bottom surface, and side surfaces should be as vertical as possible so dust will not readily collect. Luminaires suspended from the ceiling in relatively dust-free areas should have an opening above the lamp; the opening creates air circulation because the heated air within the luminaire rises through the opening, carrying dust away. Luminaires in areas with a lot of dust or moisture (flour dust in kitchens or moisture in dishwashing areas, for example) should have dust-proof or vapor-tight luminaires—luminaires that completely enclose the lamp.

Color Rendition. Since the color of the light emitted by various types of lamps differs, the types of lamps used by a property have a great impact on the appearance of the surfaces, finishes, and furnishings within the building. For example, restaurants should have lamps in their dining areas that give off a sufficient amount of light in the red and orange frequencies, or foods such as beef and tomatoes that are rich in red and orange colors will appear dull, dark, and unappetizing. As mentioned earlier in the chapter, the color rendering index (CRI) is used to rate the relative performance of artificial light sources (see Exhibit 4). Generally speaking, the higher the CRI value, the truer the colors.

Safety. Designers must keep safety as well as costs and aesthetics in mind when designing a lighting system. Compliance with local safety code requirements is a

Exhibit 4   Typical CRI Values of Various Light Sources

Source	Typical CRI Value
Incandescent/Halogen	100
Fluorescent	
Cool White T12	62
Warm White T12	53
High Lumen T12	73–85
T8	75–85
T10	80–85
Compact	80–85
Mercury Vapor (clear/coated)	15/50
Metal Halide (clear/coated)	65/70
High-Pressure Sodium	
Standard	22
Deluxe	65
White HPS	85
Low-Pressure Sodium	0
Light-Emitting Diode (LED)	75–85

must. Plastic fixtures should only be used if the plastic materials are slow-burning or self-extinguishing and have low smoke-density ratings and low heat-distortion temperatures. (For aesthetic reasons, long-term durability of plastic fixtures when exposed to ultraviolet light should also be investigated to ensure that yellowing or embrittlement will not occur.) Fixtures should always be installed according to the manufacturer's recommendations, with adequate ventilation and clearance to avoid heat build-up. Luminaires should always be used with lamps with the proper (rated) wattage.

Light sources in locations where the breakage of a lamp could pose a likely health hazard (such as kitchens and pool areas) must have either a luminaire with an acrylic diffuser to retain glass and lamp phosphor materials or (for fluorescent lamps) a tube safety shield around the lamp. This is usually required by local health codes.

Light itself—or the lack of it—can be the culprit or at least a contributing factor in employee and guest accidents. Insufficient lighting is an obvious hazard, but other light conditions can cause trouble as well—glare from lights that are too bright, blinding reflected glare from polished surfaces, harsh shadows, and so on. Guests who move from a bright hotel lobby into a dark restaurant just off the lobby may stumble or even fall if there is a change in floor level between the areas. This is caused by the delayed eye adaption that individuals experience when they move from bright surroundings into dark ones. For that reason, guests should not be confronted with widely varying light levels between adjacent hotel areas.

Care should be exercised in the maintenance of lighting systems. Failed lamps can have cracked glass or may be subject to breakage while being removed; workers may need to wear eye protection and gloves in some situations. Some public-space lighting systems operate at 277 volts; lockout/tagout requirements should be considered when working with these systems.

Emergency Lighting. Emergency lighting requirements for a property will be specified in the local community's building codes. Local codes must be complied with. This discussion will draw on the requirements found in the Life Safety Code[4] and the *National Electrical Code (NEC)*.[5] Local building codes usually follow these two standards.

The *NEC* states that

> emergency illumination shall include all required means of egress lighting, illuminated exit signs, and all other lights specified as necessary to provide required illumination. Emergency lighting systems shall be so designed and installed that the failure of any individual lighting element, such as the burning out of a light bulb, cannot leave in total darkness any space which requires emergency illumination.[6]

Emergency lighting can be provided as (1) an emergency lighting system with its own power, independent of the regular lighting system, or (2) two or more separate and complete regular lighting systems with independent power supplies, each system providing sufficient current for emergency lighting purposes. In the event of a power failure, a delay of no more than ten seconds is permitted in the operation of the emergency lighting system. The system must be capable of providing a minimum of one footcandle for 1.5 hours.

It is important to note that even when hotels are up to code, they can encounter significant difficulties in providing lighting during periods of prolonged electric power outage. This was illustrated in the Northeast Blackout of 2003, after which nearly 90 percent of surveyed hoteliers cited a lack of adequate emergency lighting as a problem they faced. While codes set minimum required standards, hotels may wish to analyze and determine whether these standards will properly address their needs.

The lighting of exit signs is another emergency lighting concern. Exit signs operate twenty-four hours a day and must be kept in good repair, with lights functioning properly. That said, exit signs can be excellent opportunities for energy conservation. Exit-sign lighting options include:

- Light-emitting diodes (LEDs).
- Low-wattage incandescent lamps.
- Compact fluorescent lamps.
- Incandescent lamps.
- Electroluminescent fixtures.
- Self-luminous signs.

Light-emitting diodes are the most energy-efficient option, consuming two to five watts of energy per sign. They have the added advantage of extremely long lifetimes (twenty-five years). Low-wattage incandescent lamps (eight to eighteen watts) in a flexible "light tube" configuration also have long lives (ten years). Compact fluorescent lamps have low power consumption (ten watts or less) but only have a two-year lifetime and are somewhat costly. Incandescent lamps should be avoided, due to their high lifetime operating costs. Electroluminescent sources have relatively high initial costs ($200 per fixture) but have a low wattage (about one watt per fixture) and lifetimes of approximately ten years. Self-luminous signs require no electricity and have lifetimes of ten to twenty years but cost in excess of $200 per fixture. Also, since they utilize tritium, they require disposal as a radioactive waste.

Lighting System Maintenance

Operating problems with lighting systems can be caused by several factors. If the voltage supplied to the lamp is above or below the rated voltage for the lamp, the lamp's output and life will be affected. Fluorescent and some HID lamps may not operate properly if placed in an operating-temperature environment for which they are not rated. Choosing ballasts that are not compatible with the lamps can also result in operational problems. Managers should always remember that they are dealing with a lighting system, all of whose components and interconnections must be correct if proper operation is to be achieved.

The requirements for lighting system maintenance depend on what types of lamps are used, their locations, and the purpose served by the lighting. The two major activities of lighting system maintenance are cleaning luminaires and lamps, and replacing lamps.

Cleaning Luminaires and Lamps

How clean the housekeeping staff keeps a building's luminaires and lamps will affect light output, thereby affecting the ability of the lighting system to deliver its designed light levels. Periodic cleaning of lamps and luminaires will enable the lighting system to deliver a greater fraction of its light output than it does when the light is absorbed by dirt on the lamps and luminaires. Regularly replacing filters in the building's air-handling units can make housekeeping's job easier by removing dust and dirt from the building's air.

How often should luminaires and lamps be cleaned? Semi-annual cleaning is sufficient in many locations; in dustier or dirtier areas, more frequent cleaning may be necessary. Each hotel must establish a cleaning program that works for it.

To prevent them from attracting dirt, plastic luminaires should be de-staticized when they are cleaned (often, a destaticizer is included in the cleaning solution). Plastic luminaires should be air-dried; wiping them would give them a new static charge. Employees should wear clean gloves when handling the cleaned luminaires; otherwise, oil from their hands will leave marks on the plastic and destroy the de-staticization there.

Replacing Lamps

Replacing lamps can be as simple as screwing a light bulb into a guestroom table lamp or as difficult as climbing into a bucket truck to replace a pole-mounted high-pressure sodium lamp and its ballast in the middle of a parking lot. Two factors that help determine how lamps are replaced at a property are lamp characteristics and the property's replacement policy.

Lamp Characteristics. As mentioned earlier, incandescent, electric discharge, and LED lamps have different life expectancies. Incandescent lamps need to be replaced much more often. For example, if we assume an incandescent lamp life of 1,000 hours (some may have a life of only 750 hours), a fluorescent lamp life of 12,000 hours, and an LED lamp life of 25,000 hours (or more), the incandescent lamp could require as many as eight or nine replacements per year if burned continuously (there are 8,760 hours in a year), the fluorescent lamp would be replaced about once every 1.5 years under such circumstances, and the LED lamp would last for almost three years.

A consideration when replacing fluorescent lamps is maintaining the desired color rendition. Replacing a fluorescent lamp with a lamp that has a markedly different color rendition (warm white with cool white, for instance) results in a mottled lighting effect on the interior design that can be disastrous. Similar concerns can exist with LED lamps, especially since they may be installed in large ceiling areas where many lamps will be visible at the same time. Group relamping in such circumstances will help maintain a uniform appearance and cut down on replacement labor costs as well.

If a property's lighting system maintenance program is designed to maintain the lighting system and its light levels as closely as possible to its initial condition, then the lumen depreciation of the system's lamps is also of concern. **Lumen depreciation** is a measure of a lamp's tendency to decrease its light output over time. With mercury vapor lamps and some other types of fluorescent lamps, light output drops off dramatically as the lamps' operating hours approach the lamps' rated life. Unless the lighting system is greatly overdesigned, it may be desirable to replace lamps before they fail entirely because their light output has fallen so far below what it should be.

Other characteristics of lamps that affect maintenance needs are the average burning time of the lamp and the voltage of the electrical supply to the lamp. Incandescent and fluorescent lamps that are frequently cycled (turned on and off) will have greatly reduced lifetimes, resulting in greater maintenance costs in terms of lamps and labor. Lamps that are supplied electricity at a voltage different from the lamp's rated voltage (even by only a very low percent) will have a reduced life if the voltage is above the lamp's rated voltage, an increased life if the voltage is below the lamp's rated voltage. Electrical system or circuit voltages can change for a variety of reasons, including loads being added or removed, changes in electric utility supply voltages, and malfunctions of electrical equipment.

Replacement Policies. Most discussions of lamp replacement policies include a discussion of group relamping versus replacement upon burnout. Group relamping advocates suggest that wholesale replacement of all of the lamps in the lighting system (or a portion of the system) after some prescribed number of operating hours will result in significantly reduced lamp replacement costs. Cost reductions are possible primarily through a labor cost reduction, although it may be possible to reduce lamp costs as well by purchasing them in bulk. One lamp replacement policy is shown in Exhibit 5.

A group relamping policy does not mean that the visual appearance of the space is compromised by not replacing burned-out lamps, as Exhibit 5 illustrates. Lamps that burn out are replaced as they fail, but rather than doing the relamping on a "failure" basis indefinitely, a group relamping program is proactive with regard to failure—that is, it anticipates failure. When the lamps in a given area reach a portion of their rated life (80 percent in the instance of Exhibit 5), they are all replaced. The result is a space that enjoys a uniform light level, with fewer instances of burned-out or malfunctioning lamps. Group relamping can save the property money as well. Group relamping is particularly appropriate in any area (for example, a convention hall or parking lot) that requires a significant number of labor hours simply to gain access to the lamps or where special equipment is required.

Labor costs for lamp replacement can vary considerably, depending on the length of time required to replace a lamp and the wages of the individual replacing it. For example, if burned-out lamps in guestrooms can be replaced by housekeeping employees as part of their normal rounds, the cost of lamp replacement in guestrooms will be low. However, if every time a lamp burns out it's replaced by a member of the engineering staff dispatched via radio, the labor cost to replace a single lamp can approach $5 to $10.

Lamp and Ballast Disposal. Replacing lamps and ballasts brings up waste disposal issues. This is especially true during lighting system upgrades or a group relamping effort; both can result in the accumulation of large numbers of lamps

Exhibit 5   Sample Lamp Replacement Procedures

P.M. PROCEDURES: Planned Lamp Replacement
MAINT. ACTION #23
FREQUENCY: Annually

Maint. Action #23A

How to set up this program:

1. List all your lamps by area, such as:

   - Coffee Shop—50 lamps
   - Restaurant—100 lamps
   - Corridors—200 lamps

2. Doing one area at a time, replace all the lamps with new ones. Save 20 percent of the best-looking lamps in a "replacement" box with the area the lamps came from clearly marked on it.

3. Now, let's take the coffee shop with 50 lamps as an example. If you saved 20 percent of the old lamps, you have 10 lamps in a box marked "Coffee Shop."

4. As the lamps in the coffee shop burn out, replace them with the ones you have in their replacement box. When there are no lamps left in the box, you have achieved 80 percent of the coffee shop lamps' life and it is time to re-lamp this area with 50 new lamps, once again saving 20 percent (10) for the replacement box.

<u>EASY, ISN'T IT?</u>

P.S. Don't forget to maintain an inventory of lamps sufficient for complete lamp changes.

Source: Adapted from Maintenance Operating Manual, Days Inns of America, Inc., Atlanta, Georgia.

and ballasts that must be disposed of properly. Legal as well as environmental issues must be considered.

Because fluorescent lamps contain mercury, there are regulations regarding their disposal. Within the United States, the federal Universal Waste Rule (UWR)[7] establishes required disposal practices. The UWR is superseded by more stringent regulations in some states.[8] With the European Community, the Waste Electrical and Electronic Equipment Directive[9] sets forward collection, recycling, and recover targets for all types of electrical goods, including fluorescent lamps. Specific implementation is done by each EU member country.

Mercury vapor, metal halide, and low-pressure sodium lamps all contain mercury as well, so their disposal must follow established regulations. Since replacement of these lamps is often done on a group relamping program (which may be done by contractors with special equipment), care should be taken to ensure that this large quantity of lamps is disposed of properly.

All ballasts manufactured through 1979, and some after this date, contain PCBs. There is legislation in the United States (at both the state and federal level) and in many other countries that specifies proper handling and disposal practices for PCB ballasts. These laws must be followed by the property or the contractor retained by the property. Options for ballast disposal include incineration, recycling, and disposal in a landfill. Information about lamp recycling can be found at www.lamprecycle.org.

A Final Word on Replacing Lamps. A major change impacting the replacement of lamps has occurred in recent years. Governmental legislation throughout the world has established efficiency standards for lamps and has prohibited the manufacture (and, eventually, the sale) of lamps that do not meet those standards. In the United States, efficiency standards for lamps were established as part of the Energy Independence and Security Act of 2007 (EISA). As a result of this legislation, typical incandescent light bulbs are ceasing to be manufactured in the United States and will no longer be available for sale once current supplies are sold. However, specialty incandescent lamps will continue to be available, and manufacturers are working on higher-efficiency incandescent light bulbs that meet EISA standards.[10]

Energy Conservation Opportunities

For lighting systems, the two primary energy conservation opportunities are the use of more efficient lighting sources and the control of operating hours. Secondary benefits may be possible by reducing lighting in overlit spaces, but this must be approached with caution since lighting reductions may affect safety, productivity, or guests' perceptions of the property.

One way to achieve more efficient lighting (fewer watts per lumen) is to replace incandescent lamps with fluorescent or LED lamps in as many locations as possible. Compact or screw-in fluorescent lamps and LED lamps are available that can be substituted for incandescent lamps in downlights, table lamps, and ceiling-mounted lighting fixtures of various designs. The result will be a reduction of up to 75 percent in the electricity consumed by the lamp. In addition, there will be substantial labor savings due to the longer life of the fluorescent and LED lamps. Replacing inefficient exterior lights with more efficient ones usually has a short payback period, since the operating hours of exterior lighting are very long.

Efficiently controlling the operating hours of lights results in fewer operating hours, lower energy usage, and lower costs. The easiest control method is to simply turn off lights that are not needed. This is something everyone employed at a property can do that requires no additional training, investment, or labor hours, and has immediate benefits. Since motivating employees and managers to take this responsibility seriously has sometimes proven difficult, many operations use mechanical methods whenever possible to turn off unneeded lights. Microprocessors can also be used to turn lights on and off on a predetermined schedule. In addition to saving electricity, reduced operating hours also increase the time between lamp replacements.

One area that certainly lends itself to mechanical control is exterior lighting, including parking lot lighting. Photocell control for exterior lighting is highly recommended and, in comparison to either manual or time clock control, should result in substantial energy savings with a minimal initial investment. (Time clock control for this lighting must frequently be reset in order to operate the lighting only when needed.) In locations within the property that benefit from natural light, management may wish to install photocell control as well. In these instances, the photocell control acts to maintain a preset light level in the area and either dims or turns off lamps as the amount of natural light increases, or turns on and brightens the lamps as natural light decreases. This can be quite effective in reducing energy costs.

To control the operation of lights in meeting rooms, storerooms, and other areas where lights do not need to operate continuously, the use of ultrasonic or infrared sensors or twist timers may be appropriate. Sensors turn on lights when they sense movement in the room. Following a preset period of inactivity in the room, the lights are switched off. Twist timers are manually activated by the person wanting to use the space; they automatically turn off after a period of time. The length of time lights stay on is dictated by the type of timer and the degree to which it is turned.

It is common practice in hotels and many commercial buildings to operate corridor and stairwell lighting at full light output 100 percent of the time. With the use of energy-efficient lamps, the cost of full-time operation is reduced, but there are ways to further reduce operation costs through the use of occupancy sensor controls on corridor and stairwell lighting. For example, half of a corridor's lights can be wired with occupancy sensors, so that they only turn on when an individual enters the corridor and 100 percent of the lighting is needed; the rest of the time they are off, saving electricity costs. For a stairwell (a location less frequently used in hotels than a corridor), bi-level lighting fixtures are being developed that significantly reduce energy use by shifting stairwell lighting to greatly reduced light levels when the stairwells are not in use. Other creative ideas may provide opportunities for further improvement of energy efficiency while maintaining satisfactory lighting system operation.[11]

Life Cycle Cost Estimating

A life cycle approach to the selection of lamps (and lighting systems) is certainly appropriate. Life cycle approaches consider all costs associated with a certain piece of equipment or system. For lighting systems, this typically means the lamps (and, if appropriate, the ballasts), labor to replace the lamps, energy to operate the lamps (and possibly energy to remove the heat generated by the lamps), and the cost of lamp disposal. Lamps that have low initial costs (such as incandescent lamps) can have large energy costs and significant replacement labor costs. The U.S. Environmental Protection Agency has placed analysis programs on its Energy Star website to assist people in evaluating the life cycle costs of lighting options. Lamp manufacturers also have calculators on their websites.

Endnotes

1. Walter A. Rutes, Richard H. Penner, and Lawrence Adams, *Hotel Design, Planning, and Development* (New York: W. W. Norton, 2001), p. 338.

2. An excellent glossary of lighting terms can be found at http://www.gelighting.com/LightingWeb/emea/resources/world-of-ge-lighting/glossary/.

3. The source for this section on LEDs is http://www.energystar.gov/index.cfm?c=lighting.pr_what_are#what_are.

4. NFPA 101—Life Safety Code (Quincy, Mass.: National Fire Protection Association, 2012).

5. NFPA 70—National Electrical Code (Quincy, Mass.: National Fire Protection Association, 2014).

6. Reprinted with permission from NFPA 70-87—National Electrical Code, copyright 1986, National Fire Protection Association, Quincy, Mass., 02269. This reprinted material is not the complete and official position of the NFPA on the referenced subject, which is represented only by the standard in its entirety.

7. http://www.epa.gov/osw/hazard/wastetypes/universal/lamps/faqs.htm.

8. http://www.epa.gov/osw/hazard/wastetypes/universal/statespf.htm.

9. http://ec.europa.eu/environment//waste/weee/index_en.htm.

10. http://www.energystar.gov/ia/products/lighting/cfls/downloads/EISA_Backgrounder_FINAL_4-11_EPA.pdf.

11. The PIER Lighting Research Program (at http://www.archenergy.com/lrp/final-reports/deliverable_1.1.9_LRP-FINAL_RPT-09-21-05.pdf) and the Lighting Research Center (at www.lrc.rpi.edu) are excellent sources of information concerning innovative research in lighting.

⚷ Key Terms

artificial light—Light other than sunlight.

ballast—A piece of equipment that controls the starting and operation of electric discharge lamps and acts as a small transformer in the lighting circuit.

coefficient of utilization—The efficiency factor that combines the luminaire efficiency (light delivered from the luminaire divided by the light produced by the lamp) with the room characteristics and the light distribution in the room.

color rendition—A light source's ability to provide a perceived color similar to that which results from sunlight.

electric discharge lamp—A lamp that generates light by passing an electric arc through a space filled with a specially formulated mixture of gases. Types of electric discharge lamps include fluorescent, mercury vapor, metal halide, and high- and low-pressure sodium.

efficacy—A measure of how effective the light source is in converting electricity to lumens. Expressed in lumens per watt.

footcandle—A measurement of illumination. One footcandle denotes a light intensity of one lumen per square foot.

high-intensity discharge (HID) lamp—A lamp requiring a ballast that generates light by passing an electric arc through a space filled with a specially formulated mixture of gases. HID lamps are types of electric discharge lamps that are characterized by high lumens per watt and long strike and restrike times.

illumination—Light that is incident on a surface.

incandescent lamp—A lamp that consists of a filament inside a sealed glass bulb. Current passing through the filament heats it to incandescence, producing light.

lamp life—The expected operating lifetime of a lamp, defined as the time it takes half of the lamps in a given sample to fail.

light-emitting diode (LED) lamp—A lamp that consists of semiconductor devices that produce visible light when an electric current is passed through them. LEDs are a type of solid-state lighting.

lumen—The most commonly used unit of light.

lumen depreciation—A measure of a lamp's tendency to decrease its light output over time.

lumen maintenance—A lamp's ability to maintain its output.

luminaire—A lighting appliance that consists of a lamp, lamp socket, ballast (for luminaires using electric discharge lamps), reflective material, lenses or louvers, and a housing. Also called a fixture.

lux—Metric system measurement of illumination. One lux denotes a light intensity of one lumen per square meter.

natural light—Sunlight.

strike time—The time required for an electric discharge lamp to reach full output from a cold start.

visible light—Radiated energy that can be seen by the human eye.

Review Questions

1. What are the advantages of natural light?
2. What are the advantages and disadvantages of incandescent lamps?
3. How do incandescent lamps, electric discharge lamps, and LED lamps produce light?
4. What are the various types of electric discharge lamps and their characteristics?
5. Why is a lighting system's design an important element of a building's overall design?
6. What are some safety considerations designers must keep in mind when designing a lighting system?
7. How does the type of lamps used at a property affect lamp replacement?
8. What is group relamping?
9. What are some ways lighting systems can conserve energy?

10. When considering the life cycle cost of a lighting system, what are the major costs that should be considered?

Internet Sites

For more information, visit the following Internet sites. Remember that Internet addresses can change without notice. If the site is no longer there, you can use a search engine to look for additional sites.

American Lighting Association
www.americanlightingassoc.com

American Society of Heating, Refrigerating and Air-Conditioning Engineers
www.ashrae.org

Consulting-Specifying Engineer
www.csemag.com

Energy Star Lighting
www.energystar.gov

General Electric
www.gelighting.com

Illuminating Engineering Society of North America
www.iesna.org

International Association of Lighting Designers
www.iald.org

Lighting Research Center
www.lrc.rpi.edu

U.S. Department of Energy—Solid-State Lighting
http://www1.eere.energy.gov/buildings/ssl/ledlightingfacts.html

Additional Information

Useful descriptions can be found at HowStuffWorks.com:
http://home.howstuffworks.com/light-bulb3.htm
http://home.howstuffworks.com/fluorescent-lamp.htm
http://electronics.howstuffworks.com/led.htm
http://home.howstuffworks.com/question337.htm

Chapter Appendix:

Energy-Efficient Interior Light Bulbs

Interior lighting represents about one-third of electricity consumption in typical hotels. Installing energy-efficient light bulbs can significantly reduce electricity consumption and result in energy and cost savings. Energy-efficient light bulbs such as compact fluorescent lights (CFLs), light-emitting diodes (LEDs), and T8 fluorescents use less electricity than traditional bulbs such as incandescent and T12 fluorescent lighting.

A CFL is a spiral-shaped white bulb that uses the same socket as an incandescent bulb. CFLs use approximately 75 percent less energy than incandescent bulbs and have a life span of approximately 10,000 hours. Replacing existing incandescent lamps with CFLs is an excellent way to lower energy usage, generate less heat throughout the interior of the hotel, reduce labor replacement costs, and generate cost savings.

LEDs are similar in size to an incandescent bulb and use the same socket. LEDs use approximately 87 percent less energy than halogen lamps and have a useful life span of 25,000–50,000 hours. That means that if an LED lamp is on for twenty-four hours a day, you may not have to replace it for almost six years. (The same fixture using a halogen lamp would have to be replaced once a year.) Replacing existing lamps with LED lamps can give hotels efficient and durable lighting for their lobbies, hallways, guestrooms, and banquet spaces. Not only do LEDs use less electricity, generate less heat throughout the interior of the hotel, lower labor replacement costs, and generate savings, they also result in less pollution upon disposal.

Fluorescent lamps are long white cylindrical bulbs that provide fluorescent lighting. There are three types of fluorescent lamps currently in use, labeled T12, T8, and T5 lamps. T12 lamps are 1½" in diameter and have a life span of 7,000+ hours. T8 lamps are 1" in diameter and have a life span of 15,000+ hours. T5 lamps are 3/8" in diameter and have a life span of 20,000+ hours. The smaller the diameter, the more efficient the bulb.

High-performance T8 lamps, along with electronic ballasts, are setting new standards for low power consumption, low life-cycle costs, and illumination that more closely resembles natural light. The slim profile of the T8 lamps enables them to function more efficiently. They are available in linear and U-shaped configurations.

Electronic ballasts are designed to provide the right voltage and current to fluorescent lamps. Newly designed ballasts use high-frequency and solid-state circuitry instead of heavy copper to perform this task.

Installing energy-efficient lighting systems is an important part of any hotel's electric lighting strategy. Maximizing lighting quality while minimizing lighting costs should be top priorities for lodging managers.

Sample Business Case

The Blue Sky Hotel, a 300-room hotel, believes that it may have a potential opportunity to reduce energy consumption by replacing the existing MR16 halogen 50-watt lighting it has on dimmers in most of the hotel's public spaces with 7-watt

LED lamps. Before taking any action, the managers of the Blue Sky Hotel want to calculate the return on their investment. The computations listed below shows the annual savings, investment costs, and the payback period for the installation.

Energy costs saved are taken from the EPA's Energy Star calculator. The cost of an LED bulb varies depending on its wattage and use. Many local utility companies have LED replacement lamp incentives in their rebate programs. Hotel managers should be sure to contact their local utility company to determine if rebates are offered before starting any lamp-replacement project.

Calculations

For this calculation, the cost per Kwh is $.12 (obtained from the Blue Sky's electricity bills). The cost to install one MR16 LED 7-watt lamp is $39, including labor:

Number of Lamps		Reduction in Wattage		Hours Used Daily		Total Days		Kwh Multiplier		Total Kwh Saved
480	×	43w	×	24	×	365	×	.001	=	180,806

Annual Savings

Annual Kwh Electric Savings: 180,806 × $.12 = $21,696.72
    Total Annual Savings: $21,696.72

Investment

Cost per LED Lamp Installed (including labor): $39
Number of LED Lamps: 480
    Total Investment: $18,720

Payback

Investment: $18,720
Annual Savings: $21,696.72
    Payback: .86 years

Resources

Learn more about commercial LED lighting from Energy Star at energystar.gov. Hotel managers and others can use the Energy Star Portfolio Manager tool to record their energy usage and receive additional information that compares their hotels to similar hotels.

The federal government operates an Environmentally Preferable Purchasing program. Information about this program, its standards, and program products can be found at http://www.epa.gov/epp/.

In many states as well as at the federal level, loan, rebate, and tax incentive programs exist for the purchase of energy-efficient equipment as well as the installation of renewable-energy equipment. Hotel managers should be aware of these programs and incorporate the savings they offer into any purchase evaluations.

Source: Adapted from "Install Energy Efficient Interior Light Bulbs," American Hotel & Lodging Association, 2014; http://www.ahla.com/Green.aspx?id=35746.

Competencies

1. Explain how hotels deal with laundry, and describe laundry transport equipment. (pp. 335–338)

2. Distinguish a washer-extractor from a tunnel washer. (pp. 338–340)

3. Describe extractors and dryers. (pp. 340–342)

4. Describe flatwork ironers, folders, and valet equipment. (pp. 342–345)

5. Explain factors in designing a laundry and selecting laundry equipment. (pp. 345–354)

6. Outline laundry maintenance. (pp. 354–356)

7. Describe emerging trends in laundry operations. (pp. 356–358)

Laundry Systems

Significant contributions to this chapter for this edition have been made
by Tom Mara Sr., President of the Victor Kramer Company,
Oceanport, New Jersey.

*The Wyndham Wind Watch Hotel doesn't try to put any marketing
spin on its laundry equipment — the staff just knows it works.*

*Humming behind the scenes at the Long Island hotel is an in-
house laundry system which goes unnoticed by guests who just see
the soft and clean whites and linens which make their stay comfortable and worry-free. Executive Housekeeper David Jakubowski knows
exactly how important that is to a hotel, and to its housekeeping staff.*

*The hotel uses two 150-pound machines and a single 250-pound
machine to accomplish the dirty work, while a custom-built automatic folding and ironing machine puts the finishing touches on
hotel whites. That and two industrial-size dryers round out the modest but hardworking equipment at the hotel.*

*"We haven't had any problems whatsoever with the equipment
since I came here," Jakubowski said. "We have an in-house preventive maintenance program which keeps things running smooth."*

*At a time when many hotel companies are forced to outsource
their laundry service, The Wyndham Wind Watch prefers to continue using its in-house system.*

*"It's definitely cheaper to do laundry in-house," Jakubowski
said. "But the real advantage is the convenience to the guests. It's
always right there. You don't have to worry about the laundry truck
getting stuck in a snowstorm."*[1]

DEALING WITH LAUNDRY is a fact of life for hotels. Guestrooms, restaurants, room
service, banquets, spas, recreational facilities (fitness centers, pools, etc.) and
employees all give rise to soiled linens, towels, tablecloths, and uniforms that must
be cleaned. Hotels have several choices in how they handle this chore. They can:

- Rent linens from commercial linen and uniform rental companies.

- Buy their own linens and use a commercial laundry for processing services.

- Buy their own linens and send them to a centralized laundry (either free-
  standing or within a hotel) run by the hotel chain or some other group of
  affiliated hotels for processing linen and uniforms.

- Buy their own linens and use their own on-premises laundry for processing.

- Use a combination of these options.[2]

Most lodging properties in the United States operate an on-premises laundry for processing their soiled linen. In contrast, lodging properties in Europe usually have their linen processed by outside contractors. Some U.S. chains operate regional laundry facilities where linen from several of the chain's hotels is processed, providing an off-site laundry similar to a commercial laundry but retaining corporate control over linen quality and service. For example, Walt Disney World processes linen from its over 23,000 guestrooms plus a number of other facilities in a centralized facility separate from its Orlando, Florida, hotels. In Edison, New Jersey, Marriott International processes textiles from more than 134,000 rooms. Hilton Worldwide operates large central laundry facilities in Piscataway, New Jersey, to process linen from their 6,500 guestrooms in New York and New Jersey. These mega-facilities include state-of-the-art laundry equipment and systems, particularly tunnel washing systems and high-speed flatwork ironers, and are designed to be highly efficient operations.

There are several advantages to operating an on-premises laundry, such as more control over linen quality, service, and costs. When an on-premises laundry is operated efficiently, many properties enjoy significant savings in comparison to the cost of outsourcing linen to a commercial provider. In addition to control over quality and service, properties with on-premises facilities require lower linen par levels, which means fewer dollars tied up in linen inventory. Proper on-premises processing extends the life cycle of linen items, which reduces the cost of linen replacement due to premature wear out, unaccountable loss, and damage. Additionally, the quality of the finished linen is oftentimes higher. For these reasons, many hotels and hotel companies prefer to operate their own laundries and not be dependent on outside commercial providers.

Laundry Equipment

It takes a significant amount of different types of equipment to outfit the laundry of a large hotel, especially one that offers in-house valet service to its guests. Laundries at small properties can usually get by with the basics—washers and dryers. In the section that follows, we'll discuss a full range of commercial laundry equipment. Keep in mind that the number and type of equipment a hotel has depends on the hotel's size, level of guest service, and other factors.

Laundry Transport Equipment

Employees have to get soiled linens to the laundry. At small properties, linen is usually transported in a hamper bag carried by employees. At larger properties, carts or chutes are used to move large amounts of linen quickly and efficiently. Some hotels have automated overhead monorail systems to carry linen to the washers and then to the dryers after washing.

Carts. If the property does not have linen chutes, hamper carts are used to transport linen to the laundry, within the laundry, and to storage areas outside the laundry.[3] There are basic carts, carts with shelves, carts with bars or hangers, and "raising platform" carts—the bottom of the cart rests on springs, so that as workers unload the laundry, the bottom rises and workers don't have to bend over as much. There are open carts, carts with covers, and lockable carts. Other cart options include tow hitches (so a worker can pull more than one cart at a time), wheel brakes, special casters, and caster swivel locks.

Laundry carts are available in various sizes—common sizes carry 100 to 300 pounds of linen. There are many color options so that hotels can choose carts that match their décor. Carts range from heavy-duty canvas to one-piece plastic types with drain holes for easy washing.

Carts should not have protrusions that can snag or tear linen. They should move easily, and employees should be able to load and unload laundry without excessive bending and stretching. Carts should be cleaned and sanitized on a regular basis. It is a good idea to keep carts for soiled laundry separate from those for clean laundry. The clean-linen carts can be a different color or made from a different material so that they are not mixed in with the soiled-linen carts.[4]

Chutes. Laundry chutes are usually located on each floor of a hotel inside the housekeeping storage area. They are a convenient way to get guestroom linen to the laundry room. Laundry chutes should be cleaned regularly to remove lint and dust. Any fire detection or suppression equipment in the chute should be checked periodically to ensure proper operation in case of fire. Laundry chutes should be kept locked to reduce the risk that they will be used by a prankster or an arsonist. The locks should be on the engineering department's preventive maintenance schedule to ensure that they are kept in working order.

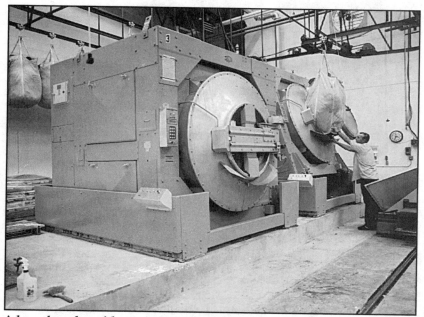

A large laundry with an automated overhead monorail system. (Courtesy of the Pellerin Milnor Corporation, Kenner, Louisiana)

Employees in other areas of the hotel (food and beverage outlets, fitness centers, spas, recreational facilities, etc.) use linen carts to transport soiled and clean linen in these areas to and from the laundry.

Automated Overhead Monorail Systems. Some large properties have automated overhead monorail systems in their laundry rooms. With a typical system, employees sort laundry items and place them in bags that travel on overhead rails to the washers. When a washer is ready for another load, an employee opens the bottom of the bag (or the bag automatically opens) and drops the laundry into the washer. Some machines tilt backward to make this easier. If the transport system is computerized, the computer can keep track of which linen goes where and make sure it is properly processed.

Washers

There are two commercial washer types—conventional washer-extractors and tunnel washers. Conventional commercial washer-extractors range in size from 25 to 700 pounds per load, whereas tunnel washers range in size from five chambers (accommodating 100 to 150 pounds of linen per chamber) to twelve chambers.

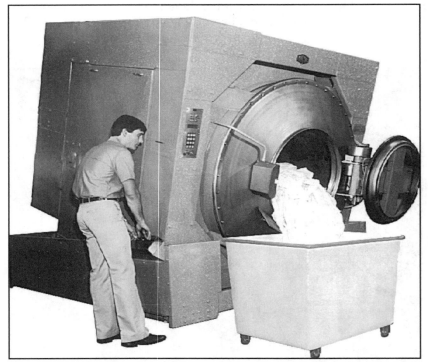

This washer-extractor handles up to 450 pounds of laundry per load. Machines of this size would only be found in large hotels. (Courtesy of the Pellerin Milnor Corporation, Kenner, Louisiana)

Washer-Extractors. Washer-extractors are free-standing units made of stainless steel used to clean linen and extract water from it to prepare it for drying. Washer-extractors may be front or side loaders. The type of machine a manager chooses depends on the property's laundry operation, floor space, and ceiling height. Side loaders, for example, are usually used in laundries that deliver soiled items to the washers by way of an overhead transport system.

Once soiled linen is loaded into the washer-extractor, an operator selects, based on the items being washed, the proper computerized washing formula, which includes a series of washing cycles (wash, bleach, sour, rinse(s), and extraction). The formulas programmed into the machine are developed by chemical technicians who take into account the chemicals required, the typical degree of soiling of the various types of linen, desired water temperatures, and the condition of the water itself (i.e., the degree of hardness).

The wash times of standard washing formulas vary in length depending on the items being processed. For example, flat linen (sheets and pillowcases) may be washed for thirty to thirty-five minutes, terry for thirty-five to forty minutes, and food and beverage linen from forty to forty-five minutes from the start of the wash to the finish (extraction).

Some large washer-extractors tilt forward to help with unloading. Once the machine is tilted, an employee can position a laundry cart under the door and push a button to rotate the cylinder, causing the clean laundry to tumble into the cart. The machine can also unload the linen onto a conveyor that transports it to a dryer. Some washer-extractors also tilt back to help employees load laundry.

Tunnel Washers. Tunnel washers, also called batch washers or continuous batch washers, have characteristics that make them different from conventional washer-extractors. As you can see from Exhibit 1, a tunnel washer is, in effect, a series of interconnected chambers. As mentioned earlier, each chamber can accommodate 100 to 150 pounds of laundry, depending on the manufacturer.[5]

In both conventional washer-extractors and tunnel washers, laundry is subjected to successive "baths"—some with chemicals—to loosen, suspend, and rinse away soil. These baths are followed by finishing operations (sour, softener, etc.). A conventional washer does this in a single cylinder; baths are changed by draining and refilling the cylinder. A tunnel washer, on the other hand, keeps each bath in a different cylinder and moves the linen from one cylinder to the next. The laundry is separated into batches, just as with a conventional washer. Computerized tunnel washers can keep track of each batch as it moves through the tunnel and automatically adjust water temperatures and chemical formulas so that each batch receives the treatment it needs for optimum cleaning.

Two basic types of tunnel washers are top-transfer machines and bottom-transfer machines. **Top-transfer machines** lift the laundry out of the water and drain it before transferring it to the next bath; **bottom-transfer machines** transfer both the laundry and the water along the bottom of the washer. Top-transfer machines offer the advantage of draining laundry before moving it along to progressively cleaner baths; this process makes for cleaner laundry. In bottom-transfer machines, dirty water moves forward with the load, so laundry is not as clean.

Exhibit 1   Diagram of a Tunnel Washer

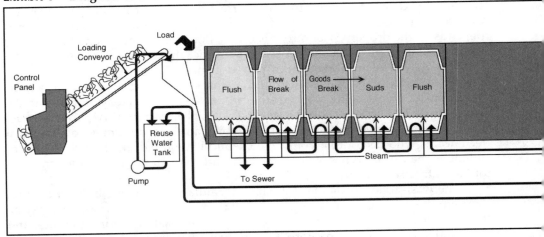

Courtesy of the Pellerin Milnor Corporation, Kenner, Louisiana

Tunnel washers are extensively used in the United States and throughout the world for a number of reasons. One is that it takes fewer employees to operate them. Tunnel washers are connected to an extractor, and conveyors can automatically move the linen from the extractor to the dryers, so that instead of a number of employees loading and unloading separate washers, extractors, and dryers and transporting laundry between these machines, only one employee is needed to load the washer. (After extraction, the linen is automatically transported by conveyor to the dryer. After full drying, the items are transported by a conveyor, an overhead monorail system, or by carts to the finishing areas to be ironed and folded.) In addition to labor savings, there can be significant energy and water savings. Where conventional washers can use as much as three to four gallons of water per pound of linen, tunnel washers use just one gallon or less per pound. By extension, energy is saved because less water needs to be heated, and using less water lowers the laundry's water and sewer charges.

Tunnel washers have other advantages as well. Linen is processed faster because there are no delays for filling and draining cylinders. Because water and energy demands are constant, support systems—water heaters, water softeners, drains, and so on—do not have to be sized to cover peak demands. Since tunnel washers process linen steadily in small batches, morning startup time is quicker and throughput is at a steady level. Employees in the finishing sections don't have to wait a long time to get started, only to be buried under hundreds of pounds of laundry all at once.

Extractors

As the name implies, **extractors** extract water from laundered fabrics. Standalone extractors are used in laundries with tunnel washers; as noted earlier,

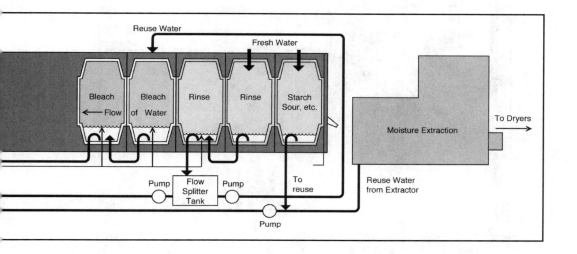

washer-extractors do their own extracting, and many laundries don't need a separate extractor.

Dryers

Dryers are machines that dry linen by tumbling it in a basket exposed to circulating hot air. The heat is generated by gas, propane in areas without access to natural gas, or steam. Although dryers heated by electricity are available, the cost to produce the required heat is cost-prohibitive for most laundries. Gas is generally the most economical heat source; steam dryers are best suited for locations where steam power is already available. Dryer capacities range from 25 to 400 pounds.

Today's dryers are more sophisticated than their counterparts of yesteryear because (1) there are more types of fabrics now, some of which have special drying needs, (2) saving energy is of greater concern, and (3) managers are seeking simpler machines that can reduce energy, training, and labor costs.

Most dryers now have microprocessor-driven control systems. All an employee has to do is push the button on the control panel that corresponds to the type of laundry being dried, and the dryer goes through a cycle that has been pre-programmed by the laundry manager or by the dryer's manufacturer (usually with input from the laundry manager). Some dryers dry the load for a set number of minutes recommended for that fabric; others have sensors linked to their microprocessors that can sense moisture in the load and turn the dryer off automatically the moment the laundry is dry. Many dryers then go through a **cool-down cycle** so that wrinkles are not set into no-iron fabrics. Some also have an anti-wrinkle feature that automatically tumbles the load without heat at pre-selected intervals—managers may program the dryer to tumble the load for twenty seconds every two minutes for ten minutes, for example. If an employee is busy and can't

Two 50-pound washer-extractors. (Courtesy of the Pellerin Milnor Corporation, Kenner, Louisiana)

get to the laundry right after a cycle is completed, the anti-wrinkle feature keeps clothes from sitting at the bottom of the dryer basket and wrinkling.

Energy-saving features on dryers include an ignition system for gas dryers rather than a standing pilot light. Some manufacturers build extra insulation into their energy-saving models. One manufacturer offers a "heat reclaimer package," in which a portion of the hot exhaust air is recirculated into the dryer, saving energy and reducing drying time. Another dryer saves time and energy by using a permanently tilted basket and gravity to position the wettest laundry (which is the heaviest) closest to the hot air inlet.

Dryers include signal lights indicating dryer operation, self-cleaning lint screens, reverse cylinder drives (to help prevent laundry from balling and tangling), "no-snag baskets" with extruded perforations to help protect delicate fabrics, and automatic backdraft dampers (to eliminate downdrafts that chill the dryer). Some dryers with microprocessors have diagnostic boards that allow maintenance employees to locate a problem quickly.

Flatwork Finishers

The two machines commonly used to finish linens, tablecloths, and other items are flatwork ironers and folders.

Flatwork Ironers. Flatwork ironers give linens a crisp, finished look. Flatwork ironers can be heated by gas (generally the most economical method), propane,

The Ten Most Common Drying Mistakes

Although these tips were written with large laundries in mind, many of them can also help managers of mid-size and small laundries.

1. **Not loading the dryer to full capacity.** Underloading is the most common and most costly mistake made in institutional laundries. Dryers with microprocessors can eliminate this problem with "small load" dry cycles for each fabric classification.

2. **Allowing laundry to dry too long.** Besides wasting energy and production time, overdrying creates friction, which wears out linen fibers and produces excess lint. Don't pad drying time "just to make sure."

3. **Not running the dryer at constant production rates.** It's a waste of production time to let employees dictate when a dryer is loaded. Often the machine sits idle after a load is dried because employees are engaged in other tasks. There are automatic or semi-automatic dryer loading and unloading possibilities for almost any laundry.

4. **Taking too long to load or unload machines.** Besides wasting time, this allows the dryer's cylinder to cool off between loads, resulting in the dryer having to work harder to bring the temperature back up for the next batch.

5. **Too much heat at the end of the load.** The most effective means of drying is to apply the greatest heat to laundry at the beginning of cycles. It is best to restrict heat toward the end, when goods are most susceptible to damage. Dryers with microprocessors can do this easily.

6. **Not enough cool-down.** If dried laundry is not cooled down enough during the dryer's cool-down cycle, at worst there is a chance that it may smolder—or even catch fire! At best, wrinkles are set into the fabric, which means employees must spend more time in the finishing area trying to get them out. Sometimes the laundry must be rewashed. Ideally, the cool-down cycle should occur when the laundry reaches a certain temperature, not at a pre-selected time. Microprocessors make this possible.

7. **Not keeping filters clean enough to allow the dryer to operate at optimum levels.** Although it should be a given that laundries follow the manufacturer's recommended filter-cleaning schedule, it's amazing how few do.

8. **Not maintaining the dryer's seal.** A dryer's efficiency is directly related to the condition of its seal, since the seal keeps cold air out and hot air inside the basket so it can flow through the laundry. Most seals wear out quickly because they are subjected to the reverse side of the basket's perforations (a cheese-grater effect). A worn-out seal means the dryer has to work harder and longer to dry goods. You can bypass this problem entirely with new dryers, which have an unusual placement of the seal on a smooth band around the basket.

9. **Not moving laundry to finishing stations quickly.** Optimum use of ironers, for example, relies on a specific amount of moisture in the goods before ironing. Allowing goods to sit too long makes them wrinkle; sometimes rewashing is the only cure. Besides improving scheduling, consider installing a conveyor or some other automated means of transport between dryers and finishing stations.

10. **Not keeping accurate production and cost figures for drying.** To improve anything, you need to know what you're starting with—how much time and fuel are projected for each classification versus actual numbers. New personal computer systems can provide this information in summarized reports.

Source: Mike Diedling, "Avoiding the Ten Most Common Errors in Drying Reduces Fuel Costs in Institutional Laundries," *Laundry News.*

steam, or circulating thermal fluid, and are available in several sizes. The capacity of a flatwork ironer is measured by the number, diameter size, and length of each roll. Small units may finish forty to 100 pounds of laundry per hour; large units can finish up to 1,500 pounds per hour.[6] Modern flatwork ironers (up to 136 inches in length) are wide enough to finish tablecloths and king-size bed linens. Some ironers also automatically fold and stack linens after finishing.

Flatwork Ironer Maintenance

Effective care and maintenance of the laundry's flatwork ironer(s) is an important element of any conservation and utilities-cost-containment program, particularly since the flatwork ironer is the most expensive machine in the laundry. Flatwork ironer maintenance activities include the following:

- Keep the surfaces of all ironer chests or heated rolls clean and properly lubricated.

- Lubricate the chests regularly but sparingly (two to four times per shift).

- Operate the ironer at reasonably high speeds but, generally, do not exceed the speed at which the operators can feed product into the machine.

- Regularly check ironer roll padding thickness and compaction to assure maximum contact area under pressure; replace padding and covers whenever the contact area is substantively diminished as a consequence of padding compaction.

- Ensure that each roll is padded such that the rolls are sequentially larger in diameter, or that the roll drives operate such that each successive roll revolves at a slightly greater pace, so that the goods are "stretched" as they travel through the chests.

- Ensure that the longitudinal axis of each roll remains at a perfect right angle to the direction of the flow of goods through the chests.

- Regularly replace the feed board ribbons to ensure they remain in top condition.

- Regularly replace the cover and/or padding of the doffer (or "finger") roll to ensure that its ability to hold down the flat goods, as they transition in the machine, remains effective.

- Ensure that all washed goods are thoroughly rinsed and pH neutralized, so that chemical accumulations on the ironer chest or roll surfaces do not occur.

- Install ironer guide tapes properly (join tape ends carefully so as to avoid "lumpy knots" that will degrade the roll covers and compact the padding); consider using an appropriate adhesive product for this purpose, since knots or staples should be avoided.

- Move the guide tape spools and spindles across the width of the ironer on a regular basis so as to minimize compaction of the padding and covers at set intervals across their surfaces.

Microprocessors on large units monitor temperatures, roll pressure, and production speed. Large-diameter ironers can fully dry linens directly from washer-extractors, eliminating the drying step.

Folders. Folders can be very simple devices that function like an extra pair of hands to help an employee fold laundry manually. Folders can also be large, rectangular machines that look much like ironers and fold laundry automatically. Linens coming off the flatwork ironer are automatically fed into these latter types of folders; items are folded using blasts of air for the primary folds. There are primary folders and cross-folders. Some machines combine both functions. Some folders have infrared photo sensors that measure the linen as it is fed into the machine; a microprocessor then makes the calculations that determine the fold points and trigger the air blasts. Counters display the number of linens that have been folded. Grading devices signal employees when soiled or torn linens go through the machine. Some folders have attachments that stack folded linens on a conveyor belt; the belt then moves the stacks to the next laundry station. Due to the quantity of belts and sensors in automated folders, it is important that these folders be cleaned regularly and properly maintained via daily and weekly preventive maintenance procedures performed by the hotel's engineering department.

Small piece folders. Small piece folders, also known as towel folders, are typically used in large hotels to fold towels (bath, hand, pool, and beach). Small piece folders can fold 600–900 terry pieces per hour, depending on the items. Small piece folders are easy to operate: one employee feeds the item into the machine, where it is folded, cross-folded, and dropped onto a conveyor in piles of ten (large items) or twenty (small items). Since they can out-produce employees folding items manually by a ratio of three to one, small piece folders reduce payroll hours and costs. However, like sheet folders, these units require routine preventive maintenance and cleaning.

Valet Equipment

Valet services require many types of equipment.[7] There are body presses, sleeve finishers, collar-yoke-cuff presses, vacuum spotting boards, form finishers, utility presses, mushroom presses, pants toppers, and others. Presses are heated with steam and come in automatic, semi-automatic, and manual models. Presses greatly increase employee productivity. For example, an employee can finish twenty to thirty-five shirts per hour with a good shirt-finishing press.

Finishing cabinets and tunnels are used to get wrinkles out of no-iron employee uniforms and other garments. Garments are put on hangers and placed in a cabinet or on a conveyor that pulls laundry through a tunnel where wrinkles are steamed out.

Hand irons (electric or steam), water spray guns, and sewing machines are also part of a good valet department.

Laundry Design

Obviously, to run smoothly a laundry needs to be well-designed and have the right equipment, properly installed. What may be less obvious is that such laundries

Utilities Usage and Conservation

Even though hotels do not typically meter the utility services used by their on-premises laundries and do not allocate costs to the laundry department, it is incumbent on the laundry manager to be mindful and proactive regarding conservation so that the hotel does not pay unnecessarily high utility costs because of inattention to such matters in the laundry department. After payroll expenses and linen replacement costs (another expense not charged to the laundry department), utility costs commonly rank as the third highest cost center for a lodging operation, and can amount to as much as $60,000 per year at a typical 200-room hotel, or even more in locations where utility rates are significantly higher than national averages.

Taking steps to conserve energy in the laundry operation can reduce utility costs and have a positive impact on the environment:

- Proper hot water temperature means reduced or eliminated heating in the washers via direct steam injection; this speeds washer production by reducing average formula run time, reduces boiler feed-water-treatment chemical usage and cost, and reduces electrical consumption as a direct result of shortening the average cycle time.

- Tightly fitting door and drain seals, and the absence of any leaks in the piping for the washers, reduce water usage and improve formula effectiveness by helping to ensure the maintenance of proper water levels during each step of the washing cycle.

- Proper operation of all burner and temperature control components in dryer tumblers means more efficient utilization of natural or LP gas, faster drying, and improved quality; this also reduces electrical consumption as a direct result of shortening the average cycle time. For steam-heated dryers, the same results will accompany the proper maintenance and operation of steam traps and steam inlet valves.

- A properly ventilated and well-maintained flatwork ironer will increase ironing productivity (and linen quality); this translates into faster throughput, improved energy utilization, and reduced electrical consumption.

- Properly maintained piping insulation will reduce energy losses due to radiation.

- Elimination of all leaks in the steam, condensate return, water, and compressed air piping systems will enhance efficient utilization of these services, lower consumption, and save money; this can also help to improve equipment productivity.

- Proper maintenance of all steam traps is essential and can save much more than the cost of a regular trap inspection and maintenance program; it will also improve the operation of equipment, throughput rates, and the finished quality of the goods.

- When laundry equipment functions properly and efficiently, linen can be processed in less time and work schedules can be shortened (sometimes dramatically). When this occurs, energy used to ventilate, cool, and light the laundry plant can be reduced as well.

have lower equipment maintenance costs. By having a well-designed facility with correctly installed equipment, equipment modifications and equipment break-downs due to overuse and misapplication will be minimized.

Managers at many properties have their on-premises laundries designed by outside contractors. These contractors should be aware of guestroom occupancies, food and beverage covers, laundry employees' schedules, and the quantities of soiled linen and uniforms typically laundered. Guestroom laundry includes sheets, pillowcases, and duvets, plus terry items—towels, mats, bath rugs, bath robes, and wash cloths. Laundry from food and beverage operations includes tablecloths and napkins. Depending on a hotel's facilities, laundry may come from other sources such as spas, a health club facility, and recreation areas (pool and beach).

There may be a time in a lodging manager's career when he or she will be asked to help design or redesign an on-premises laundry. There are several signs that a laundry is inefficient and may need to be redesigned:

- Too many last-minute rush jobs

- Persistent linen shortages

- Excessive overtime (above 3 percent of normal laundry staff payroll hours)

- The laundry never seems to catch up

- Work space is tight; often there seem to be too many employees, carts, and equipment for the space[8]

Managers should ask questions before redesigning a laundry, however:

- Can the flow of linen be changed to avoid last-minute rush jobs? Would a change in the laundry's operating hours solve the problem?

- Are linen shortages due to inventory depletion because linens have been mis-used, prematurely worn out, or unaccountably lost or pilfered? Is the linen replacement budget adequate to maintain par levels? Typically, the hotel can expect to replace at least one par per year. In the event losses are greater, it is likely the hotel has a linen control problem. Are you taking monthly physical linen inventories for all linen items? Are you recording linen discarded due to stains or fabric damage? All hotel properties should conduct monthly inventories of all linen items, not just guestroom linen. Do your linen inventories compare current stock to par levels, show quantities removed from circulation due to wear-out, and quantities unaccountably lost? And, most importantly, are you routinely bringing linen levels up to the established par?

- If there is an overtime problem, is it due to improper scheduling, inadequate linen, frequent equipment breakdowns, incorrect washing formulas, lack of training, not holding the staff accountable to production standards, poor laundry management, or all of the above? Efforts should be taken to fix any overtime issues by looking into these areas and addressing any problems that are revealed rather than leaping to the conclusion that a big investment is needed to redesign the laundry.

- If the laundry is always running behind, is it because employees are not scheduled correctly? Do you simply need more equipment? Is linen being washed or dried too long, causing unnecessary delays? Is equipment operating at peak efficiency?[9]

- If the laundry cannot process in a timely manner the linen required by the hotel, is it due to equipment breakdowns? You should ensure that the maintenance department is providing routine preventive maintenance according to the manufacturers' manuals. Additionally, the maintenance department should keep a log for all equipment repairs and the cost of replacement parts. Washers, dryers, and folding equipment should last at least fifteen years (unless the laundry is operating multiple shifts); the flatwork ironer should last twenty to twenty-five years, assuming it is properly maintained. If the age of your equipment exceeds these time frames, it is probably time to redesign the laundry.

- Even if the work space is tight, a redesign of the laundry may not be necessary. Are laundry operations properly scheduled? Is there an efficient flow of laundry into and out of the facility? If space is an issue, can an area outside the laundry, easily accessibly and secure from linen theft, be used for storing soiled laundry?

If managers look into these questions and decide that pursuing the lower-cost options mentioned above would not bring the laundry's efficiency up to an acceptable level, then a redesign of the laundry may be in order. However, a cost analysis should be conducted to include all direct and indirect operating costs (salaries, supplies, maintenance, repairs, utilities, depreciation, and so on) and compared to the cost of outsourcing the laundry function (assuming that there is a quality commercial laundry provider in your area). It is essential that managers not only know the total cost of operating the laundry, but also the cost per pound and cost per occupied room of processing linen in-house. When an on-premises laundry is operated properly and efficiently, it is typically less expensive to process linen in-house than to outsource that function. For the cost analysis, managers should determine the cost for outside processing (per pound and per occupied room), and be sure to include the cost of internal staffing for handling clean and soiled linen, and the investment cost for an additional linen par (add 15 percent to the hotel's annual linen replacement expense, too). The cost difference between an efficiently operated on-premises laundry versus outsourcing will enable managers to determine the return on investment (most hotel owners or asset managers expect no more than a four-year return on investment). Lastly, managers should solicit competitive bids from equipment vendors for replacing all or some of the laundry equipment, and be sure to include the costs associated with equipment removal; new equipment rigging into the building; equipment delivery, installation, and startup; and sales tax. The numbers may very well reveal that a redesign of the property's on-premises laundry is the most cost-effective solution in the long run.

Principles of Laundry Design and Equipment Selection

A basic understanding of the principles of laundry design and equipment selection will benefit hotel managers and their properties in two ways. First, a knowledge of how the laundry should be designed will help general managers understand the deficiencies that may exist in any plant for which they have the ultimate operational responsibility as the hotel's top executive. This knowledge will help them guide their laundry managers to develop operating methods that take into account those deficiencies and, thus, foster improved productivity and lower operating costs. Second, it is likely that at least once in a general manager's career he or she will encounter an opportunity to participate in the design of a new or renovated on-premises laundry facility, and knowing about laundry design and equipment will help the manager to create a more efficient laundry operation.

Location and Size Considerations. If managers are planning to redesign an existing laundry, the location of the laundry has already been decided. But since most laundries are expanded when they are redesigned, there is still the question of where to find the additional space. For optimum efficiency, it is ideal to expand into adjacent space. For example, one hotel moved the valet section of its laundry into an adjacent locker room, freeing up space in the laundry for additional equipment.

If managers are planning a new on-premises laundry, they should make sure to locate it far enough from guestrooms so that guests won't be disturbed when laundry equipment is running. Another important consideration: are utilities and drains readily available at the proposed location? If so, installation costs will be lower. Very hot water—160°F to 180°F (71°C to 82°C), cold water, steam, gas, and large sewer drains and water lines are essential plumbing requirements.

Getting carts into and out of the laundry is easier if the laundry is located on the main floor. Remodeling costs can be kept down if the laundry is located in or near the current linen distribution area. And last but certainly not least, ideally a laundry should be located in an area with an outside wall, since dryers and other equipment need to be vented to the outside.

If a hotel has a basement, the laundry is usually located there because (1) laundry equipment can be very heavy, and (2) vibrations from the equipment are better absorbed. There are exceptions to this, however. One hotel chose to expand its laundry by taking space above the laundry rather than alongside it. The floor of the new laundry was structurally reinforced to bear the added weight, and vibration was not a problem since the new equipment had anti-vibration features such as shock absorbers and self-balancing baskets. In Hawaii, where flooding can be a problem, the Hawaii Prince Hotel in Waikiki located its laundry well above the basement. If an upper floor has not previously supported laundry equipment, it is important for management to consult a structural engineer before moving equipment to that floor.

Wherever the laundry is located, the laundry room's walls should be durable and moisture-resistant, and ceilings should resist moisture and absorb sound. An eight- to ten-foot ceiling is usually sufficient. A cement floor with easily cleanable floor drains and no low spots where water can pool is ideal.

The size for a hotel laundry is dependent on a number of variables: the types and amounts of linen used; the average number of guests per day; the number of restaurants in the hotel; the types and capacities of laundry equipment; and whether employees wear uniforms and, if so, whether those uniforms are laundered at the hotel. Laundry equipment manufacturers and laundry design consultants can help managers determine the correct size and space allocations for their hotel's specific needs. (See Exhibit 2 for sample laundry space allocation guidelines.)

Functional Requirements. To start with, a clear understanding of the functional requirements of a laundry facility is an essential prerequisite to effective design. These requirements are discussed in the following sections.

Workload and operating schedule. Managers should determine the average weekly workload and how many days per week the new laundry plant will operate. An accurate understanding of the workload is essential. Therefore, the

Exhibit 2   Sample Laundry Space Allocation Guidelines

The following table should serve as a guide for managers and others who are help-ing to design the component areas of a new laundry facility. In some cases, the space allocation is given; for others, the allocation must be calculated based on laundry workload. Managers should use a known value for linen usage, if avail-able (overall pounds per occupied room night, for example). For a business-class hotel located in an urban setting, a typical value for linen usage is twelve to fifteen pounds per occupied room night; for a resort hotel without beach facilities, a typical value is twenty to twenty-five pounds per occupied room night; for a resort hotel with a beach area and large spa facilities, a typical value is thirty pounds per occupied room-night.

In the following table, the abbreviation "PPD" stands for "pounds-per-day" and can be calculated as follows: number of guestrooms times average occupancy times the pounds of linen per room night. For a 300-room hotel with 80 percent average occupancy and twenty-five pounds of linen per room night, the calculation would be: 300 × 240 (300 × .80) × 25 pounds = 6,000 pounds per day.

Laundry Space Allocations

1.	Laundry Manager's Office	100 square feet
2.	Soiled Linen Storage and Sorting	0.085 square feet × PPD
3.	Washing and Finishing	0.425 square feet × PPD
4.	Clean Linen Storage and Cart Packing	0.13 square feet × PPD
5.	Valet (Garment Shop)	800–850 square feet
6.	Uniform Storage, Issue, and Tailoring	0.05 square feet × PPD
7.	Mechanical (including dedicated laundry water systems)	400–800 square feet
8.	Washing Chemical Storage and Injection Systems	100 square feet
9.	Air Compressor(s) and Refrigerated Dryer	80 square feet
10.	Clean and Soiled Linen Holding Area (if laundry is off-site)	0.2 square feet × PPD

laundry manager should carefully measure and record the weights of the goods produced by the hotel's current laundry.

The average weekly workload should reflect the hotel's forecast of long-term average annual occupancy, typically anywhere from 70 to 85 percent. Managers can multiply the average of the estimated occupied room nights per week by an actual or estimated value of overall linen usage per occupied room night (guestroom, food and beverage, spa, and recreation linens) to determine the so-called "weekly design workload" for the new laundry facility. Managers can then determine the number of days (or shifts or hours) that the plant will operate each week in order to produce the average weekly design workload.

Soiled linen storage. To be productive, the laundry must have a consistently ready supply of soiled linen whenever the laundry staff is present (availability of soiled linen may have an effect on the daily shift starting time or the order in which goods are processed). Typically, then, the laundry will require storage space for some portion of the daily workload. Space allocation guidelines such as those shown in Exhibit 2 can help managers determine how big this space should be.

Clean linen storage. For the same reason (productivity), the laundry must have adequate space in which to store a suitable supply of clean linen and park delivery carts. Space allocation guidelines can help managers determine the proper amount of clean linen space needed. If an optimally sized clean linen space is not possible, managers may have to develop special operating procedures and look for other storage solutions (e.g., multiple daily deliveries instead of one overnight delivery to each linen closet, utilizing outlying storage rooms, etc.).

Process machinery. Space allocation guidelines also stipulate the amount of space required for installation of washing machines, dryers, an ironing system, and an optional towel folder. A properly configured laundry will provide space at each station in the laundering process for the staging of work-in-progress (usually at least about two hours' worth of work).

Valet (garment shop). Except for those hotels that do not perform the valet function or in certain rare cases where the valet task is extraordinarily large, an allocation of 800–850 square feet of space is usually set aside for this function.

Uniform storage and issue. For properties that provide uniforms to employees and process them in the on-premises laundry, a separate room is ideal for the installation of a uniform storage carousel, an issue counter, and sewing/tailoring stations.

Auxiliary activities. Design standards typically call for an allocation of 100 square feet of space for the laundry manager's office. Separate rooms of 100 and 80 square feet, respectively, are specified for chemical storage and air compressors. If the laundry will have dedicated water and/or steam systems, then a separate room of 400–800 square feet will be required (depending on the nature and size of these equipment systems). There is a growing trend for hotels to include laundry water or heat conservation and recovery systems; if managers are contemplating installing such systems, they must allocate space for them.

Adjacencies and workflow. The garment shop and the uniform storage room should be immediately adjacent to each other so that employee uniforms processed in the former may move directly into the latter for storage and issue. For this same reason, the garment-finishing tunnel should be installed in the garment shop and not in the laundry. The uniform room should be near employee locker rooms, the time clock station, and the employee entrance, and all should have direct connectivity with the main service corridor. The uniform issue counter should be set into an alcove so that employees awaiting service do not block other traffic in the main service corridor.

For the sake of management expediency, it is desirable (but not mandatory) that the laundry also be located adjacent to the valet shop and uniform room.

In the laundry, which also should be located adjacent to the main service corridor, a "U" shaped flow is desirable, thus allowing soiled goods to enter at one location and exit at another. The layout of the processing machinery should facilitate this flow, and care should be exercised to avoid any instance where "flow ways" cross each other. For example, the equipment design should make it possible for work leaving the washers to flow to the dryers without crossing other work flows.

The soiled and clean linen storage spaces should be located immediately inside and adjacent to each of the two principle laundry entrances, and configured to facilitate an efficient flow of goods either to the washers (in the case of soiled linen) or from the finishing equipment (in the case of clean linen). The soiled linen scale should be installed just inside the soiled linen entrance so that goods may be weighed as soon as they enter the plant; if possible, the scale's location should also readily serve the washer-loading function.

Owing to the nature of the "U"-shaped workflow, it is desirable that any laundry manager/supervisor offices and/or the chemical storage and air compressor rooms be located at the top of the "U" and along the main service corridor so that each of these spaces can be accessed from the main corridor as well as inside the laundry room. The two aforementioned laundry facility entrances then can be positioned on either side of this suite of rooms, and the processing machinery lined up along the lower curve of the "U."

The ultimate shape and configuration of the laundry facility obviously will be influenced by other nearby hotel facilities and their space requirements. Therefore, the ideal laundry facility may not always be achievable, so laundry designers and others involved in the laundry design process must be ready to compromise and find creative solutions to laundry design challenges.

Equipment Selection. Equipment should be selected to provide an overall sustainable capacity equal to at least 115 percent of the average expected weekly workload.

Washer-extractors. Managers should select solid-mount units unless the laundry floor is above grade, in which case suspended-mount units must be specified. Four washer-extractors is a typical number for a hotel to have but it may be necessary to plan for five or even six, depending on the workload and the washer-extractor capacities. Open-pocket machines in the range of thirty-five to 150 pounds are preferred, but the mix of sizes should be restricted to no more than three. At least one small machine is required in order to efficiently process small or odd lots of goods. Steam and liquid chemical injection are mandatory options. A third water inlet may be needed if water reuse or reclamation is planned. Solid-mount washer-extractors require an eighteen- to twenty-inch-deep isolated

Washer-Extractor Capacities

	Double sheets	Pillow cases	54 × 54 table cloths	20 × 20 napkins	Bath towels	Shirts	Pants	Uniforms	Mop-heads
35 lb. model	23	116	37	206	61	74	29	38	23
50 lb. model	33	170	54	295	88	106	42	55	33
75 lb. model	50	250	81	442	130	159	63	82	50
95 lb. model	62	315	102	560	165	200	80	105	63
135 lb. model	90	450	145	795	235	256	113	148	89

These sample laundry capacities provide a general idea of how much laundry can be placed in small to mid-size washer-extractors. Of course, the amount of laundry a given size washer-extractor can process will vary from manufacturer to manufacturer (these numbers were provided by the Pellerin Milnor Corporation). How much laundry can be washed per cycle also depends on a number of other factors, including how much the individual laundry items weigh, the type of fabric they are made of, and their degree of soiling.

concrete pad, six inches of which should protrude above the adjacent floor surface.

Ironing system. The ideal ironer will be of the chest-type design and will have a minimum of three rolls at least thirty-two inches in diameter and at least 130 inches long. Steam heat is preferred but, if not available, a self-contained gas-heated or thermal-oil-heated ironer is acceptable. Gas-heated cylinder-type ironers do not produce as high a level of linen quality and do not ordinarily provide a similar level of capacity. An automatic sheet spreader/feeder is optional and should not be included unless the flatwork ironing task exceeds 500 pounds per hour. The folder should include four primary lanes, a single cross-folding lane, a multi-lane small-piece accumulator, and at least one large-piece stacker. Managers should be careful that the "eject" side of the folder is on the correct side in terms of the laundry layout.

Dryers. There should be at least one dryer for each size of washer, and each dryer should be sized at least 35 percent larger than the washer (e.g., a 170-pound dryer should be mated with a 125-pound washer). Overall dryer capacity should be determined on the basis of full-drying all terry and other non-ironed goods and pre-conditioning of all flatwork and uniforms. A separate lint filter is to be avoided, since all cabinet-style dryers are equipped with an internal filter and all larger dryers (200 pounds or more) can be ordered with integral filters. Dryers should be ordered with fire suppression systems. Steam heating is preferred for units having a capacity of less than 200 pounds, although gas heating is acceptable.

Towel folders. Tower folders are not usually necessary unless hourly towel and bath mat folding capacity exceeds 400 pounds per hour.

Valet shop equipment. For properties requiring valet facilities for on-premises processing of employee uniforms and guest valet items, the following list of equipment is recommended as a minimum: (1) a check-in table with shelves and/or drawers; (2) a marking machine; (3) a final assembly and check-out table with sorting and storage cubicles above the work surface; (4) at least one dry cleaning machine in the 35–45 pound range, or two units with 20–25 pounds of capacity each; (5) a spotting board; (6) a three-piece shirt finishing unit (single-buck body finishing cabinet, a sleeve finishing cabinet, and a collar-cuff-yoke press); (7) a utility dry clean finishing bay (with utility dry clean finishing press, a trouser leg press, a trouser top finisher, a form finisher, and a three-head puff finishing unit); (8) a garment finisher for wet-washable poly-cotton work wear (uniforms); (9) a utility laundry press unit composed of one or two forty-eight-inch tapered and one mushroom hot-head presses; (10) a central vacuum unit; (11) a forced-air finishing board, a shirt folder, and a bagging stand; and (12) hamper carts, garment racks, and at least one basket scale.

Other laundry room equipment. The laundry equipment list should include at least one weighing scale having a platform size of a minimum of forty-eight inches by forty-eight inches (forty-eight inches by sixty inches is preferred). There should also be at least one rotary-type air compressor with a minimum motor size of ten horsepower, and a refrigerated compressed-air dryer. A barrel or drum truck is helpful for moving chemical drums. To handle uniform storage, managers should consider a double-tiered uniform storage carousel having a number of slots equal to at least 130 percent of the number of hotel guestrooms (200 percent would be ideal). As far as carts are concerned, a laundry will need large-capacity soiled linen carts and large-capacity clean linen carts, with shelving; hamper carts in various sizes with spring-lift platforms; and open-ended sheet-feeding carts.

Laundry Maintenance

The lodging property's general manager has the ultimate responsibility for correctly operating and maintaining the on-premises laundry. Direct responsibility is shared by the housekeeping department and the engineering department. Engineering is responsible for maintaining laundry equipment and keeping the laundry's utility and water costs within limits set by upper management. The laundry manager or supervisor reports to the housekeeping director and is involved in a number of day-to-day decisions and actions that have an impact on how much maintenance a laundry needs.

A laundry's maintenance and operating needs depend in part on its size and equipment. In a hotel that processes laundry for other hotels as well as its own, the laundry's size is much larger and it has more equipment than is required just for the hotel itself. The type of equipment in the laundry depends on whether the facility provides all possible laundry services or only the basics. For example, a hotel laundry may do dry cleaning for the hotel or may send it to an outside commercial establishment.

Exhibit 3 contains sample maintenance actions for washers and dryers. Maintenance actions are usually not complex, although troubleshooting and repair of

Exhibit 3   Sample Maintenance Actions for Laundry Equipment

CLOTHES WASHER

DAILY

1. Inspect washer and check operation.
2. Wipe door gasket to remove soap buildup.

MONTHLY

1. Check and tighten base hold-down bolts.
2. Vacuum lint and dust from control housing.
3. Check for loose wires and connections. Tighten.
4. Check belt for wear and tension.
5. Check drain assembly. Clean out rubbish.
6. Lubricate drain solenoid linkage.
7. Lubricate bearings per manufacturer's specs and frequency (may be annually rather than monthly).
8. Clean machine.

ANNUALLY

1. Conduct all actions listed under monthly heading.
2. Check pulley alignment. Adjust as required.
3. Open front loading door. Check rotating drum for clearance. Adjust from rear as required.
4. Check all safety devices.

CLOTHES DRYER

DAILY

1. Inspect machine and check operation.
2. Clean lint trap.

MONTHLY

1. Check and tighten base hold-down bolts.
2. Vacuum dust and lint from top compartment and burner assembly.
3. Blow out dust and lint from lower electrical compartment.
4. Check for loose wires and connections.
5. Check belt for wear and tension.
6. Lubricate chain per manufacturer's specs and frequency (may be annually rather than monthly).

ANNUALLY

1. Carry out maintenance actions listed under monthly.
2. Lubricate bearings per manufacturer's specs and frequency (may be monthly rather than annually).
3. Open front loading door. Check rotating basket for clearance. Use adjustment bolts in rear if required.
4. Thoroughly clean dryer.
5. Check pulley alignment. Adjust as required.

Source: Adapted from materials supplied by the Pellerin Milnor Corporation and Jay D. Chase, "Laundry Service: Consider the Options," *Lodging,* May 1986, p. 34.

today's computerized equipment can become so. For large laundries, some maintenance employees may be assigned virtually full-time to the laundry, or contract maintenance services may be used. A good preventive maintenance program for laundry equipment is a must, since a breakdown can have immediate effects on many aspects of the hotel. Exhibit 4 is a sample of the type of general maintenance checklist that can be helpful for the hotel's engineering and maintenance department.

Equipment is not the only maintenance concern in a laundry. Because of the heat, humidity, and chemicals present in laundries, the only way most laundries can be kept habitable is by using an HVAC system. For this reason, maintenance staff should give any HVAC maintenance request by laundry personnel a priority.[10]

Emerging Trends in Laundry Operations

Despite the preference of many hotels and hotel companies to operate their own on-premises or centralized laundries, there is a growing trend among hotel owners and asset managers in favor of outsourcing the laundry function in order to avoid the capital investment needed to install or upgrade laundry facilities. Although there are some quality commercial providers in certain markets in the United States, there is a fundamental absence of such commercial companies in many areas of the country, which forces owners and asset managers to closely consider all options, including the continuation of on-premises processing while "in-sourcing" the laundry to a third party. With the in-sourcing option, a third-party company assumes the day-to-day operation of the laundry and provides the management, labor, supplies, equipment maintenance, and, in some cases, the investment dollars to install or upgrade the laundry. In-sourcing of laundry services is growing in North America and is already widely accepted in India.

Exhibit 4   Sample General Maintenance Checklist for a Laundry Facility

- Repair all known plumbing leaks.
- Repair or replace all leaky water hoses on the washers.
- Repair all leaky washer door and drain seals.
- Ensure that steam traps always operate properly.
- Keep steam shut off to machinery not in use.
- Maintain the boiler and dryer burner systems in good condition.
- Keep dryer exhaust ductwork and lint-filtering systems clean.
- Maintain steam and condensate piping insulation in good condition.
- Maintain ironer padding and ironer vacuum exhaust systems in good condition.
- Maintain all components of the water systems in good working condition.
- Repair all leaks in the compressed-air piping systems.
- Conduct an infra-red scan of all motors, and repair or replace inefficient units.

Due to the continued high cost of linen and uniform replacement, there is growing interest within the hotel industry in tracking linen and uniforms via the insertion of radio frequency identification (RFID) tags onto linen and uniform items. The use of RFID technology has already become a common practice in the uniform rental industry. Essentially, every uniform item is tracked while being processed at uniform rental plants, and when it is shipped to and returned from a customer. Not only does this technology assist in monitoring production within a plant, it helps track uniform losses by customers so that they can be charged accordingly.

Manufacturers of laundry equipment continuously strive to improve their equipment and the processes of design and installation. And, as mentioned at the beginning of the chapter, some lodging companies are moving from the long-established practice of doing laundry on-site in favor of constructing centralized laundry operations serving a number of hotels in urban areas. These emerging trends are potentially important both for the operation of existing facilities and the design of new operations. Other emerging trends are the use of ozone for bleaching and sanitizing, and the installation of water recycling equipment.[11]

The use of ozone for bleaching and sanitizing in place of chlorine-based bleaches can have a number of benefits. Chlorine-based bleach materials are potentially toxic and can damage linens and towels. Ozone-based bleaching and sanitizing uses no toxic chemicals and the ozone has little effect on linen and towel fabrics. In addition, ozone allows for modifications to the washing cycle that can reduce the quantity of water required, the amount of hot water required, and the length of the washing cycle (all of which helps to reduce utility costs). Ozone equipment also requires relatively little space and can be retrofitted to many existing laundry operations relatively easily and cost-effectively. Because of all these benefits, replacement of chlorine bleaches with ozone is worth considering for many operations. However, some types of soil (such as food stains and makeup) may require treatment other than ozone.

Water recycling equipment potentially holds great promise for operations interested in reducing not only water usage but also water heating costs. Hotel laundry operations that have installed this equipment have seen water savings of 60 to 65 percent. The equipment required to do this is substantially larger than the ozone systems just discussed, so more space and engineering will likely be necessary for installations. Current installations are generally in large laundry operations, with installation costs of around $100,000–$200,000 (depending on the size of the laundry) and paybacks of two to three years.[12] Some operations are also investigating the recovery of heat from dryer exhaust as well.[13] As with laundry equipment, it is essential that ozone and water recycling equipment be properly maintained by the hotel's engineering and maintenance department.

Most hotels and hotel companies have developed and implemented "green initiatives" to reduce the volume of linen used in hotels. For example, many hotels are no longer routinely changing bed linens on a daily basis. The widely accepted practice today is to change bed linens every third day or upon check-out. Many hotels place cards with slogans such as "Help Us Save the Environment" in their guestrooms. Such cards might also ask guests to hang their towels on a hook in the bathroom to be used for a second time, and inform guests about the significant volume of water saved and the reduced amount of chemicals introduced into the environment because of such actions.

Recycling is a major component of any "green" program and is widely accepted by the general population. As it relates to laundries, recycling extends much further than most people ordinarily are aware of. For example, metal hangers may be retrieved from guestrooms and from employees to be reused for handling employee uniforms. Laundries typically return their empty plastic chemical drums to their chemical vendors. Old or damaged equipment parts may be transported to metal recyclers. And the cardboard shipping boxes that many laundry supplies are shipped in are collected by many hotels and bundled for collection by recycling companies.

Endnotes

1. Nick Raio, "Wyndham Wind Watch In-House Laundry Custom Fit for Hotel Needs," *Hotel Business,* July 7–20, 1998, pp. 32–33.

2. Adapted from Frank D. Borsenik and Alan T. Stutts, *The Management of Maintenance and Engineering Systems in the Hospitality Industry,* 2nd ed. (New York: Wiley, 1987), p. 442.

3. Some of the following information was found in "Poly-trux: Seamless One-Piece Molded Polymer Trucks," a brochure from Meese, Inc., Leonia, New Jersey.

4. "Commissioning Milnor 35 and 50 lb. Machines," a brochure by the Pellerin Milnor Corporation, Kenner, Louisiana, p. 30.

5. Much of the information in this section was found in "Questions People Ask About Tunnel Washing," a brochure by the Pellerin Milnor Corporation, Kenner, Louisiana.

6. From "Chicago's All Star Lineup," a brochure by the Chicago Dryer Company, Chicago, Illinois.

7. Much of the material in this section is drawn from brochures and other materials from the Cissell Manufacturing Company, Louisville, Kentucky.

8. This list and much of the information in this section are based on "How to Spot and Remedy Growing Pains," by Charles A. Emling, Jr., *Laundry News.*

9. For example, is the laundry equipment producing one load per hour for washer-extractors, and 1.5 loads per hour for the dryers? If the washers are not producing one load per hour, the washing formulas may be too long or the staff may not be loading and unloading the machine efficiently. If the dryers are not producing 1.5 loads per hour, make sure there are no restrictions in the exhaust ducts causing back pressure, and the staff is promptly unloading and loading the dryers.

10. Two sources for more information about on-premises laundries and laundering are the National Association of Institutional Linen Management and the American Laundry and Linen College, both in Richmond, Kentucky.

11. The use of ozone systems is actually a re-emerging trend. When the technology was first introduced, there were a glut of start-up companies producing and selling ozone systems. Many of these companies did not have the proper funding to sustain the required service support network, and ultimately went out of business, which soured the industry on the use of ozone. However, at present the companies that sell and support ozone systems are solid businesses, and interest is returning for this technology.

12. "New Technology Lowers Laundering Costs," *Energy News* 8 (July 2004). Composed for the Four Seasons Hotels and Resorts by Siemens Building Technologies, Inc., Canton, Mass.

13. "Too Good to Be True? Not Always. Ramada Achieves 50% Fuel Reductions with Laundry Dryer Heat Recovery." Reprinted at www.rototherm.net from HMEA Hotel/ Motel Engineers Association, 2000.

Key Terms

bottom-transfer machine—A tunnel washer that moves the laundry and the water along the bottom of the washer.

cool-down cycle—A washer cycle in which cold water is slowly injected into the wash to prevent blended no-iron fabrics from going into the "thermal shock" that causes wrinkles.

dryer—A machine that dries laundry by tumbling it in a basket exposed to hot air.

extractor—A machine that extracts water from laundered fabrics, usually by spinning the laundry in a basket, though very large extractors may press the water out. Extractors cut down on drying time and costs.

flatwork ironer—A machine that uses rollers to iron linens, giving them a crisp, finished look. Some ironers also fold and stack linens.

folder—A machine that folds laundry. Folders range from simple devices that help employees fold laundry manually to huge rectangular machines that fold laundry automatically, taking linens fed into them manually or directly from the ironer.

top-transfer machines—A tunnel washing machine that lifts the laundry out of the water and drains it before transferring it to the next bath.

tunnel washers—Also called batch or continuous washers, tunnel washers are, in effect, a series of interconnected washers in which each bath, or cycle, is kept in a different cylinder and laundry is moved from one cylinder to the next.

washer-extractors—Sometimes called conventional washers, these free-standing units are used to both clean laundry and then extract water from it in preparation for transfer to dryers.

Review Questions

1. How can laundry be transported to and within the laundry room?

2. What are the differences between a washer-extractor and a tunnel washer?

3. How do top-transfer and bottom-transfer tunnel washers differ?

4. What are some of the features available on today's sophisticated dryers?

5. What are some signs that a laundry may need to be redesigned?

6. What are some of the principles of laundry design and equipment selection?

7. What are some of the maintenance issues for a laundry?

8. What emerging trends are affecting laundry operations in hotels?

Internet Sites

For more information, visit the following Internet sites. Remember that Internet addresses can change without notice. If the site is no longer there, you can use a search engine to look for additional sites.

G. A. Braun
www.gabraun.com

International Fabricare Institute
www.ifi.org

Laundry Today
www.laundrytoday.com

NAILM: American Laundry & Linen College
www.nailm.com

Pellerin Milnor Corporation
www.milnor.com

Textile Care Allied Trades Association
www.tcata.org

Chapter 10 Outline

Exterior Building Structure
    Foundation
    Structural Frame
    Exterior Walls
    Windows and Doors
    Roof
Building Interiors
    Ceilings and Wall Coverings
    Carpet Materials
    Hard Surface Flooring
    Elevators
Exterior Facilities
    Parking Areas
    Storm Water Drainage Systems
    Utilities
    Landscaping and Grounds

Competencies

1. Describe a building's foundation, structural frame, exterior walls, windows and doors, and roof, including typical problems that each of these building elements have, and preventive maintenance measures that hotel managers can take to keep these building elements in good shape. (pp. 363–370)

2. Identify the characteristics of various ceiling and wall coverings, carpet materials, and hard surface flooring. (pp. 370–376)

3. Describe the components of, and maintenance concerns associated with, elevator systems. (pp. 376–378)

4. Describe parking areas, including the materials parking structures are made of (concrete and/or asphalt), structural features, layout considerations, maintenance issues, and ADA requirements. (pp. 378–390)

5. Describe storm water drainage systems, utilities, and landscaping and grounds, including preventive maintenance strategies and inspection tips. (pp. 390–398)

Building Structure, Finishes, and Site

The building exterior and interior, grounds, and parking areas of hospitality businesses are the first places seen and experienced by guests. Hospitality businesses strive for a pleasing curb appeal and need to maintain it. In addition, the building exterior represents the barrier between the conditioned interior of the facility and the varying and sometimes harsh conditions found in the natural environment. Within the structure, interior finishes such as paints, wall coverings, and carpets need to be properly selected and maintained as well.

IN THIS CHAPTER we will discuss the building itself—the shell that shelters employees and guests and houses the electrical, HVAC, lighting, telecommunication, and other systems. We will also discuss the facilities exterior to the building—parking areas, storm water drainage systems, utilities, and landscaping and grounds—that provide parking spaces for staff members and guests, protect the building, provide the building with power and other services, and enhance the building's value.

Exterior Building Structure

The building envelope consists of all the building's exterior elements: the foundation, structural frame, exterior walls (including doors and windows), and roof. The various parts of a building must work together. If any one part is neglected, it can have an adverse effect on the others.

The functions of a building are to provide usable space and shelter people, equipment, fixtures, and furnishings from the weather. Wind, rain, snow, heat, and cold are excluded or managed by the building envelope.

Foundation

Foundations are traditionally constructed of masonry and/or reinforced concrete supported by a solid, underground footing. If firm foundation material is not available at a reasonable depth, it may be necessary to go deeper by using piles. The decision on footing depth and type is usually left to the architect and structural engineers.

Frost walls commonly surround a building in cold climates and are usually part of the foundation system. Their primary purpose is to exclude entry of frost into the foundation, and their structural uses are normally very limited.

The foundation of a building is structurally designed to carry the various loads of the building: **dead load** (the weight of the building itself), **live load** (the weight of the people, equipment, furnishings, and so on within the building), and loads and stresses imposed by nature (wind, rain, snow, earthquakes). Frequent inspections and a preventive maintenance program are recommended to keep the foundation intact. If maintenance is neglected until it becomes remedial in nature, it is usually too late, and serious problems probably already exist.

Foundation walls commonly also serve as basement walls. In these cases the foundation walls take on the added load caused by lateral pressures from the soil. Normal construction techniques require that foundation walls serving as basement walls be waterproofed. However, many old structures have no waterproofing, and many new structures have inadequate waterproofing and foundation drainage systems.

Preventive Maintenance. Preventive maintenance on foundations and footings is difficult because these structural elements are mostly hidden and inaccessible. However, there are some things that can be done:

- If there are foundation or footing drains, keep the outlets open, so that no water stands in the drains.
- Keep rodent covers over all drain tiles.
- Relieve excessive water pressure from the outside.
- Maintain the integrity of the exterior waterproofing. If any excavation is done near the foundation, be sure the waterproof membrane is not disturbed.

Inspections. Foundations are often difficult to inspect, and generally it is impractical to inspect the underground portion of the foundation system. However, it is essential that the upper portion receive an annual inspection. The inspector should look for at least the following:

- Cracks through the foundation wall
- Evidence of water flowing adjacent to the foundation
- Spalling or crumbling concrete
- Moisture penetrating the foundation walls into basement areas

Structural Frame

The structural frame of a building is normally thought of as the "skeleton" that provides support for the entire building. If there is failure in the structural frame, the entire building has serious problems. Typical construction materials used in structural framing include steel, concrete (reinforced, pre-stressed), and ordinary or heavy timber.

Preventive Maintenance. Preventive maintenance efforts needed for the structural frame include:

- Inspecting visible structural members.
- Inspecting other building features that might give telltale signs of structural problems (for example, cracks in walls, floors, or ceilings).
- Checking doors and windows for proper alignment and closure.
- Tightening all connections.
- Weatherproofing (including painting) structural elements.
- Maintaining fireproofing materials. (Sometimes maintenance on building systems will result in damage or removal of structural fireproofing.)
- Checking reinforced concrete members.
- Preserving structural steel members.

Inspections. The structural frame is usually not exposed to view, but can be inspected fairly easily through access panels and by going into "behind-the-scenes" areas. This inspection should take place at least once a year, and answer at least the following questions:

- Have there been any changes since the previous inspection?
- Are bolts tight and welds intact?
- Is there unusual or unexpected evidence of corrosion?
- Are structural beams deformed or bent?
- Are fireproofing materials in good condition?
- Are anchors and attachments in good condition?

For multi-story buildings, this inspection should be supervised by a structural engineer.

Exterior Walls

Exterior building walls have two basic functions:

1. To enclose the usable parts of the building
2. To provide support for higher floors and the roof system

For walls to function as intended, they must be built to provide protection against the weather and have enough structural strength to support the building.

Exterior walls are constructed of a variety of materials, such as timber, concrete, and steel. A wall may be an integral unit, or be constructed in pre-assembled units and joined together on the job site. A wall's materials and method of construction and assembly have a pronounced effect on maintenance. In recent years, some hotels have been constructed using exterior finish insulation systems (EFIS, also known as exterior insulation finish systems or EIFS) that integrate the building insulation with a waterproof exterior surface. EFIS systems can have a number of exterior surface treatments that make them look like stone surfaces.

Walls can be classified as bearing (supporting) or non-bearing, depending on whether they support other building elements or only themselves.

The useful life of an exterior wall depends on the type of wall and the quality of construction. In general, any exterior wall, properly maintained, should survive over 100 years. Without good maintenance, a wall's useful life may be reduced dramatically.

Preventive Maintenance. Preventive maintenance activities for exterior walls include painting, cleaning, and inspecting.

Painting. Painting outside surfaces poses special problems. Wind, sun, rain, and snow can quickly take their toll if these surfaces are not properly protected. The durability of exterior painting depends on many factors, such as the quality of paint selected, the extent of the surface preparation, the skill with which the paint is applied, and local climate and weather conditions.

For the longest-lasting job, top-quality paint should be selected. Some measures of paint quality include hiding power, color retention, chalking resistance, and blister resistance. Surface preparation is also very important. It is a good idea to inspect for difficult areas, such as peeling paint under roof eaves or on gutters and downspouts. If the surface is not correctly prepared, the new paint will not adhere properly. Surface preparation should include scraping the outside surfaces clean of peeling paint and rust, and making sure that oil, grease, and dirt are removed.

Graffiti on exterior walls can be a serious problem, especially for masonry walls. The most practical method of minimizing graffiti damage to masonry walls is to apply clear sealers. When masonry pores are sealed, paint and other materials used for graffiti are prevented from penetrating the surface, making cleanup relatively easy. Acrylic sealers are the most promising of many sealers available solely for protection against graffiti.

Cleaning. Cleaning is an important part of the preventive maintenance program for exterior walls. Dirt provides a much greater surface area than clean building materials, and the more surface area that is exposed to atmospheric pollutants, the greater are the possibilities that destructive chemical reactions will start. Dirty areas remain wet longer, resulting in more severe freeze/thaw cycles. And wet, dirty areas can support microorganisms that may cause disintegration, destruction, and staining.

Selecting an appropriate cleaning method can be challenging, because the composition of dirt is so complex. Acidic cleaners can be very damaging, particularly to stone such as marble and limestone, and alkaline cleaners can also be harmful. Test a cleaner on a small area to make sure it will not damage the wall.

Often, high-pressure water washing with no cleaning agent is sufficient. Power washing is the cleaning of surfaces using high-pressure water. Power washing is an effective and inexpensive cleaning method. It may also expose deterioration that needs repair.

When cleaning a sealed masonry surface that has been marked with graffiti, first try the gentlest treatment, such as water mixed with a detergent. A stiff scrub brush, such as a roofing or whitewash brush, is a recommended tool. If this treatment is ineffective, a mild organic solvent, such as mineral spirits, may be used. If the markings still won't come off, stronger solvents are necessary. These include xylol, lacquer solvents, and paint strippers. These materials may remove some of the acrylic sealer along with the markings. However, as long as the sealer keeps the markings from penetrating the wall's pores, it has served its purpose.

Inspections. Exterior walls should be inspected at least semi-annually. Inspections should look for cracks, loose mortar, mildew, inflow or outflow of water, paint and sealant deterioration, and evidence of wall or building movement. Changes noted since the previous inspection should be investigated to determine why the change occurred. Any evidence or suspicion of wall movement should be thoroughly checked by a structural engineer.

Windows and Doors

Openings in the building's exterior walls include windows, doors, louvers, vents, openings for "through the wall" air conditioning equipment, etc. These openings require perimeter sealants around frames and adjoining dissimilar materials. Weather stripping is used at doors and windows to prevent heat loss or gain. Buildings can lose significant amounts of heat in cold months and cool air in hot/humid months if windows and doors are not properly designed and maintained.

Windows in new buildings are often fixed (not operable). Casement windows open either outward or inward like a door, while vertically hung windows open by sliding the lower half up. The window glass and seal is referred to as glazing. Single-glazed windows have one pane of glass; double-glazed windows have two sheets of glass designed with a sealed space of air or gas in between. Multiple glazing provides better temperature and noise insulation than single-glazed windows. Tinted glass has a coating that is designed to reflect heat and to maintain a cooler building in summer and a warmer one in winter.

Doors may be wooden or metal, solid or hollow. Some doors are all or mostly glass with wood or metal frames, such as revolving doors. Revolving doors are used at some hospitality properties because they don't get the wear regular doors receive from constantly being opened and closed, and because they reduce the amount of outside air that enters the building. Fire safety codes may stipulate that a hinged door with an automatic closer and exit hardware be installed next to a revolving door as an emergency exit.

Inspections. Windows should be inspected regularly for ease of opening and closing, loose-fitting frames, cracked glazing, damaged hardware, deteriorated sealants, and corrosion (for windows with metal frames). Operable windows should have pins or restraining devices in place to prohibit the windows from opening beyond a certain point, to reduce potential safety concerns. Doors should be inspected for surface deterioration; damage to hinges, locks, and frames; and improper door-to-frame alignment.

Roof

The roof is a critically important part of any building. Unfortunately, the roof is often ignored until it leaks. If water gains access to the building through the roof, great damage can result, first to the roof and later to the structural elements of the building. Interior finishes are also quickly destroyed by roof leaks. For example, a new paint job is ruined by just a few minutes of water leakage.

It is not uncommon to find roofs with very few problems over a twenty- to thirty-year period. On the other hand, some roofs suffer partial or total failure in the first year of a building's operation. A roof's life expectancy depends on the quality of the construction materials, the skill of the builders, and the effectiveness of the preventive maintenance program.

A major roof repair can be a very substantial investment that has a profound effect on cash flow as well as day-to-day operations. Therefore, serious efforts should be made to maintain a roof properly and extend its service life.

Basic Structure. A roof is composed of a deck and a covering. The deck is the structural material the covering is placed upon. The deck is usually made of wood, metal, or concrete. A roof system is the combination of all the components of the roof that act together to create a weather and climate barrier for the building.

There are several common types of roofing materials, including asphalt or fiberglass shingles and roll roofing, split wood shakes, sawn wood shingles, clay and concrete tile, steel and aluminum, and various types of built-up and single-ply materials. The roofing material chosen for a building will depend on factors such as economics, the shape of the roof, climate, fire resistance, durability, and aesthetics. Even marketing may play a factor—some hospitality properties have distinctive colors or shapes to their roofs that serve to identify the product to prospective guests.

The primary purpose of all of these roofing systems is to keep water from penetrating the roofing material. For some systems, this is accomplished by having overlapping layers of roofing material oriented on the roof so that water running down the roof will not penetrate under the layers. This is the method used on many homes. For added protection, a layer of asphalt- or tar-impregnated paper called **roofing felt** is installed directly on the roof's deck.

When roofs are relatively flat, multiple layers of felt may be sealed together to form a moisture barrier. These layers are then covered with a surface material—often a gravel washed layer (referred to as a ballast) that can (1) help reduce damage due to ultraviolet rays, (2) provide weight to hold down insulation materials, and (3) provide a greater degree of fire protection. This type of roofing system is referred to as a **built-up roof** (see Exhibit 1).

Many flat roofs are built today with **single-ply roofing** systems. These systems are a membrane roofing system composed of large pieces of roofing material that are bonded together using heat or chemicals to form a one-piece roof system. The roofing material may adhere to the deck by mechanical means or adhesives. There are many different materials used for single-ply roofing systems, each of which has particular properties, installation requirements, and maintenance needs.

Most roof structures are pierced by a variety of building mechanical systems and mounting locations for various equipment, and are subject to foot traffic for periodic inspections, the removal of debris, and the maintenance of equipment. In addition, most flat roofs have internal roof drains for the removal of water. All penetrations of the roof structure must be adequately sealed so that water does not enter below the roofing material at these locations. **Flashing** is installed under the roofing and up the sides of equipment and where roofs contact walls. Flashing is

Exhibit 1 Built-Up Roof

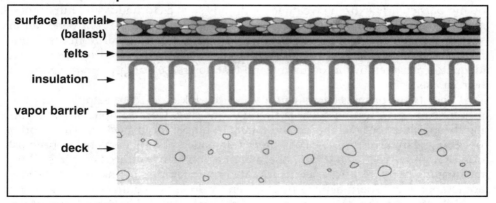

usually formed from sheets of aluminum or copper with edges and joints sealed with elastomeric materials.

It is important that roof drains be kept free of debris. This means regular inspections are needed, especially during times when leaf or snow buildup may occur. In recent years, several areas of the United States have been experiencing unusually heavy rain and/or snow, which can result in water buildup on roofing. If strong winds are also occurring, inspection of roofs for damage in the aftermath of high winds is also needed.

In addition, many roofing systems include insulation as part of the roof system. In these instances, the roofing system also plays a key role in controlling the building's energy usage. The use of white or light-colored roofing also reduces energy usage by reflecting sunlight and maintaining lower roof temperatures.

Preventive Maintenance. A preventive maintenance program for a roof should include regular inspections (before and after the most severe climatic season each year, and after each major storm), removal of all foreign objects (tree limbs, leaves, dirt, and so on), repair of blisters (pockets of air or water between layers of the roof system), exclusion of ponded water, maintenance of all flashing, and maintenance of the ballast. Just because a roof is under warranty does not mean that it should be neglected. Indeed, failure to routinely inspect the roof may void the warranty.

Inspections. As part of the inspection process, the condition of the roof should be documented with photographs. This is especially true if a leak is found. It is then important to determine the location of the leak and document the conditions when the leak occurred (such as temperature, wind direction and velocity, and so on). It should also be noted if anyone was on the roof prior to the first time the leak was noticed. A more thorough and detailed inspection by building or roofing professionals is often required.

Visual inspections of roof areas should be conducted at least twice a year. Inspecting toward the end of the summer will help to identify possible problems caused by high heat and UV exposure over the summer months and, if inspections are made early enough, time will still be available for needed repair before winter. Inspections should also be conducted in early spring to assess whether damage occurred over the winter. In addition, it is important to conduct inspections following particularly extreme weather conditions such as tornados and hurricanes. Special attention should be paid during inspections to areas of roof penetration (such as for exhaust fans) as well as areas where discharges of air from the building occur. Kitchen exhaust hoods should be carefully inspected to ensure that adequate grease removal is occurring and that no grease buildup is happening on the roof itself.

Other types of inspections can involve the taking of core samples and use of non-destructive testing such as **thermal imaging**. Core samples involve cutting through the roof membrane and taking a sample for inspection. The priority concern here involves presence of water or damaged roofing elements. A primary form of non-destructive testing is thermal imaging using infrared cameras. Thermal imaging can detect water in deteriorated roof materials by measuring the surface temperature. Thermal imaging is generally done as a contract service.

Asbestos may be present in roofing materials (as well as other areas of the hotel). Its use in building materials was phased out in the late 1970s/early 1980s, but it may be present in older buildings today. There are many regulations involving the proper handling of asbestos-containing materials that need to be followed, including OSHA 1926.1101, "Toxic and Hazardous Substances: Asbestos."

Building Interiors

A building's interior components are among the most visible elements of the facility to hotel guests. Ceilings, walls, carpets, and hard surface flooring surround guests during their visits, and the visual appearance of these elements is an important part of the guest experience. Proper initial selection of these materials coupled with their ongoing care will help to ensure a positive guest reaction. While the ongoing care of many of these interior surfaces is the responsibility of housekeeping, engineering is typically responsible for periodic repairs and for the extensive refurbishments of these surfaces as needed or as part of a property renovation. Engineering will also have responsibilities for certain aspects of the elevator system.

Ceilings and Wall Coverings

Ceiling, wall, and window coverings date back to the Middle Ages, when the residents of castles hung intricately woven tapestries and bed curtains to brighten up rooms and keep out drafts.[1] Today, ceiling, wall, and window coverings are chosen more for their acoustical properties, safety, and appearance than for their insulation against the cold.

There is a wide variety of ceiling surfaces and wall coverings on the market today. Paint is by far the most common. However, vinyl manufacturers have introduced a wide variety of practical and attractive products in recent years, making vinyl a popular alternative to paint in properties of all types.

Ceiling surfaces and wall coverings include various kinds of wood surfaces such as laminated plywood, veneer, and paneling; synthetics such as carpet, paneling, and spray-on textured coatings; wallpaper; and stone such as ceramic tiles or marble. The following sections discuss more common surface coverings—paint, vinyl, and fabric.

Painted Surfaces. Much of paint's appeal derives from the fact that it is relatively inexpensive to purchase and apply to both walls and ceilings. It can also be cleaned easily with mild soap and water. In recent years, manufacturers have greatly improved the durability and cleanability of paint by decreasing its porosity. In general, the less porous the paint, the more durable and stain-resistant.

Vinyl Surfaces. Vinyl is now widely used as a wall covering and also as a surface for ceiling panels. Vinyl wall coverings are made by laminating vinyl to a cotton or polycotton backing. Polycotton-backed vinyl is recommended more often than cotton-backed vinyl because it is more durable and less flammable than cotton-backed vinyl.

Like wallpaper, vinyl comes in rolls and is applied with a special adhesive. Vinyl wall coverings should be applied with adhesives that contain mildewcides—especially in areas with hot, humid climates. Mildew causes the wall covering to loosen from the adhesive, creating ripples in the surface of the vinyl. Installing wall coverings is the job of maintenance personnel or an outside contractor. Housekeeping staff may be faced with cleaning adhesive seepages off the wall, especially around seams. A solvent recommended by the manufacturer can be used to remove the adhesive.

Vinyl was once chosen strictly for practicality; it can be scrubbed with a brush and soap and water or harsher cleaning agents if necessary. Today, however, vinyl wall coverings come in a wide assortment of colors and textures, which adds aesthetic appeal to practicality.

The federal government classifies vinyl wall coverings into three types. Type II vinyl is the most practical for public areas because of its durability and appearance. It usually lasts about three times as long as paint. However, it is vulnerable to tears and rips from accidental bumping. Highly textured vinyls may not be scrubbable.

Fabric Surfaces. Fabric wall coverings are considered among the most luxurious. They are also expensive, tricky to install, easily damaged, and hard to clean.

Linen, once the material of choice for fabric wall coverings, is giving way to a wider variety of materials—cotton, wool, and silks. Sometimes two or more materials may be combined to make the texture of the covering more appealing.

Fabric wall coverings may be paper- or acrylic-backed. Paper-backed wall coverings ravel less at the seams and are easier to install than acrylic-backed coverings. But acrylic-backed coverings are less vulnerable to wrinkling and can be adjusted more easily on the wall during installation. All fabric wall coverings should be vacuumed regularly. Stains and spots should be removed with a cleaner recommended by the manufacturer. Water should *never* be used on fabric wall coverings, because shrinking can occur.

Carpet Materials

Carpeting offers a number of benefits over other types of floor coverings. Carpeting reduces noise in halls and guestrooms, prevents slipping, and keeps floors and rooms warmer. Carpeting is also easier to maintain than many other floor coverings. Most lodging properties use commercial-grade carpet specially designed to withstand more wear and tear than the retail- or consumer-grade carpets people install in their homes.

In general, carpets have three components: the **face**, the **primary backing**, and the **secondary backing**. Exhibit 2 shows a cross section of these components.

The face or **pile** of the carpet is the part you see and walk on. The face may be made of synthetic fibers or yarns such as polyester, acrylic, polypropylene (olefin), or nylon. The face may also be made of such natural fibers as wool or cotton, though cotton is seldom used as a **face fiber** today. Some carpets are made of blends of synthetics and natural fibers, or blends of different kinds of synthetics. The carpet's face fibers, as well as its density, height, twist, and weave, will affect the carpet's durability, texture retention, and serviceability.

The density of the carpet's face fibers is the best indicator of durability. In general, the greater the density, the better grade of carpet. Dense carpets retain their shape longer and resist matting and crushing. They also keep stains and dirt at the top of the fibers, preventing deeply embedded soiling. To determine how dense a carpet is, bend a corner of the carpet and see how much backing shows underneath the pile. The less backing that shows, the denser the carpet.

In carpets of equal density, the one with the higher pile and tighter twist will generally be the better product. Carpet that is more tightly twisted is more resilient and will retain its appearance better. When examining a carpet, you should be able to see the twist. The tips of the fibers should not be flared or open. Good quality cut pile carpets have a heat-set twist.

Pile weight, while not as important as density, can affect the carpet's durability. Pile weight is measured in **face weight**—the weight of the face fibers in one square yard of carpet. The greater the weight, the more durable the carpet.

Face fibers are attached to a primary backing that holds the fibers in place. This backing may be made of natural material (typically jute) or synthetic material such as polypropylene. Jute backings are durable and resilient but may mildew under damp conditions. Polypropylene has most of the advantages of jute and is

Exhibit 2   Cross Section of Carpet Components

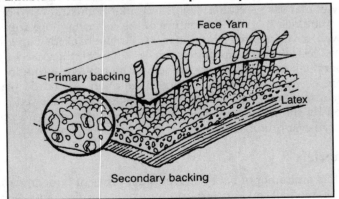

mildew-resistant. Both jute and polypropylene are suitable for tufted or woven carpets.

Usually, the primary backing of the carpet has a backsize. A backsize is a bonding material made of plastic, rubber, latex, or other adhesive that holds the fibers in place. This material is spread in a thin layer over the back of the primary backing and prevents the carpet tufts or loops from shifting or loosening after installation. Some carpets have a secondary backing that is laminated to the primary backing to provide additional stability and more secure installation.

In the past, all carpeting was installed over a separate pad. Today, carpeting may be glued directly to the floor or installed over one of a variety of pads. Sometimes, particularly with carpet tiles, a pad may be bonded directly to the backing in the manufacturing process.

In general, pads should be chosen with as careful an eye toward quality as toward the carpet itself. A cheap pad will reduce the life of the carpet as well as its insulating, sound-absorbing, and cushioning abilities. A thick pad will prevent the carpet from shifting *unless the carpet is installed in an area where heavy equipment will be rolled over it frequently;* in this case, a thinner pad is preferred.

Tufted Carpet. Nonwoven or tufted carpet is constructed with either **staple** or **bulk continuous filament (BCF)** fibers. Staple fibers are short (approximately seven to ten inches long) and are twisted together to form long strands. BCF fibers form one continuous strand. Of course, wool and other natural fibers are only available as staple fibers. The reason some carpets shed or pill (pills are small, round fibers appearing at the tips of the tufts or loops) is that not all the fibers in a staple construction are attached to the primary backing as well as the fibers in a BCF construction. Carpets that do not shed are almost always made of BCF fibers.

In tufted construction, needles on a large machine pull the face fibers through the carpet's backing to form tufts or loops. These tufts or loops form a thick pile or plush. Cut pile may be long, short, or cut in various lengths to provide a sculpted effect. Or, the tufts may be pulled to different lengths and left uncut to give a pattern to the finished carpet. Sometimes, both methods are used to create a cut-and-loop effect.

Berber carpets have short, nubby tufts and are available in a variety of textures. Level loops are the most common commercial carpets, usually tufted in short continuous rows. Lodging properties typically use a level-cut pile carpet in guestrooms to approximate the appearance of residential carpet. Other types of carpeting may be used in public areas, depending on the individual design requirements of the property.

Woven Carpet. In a woven carpet, a machine or loom weaves the face fibers and backing together as the carpet is being made. Generally, woven carpets are available only in narrow widths or strips that are attached or seamed together. Woven carpets do not have secondary backings, but they can perform as well as or better than tufted carpets if properly installed and maintained.

The weaving consists of warp (lengthwise) and weft (widthwise) yarns interwoven to form the face pile and backing at the same time. Different weaves include Velvet, Wilton, and Axminster. Many variations are available with the Velvet weaving method, including plushes, loop pile, multilevel loop, and cut-and-loop styles. Wilton refers to the special loom used to produce intricate patterns (sometimes multicolored) using perforated pattern cards. Axminster weaves are made from prearranged spools of different colored yarns that are fed into a mechanical patterning device. This method places most of the pile yarn on the surface and leaves a ribbed back.

Different types of carpets and various characteristics are shown in Exhibit 3.

Face Fibers. In general, synthetic fibers are more durable, more sanitary, and less expensive than natural fibers. These advantages help explain why synthetic fibers make up 90 percent of the carpets used in commercial operations. Face fibers are judged on their appearance, springiness and texture retention (ability to hold their shape), resistance to wear, resistance to soil, and cleanability. Typical face fibers include wool and other natural fibers, and nylon and other synthetics.

Wool and other natural fibers. People who buy and sell carpets agree that wool is good-looking, resilient, durable, and easily cleaned. It is also expensive.

Exhibit 3   Typical Carpet Types and Characteristics

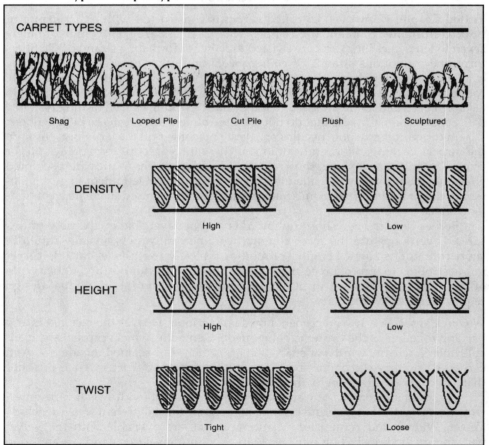

Despite the cost, wool is especially well-suited for lodging properties because of its natural resistance to flame and its ability to shed soil. Indentations caused by furniture legs, sometimes permanent on synthetic carpet, can be removed easily from wool by applications of moisture and low heat.

Wool fibers are also water-loving, which means they are responsive to wet cleaning. Unfortunately, this also means that they provide a better breeding ground for microorganisms than do synthetic fibers. Molds, mildew, bacteria, and other growths can mar the carpet and/or cause odors. Cleaning solutions for wool should be chosen carefully; ammonia, salts, alkaline soaps, chlorine bleach, or strong detergents can damage the fabric.

Other natural fibers available but rarely used today are cotton, sisal (hemp), and silk.

Nylon. More than 80 percent of all carpets manufactured in the United States are nylon. Nylon holds its shape and color well, cleans easily, and costs much less than wool. When properly maintained, nylon carpet fibers are less likely to promote bacterial growth than wool ones; they are easily treated for resistance to mold, mildew, and other organic growth. Nylon is particularly attractive because of its durability and its flexibility in construction and design. It is also comfortable underfoot and is more resistant to stains and soil than wool.

Nylon fibers normally have a shiny appearance. However, a "baking" process is now available that gives the carpet a duller or **delustered** finish that looks more like wool. Delustered carpets have the added advantage of soiling less quickly.

Other synthetics. Acrylic fibers were developed in the 1950s to approximate the appearance and durability of wool. Generally, acrylic carpet is not as easily cleaned or as resilient as other synthetics. It can also turn brown during cleaning. It has poor resilience and a tendency to pill and fuzz. Oil may leave permanent stains if not treated quickly. Acrylic does, however, resist most acids and solvents. **Modacrylic** is similar to acrylic, but has less resistance to stains and abrasions than acrylic.

Olefin (or polypropylene) fibers wear very well. They can be cleaned very aggressively without damage and are not as susceptible to sun fading as nylons and wools. Olefin carpets are solution-dyed, which means that color is added to the olefin in its liquid state. Olefin resists acids, solvents, and static electricity buildup. Olefin is, however, susceptible to heat or friction damage and is not as comfortable to walk on as other fibers.

Polyesters offer an appearance similar to wool. They are also very durable and clean easily. They do, however, have a tendency to mat under heavy traffic and are not very resilient.

Acetate is a low-cost silky fiber. It is colorfast and resistant to mildew, but it is relatively easy to soil and is vulnerable to abrasion. Spot-cleaning should be handled with care, because acetate may dissolve when dry-cleaning fluid or solvents are applied.

Rayon has many of the same characteristics as acetate—poor resistance to soil and abrasion but good color retention and resistance to mildew. Dense, high-grade rayons have adequate resilience for hotel use. Rayon is vulnerable to oil stains.

Hard Surface Flooring

Certain areas of hotels (guest baths, public space, back-of-the-house areas) are typically constructed using various types of hard surface flooring. In general, the materials used for hard surface flooring are noisier, harder, and slipperier than carpeting. However, they also have some advantages, in that they can be more durable, more sanitary, and do not conduct static electricity. There are three basic types of hard surface flooring: resilient, wood, and hard floors.

Resilient floors are easier to stand and walk on and may reduce noise better than hard floors. Types of resilient floors include vinyl, asphalt, rubber, and linoleum.

Wood floors are often made from oak (for durability and attractiveness), with maple, walnut, and teak also used (these woods are more expensive). In recent years, bamboo has become popular as an eco-friendly wood floor product. Proper installation, sealing, and finishing are essential to the durability of a wood floor. A laminate wood floor creates the look of a solid wood floor at a fraction of the cost.

Hard floors may be made of concrete, terrazzo, ceramic tile, and natural stone. Concrete flooring may be found in parking areas, garages, and trade show areas. Concrete floors may be covered, painted, or sealed. Terrazzo floors mix marble or granite rubble with mortar to form a mosaic. Ceramic tile is made with various materials and is very durable and easy to maintain. Natural stone flooring may be made of slate, marble, limestone, or granite.[2]

Elevators

Any hospitality building must make allowances for the building's "transportation system"—the hallways, stairways, and elevators that are an integral part of the physical facility.[3] Because of the elevator's importance and cost, we will discuss elevators and elevator maintenance in this section.

Components. Elevator systems are made up of several components. A cable elevator system has an elevator shaft, a car or cab, guide rails, cables, counterweights, safety devices, and an elevator motor that supplies the electrical power (see Exhibit 4).

The car is the only component of an elevator system guests see. The car moves passengers and goods up and down within a vertical shaft. Guide rails are positioned in the shaft; the elevator rides on wheels along the guide rails. Cables attach the car to counterweights that move in the opposite direction of the car; counterweights help offset the weight of the car and its passengers, so less energy is needed to move the car. Safety devices keep the car from moving past the lowermost and uppermost floors it serves and properly level the car at each floor. Should the cables holding the car break, rail clamps will slow or stop the descent of the car, and bumpers installed at the bottom of the shaft will absorb the impact, limiting passenger injuries and physical damage to the car.

There are two basic types of elevator systems: **cable** and **hydraulic.** The basic difference between them is that cable elevators move up and down with the help of cables and counterweights; a hydraulic elevator has no cables or counterweights. Instead, the car is mounted on a giant piston inside a cylinder. The

Exhibit 4   Cable Elevator System

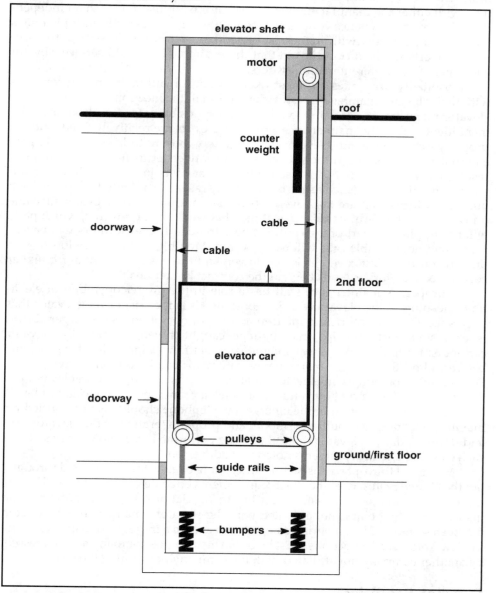

cylinder extends into the ground to a depth equal to the height the elevator will rise. An electric pump forces oil into the cylinder, displacing the piston and raising the car. The oil pours out of the cylinder through valves when the car goes down. Hydraulic elevators can only be used in buildings of six stories or less. Cable elevators are used in buildings with more stories.

Maintenance. To maintain their elevators, hospitality properties generally contract with either the manufacturer of the elevator equipment or with an independent elevator maintenance company. Hospitality companies with multiple hotels may sign agreements with maintenance companies to provide service to all of their properties, which could mean that these companies would service elevator equipment from different manufacturers.

Hospitality properties are most likely to opt for full-maintenance contracts with their elevator maintenance provider. Full-maintenance contracts obligate the elevator maintenance company to take total responsibility for the elevator equipment identified in the maintenance agreement. Costs are relatively fixed, and the property's concerns about elevator liability and exposure to lawsuits are largely eliminated with these contracts. Contracts for longer terms (e.g., five years) can result in lower costs. There are also contracts that cover just the minimum maintenance requirements (such as parts, oil, and grease); such limited contracts list a number of items that are *not* covered (such as controllers and elevator machine units) and need to be quite clear in stating what work will be covered, which parts will be supplied as part of the contract, how frequently the elevators will be serviced, and how trouble calls will be answered. Monthly costs may be lower with limited contracts, but coverage is also lower, and there is the potential for higher costs if needed work extends beyond the contract limitations.[4]

A property's maintenance staff has a role in the proper operation of elevators. Cleaning of the elevator car is important—it is the part of the elevator that guests see. Dirt and debris can interfere with door operation, as can larger objects (such as small rocks or coins) that might get caught or wedged under the elevator car doors. Having the property's maintenance staff investigate elevator problems before calling the elevator maintenance contractor can be a money-saving step. For example, sometimes an elevator "malfunction" is as simple as an elevator car that has been "keyed off" by vendors or hotel staff members who forget to key it back on. Proper operation of the emergency telephone should also be verified by maintenance staff, as should the smooth and proper operation of the elevator cars and doors. A daily "elevator ride" should be performed by maintenance staff on each elevator, and any problems noted and addressed.

An annual third-party inspection and testing of elevators is required throughout the United States, with the exact requirements often determined by local building codes or occupational safety and health regulations. Using a contractor for inspection/testing that is not affiliated with the elevator's maintenance contractor has been suggested by some as a safeguard to ensure a more valid inspection/test. In New York City, inspections must be performed by one company and witnessed by another company not affiliated with the company performing the test.

Exterior Facilities

Some essential facilities are located exterior to the main building. Many of these are underground, and, in a classic illustration of "out of sight, out of mind," are not thought about until there are problems. The function of exterior facilities is to provide essential support services to the building(s). Common types of exterior facilities are:

- Parking areas.
- Storm water drainage systems.
- Utilities.
- Landscaping and grounds.

Parking Areas

Almost every hotel has a parking area of some description for guests and employees. Some center-city hotels may rent space in a municipal parking garage that is maintained by the city. But most hotels are on their own when it comes to parking area maintenance. This section will provide some useful tips on how to properly maintain a parking area. Since most parking lots and garages are built of concrete or asphalt, the section will open with a discussion of these materials and what causes them to deteriorate. Next there are sections on parking lots and garages and the activities necessary to properly maintain them. The section concludes with a discussion of parking lot accessibility requirements mandated by the Americans with Disabilities Act.

Concrete. Concrete is a simple building material formed by a somewhat complex chemical process. Concrete's durability, versatility, and economy have made it the most used construction material in the world.[5] It's no wonder that many developers, builders, and building owners use it to construct their parking lots.

Fundamentals of concrete. Concrete is basically a mixture of paste and aggregates.[6] The paste is composed of portland cement, water, and entrapped air. Portland cement combines slowly with water to form a hard solid mass. Aggregates are the inert materials in the concrete such as sand, gravel, and crushed stone. Aggregates make up 60 to 75 percent of the volume (70 to 85 percent by weight) of most concrete mixes. Fine aggregates generally consist of natural sand or crushed stone with most particles smaller than .2 inches (.51 centimeters). Coarse aggregates consist of gravel or crushed stone with particles generally between ⅜ and 1 ½ inches (.95 and 3.8 centimeters). The quality of concrete depends to a great extent on the quality of the paste. In properly made concrete, each particle of aggregate is completely coated with paste and all of the spaces between aggregate particles are completely filled with paste.

Hardening of concrete is a chemical process called "hydration." Hydration is the chemical reaction between cement and water that forms a rocklike material that bonds to aggregate particles, steel, and other materials. Hydration is not the same as drying. In fact, dry cement does not hydrate because with no water the chemical reaction cannot take place. The more cement hydrates, the stronger it becomes.

Hardened concrete becomes a strong, non-combustible, durable, and abrasion-resistant building material that requires little maintenance. However, concrete's relatively low **tensile strength** (the greatest longitudinal stress it can bear without tearing apart) causes it to crack. Exhibit 5 illustrates how cracks can result from shrinkage. Think of a concrete slab as made up of a series of thin vertical segments. Because the top shrinks more than the bottom, each segment becomes slightly

Exhibit 5   Concrete Shrinkage and Curling

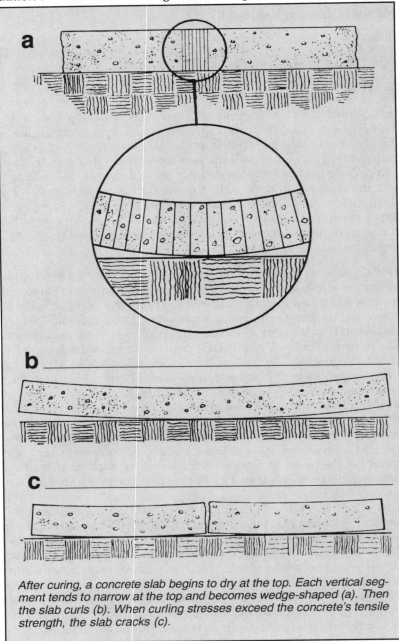

After curing, a concrete slab begins to dry at the top. Each vertical segment tends to narrow at the top and becomes wedge-shaped (a). Then the slab curls (b). When curling stresses exceed the concrete's tensile strength, the slab cracks (c).

Source: American Concrete Institute, *Concrete Craftsman Series—Slabs on Grade* (Detroit, Mich.: American Concrete Institute, 1982), p. 6.

narrower at the top than at the bottom, so the segments become slightly wedge-shaped. Because the segments remain in full contact with each other, the slab tends to curl at the edges. This creates enough stress to cause the concrete to crack when loads are applied to its surface.

The existence of a crack usually does not mean the concrete is in danger of collapse or disintegration. Cracks are of serious concern only when they are of a type or frequency that cannot be considered typical for a particular structure. Since a certain amount of cracking is usually unavoidable, builders have developed ways to reduce and control cracking. Joints are the most effective method of controlling unsightly cracking. Joints do not eliminate cracking; they are used to predetermine and control the location of cracks. Cracks along neat, straight joints are much easier to seal and maintain than are random cracks.

Many concrete problems, especially in concrete parking lots, decks, and ramps, can be avoided by applying a high-quality sealant. Sealants fill the pores of the concrete surface and protect it against penetration by waterborne de-icing salts and other contaminants. There are many sealants on the market. Professional advice should be sought as to which is best suited for a particular use and a particular concrete area's exposure conditions.

Concrete deterioration. Concrete deterioration includes crazing, leaching, the deterioration caused by freeze/thaw cycles, and spalling. Most of these problems can be controlled, or at least reduced, by the periodic application of a high-quality protective sealant.

Crazing refers to fine hairline cracks that form a map-like pattern on the surface of concrete. Just as with many other concrete cracks, crazing is caused by shrinkage. These tiny cracks generally do not seriously affect the usability of a concrete floor. However, if the cracks are wider than hairline width the problem may become quite severe and lead to the concrete's disintegration.

Leaching is caused by frequent water migration through a cement floor or through the cracks in the floor. As water migrates through, it takes along part of the cementing constituents and deposits them as a white film, stain, or stalactite on the underside of the concrete. Over a period of years, this process weakens concrete and is accelerated by porous or perpetually moist concrete.

Successive freeze/thaw cycles and the resulting disruption of paste and aggregate eventually will damage concrete. In northern climates, freeze/thaw cycles can cause substantial damage. As the moisture in concrete freezes, the concrete expands. When spring thaws start, the concrete's surface thaws first, and has a tendency to shrink back to its original volume, but the frost continues to hold the expanded concrete below the surface in place. This uneven thawing causes the beginning of surface cracks that allow spring rains to penetrate the concrete. When freezing temperatures return, these cracks are widened because the moisture in the cracks freezes and expands. The freeze/thaw cycles are repeated, with cracks continuing to grow wider. Finally, the surface area breaks free of the underlying material and begins to break up during a thaw period. The weakened material breaks loose under the movement of traffic and a pothole is formed.

Reinforced concrete contains embedded bars, wires, or strands made of steel or other materials. Corrosion of the embedded reinforcement can lead to dish-shaped cavities called **spalls.** Metallic corrosion is an electrochemical process that induces progressive deterioration of reinforced concrete. Rust, a byproduct of corrosion, occupies a volume at least 2.5 times that of the parent metal. Therefore, as rust develops on metal surfaces, the metal expands, causing pressure that forms cracks in the concrete surface.

The depth of concrete over and below embedded reinforcement is perhaps the single most important aspect of design and construction that can help prevent spalling. Floor slabs with less than recommended cover over reinforcement, and subject to a lot of de-icing salts, undergo rapid and severe spalling. When preparing maintenance programs for parking facilities, maintenance managers should pay special attention to the areas where reinforcement occurs near the concrete's surface.

Repairing concrete. Repairs to deteriorated concrete range in complexity from simple cleaning and sealing to complete reconstruction. If done properly, patching is generally an effective method of repairing isolated spalls or potholes (see Exhibit 6). A good patch must be durable and must bond well to the concrete surrounding it. Although many patching materials have been tried, the most widely used and effective are generally of portland cement concrete. Other patching materials include epoxy and polymer concretes.

When the area to be patched covers a significant part of the concrete's surface area, an overlay may be more cost-effective than isolated patching. In the case of a concrete floor within an enclosed structure (such as a parking garage), overlays add thickness to the original floor, reduce headroom, and increase the floor's weight. Poorly planned overlays can also cause serious drainage problems. Consulting a qualified engineer can help ensure that the overlay does not cause more problems than it solves.

Asphalt. Asphalt is a dark brown or black thermoplastic material refined from petroleum. Asphalt cement is asphalt that is further refined to make a semi-solid material suitable for paving and other industrial uses. Asphalt is valued because it is strong, durable, waterproof, and resistant to the action of most acids and salts.

Fundamentals of asphalt. Asphalt concrete is asphalt cement combined with aggregate to make a dense paving material. Just as with the aggregate used for cement, there are various types of aggregate, from fine to coarse, used with asphalt. The asphalt cement and aggregate must be heated before they are combined—the asphalt cement to make it fluid, the aggregate to make it dry and hot enough to keep the asphalt cement fluid while it is coating the aggregate particles.

Asphalt paving mixes may be designed and produced from a wide range of aggregate blends, each suited to specific uses or localities. Different types of mixes are preferred, depending on the geographic area. Specifications for asphalt mixes have been created by the American Association of State Highway and Transportation Officials and the American Society for Testing and Materials.

The soil base must be carefully prepared before the asphalt mix is spread. Once spread, the asphalt must be compacted with steamrollers or other heavy equipment. Squeezing out the air in the asphalt mixture and compressing the aggregate and asphalt together strengthens the pavement and makes it more waterproof. In fact, compaction is the single most important factor affecting the quality and life of an asphalt pavement.

Exhibit 6   Concrete Patching

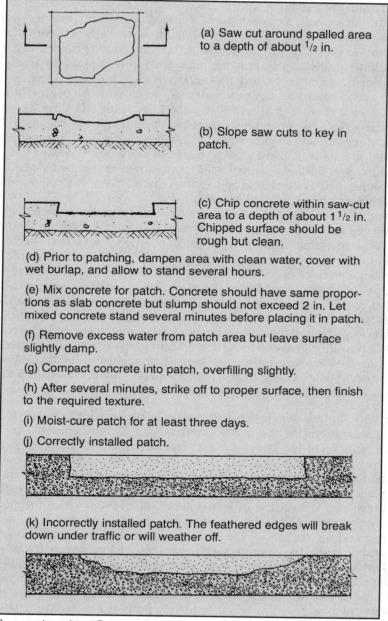

(a) Saw cut around spalled area to a depth of about $\frac{1}{2}$ in.

(b) Slope saw cuts to key in patch.

(c) Chip concrete within saw-cut area to a depth of about $1\frac{1}{2}$ in. Chipped surface should be rough but clean.

(d) Prior to patching, dampen area with clean water, cover with wet burlap, and allow to stand several hours.

(e) Mix concrete for patch. Concrete should have same proportions as slab concrete but slump should not exceed 2 in. Let mixed concrete stand several minutes before placing it in patch.

(f) Remove excess water from patch area but leave surface slightly damp.

(g) Compact concrete into patch, overfilling slightly.

(h) After several minutes, strike off to proper surface, then finish to the required texture.

(i) Moist-cure patch for at least three days.

(j) Correctly installed patch.

(k) Incorrectly installed patch. The feathered edges will break down under traffic or will weather off.

Source: American Concrete Institute, *Concrete Craftsman Series—Slabs on Grade* (Detroit, Mich.: American Concrete Institute, 1982), p. 65, and Steven H. Kosmatka and William C. Panarese, *Design and Control of Concrete Mixtures*, 13th ed. (Skokie, Ill.: Portland Cement Association, 1990), p. 118.

Asphalt deterioration. Asphalt problems can result from poorly compacted soil underneath the asphalt or from surface failures caused by weathering or wearing, insufficient asphalt, too much asphalt, unstable mixtures, or poor drainage.

Repairing asphalt. Small asphalt cracks should be cleaned with a broom or a leaf blower to get rid of surface debris. If there are plants growing in the cracks, they should be pulled out (if possible) and weed killer should be applied to the cracks. It may be necessary to flush the cracks with water to remove coatings of clay or dirt. The cracks must be completely dry before repair work begins, however.

Once clean, small asphalt cracks can be filled with a hot, rubberized crack filler. Squeegeeing the filler into the crack strengthens the repair and makes for a smoother surface. If there are only a few small cracks to repair, they can be repaired manually. If there is a large area of cracking, it may be necessary to apply a slurry seal instead. A slurry seal is a mixture of emulsified asphalt (asphalt cement thinned with water), fine aggregate, mineral filler, and water applied in a uniform, thin coat to an existing pavement.

Repairing large cracks and potholes in asphalt is similar to repairing potholes in concrete. First, the edges of the hole should be squared vertically, and all damaged or loose material removed from the hole. Then a tack coat—a thin, sticky layer of emulsified asphalt—should be applied to the sides and bottom of the hole. The hole can then be filled with an asphalt patching mix and compacted.

The patching mix should be soft and pliable for easy shoveling, raking, and shaping. If possible, the hole should be dry before the tack coat and patching mix is applied. If the hole is wet, the tack coat or patching mix may not stick and the mix will be forced out of the hole by traffic. That is why many potholes repaired in wet winter conditions have to be repaired again in the spring or summer.

Skin patches are generally used to re-level asphalt areas that have settled. Again, the edges of the area to be patched should be squared vertically and the area sprayed with a tack coat to make the asphalt mix stick to the existing pavement.

Parking Lots. In this section we will discuss a parking lot's structural features, layout considerations for parking lots, and parking lot maintenance.

Structural features. The structural features of a ground-level parking lot include the subgrade, subbase, and surface course (see Exhibit 7). The **subgrade** is the soil that has been prepared and compacted to support the surface course. The **subbase** is a layer of sand, gravel, crushed stone, or other granular material that is sometimes placed over the prepared subgrade to enhance uniformity of support, bring the site to the desired grade, and serve as a cushion between the surface course and the subgrade. The **surface course** usually consists of concrete or asphalt and provides the wearing surface for vehicles to drive on. It also functions as a sealant, preventing moisture from entering the subbase and the subgrade.

The performance of a ground-level parking lot depends in large part on the strength and uniformity of the subgrade. Cracks, slab settlement, and structural failure can often be traced to an inadequately prepared subgrade. The subgrade should be well drained; of uniform bearing capacity; level or properly sloped; and free of sod, organic matter, and frost.

The surface of a parking lot will be subjected to varying, but predictable, vehicle loads throughout its lifetime. To help the parking lot designer determine the

Exhibit 7   Structural Features of a Ground-Level Parking Lot

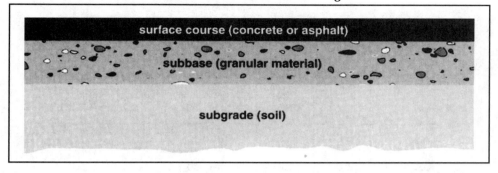

optimum thickness of the surface course, the facility's general manager or maintenance manager must supply the designer with estimates of:

- The types of vehicles that will use the parking lot (for example, passenger
  cars, light trucks, heavy trucks).
- The number of vehicles of each type.
- Typical vehicle loads.
- The number of vehicles expected in the parking lot each day.

These estimates, and traffic studies done for similar types of facilities, can help a
designer establish structural design requirements. Exhibit 8 indicates concrete slab
thicknesses appropriate under various traffic loads.

Surface parking lots should be designed and constructed to drain well, dry
quickly, and be puddle-free. If possible, the grounds surrounding a parking lot
should be sloped so that rain water drains away from the lot rather than toward it.
In addition, the lot should be designed to provide adequate drainage in all gutters,
around all traffic islands and structures, and especially in intersections and pedes-
trian walkways. Roof drains should not discharge large amounts of water onto a
parking lot, because maintenance problems can result, such as erosion of surface
materials, build-up of algae growth (under certain conditions), and the creation of
icy spots in cold weather.

Layout considerations. Layout considerations for parking lots include determining parking dimensions and establishing parking controls to channel and seg-
regate traffic. Parking lot entrances and exits should be well-defined and located so
as to have as little effect as possible on traffic movement on adjacent streets. Local
standards usually prescribe lengths of acceleration/deceleration lanes at entrances
and minimum distances from intersections. Local zoning regulations usually dictate the minimum number of parking spaces required for various types of buildings. Many local regulations also specify minimum sizes of parking spaces.

A parking lot is not usually expected to serve the broad spectrum of traffic—from very light vehicles to the heaviest trucks—that highways and streets
must serve. When parking lots are planned to serve heavy delivery trucks as well
as light vehicles, traffic controls are usually imposed to separate and channel

Exhibit 8   Recommended Concrete Thickness for Various Traffic Loads

Allowable Load Applications for Various Slab Thicknesses (20-yr. life)

Type of vehicle	Representative axle loads (lb)		Allowable number of passes per week for indicated slab thickness				
	Front	Rear	4 in.	5 in.	6 in.	7 in.	8 in.
	2,500	2,500	Unlimited				
	2,500	2,500	Unlimited				
	9,000	18,000	•	4	40	Unlimited	
	8,000	32,000	•	•	20	Unlimited	
	8,000	32,000	•	•	10	Unlimited	

•Occasional loads only - consult pavement design manuals.

Source: *Concrete Parking Areas: By Definition—A Classic,* a brochure produced by the Portland Cement Association, Skokie, Illinois.

the heavy trucks away from areas designed for automobiles and light trucks. If vehicles carry loads beyond those allowed for in a parking lot's structural design, structural failures result. A common cause of structural failures is the garbage truck, which is very heavy and must usually cross the entire parking lot to reach refuse containers at the rear of the property. Some properties install a separate cement pad near the refuse containers for garbage trucks, designed especially for the loading conditions imposed.

Maintenance. A well-designed and well-maintained surface parking lot should have a service life expectancy of fifteen to twenty years. The following list indicates typical parking lot maintenance tasks and the frequency with which they should be performed:

Maintenance Task	Frequency
Surface cleaning	Daily
Security inspection	Weekly
Drainage inspection	Monthly
Parking control inspection	Monthly
Waterproofing	Monthly
Minor repair of surface cracks	Monthly
Structural repairs	Monthly
Snow and ice removal	As needed

Each of these tasks should be incorporated into an overall preventive maintenance program.

Parking Garages. Parking garages are commonly constructed of reinforced concrete, prestressed concrete, or concrete surfaces over a steel frame structure. A parking garage is not just a series of concrete floors for parking vehicles. A parking garage also has drainage structures, underground drainage systems, exhaust and ventilating fans, lights, traffic control markings, guardrails, and access ramps.

Maintenance. A well-designed and properly maintained parking garage should have a service life expectancy well in excess of thirty years. The maintenance plan for a parking garage should include regularly scheduled cleaning, inspections, and maintenance activities. In addition, the plan should specify how managers evaluate the effectiveness of the maintenance program.

Parking garage maintenance can vary widely because of features unique to some garages that require special maintenance care. The following items indicate typical maintenance tasks and the frequency with which they should be performed:

Maintenance Task	Frequency
Cleaning	Daily
Parking control equipment inspection	Daily
Safety checks	Daily
Security system inspection	Daily
Painting and striping	Annually
Snow and ice removal	As needed

Each of these tasks should be incorporated into an overall preventive maintenance program.

ADA Accessibility Requirements for Parking Areas. The Americans with Disabilities Act (ADA) requires hospitality businesses to modify their parking areas to make them accessible to people with disabilities.[7] The law requires that modifications must be made that are "readily achievable." However, there are no clear guidelines defining what is meant by readily achievable. In general, it is recommended that any modifications be completed in accordance with the Justice Department's appendix to the law, called the Americans with Disabilities Act Accessibility Guidelines (ADAAG).

Accessible parking spaces. The ADAAG calls for a sliding scale of **accessible parking spaces** from 4 percent in parking lots with one to 100 spaces down to 2 percent when there are more than 1,000 spaces (see Exhibit 9).

Accessible parking spaces serving a particular building must be located on the shortest accessible route of travel from adjacent parking to an accessible entrance. Accessible parking spaces are reserved by a sign showing the international symbol of accessibility. Signs designating parking spaces for disabled people should be at the front of accessible parking spaces and mounted high enough above the ground so they can readily be seen from a driver's seat. Also, signs must be located so they cannot be obscured by a vehicle parked in the space.

Accessible parking spaces must be wide enough to allow a wheelchair user to open the vehicle door, transfer to a wheelchair, and easily exit to the walkway.

Exhibit 9   Guidelines for the Number of Accessible Parking Spaces

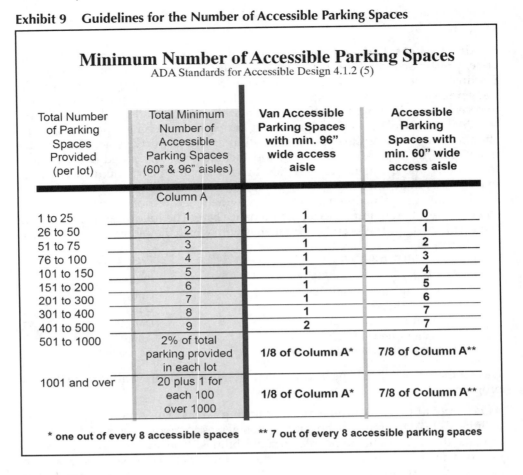

Minimum Number of Accessible Parking Spaces
ADA Standards for Accessible Design 4.1.2 (5)

Total Number of Parking Spaces Provided (per lot)	Total Minimum Number of Accessible Parking Spaces (60" & 96" aisles)	Van Accessible Parking Spaces with min. 96" wide access aisle	Accessible Parking Spaces with min. 60" wide access aisle
	Column A		
1 to 25	1	1	0
26 to 50	2	1	1
51 to 75	3	1	2
76 to 100	4	1	3
101 to 150	5	1	4
151 to 200	6	1	5
201 to 300	7	1	6
301 to 400	8	1	7
401 to 500	9	2	7
501 to 1000	2% of total parking provided in each lot	1/8 of Column A*	7/8 of Column A**
1001 and over	20 plus 1 for each 100 over 1000	1/8 of Column A*	7/8 of Column A**

* one out of every 8 accessible spaces   ** 7 out of every 8 accessible parking spaces

These parking spaces should have a minimum width of eight feet (2.4 meters) for the vehicle and five feet (1.5 meters) for an access aisle (see Exhibit 10).

Access aisles allow guests to exit and enter vehicles with a device, such as a wheelchair, and travel to the sidewalk or entrance. Access aisles cannot be restricted by planters, curbs, or wheel stops. As shown in Exhibit 10, adjoining accessible parking spaces may share a common access aisle. An essential consideration for any design is having the access aisle level with the parking space. Since a person with a disability must maneuver within the access aisle, the aisle cannot include a ramp or sloped area. The access aisle must either be level with the accessible route or have a curb ramp that allows for easy access to the route.

An **accessible route** is an obstruction-free route that connects the parking area to an accessible entrance of the facility. Curb ramps must be provided wherever an accessible route crosses a curb. The minimum width of a curb ramp is three feet (ninety-one centimeters), exclusive of flared sides. Transitions from ramps to walks, gutters, or streets must be flush and free of abrupt changes. Also, no

Exhibit 10   Features of Accessible Parking Spaces

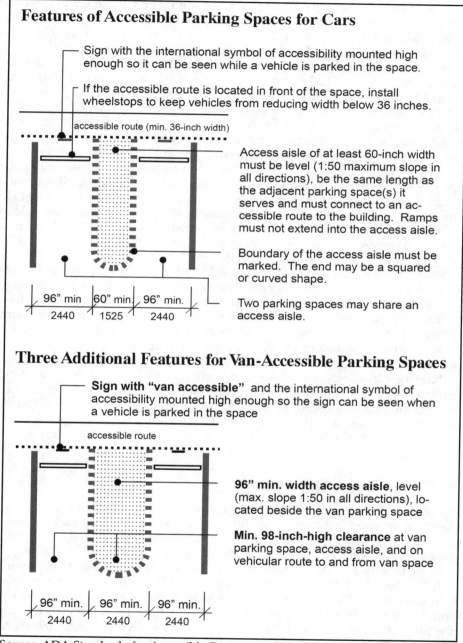

Features of Accessible Parking Spaces for Cars

Sign with the international symbol of accessibility mounted high enough so it can be seen while a vehicle is parked in the space.

If the accessible route is located in front of the space, install wheelstops to keep vehicles from reducing width below 36 inches.

accessible route (min. 36-inch width)

Access aisle of at least 60-inch width must be level (1:50 maximum slope in all directions), be the same length as the adjacent parking space(s) it serves and must connect to an accessible route to the building. Ramps must not extend into the access aisle.

Boundary of the access aisle must be marked. The end may be a squared or curved shape.

| 96" min. | 60" min. | 96" min. |
| 2440 | 1525 | 2440 |

Two parking spaces may share an access aisle.

Three Additional Features for Van-Accessible Parking Spaces

Sign with "van accessible" and the international symbol of accessibility mounted high enough so the sign can be seen when a vehicle is parked in the space

accessible route

96" min. width access aisle, level (max. slope 1:50 in all directions), located beside the van parking space

Min. 98-inch-high clearance at van parking space, access aisle, and on vehicular route to and from van space

| 96" min. | 96" min. | 96" min. |
| 2440 | 2440 | 2440 |

Source: ADA Standards for Accessible Design (28 CFR Part 36): § 4.1.6 Alterations; § 4.1.2 Accessible Sites and Exterior Facilities: New Construction; and § 4.1.6 Parking and Passenger Loading Zones.

obstructions should hang over the accessible route that would present hazards to a person who has a visual impairment. The route should be a minimum of three feet (ninety-one centimeters) wide to allow for people who use crutches or wheelchairs and individuals carrying bags. Exhibit 11 shows clearances for accessible walks and other walking surfaces that meet minimum ADA requirements.

When accessible parking spaces are designed to meet minimum requirements, at least one (and 12.5 percent of all accessible spaces) must be designated as "van accessible." The access aisle for a van-accessible space must be eight feet (2.4 meters) wide. A sign is needed to alert van users to the presence of the wider aisle, but the space is not intended to be restricted only to vans. (It should also be remembered that high-top vans, which disabled people or transportation services often use, require higher clearances in parking garages than automobiles.)

An alternative to providing a percentage of van-accessible parking spaces is the use of "universal" parking space design. With this design, all accessible spaces are eleven feet (3.4 meters) wide with an access aisle that is five feet (1.5 meters) wide. With this design, no "van-accessible" signs are needed, because all spaces can accommodate a van with a side-mounted lift or ramp. Also, there is no competition between cars and vans for spaces, since all spaces can accommodate either.

Valet parking. Not all disabled individuals can use valet parking services. For instance, a disabled individual may use vehicle controls that render the regular controls inoperable, or the driver's seat in a van may be removed. In these situations, another person cannot park the vehicle. It is recommended that some self-parking spaces be provided at valet parking facilities for individuals whose vehicles cannot be parked by another person, and that such spaces be located on an accessible route to the entrance of the facility.

Passenger loading zones. Passenger loading zones are typically located outside the main entrance of a hospitality facility. Accessibility requirements for these zones include an access aisle at least five feet (1.5 meters) wide and twenty feet (6.1 meters) long adjacent and parallel to the vehicle pull-up space. If there is a curb between the access aisle and the vehicle pull-up space, then a curb ramp should be provided.

Storm Water Drainage Systems

Storm water drainage systems are designed to carry rain water away from the property. Rain water can also be controlled by allowing it to seep into the soil. If the water is not contained through seepage, it must be transported to a place of storage on the property or discharged from the property.

Sheet flow is a uniform flow of water across the ground until it has ultimately reached its storage point or has been discharged from the property. It is not directed into definite channels of flow. An example of a sheet flow is the flow of water over a surface parking lot. The direction of flow always follows the slope of the ground. Depths of sheet flow seldom exceed ½ inch (1.3 centimeters) and can be controlled by changes in the ground's surface. Sheet flow can cause erosion.

Open-channel flow is water that flows into a defined channel such as a roadside ditch.

Exhibit 11   ADA Guidelines for Walking Surfaces

403 Walking Surfaces

403.1 General. Walking surfaces that are a part of an accessible route shall comply with 403.

403.2 Floor or Ground Surface. Floor or ground surfaces shall comply with 302.

403.3 Slope. The running slope of walking surfaces shall not be steeper than 1:20. The cross slope of walking surfaces shall not be steeper than 1:48.

403.4 Changes in Level. Changes in level shall comply with 303.

403.5 Clearances. Walking surfaces shall provide clearances complying with 403.5.

EXCEPTION: Within employee work areas, clearances on common use circulation paths shall be permitted to be decreased by work area equipment provided that the decrease is essential to the function of the work being performed.

403.5.1 Clear Width. Except as provided in 403.5.2 and 403.5.3, the clear width of walking surfaces shall be 36 inches (915 mm) minimum.

EXCEPTION: The clear width shall be permitted to be reduced to 32 inches (815 mm) minimum for a length of 24 inches (610 mm) maximum provided that reduced width segments are separated by segments that are 48 inches (1220 mm) long minimum and 36 inches (915 mm) wide minimum.

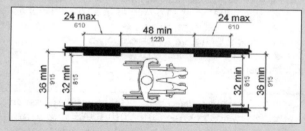

Figure 403.5.1 Clear Width of an Accessible Route

403.5.2 Clear Width at Turn. Where the accessible route makes a 180 degree turn around an element which is less than 48 inches (1220 mm) wide, clear width shall be 42 inches (1065 mm) minimum approaching the turn, 48 inches (1220 mm) minimum at the turn and 42 inches (1065 mm) minimum leaving the turn.

EXCEPTION: Where the clear width at the turn is 60 inches (1525 mm) minimum compliance with 403.5.2 shall not be required.

(continued)

Exhibit 11 *(continued)*

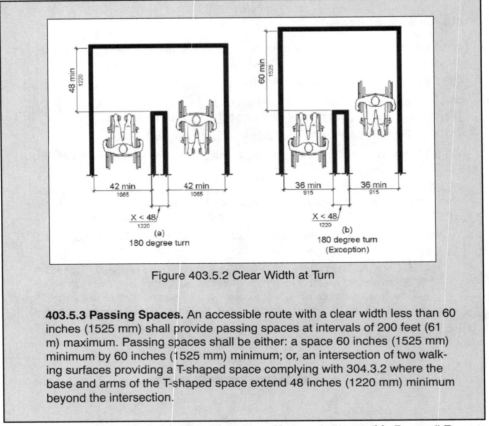

Figure 403.5.2 Clear Width at Turn

403.5.3 Passing Spaces. An accessible route with a clear width less than 60 inches (1525 mm) shall provide passing spaces at intervals of 200 feet (61 m) maximum. Passing spaces shall be either: a space 60 inches (1525 mm) minimum by 60 inches (1525 mm) minimum; or, an intersection of two walking surfaces providing a T-shaped space complying with 304.3.2 where the base and arms of the T-shaped space extend 48 inches (1220 mm) minimum beyond the intersection.

Source: *2010 ADA Standards for Accessible Design,* Chapter 4, "Accessible Routes," Department of Justice; http://www.ada.gov/regs2010/2010ADAStandards/2010ADAstandards.htm#c4.

An underground drainage system collects surface water through a catch basin or some other type of inlet structure and transports it down through an underground piping system to its ultimate point of discharge from the property.

Usually, the drainage from even a small property is a combination of all these types of flows. The goal of a drainage system is to control the flow of water so that it is not a problem for guests and does not damage the property.

Traditional design of storm water drainage has focused on removing rainwater from the property either immediately via storm drains or more slowly over time through the use of retention basins. There is growing interest in parking lots and other areas that use permeable paving systems and other methods of storm water retention. Permeable paving systems allow water to reenter underground areas on the site itself rather than being diverted to runoff into adjacent lands or storm water systems. Permeable paving systems can be used over the entire surface area or may be incorporated into swales or drainage areas receiving water from runoff from impermeable areas.

Another area of recent interest regarding the management of storm water involves the use of green roof systems. Green roof systems have vegetative covers installed to retain rainfall and improve the quality of the runoff that does occur. Green roofs are also credited with reducing energy costs for the structures on which they are installed, reducing the amount of heat in urban areas due to roof heating, and providing a more aesthetic roof surface. A variety of options exist for the actual design of the systems as well as for the various types of plants that can be grown. It is possible to use these systems to produce fresh herbs for food and beverage operations, for example. Green roofs can be retrofitted to existing roofs in many instances.

Due to the nature of the type of construction required, no underground drainage facilities should be constructed or installed with a life expectancy of less than fifty years. Extensive earth excavation is necessary to install an underground drainage system. This excavation almost invariably results in conflicts with other existing or planned utilities. Temporary repairs and alterations usually result in so many problems that their value must be questioned. If changes are needed, it is probably best to do all needed work in a permanent manner, and limit the number of times the ground must be opened.

Preventive Maintenance. Preventive maintenance of drainage facilities includes routine inspections after every rain. Were there blockages at any points? Did the water pond or back up during the rain? Did the flow seem sluggish? These are typical questions that should be answered. The answers usually determine the preventive maintenance that is needed. Leaves, twigs, and discarded rubbish and trash that block or clog the drainage system are the causes of most problems. They should be promptly removed.

Manhole and catch basin covers and grates should be kept in place. They are usually set in a frame, but are anchored only by their substantial weight. If the frame is loose, it should be tightened; this usually requires the use of a welding machine. If grates or lids make excessive noise when vehicles cross over them, it may be necessary to anchor or secure them in some way. Do not weld them shut; ease of access is important. Likewise, do not allow manholes to be covered by asphalt or concrete. This may easily happen if a parking lot or driveway is repaved.

Inspections. Inspections of storm water drainage systems should include a thorough visual inspection of the entire system after every hard rain. Problems will usually show up then. Look especially for spots where water is going through a hole into the ground, other than at a catch basin or inlet. These holes are always signs of underground voids. Left uncorrected, these voids will grow larger. Often the water will enter the ground in a swirling motion.

Inspect for blocked or partially functioning inlets. Often they are clogged with debris or leaves. Fast heavy rains closely following grass mowing can carry a significant amount of clippings into the inlet, causing clogs. Look down into the inlets and catch basins while it is raining to see if the water is flowing away smoothly or if it appears to be impeded by something.

Utilities

Typical utilities used in a hospitality facility include water, sewer, oil, gas, electricity, steam, chilled water, telephone, and cable television.

Externally supplied or purchased utilities are normally brought to a distribution point somewhere on the property. For example, in the case of the water supply, the distribution point is commonly at the property's water meter. Electricity is normally brought to an electric meter's distribution panel.

Ideally, utilities enter the property and are distributed by an underground system to various parts of the property. However, some utilities, such as cable television, telephone, and electric service, are carried above ground at some properties. These above-ground lines are easier to inspect and maintain than underground lines, but they are not as aesthetically appealing.

Normally it is necessary for the facility to maintain the utilities from the facility to their final delivery point. The final delivery point is usually considered to be the meter recording the quantity or volume consumed of the particular utility being provided.

Extreme caution should be used when working around any of the public utilities. Dangers from electrical shock and earth cave-ins are but a few of the problems that can occur. Any time underground digging takes place, the potential for striking an underground utility line is present. Workers should never be allowed to work alone under dangerous conditions.

Preventive Maintenance. Water lines, both potable and non-potable, are normally equipped with valves for control purposes. These valves not only shut off the water, but control the direction and quantity of flow as well. Water control valves should be "exercised" annually—that is, they should be fully opened and closed, to be sure they seat properly and still perform their intended function. If left too long in one position, valves have a tendency to stick in that position, rendering them useless in time of need. A record should be made each time a seldom-used control valve is exercised. Any problems should be noted and taken care of.

Sanitary sewer lines can become clogged by a buildup of solids. This can be caused by the flow being too slow (the sewer grade being too flat), or by the sewer grade being too steep, allowing the liquids to outrun the solids, leaving the solids behind. Obviously, sewer slopes should be neither too steep nor too flat.

Sewers that are partially or completely blocked should be rodded or flushed out. Flushing can be done with a high-pressure hose, such as a fire hose. A typical garden hose is usually not capable of supplying the quantity of flow or the pressure needed. Rodding is done by mechanical means, usually by inserting a flexible rod into an opening such as a manhole and pushing it through to the next opening. A roto-rooter is a piece of equipment that rotates a cutting bit through the sewer or drain pipe, "rooting" its way through the blockage. The cutting bit is attached to a flexible cable that is rotated by a power source. This equipment is fairly easy to use and is effective in removing blockage. Roto-rooter equipment comes in various diameters and is capable of accepting different turning forces.

Inspections. Inspection of underground utilities is usually limited to observing the surface of the ground above them and looking at the lines themselves through access points such as manholes. Tools are available to do scientific analysis, such as natural gas detectors, moisture and water detectors for water mains, and sewer gas analysis equipment. The necessary equipment ranges from hand-held, reasonably user-friendly equipment to very sophisticated electronic analyzers.

Overhead electric, cable television, and telephone lines can be more easily inspected. If necessary, ladders and lift trucks can be used for detailed inspections.

Landscaping and Grounds

A property's landscaping and grounds set the visual tone for the entire property; they are a large part of the first impression guests receive. Allowing the grounds to decline into mediocrity will severely diminish the property's attractiveness, which may result in lower revenues. To keep the property's curb appeal high, the grounds should always be kept at their best.

As landscaping and grounds are planned, consideration should be given to entrances, the location and types of driveways, the first or principal view guests see, drainage conditions, existing trees, the direction of the prevailing wind, underground and overhead utility lines, recreational facilities, the direction of the sun, watering facilities, and—of course—the initial cost of the landscaping and the cost and ease of maintaining it.

Preventive Maintenance. The most common maintenance activities for grounds are mowing, fertilizing, and pruning. Mowing is necessary to keep a lawn attractive and healthy. The mower's blades should be sharp so that grass blades are cut cleanly, not ripped; ripped, frayed blades invite disease. The grass should be cut when it needs cutting, not according to some arbitrary timetable. Only one third or less of the grass blades should be cut at any one time, otherwise the roots may be starved for nutrients and grass health is damaged. Lawns should not be mown too close to the ground, because short grass makes it easier for moisture to evaporate and weeds to invade the lawn.

Lawns, plants, and trees usually need fertilization to maintain the healthy appearance guests have come to expect from landscaped grounds. Commercial fertilizers usually contain nitrogen, phosphate, and potash. The amount of each element that is needed depends on the type of soil, the vegetation, and the climate. The manufacturer's instructions should be followed carefully when applying fertilizer.

Trees and shrubs must be pruned with care. Using the wrong technique or pruning at the wrong time of year can ruin or kill a plant. When is the right time to prune? It depends on the plant. For example, deciduous trees should be pruned in winter when they are dormant; evergreens can be pruned in April before new growth begins or in July after new growth has matured. Maintenance employees should consult the Internet, reference books, or call a lawn and garden center if they are unsure of when or how to prune a particular plant.

Regardless of the kind and extent of landscaping work, the maintenance manager is faced with the decision of who should do the maintenance. Many otherwise competent persons in a maintenance department lack the skills to do an acceptable job on landscaping. Extensive training may be necessary. The alternative to training the in-house maintenance staff is to hire a landscaping maintenance service.

Attractive landscaping adds to a property's appeal. (Courtesy of The Greenbrier, White Sulphur Springs, West Virginia.

The amount of landscaping work varies significantly with the seasons and climate. It is usually best to organize maintenance activities for the grounds into monthly cycles and to subdivide these further into weekly and daily tasks. When rainy days prevent outside work, the landscaping staff must be rescheduled. Following extended rainy periods the landscaping workload may be very heavy.

Inspections. Landscaping and grounds are relatively easy to inspect, since they are readily visible and accessible. The inspector should walk the entire grounds, noting any problems or changes since the last inspection. Problems often develop slowly over a period of time, so detailed notes should be kept. Preferably a scaled drawing should be used to help managers and others keep track of issues. Inspections should be done at least quarterly, and following any significant departure from normal weather.

Irrigation Systems. Many hospitality facilities use irrigation systems to maintain their grounds. The need for irrigation is not universal. It is not necessary in areas where rainfall is equal to the needs of plant life.

In the hospitality industry, the function of irrigation is to artificially provide a reliable source of water for a building's landscape. In some cases the irrigation water is also used as the transport vehicle for soil and plant nutrients. A successful irrigation system not only furnishes water to plants and trees, it supplies the water at the proper time and in the proper quantity.

All irrigation systems must take the following elements into account:

- Rate of water loss through evaporation

- Rate of water infiltration into the soil

- Water-absorption capacity of the soil to which the water is applied

- Depth of infiltration (usually related to depth of the topsoil)

- Depth of plant roots

Lawns and trees usually need large amounts of water. However, it is prudent to stretch the interval between waterings as much as possible, since overwatering wastes water and can have a negative effect on plant life.

The supply or source of water can be one of the following:

- The treated, potable water system of the facility

- A stored supply, such as in a lake or underground tank

- A nearby stream or river

- Gray water

Water that comes from the potable water system must be paid for, and thus carries a significant cost. Potable water used for irrigation should be metered separately. It commonly has had many of the most desirable nutrients removed in the purification process, and often has had chemicals added that are detrimental to plants. It is typically the most readily available source, but is the least desirable. Backflow prevention devices must be used if the irrigation system is connected to the potable water supply.

Water for irrigation can be stored on the surface or underground. Surface storage can either be natural (a lake) or artificial (a tank or a constructed pond). Underground units include cisterns and other underground tanks. These tanks are usually small because of the cost of building a large underground tank.

Gray water is obtained from selected parts of the facility's plumbing system. It originates from the laundry, kitchen, and bathroom sink areas. Its primary pollutants are dirt, food wastes, and laundry detergents. Most of these can be successfully removed by a simple clarification process. The heaviest pollutants settle to the bottom of the clarifier and can be retrieved and dumped into the sanitation sewer. The remaining gray water is rich in nutrients, such as phosphate and nitrogen, and makes excellent irrigation water. Because of the danger of contaminating pathogens, the gray water should be disinfected. Common methods of disinfection include chlorinating and applying ultraviolet light.

A typical irrigation system consists of sprinkler heads or mist applicators. Sprinkler heads are located at the terminals of a piping system. When the water pressure reaches a certain point, the heads begin to spray water. Sprinkler heads are, in general, pressure dependent; the greater the pressure, the greater the flow of water and the greater the area of coverage. Three common types of sprinkler heads are fixed, pop-up, and pulsating.

Mist applicators are similar to the other types of sprinkler heads, except that the nozzle is designed to create a fine mist. Because the discharge nozzles of mist applicators are smaller in diameter, they are easier to clog and thus require more maintenance.

Preventive maintenance. Irrigation systems should be observed daily when in use and inspected in detail monthly. Observers should make note of any sprinkler units that do not seem to deliver the correct quantity of water (either too much or too little). If too little water is delivered it can be a sign of clogged pipes or nozzles, partially closed valves, inadequate water pressure, or other problems.

As part of preventive maintenance, the following should be looked for each day:

- Pump problems
- Leaks in the distribution system
- Sprinkler heads not functioning

All control valves in the irrigation system should be exercised (completely opened and closed) semi-annually. Valves and control devices should be marked with an identifiable code and special paint color. Their location should be documented for easy access.

Irrigation systems located in cold climates must be protected against freezing. As the water in a system freezes, it expands, bursting pipes and valves. To winterize the system it is usually necessary to remove the water.

Endnotes

1. This discussion of ceiling, wall covering, and carpet materials is taken from Aleta A. Nitschke and William D. Frye, *Managing Housekeeping Operations*, Revised Third Edition (Lansing, Mich.: American Hotel & Lodging Educational Institute, 2008).

2. Recommended floor care for a variety of flooring options (as well as for other building interior components) can be found in Aleta A. Nitschke and William D. Frye, *Managing Housekeeping Operations*, Third Revised Edition (American Hotel & Lodging Educational Institute, 2008).

3. Some of the information in this section was adapted from Frank D. Borsenik and Alan T. Stutts, *The Management of Maintenance and Engineering Systems in the Hospitality Industry*, 3d ed. (New York: Wiley, 1992), pp. 399–403; and Mel A. Shear, *Handbook of Building Maintenance Management* (Reston, Va.: Reston Publishing Company, 1983), pp. 508–514.

4. Elevator maintenance contracts have numerous options and provisions. Careful review of the contracts is needed to be sure that correct levels of service are purchased at a reasonable price, with liability and legal issues properly addressed. The following references are a useful start for further background on these issues: www.elevatorsource.com/elevator-contracts.html; and http://elevatorcsi.com/index.php?option=com_content&view=article&id=14&Itemid=10.

5. Steven H. Kosmatka and William C. Panarese, *Design and Control of Concrete Mixtures*, 13th ed. (Skokie, Ill.: Portland Cement Association, 1990), p. vii.

6. Much of the material in this section was adapted from Steven H. Kosmatka and William C. Panarese, *Design and Control of Concrete Mixtures*, 13th ed. (Skokie, Ill.: Portland Cement Association, 1990); ACI Committee 330, *Guide for Design and Construction of Concrete Parking Lots* (Detroit, Mich.: American Concrete Institute, 1988); and the American Concrete Institute, *Concrete Craftsman Series—Slabs on Grade* (Detroit, Mich.: American Concrete Institute, 1982).

7. For more information, refer to the 2010 ADA Standards for Accessible Design, Chapter 4, "Accessible Routes," at www.ada.gov/regs2010/2010ADAStandards/ 2010ADAstandards.htm#c4.

🔑 Key Terms

access aisle—An aisle next to an accessible parking space that allows disabled individuals to exit and enter vehicles with a device, such as a wheelchair, and travel to the sidewalk or building entrance.

accessible parking space—A parking space specially designed for disabled persons that meets or exceeds the requirements of the Americans with Disabilities Act.

accessible route—A route that connects the accessible parking area to an accessible entrance of the building the parking lot serves. An accessible route should be a minimum of three feet (91 centimeters) wide and have no abrupt surface transitions (from sidewalks to streets, for example) or obstructions that would present hazards to a visually impaired person.

acrylic—Synthetic material used in making fabric or molded transparent fixtures or surfaces.

asphalt—A dark brown or black thermoplastic material refined from petroleum that is often used in parking lot construction.

bulk continuous filament (BCF) fibers—Continuous strands of fiber that are used to construct non-woven or tufted carpet.

built-up roof—A roof system comprising multiple layers of overlapping roofing materials.

cable elevator system—An elevator system in which an elevator car moves up and down with the help of cables and counterweights.

crazing—Fine hairline cracks that form a map-like pattern on the surface of concrete.

dead load—A structure's own weight.

delustered—A process used on nylon carpet to lessen the carpet's shine and give the surface a duller finish that looks more like wool.

face—In the carpet industry, a term for the pile of the carpet.

face fibers—Yarns that form the pile of the carpet.

face weight—The measure of a carpet's pile, equal to the weight of the face fibers in one square yard of carpet.

flashing—Copper, aluminum, or fiber sheeting that joins the roof covering to the building structure where the roof meets a wall, chimney, etc.

hydraulic elevator system—An elevator system with no cables or counterweights. Instead, the elevator car is mounted on a giant piston inside a cylinder that extends underground to a depth equal to the height the elevator will rise.

leaching—The subtraction of cementing constituents from cement due to water migration through the cement.

live load—The weight of the people, equipment, furnishings, and so on within a building.

modacrylic—Acrylic fiber that is less resistant to stains and abrasions.

pile—In the carpet industry, a term for the surface of a carpet; the pile consists of fibers or yarns that form raised loops that can be cut or sheared.

primary backing—The part of the carpet to which face fibers are attached and which holds these fibers in place.

roofing felt—Fiber-filled paper impregnated with asphalt or tar.

secondary backing—The part of a carpet that is laminated to the primary backing to provide additional stability and more secure installation.

single-ply roof—A roof system using large pieces of roofing material that are bonded together using heat or chemicals to form a one-piece roof system.

spall—A surface cavity of a cement slab, caused by corrosion of embedded metals.

staple fibers—Fibers approximately seven to ten inches long that are twisted together into long strands and used to construct non-woven or tufted carpet.

subbase—In parking lot construction, a layer of sand, gravel, crushed stone, or other granular material that is sometimes placed between a prepared subgrade and the surface course.

subgrade—In parking lot construction, soil that has been prepared and compacted to support a layer of concrete or asphalt.

surface course—A wearing surface for vehicles to drive on, usually made of concrete or asphalt.

tensile strength—The strength to bear longitudinal stress.

thermal imaging—Use of an infrared camera to detect water leaks by identifying insulation deterioration.

Review Questions

1. What should an inspector look for when checking a foundation?

2. What are some preventive maintenance strategies for a building's structural frame?

3. What are typical preventive maintenance activities for exterior walls?

4. What is the basic structure of a roof?

5. Elevator systems are made up of what basic components?

6. What are some of the structural features and layout considerations for parking lots and parking garages (including ADA requirements)?

7. What are some preventive maintenance strategies for storm water drainage systems?

8. What are some preventive maintenance strategies for utility systems?

9. What are some typical maintenance activities for landscaping?

10. Water for irrigation can come from what sources? What issues are associated with each source?

Internet Sites

For more information, visit the following Internet sites. Remember that Internet addresses can change without notice. If the site is no longer there, you can use a search engine to look for additional sites.

American Concrete Institute
www. concrete.org

American Concrete Pavement
  Association
www. pavement.com

Asphalt Emulsion Manufacturers
  Association
www. aema.org

Asphalt Institute
www.asphaltinstitute.org

Asphalt Roofing Manufacturers
  Association
www.asphaltroofing.org

Association of Asphalt Paving
  Technologists
www.asphalttechnology.org

ASTM International
www.astm.org

Concrete Reinforcing Steel Institute
www.crsi.org

Construction Specifications Institute
www.csinet.org

Ecological Landscaping Association
www.ecolandscapingassn.org

Elevator Escalator Safety Foundation
www.eesf.org

European Asphalt Pavement
  Association
www.eapa.org

RCI, Inc.
www.rci-online.org

International Code Council
www.iccsafe.org

International Union of Laboratories
  and Experts in Construction Materials, Systems and Structures
www.rilem.org

Irrigation & Green Industry Network
www.igin.com

Irrigation Association
www.irrigation.org

Irrigation Tutorials.com
www.irrigationtutorials.com

National Asphalt Pavement
  Association
www.asphaltpavement.org

National Association of Elevator
  Contractors
www.naec.org

National Gardening Association
www.garden.org

National Roofing Contractors
  Association
www.nrca.net

Portland Cement Association
www.cement.org

Professional Landscape Network
www.landcarenetwork.org

Part III

Facility Design

Chapter 11 Outline

Competencies

Lodging Planning and Design

This chapter was written and contributed by Stephani Robson, Ph.D., Senior Lecturer, School of Hotel Administration, Cornell University, Ithaca, New York; and Richard H. Penner, Emeritus Professor, School of Hotel Administration, Cornell University, Ithaca, New York.

"Today's hotel is not merely a destination, but is also a convergence of an incredible array of experiences."
— *David Rockwell, Founder and CEO, The Rockwell Group*

CREATING A HOTEL OR RESORT is an integrative process that brings together the skills and expertise of owners, brand managers, property managers, architects, builders, and a host of others to conceive and construct a building to meet a variety of objectives. Owners see a hotel primarily as a real estate and investment opportunity; brand managers expect a hotel project to meet certain strategic goals and to provide revenue; property managers require the hotel to be both functional and attractive to maximize revenues and minimize expenses; and design professionals make their living and their reputation by creating effective and noteworthy physical assets. Of course, there are the future building users themselves—guests and employees—who are not part of the development team but whose interests and expectations must be considered throughout the hotel development process.

While service and pricing are the key components of guest satisfaction once a hotel opens, decisions made during the planning and design process are enormously influential to the guest purchase decision. Where precisely should the hotel be located? Should the hotel be branded, and, if so, which brand? What physical amenities should the property offer to best meet the needs of its target market(s)? All of these factors—location, brand, and amenities—are part of what a guest considers when choosing a lodging property, but, given that the vast majority of travelers do their hotel research and booking online, and that most consumers are heavily reliant on the images they see on their computer screens when choosing a hotel, hotel design has become a particularly important driver of demand and a critical differentiator among hotels and resorts. A well-designed hotel is one that balances the financial and operational needs of owners, brands, and managers with the experiential preferences and desires of guests.

In this chapter, we will discuss how an individual hotel is developed and present planning and design guidelines for typical hotel types. The development, design, and construction phases may take up to two years for a relatively small hotel and four or more years for a large urban or resort property. It is important that owners and hotel managers understand the discipline and control needed to organize and manage such a lengthy process, which includes such steps as confirming the hotel's feasibility; selecting the project team; establishing space requirements, operational standards, and construction and engineering criteria; and preparing the budget and schedule. These are only part of the process. The owners and managers also must be familiar with planning and design guidelines for guestrooms and suites, lobbies, food and beverage outlets, function space, recreational facilities, administration offices, food production areas, and back-of-the-house spaces. A hotel's design is instrumental in attracting business, pleasing guests, and enabling managers and staff to operate effectively and efficiently.

The Development Process

Lodging development can be broken down into several steps but typically begins with a conceptual phase during which the first idea for a project is envisioned. If some initial analysis demonstrates that there is proven demand and sufficient resources to develop the project, the development process continues through a series of planning, design, and coordination steps that together can take as long as several years until the hotel finally opens. Even a relatively simple limited-service hotel development using an established design from a hotel brand can take well over a year to execute.

The development and design process brings together many specialists in an intensive, cooperative effort. The hotel developer plays the key project role of initiator and coordinator, and is often also the owner of the real estate being developed. The early stages of the process require the assistance of legal and financial experts as well as marketing consultants who are retained by the developer to test and further refine the project's concept. The developer also assembles a design team, including architects, engineers, interior designers, kitchen specialists, and other design consultants; establishes an agreement with a hotel brand and/or hotel management company and involves them in strategic and operational decisions for the property; negotiates both construction and permanent financing agreements; and contracts with a construction firm to build the property. As you can see, the developer must have a clear vision for the project and the leadership and coordination skills to bring the project to life.

Hotel development and design is a mammoth effort, one that brings great satisfaction when it is successful and great frustration when problems arise. Critical to a successful project is the organization of the pre-design phase, during which criteria are set, the development team is brought together, and preliminary budgets and schedules are established. Some of these tasks are identified in Exhibit 1.

Perhaps the most important factor in ensuring development success is clear and frequent communication. The various members of the development team must understand what the others are doing and, especially, the point of view that each person brings to the effort. One effective way of initiating the project is to insist that the full team assemble for a "kick-off meeting," during which team members consider different approaches to meet the overall objectives of the owner and, if relevant, the hotel brand. This meeting leads to a number of planning and design activities—many occurring simultaneously—that will give shape to the future lodging property.

Exhibit 1 Development Team Member Responsibilities During the Pre-Design Phase

Owner/Developer Responsibilities

- Establish project objectives (financial, developmental, operational).
- Assemble project team (architect, design consultants, hotel brand, hotel management company, and joint-venture partners if needed).
- Identify developmental issues (regulatory, environmental, legal).
- Commission feasibility study.
- Establish preliminary project budget.
- Establish project schedule.
- Obtain option on land (If not already acquired).
- Investigate potential financing.
- Negotiate joint-venture and hotel-management agreements.
- Schedule "kick-off" meeting for the full team.

Hotel Brand and/or Management Company Responsibilities

- Confirm feasibility recommendations.
- Recommend architect and consultants.
- Prepare space allocation program.
- Share brand architecture and construction design standards.
- Prepare budget for operating supplies and equipment.

Architect Responsibilities

- Select consultant team.
- Analyze site.
- Prepare conceptual design.
- Review program and budget.

The Feasibility Study

Among the first steps that the developer takes is to study the feasibility of the proposed hotel. The **feasibility study** (also called a market study) is usually prepared by a consulting firm that specializes in lodging and is reviewed by the hotel brand and/or management company as well as by the developer who commissioned the work. This study's purpose is threefold: One, it assesses present and future demand for lodging and such hotel services as food and beverage offerings, meeting rooms, and recreational facilities. Two, it recommends a basic mix of facilities and positions the future hotel against its primary competitors. And three, it estimates the proposed hotel's operating income and expenses for five to ten years after the hotel opens.

A hotel developer has many reasons for commissioning a feasibility study. Most will use the study to help obtain permanent financing; others may use it to gain a franchise or management agreement, attract equity partners, or support a request for a zoning change. Interestingly, despite the fact that they are often referred to as feasibility studies, only infrequently do these studies actually assess a proposed project's feasibility, which may largely depend on the owner's investment strategies and tax status. Instead, the feasibility study provides a description of the local area and potential markets, recommends proposed facilities, and projects cash flow. The typical report usually covers the following components:

- *Local area evaluation:* Analyzes the economic vitality of the city or region and describes the suitability of the project site for a hotel.

- *Lodging market analysis:* Assesses the present demand for lodging and other revenue generators and future growth rates for each of several market segments, and identifies the existing supply of competitive properties and their probable growth.

- *Proposed facilities:* Proposes a balance of guestroom and revenue-generating public facilities (restaurants and lounges, function rooms, retail stores, recreational facilities) and assesses the competitive position of the property.

- *Financial analysis:* Estimates income and expenses for the hotel over a five- or ten-year period to show its potential cash flow after fixed charges (before debt service and income tax).

When seeking a feasibility consultant, owners and managers should look for a firm with experience and high credibility within the hospitality industry. The consultant must be neutral and objective in order to meet lender requirements and should be prepared to provide explanations and documentation to support the underlying assumptions in the report. The time frame and cost of the consultant's work varies, depending on the complexity of the project.

The Program

Following a positive feasibility assessment, the development team establishes the program for the proposed hotel. The **program** is a document that lists the design requirements for a project. This is a cooperative effort, with input from the owners, based on the feasibility report and the owners' objectives, as well as the objectives of the brand, the operating company, the architect, and other consultants. Most programs consist of two components: a clearly articulated description of what each area of the hotel needs to include, and an allocation of space for each area.

The program serves a vital role early in the development process, as it forms the "road map" for the design team. Clear direction about features that are desired by the owner, brand, and/or operator streamlines the design process and minimizes the potential for miscommunication or disagreements later on that can delay the project or result in cost overruns.

The allocation of space among the principal functions in a hotel varies from property to property. The most obvious difference among properties is the ratio of guestroom space to public and support space. This varies from over 90 percent guestroom space in economy properties and many motels (where there are limited or no food and beverage, meeting, and back-of-the-house areas) to less than 65 percent guestroom space in large convention and resort properties, where generous public and support functions are essential to the property's ability to gain or keep market share. Exhibit 2 shows the percentage of total hotel space allocated to guestrooms for a range of lodging property types.

For each type of hotel developed at a particular location to meet the needs of a specific target market at a given price range, the hotel brand or operating company can provide a tentative list of facilities and an early estimate of space requirements. Until a more detailed space allocation program is established, this gross approximation of the proposed hotel's size is the basis for all cost estimates. Exhibit 3 shows fairly typical guestroom space allocation requirements for five different types of lodging properties. Of course, market conditions and brand standards will influence these allocations significantly for any given project.

The development of the architectural space program does not occur solely at one time nor does it result in a static document. Usually, at the beginning of the first phase of the design process—**schematic design**—the architect develops a list of required spaces and later refines it into a more detailed program as more information about the intended uses and requirements of the hotel are determined. In the case of a branded hotel, detailed planning and space requirements are transmitted through a comprehensive design guide, developed by the hotel brand, that steers the overall design work and may be adapted for the specific needs of a given hotel project. For branded hotels, detailed space allocation information can be issued to the development and design team early in the process and updated as required.

Exhibit 2   Guestroom Space Requirements per Type of Lodging Property

Lodging Type	Service Level	Proportion of Space Allocated to Guestroom Areas*
Economy	Limited service	90–95%
Mid-Price (no F&B)	Limited service	85–90%
Mid-Price w/F&B	Full service	75–85%
Upscale Transient	Full service	70–75%
Conference Center	Full-service	55–65%
Convention	Full service	60–65%
Luxury Transient	Full service	60–65%
Resort	Full service	<65%

* Includes guestroom corridors, stairs, elevators, and storage areas on guestroom floors.

Exhibit 3   Representative Hotel Space Allocation for Guestrooms

	Economy	Upscale Limited-Service	Upscale Full-Service	Convention	Resort
Number of Keys*	60	100	200	600	200
Key Size	250	325	350	350	450
Gross Guestroom Area per Key**	300	425	475	490	630
Total Guestroom Area	18,000	42,500	95,000	285,000	126,000
Typical % of Hotel Dedicated to Guestrooms	90%	75%	70%	60%	65%
Total Hotel Area	20,000	56,000	136,000	475,000	194,000
Total Hotel Area per Key***	330	560	680	790	970

*   Rentable units (guestrooms, suites)

**   Includes an allowance for guestroom corridors, stairs, elevators, linen closets, and other supporting spaces and walls on guestroom floors

*** Determined by dividing total keys by total hotel area (which includes public spaces and back-of-the-house areas not included in the "gross guestroom area per key" calculation)

Operational Criteria

In addition to a space allocation program, the complete hotel development program requires a second major element: a thorough description of the future property's operations, including food and beverage concepts, front office procedures, housekeeping systems, typical guest amenities, and so forth. Among the most challenging aspects of hotel design is the need to develop a plan that accommodates several potential guest markets as well as the operational requirements of the hotel, the identity and strategic initiatives of the hotel brand, and the specific needs of the proposed project's site and other development issues. As might be expected, these requirements often conflict and the cost of providing for every need is likely to be prohibitive. Experienced developers work closely with the brand and the operating company to ensure that the eventual project meets as many needs as possible within the limitations of the project budget, which requires that there be good communication among all parties from the very beginning of the development process.

The labor-intensive nature of the hotel industry forces managers to establish creative new procedures and systems to reduce or streamline repetitive tasks while maintaining an appropriate level of service for the hotel's price point. Major brands and management groups such as Starwood and Hyatt are centralizing many services to increase efficiency. Reservations, revenue management, and/or the purchasing function for several hotels in one region might be handled at one location rather than duplicated at each property; urban properties are outsourcing many traditional hotel departments or eliminating them altogether.

The following list identifies some of the operational decisions affecting the proposed hotel's design and layout that the development team must make as early in the design process as possible:

- *Front desk:* Determine which functions will be performed by staff versus by technology; select information systems and interfaces; and determine the need for guest services, safety deposit areas, and/or concierge services.

- *Luggage handling:* Decide how luggage will be moved to and from guest-rooms and by whom, estimate the volume of stored luggage during typical operations, and plan a location for luggage storage.

- *Receiving and storage:* Determine responsibilities for purchasing, receiving, and issuing food and other goods, and identify the frequency with which goods will be delivered and/or removed from the property. The desired handling of temperature-sensitive goods needs to be considered at this time.

- *Trash and garbage:* Study waste-holding and collection alternatives; the need for room refrigeration or other special handling; and requirements for composting, reuse, and material recycling.

- *Housekeeping:* Consider which services (e.g., evening turn-down, daily linen replacement) are expected by customers, as well as anticipated bedding programs.

- *Administration:* Identify which administrative functions will be performed on-site and which will require direct access from the hotel's public spaces.

- *Food and beverage:* Establish concepts for each food and beverage outlet and for room service, including hours of operation and production needs. Identify unique facility requirements such as open kitchens, in-house baking or other specialty food production, and on-site kitchen gardens or apiaries.

The food and beverage program is one of the most complex operational components of a full-service hotel. Many hotel operators create a detailed description of each outlet early in the design process, not only establishing its theme and capacity but specifying service methods, tabletop design, special equipment requirements, and even interior finishes. This level of detail is of great assistance in sizing storage and warewashing areas, and placing key engineering features such as grease traps and ventilation ductwork. (Later in the chapter, these issues are described in more detail in the discussion of planning food and beverage outlets.)

Construction and Engineering Criteria

In addition to estimating and refining space requirements and defining the operational aspects of the proposed hotel, the development team needs to establish preliminary standards for construction and engineering systems. While these might not be so prescriptive as to dictate, say, a steel frame versus a reinforced concrete structural system, the team should establish outline specifications that identify such construction details as the primary exterior materials, type of window glass, and quality of interior finishes.

All hotels are subject to a wide variety of regulations, from zoning codes to health standards to sign ordinances. Once the proposed hotel meets the site's zoning requirements regulating use, height, setbacks, and total size of the building, the detailed design must comply with local building and fire codes. The intent of these codes is to protect the public against faulty design or construction by ensuring that a building will resist fire and other emergencies and protect the occupants until they can exit safely from the premises. Local health codes also may play a role in early design decisions.

The development team should also confirm compliance with the Americans with Disabilities Act (ADA). Specifically, developers should obtain copies of the most recent ADA requirements and ensure the design and contracting teams are referring to current regulations. Common ADA errors that can be costly to remedy can be identified and eliminated if the development team is conscientious about considering ADA requirements early in the design process. Exhibit 4 lists some of the common ADA-related mistakes that hotel owners, designers, and builders can avoid through good initial planning.

The development team also needs to establish engineering standards, in part to meet building and other code requirements but also to establish the desired level of quality in the interior environment. Engineering criteria must be established for heating, air conditioning, ventilation, water, power, lighting, fire protection, and information technology and communications systems, all of which can lead to immense detail. The team might dictate exact requirements for each guestroom and guest bathroom, for instance, including lighting levels, water flow, bathroom ventilation, guestroom heating and air conditioning, in-room entertainment, wireless and other data networks, smoke detectors, and fire alarms. More detail early in the development process helps the team better define quality levels, establish the project budget, identify which specialists will be needed, and ensure that critical elements aren't forgotten or ignored. Exhibit 5 lists some of the many building systems that may be found in a hotel.

The Project Budget

Among the most important elements of the pre-design phase is establishing a project budget. Too often, grossly inaccurate budgets are established by inexperienced or ill-informed developers and the inadequacy of the cost estimates only becomes apparent when the design is refined or when prospective contractors submit construction bids. Then, the owner or developer and the hotel operating company have to make difficult decisions on which features to eliminate or defer, or they may attempt to seek new equity financing, thereby lowering their share of building ownership.

It is a mistake to rely wholly on a generic cost per room or cost per square foot estimate for the construction budget. It is only when the hotel design is fully established and the building materials, systems, and level of detail are clearly defined that the actual project costs can be accurately estimated. A preliminary budget

Exhibit 4   Key ADA Accessibility Planning Requirements for Lodging Properties

Guestrooms

- Guestroom and guest bathroom doors must have a clear opening width of at least thirty-two inches (eighty centimeters).

- Accessible guestrooms and suites should be dispersed among the various classes of rooms available at a property and provide people with a variety of disabilities the same range of amenities available to others.

- In properties with fifty or more sleeping rooms, a proportion of guest bathrooms must be provided with a roll-in shower.

- ADA-compliant guestrooms and suites, including an additional number of rooms specifically for individuals who have hearing impairments, should be equipped with visual alarms and other visual notification devices.

Operating Hardware

- Hardware on accessible doors and on faucets, fixed lamps, drapery controls, and heating and air conditioning controls must conform to ADA standards for ease of use by those with grasping or mobility impairments.

Signage

- For permanent rooms and spaces, identification signage must be mounted at a convenient height and supplemented with raised lettering and braille identification.

Accessible Routes

- All spaces of public accommodation, including lobbies, food and beverage outlets, meeting spaces, and recreational areas (including pools) must have wheelchair accessibility.

- An elevator is necessary if the hotel has more than two floors or if there are no guest accommodations on the ground floor.

- There should be no protuberant or low-hanging obstacles along corridors or other walkways where the public is expected to pass.

Source: *"Common ADA Problems at Newly Constructed Lodging Facilities,"* www.usdoj.gov/crt/ada/comhotel.htm.

must include contingency funds (typically 5 to 10 percent of the total development budget), consider inflation, and accurately reflect the final quality standard for the hotel. The developer needs to realize that the construction cost is only about 60 to 65 percent of the total project budget and does not include the costs of furniture, fixtures, and equipment (FF&E), professional fees, financing, and pre-opening expenses, among other development costs (see Exhibit 6).

Because total hotel project costs vary tremendously, from as little as $70,000 per guestroom to $500,000 per guestroom and beyond, strict budget control throughout the entire process is critical. Budgeting is made more difficult by the common practice in hotel work of using separate architectural and interior design

Exhibit 5   Typical Hotel Building Systems

HVAC
- Heating
- Ventilation
- Air conditioning
- Exhaust

Electrical
- Power
- Light
- Emergency power and lighting
- Communications cabling
- Data and network cabling, including Wi-Fi
- Entertainment system cabling
- Security systems
- Audiovisual and public address systems
- Site lighting

Vertical Transportation
- Elevators
- Escalators

Plumbing
- Water supply
- Domestic cold and hot water
- Sanitary waste and vent piping
- Special waste piping (grease traps, etc.)
- Storm water drainage
- Site drainage
- Lawn irrigation system

Fire Protection
- Portable fire extinguishers
- Smoke detectors
- Fire alarm system
- Standpipe/site hydrant system
- Sprinklers
- Fire pumps

Special Systems
- Energy management
- Co-generation
- On-site power generation (solar, wind, or other)

Source: International Facilities Management Association, www.ifma.org.

firms—in some cases, multiple firms of each type may work on the same large project. Therefore, the developer must define precisely the design and budget responsibilities of each member of the team—for example, differentiating costs between the general construction budget and the FF&E budget.

As the project moves through the design phases, the developer modifies the allocation of the contingency funds. Early in the process at least 10 percent should be added to estimates to allow for later changes or refinement. (For projects that involve upgrading or adapting an old building, a 15 percent contingency allocation is not unreasonable.) By the time construction begins, the contingency may be reduced to as little as 5 percent, but monies still need to be reserved to deal with unforeseen expenses. Some construction managers like to separate the contingency into specific accounts so that FF&E or legal expenses, for example, maintain their own cushion against cost overruns.

The development budget also should include a "reserve against operating shortfall" to offset operating losses during the hotel's first one or two years, before revenues are sufficient to meet day-to-day expenses and cover debt.

Exhibit 6 Typical Budget Allocations for Hotel Development Projects

Budget Category	Proportion of Budget
Land (varies greatly by location)	2–15%
General construction (includes building and site work)	60–65%
Furniture, fixtures, and equipment (FF&E)	15–18%
Development costs, including:	8–12%

Architectural/engineering fees
    Design consultant fees (interiors, kitchens, lighting, etc.)
    Purchasing fees
    Financing
    Developer's fee
    Insurance during construction
    Real estate taxes
    Legal, permits, surveys, etc.	

Interest during construction	4–8%
Pre-opening expense and working capital	4–8%
Reserve against operating shortfall	2–4%

The Preliminary Schedule

The owner or developer must prepare a preliminary schedule for the development and design phases of the project and establish a target date for the hotel's opening. The schedule should identify the myriad pre-design and design tasks, identify the members of the development team who are responsible for each one, and set realistic completion dates.

Hotel projects vary greatly in their duration. Factors that influence the schedule include the existing conditions on the site, the complexity of the design, the ease and speed with which permits and inspections can be obtained, and the status of project financing. Perhaps the key factor necessary for staying on schedule is good advance planning by skilled and experienced managers who understand and have a background with hotel projects. A strong and open relationship with the hotel brand and operator also helps ensure that the right decisions are made in a timely fashion.

Many steps during the development process occur simultaneously. For example, the site owner may be negotiating the final hotel management contract or pursuing various financing alternatives at the same time that the developer is selecting the design consultants and the architect is developing the initial building designs. Usually, the owner's legal and financial responsibilities continue through the design and construction phases.

The design phases in a hotel project are sequential and relatively straightforward. The architect typically works through three phases: schematic design, in which alternative plans are studied and a design direction is established for the hotel, along with a preliminary budget; design development, in which the plan is firmly set, materials and finishes are selected, interior design and engineering systems are coordinated, and a more detailed construction budget is outlined; and construction or contract documents, in which the complete architectural and engineering drawings and specifications are prepared for bidding and construction. The engineers and all other design professionals on the project follow the same sequence, although typically slightly later than the architect, because they must base their work on the architect's drawings. At the end of each design phase, the owner should approve the architect's and other consultants' drawings and authorize the team to continue with the next stage.

The Planning and Design Process

Once the hotel design team is assembled, among the first architectural tasks is to develop an initial conceptual design for the hotel. In fact, architects often are called upon to prepare a schematic design even before the developer has a hotel brand or operator on board, in part to test the site capacity, generate preliminary construction estimates, and add credibility to a lender's package. While these conceptual studies may occur early in the project schedule, they do make and follow some preliminary assumptions about the number of guestrooms, amount of food and beverage and function space, relative emphasis of such architectural spaces as the lobby, and general massing of the building. As noted earlier, it is vital to the eventual success of the project that hotel operators be brought onto the project team as early as possible and certainly before the project proceeds to the design development phase.

Site Planning

During the one or two months that might be devoted to the initial concept, the architect has to balance preliminary program and operational requirements with a number of site-related and construction issues. The first step is to analyze the site and its constraints and opportunities. The architect is responsible for coordinating the site planning with engineering consultants, who deal with such issues as site drainage and exterior lighting, and the interior designer and/or landscape architect, who may select paving materials and outdoor furnishings.

The architect should consider how guests arrive at the site and how they might best approach the building, especially at suburban and resort hotels where the building is not crowded by nearby structures. Even before guests enter the lobby or are greeted by staff, they will have formed an impression of the hotel based on their approach and arrival. Are the grounds landscaped? Does adequate and convenient parking exist? What types and numbers of vehicles must be accommodated? Is there clear signage? Is the building illuminated at night? Does the entrance canopy provide sufficient shelter?

The architect should explore different ways to organize the hotel spaces. Should the hotel be a high-rise structure or a series of low-rise wings? Should the building enclose a public entry plaza or a private garden courtyard? While a flat, treeless **greenfield site** may offer certain advantages—mostly through reductions in construction costs—the guest experience may be enhanced when the architect is challenged to creatively design a hotel on a more difficult site.

Thus, the architectural team needs to investigate and consider the site carefully before it can begin to develop the building's form and organization. The following list identifies some of the ways that site characteristics can influence an architect's task:

- *Visibility and accessibility:* Consider surrounding street patterns, road access, and adjacent buildings (existing and proposed).

- *Surface conditions:* Analyze terrain, vegetation, utilities, existing buildings and roads, drainage patterns, and environmental constraints.

- *Subsurface conditions:* Investigate the water table, bearing capacity of the soil, underground utilities, and environmental hazards.

- *Regulatory restrictions:* Research applicable zoning, parking, building, and other codes.

- *Site character:* Study surface conditions, adjoining uses, and views.

- *Orientation and climate:* Position building and recreational facilities for sun exposure; analyze microclimate and surf conditions (for resorts).

- *Adaptability:* Determine the site's potential for expansion or development for other uses.

Site planning is concurrent with building design: some of it takes place very early in schematic design when the architect is exploring alternative concepts for the hotel and its siting, while other aspects of the site plan occur much later when the final construction documents are produced. For urban hotels and branded hotel projects on small, simple sites, the architect may complete these planning and design tasks with a minimum of help from consultants, perhaps hiring only a local nursery to help select proper plantings for the area. But for more complex projects, the design team may include land planners who assist the architect with early site analyses and the development of a comprehensive master plan; landscape architects; traffic or transportation specialists; golf course architects; mountain resort planners; and other specialists.

Architects designing a large hotel may develop a number of different entrances to help separate overnight guests from visitors to meeting spaces or recreational facilities, reduce the amount of unnecessary traffic through the building, and establish a distinct identity for a restaurant or spa. Additional entrances, however, may create additional security concerns. Designers should assess the relative need for the following public entrances (in addition to the necessary back-of-the-house entrances for service vehicles and employees):

- Main hotel guest entrance

- Meeting space/banqueting entrance

- Restaurant/bar entrance

- Entrances to special facilities such as a spa or casino

- Retail entrance

- Tour bus/airport bus drop-off entrance

- Condominium entrance

Among the most prominent entry features in a hotel is the **porte cochère**, the entry canopy designed to protect guests from inclement weather and provide visual emphasis to the entrance. The architect's design for the porte cochère should incorporate lighting and signage and be of sufficient height for buses and emergency vehicles. The driveway beneath the porte cochère must be at least two lanes wide, preferably three lanes or more, to facilitate peak numbers of arriving and departing guests. (Large resorts such as casino hotels may have six to eight lanes for vehicles at their main entrances.) The sidewalk must be wide enough to accommodate groups waiting for taxis or tour buses and allow for the easy loading and unloading of large quantities of baggage.

Parking areas, including the approach, driveways, sidewalks, receiving area, and emergency access, are perhaps the most important entry features for many limited-service lodging properties and perhaps for full-service hotels in suburban areas. Parking requirements usually are specified in the local zoning ordinance and may specify more than one parking space per guestroom, especially in small cities and suburban locations. In major urban areas, where a large number of guests will arrive by cab, the final parking agreement may be negotiated between the developer and the city and may not even be part of the design itself but rather outsourced to a nearby garage. Providing sufficient parking is critical if a hotel intends to attract food and beverage or meetings business, so the developer must carefully analyze and balance the need for parking against its cost.

All of the major hotel "brand families" continue to develop new concepts and brands, each with one or more prototype designs. Usually there will be a typical site plan for a given brand, illustrating requirements for landscaping, parking, and service access. In developing a recent prototype for Sheraton, for example, the Starwood development team focused the site plan largely on the arrival sequence. Sheraton brand executives insisted that arriving guests not drive through a parking area to reach the front door. The design solution, then, included signage and landscaping that guided customers to the porte cochère and hotel entrance, and placed all of the parking on the other side of the hotel and to the rear of the assumed entrance. Of course, each project will have a somewhat different site plan, but the design criteria should be clear and key expectations established.

Hotel Planning

Once the influence of the site on the building program is understood, the architect can begin to design the hotel in much greater detail. Architects initially must resolve such conceptual design issues as building height, massing, exterior materials, location of entrances, and façade details, while at the same time accommodating structural and engineering systems, satisfying the building codes, and working with typically stringent budgets. Sometimes these plans are influenced primarily by the context: a twenty-story mirrored glass tower fits into a downtown location both physically and economically, while a cluster of villas and low-rise public space

The Peninsula Hotel, New York City. The architects for the luxury Peninsula Hotel used lighting to emphasize the scale and grandeur of the historic façade and added an understated porte cochère to shelter arriving guests from rain and snow. (Courtesy of Brennan Beer Gorman Architects)

and administrative structures would be more appropriate for a remote Caribbean island. The architect must create a building concept and organize the hotel's functions so that they meet the owner's objectives, the operator's functional requirements, and the future guests' expectations. The following sections discuss the variety of planning and design principles that help the design team to meet these demands, beginning with guestrooms and suites, then continuing with public and back-of-the-house areas.

Guestrooms and Suites

The guestroom has a tremendous influence on the guest's experience while at the hotel, but, because of the popularity of selecting a hotel based on reviews and images posted online, a guestroom's design and appearance are also key components in a guest's purchase decision. A well-planned and well-executed guestroom design adds value for guests and may even allow the hotel to increase its rates. But one of the difficulties is that any feature added to a guestroom must be duplicated many times: a decorative valence added to the drapery treatment must be added in every room, a marble vanity counter for the guest bath appears in every guestroom bathroom, a more expensive nightstand or bedside lamp appears in every guestroom, and so forth. While each item may add less than $100 to the development cost of a single guestroom, this cost soon becomes many thousands of dollars as the item is added to all the guestrooms. This fact, coupled with the costs of cleaning and maintaining each guestroom on a regular basis, means that good design must consider cost and value to the hotel owner and operator as well as aesthetics and functionality for the guest.

Effective suite design requires creating distinct zones of activity while retaining a distinctive character across the entire space. Created in partnership with Bentley Motors, this luxury suite—the Bentley Suite in the St. Regis New York in New York City—uses a floor covering to delineate the sitting area from other parts of the room, and marries modern and traditional elements by harnessing simple shapes and bold, contrasting finishes. This suite also reflects an emerging trend in hotel development: the branding of high-end guestrooms by prominent consumer brands. Courtesy of WATG.

To maximize the efficiency and revenue-generating potential of the guestroom portion of a hotel, a major planning goal should be to keep corridors, elevators and stairs, and service areas on guestroom floors to the minimum necessary to meet building and safety code requirements and support the desired guest experience. Guestroom size also must offer a balance between market expectations, brand standards, and the economics of the development project.

Guestroom Floor Planning. The planning requirements for the guestroom floors are relatively few: there must be a designated number of guestrooms or suites, guest and service elevators should be conveniently located, exit stairways must meet building codes, adequate linen storage and vending areas should be provided, and small electrical and data equipment closets are usually necessary. But the way all of these components are arranged can easily affect the total floor area by as much as 15 percent. Therefore, skillful planning can make a substantial impact on the efficiency of the guestroom areas. For example, essentially the same 250-room hotel could vary by 10,000 to 15,000 gross square feet (930 to 1,359 square meters) due entirely to the level of planning efficiency for the guestroom floors; the additional floor area can translate into $1 to $2 million in additional project costs, depending on the location and quality level of the hotel. The money saved in construction due to efficient planning of the guestroom floors may be enough to make a marginal project profitable; or those dollars might be diverted to pay for larger guestrooms or better-quality furnishings in the rooms or elsewhere in the hotel. The hotel developer and management group should insist that the architect refine and modify the guestroom floor design until it meets a sufficiently high standard for efficiency and effectiveness.

Common hotel guestroom floor configurations include the **double-loaded slab**, where rooms are laid out on both sides of a central corridor; the **tower**, in which rooms are grouped around a central vertical core; and the **atrium**, which features rooms off a single-loaded corridor encircling a multi-story lobby space (see Exhibit 7). In general, the double-loaded slab is the most efficient floor design, with about 70 percent of the gross floor area devoted to guestrooms; the amount of saleable space drops to 65 and 60 percent, respectively, in the tower and atrium configurations. In general, the more guestrooms there are on a given floor, the greater that floor's efficiency will be.

In addition to other planning considerations, the architect must recognize a number of programmatic requirements established by the brand or the operating company. These include, for example, the room mix, which is the number of rooms of each type (king, double queen or **double-double**, multi-**bay** suites, etc.), the number of connecting rooms, guest bathroom standards, and necessary features and amenities to meet brand standards. Room mix is often a function of the particular market for the project and may vary from what the brand or operator might offer in a different location, but the layout of the rooms themselves and the provision of particular elements of the guestroom floor design are generally dictated or at least carefully controlled by the brand.

Guestroom Layout. The layout of hotel guestrooms is intertwined with decisions that the architect makes during schematic design when he or she determines the dimensions of the typical guestroom, non-typical room shapes to make best use

Exhibit 7   Guestroom Floor Configurations

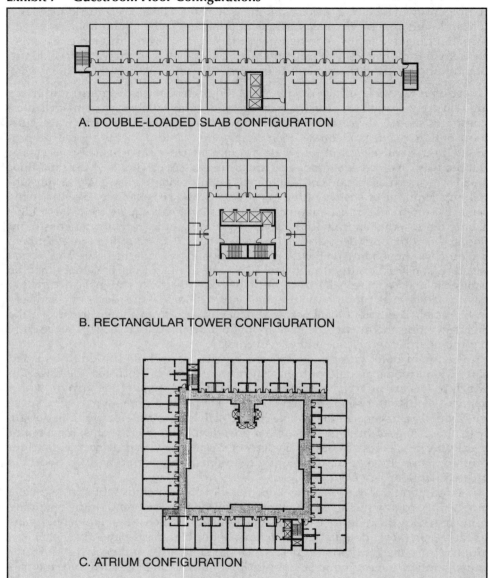

Each hotel project is designed to meet the specific requirements of its market and the site, but there are typical floor configurations that are efficient for hotel use. The double-loaded slab (A) is the most efficient use of space for a hotel floor; ideally the elevators should be as close to the middle of the floor as possible. Tower configurations (such as B) are more suitable for small urban sites; while less efficient in terms of floor use, they are effective because they centralize all of the support functions. Atrium plans (C) are the least efficient, with single-loaded corridors overlooking the lobby.

of corners or space behind elevators or fire stairs, and the design of the guest-room bathrooms. These decisions, along with the target room mix, provide the project's interior designer with the framework within which to design the various guestrooms and suites. This task includes designing the furniture layouts, select-ing interior finishes for the floor and walls, choosing fabrics and colors, speci-fying lighting, and so forth. For many hotel brands, this work has already been done by the brand at corporate headquarters: furniture, fixtures, and equipment (FF&E) layout and specifications will be part of the technical services provided to the developer or owner as part of the brand's fees. Higher-end hotel brands tend to be less prescriptive in terms of guestroom layout and material choices but will still be actively involved in ensuring that the interior designer's work conforms to the brand's overall strategy and positioning.

Room designers need to understand the hotel's typical guests and their needs, establish and respect a furnishings budget, and create a design concept that gives the guestrooms a distinctive character, yet one that is consistent with the hotel's public areas. One approach is to consider breaking the guestroom into distinctive areas or "zones," accommodating such overlapping functions as sleeping, work-ing, lounging, dressing, and hygiene (see Exhibit 8).

Exhibit 8   Guestroom Zoning

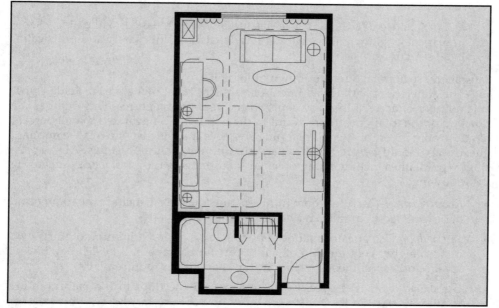

Good planning divides the guestroom into five "zones": a space for sleeping that has a view of the flat screen TV; a lounging or sitting area that likewise can view the TV; a working area with adequate space for using a laptop as well as spreading out papers; a dressing area with access to a full-length mirror and storage for both folding and hang-ing clothes; and the bathing area with a sink, ample counter space, a discreetly located toilet, and a shower stall or tub/shower combination.

Furnishing choices within each zone should meet a number of basic design criteria:

- *Beds:* Determine the exact room mix for the hotel; provide adequate spacing around the bed for easy access for guests and hotel staff; include bedside tables with flexible lighting and ample electrical outlets; consider TV viewing angle.

- *Work area:* Provide some form of desk or table space; consider chair comfort and adjustability; provide adequate task lighting and multiple outlets at desk height; consider TV viewing angle; provide ports for connecting to entertainment systems and building networks.

- *Lounge area:* Provide soft seating of some type; consider comfort, lighting, electrical outlet access, TV viewing angle, and (where appropriate) adequate space for foldout sofa and/or a minibar.

- *Clothes storage/dressing area:* Determine requirements for drawer space, the size of the closet, and luggage storage needs; provide full-length mirror and adequate lighting; consider proximity to the bathroom.

- *Bathroom:* Select bathroom fixtures and accessories; consider lighting, outlets, amenity placement and storage, counter space, towel hooks, ventilation, and resilient finishes.

- *Decor:* Choose FF&E that expresses the intended message while at the same time meets maintenance and budgetary goals; consider safety and practicality in all selections.

Sample guestroom layouts are shown in Exhibit 9.

The Americans with Disabilities Act requires hotel owners to provide a specific number of accessible guestrooms with a variety of features. This number is a function of the total guestroom count in the hotel, but is never less than 2 percent of guestroom inventory. Good planning suggests that at least one ADA-compliant guestroom should be provided in each room type, including suites. ADA accessibility guidelines include many detailed requirements for guestrooms, including the following:

- *Room signage:* Corridor room numbers must be raised, include the room number expressed in braille, and be precisely located.

- *Entry door:* The guestroom door opening must offer a minimum of thirty-two inches (eighty centimeters) of width for the passage of wheelchairs, have a lever handle, and meet specific clearance and other requirements.

- *Guest bathroom:* The access requirements for the door to the bathroom are similar to those for the guestroom entry door. There are also requirements for clearance around the bathroom fixtures, grab bars at the tub or shower, and other specifics.

- *Guestroom interior:* Guestrooms must meet ADA requirements for ease of movement through the room and heights of switches and thermostats, closet rods, and other features.

Exhibit 9   Sample Guestroom Layouts

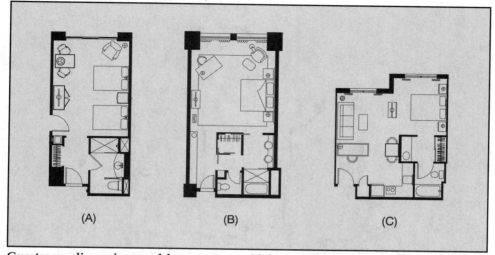

(A)   (B)   (C)

Guestroom dimensions and layouts vary widely among hotels, depending on market needs and real estate costs. A typical guestroom in a convention hotel (A) might feature two full-size beds and a connecting door, with a stall shower rather than a bathtub to reflect the preferences of most business travelers. Luxury hotels (B) tend to have wider guestrooms that offer abundant space and the potential for more variety in FF&E placement. The bathrooms in these hotels are much larger than in other hotel types and often have a compartmentalized toilet. Extended-stay guestrooms (C) are more like miniature apartments with a kitchenette, a separate small table for dining, and often a sink and vanity that is outside of the toilet and bath.

- *Hearing-impaired room:* A certain number of guestrooms must have text displays on entertainment and communication devices, visual alarms, and related features.

Suite Layout. There is no standard definition or layout for a hotel suite, but, generally speaking, a hotel suite refers to a guestroom in which the sleeping space is distinctly separated from the remainder of the room (see Exhibit 10). Through the mid-twentieth century, hotel suites traditionally made up a relatively large part of urban hotels and frequently were occupied by permanent residents, a model we still see in the condo-hotel mixed-use developments that are popular in many markets. Today, suites are popular inclusions in almost all hotel types. Large hotels provide a hierarchy of suites, from those with a simple living room and an adjacent sleeping alcove, to grand suites with an oversized living room and as many as four or more adjoining rooms, including a dining or conference room and several bedrooms. Presidential or other deluxe suites can fill most of a floor; at the ARIA Resort in Las Vegas, the largest Sky Villa suite is much larger than most homes at 7,000 gross square feet (650 square meters) spread over two top floors of the building. Suites are popular with business travelers and traveling families, as well as

Exhibit 10   Sample Suite Layout

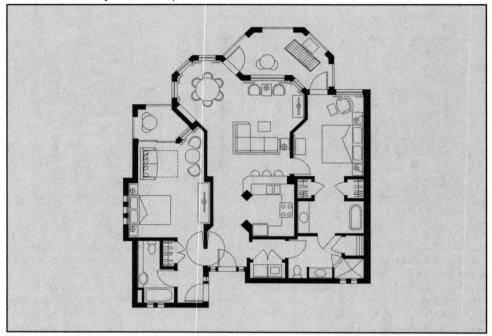

Suite quantities and configurations are driven by the hotel's market. In this suite lay-out, there are two rentable units or "keys": this room may be sold to a single party, or the smaller guestroom on the left may be sold individually. This kind of flexibility adds significant value to the hotel asset. This particular suite represents a vacation own-ership unit, offering condo-like amenities such as a full kitchen and a washer/dryer. Note the generous closet space, which is important for properties with a relatively long length of stay.

with hotel operators who wish to reward loyal guests with upgraded rooms when possible.

The number and mix of suites in a hotel should be driven by the hotel's market(s). In recent years, the demand for suites has increased in many hotel types—particularly in the resort segment—so it is not unusual for new hotels to have well over ten percent of their rental accommodations designated as suites. Good hotel planners strive to intersperse suites with typical guestrooms that can be sold as connecting rooms to offer greater flexibility.

In most urban hotels, the suites are placed on the upper floors. Sometimes suites are stacked vertically in the same location on each floor, especially where they take advantage of an unusual architectural configuration. Many hotel brands have established premium-priced "club floors" with upgraded suites and guest-rooms, and such additional features as express check-in; concierge services; lounge and conference areas; and complimentary breakfast, tea, and/or cocktails. While in smaller properties the lounges on club floors may be no larger than about 1,000 square feet (93 square meters), in luxury and convention hotels they may be two or three times bigger. Typically, a club floor lounge requires a small pantry for food preparation, associated storage, and data and phone systems to connect the staff with other hotel areas.

Suite design criteria shares much with typical guestrooms: there must be zones for specific guest activities and functions, and each zone must convey part of a consistent concept or design idea. Suites tend to have more amenities than guestrooms and, because of the larger floor space, there are more challenges in dividing a suite into comfortable and useful sub-areas. While certainly full-height partitions can be used for this purpose, part of the appeal of a suite is the sense of spaciousness it affords, particularly at the entry when the guest sees the space for the first time. Floor finish changes, dropped ceilings, screens and other semi-opaque room dividers, or even treated glass can help to break up the space visually while retaining the oversized appearance that suite guests value.

In addition to hotels that have a mixture of guestrooms and suites within them, there are hotels whose guest accommodations consist entirely of suites. Beginning in the mid-1970s such chains as Guest Quarters and Granada Royale recognized the opportunity to provide specialized suite hotels for the extended-stay market and created the first all-suite hotels for business travelers. Later, in the early 1980s, Holiday Inn established its Embassy Suites brand; other major management companies soon followed with their own suite hotel brands. Although there are many variations, the typical extended-stay suite unit is between 400 and 500 square feet (37–46 square meters), or about 30–40 percent larger than a typical hotel guestroom, and consists of a separate bedroom and living room, guest bathroom, and wet bar or kitchenette. Some of these extended-stay suites are "studio" suites that don't have a distinct separation between the sleeping area and the other parts of the room and may actually not be substantially larger than a typical hotel guestroom, but still offer most of the amenities of a more traditional suite layout.

There are two common models for suites in all-suite properties, with dozens of variations for each. One is the narrow "front-to-back" or "**shotgun**" arrangement in which the living room faces an atrium or outside corridor, the bathroom is in the middle, and the bedroom is in the rear, with windows to the outside. The other model, the "**side-by-side**" configuration, is organized along a double-loaded corridor and consists of two smaller rooms parallel to each other, each with windows to the outside. The hotel brand and architect have a number of choices for the design of the bathroom and for the connection between the living and sleeping areas: sliding panels, pocket doors, glazed French doors, or just simple partitions with a standard door may be used.

The Lobby

The lobby is the most prominent public space in most hotels. In addition to establishing the image of the hotel, the lobby serves many obvious functional requirements: it provides a space for welcoming and processing arriving guests; it provides social space for hotel guests and, in some urban hotels, for the general public; and it helps orient and direct users of the hotel's function spaces, restaurants, bars, and other facilities. One of the key planning objectives for hotel architects is to cluster the public facilities around the lobby, ensuring that hotel guests and others can find the various facilities with a minimum of difficulty. The lobby also should function as a control point, with the staff visually overseeing access to guestroom elevators.

The development team must establish criteria for the planning and design of the lobby based on the hotel's concept and the guest markets it will attract. These criteria might include the following:

- *Circulation:* Provide clear paths to the front desk, elevators, food and beverage outlets, function space, etc.

- *Front desk:* Make the front desk visible to entering guests. It should overlook the elevators, have sufficient space for check-in/check-out lines, and have direct access to the front office. Even if there are kiosk or mobile applications for the check-in function, some form of front desk is still needed for addressing guest requests and providing other guest support.

- *Luggage:* Provide areas for bellpersons, luggage storage, and other locked storage.

- *Seating:* Provide seating near the front desk and entrance, with more private seating nearby, and determine the need for a lobby lounge. Seating should vary in type and functionality: soft seating, communal tables for co-working, and perhaps even casual-dining seating may be needed.

- *Support functions:* Conveniently locate retail outlets, the concierge desk, public restrooms, coatrooms, directory screens, tour desks, and other supporting functions.

- *Decor:* Establish the hotel's image with millwork, furnishings, artwork, lighting, signage, and so forth that are appropriate to the locale, the brand, and the hotel's price point. Some kind of focal point to serve as an orienting device is often a good choice, particularly for large properties.

As they are areas serving the public, lobbies and related spaces such as parking areas and the hotel's entrance need to meet ADA accessibility requirements.

Food and Beverage Outlets

Hotel food and beverage service varies greatly based on the market, the brand of the hotel, and the philosophy of the hotel's management and ownership. While pretty much all full-service hotels have some kind of restaurant offering, the traditional hotel-operated three-meal dining room is now only one of many possible options. Many urban hotels outsource one or more of their restaurants to a third-party operator, while limited-service hotels are including fast-casual food operations as part of a lively lobby "living room." Large resorts and casino hotels may have dozens of food and beverage outlets, whereas boutique hotels may have one or even none. An early development decision for any hotel should be how many and what types of food and beverage outlets will be appropriate for the project, and who will operate them.

The design of hotel food and beverage outlets depends on these key decisions. The initial feasibility study, which investigates the demand and supply characteristics of the market and projects revenues and expenses, is the basis for recommending the number and capacities of food and beverage outlets for the proposed hotel. However, it is necessary for the development team to confirm these recommendations and establish concepts for the food and beverage outlets. Hotel brands will have a corporate-level team that will translate operational needs into design requirements and can support the architect and other designers as they work through space planning, layout, and FF&E selections. Third-party restaurant operators may also offer this service to the development team. There are also specialty consultants whose expertise in restaurant concept development, interior design, and kitchen planning are all important to the smooth incorporation of the food and beverage outlets into the hotel's architectural and engineering plans.

Because they face such severe outside competition, hotel restaurants and lounges create the greatest operational and design challenges. Whatever the concept, the food and beverage outlets must incorporate some generally accepted design criteria:

Hotel restaurants are challenging to design because they need to be attractive and effective during all three meal periods (breakfast, lunch, and dinner). This luxury buffet restaurant uses the space's soaring columns to good effect, creating more intimate dining areas within a very large room. The designers have also used banquettes to break up the main dining area, making the space more attractive to guests and more productive for the operator. The Grand Brasserie, Waldorf Astoria Shanghai on the Bund, Shanghai; courtesy of Hilton Worldwide.

- *Location:* Position the hotel's main three-meal restaurant convenient to the lobby. Consider locating any specialty restaurants with direct exterior access to capture patrons from the street as well as in-house. Lounges should be easily seen and/or accessed from the lobby.

- *Service:* Any outlet that serves food should have direct access to some form of kitchen or pantry, and ideally all outlets should have easy access to a central main production kitchen. This access can be via vertical circulation but should be as direct as possible.

- *Flexibility:* Design large restaurants and bars so that sections can be closed during slow periods. Consider designs that allow the scope of food and beverage service to change as volume varies across meal periods, days of the week, or seasons.

- *Layout:* Provide a desk for the host, service stations, and a flexible mix of tables to accommodate different party sizes. Minimize or eliminate floor-level changes to better accommodate disabled guests and simplify service.

- *Support areas:* Place public restrooms, coatrooms, and telephones nearby.

Hotel Restaurants. The staid traditional dining room of yesteryear is a rarity in today's hotels. Hotel restaurants may be full- or limited-service, but generally there should be at least one dining option for every meal period (breakfast, lunch, dinner). Flexibility in the design is important to allow the same space to be suitable for breakfast, lunch, and dinner in hotels that offer a single three-meal restaurant option. To speed service and keep labor costs down, many hotels choose to operate buffet service in these spaces during breakfast and possibly lunch, while others have been experimenting with multiple-concept food halls or extensive self-service facilities. The New York Hilton Midtown made headlines by adding a 24/7 "grab and go" food and beverage outlet with staffed stations for salads, sandwiches, and pizza, as well as a barista for specialty coffees and an extensive bank of pre-prepared items that can be eaten on-the-go or taken back to the guestroom. In addition to a high-quality "three-meal restaurant," luxury hotels will often have one or more signature restaurants—often operated by a well-known chef—that may have their own entrances off the street. Because of their orientation toward the group market segment, convention hotels may have large, convivial casual restaurants that emphasize a particular cuisine or beverage type.

Restaurants tend to require updating or even full conceptual overhauls much more frequently than most other spaces in a hotel, so good designers take care to ensure that the budget for the hotel's food and beverage outlet(s) and the complexity of the design are both reflective of the likelihood that these spaces will probably need to be changed in three to five years.

Hotel Lounges. Using a process similar to that used for restaurants, the brand or operator establishes the bar and lounge program, the architect prepares preliminary plans to accommodate these requirements, and the interior designer develops the concepts more fully and details the desired FF&E. Early important decisions include the scope of the beverage program, the degree to which non-guests are to be targeted as customers, and the overall atmosphere being sought: serene, lively, sophisticated, romantic, or club-like.

The lobby bar grew in popularity in the 1970s as a method of creating activity and excitement in hotels with open atrium space. After the success of lobby bars as revenue generators was proven, developers began to place lobby bars in more traditional hotel lobbies. Open to the lobby space, a lobby bar or lounge typically provides a small service bar, limited food service, occasional entertainment, and soft-seating groupings that can be used flexibly to expand seating in the lobby.

The popularity of mixology has given a rebirth to the classic hotel cocktail bar, albeit with a stronger emphasis on the technique and creativity of the staff. Large hotels may have additional bars that capitalize on exceptional settings, notably those out of doors or at the top of the building to take advantage of a city view. Poolside bars require special planning to ensure they can be adequately stocked and supported. Lounges and bars featuring live entertainment are more typical of the casino and (to a lesser extent) the resort segments of the industry, but live entertainment may also be a feature of urban full-service hotels.

Room Service. Generally, a full-service hotel includes some form of room service. Many operators view room service as a separate food and beverage outlet, while others tack on room service as an amenity provided by the three-meal restaurant using a subset of the same menu. In recent years, some hotel operators have been questioning the sustainability of room service as a business model for many hotel types, particularly in locales where there are many other dining options for late-arriving guests.

Function Space

Perhaps the clearest distinguishing feature among the different types of lodging properties is the size and mix of their **function space**: the ballrooms, smaller meeting and banquet rooms, reception and exhibit spaces, and dedicated conference and board rooms (see Exhibit 11). First introduced in the mid-nineteenth century to accommodate important civic and social gatherings, function space in hotels is now utilized most often for a variety of corporate and association meetings and, in some hotels, social events such as weddings. These types of groups have different needs. Corporate groups require relatively small but high-quality spaces for sales and management meetings, new product introductions, and continuing-education programs for executives. The association market primarily needs extensive exhibition space, facilities for large group meetings, and small rooms for seminars and workshops. The wedding segment seeks unique venues and a great deal of flexibility in offerings. Local organizations use hotel function space for a variety of meetings, banquets, and receptions, while nearby residents use it for special occasions and community events of all types.

Generally, the feasibility study for a new hotel will suggest a mix of function space based on an analysis of the demand for different types of business and social uses. For example, small mid-price properties generally offer a single multi-purpose meeting room, simply decorated and equipped to accommodate a full range of small meetings, civic lunches, bar and bat mitzvahs, wedding receptions,

Exhibit 11   Schematic Plan of Function Space Area

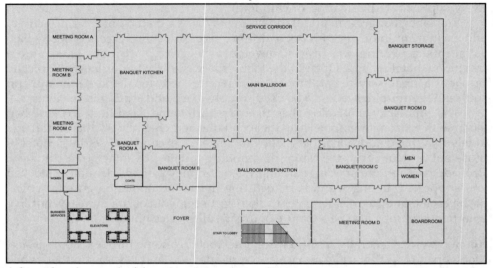

A key planning goal of function spaces is to offer easy and secure access from service areas, particularly for ballrooms and banquet rooms where meals will often be served. In the plan above, notice the compact service corridor that connects many of these spaces together. Many of the function spaces can be subdivided to offer the hotel's sales team greater flexibility in booking events. Guest support areas—restrooms, a coat check area, and a business services area where guests can get copies made, send or receive shipments, and print out documents—are conveniently clustered together near the elevators.

and local product displays. It is only infrequently used to attract groups booking large room blocks.

On the other hand, convention hotels might include a major ballroom for 1,000 to 3,000 people, smaller junior ballrooms, and dozens of smaller multi-purpose meeting and breakout rooms of varying sizes. The ballrooms are designed for major banquets and social functions but include projection, sound, and other technical support systems for presentations of all types. The secondary meeting rooms often are designed to be combined in numerous configurations and to provide a high level of technical services. Throughout the function spaces, key factors are flexible lighting systems, excellent noise dampening to prevent disruption from neighboring events, and very robust high-speed Wi-Fi.

Conference centers are different still. These hotels are designed for much smaller groups (no larger than 200 to 300 people) and feature dedicated single-purpose banquet, meeting, conference, and boardrooms so that each client has specialized rooms to meet particular needs. Conference centers offer such amenities as extensive foyer and gathering areas, twenty-four-hour use of meeting rooms, additional conference services, and, like their convention hotel cousins, high-quality Wi-Fi and presentation systems.

Because of the differences among the many types of lodging properties and the markets they serve, coupled with the highly competitive nature of the meetings business, the design team must review carefully the programming and design criteria for the hotel's proposed function areas. In smaller, less-sophisticated hotels, the function space may only total ten to twenty square feet (.93 to 1.86 square meters) per guestroom. However, in convention hotels and dedicated conference centers it commonly reaches sixty and 100 square feet (5.6 and 9.3 square meters) per room or more, respectively. Considering the additional kitchen and back-of-the-house areas needed to fully support a first-class convention facility, the potential investment in the hotel function space is substantial. Therefore, most successful developers carefully consider the appropriate balance between large and small function rooms, their decor, and equipment. Where a hotel project shares a site with a civic convention center, many of these function spaces are omitted from the program of the hotel itself and instead is incorporated into the civic facility's program. Hotels with access to large outdoor spaces such as terraces, pool decks, and lawns often treat these as potential meeting spaces as well, requiring adequate support and storage facilities to garner maximum utility from every possible rentable space.

Just as restaurants have dedicated consultants to deal with specific elements of restaurant concept development and design, the planning of the function space may require special consultants such as acoustic and audiovisual specialists, information technology consultants, and lighting designers. For large properties, the brand or operator may assemble focus groups consisting of meeting and event planners to discuss meeting space features that are most critical to them. Such discussions have led to a number of recommended planning and design criteria for hotel function space:

- *Location:* Group all function areas in a location easily accessible from the lobby, either on the same level or by dedicated vertical circulation; in major convention hotels, designers should consider creating two or more separate function zones.

- *Flexibility:* Include moveable partitions in large rooms, determine the need for multi-purpose versus dedicated rooms, and create multiple pre-function areas for receptions and breakouts.

- *Access:* Provide a separate entrance to the function area from the street or parking lot, provide public and service access to each function room, and consider the access needs for moving bulky goods and display materials into the ballroom and exhibit areas.

- *Support areas:* Include sufficient restrooms, coatrooms, and refreshment areas for the public, and provide banquet pantry, furniture, and audiovisual storage in back-of-the-house areas. Provide charging stations for mobile devices and access to power outlets for all occasional-seating groupings.

- *Structure:* Provide column-free function spaces and locate the ballroom and large meeting rooms independent of the guestroom tower to simplify the hotel's structure.

- *Ceiling height:* Determine the need for projection in each function space and consider how the high ceilings in these rooms will affect the floor above.

- *Windows:* Determine the need for natural light in function and assembly areas.

For new projects, the architect must address these planning issues early in schematic design because they have a major impact on the hotel's ability to attract group business, which is obviously essential in the major convention markets. In existing hotels, the owners must assess the scope of any potential renovation to make the meeting and banquet areas more functional both for the public and for the hotel staff. Although it is expensive to modify function space, an older hotel may need to undertake a major renovation of its function space to remain competitive.

Once the schematic design is accepted, the architect, interior designer, other consultants, and management staff need to focus on the details of future operations. For example, they should consider where meeting registration desks or refreshments will be set up in the pre-function area and how guests will move through the space, particularly when there are multiple concurrent events in-house. The design team should study alternative furniture layouts for each individual meeting or banquet room; that is, test whether the room dimensions accommodate various meeting or banquet configurations efficiently. Such function plans, developed relatively early in design, often show that a minor adjustment to the planning will offer substantial improvement in flexibility or increased capacity.

Experienced designers are familiar with many simple features that result in a better experience for the banquet guest or meeting attendee or that offer operational advantages. Most of these do not cost any more to implement if incorporated into the design at an early stage. For example, some designers typically use a ballroom carpet with an approximately twenty-two-inch (fifty-six-centimeter) pattern repeat to help hotel staff quickly arrange chairs in straight rows. Consider the potential problems if banquet guests have unscreened views into the service corridor or if inadequate directional and room signage are provided. The design team must address many of these seemingly insignificant design issues:

- *Floors:* Select a carpet pattern to aid in room setup; use a portable dance floor.

- *Walls:* Apply a chair rail to walls to protect their finish; add fabric panels to improve acoustics and upgrade room appearance.

- *Ceiling:* Organize HVAC, lighting, sound, fire protection, and other systems into a unified design.

- *Windows:* Add full blackout capability.

- *Furniture:* Select risers, lecterns, stacking chairs, and a balance of rectangular classroom tables and round or oval banquet tables; select high-quality chairs for upgraded conference rooms.

- *Lighting:* Provide a fully dimmable system including, as appropriate, chandeliers, downlights, LED lighting, rails for stage lighting, and decorative wall fixtures.

- *HVAC systems:* Provide separate mechanical, electrical, and sound systems for each room division. Consider vibration and noise when HVAC systems are operating.

- *Technology:* Provide high-bandwidth Wi-Fi that is extremely stable and robust, as there could be hundreds or even thousands of individuals accessing the hotel's Wi-Fi system concurrently. Consider special projection needs for teleconferencing.

Recreational Facilities

A generation ago, the only recreational amenity most lodging properties had was a swimming pool and perhaps a simple fitness room. Over time, developers realized the competitive advantage of more expansive fitness and wellness facilities, so that today it is common for first-class or luxury hotels to include a full-size spa to complement fully equipped fitness rooms; even limited-service hotels may now offer a small gym area and a pool suitable for laps. In-room fitness amenities such as yoga mats or Pilates props are also becoming more common, particularly in hotels catering to female business travelers.

Determining the appropriate mix of recreational facilities is based on an understanding of the market needs and a competitive analysis of other properties in the area. The development team also may consider the potential revenue that can be generated by selling fitness-facility memberships to people in the local community. Among the planning issues are considerations for guest access to the facilities and the need to isolate them from other building elements. In upscale properties, the architect should try to separate the pool area so that guests don't need to pass through the lobby or other major public areas in swimwear or robes. Also, the development team should keep in mind that non-guests who use the fitness facilities will want convenient access to the facilities from parking areas.

Some recreational facilities can get noisy, so they should be separated from the public areas and guestrooms if possible. For example, meeting rooms should not be near recreational space (although, as alluded to previously, the pool deck can double as very effective function space for many types of events). The chlorine odor and high humidity of indoor pools generally require that they be fully enclosed and not combined with non-recreational areas.

Administration Offices

The hotel's design must include office space for the executive staff and front office, accounting, and sales departments. Not only does the design of these offices influence the productivity of the staff, it has a direct influence on guests as well. Many guests deal with the general manager or with sales and catering staff, so the placement of these offices should be undertaken with ease of public access in mind.

Typically, the administration offices are clustered into four groups: front office, accounting, executive, and sales and catering. Even with the advent of self-service, mobile, or tablet check-in technology, it still remains imperative that the front office be located within easy reach of the check-in function. The front office typically includes space for the front office manager, reservations personnel, perhaps a revenue manager, and a general work area. The accounting area includes offices for the controller and other staff members who take care of payroll, accounts payable, accounts receivable, and management information systems. As fewer and fewer guests use cash for any transactions, the need for a secure and accessible location for the accounting function has become much less acute, and some hotels have located their accounting offices in another building altogether. Information systems and IT support are best located on-site.

In many hotels it is not possible to provide sufficient space near the lobby for the executive and the sales/catering offices. These easily can be located a few floors away, often near function space. An advantage of grouping these together is that executive and sales personnel can share a reception area and conference room(s). If that is not a necessity, these offices can be separate from each other. The executive suite includes offices for the general manager and the assistant general manager(s), and often the division managers for rooms and for food and beverage, as well as the administrative support staff. The sales and catering area commonly includes offices for the marketing and sales directors, several sales and banquet managers, conference services staff, and general support space.

Food Production Areas

Of all the service areas in a hotel, the kitchens and related food production areas require the most design attention, in part because of the extent to which the mechanical, electrical, and plumbing services must be integrated with the functional layout of these spaces. In addition, the design of the kitchen, usually the largest single back-of-the-house area, critically influences labor and energy costs for the life of the building. Distances within the kitchen should be as short as possible, related activities should be located close together, and layouts should be flexible to accommodate menu or concept changes in the food and beverage outlets. Therefore, the planning and design aspects of the kitchens require the coordinated attention of a variety of specialized food service and engineering consultants.

Among the many planning requirements that the architect should address during conceptual design, the most important is to locate the receiving and food storage areas, the kitchen(s), the restaurants, and the banquet rooms on a single floor whenever possible. When this is not achievable, the designer must assess the relative merits of alternate groupings of service and public functions. The design team should make every effort to link the following areas:

Essential food service connections

- Food storage to main kitchen
- Main kitchen to restaurants
- Room service area to service elevators
- Kitchen or banquet pantry to ballroom

Desirable food service connections

- Receiving to food storage
- Main kitchen to banquet pantry

- Banquet pantry to smaller banquet rooms

- Banquet pantry to pre-function rooms

- Kitchen (either main kitchen or restaurant kitchen) to room service area

- Kitchen to bar areas

- Beverage storage and ice production to beverage outlets

- Kitchen to waste-handling areas

- Kitchen to employee dining or breakroom(s)

The amount of floor space required in the kitchen and food and beverage storage areas depends on the number of meals served, the complexity of the menu(s), the degree of preparation needed for incoming ingredients, and the food delivery schedule. Because of the high cost of equipment, energy, and labor, one goal should be to design the smallest kitchen that meets the hotel's operational objectives. For example, many downtown hotels, where space is at a premium because of high land costs and where most foods are readily available, operate with minimal food storage space and emphasize multifunctional equipment.

After the food production space has been allocated during the early design phases, a specialized food service consultant can propose a preliminary kitchen design. Assuming that the major planning criteria are met and the budget allocated to food production areas has been accommodated, the design plan is then coordinated with the architect and engineers so that they might incorporate key kitchen features and requirements in their own plans.

While kitchen layouts will vary substantially depending on the concepts being supported and the scope of the hotel's food and beverage program, there are some basic kitchen planning criteria that apply in most cases:

- Locate food and beverage storage areas adjacent to either the receiving area or the kitchen, with the latter arrangement preferred. When receiving and the kitchen are on separate floors, ensure that there is adequate temperature-controlled storage in both locations to ensure food safety.

- Provide for a forward flow of food from storage through preparation and service areas; avoid backtracking or cross traffic.

- Minimize the distance between the kitchen serving area and restaurant seating. Many planners rely on a "sixty-foot rule" and try to limit the travel distance from the kitchen door to the farthest dining seat to a maximum of sixty feet (eighteen meters) for restaurants.

- Arrange compact work centers. Maintain an aisle of thirty-six to forty-two inches (ninety to 100 centimeters) between banks of cooking equipment and prep or plating tables for maximum ergonomic efficiency.

- Ensure that equipment such as ice makers, coffee brewers, and prep tables with sinks have an indirect drain to prevent wastewater from backing up into food contact areas.

- Locate secondary ambient (room temperature) and refrigerated storage areas near each service station as required.

- Place shared facilities such as warewashing centrally. Work with engineering to ensure that the grease trap is positioned to effectively prevent fats, oils, and grease from settling in drain lines.

- In all areas, consider sanitation and employee safety. Select flooring that is non-slip and has coved corners where the floor meets walls.

- Plan for the efficient use of all utilities by grouping floor drains or cooking equipment that requires gas service together, and combining warewashing and potwashing into a single section.

- Minimize the length of ventilation hoods wherever possible. Consider which pieces of equipment must be under a Class I ventilator for removing grease-laden vapor, and which items merely require heat and/or humidity removal.

- Group all walk-in refrigerators and freezers together to share common walls and floor depressions. Weigh the costs and benefits of remotely located condensing units and recirculated water for heat removal.

- Plan for recycling and composting, with labeled receptacles placed at each waste-generation point in the kitchen.

- Comply with all national, state, and local codes relating to health, safety, and fire protection.

Other Back-of-the-House Areas

Although the kitchen may be the most critical of the service functions in a hotel, it typically occupies only about 3 to 4 percent of the total hotel area; together, the other back-of-the-house functions require approximately twice that amount of space. Many of these other back-of-the-house areas tie directly into the kitchen, such as the receiving area and employee dining area. Others areas, such as the laundry and housekeeping areas, are more directly associated with the rooms operation.

Too often the architect and other members of the development team defer decisions on the planning of back-of-the-house areas until the design development phase, well into the design process. Because these areas are so important to the efficient functioning of the hotel, including its ability to operate within labor budgets, the development team should establish the back-of-the-house program as soon as the hotel is deemed feasible, and the architect should consider its planning implications early in schematic design. Throughout the design phase, the hotel operator must carefully review the plans as the architect refines and adds detail to the back-of-the-house areas. Key considerations for these areas include the following:

- Plan the receiving area to accommodate at least two trucks at one time (more for larger operations). Consider the size of the vehicles that will be needing access to the dock area.

- Enclose the receiving area so that it is secure and protected from the weather.

- Separate waste-holding areas from the receiving dock.

- Position receiving and security offices so that there is visual oversight of the loading dock and employee entrance.

- Establish employee lockers based on the staffing program for the hotel and the expected male/female ratio.

- Design employee lounge or dining areas with serving lines, dining tables, lounge seating, vending, etc. in mind. If possible, provide windows for natural light.

- Provide a linen chute from guestroom-floor service areas to a generous soiled linen area with adequate space for linen sorting.

- Establish separate locked linen storage for particular hotel areas (food and beverage outlets, the pool, etc.).

- Group the engineering offices, maintenance shops, and support spaces around a central work area.

- Locate mechanical areas so that noise and vibration don't negatively affect guest areas.

- Design mechanical rooms to allow for eventual equipment replacement.

Further specific requirements for other key hotel back-of-the-house areas—receiving and waste handling, general storage, employee areas, laundry and housekeeping, and maintenance and engineering—will be discussed in the following sections.

Receiving and Waste Handling. The hotel's receiving and waste-removal areas should be located so that they accommodate the necessary movement of trucks without disrupting guest parking, yet are hidden from the hotel guestrooms and such public areas as restaurants, lounges, and recreational areas. Sufficient space must be available in the receiving area to inspect goods before moving them to the kitchen(s) or storage areas. Often, purchasing/receiving staff work in an area overlooking the receiving dock to provide security at the dock.

The hotel's recycling and composting programs should be considered when planning the waste-handling areas. It may be necessary to provide secure storage for waste or recyclables that have value, such as empty beer bottles and kegs. Food waste should be held in a separate room that has multiple air changes an hour and can be easily accessed from kitchen areas. The design team should consider the type of waste receptacles that will be used—either bins that are lifted for emptying by the waste hauler or roll-off containers that are pulled onto the hauler's truck—and plan dock areas accordingly.

General Storage. Hotels require large amounts of storage areas. Most storage is associated with specific functions: food storage near the kitchen, furniture storage near the ballroom, and linen storage on guestroom floors, for example. However, hotels also require space for storing miscellaneous items such as records, decorations, and extra furnishings and equipment. The general storage area sometimes is located near the receiving area but it can easily be located in a more remote area. It should be secured and perhaps include two or three caged areas so that different operating departments can control separate sections of the room.

Employee Areas. Employee areas form another major part of the back of the house. The usual support functions for employees—the human resources office, staff lockers, and an employee dining area—are somewhat independent from each other and relate to other service areas as much as they do to each other. For example, the human resources function is related closely to the employee entrance, the lockers are related to the uniform issue area, and the employee cafeteria should have reasonable access from the main kitchen. In some destination resorts, the operator may have to provide employee housing as well. Although employee areas may be limited in small properties, it is essential that adequate locker and other space be provided in full-service hotels. During the early stages of design, the architect usually designates large blocks of space to the individual back-of-the-house functions, such as locker rooms. Often, though, these preliminary space allocations aren't tested to see whether the required functions can be accommodated in the actual spaces, which might have columns, irregular shapes, or other constraints as design plans are firmed up. To avoid potential problems, by the end of the schematic design phase the architect, with additional program information provided by the hotel operator, should develop a level of detail to confirm that lockers, restrooms, and so on can be accommodated in the space provided.

Laundry and Housekeeping. The laundry and housekeeping areas are another major back-of-the-house component. Even the smallest motel needs some space for storage and control of guestroom linen; in larger hotels in resort destinations where off-site laundry service may not be available, the laundry and housekeeping areas may total more than 5,000 square feet (465 square meters). Among the key decisions the development team must make is whether to have an in-house laundry. For many properties, the high cost to build and equip a laundry may make it more economical to use a commercial laundry service rather than handle laundry chores in-house. Regardless of whether laundry is washed in-house or sent out, there must be adequate space for sorting soiled linens, loading and moving two sets of linen carts (one set for clean linens and one for soiled), and storing linens ready for use. Early on, it should be established how and where uniforms and guest laundry will be handled, and whether on-site dry cleaning is necessary.

If the hotel is to have an in-house laundry, the laundry layout may be designed by the technical services staff of the hotel operating company or by the laundry equipment supplier. An in-house laundry preferably should be located on the hotel's lowest floor to prevent noise and vibrations from disturbing guest areas. Other housekeeping areas, notably office space and amenity storage areas, should be in the same vicinity as linen-handling areas.

Maintenance and Engineering. A final back-of-the-house component includes the engineering offices, repair and maintenance shops, and mechanical and electrical areas. Too often these activities are given insufficient space, often no more than the areas left over after schematic design. The amount of space needed varies by hotel type and location, but should consist of at least one or two office spaces for coordinating maintenance functions and keeping records, and spaces for paint supplies, electrical and plumbing repair, and extra equipment such as televisions.

The engineering function operates twenty-four hours a day and must be centrally located so that the engineering staff can respond readily to both routine and emergency calls.

The mechanical equipment areas may be scattered throughout the building. They do not need to be immediately adjacent to the engineering offices but, whenever possible, they should be located in proximity to the laundry, kitchen, and other high-energy-use areas for most effective operation. For example, it is common to install ballroom air-handlers on a mezzanine or within a separate roof enclosure above the ballroom to put them as close as possible to the function space and reduce the substantial amount of space required for supply and return ducts. Also, additional mechanical equipment is usually placed on the roof of the guest-room tower.

Key Terms

atrium—A guestroom floor configuration in which rooms are laid out off a single-loaded corridor encircling a multi-story lobby space.

bay—The space equivalent of a standard guestroom for a given property.

double-double room—A guestroom featuring two full-size beds. Also common are double-queen rooms. (Rooms with two single-size beds are called twin rooms.)

double-loaded slab—A guestroom floor configuration in which rooms are laid out on both sides of a central corridor.

feasibility study—An analysis that assesses present and future demand as well as development costs and the projected financial performance for a proposed hotel.

function space—Rentable space such as ballrooms, meeting and banquet rooms, reception and exhibit spaces, and dedicated conference rooms and boardrooms designed to accommodate meetings and a variety of corporate and association conferences. Often called meeting space.

greenfield site—A parcel of land that has not been developed previously and is free from existing structures.

porte cochère—A canopy designed to protect hotel guests from inclement weather and provide visual emphasis to the main entrance.

program—A document that spells out in detail the design parameters for a hotel project, including functional needs and space allocation requirements.

schematic design—The first phase of hotel design in which the architect and other designers block out how the spaces and functions defined in the program will be organized on the site and how circulation will work between spaces.

shotgun suite—A suite in which the living room faces an atrium or outside corridor, the bathroom is in the middle of the bay, and the bedroom is in the rear, with an exterior orientation.

side-by-side suite—A suite that consists of two regular guestroom bays positioned beside one another, each with windows to the outside. One bay is typically the living room of the suite and the other is usually the bedroom and bathroom.

tower—A guestroom floor configuration in which rooms are grouped around a central vertical core.

 Review Questions

1. What are the key steps of the development process?

2. What does a feasibility report typically cover?

3. Why is a program document important? At what stage in the process should it be prepared?

4. What are the three design phases the architect typically works through?

5. What are some of the site characteristics an architect must investigate before designing a hotel?

6. What are some of the planning considerations for guestroom floors?

7. What are some of the design criteria for food and beverage outlets?

8. What are some examples of hotel function spaces? How do they differ in terms of design?

9. What areas should be adjacent to the hotel kitchen?

10. What administrative office clusters are typical in a hotel?

Chapter 12 Outline

Competencies

1. List typical reasons for renovating a hotel, summarize the life cycle of a hotel, and describe types of renovation. (pp. 445–451)

2. Describe how a renovation plan is created. (pp. 451–462)

3. Explain how a renovation plan is implemented, including the design phase and construction phase. (pp. 462–475)

4. Describe issues that must be addressed after a renovation project is completed, if not before. (pp. 475–477)

12

Renovation and Capital Projects

This chapter was revised and contributed by Jeanne Varney, M.B.A., LEED Green Associate, Green Globes Professional, and Lecturer at the School of Hotel Administration, Cornell University, Ithaca, New York; and Jan deRoos, Ph.D., Associate Professor, School of Hotel Administration, Cornell University, Ithaca, New York.

The Loews Regency Hotel has been a classic New York icon for over 50 years. Sitting at the corner of 61st and Park Avenue, the Loews Regency Hotel looms 21 stories high and is the epitome of luxury. Over its long history, the hotel has hosted a who's who of celebrities, politicians, dignitaries, and is home to New York's famous "power breakfast." The hotel is an institution, but it needed a fresh look that embraced both the past and the future.

In January 2013, after much deliberation on how to best perform the renovation, it was decided that the Loews Regency would close its doors for a year-long, $100 million renovation. The only way to totally renovate the hotel from the structure to the finishes was to shut the hotel down, perform the renovation, and then open to the public as a completely modernized facility. The entire hotel—lobby, guestrooms, restaurant, bar, fitness center, salon—would be overhauled. Loews Hotels brought in Jonathan Nehmer + Associates, Inc. (JN+A) for Architecture, and Rottet Studios and Meyer Davis Studio for Interior Design to transform the property. The owners also brought in an established restaurateur, Sant Ambroeus, and salon operator, Julien Farel, to further elevate the hotel.

The lobby and sense of arrival underwent a major transformation. The concept for the renovation was to open up the entire public area so that the front desk was prominent and much more friendly and approachable. The walls between the restaurant and the lobby were removed to make them more visible and inviting to the guests upon entry. The former, dark, inward-focused restaurant was transformed to include a bar and lounge space at the front corner of Park Avenue and 61st street, inviting New York in. The use of front desk "pods" provide for a more personal check-in experience with better interaction between the guest and hotel associates.

The tired guestrooms needed a refresh as well. Every guest-room was completely redone, including all-new FF&E and new bathrooms.... [T]he key count was increased from 354 to 379 by splitting up lesser-used larger suites. One of the most important upgrades was to replace all of the windows in the hotel to negate the New York City traffic noise.

The behind-the-scenes infrastructure of the hotel had to be updated. This included modernization of the elevators and upgrading the fire alarm and mechanical systems. All of the risers and distribu-tion lines were checked and either replaced or repaired. Technology improvements were made to every system including an abundance of places to plug in and get connected to the Internet, energy manage-ment, telephone, data, HDTV, security, and more.

This was truly a restoration from the "bones" of the hotel up to the finishes. The Loews Regency is truly a sophisticated boutique. It features clean, contemporary lines, with touches of elegance to create a sense of place and comfort. This is the next era for the Loews Regency as it strives to be modern, but yet remains classic and timeless.[1]

Renovation of lodging facilities requires significant resources, including finances, materials, and labor. It is estimated that the annual volume of lodging-related renovation work in the United States averages between $3.5–$5.5 billion per year, depending on the economic cycle of the industry.[2] Virtually every hotel undertakes an annual capital-expenditure planning process in which managers develop the upcoming year's budget, and then a five-, ten-, or possibly even a twenty-year capital expenditure budget forecast. Given the competitive nature of the industry, renovation is necessary to maintain and enhance business volume and hence the financial health of individual hotels.

There are many terms used in the industry to describe where the money comes from to pay for renovation, including "reserve for replacement," "capital expenditures," "Escrow Fund," "CapEx," and "FF&E reserve." In fact, there is a debate within the industry over accounting and valuation rules related to the clas-sification of renovation expenditures. In this chapter, we distinguish renovations from other expenditures by categorizing renovations as work on the property for which the work's useful life extends over a multi-year period. This includes not only work that simply replaces furniture, fixtures, and equipment (FF&E) that are worn out, but also work performed on major building systems such as HVAC systems and roofs, work performed to reposition a property or an area within a property, work performed to meet new government regulations, work performed to meet new market demands, and work performed to keep the property up-to-date in the technology arena.

In this chapter we examine why hotels should renovate and discuss the life cycle of elements that make up a hotel. We also discuss different types of renovation and the planning, design, and construction phases of the renovation process. The chapter concludes with a section on after-renovation best practices. Although the chapter will focus on hotels, much of the material applies to res-taurants as well.

Hotel Renovation

Generally speaking, **renovation** is the process of renewing, refurbishing, and updating a hospitality property, usually to offset the consequences of use or modify spaces to meet the needs of changing demand in markets. Renovations modernize the look and feel of interior spaces; they provide a means to bring up to date the engineering systems that provide a safe, comfortable, and convenient interior environment; and they allow managers to change the mix and type of services and facilities offered to the public.

It is important that the processes and resources used in hotel renovations evolve with the ever-changing trends within the industry. These trends include the following:

- Increased market segmentation and expansion will continue. New brands will always be under development, whether by large, international brands or start-up lodging companies. This means that as market segments are further refined, so too must design schemes, technologies, and amenities be further refined to capture those segments.

- An increase in customer choice typically leads to a more complex and competitive environment for hotels to navigate. This may place significant pressure on properties to seek ways of differentiation. They must not only maintain their expected level of furnishings and services, but continuously seek ways to upgrade their offerings.

- Over the last decade, customer expectations about lifestyle services, technology and technology access, and in-room services have changed significantly.

These factors combine to produce a much more competitive environment for hotels. Existing hotels must renovate or become the physically and functionally obsolete properties within their markets. A hotel can no longer plan to use its systems and interior finishes without change for fifteen to twenty years. Technological, functional, and stylistic obsolescence forces most hotel managers to introduce changes within five to seven years of opening a new facility, with extensive changes taking place over a typical twelve- to fifteen-year cycle.

Reasons to Renovate

There are many reasons to renovate a hotel. Some of the most common are:

- Equipment reaches the end of its useful life.

- Building system elements reach the end of their lives and must be replaced. If the roof, for example, is not replaced at the proper time, the hotel risks significant business interruption due to serious leaks in revenue-generating areas that force those areas to shut down for repairs.

- The furnishings and finishes within the facility are worn out, leading to a competitive disadvantage.

- The interior design is out-of-date and a source of embarrassment or is directly linked to declining revenues.

- The management identifies a more profitable use of space within a facility. Over time, demand for services can change and physical alterations within a section of the building may be required to take advantage of this demand. Examples include converting a restaurant to meeting space, or adding retail space.

- Present or previous ownership has not spent the funds necessary to keep the hotel in a fully updated condition, and the physical plant has deteriorated. As a direct result, business volume has declined to a point where revenues do not support the hotel's level of debt. In this case, a decision must be made to hold and renovate versus sell the property.

- New technology must be installed to meet customer needs.

- The property has physical or environmental issues that must be dealt with. For example, a hotel might need to renovate to meet Americans with Disabilities Act (ADA) requirements, or to cure indoor-air-quality problems.

As a property ages, the renovation strategy needs to change. Maintaining the original design is important in the early years; making extensive changes to meet changing guest needs and expectations becomes important in later years. It is tempting to accelerate the process of changing the original design, but few facilities can justify speeding up major changes on a return-on-investment basis.

Most owners of lodging facilities want the funds they spend on renovations to provide a return on their investment. The question for an owner is, "Which makes the most sense financially—should I put money into the hotel (renovate it) and keep it, or should I sell it?" For this and other reasons, most owners today require a detailed financial analysis of each major renovation project. This change has occurred slowly, but conducting a financial analysis for a proposed renovation is now the norm, not the exception, for most renovation projects. Major responsibilities of the owner's asset manager are to (1) ensure that renovation projects indeed add value to the property, (2) assist property managers in setting a strategic direction for the renovation plan over the anticipated ownership period, and (3) monitor/direct the renovation planning and execution process.

Someone at the property must take responsibility for creating and maintaining a long-term renovation plan. Such a plan provides for continuity over time, provides a linkage between a property's business plan and the physical condition the property must maintain to achieve the business plan, and becomes a repository of wisdom regarding project economics. Increasingly, the decision-making responsibility is shared between the owner's asset manager and the owner's property manager, who work within a set of brand standards to craft a short- and long-term strategy for the property.

Acquiring and renovating an existing hotel presents an opportunity that is often superior to constructing a new hotel in terms of location, timing, and costs. Typically these purchased hotels require physical improvements (renovations) through the use of property improvement plans, commonly referred to as PIPs. A PIP is a document generated by the hotel owner or brand that will be in place after the purchase. Brand design and construction representatives tour the hotel to determine what changes or upgrades are necessary for the hotel to be compliant with the brand's quality and brand standards. Areas typically scrutinized include guest-access locations (lobby, guestrooms, restaurants, meeting spaces, fitness center, etc.) and fire and life safety systems. The PIP document is contractually binding and must be executed by the hotel owner that will be in place after the transaction. There are specific deadlines of completion required for each renovation project (typically phrased in the PIP document as "Renovation X is to be completed by X date") and the renovations typically fall within a three-year window following the date of the transaction. Completion of the specified PIP renovations is required to retain the flag of the brand writing the PIP. Failure of the hotel's owner or ownership group to fulfill the PIP could result in the removal of the brand flag from the hotel.

The Life Cycle of a Hotel

All commercial businesses have an identifiable life cycle, and hotels are no exception. In many cases, the cycle is typified by the following scenario:

> *A hotel is constructed to meet the needs of a growing community and becomes a dominant force in the market for a number of years, enjoying higher occupancies and rates than its competitors. During this robust first phase, the property may be the preferred site for local social and business functions. Other hoteliers, seeing this hotel's success, enter the market with equal or superior products, especially in communities that are growing in population and business activity.*
>
> *In the second phase, the hotel's occupancy and average daily rate decline over time as new competitors enter the market and "steal" market share from existing properties. This process is hastened if ownership and management do not invest in the renovation of the hotel.*
>
> *In the third phase, the market changes as well, demanding new services different from those the hotel is capable of offering in its current state. If the hotel is part of a chain, in many cases the franchise is lost or changed during this phase. Over time it becomes apparent that revenues will not support the property's required returns. The hotel's decline has two possible outcomes: disposal of the hotel (by selling it, for example) or a change in its focus, meaning repositioning or rehabilitation. The critical factor at this point is whether investments in the facility will bring higher returns than the returns associated with selling the hotel and reinvesting the money elsewhere.*

This process of dominance, decline, and rehabilitation or reuse is illustrated in Exhibit 1. Renovation work should be used to extend the phase-one period of strong performance and minimize any periods of decline. Renovating early in a hotel's life preserves and extends its healthy phase-one period. Renovations in the second phase incorporate changes in response to market forces. Third-phase renovations involve significant changes to the building to reposition it within the market and upgrade support systems (such as mechanical, life-safety, or technology systems) that are outdated.

Types of Renovation

Renovations typically fall into five categories, depending on the scope of work performed: minor renovation, major renovation, restoration, special projects, and discretionary.

Exhibit 1   The Life Cycle of a Hotel

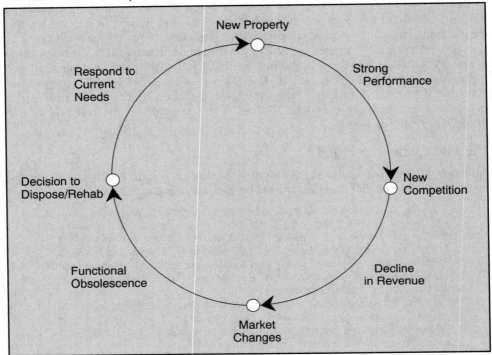

Minor Renovation (Six-Year Cycle). The scope of a **minor renovation** is to replace or renew the non-durable furnishings and finishes within a hotel space without changing the space's use or physical layout. For example, minor renovation of a meeting room would include replacing carpets and wall coverings, repainting doors and frames, and other minor work. Minor renovation of a guestroom would include replacing carpets, wall coverings, drapery, and bedspreads; minor painting; and touching up the furniture.

Major Renovation (Twelve- to Fifteen-Year Cycle). The scope of a **major renovation** is to replace or renew all furnishings and finishes within a space, and may include extensive modifications to the use and physical layout of the space itself. For example, major renovation of a restaurant can include changing the concept; changing the location of the entrance(s); replacing all seating and tables; replacing all floor, wall, and ceiling treatments; changing mechanical, electrical, and lighting systems; and installing an up-to-date point-of-sale (POS) system. Major renovation to a guestroom would include everything involved in a minor renovation plus replacement of all furniture, bedding, lighting, and artwork. In many cases, the bathroom also is upgraded, which might include replacing ceramic tile with marble or granite; replacing the vanity, lavatory, and bathing fixtures; and installing new lighting.

Restoration (Twenty-Five- to Fifty-Year Cycle). The scope of a **restoration** is to completely gut a space and replace systems that are technically and functionally obsolete, while restoring furnishings and systems that can still be used, given the current needs of the facility. Examples include wholesale replacement of kitchen and laundry facilities; interior demolition of entire guestroom floors to reconfigure the mix of rooms and placement of bathrooms; replacement of all mechanical, electrical, and plumbing systems; and restoration of a ballroom, including plaster filigree work, crystal chandeliers, and ornamental woodwork.

Special Projects. The scope of a **special project** is to perform work related to a specific system upgrade that can be handled without changing the hotel's interior design in any substantial way. As such, special projects have typically been related to technology or engineering systems. Examples include installation of electronic locking systems, installation of equipment for high-speed Internet access, work in the realm of ADA compliance, and fire sprinkler system retrofits.

Discretionary. Discretionary renovations are projects that are not customary or required by law. They are typically value-enhancement projects such as converting a restaurant to meeting space or adding a coffee kiosk, spa, or some other new service area for guests. Discretionary renovations typically require a strong return on investment to obtain the necessary funding.

Creating the Renovation Plan

The planning process for renovation work is often called the capital budgeting process. Traditionally, the planning process for renovation projects starts by establishing a budget that is some percentage of total property revenues. Historically, this percentage was set at 3 percent, but has moved to 4 percent (5 percent for full-service properties) during the past two decades. This does not mean that 3 or 4 percent of property revenues actually provided adequate funding for all capital projects, but it was seen as a benchmark measure. This percentage may or may not be adequate to fund a particular property's CapEx needs.

Two organizations historically have studied and provided findings to the lodging industry concerning hotel CapEx cost estimates. JN+A/HVS Design provides an annual report that details up-to-date cost estimates not only on the hotel-chain scale, but also provides a low, average, and high range of the cost estimates; it is an excellent resource for system-level estimating (discussed in detail later in the chapter). The second study is conducted by the International Society of Hospitality Consultants (ISHC). This is a collaborative industry effort of data collection and analysis. Three studies have been published, in 1995, 2000, and most recently in 2007. It is acknowledged that data sources vary (depending on which hotels report) in each year of the CapEx study publications.

When looking at the historical data, the average CapEx expenditure per hotel has been declining over the past several decades (see Exhibit 2). This is an appropriate time to discuss the impact of economic cycles on CapEx spending. Average CapEx spending in the 2007 IHSC study was 5.1 percent of sales for all hotels (the actual time frame of the data was from 2000–2005). In the 2014 JN+A/HVS Design data, average CapEx spending was 3.6 percent of sales (actual time frame of data

Exhibit 2   CapEx Spending per Hotel

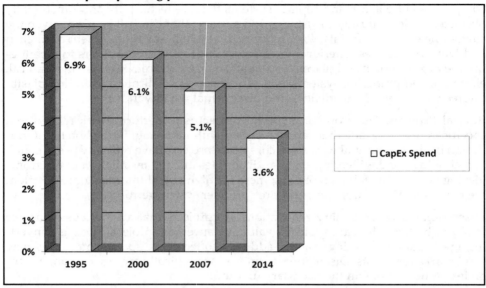

Sources: *CapEx 2007: A Study of Capital Expenditures in the U.S. Hotel Industry* (Memphis, Tennessee: International Society of Hospitality Consultants, 2007); and *2014 Hotel Cost Estimating Guide* (Bethesda, MD: JN+A/HVS Design, 2014).

was from 2007–2012). Why the significant difference? The Great Recession in the United States caused a severe decline in both occupancy and average daily rate (ADR) from 2008–2011 (see Exhibit 3). From 2007 to 2009 the industry lost over $12 in revenue per available room (RevPar). This translated into a significant drop in CapEx and/or FF&E fund contributions. Simply put, there was less money available to spend, so many CapEx projects were either delayed or cancelled.

Exhibit 3   U.S. Hotel Statistics, 2007–2012

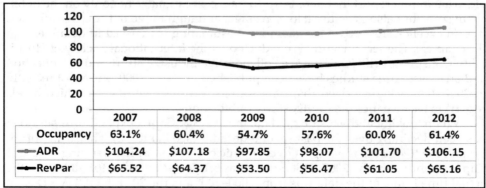

	2007	2008	2009	2010	2011	2012
Occupancy	63.1%	60.4%	54.7%	57.6%	60.0%	61.4%
ADR	$104.24	$107.18	$97.85	$98.07	$101.70	$106.15
RevPar	$65.52	$64.37	$53.50	$56.47	$61.05	$65.16

Source: American Hotel & Lodging Association, www.ahla.com.

The CapEx studies have also demonstrated several other notable facts:

1. A property's capital needs vary widely over time and can only be approximated each year by a percentage of revenues.

2. Capital needs tend to "lump" in certain years and increase significantly as properties age.

3. There are significant differences in capital spending across property types.[3]

Exhibit 4 provides capital expenditure summary data from HVS Design; Exhibits 5 through 7 give some other capital expenditure information from the same report.

There is significant debate over the long-term adequacy of the 4 to 5 percent yearly FF&E fund that hotels typically maintain. The CapEx 2007 study noted the following: "Capital spending increased in conjunction with the age of the property. As a ratio of total revenues, hotels older than 15 years spent 10.5 percent, versus 3.1 percent for hotels between 5 and 15 years old and 0.7 percent for hotels

Exhibit 4   Capital Expenditures Spending from 2007–2012

	Percentage of Total Revenues	Dollars per Available Room per Year
All Hotels	3.6%	$5,102
Full-Service Hotels	2.1%	$5,596
Select-Service Hotels	3.4%	$4,092
Extended-Stay Hotels	4.1%	$5,660

Source: Jonathan C. Nehmer, AIA, ISHC, HVS Design, 2014.

Exhibit 5   Composition of Capital Expenditures

Component	Full-Service Hotels	Select-Service Hotels
Rooms and Corridors	34%	50%
Food & Beverage	6%	2%
Other Public Space	17%	19%
Building	19%	13%
Technology	7%	5%
ADA/Life Safety	2%	1%
Meeting Space	6%	8%
Other	9%	2%

Source: Jonathan C. Nehmer, AIA, ISHC, HVS Design, 2014.

Exhibit 6   Capital Expenditures by Hotel Location, 2008–2012

Location	Full-Service			Select-Service Hotels			Extended-Stay		
	Avg. Age	CapEx %	CapEx/ Rm	Ave. Age	CapEx %	CapEx/ Rm	Avg. Age	CapEx %	CapEx/ Rm
All Properties	17.3	2.1%	$5,596	14	3.4%	$4,092	12.7	4.1%	$5,660
Airport	16	6.7%	$1,321	13.6	1.9%	$2,555	10.2	6.0%	$6,677
Urban	30.7	2.2%	$6,613	16.8	2.2%	$3,731	9.1	5.7%	$9,238
Resort	28.4	1.2%	$4,383	20.5	3.8%	$6,679	16.5	5.0%	$6,194
Highway/ Small City	17.8	0.1%	$1,374	15.6	5.2%	$5,080	15.1	3.8%	$3,546
Suburban	12.8	3.2%	$3,307	11.6	3.8%	$3,772	11.2	3.4%	$4,893

Source: Jonathan C. Nehmer, AIA, ISHC, HVS Design, 2014

Exhibit 7   Capital Expenditures by Hotel Age

	Full-Service		Select-Service		Extended-Stay	
	CapEx %	CapEx/ Rm	CapEx %	CapEx/ Rm	CapEx %	CapEx/ Rm
All Properties	2.1%	$ 5,596	3.4%	$ 4,092	4.1%	$ 5,660
Before 1997	2.3%	$ 6,331	3.6%	$ 4,486	9.0%	$14,591
1998–2007	1.5%	$ 4,087	4.3%	$ 5,742	3.2%	$ 5,015
After 2007	0.2%	$ 335	0.5%	$ 423	30.0%	$ 264

Source: Jonathan C. Nehmer, AIA, ISHC, HVS Design, 2014

of less than 5 years of age." With the average age of hotel buildings in the United States at approximately forty years old, and 70+ percent of hotels over fifteen years old, the level of FF&E funding certainly appears to be cause for concern.[4]

Increasingly, the industry is recognizing that the most correct way to forecast capital expenditures is to establish a space-by-space schedule of renovation needs over a very long time horizon, such as twenty to thirty years. Such a schedule is based on the expected life of various components within each space and the cost to replace them at the end of their expected life. By proceeding in this manner, management obtains a more accurate view of the property's capital needs over the long term. A space-by-space schedule provides a guide for both project timing and the approximate financial needs of the building over the horizon period. **Facility life-cycle cost studies** are commonly used by asset managers of long-term-hold assets (assets that will likely remain in the portfolio for ten+ years).

It should be noted that facility life-cycle cost studies do not need to use the physical life of building components as the basis for the replacement cycle; indeed, in many cases they should not. For example, it is widely recognized that the economic life of a cocktail lounge is considerably less than its physical life. Scheduling the replacement of a cocktail lounge's furnishings and finishes on a three-year cycle but the replacement of its equipment on a six-year cycle recognizes that some items that are still in good shape physically must be replaced to maintain the lounge's appeal and therefore its ability to generate income; others items (behind-the-scenes equipment) can wait to be replaced when they are worn out.

By producing a well-thought-out facility life-cycle cost study, management will come to understand that the property will require, for renovation purposes, perhaps 4 percent of revenues during the first decade of business, 6.5 percent during the second decade, and 7.5 percent during the third. Such a study provides managers with a benchmark based on the business and the physical needs of the property. The process is not perfect, because, among other reasons, it is not possible to predict changes in building codes or where technological advances may take us.

The Planning Phase

The planning phase for property renovation consists of several steps:

- Conduct a strategic review.
- Survey the property and create a preliminary project list.
- Estimate project costs and benefits.
- Set priorities and choose projects.

We'll take a look at each of these steps in the following sections.

Conduct a Strategic Review. The annual renovation process should begin with an understanding of the hotel's long-term needs, ideally arrived at through a facility life-cycle cost study. However, this plan is normally based on the typical life of building components, without regard to current competitive pressures. Therefore, in addition to this long-term plan, management must have a strategy to contend with the property's immediate competitive environment. Thus, consulting the hotel's overall strategic plan is strongly advised.

Owners and managers should take a step-by-step approach to the assessment of the property's current and desired operational mission. There should be a rigorous periodic evaluation of the property, a **strategic review**. In most organizations, this step is usually handled as a joint effort between management and ownership, typically conducted by the property's general manager and the owner's representative or asset manager. In large hotel chains, regional or divisional managers are also involved. Steps in this strategic review are as follows:

1. Conduct an honest evaluation of the hotel's current market position. Using historical performance data and information from competing properties, evaluate the existing reputation of the property and its strengths, weaknesses, opportunities, and threats.

2. Identify the key trends in the local area that will drive the lodging market as a whole for the foreseeable future.

3. Combine the above analyses to formulate the best market position for the property, consistent with constraints such as location. In many cases it will become obvious that the property should change its positioning within the market, while in others, maintenance of the current market position is optimal.

By subjecting the property to a rigorous strategic review and seeking to understand both the current and desired market position, management will then be prepared to craft the renovation plan in a manner that brings the most value to the property. This step should establish consensus about the property's main renovation concerns and create a preliminary phasing plan. It is wise to remember that renovation is not the objective itself, only the means to greater objectives: to increase a property's competitive position and maximize its value. Every renovation, large or small, must also be appropriate to the property's rate structure, target markets, franchise affiliation, sales strategy, and level of service. The next job is to identify the renovation projects that will best support the findings of the strategic review. This is done through a property survey.

Survey the Property and Create a Preliminary Project List. The need to properly survey the property is difficult to overemphasize. A thorough physical survey of the property helps management determine what areas and facilities need to be renovated. A proper survey also includes qualitative input from employees, department heads, and guests. The survey process is meant to identify needs and stimulate ideas.

Employees occupy the hotel's spaces every day and typically interact with guests. Employees likely will be able to identify hotel spaces that can be improved in terms of functionality and be able to convey anecdotal guest feedback. Department heads will also have feedback on hotel spaces that can be improved, and participating in the survey will compel these managers, who may share in renovation responsibilities, to physically inspect the spaces to be renovated. Lastly, guests have the perspective of the end-users of most hotel spaces and will inevitably have feedback for improvements. Repeat guests typically are excellent resources for feedback because they know the hotel well and often are interested in its improvement. Exhibit 8 contains a checklist of hotel areas that should be surveyed on a regular basis.

In many cases, two survey phases are appropriate. The first survey is typically performed by the hotel's management to identify needs. There should be both a physical examination of hotel spaces as well as qualitative research performed to determine functional needs (by surveying guests, employees, and managers). Once potential renovation projects have been determined, a follow-up survey is done by the manager in charge of the renovation along with the hotel's designer(s) and/or engineer(s) to determine the exact scope of the renovation work.

When surveying the property for the first time, managers should keep in mind the relationship between the economic life of building systems and the physical life of these systems. In most cases the physical life exceeds the economic. Most

Exhibit 8   Hotel Survey Checklist

FRONT-OF-THE-HOUSE SPACES

Rooms Division
- ☐ Guestrooms, guestroom baths, suites, and corridors
- ☐ Guestroom amenities and accessories—safe, mini-bar
- ☐ Guestroom technology—Internet access, in-room movies, DVD/Blu-ray, radio, bedside controls
- ☐ Bathroom accessories-pulsating shower heads, lighted mirrors, towel warmers, shoe polishers, whirlpools, and steam baths
- ☐ Support areas—front desk, reservations, guest services areas

Food and Beverage Outlets
- ☐ Restaurants and lounges—concepts, condition, consistency, competition
- ☐ Support areas—coat check room, entrances, restrooms

Public Areas
- ☐ Ballrooms, meeting rooms, banquet rooms, lobbies
- ☐ Pools, health and recreation facilities
- ☐ Elevator interiors

ENGINEERED SYSTEMS

Heating, Ventilating, and Air Conditioning Systems
- ☐ Temperature, humidity, fresh air, and odor control
- ☐ Mechanical noise and vibration control

Life Safety Systems
- ☐ Sprinklers, standpipes, hose racks, fire extinguishers
- ☐ Smoke detectors, fire alarms, voice communication system, command post
- ☐ Emergency power generator, lighting, fire pumps, elevators
- ☐ Kitchen hood protection, computer protection

Energy Conservation Systems
- ☐ Computerized energy management systems
- ☐ Heat recovery systems (kitchen and laundry hot water and exhaust)
- ☐ Exhaust recirculation (air purifying systems)
- ☐ Insulating windows (double and solar glazing)

Telephone and Communications Systems
- ☐ Computerized least-cost routing, accounting, wake-up call

MANAGEMENT SYSTEMS

Computerized Property Management Systems
- ☐ Reservations, room status, guest histories
- ☐ Accounting, auditing, inventories
- ☐ Point-of-sale billing

SECURITY SYSTEMS

- ☐ Card-locking systems, peepholes, secondary locks
- ☐ TV surveillance of entrances, service dock, elevators, escalators
- ☐ Alarms for exit stairs, cashier
- ☐ Cashier's vault, safe-deposit boxes

Source: Adapted from Walter A. Rutes, Richard H. Penner, and Lawrence Adams, *Hotel Design, Planning, and Development* (New York: W.W. Norton, 2001).

owners can easily see the wisdom of replacing a still-functioning but obsolete manual front office system with a computerized front office system, even though the old equipment is still working. The same analysis can be applied to laundry equipment, kitchen equipment, and engineered systems, to achieve both labor savings and energy savings. Thus, when identifying opportunities for renovation, management has to do more than just identify those items that are worn out.

Identifying renovation opportunities requires sensitivity to the available range of options for the property, including financial. It is here that the previous work of evaluating the hotel's market position becomes valuable, because managers can eliminate renovation options that are clearly inconsistent with the goals of the property, and can focus attention on those choices that are most promising.

At the end of the property survey, the hotel's management has generated a list of potential renovation projects. Senior management should take a close look at the list to determine which projects are consistent with the strategic review. Those that aren't should be discarded or tabled. This step is important to communicate to the hotel staff, so that there is a clear understanding of which projects will proceed, the priority of those projects, and the reasons for discarding certain projects. Once this step is completed, management is left with a list of appropriate renovation projects that must be evaluated further.

Estimate Project Costs and Benefits. Concurrent with generating the project list, management should estimate the costs and benefits of each project. This process will identify projects that should be dropped from the list because their costs exceed their benefits.

Estimating costs. In new construction, managers have the advantage of being able to completely plan and analyze projects before construction begins. There are relatively few unknowns on the cost side. Because renovations involve work that will be performed (in most cases) in a property that will remain open for business, they pose a different set of problems, such as maintaining public circulation while the renovation work goes on, being able to change floor-to-ceiling clearances, and finding ways to reuse existing mechanical and electrical systems. Without proper estimating and analysis, management can make poor decisions, leading to delays and cost overruns.

In many renovation projects, the choice is not whether to proceed but how to choose among alternative ways to proceed. For instance, when renovating a lounge, at what point does it make sense to move the bar to improve guest traffic circulation? Only an objective analysis of the benefits and costs associated with this move can answer the question. If revenue can be greatly enhanced by moving the bar (an expensive option due to the plumbing work involved), the idea merits consideration.

All cost-estimating methods are based on breaking projects into various components and estimating the cost of each component. For managers, the question is: What estimating technique should I use, given my current decision needs? There is a direct relationship between the amount of time and information needed to prepare an estimate and the accuracy of the estimate. Four commonly used estimating methods are:

1. *Order of magnitude.* Order-of-magnitude estimates are commonly called "ball-park" estimates. This is the quickest and least accurate (plus or minus 30 percent) method of estimating. The purpose is to create only an approximate estimate of costs. It is common to estimate by a percentage of revenues—for example, a lounge renovation will cost 50 percent of annual revenues; or by a percentage of physical value—for example, a restoration of a guestroom costs approximately 75 percent of the per-room cost of new construction.

2. *Occupancy-based estimates.* Occupancy-based estimates produce more refined estimates (plus or minus 20 percent) of project costs. These estimates are prepared by using standard units, such as cost per room for guestrooms, cost per seat in food and beverage outlets, or cost per square foot in meeting rooms (adjusted for known complicating factors).

3. *Systems estimates.* Systems estimates are created by estimating the cost of the different construction systems used in a renovation. This estimating method gives a more detailed cost estimate than occupancy-based estimates (plus or minus 10 percent). For example, a systems estimate for a guestroom includes the installed cost of a new vanity top, the removal of old wall vinyl, the installation of new wall vinyl, and so on, with a complete estimate being the total cost of all the items that will be involved in the renovation. This estimating method is very appropriate during the design phase of a project.

4. *Unit-price estimates.* This is the most detailed and accurate (plus or minus 5 percent) method of estimating. With unit-price estimates, the estimator prices materials, shipping costs, taxes, and labor separately for each item, and then adds up the totals for the items. For example, a drapery system would be estimated by pricing the cover material, liner material, the cost of flame-proofing, the cost of new drapery rods, shipping costs, taxes, and the cost of installation. This method takes considerably longer than the other methods and requires complete information about the project. This method is suited for the preparation of construction bids and for securing furnishings bids.

Order-of-magnitude estimates are useful for preparing a renovation wish list or quickly comparing the costs of different projects. Occupancy-based estimates are appropriate when you only need to select among alternatives. Once a project is approved and is moved to the design phase, it should be estimated using a more accurate method, which requires higher levels of estimating expertise.

Information for making occupancy-based estimates for the major spaces in economy, extended-stay, midscale, upscale, upper-upscale, and luxury properties is presented in the chapter appendix.[5] The price differences among property types are due to differences in the quality of the materials used, size of rooms, amount of furniture, and level of customization of the furnishings. The appendix guidelines can provide a reasonable basis for preliminary budget decision-making at most properties, especially if they are modified by the particular circumstances at a specific property. For example, the chapter appendix shows that a full renovation of a guestroom (not including the bathroom) can cost up to $19,990 per room at a luxury hotel. If, however, you know that the rooms need new televisions but not bedding, you can simply adjust the per-room price for these two items and then multiply by the number of rooms.

Many times the indirect costs of a renovation project are not included in the estimate. Examples of indirect costs include:

- Extra cleaning of all hotel areas due to construction dust and dirt.

- Complimentary goods and services or billing adjustments to soothe unhappy guests (typically, managers comp drinks or meals, but may even comp guestrooms if that is necessary to keep goodwill).

- Loss of revenue due to out-of-service facilities.

- Loss of valued employees (if the hotel closes down for remodeling), and the hiring and training costs to replace them.

In many cases, simple changes to the renovation plan can significantly reduce these indirect costs. These and other operational issues are discussed later in the chapter.

Estimating benefits of a renovation. There are two types of benefit analysis: one for projects directly affecting revenues, and the other for projects that support revenues. An example of a project directly affecting revenues is the renovation of a lounge; an example of a project that supports revenues would be replacing the roof. It is important to note here that renovations that affect revenues may not be contemplated to enhance revenue but simply to preserve revenue. For example, if a hotel has tired FF&E in its guestrooms it is at risk to lose business to a competitor with a superior room product. In this case, the renovation project's goal may be to enable the hotel to retain its current revenue level (and current guests).

To evaluate the potential benefits of a renovation project, managers must prepare an estimate (over some reasonable time period) of the operational revenues the hotel will earn without the renovation. This "base" revenue estimate is compared with an estimate of the revenues the hotel may earn over the same time period if the renovation is undertaken. The difference between these estimates is the estimate of the net revenues that will be gained by renovating. The net revenues are then compared with the cost of performing the renovation, to determine if the renovation produces the desired returns. It is very typical to use a net present value analysis as an aid to make decisions. Projects for which the present value of the benefits is greater than the present value of the costs are typically considered for funding.

The purpose of analyzing projects that support revenue is to identify those projects that will produce the greatest savings for the property. The methodology is very similar to that for projects affecting revenues, but the orientation shifts from estimating potential revenues to estimating the total cost of each alternative under consideration.[6]

As shown in Exhibit 9, life-cycle costing involves comparing the total cost of ownership for each alternative under consideration. The example in Exhibit 9 is generic, but illustrates the point that the life of each alternative need not be the same. In the example, Alternative A has a higher initial cost than Alternative B, but has the lowest annual total cost of ownership. In essence, the longer life and

Exhibit 9   Total Cost of Ownership Example

Alternative A

| | | Inflation Rate | | 3% |
| | | Opportunity Cost of Capital | | 10% |

Year	Initial Cost	Operating Cost	Salvage	Total
0	$ (12,000.00)			$ (12,000.00)
1		$ (1,500.00)		$ (1,500.00)
2		$ (1,545.00)		$ (1,545.00)
3		$ (1,591.35)		$ (1,591.35)
4		$ (1,639.09)		$ (1,639.09)
5		$ (1,688.26)		$ (1,688.26)
6		$ (1,738.91)		$ (1,738.91)
7		$ (1,791.08)		$ (1,791.08)
8		$ (1,844.81)	$1,500.00	$ (344.81)
			NPV =	$ (20,065.43)
		Annual Total Cost of Ownership =		$ (3,761.15)

Alternative B

| | | Inflation Rate | | 3% |
| | | Opportunity Cost of Capital | | 10% |

Year	Initial Cost	Operating Cost	Salvage	Total
0	$ (7,000.00)			$ (7,000.00)
1		$ (2,500.00)		$ (2,500.00)
2		$ (2,575.00)		$ (2,575.00)
3		$ (2,652.25)		$ (2,652.25)
4		$ (2,731.82)		$ (2,731.82)
5		$ (2,813.77)	$1,000.00	$ (1,813.77)
			NPV =	$ (16,385.58)
		Annual Total Cost of Ownership =		$ (4,322.47)

lower operating costs of Alternative A outweigh its higher initial cost. The lodging industry has many opportunities to use this analysis. Common examples include:

- Equipment replacement—laundry, kitchen, engineering.
- Lighting replacements—especially replacement of incandescent lamps with fluorescent, or even better, LED lamps.
- Repair versus replacement decisions—hotel van, kitchen equipment, roof.
- Replacement/retrofit of chillers and refrigeration equipment with machinery that uses refrigerants that are better for the environment.

- Replacement of through-wall HVAC units using electric heat with heat pump units.

- Installation of a micro turbine to generate electricity.

In many cases, the higher initial costs of a given alternative are more than offset by much lower operating costs, including both energy and labor savings.

Set Priorities and Choose Projects. At the completion of the estimating process, management has a list of projects ranked from most beneficial to least beneficial to the property. The list of prioritized projects is then typically presented to owner-ship for final approval in the form of the annual CapEx budget. Decision-makers usually pick those projects that offer the greatest economic returns or fulfill the most pressing needs. Good judgment is required to create this final list, because, from this point on, most approved projects are constructed. If poor projects are included, or good projects excluded, management has wasted opportunities.

Implementing the Renovation Plan

Once the planning process is complete and renovation projects have been approved, the hotel's managers can move on to the implementation of the renovation plans. Before implementation begins, one of the most important renovation team members must be appointed or hired—the project manager. This individual is responsible for coordinating all of the members of the renovation team to meet stated project objectives. Some specific responsibilities of the project manager include project scheduling, Request for Proposal (RFP) processing, communications, budget tracking, coordinating service providers, and more. In new construction, the essence of project management is to simultaneously maximize project quality, minimize project time, and meet the project budget. In renovation work, the further objective of minimizing disruptions in operating sections of the hotel is added. Achieving all four objectives is a tall order, but not impossible. It requires dedication, attention to detail, and a willingness to confront minor problems before they become major ones.

Once the project manager is in place, implementation of the design and construction phases begins.

The Design Phase

The renovation plan's first implementation step is to prepare, for each approved project, a design—or more precisely, a set of design documents—that serves as:

- The visual embodiment of the desires of ownership and management.

- A tool to secure building permits and licenses.

- A means to communicate to contractors the scope and detail of the work to be completed.

- A set of specifications that can be used to purchase furnishings.

While it may seem unlikely that one set of design documents can serve all these functions, in the end it must, for failure in any of these areas renders the documents virtually useless. For example, if the design is complete but does not meet local building codes, the renovation project will not receive the building permit and therefore not proceed. In this instance, the plans must be modified until the code requirements are met.

The extent and level of detail required in the design vary widely from project to project. Some projects may require only a simple sketch and some performance specifications, while complex renovations involve a complete set of construction plans, specifications, and schedules.

The Design Team. Whether the renovation is large or small, the design work for the renovation is usually the product of a team. The number of team members will vary widely from property to property and project to project, but all renovation projects should have a team composed of:

- Property managers.
- Project manager.
- Design professionals.
- Contractors.
- Purchasers.

To achieve success, these team members must integrate their respective needs and responsibilities while keeping in mind, "Good design costs no more than bad design." Exhibit 10 lists the responsibilities of team members and shows where those responsibilities overlap.

Because of the nature of renovation work, many renovation designers are specialists. Some specialize in the restoration of historic properties, others in southwest mission–style design, others in lighting systems, still others in life-safety system retrofits. Managers should interview designers to probe for their strengths and weaknesses before hiring them. If a design firm has experience with your type of facility or the specific nature of your project, it should be better able to understand your needs and those of your guests.

Bringing in professional designers is justified for all but the very smallest renovation projects. Designers bring a breadth of experience to the project and have access to the most current materials, furnishings, and construction technology. They see to it that the designs meet building code requirements, and provide the documents needed by local building officials. A design firm's services are usually paid for through a fixed-price contract based on a specific amount of work called "Basic Services," with payments made according to a schedule of completion. The client (in most cases, the hotel owner) usually reimburses the design firm for the costs of travel, drawing reproduction, and other reimbursables. Fees are usually based on a percentage of the work to be performed. A typical fee schedule for renovation work is shown in Exhibit 11.

In many renovations, the choice of one particular designer—the interior designer—is a key decision. The interior designer sets the boundaries of the project in a physical, aesthetic, and economic sense. The interior designer's decisions will affect the renovation budget, the renovation schedule, and the appearance of the facility for many years.

Exhibit 10   Responsibilities of the Design Team

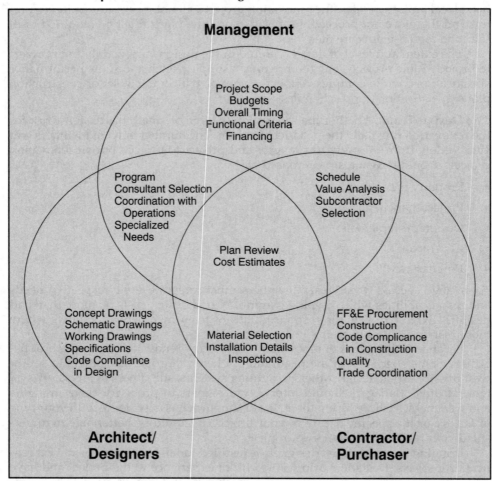

Exhibit 11   Typical Renovation Fee Schedules

Service	Fee
Architectural Design	3% – 7% of construction costs
Structural Design	2% – 4% of construction costs
MEP Design	1% – 4% of construction costs
Interior Design	3% – 7% of FF&E costs
Specialty Design	5% – 10% of specialty works cost

Source: Jonathan C. Nehmer, AIA, ISHC, HVS Design, 2014.

The Design Process. Design work has many phases, and in each phase the design firm will ask the client to approve the work before the firm goes on to the next phase. If the client has a change of heart after an approval and decides to do something different, the design firm will comply, but typically will request a fee for the additional work. By using this approach, the design firm and the client (in this case, the hotel's owner and managers) balance the need for the designer to make decisions on the client's behalf with the client's right to have ultimate control over those decisions. Done properly, the process results in completed projects that reflect the client's desires. Failure of this process results not only in bad design, but also in the creation of spaces that do not work as desired or intended, thus compromising revenue and property value.

Phase 1—conceptual design. Conceptual design sets the bounds and scope of a renovation project. It begins with the hotel's written renovation program being delivered to the design firm, and ends with the hotel's approval of concept documents prepared by the designers. The renovation program comes from the property survey process. The designers' work includes drawings; models; presentations of interior fabrics, colors, and materials; and sets of outline specifications. Through these documents, designers at the design firm demonstrate their understanding of the owner's needs and desires. In many cases, the design team will also produce a set of measured drawings that document existing as-built conditions. Especially in older buildings, this work can significantly reduce project uncertainty and lead to much better results.

Phase 2—schematic design. This phase fleshes out the conceptual design, fixing the location of design elements—a bar, front desk, or entry door, for example—establishing rigid boundaries, and showing the limits of demolition. This phase ends when the schematic design drawings are approved. The approved drawings show final colors and the final choices of the materials the major design elements are made of—stone rather than tile, vinyl rather than paint, wood rather than laminate, for example. Schematic design also shows how the work will be scheduled.

Phase 3—design development. Design development drawings are highly detailed, allowing the reader to determine accurate counts on numbers of seats, number of square feet, and quantities of materials. Construction materials and methods are specified, and design details between surfaces (for example, door moldings and jambs) and materials (for example, carpet to stone) are worked out. During this phase, design professionals coordinate and resolve any difficulties between each other's work, so that the completed design achieves the owner's objectives. Examples include coordinating gas and electrical service to kitchen equipment, reconfiguring duct work to accommodate ceiling changes, planning an aesthetically pleasing sprinkler-head layout in a ballroom, and incorporating all code-required changes. Approval of this set of drawings signals the client's desire to proceed with the work as designed. Changes after this point will affect construction of the work.

Phase 4—construction documents. Construction documents (also known as working drawings) constitute the final design phase. They are necessary primarily for two purposes: (1) to provide construction guidelines and guidelines for procuring materials, and (2) to secure the necessary building permits required to perform the work. This set of documents requires the highest level of detail and the longest time to prepare. It is also the most straightforward work, assuming no changes are made. Changes in the scope or nature of the renovation at this time will cause long delays in the production of the documents and will increase design costs.

Good construction documents eliminate uncertainty and result in lower costs, higher quality, and faster work. They allow the contractor to focus on the work exactly as shown on the documents and allow the purchaser to know precisely what and how much of each item to obtain.

The Construction Phase

Once construction documents are completed, contractors can be hired to begin construction. Before we move on to a discussion of construction contracts for contractors, it should be noted that some small renovation projects do not require a contractor—i.e., the work can be performed by in-house staff (an owner-as-contractor project). The risk with this approach is that the ongoing, day-to-day maintenance needs of the property tend to get pushed aside because the property's staff is concentrating on the renovation work. However, if the renovation is properly managed, this problem can be minimized.

Construction Contracts. The standard construction contract is a lump-sum contract that includes the following:

- A complete description of the work to be done (construction documents are used for this purpose)

- A description of the duties and responsibilities of hotel management, the contractor, and the design firm

- The cost of the work and the method of payment

- The date of commencement and the date of completion (for renovation work, this is particularly important and may include several interim dates as deadlines for phased work)

- The conditions that define final completion and acceptance of the contractor's work

The American Institute of Architects (AIA) has developed sample contracts that do a good job of protecting the interests of all parties. One contract in particular is well done—AIA Document A101, Standard Form of Agreement between Owner and Contractor. Although AIA's sample contracts are good places to start, you should always modify them (with the help of an attorney) for the particular work at hand. AIA Document A101 is used for large jobs with complex scopes or complex relationships between the parties. For smaller jobs, AIA Document A107—Abbreviated Form of Agreement Between Owner and Contractor—is often used.[7]

Before signing a contract, management will typically obtain bids from several contractors. In private work, one can choose the contractors allowed to bid. It is wise to prequalify contractors and create a bidder's list of firms able to perform the work. This is done via interviews and a review of each firm's technical and financial capabilities.

Each prequalified bidder receives a bid package consisting of the construction documents, a copy of the proposed construction contract, and a bid form. The bid form requests the contractor to provide a cost and a time to complete the work detailed in the construction documents. By submitting a signed form, the contractor certifies that he or she is able and willing to do the work for the price quoted in the time specified, and to abide by the terms of the contract.

Managers often neglect to use penalty and/or bonus clauses to encourage the contractor to finish on time. These clauses, coupled with good design documents, can help ensure timely completion and avoid hard feelings or litigation.

Purchasing. Purchasing furnishings, supplies, and equipment for renovation projects is a function with no uniformly defined status across hospitality firms. For some hotels, purchasing is performed by a corporate-level purchasing department, for others it is performed by a purchasing manager at the hotel, for still others it is performed by a third-party purchasing agent.

Even though much purchasing today can be done electronically, someone or some team still must take responsibility for renovation purchases. It is essential to manage renovation purchasing as a project distinct from operational purchasing. There are four key elements to success that the purchasing agent for the renovation project should keep in mind:

- Purchase materials of proper quality and durability.

- Purchase materials in the proper quantities.

- Make sure materials are on hand when needed.

- Stay within budget guidelines.

In many cases, the purchasing agent buys materials for the contractor to use during construction. Examples are kitchen and bar equipment, wall coverings, accessories (bath or closet, for example), lighting fixtures, and attached seating. In these cases, close coordination between the purchasing agent and the contractor concerning lead times, delivery dates, and handling of the material before installation are vital to maintaining the construction schedule.

One of the most difficult responsibilities of the purchaser is the expediting process. Expediting is the formal follow-up process used to ensure that goods are produced and shipped on schedule while maintaining the quality specified. A good expediting effort is often the key to meeting a renovation project's completion date. In many cases, however, expediting is performed haphazardly, leading to missed deadlines or the need to use expensive express-delivery services. The project manager should insist on being familiar with the purchasing agent's expediting procedures.

One final issue in purchasing is the question of what to do with the old furnishings. In some cases, selected pieces can be incorporated into the renovation, subject to cleaning, re-upholstering, or restoration. These pieces should be set aside for a restoration specialist to work on. In other cases, managers want the entire lot of existing furnishings to just go away. There are three ways to get rid of existing goods:

How to Deliver a Successful Construction Project:

Five Things That You As a Hotel Manager or Owner Must Do to Set You on the Right Path

1. **Select a Project Manager.** The project manager should be the first person you select for the renovation project. He or she is the conductor of the renovation orchestra and the focal point at which all information flows to and from. It's important to have the project manager on board before the renovation project begins, as this individual will be responsible for selecting the rest of the renovation team, managing the team, and, most importantly, keeping the project on time, on budget, and on quality.

2. **Establish a Clear Scope and Budget.** Understanding the extent of the scope of work and creating an approved budget before soliciting proposals from architects and other consultants is crucial. Take the time needed! Go over the renovation's scope with the project manager and the hotel's operations team. Do the "what ifs." Review the available funds and decide what are the must-haves, the want-to-haves, and the what-can-be-done-without.

3. **Select a Design Team.** Solicit Request for Quotations (RFQs) from architects and interior designers. Sending out an RFQ prior to the Request for Proposal (RFP) will allow the project manager the opportunity to review the experience and focus of interested parties and reduce the RFP list to a manageable number. The design team should be selected based on the correct qualifications for the project. Yes, price is very important, but selecting the right team for the job is more important. Once the list of pre-qualified firms is determined, a detailed RFP should be created. Make sure the RFP outlines details on the project's scope, budget, schedule, and sub-consultants necessary to complete the project. The specifics will help create a consistent response to the RFP from all bidders. Once you have the proposals back, select the appropriate design team based on the right firm/fee/experience/capabilities.

4. **Decide on a Project Delivery Method for Construction.** Once the design team has been selected, the next step is to bring on the construction team. This can be accomplished in many different ways. However, there are pros and cons for each one. We recommend selecting from the following project delivery methods:

    -   *Integrated Project Delivery.* For projects with a difficult or tight schedule, it is recommended to bring the general contractor and purchasing agent onto the team early in the process. This method allows for the entire team to be on the same page from the beginning, which can mitigate issues further along in construction. The design team is able to draw on the expertise of the contractor during the design phase, which can minimize mistakes and be helpful in identifying alternative means and methods of construction and installation. Collectively, the design, purchasing, and construction entities should work as a close-knit team to arrive at the best possible solutions. Other benefits of this method include the ability to identify and solve potential problems at a much earlier stage of the project.

- *Design/Bid/Build.* This method is more widely known as the "traditional" approach for delivering a project. The design team completes its documents and they are sent out to several contractors for bids. Once the lowest responsible bid is accepted, a stipulated-sum contract is entered into with the contractor. This competitive bid process may help you get to the lowest cost number. However, any errors or inconsistencies in either the renovation design or the building's existing conditions, or any weather delays or other unforeseen events will translate into added project costs, as the contractor has bid a very specific scope of work.

- *GMP.* GMP stands for Guaranteed Maximum Price. GMP contracts are used when speed is required to get a project started. In a GMP, the contractor is selected early in the design process and bids the work based on very early design documents. This means that there are many unknowns. Consequently, the contractor's bid contains numerous exclusions and contingencies. This form of contracting requires a much greater effort on the part of ownership to review every part of the project when final drawings are done to compare scope and cost to the original GMP contract scope.

- *Design/Build.* This delivery method also is used for speed to market. However, the major difference is that the design team is under contract to the builder (contractor). This puts more responsibility on the contractor to deliver a completed project on time and on budget, but the major drawback is that the client loses control over the design. The contractual relationship is between the contractor and designer, not designer and client.

5. **Stick to Your Plan.** Don't allow "scope creep" to derail all of the planning and hard work. One of the hardest things to control in a renovation project is the tendency to add more scope to the project. Adding scope or even changing the scope of the project can be devastating to the project budget, schedule, and quality of work. If proper planning is done at the beginning, then the necessary time has been taken to look at all of the wish list items that may be desired. Make decisions on scope and stick to them. If a change in the middle of a project is absolutely necessary, then a simple question needs to be asked prior to implementation: "Will this change in scope have a material impact on the guest's experience at the hotel?" Unless the answer is that it definitely does, then don't do it. Wait until the project is finished and then evaluate any changes or upgrades. It may be true that the proposed ideas for change are very good, but oftentimes it is best to save them for the next renovation cycle.

6. **Stick to Your Schedule.** Once the project's critical path method (CPM) schedule is established, make sure that everyone knows that it is the road map to be followed. A CPM schedule will show what to do and when to do it. When the project is stopped, changed, slowed down, or sped up, it changes the critical path. Many times during a project, opportunities can come up for the operations team to book pieces of business that would require the project to be halted. When this happens, the total impact of this change in the project's schedule must be evaluated. The stop in schedule may gain the operations team $5,000 in profit on a function or event that it books at the hotel, but the

(continued)

(continued)

> delay on the renovation project may cost $25,000. For this reason, it is never a good idea to stop in midstream during a project. Do the planning up front. It is possible to "work around" business by phasing a project properly if done in the planning stages. The word "DELAY" should always be taken seriously and avoided at all costs.

Source: Jonathan C. Nehmer, AIA, ISHC, Managing Principal, HVS Design.

1. *Have a liquidation sale at the hotel and sell as many items as possible.* While in-house staff can handle the liquidation, it is better to use the services of a professional liquidator, who in most cases will get higher prices for the goods.

2. *Contract with a furnishings handler to remove the items for a fixed price.* The agreement is usually very specific and lists all items to be removed, when they are to be removed, and payment terms.

3. *Donate the unwanted items.* There are many organizations, either local or national, that will gladly accept used FF&E. Organizations like the Furniture Bank Association of North America offer a network of affiliates that can professionally remove and reuse old materials.

The procurement and disposal of goods brings up the sustainability issue in renovation projects. There are many sustainable design and development strategies that those involved in a renovation can employ. What follows are a few of the notable sustainability issues that should be considered during all renovation projects:

- *Volatile organic compounds (VOCs).* These are toxic chemicals that are used in the manufacturing process. They are often found in paints, sealants, glues, flooring, coatings, and other additives. They off-gas over time, but breathing in the fumes is thought to be harmful. Low- or no-VOC products should be specified.

- *Nylon 6 carpet.* Nylon 6 is a chemical used for carpet fiber. The environmental benefit is that once it is produced, it may be infinitely recycled. It is estimated that more than five billion pounds of carpet enter landfills each year, so it makes great sense to specify Nylon 6 carpet whenever possible to reduce this waste stream.

- *Rapidly renewable materials.* These are materials that regenerate to maturity within a ten-year period. Examples include bamboo, cork, eucalyptus, and others. Building with rapidly renewable materials is better for the environment.

- *Locally sourced.* Although there is debate on the appropriate radius used to determine what "local" means, the U.S. Green Building Council defines locally sourced manufactured goods as those goods that can be procured within a 500-mile radius. Building with locally sourced materials minimizes carbon emissions from the transportation of those materials, and enhances the local economy through the support of local jobs and businesses.

Managing Construction. Even with excellent planning, communication, and documentation, issues still can arise during construction. Two key issues that must be dealt with by the project manager are documenting work (and changes to the work), and managing conflict. Documenting work consists of preparing a record of decisions that affect the project. Examples of documentation are:

- Approvals of sample materials, workmanship, or shop drawings.

- Written requests for interpretation of the drawings and a written reply.

- Minutes of job meetings.

- Written telephone conference records.

- Change proposals and change orders, signed and accepted by the contractor, design professionals, and renovation manager.

In short, the most important thing to remember in managing construction is to "get it in writing." Changes to the construction drawings invariably occur, and all changes should be written down and signed off on by everyone involved. Such documentation keeps conflict to a minimum.

A certain amount of conflict is inevitable in construction. It is not humanly possible for designers to foresee all possible contingencies and indicate every bit of work to be done. The owner, renovation manager, and contractor must understand that the construction drawings convey the designer's intentions, but may not show every minute detail. It is up to the individuals in charge of the project to equitably and properly work out any omissions or errors in the drawings and specifications.

Much conflict can be avoided if all parties to the renovation understand their roles and completely understand the scope of work to be completed. If all parties involved in the project work as a team, with trust and understanding, the result can be a high-quality renovation completed on time within the budget.

Issues that come up during construction that deserve special attention from the project manager include coordinating the renovation with ongoing operations, the effect of building codes and new legislation on renovations, and cost and quality control.

Coordination with operations. One of the most important decisions in any hotel renovation is the decision about what spaces will be closed and how long they will be closed. The general industry consensus is that a hotel should stay open unless renovation work cannot be completed without closing. When a property remains open, it usually engages in a set of phased closings of certain spaces. In some cases, it becomes apparent that the necessary closings are so extensive that the entire hotel should be shut down. The benefits and liabilities of closing are:

Benefits of Closing the Hotel

- Faster construction schedule, because all spaces are available

- Lower construction cost—no temporary facilities, shorter schedule, more efficient work

- Possibility of higher quality—no start/stop transitions; the ability to attract the best subcontractors

- No guests disgruntled by construction work

Liabilities of Closing the Hotel

- Loss of income during closing

- Loss of goodwill and market presence during closing

- Loss of good employees during closing (some may move on to other jobs)

There are ways to manage a renovation so that construction problems are minimized and the hotel can remain open. For example, a kitchen may be relocated to an on-site trailer if conditions require it. Spaces under renovation can be temporarily put in working order to accommodate a sell-out or high occupancy period. Employees can be informed of renovation plans and progress via town hall meetings, an in-house newsletter, an attachment to their paycheck, and frequent postings of pertinent information. Guests can be accommodated by moving a restaurant or lounge to a meeting room on a temporary basis. When a property remains open, it is important to convey to guests that the level of service hasn't changed, even though the number of services offered may be temporarily reduced.

In many cases, hotels post on their web pages advance notice to guests that certain spaces will be under renovation. This avoids blindsiding the guests with noise or disruption when they arrive at the hotel and reduces the number of complaints from guests. If the hotel remains open (albeit with some of its spaces temporarily closed), the project manager must communicate often and clearly with the sales staff, so the staff can properly manage the inventory of rooms and meeting space. Sales employees should treat the project manager like a client and block space to be renovated in the same manner they do with other clients; the project manager then has the responsibility to vacate the space on the agreed-upon date, like with any other client.

Another management concern during a renovation is temporary facilities. Temporary facilities take the form of physically moved or relocated facilities and constructed physical barriers. When considering temporary facilities, you should take the attitude that something worth doing is worth doing right. When relocating facilities, guests will tolerate some inconvenience, but you run the risk of asking so much of guests that they are alienated. It is here that friendly, competent service will greatly assist the renovation effort, for if guests perceive that the staff is not in control of the situation, they will become irritated and may not return. It is important to finish temporary barriers properly. A wall of unpainted plywood or drywall is ugly and intimidating. Usually, temporary walls can be used to display plans and colored drawings of the work being performed. In addition to separating construction from guests, barriers should control noise and dust.

A further factor in coordinating renovation work with ongoing operations is accommodating construction crews. The attitude of most hotel managers is that construction tradespeople are a necessary evil of renovation. Most tradespeople are not used to working on jobs that involve an operating business, and bring with them habits developed from years of work on new construction. It is important that the hotel's renovation manager establish **house rules**—clear and precise rules for the workers to follow while working on the property. Most construction workers will comply with reasonable rules. Rules should address parking, entrances and exits, restroom facilities, lunch facilities, smoking, use of radios, hours of work, and identification of workers. To maintain discipline and order on the job, violations should be quickly dealt with. It should be made clear to construction workers that these rules are not designed to infringe on their ability to do their jobs; rather, they are designed to facilitate the delivery of services to the hotel's guests and address the safety concerns of guests and the construction crew.

Building codes and new legislation. A critical factor to consider for any renovation project is the impact that building codes and new legislation will have on the work. Most buildings were built to meet the codes in effect at the time they were first constructed and are typically not required to be upgraded to meet code changes as they are adopted and applied to new construction over the years. However, upon renovation, many of the new codes could come into play, requiring changes to:

- Entrances and exits (configuration, location, and number)
- Life-safety systems
- Parking areas
- Construction materials (an upgrade in fire-resistance levels, for example)

Due to federal legislation, one area of particular interest continues to be building codes designed to accommodate disabled individuals. The Americans with Disabilities Act was originally passed in 1990 and was subsequently updated in 2010. Although the 2010 changes were not dramatic, there are some new accommodation standards that hotels must design into their future renovation projects.

The ADA itself applies a broad definition of "disabled." According to the ADA, people with arthritis, heart conditions, emphysema, shortness of stature, amputated limbs, AIDS, and other conditions are considered to be disabled people along with those individuals commonly associated with the term, such as people using wheelchairs. Most lodging and restaurant facilities are compelled to comply with ADA requirements because they fall under Title I and Title III of the ADA:

- *Title I of the Americans with Disabilities Act of 1990 prohibits private employers, state and local governments, employment agencies, and labor unions from discriminating against qualified individuals with disabilities in job application procedures, hiring, firing, advancement, compensation, job training, and other terms, conditions, and privileges of employment. The ADA covers employers with 15 or more employees.*

- *Title III prohibits discrimination on the basis of disability in the activities of places of public accommodations (including restaurants and hotels) and requires newly constructed or altered places of public accommodation—as well as commercial facilities to comply with the ADA Standards. It states that no individual may be discriminated against on the basis of disability with regards to the full and equal enjoyment of the goods, services, facilities, or accommodations.*

Complying with the ADA is not optional; it is a federal building code. All newly constructed buildings must fully comply with the 2010 code. Existing buildings are required to be compliant at the time of material renovations to specific spaces.[8] As with other specialty services that are required for renovations, hiring an ADA specialist for a renovation project may be prudent to ensure compliance.

Cost and quality control. Achieving the proper balance between cost and quality requires skill, attention to detail, and vision. There never seems to be enough funds for renovation. Good project managers spend endless hours revising budgets, seeking alternatives, and surgically adjusting the renovation's scope to achieve the most renovation for the funds expended. But cost-cutting is not always the answer and should not be overdone. After the renovation is complete, the brief satisfaction of saving a few dollars fades quickly if it turns out that quality was sacrificed to achieve budget objectives, for the facility must live with the renovated space until the next renovation cycle. Mistakes to avoid include:

- *Not hiring design professionals.* Although it is less common that this would occur for a large project, with smaller renovation projects it can be difficult for many people to see the value of design professionals. Competent designers save their fees many times over by specifying the correct materials for the job, fixing problems on the plans rather than working them out in the field, knowing where to find competent manufacturers and contractors, achieving a consistent look to a space, and—most importantly—creating spaces that work aesthetically and functionally.

- *Allowing unqualified contractors to bid or work on a project in an attempt to lower construction costs.* This is perhaps the most destructive form of pennywise, pound-foolish judgment. It is the project manager's responsibility to select competent contractors and tradespeople and pay them a fair price for the work. Some facilities have been ruined by contractors who did not have the ability to do the work properly. While the manager received a low price for the work, the end result was not worth the savings.

- *Reducing the renovation's scope to the point that the renovation becomes meaningless.* "Value engineering" or scope reduction may lead to mismatched materials, dysfunctional spaces, and frustrating results. One does not renovate a lobby by replacing the drapes and reupholstering the furniture. If this work is all that needs to be done, it should be performed in harmony with the existing interior design, and not be called a renovation. This does not mean that this type of work should be avoided, but one should make decisions based on the needs of the space, not simply apply a few dollars to a space and call it "renovated."

When considering renovation, managers should look for ways to save money without sacrificing quality. Some examples are:

- Asking food and beverage purveyors to supply equipment at no cost or reduced cost, if you use their products. Examples include coffee makers, juice dispensers, and soda equipment.

- Purchasing used equipment that has been refurbished. This is an especially appropriate idea for kitchens, laundries, and engineered systems.

- Buying equipment that may be show samples, prior-year models, or discounted because of superficial damage during shipping.

- Allowing renovation funds to build in a bank account; the funds will grow as interest is added. This may require delaying renovation projects for several months or even years, a trade-off that should be considered if funds are especially scarce.

- Refinishing or reupholstering existing furniture if the quality and style are appropriate for the renovation.

While these ideas may make some people cringe, they should be considered, along with other money-saving ideas, if the renovation budget is tight.

Final Completion and Acceptance. Final completion and acceptance is an important phase of all renovation projects. It signifies both physical acceptance of the work, as completed, and compliance with the legal requirements of the construction contract—meaning that the contractor is entitled to full payment of money owed.

It is common to formalize acceptance of the contractor's work by using a document called the Certificate of Substantial Completion. The essence of this document is that the renovation manager, design professional(s), and contractor agree that the work is fit for its intended purpose, that it meets the requirements of the construction contract, and that it is ready for occupancy. The renovation manager usually does not sign this document unless he or she has secured a Certificate of Occupancy from the appropriate local authorities and (if necessary) has attached a list, called a **punch list**. The punch list details items that require corrective action or completion in order to meet contract specifications. Once the punch list items are resolved, the contractor is paid in full.

While the standard AIA contracts call for the contractor to prepare the punch list, this is not common in practice. The project manager should be in charge of preparing the punch list. Typically the project manager inspects all areas included in the renovation with the contractor, designer, and property representative. If the project is large, many times the asset manager will participate as well. The punch list is then presented to the contractor for review. If the contractor disagrees with some of the items, those items must be negotiated.

Another issue during the final-completion-and-acceptance phase is clean-up. In many cases, the hotel's housekeeping staff will assist the contractor in the clean-up effort, in order to help meet the schedule and ensure proper housekeeping standards. The amount of cleanup the housekeeping staff will do should be worked out before signing the Certificate of Substantial Completion. Once the construction crew is gone, housekeeping staff must outfit the newly renovated areas for guest use (which may involve the placement of linens, towels, amenities, soaps, etc.).

After the Renovation

Even after the renovated areas of the hotel are finished and open for business, the renovation is not yet complete. Several items should be addressed at this point (if not before), including:

- The post-audit.
- Employee training.
- Grand reopenings.
- Impact of the renovation on operating budgets.

Post-Audit. Once the renovation project is complete, it is important that the renovation team complete the **post-audit** process. All renovation team members should participate in this process, which involves documenting best-practices, outlining lessons learned, and noting the unique challenges or attributes that the physical facility presented. The post-audit is also an appropriate time to note the performance of the service providers—the architects, designers, project manager, FF&E manufacturers, etc. This post-audit information should be used as a reference for future property renovations.

Employee Training. Employee training is often neglected or ignored until a renovation is complete and management suddenly realizes that the employees who work in the renovated space need reorientation and training to maximize the benefit of the renovation. The interior designer should take part in the training to ensure that employees work within the space and maintain it as envisioned by the renovation manager and designer. Training should address:

- New or changed service standards.
- New or changed methods of production, holding, and presentation of food and beverage items.
- How to operate new equipment, especially electronic systems (training requirements should be written into purchasing contracts with suppliers of this equipment).
- How to present the new product/technology/service to guests.

One often hears the refrain, "Oh, I didn't know we could do that!" months after a renovation is complete. Managers and employees discover by accident or from suppliers how systems or equipment work or should be maintained. Examples include discovering capabilities in the new sound systems or lighting systems that managers and employees knew nothing about, or continuing to maintain a floor in the same old way when the new floor requires much simpler maintenance procedures. In these cases, management has lost opportunities and the employees have been done a disservice by a lack of proper training.

Grand Reopenings. Often it is appropriate to involve the hotel's marketing department or even the corporate office (if the hotel is part of a chain) in a public celebration of the renovation. The objective of the celebration should be to build awareness among potential guests, travel agents, and meeting planners that the new and improved facilities are available for use. The reopening is often a grand occasion, with dignitaries and the media invited. These events should be planned and budgeted as part of the original scope of renovation work.[9]

Impact of the Renovation on Operating Budgets. As mentioned earlier in the chapter, the feasibility of renovation projects is based in part on projections of future revenue or future cost reductions. Once projects are completed, there should be a formal tracking procedure to determine whether each renovation project has the financial impact management projected. This tracking will be valuable for future renovations, providing managers with solid information with which to base future decisions.

Conclusion

Renovations are a complex, time-consuming, and capital-intensive process. Executing a successful renovation project takes detailed planning, talented professional service providers, and excellent management. Just like no two hotels are exactly the same, neither are any two renovation projects. Vigilant attention to detail is required at every turn, for every project. However, with the utilization of proper strategies, the renovation will yield a high-quality product that will enhance the hotel's functionality and value.

Endnotes

1. Jonathan C. Nehmer, AIA, ISHC, Managing Principal, HVS Design.

2. Bjorn Hansen, "SCPS' Bjorn Hanson Finds U.S. Lodging Industry Capital Expenditures Increase to a Record Level in 2013," www.nyu.edu, August 2013.

3. *CapEx 2007: A Study of Capital Expenditures in the U.S. Hotel Industry* (Memphis, Tennessee: International Society of Hospitality Consultants, 2007).

4. See "The Ages Of U.S. Commercial Buildings By Type, As of Mid-2011."

5. This information is based on national average costs in 2013 and represents system-level costs.

6. For a detailed discussion, see Rosalie T. Ruegg and Harold E. Marshall, *Building Economics: Theory and Practice* (New York: Van Nostrand Reinhold, 1990).

7. For these and other forms, see www.aia.org. There are several variations to the standard owner-contractor agreement that have been used with success, such as Integrated Project Delivery, Design/Bid/Build, Guaranteed Maximum Price, and Design/Build.

8. Adapted from U.S. Department of Justice, *Guidance on the 2010 ADA Standards for Accessible Design*, Volume 2, 2010.

9. See Richard H. Penner, Lawrence Adams, and Stephani K. A. Robson, *Hotel Planning, Design, and Development*, 2nd ed. (New York: W. W. Norton & Company, 2012) for an excellent resource with illustrations that visually demonstrate what is possible through renovation.

Key Terms

facility life-cycle cost study—A space-by-space schedule of the projected renovation needs for a given building over a very long time horizon (such as twenty to thirty years), based on the expected life of various components within each space and the cost to replace them at the end of their expected life.

house rules—Rules for the construction crew to follow while working in the hotel during a renovation. For example, one house rule might be that construction workers cannot use the hotel's public restrooms, but instead must use employee restrooms.

major renovation—Replacement or renewal of all furnishings and finishes within a space, and, in some instances, extensive modifications to the use and physical layout of the space.

minor renovation—Replacement or renewal of non-durable furnishings and finishes within a space, without changing the space's use or physical layout.

post audit—The process of reviewing all of the activities related to the just-completed renovation, including strategic analysis, team performance, design, materials, and execution.

punch list—A list of non-conforming construction work, attached to the Certificate of Substantial Completion, that a contractor must correct before receiving full payment for the work.

renovation—The process of renewing and updating a property, usually to offset the ravages of use or modify spaces to meet the needs of changing markets.

restoration—A complete gutting of a space that involves replacing systems that are technically and functionally obsolete, while restoring furnishings and systems that can still be used.

special project—A renovation task related to a specific upgrade, service, or system that can be handled distinctly from renovation work that is tied to changing an interior design. As such, special projects in hospitality businesses have usually been related to technology or engineering systems.

strategic review—A periodic, rigorous evaluation of a property, usually by the property's general manager and the owner's representative or asset manager (in large organizations, regional or divisional managers may also be involved); in this evaluation, managers and ownership representatives conduct an honest evaluation of the hotel's current market position, identify key trends in the local hospitality market, and combine the above analyses to formulate the best market position for the property and plan for future renovations.

Review Questions

1. Why should a hotel renovate?

2. What are the differences among the five types of renovation?

3. What is a facility life-cycle cost study?

4. The planning phase for property renovation can be broken down into what four steps?

5. How are renovation costs and benefits estimated?

6. What are the four phases of design work?

7. What is included in a standard construction contract? What are some variations to a standard owner-contractor agreement?

8. What are some issues hotel managers should keep in mind while managing construction work?

9. What are some of the benefits and liabilities of closing a hotel while it is being renovated?

10. What are some areas that managers should address after a renovation is complete (if not before)?

Internet Sites

For more information, visit the following Internet sites. Remember that Internet addresses can change without notice. If the site is no longer there, you can use a search engine to look for additional sites.

American Institute of Architects
www.aiaonline.org

Americans with Disabilities Act Guide
www.ada.gov/regs2010/2010ADAStan
dards/Guidance2010ADAstandards.
htm#titleIII

American Society of Interior Designers
www.asid.org

Associated Builders and Contractors,
Inc.
www.abc.org

Association of Restorers
www.assoc-restorers.com

Association of Specialists in Cleaning
& Restoration
www.ascr.org

Construction Management Association
of America
www.cmaanet.org

Furniture Fixture Services
www.hotelrenovators.com

HVS Design
www.hvsdesignservices.com

International Society of Hospitality
Consultants
www.ishc.com

Case Study

A Renovation in Retrospect

"This was not the reaction I was hoping for," thought Mitch Scaparelli as he stared at the e-mail on his computer screen. Mitch was the general manager of the GreenTree Hotel, a 400-room suburban chain property that had just completed the first phase of a major guestroom renovation. The e-mail was from Ted North, the GreenTree's owner representative. Ted wanted to meet with Mitch to talk about the project's delays and cost overruns. As Mitch scanned the e-mail again, ominous phrases jumped out: "deeply concerned," "unexpected costs,""adverse impact on the hotel's revenue stream," and so on. Mitch could read between the lines. Stated simply, Ted's message was, "I'm disappointed, and you've got some explaining to do."

Thankfully, Mitch had a good relationship with Ted, and he didn't think his job was in serious jeopardy. But he wasn't about to win the general manager of the year award, either. "How did I get into this mess?" Mitch thought. "Why didn't the renovation go as smoothly as I thought it would?"

Mitch leaned back in his chair and reviewed the project in his mind. It was almost a year ago that the hotel staff was putting the last pieces of the renovation plan together. The GreenTree, built twenty years ago, didn't have any major maintenance and engineering issues, but its guestrooms definitely needed some attention, and it was decided to complete the renovation project in two phases: 250 rooms the first year, the rest of the rooms the year after. With a budget of $10,000 per guestroom, it was costing the hotel $2.5 million in the first year alone, so it was important that the project be managed properly. Mitch remembered wrestling for quite a while with whether to save some money and let Bill, the hotel's chief engineer, manage the project, or spend the money to hire an outside firm to manage it.

To help him make that decision, Mitch had traveled to the chain's recently renovated 1,200-room flagship hotel to talk to Soo Landry, the general manager there. "As you know, most hotels in our chain hire the Glazer Corporation to manage major renovation work," Soo had told him, "but my director of engineering, Arjun Singh, has twenty years' experience in maintenance and engineering, and he not only knows our property inside and out, he has worked on major renovation projects before.

"He did a fantastic job," she continued. "He kept in close contact with the contractors all the way, and the project was completed on budget and on time. He didn't forget about the eighty people in the engineering department, either, so they never missed a beat with the hotel's regular maintenance work. Arjun kept the needs of our guests in mind all the way through the renovation, and the hotel looks great!"

After talking with Soo and hearing how well Arjun had done, Mitch had decided to let Bill take on the GreenTree renovation. After all, Bill had been the property's chief engineer for the past five years and had overseen GreenTree's lobby renovation three years ago, as well as other minor renovation projects, so he had some experience. Plus, Bill's twelve-person staff had a couple of engineers on it, so they could probably help him out if there were parts of the renovation he couldn't handle. Mitch liked the idea of giving Bill a chance to manage the project; Bill had been with the property for twelve years, arriving fresh from trade school and starting out as a mechanic before working his way up to chief engineer. This would be an opportunity for Bill to stretch and grow professionally. Best of all, Mitch remembered thinking, was that Ted North, who was always preaching cost containment, would love the idea of not hiring the Glazer Corporation, thereby saving money. Typically, hiring an outside project management company could cost upwards of 10 percent of the project's budget, so, with Bill in charge, that would free up $250,000 for the hotel to spend on better guestroom upgrades.

Mitch remembered announcing his decision at the end of a Monday morning staff meeting. He had expected it to be greeted with smiles and approval all around, but the news received a mixed reaction. The controller had frowned and said, "Bill runs a good department, but are you sure we shouldn't bring in an outside guy, someone with expertise in this area? Cost overruns and guestrooms that aren't finished on time could really bust our budget this year." The food and beverage director said he didn't care who managed the project, as long as they stayed out of the restaurant and kitchen. The executive housekeeper smiled and said she was confident Bill would do a good job. But perhaps most puzzling of all had been Bill's reaction. "I appreciate the vote of confidence," he had said, smiling, but there was a worried look in his eyes.

In the weeks and months that followed, it turned out that Bill's worried look had been justified, as the project hit snag after snag::

- On the first day of the project, the construction workers arrived at 7:00 a.m. to get started. Soon the phones were ringing off the hook at the front desk, from angry guests calling about the noise. Bill forgot that construction crews like to start early, and he therefore also forgot to stipulate a 9:00 a.m. start time in the contract.

- There were issues with the elevators throughout the project. Employees complained about elevator wait times when construction workers used them to move materials. At times, the contractor forgot to lock out the floor on which the construction crews were working, so that guests sometimes found themselves looking at scaffolding and dusty tarps when the elevator doors opened.

- The water supply for sixteen rooms was disrupted when the contractor began renovation work on the vacated ninth floor; he didn't realize that the water supply lines ran vertically in the building, serving adjacent rooms, so some guests on every floor found themselves without water until the issue was resolved. Again, the front desk was besieged with complaint calls and the hotel had to give out many rebates and refunds to disgruntled guests.

- Some of the heavy equipment that the contractor used at times caused electrical circuit breakers to blow, which interrupted electrical service to guestrooms and resulted in more complaint calls to the front desk and numerous maintenance calls for the engineering staff.

- The periodic electrical power disruptions caused the hotel's bedside alarm clocks to temporarily lose power, so many of them would be blinking "12:00" when guests checked into their guestrooms. Some guests could reset their own clocks and some could not, but none of them was happy about it. This added to the number of calls the front desk had to take from irritated guests.

- Twice during construction, the hotel's fire alarm went off and the entire hotel had to be evacuated. Bill didn't realize that the dust generated when the construction workers were sanding the new drywall could get thick enough to set off the alarms.

- The hotel's regular maintenance work suffered as Bill's staff of twelve struggled to move the old furniture out of, and the new furniture into, the affected rooms. Haste and fatigue led to damaged walls and dropped furniture, which led to more costs because of change orders to get the walls repaired and the need to order replacement furniture for some items.

- Bill was glad to see the 250 new television sets arrive one morning, but he was confused when, an hour later, he found all of them still sitting in the receiving area. Bill called the contractor, who reminded Bill with sympathy—well-feigned but for the twinkle in his eye—that, according to the contract, TV installation was not part of his scope of work. He helpfully offered to write up a change order and install and program the TVs for an additional $10,000. Not wanting to add another burden to his already overworked engineering staff, Bill reluctantly agreed to the change order.

- The 250 remotes that came with the televisions did not have a button for close captioning; they had to be shipped back to the company for replacement, causing a delay and more costs. When the new remotes arrived, Bill discovered that none of them had batteries—an oversight that he failed to catch when the wrong remotes arrived the first time. It took one of the hotel's shuttle drivers all afternoon to go from store to store and buy up enough batteries for the new remotes.

- Bill didn't notice that the contract specifications called for custom carpet from China. Not only did this special carpet have a sixteen-week delivery time instead of the usual six to eight weeks, it was also delayed in customs. Due to this unexpected variable, some of the guestrooms that otherwise were finished could not be rented to guests, because the carpet was still in transit.

- Bill forgot to stipulate in the contract that the contractor was supposed to clean the guestrooms after construction work was completed, so the Green-Tree's housekeeping staff had to clean up the dust and construction debris in each renovated guestroom, causing delays and affecting the housekeeping staff's morale.

- As the renovation dragged on, overtime costs mounted as the harried engineering and housekeeping staffs tried to keep up with the extra demands.

Despite all the problems, Phase 1 of the renovation was eventually completed and the new guestrooms looked great. Bill did grow professionally as he recovered from his mistakes and learned how to better deal with the extra workload and the contractors. However, the project came in late and over budget. Mitch was disappointed about that, to say the least. And, judging by this morning's e-mail, so was Ted North. "Maybe I made a mistake in letting Bill manage the project," Mitch thought glumly as he started gathering documents to prepare for his meeting with Ted.

Discussion Questions

1. Did Mitch make a mistake in letting Bill manage Phase 1 of the guestroom renovation project? Why or why not?

2. Should Bill be allowed to manage Phase 2 of the project, or should the Glazer Corporation be hired to manage it?

Case Number: 28114CA

The following industry experts helped generate and develop this case: Richard Manzolina, Director of Property Operations, Capital Hilton, Washington, D.C.; Ed Pietzak, RPA, FMA, CEOE, Director of Engineering, New York Marriott Marquis, New York, New York; and David M. Stipanuk, Associate Professor, School of Hotel Administration, Cornell University, Ithaca, New York.

Chapter Appendix: Renovation Cost Guidelines

	Economy		Extended-Stay		Mid-Scale	
Guestrooms & Corridors						
Guestroom Only Softgoods Reno.	$1,919 to $2,922	Per Guestroom	$5,147 to $7,402	Per Guestroom	$4,209 to $6,312	Per Guestroom
Add for Full Reno.	$1,662 to $2,076	Per Guestroom	$7,744 to $10,597	Per Guestroom	$4,274 to $5,509	Per Guestroom
Bathroom (1) Softgoods Reno.	$563 to $981	Per Guestroom	$1,154 to $1,939	Per Guestroom	$1,178 to $2,103	Per Guestroom
(2) Add for Full Reno.	$2,770 to $4,294	Per Guestroom	$4,813 to $6,618	Per Guestroom	$4,245 to $6,136	Per Guestroom
Guestroom Corridors (3,4)	$403 to $617	Per Guestroom	$1,033 to $1,482	Per Guestroom	$940 to $1,289	Per Guestroom
Public Spaces						
Reception Area (5) Softgoods Reno.	$22 to $35	Per SF (180)	$11 to $18	Per SF (1400)	$8 to $13	Per SF (2500)
Add for Full Reno.	$89 to $131	Per SF (180)	$65 to $110	Per SF (1400)	$50 to $87	Per SF (2500)
Public Restrooms Softgoods Reno.	$5 to $9	Per SF (80)	$7 to $11	Per SF (480)	$7 to $12	Per SF (480)
Add for Full Reno.	$50 to $78	Per SF (80)	$68 to $102	Per SF (480)	$70 to $108	Per SF (480)
F & B Facilities						
Restaurant Softgoods Reno.	$17 to $26	Per SF (400)	$34 to $47	Per SF (1400)	$36 to $48	Per SF (1296)
(Economy: Breakfast Bar Only)	$570 to $881	Per Seat (12)	$627 to $869	Per Seat (76)	$683 to $909	Per Seat (68)
Add for Full Reno.	$38 to $60	Per SF (400)	$55 to $90	Per SF (1400)	$81 to $138	Per SF (1296)
	$1,263 to $2,013	Per Seat (12)	$1,008 to $1,650	Per Seat (76)	$1,539 to $2,633	Per Seat (68)
Bar & Lounge Softgoods Reno.	N/A		N/A		$45 to $60	Per SF (720)
	N/A		N/A		$605 to $799	Per Seat (54)
Add for Full Reno.	N/A		N/A		$114 to $187	Per SF (720)
	N/A		N/A		$1,519 to $2,500	Per Seat (54)
Kitchen (6) Excl. Equipment	N/A		$48 to $87	Per SF (80)	$15 to $23	Per SF (1600)
(Economy: Storage Pantry Only) Select Kitchen Equipment	N/A		$21 to $30	Per SF (80)	$13 to $19	Per SF (1600)

(continued)

Chapter Appendix: Renovation Cost Guidelines *(continued)*

		Economy	Extended-Stay	Mid-Scale
Function Spaces				
Prefunction	Softgoods Reno.	N/A	N/A	$16 to $23 Per SF (750)
	Add for Full Reno.	N/A	N/A	$43 to $79 Per SF (750)
Ballroom	Softgoods Reno.	N/A	N/A	N/A
	Add for Full Reno.	N/A	N/A	N/A
Meeting Rooms	Softgoods Reno.	N/A	$11 to $16 Per SF (552)	$11 to $16 Per SF (2964)
	Add for Full Reno.	N/A	$62 to $91 Per SF (552)	$58 to $92 Per SF (2964)
Board Rooms	Softgoods Reno.	N/A	N/A	N/A
	Add for Full Reno.	N/A	N/A	N/A
Guest Amenities				
Exercise Facility	Softgoods Reno.	N/A	$14 to $27 Per SF (400)	$18 to $36 Per SF (728)
	(7) Add for Full Reno.	N/A	$65 to $95 Per SF (400)	$58 to $88 Per SF (728)
Spas	Softgoods Reno.	N/A	N/A	N/A
	Add for Full Reno.	N/A	N/A	N/A
Outdoor Swimming Pool (8)		N/A	$12 to 27 Per SF (2,106)	$15 to $32 Per SF (2,106)
Indoor Swimming Pool (8, 9)		N/A	$47 to $74 Per SF (2,106)	$49 to $77 Per SF (2,106)
Outdoor Amenities		N/A	$41,113 to $77,794 Allowance	$47,709 to $87,717 Allowance
Infrastructure				
Outdoor Parking (Seal Lot & Stripe Spaces)		$90 to $141 Per Space (100)	$90 to $141 Per Space (175)	$90 to $141 Per Space (150)
Indoor Parking Structure Renovation		N/A	N/A	N/A
Landscaping (10)		$10,389 to $21,298 Allowance	$20,779 to $31,687 Allowance	$20,779 to $31,687 Allowance

(continued)

Chapter Appendix: Renovation Cost Guidelines *(continued)*

		Upscale		Upper-Upscale		Luxury	
Guestrooms & Corridors							
Guestroom Only	Softgoods Reno.	$5,556 to $8,000	Per Guestroom	$8,379 to $11,751	Per Guestroom	$12,503 to 17,703	Per Guestroom
	Add for Full Reno.	$7,580 to $9,979	Per Guestroom	$9,781 to $12,921	Per Guestroom	$15,207 to $19,990	Per Guestroom
Bathroom	(1) Softgoods Reno.	$1,314 to $2,265	Per Guestroom	$1,973 to $3,269	Per Guestroom	$3,180 to $5,074	Per Guestroom
	(2) Add for Full Reno.	$4,854 to $8,121	Per Guestroom	$8,002 to $12,239	Per Guestroom	$13,621 to $22,305	Per Guestroom
Guestroom Corridors (3, 4)		$977 to $1,312	Per Guestroom	$1,646 to $2,167	Per Guestroom	$2,004 to $2,696	Per Guestroom
Public Spaces							
Reception Area	(5) Softgoods Reno.	$11 to $17	Per SF (3500)	$12 to $19	Per SF (4800)	$26 to $51	Per SF (4000)
	Add for Full Reno.	$95 to $169	Per SF (3500)	$108 to $195	Per SF (4800)	$165 to $276	Per SF (4000)
Public Restrooms	Softgoods Reno.	$11 to $17	Per SF (1440)	$17 to $32	Per SF (1440)	$26 to $46	Per SF (1920)
	Add for Full Reno.	$104 to $195	Per SF (1440)	$109 to $204	Per SF (1440)	$120 to $205	Per SF (1920)
F & B Facilities							
Restaurant (Economy: Breakfast Bar Only)	Softgoods Reno.	$42 to $54	Per SF (3000)	$39 to $53	Per SF (4560)	$53 to $68	Per SF (3200)
		$901 to $1,165	Per Seat (140)	$921 to $1,244	Per Seat (195)	$1,400 to $1,816	Per Seat (120)
	Add Full Reno.	$90 to $151	Per SF (3000)	$86 to $144	Per SF (4560)	$100 to $186	Per SF (3200)
		$1,933 to $3,230	Per Seat (140)	$2,020 to $3,367	Per Seat (195)	$2,932 to $4,969	Per Seat (120)
Bar & Lounge	Softgoods Reno.	$42 to $55	Per SF (1600)	$50 to $66	Per SF (1200)	$50 to $64	Per SF (1200)
		$752 to $976	Per Seat (90)	$861 to $1,126	Per Seat (70)	$1,156 to $1,484	Per Seat (52)
	Add for Full Reno.	$119 to $196	Per SF (1600)	$191 to $312	Per SF (1200)	$228 to $395	Per SF (1200)
		$2,116 to $3,493	Per Seat (90)	$3,282 to $5,344	Per Seat (70)	$5,266 to $9,104	Per Seat (52)
Kitchen (Economy: Storage Pantry Only)	(6) Excl Equipment	$25 to $39	Per SF (4200)	$18 to $28	Per SF (7200)	$18 to $28	Per SF (7200)
	Select Kitchen Equip.	$14 to $21	Per SF (4200)	$16 to $23	Per SF (7200)	$17 to $25	Per SF (7200)

(continued)

Chapter Appendix: Renovation Cost Guidelines *(continued)*

		Upscale	Upper-Upscale	Luxury
Function Spaces				
Prefunction	Softgoods Reno.	$16 to $22 Per SF (2000)	$22 to $31 Per SF (1200)	$31 to $91 Per SF (960)
	Add for Full Reno.	$61 to $112 Per SF (2000)	$75 to $141 Per SF (1200)	$141 to $263 Per SF (960)
Ballroom	Softgoods Reno.	$10 to $14 Per SF (8550)	$13 to $19 Per SF (4500)	$14 to $20 Per SF (4800)
	Add for Full Reno.	$82 to $141 Per SF (8550)	$98 to $175 Per SF (4500)	$141 to $245 Per SF (4800)
Meeting Rooms	Softgoods Reno.	$12 to $17 Per SF (11900)	$17 to $23 Per SF (8400)	$28 to $54 Per SF (3000)
	Add for Full Reno.	$61 to $98 Per SF (11900)	$88 to $137 Per SF (8400)	$137 to $239 Per SF (3000)
Board Rooms	Softgoods Reno.	$28 to $37 Per SF (728)	$28 to $37 Per SF (1456)	$32 to $42 Per SF (1456)
	Add for Full Reno.	$80 to $134 Per SF (728)	$91 to $152 Per SF (1456)	$129 to $282 Per SF (1456)
Guest Amenities				
Exercise Facility	Softgoods Reno.	$22 to $41 Per SF (1092)	$27 to $48 Per SF (1456)	$31 to $54 Per SF (1820)
	(7) Add for Full Reno.	$98 to $155 Per SF (1092)	$126 to $185 Per SF (1456)	$118 to $210 Per SF (1820)
Spas	Softgoods Reno.	$46 to $64 Per SF (592)	$50 to $69 Per SF (1014)	$67 to $97 Per SF (1740)
	Add for Full Reno.	$121 to $257 Per SF (592)	$140 to $305 Per SF (1014)	$151 to $334 Per SF (1740)
Outdoor Swimming Pool (8)		$16 to $30 Per SF (3,500)	$15 to $30 Per SF (4,800)	$12 to $22 Per SF (10,350)
Indoor Swimming Pool (8, 9)		$61 to $94 Per SF (2,816)	$71 to $110 Per SF (3,996)	$77 to $126 Per SF (7,326)
Outdoor Amenities		$92,177 to $187,557 Allowance	$62,336 to $98,698 Allowance	$93,504 to $148,047 Allowance
Infrastructure				
Outdoor Parking (Seal Lot & Stripe Spaces)		$90 to $141 Per Space (486)	N/A	N/A
Indoor Parking Structure Renovation		N/A	$904 to $1,342 Per Space (347)	$971 to $1,437 Per Space (352)
Landscaping (10)		$41,557 to $77,920 Allowance	$62,236 to $98,698 Allowance	$93,504 to $148,047 Allowance

(continued)

Chapter Appendix: Renovation Cost Guidelines *(continued)*

General Notes

- This estimating information is a guideline only. Before utilizing this information for any renovation, a full budget estimate should be prepared by JN+A and HVS Design.

- Sources: JN+A historical data, misc. purchasing organization unit price information, input from U.S. General Contractors, geographically diverse.

- Costs indicated in this Estimating Guide do NOT include Professional Fees, Contingency, Operating Supplies and Equipment, Attic Stock, Freight or Sales Tax, etc.

- Costs indicated in this Estimating Guide INCLUDE the Contractor's General Conditions, Overhead and Profit. Cost for Performance Bonds and Building Permits are NOT included.

Footnotes

1. Includes vanity light, vinyl wallcovering, framed mirror, paint ceiling.

2. Adds vanity (base), vanity top, faucet, stone/tile tub surround, shower valve, tub diverter, tub drain, tub refinish, porcelain tile floor with tile base.

3. Includes carpet and double-stick pad, vinyl wallcovering, sconce lighting, artwork, window treatments, paint ceiling, painted millwork running trim, furniture, signage, and ice machines.

4. The guestroom component of a guest corridor occupies an area equal to the width of the gruestroom, full height, and one half of the corridor width.

5. Includes finishes and lighting upgrades; no electrical, HVAC, or life safety upgrades; nor any reconfiguration.

6. Allowance only; varies with site.

7. Assumes treadmills, elliptical, small free weights, small universal, towel display, dirty towel hamper, art, VWC, lighting, and flooring.

8. Resurface pool bottom, resurface pool deck, new pool furniture; includes ADA lift.

9. Includes interior finishes, lighting, pool pak HVAC.

10. Allowance only; varies geographically.

11. Costs listed in common additives section are for items not typically included in the renovation scopes for the major categories. These costs assume that a full renovation is also occurring at time of construction.

Appendix:
Engineering Principles

This appendix discusses some of the key principles of physics and chemistry and their application to commonly encountered situations in the design and operation of buildings. Many of these principles are presented in courses which hospitality students may take in food chemistry or physical sciences courses at colleges and universities. A substantial background in mathematics and the physical sciences is used in the design of building systems. An understanding of the basic principles governing engineering systems will provide a worthwhile dimension to the reader's understanding of the technical aspects of building operations.

Basic Principles

Mass, Force, Power, and Energy

Mass, force, power, and energy are key engineering concepts. Mass refers to the quantity of matter. In the English system of measurement, the unit of mass is the pound (lb). The pound is also the unit used for force in the English system, a rather unfortunate circumstance. An object with a mass of one pound will exert a force of one pound when subjected to the gravity of the earth (at certain standard conditions). In the metric system, the unit of mass is the gram (gm), a rather small unit defined as the quantity of water occupying one cubic centimeter of space. Since this unit is rather small, we often use the kilogram (kg) when speaking of mass in the metric system. One kilogram is equal to 2.205 pounds (mass).

Force is the product of mass and acceleration (or change of velocity). For example, weight, the action of the acceleration of gravity on a mass, is a force. The units of force in the English system are lb (mass)-ft/second-second or, as we have mentioned, the pound (force). In the metric system, the unit of force is the newton which is defined to be one kg-meter/sec-sec. One pound (force) is equal to 4.448 newton.

Power is defined as the rate of doing work or the work per unit time. Work can be thought of as a force acting through a distance. If a force of 1 lb acts through a distance of 1 ft, we say that 1 ft-lb of work has been performed, a basic unit of work in the English system. A power term commonly used is the horsepower, which is defined as 550 ft-lb/sec. In the metric system, the unit of work is the newton-meter (n-m) and the common unit of power the kilowatt, a term equal to 102 n-m/sec. One horsepower is equal to 0.746 kilowatt.

Energy is the capability of doing work. This capability can be present by virtue of either the condition or the position of a body. An additional form of energy is that which is due to energy chemically stored in an object such as a fuel. Energy by virtue of position means an object will do work if it is released. An example would be an object tied to a rope and suspended in the air from a pulley and connected to another weight. If the object is released, work could be performed. This type of energy is also known as potential energy. Energy by virtue of condition has as its most common form energy contained by virtue of motion or kinetic energy. In the English system, the units of energy are the British thermal unit (Btu) and the ft-lb (force). In the metric system, the units of energy are the joule and the kilowatt-hour. Since the joule is a very small unit of energy, the kilowatt-hour is more commonly used when dealing with building systems. The Btu is equal to 778 ft-lb (force) and the kilowatt-hour is equal to 3,413 Btu.

Laws of Conservation

Laws of conservation define relationships in engineering systems. Just as a proper accounting system is able to track the flow of all money entering and leaving a business, the laws of conservation account for all mass and energy in engineering systems.

The law of conservation of mass states that the mass of a body remains unchanged by any ordinary physical or chemical change to which it may be subject. Simply speaking, this law means when we start with a pound (mass) of something and process it, we are left with a pound at the end. For many normal processes, we extend this to entire systems. For example, the water which enters a building water system at the water meter should be accountable in terms of water which is used for various purposes in the building.

The law of conservation of energy states that energy can be neither created nor destroyed, but only converted from one form to another.

Application of the two laws of conservation to building systems and equipment will often provide the answers to problems relating to their operation and provide clues which will assist in optimizing their performance.

General Engineering Data and Metric Conversions

General engineering data concerning such things as the various properties of water and air and the meaning of certain terms is frequently needed by or useful to those performing the engineering function at a lodging property. Exhibit 1 contains a variety of potentially important data. For properties adhering primarily or solely to the metric system, Exhibit 2 presents a number of approximate metric conversion factors.

Water, Air, and Steam Flow

Water, air, and steam are all fluids which are commonly used in building engineering systems. Water is a non-compressible fluid under the conditions in which we normally encounter it, while air and steam are both compressible. The term compressible means that when the material is subjected to changes in pressure, its volume changes. Each of these fluids obeys basic laws of energy and mass conservation as it is used in the building. Because of the uses made of these fluids, there are some other parameters of interest which become important to the property designer and the operating engineer. These parameters include pressure, friction, and the means of providing energy to the fluid steam (pumping, compressing, or by means of fans).

Exhibit 1   Engineering Data

Water
  volume
    1 gallon = 8.33 lb = 0.134 cu. ft.
    1 cu. ft. = 7.48 gal. = 62.3 lb
  pressure
    1 lb/sq. in. = 2.31 ft. of water
    1 foot column of water = 0.4331 lb/sq. in.
  specific heat
    liquid = 1.0 Btu/lb-F°
    ice at 32°F = .487 Btu/lb-F°
    steam at 212°F; 14.7 psia = .482 Btu/lb-F°
  latent heat of fusion = 144 Btu/lb
  latent heat of vaporization = 970 Btu/lb
    (at 212°F; 14.7 psia)

Air (at 75°F; 14.7 psia)
  volume
    1 cu. ft. = .075 lb
    1 lb = 13.5 cu. ft.
  specific heat = .24 Btu/lb-F°

Power
  ton of refrigeration = 12,000 Btu/hr
  horsepower = .746 kw
  horsepower = 550 ft.-lb/sec
  boiler horsepower = 33,475 Btu/hr
  watt = 3.413 Btu/hr
  kw = 1,000 watts
  lumen = .0015 watt

Energy
  kwh = 3,413 Btu
  therm = 100,000 Btu
  MBtu = 1,000 Btu
  MMBtu = 1,000,000 Btu

Volume
  ccf = 100 cu. ft.
  mcf = 1,000 cu. ft.

Pressure

The pressure of a fluid is measured in force per unit area, with the most commonly encountered units being pounds per square inch or psi. The force which creates pressure can be developed as the result of a large mass of fluid, the storage of energy in the fluid, or fluid flow. The pressure readings which are talked about on the evening news weather report are due to the force of the mass of the column of air which extends to the end of the earth's atmosphere. The pressure which occurs inside a pressure cooker is caused by the transfer of energy into the water inside causing it to change to steam. The ability of an airplane to achieve lift is due to a difference between the forces on the top and the bottom of the wings generated by different rates of air flow over each wing surface.

The pressure caused by the atmosphere of the earth is continuously present. Rather than have this pressure show up on our measuring devices, we have calibrated most of them not to include the atmospheric pressure. If this were not true, a bathroom scale which was 1 ft square (144 square inches) would show a weight

Exhibit 2 Approximate Metric Conversion Factors

Symbol	When You Know Number of	Multiply by	To Find Number of	Symbol
	Length			
in	inches	2.54	centimeters	cm
ft	feet	.305	meters	m
yd	yards	0.9	meters	m
mi	miles	1.61	kilometers	km
	Area			
sq in	square inches	6.5	square centimeters	sq cm
sq ft	square feet	0.093	square meters	sq m
sq yd	square yards	0.836	square meters	sq m
sq mi	square miles	2.6	square kilometers	sq km
	acres	0.4	hectares	ha
	Weight (mass)			
oz	ounces	28	grams	g
lb	pounds	0.45	kilograms	kg
	short tons (2,000 pounds)	0.91	metric tons	Mg
	Volume			
tsp	teaspoons	5	milliliters	mL
Tbsp	tablespoons	15	milliliters	mL
cu in	cubic inches	16	milliliters	mL
fl oz	fluid ounces	30	milliliters	mL
c	cups	0.24	liters	L
pt	pints	0.47	liters	L
qt	quarts	0.95	liters	L
gal	gallons	3.78	liters	L
cu ft	cubic feet	0.028	cubic meters	cu m
cu yd	cubic yards	0.76	cubic meters	cu m
	Pressure			
inHg	inches of mercury	3.4	kilopascals	kPa
psi	pounds per square inch	6.89	kilopascals	kPa
	Temperature (exact)			
Btu	British thermal unit	.252	kilocalories	kcal
°F	degrees Fahrenheit	5/9 (after subtracting 32)	degrees Celsius	°C
	Other			
	Btu/sq ft	2.71	kilocalories/square meter	kcal/sq m
mpg	miles per gallon	.43	kilometers/liter	km/L
	Btu/lb	.556	kilocalories/kilogram	kcal/kg
cfh	cubic feet/hour	.028	cubic meters/hour	cmh
cfm	cubic feet/minute	.028	cubic meters/minute	cmm

Adapted from U.S. Department of Commerce, *Metric Style Guide for the News Media* (Washington, D.C.: National Bureau of Standards, 1976).

of 2,117 lbs (14.7 psi due to the atmosphere times 144 square inches). Pressure measurements which use the atmospheric pressure as a datum (zero value) are called gauge pressures and would commonly be represented by the units psig. Measurements which include the atmospheric pressure are noted by the units psia. If the units are given as psi, the assumption is generally made that gauge pressure is being used.

Exhibit 3   Pressure and Temperature for Saturated Stream

Gauge Pressure (psi)	Temperature (°F)
0	212
5	227
10	240
20	260
50	298
75	320
100	337
125	353

In water systems, we are concerned about the pressure produced by and required for tall columns of water in the piping systems in high-rise buildings. A column of water one foot high with a density of 62.3 pounds per cubic foot exerts a pressure of .433 psi. Therefore, a building which is 20 stories tall with an average floor-to-ceiling height of 12 feet has a pressure at the base of a water pipe of 104 psi due to the weight of the water. If we are to move water in this pipe to the top of the building, we must inject the water into the base of the pipe at 104 psi or greater, a pressure which is higher than that usually available from the local water utility.

In air systems, we are rarely concerned about the pressure created by tall columns of air since even for a 100-story building the resulting air pressure would be less than 1 psi. Building air-handling systems are concerned with friction and pumping (fan) requirements to move air about the building. Compressed air may be used in the building for operation of the building control system, but this is a specialized application.

Steam systems create pressure by confining water within a boiler and steam piping and by heating the water until it evaporates. The eventual steam/water temperature depends on how high the pressure is allowed to go (assuming heat is continually added). Exhibit 3 illustrates the relationship between the pressure of steam and the temperature. This relationship is true only for what is known as saturated steam—steam that has just left the surface of a pool of boiling water.

Friction

Friction represents the resistance of an object to the flow or movement of another object along its surface. The presence of friction in fluid flow results in a drop in the pressure of the fluid. Charts are available for flow systems (both pipes and ducts) which correlate the pressure drop (in psi per unit of length) with the flow rate of the fluid and the diameter of the pipe or duct. Valves and other devices installed in these systems will also create pressure losses. There are tables which list the losses in pressure associated with these devices as well.

The amount of friction in a flow system is dependent upon the characteristics of the pipe or duct, the material flowing through the pipe or duct, and the velocity of flow. Of particular concern is the velocity of flow, since the amount of friction is proportional to the square of the velocity. The Darcy-Weisbach equation illustrates these factors for liquid flow in a circular pipe where

$$\text{Loss of pressure due to friction} = \frac{f \times L \times V^2}{d \times 2g}$$

where *f* is a dimensionless friction factor derived from test data for the pipe; *L* is the length of the pipe; *d* is the pipe diameter; *V* is the velocity; and *g* is the acceleration of gravity. This equation allows us to determine the amount of energy which must be input to the fluid in order to overcome friction.

Pumping

In order to overcome friction, energy is added to a fluid. This energy addition is accomplished by pumps for water systems, fans for air-handling systems, and a combination of pumps and the addition of heat for steam systems. In each instance, the pressure of the fluid is increased in order to compensate for the losses in pressure which will occur because of friction.

For water systems, the pumps will also compensate for differences in water pressure required because of the height of water in the building piping.

Exhibit 4 illustrates the relationships between various parameters which define pump or fan performance. Capacity refers to the quantity of fluid moving through the pipe, usually expressed in gallons per minute (pumps) or cubic feet per minute (fans). Pressure refers to the discharge pressure from the pump or fan. For a pump, this term is often referred to as head in units of feet of water. For a fan, the units are psi or inches of water. Efficiency refers to the percentage of the input energy to the pump or fan which is transferred to the fluid and power is the rate of input of energy to the pump or fan. System pressure losses represents the pressure drop which is expected for the system on which the pump or fan is operating at the flow rate given on the horizontal axis.

Exhibit 4 illustrates several important factors in pump/fan selection and operation. Since a pump/fan is normally chosen for some peak level of flow (the load), a knowledge of the pressure needed to supply this load is important. For water systems, the head is a combination of the amount of lift we must give the fluid above the pump position, the friction in the pipe from the pump to the load, and the desired pressure at the load itself. Air systems will generally have systems curves which incorporate the friction in the duct work and the desired delivery pressure at the load. An increase in the overall pressure of the system which must be matched by the pump/fan will reduce the quantity of fluid delivered by the pump. In addition, there is a certain range at which the pump/fan operates with a high efficiency. When selecting equipment for a given application, consideration of its operating efficiency in the application is important. Applications with highly varying flow requirements may warrant the use of variable speed equipment capable of operating close to its maximum efficiency over a range of applications or the installation or multiple pieces of equipment with a staging capability.

Electricity

Electricity is a form of energy consisting of a quantity of electrons (measured in amperes or amps) flowing between two points of different electrical potential

Exhibit 4   Relationships Between Capacity and Maximum Values of Head, Efficiency, Power, and Pressure Losses for Flow Systems

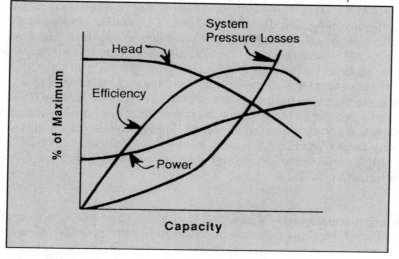

(measured in volts). One ampere represents 6.251 × 10^{18} electrons per second passing through a cross section of the conductor. The voltage between two points represents a net difference between the number of negative charges (electrons) at the two points. A point or object with more negative charges than another point or object is said to have a negative voltage. Note that voltage is a relative measurement. A voltage measurement is either made relative to ground—usually the earth at a given location—or relative to some other point, such as the voltage between two terminals of a battery.

In electrical systems, the flow of electricity does not proceed unhindered. The characteristic which measures the difficulty that electricity has in flowing through a material is called resistance. The lower the resistance of a material, the better a conductor of electricity the material is. Good conductors such as copper and aluminum are used to make building wiring. Poor conductors, such as glass, porcelain, rubber, and some plastics, are used to make insulating materials which protect us from electricity. The equipment being powered (called the load) also has resistance.

As an aid to understanding electrical systems, analogies are sometimes made between electrical and water systems. The flow of water is similar to the flow of electricity; the pressure in a water system is similar to the voltage in an electrical system; and the resistance of a wire to the flow of electricity is similar to the friction which occurs when water flows through a pipe. The analogies can further extend to pieces of equipment found in the systems as well—for example, the similarity between a pump and a battery and between a valve and a switch.

Current, Resistance, and Power—DC Systems

The discussion of the mathematical relationships which govern electricity will begin with the form of electricity known as direct current or DC. This is the type of electricity produced by a battery. It is characterized by current flow in a single direction, with the normal convention of electrical terminology showing flow from the positive (+) cell of the battery to the negative (−) cell. This rather strange convention concerning electrical flow is due to a misunderstanding of the nature of electricity which occurred hundreds of years ago. While the actual flow of electricity (electrons) is from negative to positive, the convention is to show flow from positive to negative.

When discussing DC systems and the mathematical relationships which govern these systems, the current is usually designated in equations by I, the voltage by V, and the resistance by R. Units of current flow are amps, units of voltage are volts, and units of resistance are ohms. These three terms are linked by the relationship known as Ohm's law, which states that the current in a DC circuit is directly proportional to the voltage and inversely proportional to the resistance. In equation form, Ohm's law is

$$I = V/R$$

Since our normal use of electricity is as a source of power and energy, the relationships which allow us to calculate the amount of power and energy available from an electrical source are of interest. Electrical power is measured in watts (W), where watts are the product of current (I) and voltage (V). When we couple this with the relationship for Ohm's law, we can define electrical power by the following formulas:

$$W = VI = I^2R = V^2/R$$

These formulas reveal some interesting characteristics of electrical power. If we increase the voltage (V) supplied to a constant load, denoted in the equation by the R value, the power required will increase by the square of the voltage. Therefore, if the voltage is increased by a factor of two, the power will be increased by a factor of four. A similar increase occurs if the current is doubled.

The item which we control in electrical systems is the voltage. The resistance is a physical characteristic of the load and the current results from Ohm's law given the voltage and resistance. If we think of the R value in the power equation as representing the resistance of the wires carrying the electricity, we can see why higher voltages are used to deliver higher power requirements. If we wish to provide 100 watts of power using a 20 volt source, we will need 5 amps of current. If this current flows through a wire with a resistance of 2 ohms, the resulting power loss in the line will be 50 watts. In order to deliver 100 watts, we will have to provide 150 watts due to the losses in the line. On the other hand, if we provide electricity at 40 volts, the required current will be 2.5 amps and the power loss in the line only 12.5 watts, only one-fourth of that calculated previously. Providing electrical energy at higher voltages greatly reduces line losses. It also reduces the need for large wires to carry high levels of current flow.

Energy measurements in electrical systems are made by simply multiplying the power by the length of time that level of power is used. If 1,000 watts of power are used for one hour, the amount of energy consumed is 1,000 watt hours or one kilowatt-hour.

Exhibit 5   Wave Representation of AC Current or Voltage

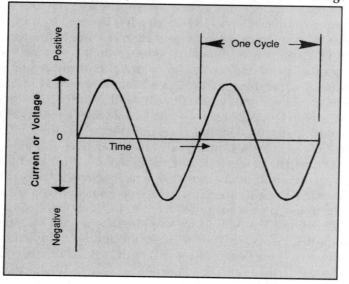

Current, Impedance, and Power—AC Systems

While the relationships and physics associated with DC power systems are relatively straightforward, the realm of AC systems is more complex and less easily grasped. Since the vast majority of our uses of electricity are in the form of AC power, an understanding of this common form of electricity is particularly helpful. Fortunately, several of the characteristics of DC electricity are also true of AC.

While the flow of electricity in a DC system is always in one direction, the direction of flow in an AC system oscillates following a generally symmetrical pattern known as a sinusoidal (or sine) wave. Exhibit 5 illustrates several waves of AC current. When the curve begins to repeat itself, we say one cycle of AC current has passed. The distance along the horizontal axis which is associated with the curve beginning to repeat itself is called a cycle. The standard North American power system operates at 60 cycles per second, also known as 60 hertz. Therefore, the time required for one cycle is 1/60th of a second. The number of cycles per second is also known as the frequency.

The voltage and the current in AC systems are sine waves with the same frequency. Because of the wave nature of AC voltage and current, it is not possible to actually assign a constant value to either of these parameters. Also, because their average value is zero, the use of an average value is useless. The value we use to measure the current and voltage is actually the peak value of each divided by 1.414 (the square root of 2). All electrical instruments commonly used to measure AC current and voltage are set up to divide the peak value of the AC sine wave by 1.414 and show this on the display of the instrument.

In AC systems, the unit of current is still the amp and the unit of voltage the volt with the symbols I and V used to denote each. The unit of resistance is somewhat more complex than in DC circuits. It is denoted by a Z and referred to as impedance, a term which incorporates both resistance as it is thought of in DC circuits and reactance, an additional type of resistance. Reactance occurs in AC circuits because of the changing (cyclic) nature of the voltage and current flows and the tendency of the material through which the electricity is flowing to resist the change in the voltage and current flows as well as the actual current flow itself.

If an AC circuit is supplying only what is known as a resistive load, the same power relationships are used for AC as are used for DC. However, if the load being supplied has any reactive resistance, as is true of such devices as electric motors, then we must calculate power in a different manner. We will find that the voltage and the current do not occur at exactly the same time due to the reactive resistance that is present. As a result, there is a time separation between their peak values which results in less power being delivered to the load than we would calculate from the calculation (W = V × I) we would perform for a DC power source. A measure of the degree of separation between the timing of the peaks of the voltage and current waves is the power factor (pf) of the load, a number with a value of 1 for purely resistive loads and less than one for loads with reactive components. For such circumstances, the equation for power is given by

$$W = V \times I \times pf$$

This equation is actually valid for both single-phase AC and DC calculations, since the power factor for DC is 1. Energy calculations are still performed by multiplying the power by the time (in hours) over which the power is used.

The world of AC power is further complicated by the presence of three-phase power systems. In three-phase systems, there are three wires, each of which functions like a single AC line. Exhibit 6 illustrates wave forms for a three-phase power supply. Within any single cycle of the power system, a load connected to a three-phase power supply will receive three impulses of current and voltage. Such a load, such as a three-phase motor, will have a wire for each of the three phases connected to separate connections on the motor and is only capable of operating properly when provided with three-phase electricity. For applications which need a single phase, such as a wall outlet, one of the three phases is used.

With three-phase power, it should be obvious that standard power relationships will not work properly since we are dealing with three lines providing power. Power calculations in three-phase circuits are governed by the relationship

$$W = V \times I \times pf \times \sqrt{3}$$

The relationships discussed and developed between current, voltage, power, and energy for AC and DC circuits are useful for property engineers when dealing with electrical systems at lodging facilities. Exhibit 7 presents sample calculations which use the relationships developed in this appendix in the context of problems which might face a property engineer. The problems are simplified for the purpose of these examples.

Exhibit 6   Wave Representations of Three-Phase AC Current or Voltage

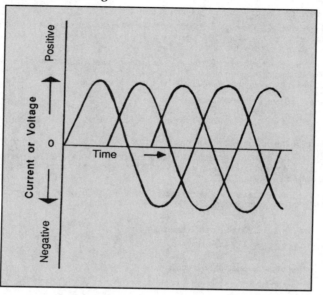

Thermodynamics

Temperature

Temperature must be defined in an indirect manner using the concept of equality of temperature. When two bodies, one hot and the other cold, are placed in contact with each other, the hot body will over time become cooler and the cold body will become warmer. Eventually, all changes in the properties of the bodies will cease and the bodies will be at thermal equilibrium (that is, they will have the same temperature). Therefore, two bodies or systems have equal temperature when no changes occur in their properties when they are brought in contact with each other.

A practical temperature scale has been developed by assigning specific, yet arbitrary, values of temperature to two easily reproducible temperatures: the freezing and boiling points of water at standard atmospheric pressure. In the English system of units, the Fahrenheit scale assigns a temperature of 32°F to the freezing point and 212°F to the boiling point.

So far, this definition of temperature only applies between the freezing and boiling point of water. But the temperature scale can be extrapolated beyond these boundaries in both directions. Therefore, the temperature in a blast freezer and a boiler can be measured as –10°F and 250°F, respectively.

Heat

Heat is a form of energy defined by temperature. When two bodies of different temperatures are brought in contact with each other, they eventually reach thermal

Exhibit 7   Sample Electrical Calculations

Problem 1: Evaluate the cost of lighting a guestwing corridor.

A corridor in the guestwing of a property is lighted by 50 lighting fixtures, each of which contains a 100-watt lamp. The lamps operate 24 hours a day, 365 days a year. The local cost of electrical energy is $.08 per kwh. What is the annual operating cost of the lamps?

The starting point for this problem is to determine the total lighting power (P) and from this to determine the energy (E) consumed by multiplying the power by the number of hours the lamps operate. The cost is then calculated by multiplying the amount of energy by the cost per unit of energy.

P = 100 watt/lamp × 50 lamps = 5,000 watts or 5 kw
E = P × time = 5 kw × 24 hrs/day × 365 days/year = 43,800 kwh/year
Cost = E × rate per kwh = 43,800 kwh/year × $.08/kwh = $3,504/year

Problem 2: Determine the current draw of a resistive load.

Determine the current draw (how many amps) of the lighting system in Problem 1. (Such a calculation may be required if additional equipment is to be connected to the lighting circuit to determine whether adequate capacity is available in the system.)

Each lamp is rated at 100 watts. Using the definition of power (P = V × I), we can calculate the current draw of each lamp. P is 100 and V is the voltage of the lamps, 120 volts being common. Solving for the current, we have

I = P/V = 100 watts per lamp/120 volts = .833 amps per lamp

The total current flow is 41.7 amps (.833 × 50).

Problem 3: Determine the efficiency of an electric motor.

An electric motor producing 5 HP (horsepower) is operated at 208 volts, single phase. The nameplate of the motor indicates the motor has a power factor of 85% and draws a full load current of 27 amps at rated horse-power. What is the motor efficiency? (A calculation of this type is necessary if a comparison is to be made between the existing motor and a new motor.)

Efficiency = Output/Input
Output = 5 HP × .746 kw/HP = 3.73 kw
Input = V × I × pf = 208 volts × 27 amps × .85 = 4.774 kw
Efficiency = 3.73 kw/4.774 kw = .78 or 78%

Problem 4: Determine the heating capacity of an electric heating element operated at other than its rated voltage.

An electric water heater installed as a booster heater for a dishwasher is rated at 4.5 kw when installed on a single phase 240 volt line. The electric service in the kitchen is 208 volts. What is the heating capability of the heater?

In this problem, the resistance of the heater is a constant value. Using a combination of a power relationship and Ohm's law, we can calculate the resistance of the heater from the following equation

P = V²/R = 240 volts × 240 volts/R = 4.5 kw

Solving for R:

R = 240 volts × 240 volts/4.5 kw = 12.80 ohm

When operated at 208 volts, the resulting power delivered by the heating element (heating capability) is

P = V²/R = 208 volts × 208 volts/12.80 ohm = 3.38 kw

equilibrium and a common temperature. The energy that was transferred between the two bodies because of their temperature difference is defined as heat. The direction of the heat flow will always be from the body with the higher temperature to the body with the lower temperature, with the convention that the flow of heat out of a body is considered negative and the flow of heat into a body is considered positive.

The amount of heat can be measured by raising the temperature of the mass of a specific material by a specific temperature difference. The Btu (British thermal unit) is defined as the amount of heat required to raise one pound of water by one Fahrenheit degree. Materials other than water require more or less heat to increase their temperatures by one Fahrenheit degree. This amount of heat is defined as the specific heat, C_p, for that material. Air, for example, has a specific heat of .24 at typical atmospheric conditions.

States of Matter

At the environmental temperatures normally associated with buildings, all matter exists in three states: solid, liquid, or gaseous. These states can be distinguished by observation of certain characteristics of the material. A solid is rigid and maintains its shape without the help of a container. Its volume changes only slightly as the environmental conditions change. A liquid takes the shape of the lower portion of its container, but maintains a horizontal upper surface. Its volume also changes only slightly as the environmental conditions change. A gas fills the entire container without maintaining shape or volume.

The same substance can exist in any of the three different states, depending on its temperature and pressure. At standard atmospheric pressure, water exists as ice (a solid) when its temperature is below 32°F, as steam (a gas) when its temperature is above 212°F, and as a liquid when the temperature is between these two values. As the pressure changes, the temperatures that identify the boundaries between the states change. At a pressure of 15 psig, water will remain in the liquid state up to a temperature of 249.7°F. At a pressure of 50 psig, the boiling point of water increases to 297.7°F.

These specific conditions of water can be observed readily in a lodging facility. The temperature of the ice in the bin of an ice maker must be lower than 32°F, while the temperature of a drink made with shaved ice is exactly 32°F. Water boiling in a stock pot is approximately 212°F. The temperature of the cooking environment or the steam in a high-pressure steam cooker is approximately 250°F because the pressure in such a unit is 15 psig. The steam being produced from a boiler set at 50 psig must be at a temperature greater than approximately 298°F.

Many of the important thermal processes that occur in a lodging property operate on the basis of a change of state for the working substance. During these changes of state, energy is either added to or extracted from the substance. Ice is produced in an ice maker by extracting heat energy from water, thus changing its temperature and state from liquid to solid. Steam is produced in a boiler by adding heat to water, thus increasing its temperature and changing its state from liquid to gaseous. A phase change in the reverse direction is used to cook food in a steamer. Water changing from the gaseous state to the liquid state as the steam is condensed in the steamer gives off heat that is used to cook the vegetables. The Freon in a guestroom air conditioner cools the room by undergoing a change from the liquid state into the gaseous state, taking the necessary heat from the room.

The two changes of state that are common are the change between the solid and liquid states and the change between the liquid and gaseous states. The first change is usually called melting or freezing, depending on the direction of the change. The latter is commonly called boiling or evaporation when the change is from the liquid to the gaseous state and condensation when the change occurs in the opposite direction. Although uncommon in a property, the third possible change of state—from a solid to a gas—is called sublimation. When dry ice (solid CO_2) is used to create "smoke" for a display, the carbon dioxide is changing directly from the solid state to the gaseous state.

An exchange of energy is always associated with any change of state. This addition or subtraction of energy does not affect the temperature of the substance, but rather only affects the form of the substance. At standard atmospheric pressure, both ice and liquid water exist at 32°F and both liquid water and steam exist at 212°F. When water at either of these two conditions changes from one state to the other, it does not change its temperature even though energy has been added or subtracted from it. The energy connected with these changes is designated latent energy, because no temperature change occurs in the process. The energy associated with the change from a solid to a liquid is called the latent heat of fusion, while the energy involved in the change of state from liquid to gaseous is called the latent heat of vaporization. For water at standard atmospheric pressure, the values are 144 Btu/lb and 970 Btu/lb, respectively.

Heat Transfer

Heat energy is transferred between two bodies that have different temperatures by three modes: conduction, convection, and radiation. In the conduction mode, energy is transferred by the direct interaction of molecules. The vibrational energy of one molecule is passed on to its neighbors by direct contact or collision, but the molecules themselves do not move a significant distance through the substance. Conduction occurs in all three states of matter, but is usually associated with solids. The heat that is transferred from the burner of a range into the stock in a stock pot is conducted through the metal container.

Heat transfer in the convection mode is accomplished through the large-scale motion of molecules in currents. Using the example of the heating of a stock in a stock pot, the molecules of the stock that touch the inside surface of the container are heated by conduction. When they are warmed, the density of the liquid decreases and the warmed molecules begin to rise through the stock. As these molecules rise, they are cooled by the surrounding cooler stock. The cooled molecules then return to the bottom of the container. This cyclical heating and cooling of the molecules sets up convection currents in the liquid. The heating of the entire liquid is accomplished by the continuous mixing caused by these currents. Convection is only associated with liquids or gases and does not occur in solids.

Radiation heat transfer occurs when energy from a hot body is converted into electromagnetic energy and is transmitted to another body with a lower temperature. This transmission of energy occurs even through a vacuum without any intermediate medium and is essentially the same as the transmission of radio or television signals. This mode of transfer usually occurs between two solids, with the color of the surfaces of the solids greatly affecting the amount of radiation transfer. Black surfaces emit and absorb energy very readily, while white surfaces inhibit the emission and absorption of radiation energy. In a radiation broiler, the heating element is heated to an extremely high temperature, and the cooking of a steak is accomplished by the radiation of heat from the element to the surface of the steak.

In most actual situations, the heat transfer between two bodies or systems is accomplished by a combination of the three modes. In the stock pot example, the heat is convected and radiated from the gas flame in the burner to the bottom surface of the container, conducted through the metal to the stock that is touching the inside surface of the container, and convected to the remaining stock through currents. For the steak, the heat is initially transferred to the surface of the meat primarily by radiation, although some convection heating also occurs. The heat is then conducted into the center of the steak. In the heating season, heat is lost through the walls of a guestroom because of the difference between the inside air temperature and the outside air temperature. The heat is convected to the inside surface of the wall, conducted through the inside surface material, convected and radiated through any air spaces in the wall, conducted through the outside surface material, and finally convected to the outside air.

In these practical situations where more than one mode of heat transfer occur, the effects of the individual modes are combined into an overall heat transfer coefficient. The total heat transfer can be determined based on the geometric configuration, material properties, and terminal temperatures. The theory for combining modes of heat transfer is based on the concept of thermal circuits or thermal resistance, a direct analogy with electrical circuits and electrical resistance.

Combining the separate effects, however, requires an understanding of the equations and terminology for each of the three modes. For the conduction of heat through a solid, three thermal properties of the material are defined: conductivity (k), conductance (C), and thermal resistance (R). The definition of conductivity is best shown by performing an experiment with a specific material in the following way.

A one-inch thick slab of the material with a surface area of one square foot is subjected to a one Fahrenheit degree temperature difference between the two flat surfaces of the slab. Heat will flow through the one-inch dimension of the material because of the temperature difference. The conductivity (k) of the material is defined as the rate of heat in Btu/hr that flows in this specific configuration, and is expressed in units of $Btu/hr\text{-}ft^2\text{-}F°\text{-}in$. Therefore, this thermal property only applies to a one-inch thick sample of the material.

Since the materials in most practical situations have a thickness different than one inch, the property of conductivity is generalized to the property of conductance (C) for a specific thickness of the material other than one inch. Conductance is defined by the following equation, where x is the specific thickness in inches, and is expressed in units of $Btu/hr\text{-}ft^2\text{-}F°$:

$$C = k/x$$

When x is one inch, then C = k as it should by definition. When x is greater than one inch, the conductance is less than the conductivity because a thicker sample of the material conducts less heat. Conversely, the conductance is greater than the conductivity when the thickness is less than one inch because a thinner sample of

Exhibit 8   Thermal Properties for Some Typical Building Materials

Building Material	k (Btu/hr-ft²-F°-in)	C (Btu/hr-ft²-F°)	R (hr-ft²-F°/Btu)
Gypsum plasterboard (.5 in)	1.11	2.22	0.45
Fiberglass insulation (4 in)	0.25	0.0625	16.0
Brick, common (4 in)	5.0	1.25	0.80
Concrete block, 3 oval cores (8 in)	----	.90	1.11
Plywood (.5 in)	0.806	1.61	0.62
Plate glass (.25 in)	2.77	11.1	0.09

Reprinted by permission from *1985 ASHRAE Handbook—Fundamentals.*

Exhibit 9   Typical Convection Heat Transfer Coefficients

Situation	h_c (Btu/hr-ft²-F°)
Still air; vertical surface	1.46
7.5 mph wind; vertical surface	4.00
15 mph wind; vertical surface	6.00
Still water; vertical surface	1.00

Reprinted by permission from *1985 ASHRAE Handbook—Fundamentals.*

the material conducts more heat. Finally, a thermal resistance (R) for the material is defined as the reciprocal of the conductance, in units of hr-ft²-F°/Btu:

$$R = 1/C$$

While the conductance is a measure of the amount of heat that flows through a layer of material, the resistance is a measure of the material's ability to resist the flow of heat. Hence, the two properties are reciprocal in nature. Values of these thermal properties for some typical building materials are shown in Exhibit 8.

For the convection heat transfer in a liquid or gas, the entire effect is expressed in a convection coefficient, h_c, in units of Btu/hr-ft²-F°. The coefficient includes the effects of the type of convection (natural or forced), the geometry of the situation, and the type of fluid (for example, water or air). Values for some common situations are given in Exhibit 9. A larger value for h_c indicates a higher rate of heat flow. The interpretation of the coefficient is analogous to that for the conductance of a solid. The resistance to convective heat flow is the reciprocal of the convection coefficient.

Similarly, the overall effect of radiation heat transfer is expressed by a radiation coefficient, h_r, with the same units. This coefficient also includes all of the effects due to the properties of material (for example, surface color) and geometry of the situation. Again, the analogy with the conductance of a solid holds, and the resistance to radiation heat flow is the reciprocal of the radiation coefficient.

Exhibit 10   Thermal Effects of Combining Building Materials

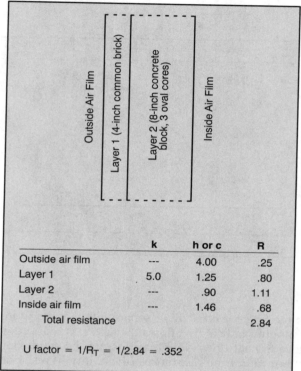

	k	h or c	R
Outside air film	---	4.00	.25
Layer 1	5.0	1.25	.80
Layer 2	---	.90	1.11
Inside air film	---	1.46	.68
Total resistance			2.84

U factor $= 1/R_T = 1/2.84 = .352$

With the heat transfer characteristics of individual layers of materials defined, they may be combined into composite assemblies that represent actual configurations that are common in hospitality properties. Refer to Exhibit 10 for this discussion. The exterior wall of a guestroom could be built of several layers of building materials (for example, wall board, concrete block, face brick), but in this example only two layers are used. The conductivities or conductances of the solid layers are obtained from tables of design values for such materials. Two additional layers of air (inside air film and outside air film) contribute to the thermal properties of the wall. The heat transfer coefficients for these layers are obtained from tables similar to Exhibit 9. In addition, the value of any radiation heat transfer coefficient should be obtained if it is appropriate. The resistances for each of these layers can then be calculated by taking the appropriate reciprocals.

The overall heat transfer capability of the entire wall may now be determined by combining the effects of the individual layers using the concept of thermal resistance. When the layers of the wall are in series (that is, all of the heat flows through each layer), the total resistance of the composite wall is the sum of the individual resistances for each layer. A common sense analysis of the situation

Exhibit 11   Spectrum of Electromagnetic Radiation

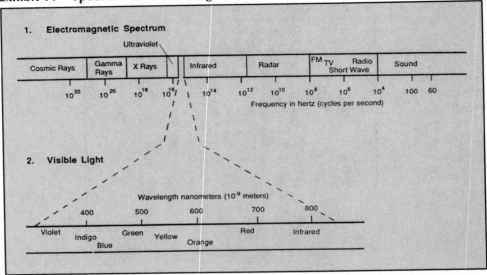

supports this method for combining separate layers. As more layers are added to a wall, the amount of heat that flows through it is reduced, thus increasing the wall's resistance to heat flow. Note that it is not the conductances (the ability to transfer heat) but rather the resistances (the ability to resist heat transfer) of the individual layers that are added together to determine the overall thermal effect of the composite wall. If the conductances were added as the number of layers were increased, then the heat flow through the wall would increase, and this effect is contrary to actual experience.

The overall thermal effect of the wall could remain expressed in terms of its resistance, but most applications require the effect expressed in terms of its ability to transfer heat. Therefore, an overall coefficient, the *U factor*, expressed in units of Btu/hr-ft^2-F°, is calculated by taking the reciprocal of the total resistance:

$$U = 1/R_T$$

This U factor represents the aggregate effect of all the layers, including the air films, on the ability of the wall or any other configuration (for example, the stock pot when heating water) to transfer heat from the higher temperature region on one side of the barrier to the lower temperature region on the other side.

Light

Light is defined most simply as radiated energy that can be seen by the human eye. Light exhibits wave properties similar to other phenomena such as radio, micro-wave, and X rays, and is part of the electromagnetic spectrum as shown in Exhibit 11.

As such, light has both wave length and frequency as do all these types of radiation. These two properties are inversely related through the constant for the speed of light as follows. With frequency in cycles per second (Hz or cps), wave length in meters (m), and the speed of light as 3×10^8 m/sec, the relationship is expressed as

$$l = c/f$$

where l represents the wave length, f the frequency, and c the speed of light. Note that metric units have been used here because most of the literature on lighting uses them.

Color

Different wave lengths or frequencies of light are interpreted by the human eye as different colors of light. The wave lengths of visible light extend from 380 nanometers (a nanometer is 10^{-9} meters) to 760 nanometers, with the former frequency corresponding to violet light and the latter corresponding to red light. Light of wave lengths in between these two values is associated with the common colors as shown in the second section of Exhibit 11. The acronym ROY G BIV identifies these colors as red, orange, yellow, green, blue, indigo, and violet. White light contains energy in equal amounts at all the wave lengths in this range.

Light Sources. Light that is produced by practical sources has different color characteristics because the light is emitted at various frequencies rather than just one. The frequencies that dominate in the spectrum cause the human eye to interpret the light as the colors associated with the dominant frequencies. Exhibit 12 shows the spectral distributions of the following common light sources: noon sunlight, a typical light bulb with a tungsten filament, and a typical fluorescent lamp that has not been corrected for color rendition.

The human eye interprets daylight as having a near-white quality, but with a slight tone of yellow, while it sees the color of the light from the artificial sources as substantially different from that of daylight. The light from the incandescent (tungsten filament) bulb is seen as yellow-orange and the light from the fluorescent lamp appears stronger in the blue range and very weak in the orange-red range. Therefore, the lamps that are used to light the interiors of buildings may not give the building's interiors the same color characteristics exhibited during the daylight hours.

Effect of Surfaces. When the light from a source strikes a surface, the light is absorbed, reflected, or transmitted in various proportions, depending on the material characteristics of the surface. Some of the light always is absorbed and converted into energy that increases the temperature of the surface. The remaining light is predominantly either reflected or transmitted, thus categorizing the material as either opaque or transparent, respectively.

The color of the light that is either transmitted or reflected by the surface depends on the interaction of the color of the incident light and the absorption characteristics of the surface material. Since the color of the transmitted or reflected light is interpreted by the eye as the color of the object, this interaction is extremely important in determining the color of objects as perceived by people in actual settings.

Exhibit 12   Spectral Characteristics of Light Sources

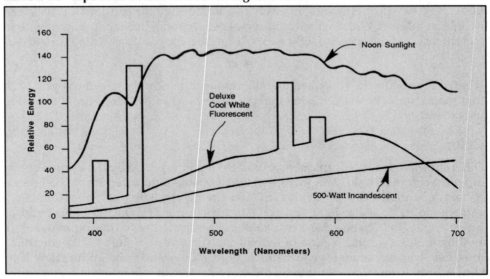

Different frequencies of light are absorbed by materials in different amounts by a process of selective absorption in which most of the light is absorbed and the remaining light is reflected or transmitted in a very narrow band of frequency. This reflected or transmitted light exhibits a distinct color or hue. For example, a red napkin absorbs almost all of the light from the visible spectrum except for those frequencies associated with the color red; yellow flowers in the atrium absorb all of the frequencies except those for yellow.

The color spectrum of the incident light is modified by the selective absorption characteristics of the surface material to determine the color of the object. When white light is incident on the surface, all colors in the spectrum are present in the incident light and the perceived color of the object is dependent on which light frequencies are absorbed by the material. For example, white light on a "red" surface appears red. When light of a specific color is incident on a surface, only light of the frequencies associated with that color is present and the perceived color of the object is dependent on which light frequencies remain after the existing light frequencies are absorbed selectively by the surface. There are two possible situations. One, when (for example) violet light strikes an object in which the material absorbs all the frequencies except those associated with the color violet, the object looks violet to the observer. Two, when the same violet light strikes an object in which the material absorbs all the frequencies except those associated with the color red, the object appears black because little or no light is reflected from the object.

Knowledge of this interaction between the color of the light source and the color absorption characteristics of an object influences many of the lighting decisions that affect the appearance of lodging facilities to their guests and employees. Foods such as beef or tomatoes that are rich in red and orange colors must be lighted by artificial sources that contain a sufficient amount of light in the red and orange frequencies or they appear dull, dark, and unappetizing to the dining room guest. Human skin must also be lighted by a source with desirable color characteristics so that it shows its natural beauty to guests as they view themselves in any of a property's mirrors.

Intensity

Power of Light Source. A standardized light source that emits radiation equally in all directions from one point is used to define the power of practical light sources. The output of the standardized light source is quantified by measuring the amount of light which strikes a spherical surface that is centered on the light source and has a radius of one foot. The unit of measurement for the total quantity of visible radiation emitted by the source is the lumen. The amount of light in a lumen is based on the light output of a wax candle, which emits approximately 12.57 lumens.

The efficacy, or the efficiency of the production of light, of a light source is expressed by an input-output ratio. For an electrically powered light source, the efficacy is measured in lumens per watt, where lumens measure the output of the light and watts measure the electrical input. While the theoretical maximum efficiency of light production is approximately 220 lumens per watt, the efficacies of actual light sources are substantially less than this value (usually 15 to 150 lumens/watt) because a large proportion (typically 75–95%) of the input energy is converted into heat which is dissipated by the light bulb.

Inverse Square Law. The light output of a light source is measured using a spherical surface centered on the light source with a radius of one foot. The extension of the measurement of light intensity to distances other than one foot requires the development of the relationship between the amount of light (lumens) and the intensity or density of light (lumens/ft^2). A *footcandle (fc)* is defined as the intensity of light of one lumen per square foot.

For a standardized light source emitting 12.57 lumens, the intensity of light measured at the surface of the unit sphere is one footcandle because the output of 12.57 lumens shines equally on 12.57ft^2 of surface area. The intensity of light on a spherical surface centered on the same light source with a radius of two feet, however, is only .25 fc because the surface area of the sphere is 50.28 ft^2, while the output of the light source is 12.57 lumens.

This reduction in the intensity of light as the distance from the light source increases is governed by the inverse square law. The relationship can be expressed mathematically by

$$fc = lm/(12.57 \times d^2)$$

where the distance *(d)* from the light source is measured in feet. For a light source of a given power, the intensity of the light decreases in proportion to the square of the distance from the source, hence the name "inverse square law."

Effect of Surfaces. When the light from a source shines on a surface, some of the light is absorbed and the remainder is transmitted or reflected, depending on whether the surface is primarily transparent or opaque. In either case, the intensity of the light that leaves the surface is dependent on two factors: (1) the intensity of the light striking the surface and (2) the material properties and geometry of the surface. The relationship among these variables can be expressed as

$$fc = fc_I \times factor$$

where fc_I is the intensity of the light incident on the surface, *factor* represents the aggregate effect of the surface on the intensity of the light, and fc is the intensity of the light leaving the surface.

The actual factors are expressed as values in percentages ranging from 0% for a surface that absorbs all the incident light to 100% for a surface that returns all the incident light, and are described in the literature as either the reflectance or transmittance of the surface, depending on whether the surface primarily reflects or transmits the incident light.

Index

A

Absorption chillers, 259, 262, 263
Access aisles, 388
Accessible
    parking spaces, 387–390
    route, 388–390
Accor, 84
Acetate fibers, 375
Acrylic fibers, 375
ADA accessibility
    requirements, 387–390, 391–392, 413
ADA Standards for Accessible Design, 133
ADAAG, 387–390, 391–392
Administration offices, 435–436
Agenda 21, 83, 117
Agenda 21 for the Travel & Tourism Industry, 83, 87, 88, 89, 117–122
AH&LA, 106, 145
AHLEI, 64, 129, 157
AIA Document A101, Standard Form of Agreement between Owner and Contractor, 466
Air handling HVAC units, 275
Alexander Hotel, 86
Algae, 191
Allergens, 255
Alternating current, 497–498
Aluminum electrical cables, 217
Ambroeus, Sant, 445
American Association of State Highway and Transportation Officials, 382
American Hotel & Lodging Association, 83
American Hotel & Lodging Educational Institute, 64, 129, 157
American Institute of Architects, 467
American National Standards Institute, 318
American Society for Testing and Materials, 134, 382
American Society of Heating, Refrigerating and Air-Conditioning Engineers, 164, 254, 255, 264, 318

American Water Works Association, 195
Americans with Disabilities Act, 10, 132, 134, 192, 255, 387, 412, 424, 473
Americans with Disabilities Act Accessibility Guidelines, 387–390, 391–392, 413
Amperes, 204
Analog phones, 237
ARAMARK, 5, 51
Architects, 415–416, 417, 418, 419, 421, 430, 434, 435, 436, 438, 440
ARIA Resort, 425
Artificial light, 310–317
Asbestos, 99
ASHRAE, 164, 254, 255, 264, 318
ASHRAE Journal, 277
Asphalt, 382–384
Asset managers, 18, 60–61
Association market, 431
Atrium floor configuration, 421, 422
Australian Institute of Hotel Engineering, 65
Automated overhead monorail systems, 338
Axminster weaves, 373, 374

B

Backflow preventers, 178
Ballasts, 312, 314, 319, 322, 324–326, 331
Ballrooms, 209, 211, 432
Banquet guests, 434
Barclay Bee, 101
Basic Services contract, 463
BASs, 280–281
Batch washers. *See* Tunnel washers
Bathroom safety, 132–135
Battery backup units (electrical), 220, 221, 223–224
Battery-operated
    faucets, 179
    flush valves, 179
Bellagio, 189
Bellevue-Stratford Hotel, 183
Benefit analysis (renovations), 460–462

Bentley Suite, 420
Berber carpets, 373
Berkol, April, 125
Bi-level lighting fixtures, 327
Biochemical/Biological Oxygen Demand, 183
Bio-fuels, 99
Blue Flag, 190
BOD value, 183
Boilers, 257–259
Bottled water, 176
Bottom-transfer machines, 339
Boutique hotels, 428
Brand
    hotels, 409, 410–411, 418, 426, 429, 430, 433, 448
    managers, 405
Breakdown maintenance, 35–36, 49
BREEAM, 65
Brundtland, Gro Harlem, 117
Brundtland Report, 83, 117
Btu/hour, 261
BTUH, 261
Budgeting, 23
Building
    area method, 318
    automation systems, 280–281
    certification, 65–66
    codes, 473
    commissioning, 21
    design, 21
    interiors, 370–378
    loads (HVAC), 251–253
    maintenance, 22
    systems, 412, 414
Building Air Quality Action Plan, 255
Building and Engineering expenses, 59–60
Building Owners and Managers Association, 64
Building Research Establishment's Environmental Assessment Method, 65
Built-up roof, 368
Bulk continuous filament fibers, 373
Bureau of Labor Statistics, 126

511

4. **Print** the information requested below. Course name and number are found at the top of your exam.

COURSE NAME: _____

COURSE NUMBER: _____

EXAM DATE: _____

Completely blacken the letter on the answer sheet that corresponds to the answer you have chosen

EXAM CONTROL NO.

⓪ ⓪ ⓪ ⓪ ⓪ ⓪
① ① ① ① ① ①
② ② ② ② ② ②
③ ③ ③ ③ ③ ③
④ ④ ④ ④ ④ ④
⑤ ⑤ ⑤ ⑤ ⑤ ⑤
⑥ ⑥ ⑥ ⑥ ⑥ ⑥
⑦ ⑦ ⑦ ⑦ ⑦ ⑦
⑧ ⑧ ⑧ ⑧ ⑧ ⑧
⑨ ⑨ ⑨ ⑨ ⑨ ⑨

DO NOT USE INK

THE EXAM CONTROL NUMBER
MUST BE FILLED IN FOR
THE EXAM TO BE GRADED

1 (A) (B) (C) (D) (E)
2 (A) (B) (C) (D) (E)
3 (A) (B) (C) (D) (E)
4 (A) (B) (C) (D) (E)
5 (A) (B) (C) (D) (E)
6 (A) (B) (C) (D) (E)
7 (A) (B) (C) (D) (E)
8 (A) (B) (C) (D) (E)
9 (A) (B) (C) (D) (E)
10 (A) (B) (C) (D) (E)
11 (A) (B) (C) (D) (E)
12 (A) (B) (C) (D) (E)
13 (A) (B) (C) (D) (E)
14 (A) (B) (C) (D) (E)
15 (A) (B) (C) (D) (E)
16 (A) (B) (C) (D) (E)
17 (A) (B) (C) (D) (E)
18 (A) (B) (C) (D) (E)
19 (A) (B) (C) (D) (E)
20 (A) (B) (C) (D) (E)
21 (A) (B) (C) (D) (E)
22 (A) (B) (C) (D) (E)
23 (A) (B) (C) (D) (E)
24 (A) (B) (C) (D) (E)

25 (A) (B) (C) (D) (E)
26 (A) (B) (C) (D) (E)
27 (A) (B) (C) (D) (E)
28 (A) (B) (C) (D) (E)
29 (A) (B) (C) (D) (E)
30 (A) (B) (C) (D) (E)
31 (A) (B) (C) (D) (E)
32 (A) (B) (C) (D) (E)
33 (A) (B) (C) (D) (E)
34 (A) (B) (C) (D) (E)
35 (A) (B) (C) (D) (E)
36 (A) (B) (C) (D) (E)
37 (A) (B) (C) (D) (E)
38 (A) (B) (C) (D) (E)
39 (A) (B) (C) (D) (E)
40 (A) (B) (C) (D) (E)
41 (A) (B) (C) (D) (E)
42 (A) (B) (C) (D) (E)
43 (A) (B) (C) (D) (E)
44 (A) (B) (C) (D) (E)
45 (A) (B) (C) (D) (E)
46 (A) (B) (C) (D) (E)
47 (A) (B) (C) (D) (E)
48 (A) (B) (C) (D) (E)
49 (A) (B) (C) (D) (E)
50 (A) (B) (C) (D) (E)
51 (A) (B) (C) (D) (E)
52 (A) (B) (C) (D) (E)
53 (A) (B) (C) (D) (E)
54 (A) (B) (C) (D) (E)
55 (A) (B) (C) (D) (E)
56 (A) (B) (C) (D) (E)
57 (A) (B) (C) (D) (E)
58 (A) (B) (C) (D) (E)
59 (A) (B) (C) (D) (E)
60 (A) (B) (C) (D) (E)
61 (A) (B) (C) (D) (E)
62 (A) (B) (C) (D) (E)

63 (A) (B) (C) (D) (E)
64 (A) (B) (C) (D) (E)
65 (A) (B) (C) (D) (E)
66 (A) (B) (C) (D) (E)
67 (A) (B) (C) (D) (E)
68 (A) (B) (C) (D) (E)
69 (A) (B) (C) (D) (E)
70 (A) (B) (C) (D) (E)
71 (A) (B) (C) (D) (E)
72 (A) (B) (C) (D) (E)
73 (A) (B) (C) (D) (E)
74 (A) (B) (C) (D) (E)
75 (A) (B) (C) (D) (E)
76 (A) (B) (C) (D) (E)
77 (A) (B) (C) (D) (E)
78 (A) (B) (C) (D) (E)
79 (A) (B) (C) (D) (E)
80 (A) (B) (C) (D) (E)
81 (A) (B) (C) (D) (E)
82 (A) (B) (C) (D) (E)
83 (A) (B) (C) (D) (E)
84 (A) (B) (C) (D) (E)
85 (A) (B) (C) (D) (E)
86 (A) (B) (C) (D) (E)
87 (A) (B) (C) (D) (E)
88 (A) (B) (C) (D) (E)
89 (A) (B) (C) (D) (E)
90 (A) (B) (C) (D) (E)
91 (A) (B) (C) (D) (E)
92 (A) (B) (C) (D) (E)
93 (A) (B) (C) (D) (E)
94 (A) (B) (C) (D) (E)
95 (A) (B) (C) (D) (E)
96 (A) (B) (C) (D) (E)
97 (A) (B) (C) (D) (E)
98 (A) (B) (C) (D) (E)
99 (A) (B) (C) (D) (E)
100 (A) (B) (C) (D) (E)

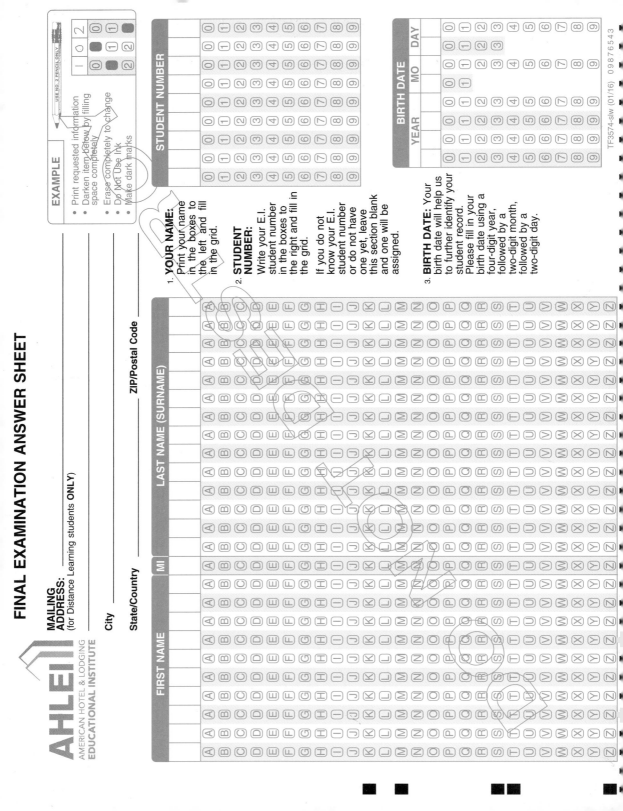

FINAL EXAMINATION ANSWER SHEET

AHLEI
AMERICAN HOTEL & LODGING
EDUCATIONAL INSTITUTE

EXAMPLE
USE NO. 2 PENCIL ONLY

- Print requested information
- Darken item below by filling space completely
- Erase completely to change
- Do Not Use Ink
- Make dark marks

MAILING ADDRESS:
(for Distance Learning students ONLY)

City _____ ZIP/Postal Code _____

State/Country _____

LAST NAME (SURNAME)   MI   FIRST NAME

STUDENT NUMBER

BIRTH DATE
YEAR | MO | DAY

1. **YOUR NAME:** Print your name in the boxes to the left and fill in the grid.

2. **STUDENT NUMBER:** Write your E.I. student number in the boxes to the right and fill in the grid.

   If you do not know your E.I. student number or do not have one yet, leave this section blank and one will be assigned.

3. **BIRTH DATE:** Your birth date will help us to further identify your student record. Please fill in your birth date using a four-digit year, followed by a two-digit month, followed by a two-digit day.

TF3574-slw (01/16)   09876543